David Yallop's previous book, *In God's Name*, was translated into nearly forty languages, sold more than 4 million copies worldwide, and won the Crime Writers' Gold Dagger Award for the best non-fiction book of the year in 1984. It was an investigation into the death of Pope John Paul I. His other books are *To Encourage the Others*, which has twice forced the British Government to reopen the Craig/Bentley murder case; *The Day the Laughter Stopped*, a biography of Fatty Arbuckle that posthumously rehabilitated him and solved a 50-year-old murder mystery; *Beyond Reasonable Doubt?*, which led directly to the release from prison of a man serving a life sentence for double murder; and *Deliver Us From Evil*, an investigation that established the truth about the Yorkshire Ripper seven months before Peter Sutcliffe was arrested.

'Read it as a thriller or reference book'
The Bulletin

'Fascinating'
Christopher Dobson, *Mail on Sunday*

'Extraordinary . . . reads like a thriller'
Sunday Express

'Assiduous attention to detail'
Weekend Telegraph

'Explodes the "myth of a cold-blooded, highly professional killer" . . . Yallop maintains the pace and heightens the drama'
Sunday Times

'Controversial'
Independent on Sunday

S0-AWG-700

Also by David Yallop

TO ENCOURAGE THE OTHERS
THE DAY THE LAUGHTER STOPPED
IN GOD´S NAME
DELIVER US FROM EVIL

and published by Corgi Books

TO THE ENDS OF THE EARTH:
The Hunt for the Jackal

David Yallop

CORGI BOOKS

TO THE ENDS OF THE EARTH:
THE HUNT FOR THE JACKAL
A CORGI BOOK : 0 552 12763 9

Originally published in Great Britain by Jonathan Cape Ltd

PRINTING HISTORY
Jonathan Cape edition published 1993
Corgi edition published 1994

The author and publishers are grateful to the following sources for
permission to reproduce illustrations: Agence France Presse, pls. 42, 45,
46, 50; Associated Press, pls. 11, 16; Deutsche Presse-Agentur, pls. 25,
33; Gamma/Frank Spooner Pictures, pls. 37, 51; the *Guardian*, pls. 24, 29;
Magnum Photos, pls. 52 (© Chris Steele-Perkins), 55 (© Micha Bar'Am);
© David Munro, pls. 40, 53, 57; OPEC, pl. 31; Popperfoto, pls. 14, 30,
32, 36, 39, 56, 62; ©*Stern*/SOA, pl. 68; Sygma, pls. 10 (© Keystone),
26 (© Alain Dejean); Topham Picture Source, pls. 12, 38, 49. All other
photographs are from the author's private collection.

'No Surrender' © Bruce Springsteen 1984 is quoted by kind permission of
Bruce Springsteen.

Excerpt from *Pity the Nation* is quoted by kind permission of Robert Fisk.

Every effort has been made to obtain the necessary permissions with
reference to copyright material, both illustrative and quoted; should there be
any omissions in this respect we apologize and shall be pleased to make the
appropriate acknowledgements in any future edition.

The right of David Yallop to be identified as author of this work has been
asserted in accordance with sections 77 and 78 of the Copyright Designs
and Patents Act 1988.

This book is set in 10/11pt Monotype Plantin by
Phoenix Typesetting, Ilkley, West Yorkshire.

Corgi Books are published by Transworld Publishers Ltd,
61–63 Uxbridge Road, Ealing, London W5 5SA,
in Australia by Transworld Publishers (Australia) Pty Ltd,
15–25 Helles Avenue, Moorebank, NSW 2170,
and in New Zealand by Transworld Publishers (NZ) Ltd,
3 William Pickering Drive, Albany, Auckland.

Reproduced, printed and bound in Great Britain by
Cox & Wyman Ltd, Reading, Berks.

For Anna
to whom this book
and its author are dedicated

'My Name is Carlos'
To the OPEC Ministers, Vienna, December 1975

'My Name is Carlos'
To the author, Lebanon, May 1985

CONTENTS

PALESTINE 1878

□ Jewish colony
• Palestinian village
● Palestinian town
○ Mixed town

LEBANON

LAKE HULEH

SYRIA

Acre

Safed

Haifa

LAKE TIBERIAS

Nazareth

Tiberias

Jenin

Beisan

Tulkarm

Qalqilyah

Nablus

MEDITERRANEAN SEA

Jaffa

Lydda

Ramleh

Ramallah

Jericho

Majdal

Jerusalem

Bethlehem

Gaza

Hebron

DEAD SEA

Beersheba

EGYPT

0   miles   50
0   kilometres   80

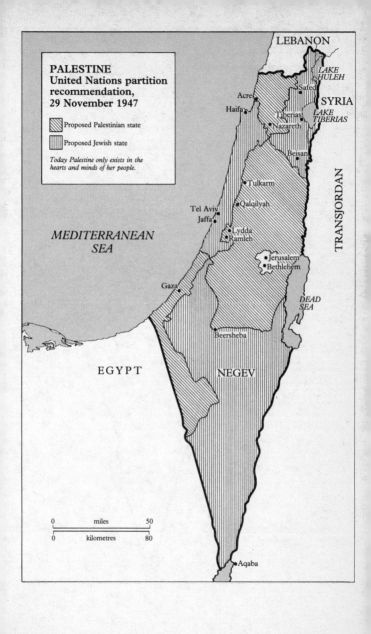

PALESTINE
United Nations partition
recommendation,
29 November 1947

Proposed Palestinian state

Proposed Jewish state

*Today Palestine only exists in the
hearts and minds of her people.*

LEBANON

LAKE HULEH

Safed

SYRIA

Acre

Haifa

Tiberias

LAKE TIBERIAS

Nazareth

Beisan

Tulkarm

Qalqilyah

TRANSJORDAN

Tel Aviv

Jaffa

Lydda

Ramleh

MEDITERRANEAN SEA

Jerusalem

Bethlehem

DEAD SEA

Gaza

Beersheba

EGYPT

NEGEV

0   miles   50

0   kilometres   80

Aqaba

ACKNOWLEDGEMENTS

Work on this book began in 1983. It was completed in early February, 1993. During the course of those ten years I received assistance, help and information from a multitude of people and from a great many sources. Many are specifically identified within the text, others are not. To relate every fact or statement with its sources would not only have resulted in a much bigger book, but also in a very cluttered manuscript. Further, copious footnotes do not necessarily mean a book is free of errors of fact. This is more than adequately demonstrated in the Appendix entitled 'The Hitler Syndrome'. As with my previous books, a number of people would only assist me on the clear understanding that their identities would not be revealed. Their reasons for insisting upon anonymity were varied, but one constant theme ran through those requests: the fear of retaliation from the man I was hunting. To those people and also to the individuals and organizations listed below I am deeply grateful.

Abu Abbas; Professor Abdullah; Dr Valentin Hernandez Acosta; Noel Adami; Bassam Afifi; Alicia Aguereverre; Pastor Heinrich Albertz; General 'Ali'; Issam El Ali; Mrs J A Allsopp; Amin; Basel Aql; Fathi Arafat; Yasser Arafat; Fayez Assayegh; Stefan Aust; Faisal Aweidah; Ambassador Raymond Baaklin; Abdul Hamid Bakoush; Anhal Barakat; Daoud Barakat; Sydney Barbara; Bommi Baumann; Jillian Becker; Mr & Mrs Ronald Beet; Gennadi Bekhterev; Nabi Berri; Dr Karl Blecha; Karl Blessing; Jonathan Bloch; Frederico Bonfanti; Mifsud Bonnici; Peter-Jurgen Boock; Barry Boxall; Argelia and Douglas Bravo; Anne Bren; Lenni Brenner; Donald

Brown; Elia Sanchez Brown; Veronica Brown; Dr Eric Buttenhauser; John Bullock; Bushra; Reno Calleja; Pascal Cariss; Jenne Casarotto; Anita Castellanos; Madame Annina Cavalho; Arnie Clayman; Dr Ray S Cline; Daniel Cohn-Bendit; William Corson; Carlos Perez de la Cova; Brian Crozier; Pauline Cutting; Rolf Cyriax; Shaban Hassan Dalul; 'Danielli'; Abu Daoud; Uri Davis; Mohamad Amine Doughan; Cheryl Drew; George Drummond; Mahmoud Ahmed Elayyan; Shaban Emsak; Erheim family; Ada Faerber; Robert Farah; Reinaldo Figueredo; Robert Fisk; Major Moshe Fogel; 'Frank'; Delia Fuentes; President Amine Gemayel; Bassam el Ghussein; Salvino Giusti; David Godwin; Timor Goksell; Wolfgang Gosch; Alan Greasely; Joe Grech; 'Gustavo'; Tarr Gyula; George Habash; Thor Halvorssen; Hassen Abu Hamdi; Maj Gen S Shahid Hamid; Mahmoud Hammoud; Maggie Hanbury; Ahmad Hariri; Alan Hart; Nayef Hawatmeh; Deborah Herrera; Pastor Heydra; Hillal family; Elie Houbeika; Samir Houlele; Greg Hunt; John Hurrell; Hani Hussan; Ibrahim Ahmed Hussein; Faisal al Husseini; Ronald Irvine; Nelly Arteaga Isaacs; Abu Iyad; Mohammed Zuheir Jannan; Patrick Janson-Smith; Ahmed Jibril; Abu Jihad; Col Jan-Erik Karlsen; Liese Katschinka; Dr Simon Kay; R E Kendall; Caroline Kennedy; Dr Francisco Kerdel-Vegas; Khalid; Abel Khatib; Samir Khatib; Mahmoud Abu El Kheir; Mrs Khusa; Mary King; Colonel Raanan Kissin; Lorissa and Marina Kovalyova; Bruno Kreisky; Vladimir Kryuchkov; Elfie Kulnig; Major Ruth La Fontaine; Saul Landau; Anne Latournerie; Michael Ledeen; Dr Werner Liebhardt; Neil C Livingstone; Christian Lochte; 'Louis'; Uri Lubrani; Alfredo and Eduardo Machado; Mahmoud; Salah Majdali; Maria; Penny Marshall; Ali Marya; Tom Maschler; Ariel Merari; Brig Gen M Meyara; Louise Middleton; Paul Mifsud; Ali Milad; Anne and Yana Mintoff; Dom Mintoff; Harvey Morris; Mousa; Abu Mousa; Rafael A Rivero Muñoz; David Munro; Nabil; Abu Nassar; Dr Jose Altagracia Ramirez Navas; Barbara Newman; Abu Nidal; Andrew Nurnberg; Odeh family;

Rezk Abou Okdeh; Olga; Nilsa Olivieria; 'Omar'; Maria Graciela Orobeza; Salway Orstwani; Paco; Alirio Parra; Dr Mauro Yanez Passarella; 'Patrick'; Maj Gen Matti Peled; Rafi Peled; Michael Penhaligon; 'Peter'; Louis Pinot; Antonio and Sonia Pittol; Astrid Proll; Bill Pugsley; Mu'ammar Abumeniar el Qathafi; Anwar Raja; Carlos and Milena Ramîrez; Dr Wiriya Rawenduzy; 'René'; Rupert Reischl; Daniel Renton; Captain Richard; Carlos Rîos; Jeffrey Robinson; John Rubinstein; Saada family; Col Ibrahim Sabouh; Said Sadani; Afif Safieh; Farag Saeti; Kemal Saiki; Abdullah Abdu Salam; Bashir Nwegy Salim; José Luis Salcedo-Bastardo; Dr Sami; Samir (Beirut); Samir (Munich Olympic Games); Samir's widow; Anthony Sampson; Lenin Ramirez Sanchez; Pastor Scheller; Kurt Schenck; Margit Schmidt; Professor Henry Schouler; Hassan Abu Sha'ban; Al Shaer family; Dr Haider Abed El Shafi; Yitzhak Shamir; Bassam Abu Sharif; Alya Shawa; Edmund H Shehadeh; Sergei Shilov; Hana Siniora; Anas Sinno; David Smith; Alenka Soukup; Josefina Spiro; Bruce Springsteen; Muhammad Sulman; Fathi Swei; Gaby Tabarini; Tarrazi family; Christine Tellner; Gabriele Tiedemann; Antony Thomas; Nydia Tobon; Isabel Torres; Mohammed Tuomi; Violetta de Vidal; Enbiea Wadi; Wolfgang Wagner; President Kurt Waldheim; Hassan Wali; Hussein M Wattar; Carlota and Jack Wigglesworth; Susan and Tony Williams; Derek Willowson; Ernest Woodhams; Barry Woodhams; Gerda Wright; Johnny Wright; Galia Y; Sheik Rashid Aby Zahoui; Zaid; Martin Zammet; Leonid Zamyatin; Elias Zananiri; Major Naim Zanika; Abu Nidal Group; Al Saqi Press; *Al Watan Al Arabi;* Amnesty International; Anglo Venezuelan Society; Arab News; Associated Press Photo Library; Austrian Airlines; Austrian Embassy, London; British Library; Crown Prosecution Services; FBI; Governor and Staff – Hamburg Top Security Prison; Institute for the Study of Conflict; Institute of Petroleum Library; International Association of Democratic Jurists; Interpol; Israeli Defence Forces; Israeli Embassy, London; Jana News Agency; Members and Staff of the

Libyan Foreign Ministry; Libyan People's Bureaux –
Paris, Malta and Vienna; Lloyds Bank; London School of
Economics; Staff of OPEC Vienna; Palestine Liberation
Organization; *Petroleum Economist Monthly Journal;* Poly-
technic of Central London; Popperfoto; Popular Front
for the Liberation of Palestine; Probsthains; Red Cres-
cent; Royal Kensington Rifle Club; Stafford House
Tutorial College; St James's University Hospital Leeds;
Members and Staff of the Syrian Foreign Ministry; United
Nations Interim Forces in Lebanon (UNIFIL); United
Nations Relief Workers Agency (UNRWA); United
States State Department; Staff of Venezuelan Embassy,
London; Westminster Hospital; Wiener Library.

Finally, I would like to thank the men and women of
the various governments, secret services and intelligence
agencies who assisted me.

PROLOGUE

The world is full of men who personally know Carlos, until you ask for an introduction.

By late 1983 I knew what the subject of this book would be. I wanted to examine certain aspects of two major world problems. One was terrorism, the other was the Palestinian issue. Research indicated a correlation between the two. Research also presented me with a powerfully dramatic catalyst – the world's most wanted man. Real name Ilich Ramirez Sanchez, better known as Carlos, or Carlos the Jackal. Here was a man inextricably linked with both issues. All I had to do was find him, interview him, tell his story.

Some said his birthplace was Santiago, Chile. Others claimed it was the Colombian capital of Bogotá. Several National Intelligence agencies recorded his country of origin as Israel. Other intelligence experts disagreed and quoted a score of homelands ranging from cities in the USA to the USSR.

Appropriate that the man should have so many homes – for many years now he has seemed to be everywhere. Simultaneously. A gun in one hand, a grenade in the other.

He has as many names as places of origin, but the man has one name that has only to be murmured down a telephone for an entire country's security forces to go onto full alert – Carlos.

I began by creating a curriculum vitae for him, based entirely on published sources.

At the age of fourteen Carlos was head of the Communist youth movement in Caracas, Venezuela. He was recruited into the KGB before his fifteenth birthday.

No man in the entire history of the KGB has apparently achieved a more successful record of spreading death and terror throughout the entire world.

May 30th, 1972. Twenty-seven people are killed and sixty-nine injured when three members of the United Red Army of Japan open fire with automatic weapons at Lod Airport near Tel Aviv. The attack was organized and planned by Carlos. Two of the attackers were killed in the exchange of fire with Israeli security. The third was captured and imprisoned. Carlos escaped.

September 5th, 1972. With the Munich Olympic Games in progress, Carlos leads the Arab group Black September in an attack on the Israeli team. Twenty-four hours later eleven Israeli athletes are dead. Though some of his colleagues are killed and others injured and captured, Carlos escapes, unhurt.

September 28th, 1973. Two Arab guerrillas board the Moscow to Vienna train, the 'Chopin Express', at Bratislava in Czechoslovakia. When the train arrives at Marchegg on the Austrian side of the border they produce automatic weapons and hand grenades and seize four hostages. They demand that Austria closes Schönau Castle, the transit camp for Jews leaving Russia. Austria submits to their demands and the two Arabs are flown to Libya. The decision by the Austrian Chancellor Bruno Kreisky to agree to the demands causes an international uproar. The man who planned and organized the attack was Carlos.

As he acquired more clients it became increasingly difficult for the rival secret services to establish exactly who he was working for. If the massacres at Lod and Munich had been on behalf of the Palestinians, who gained when the Yugoslavian Vice Consul was hit by ten machine gun bullets in Lyons in March 1974? Who was Carlos working for in Paris on December 19th, 1974, when the Uruguayan military attaché, Colonel Ramon Trabal, fell dying in an underground car park with six bullets in him? By mid 1975 counter-terrorist experts were publicly asking, with increasing urgency, 'Is Carlos the Jackal a Moscow-trained terrorist who has broken out of control?'

In December 1975 he walked through the glass doors of OPEC headquarters in Vienna at the behest of the Libyan ruler, Mu'Ammar Qathafi. The experts were puzzled as to why Carlos should have held the oil ministers of OPEC hostage. For Qathafi the fear and embarrassment suffered by the ministers was clearly all that he desired. He rewarded Carlos with a payment of twenty million dollars.

Carlos, the man with safe houses, guns and bombs and women in a dozen cities throughout the world, had need of every refuge as the hunt for him got ever hotter. A report that he had been definitely seen in Southern Chile vied for attention with another that placed him at exactly the same moment in Bogotá, a third that had him in London, a fourth that had him in Cuba, a fifth that had him in Libya, a sixth that had him in Beirut and a seventh that had him back in Israel.

Reports of positive sightings were only equalled by reports of his death. No man has read his own obituary so frequently. Few men by their actions, either real or imagined, have provoked such fear.

Carlos began 1976 by walking away from the Austrian Airlines plane at Algiers that was packed with kidnapped oil ministers; he ended the year by vanishing in the afternoon winter mists at another airport in Frankfurt. Between those two events he had not been idle.

March 23rd, 1976. Egyptian sources assert that Carlos is now in charge of Libya, with Colonel Qathafi continuing to function as token leader. The young KGB-controlled Carlos concerns himself with exporting not oil but sabotage, kidnappings and murder.

May 8th, 1976. The Royal Canadian Mounted Police distribute thousands of 'Carlos' posters throughout the country. Underneath three photos is a cryptic two-word biography – 'Extremely dangerous'. It is Olympic Games year in Canada and there is visible fear that what Carlos did in Munich 1972 he may wish to repeat in Montreal 1976.

June 27th, 1976. Air France flight 139 from Tel Aviv

to Paris with more than two hundred and fifty passengers and crew is hijacked soon after leaving Athens. The hijackers, led by German Wilfried Böse, describe themselves as the 'Che Guevara Force of the Commando of the Palestine Liberation Forces'. The entire operation has been masterminded and planned by Carlos. In a military action that electrifies the world, the Israeli Government launches a rescue operation that achieves astonishing success. Israeli paratroops land at Entebbe airport in Uganda where the hijacked plane and the hostages are being held. They storm the airport buildings and release the largely Jewish group of prisoners. Only one Israeli soldier is killed, their leader, Lieutenant Jonathan Netanyahu. Only one hostage remains captive, Dora Bloch, an elderly British woman. All the terrorists lie dead on the Entebbe tarmac. Except one. Again Carlos the Jackal escapes.

In September the news breaks that Carlos has taken delivery of a small nuclear bomb. In November US officials express fears that Carlos has now also acquired a quantity of Tabun, a deadly nerve gas. The four horsemen of the Apocalypse have a fifth companion.

It was all very bewildering, not least to the security forces of many countries. They had at their disposal budgets running into millions, the most sophisticated equipment that man could devise, unlimited fire- and man-power, yet one man continued to prove that he was unstoppable and uncatchable. As the 1970s drew to a close he continued to give astonishing examples of his unique and deadly skills. In 1979 his name was linked with the now deposed Shah of Iran. Ayatollah Sadegh Khakli announced from the city of Qom that the fundamentalists were negotiating with Carlos to have the Shah killed. Carlos was quietly advised by the CIA that the Shah's murder in his Mexican haven would be an embarrassment to them. The Shah was permitted to die a natural death.

Deposed Nicaraguan dictator Anastasio Somoza was less fortunate. Carlos caught up with him in the centre of Asuncion, in Paraguay, on September 9th, 1980, and shot him dead. In that strange way in which media morality interlocks with political expediency, many hailed this particular killing. They were less enthusiastic about Carlos's next target. Newly elected President Ronald Reagan.

Before Reagan's election Carlos had virtually single-handedly ensured that President Carter would not be elected for a second term of office. He had planned the seizure of the American Embassy in Teheran and the capture of the hostages, reducing the most powerful nation on earth to complete impotence. Public opinion in the United States reacted. The hostage crisis and President Carter's inability to resolve it were crucial to Reagan's election. Now, having materially assisted in Reagan's election, Carlos, acting on behalf of Libya's Qathafi, planned to enter the United States from Mexico in December 1981 accompanied by a small elite assassination team and kill Carter's successor. Mossad and the CIA leaked details of the plot to the American media and the resulting publicity persuaded Carlos to abandon the assassination.

Within a few months of cancelling the attempt on the President's life Carlos achieved, even by his own unique record, an extraordinary feat. In April 1982 he was in London, masterminding the attempted murder of Israel's Ambassador Shlomo Argov. The Ambassador, though grievously wounded, survived. Israel, in direct response to the attempt, invaded Lebanon. At first they stated that the reason was to establish stable and secure borders, but it soon became apparent to the watching world that the real purpose was the total annihilation of the Palestine Liberation Organization, whose headquarters were at that time in Beirut. Yasser Arafat and his supporters were eventually forced to leave the country in mid September. Subsequently the Lebanese army discovered evidence in the refugee camp of Bourj el Barajneh that among the very last Palestinian fighters to leave was Carlos, escaping on a boat for Tunisia.

As the 80s progressed, so the reputation of the legendary Carlos continued to grow. On August 14th, 1990, secret intelligence reports emanating from a number of countries revealed that Kuwait's invader, Saddam Hussein of Iraq, was preparing a terrorist offensive masterminded by Carlos. Targets included Iraqi exile dissidents based in London and other European capitals. It was revealed that the wide range of weapons at the Jackal's disposal included chemicals. Carlos, it was stated, was attending final briefings from Saddam Hussein in Baghdad.

Despite all the efforts, and contrary to many reports, Carlos continues to pose a seemingly unanswerable threat. While his many victims lie dead, Carlos goes marching on and on.

This brief history provoked so many questions, not least the authenticity of these published sources. How could one man perpetrate so much and still remain free? Who gained from this seemingly endless list of atrocities? Who protected him? Most importantly of all, was Carlos in fact guilty of having committed all these crimes? Was he guilty of any of them?

The hunt for the answers was destined to become an odyssey. Before the journey reached its conclusion and the truths were established, other far more important truths and issues were uncovered. Other revelations.

Throughout the eight years of President Reagan's terms of office there was a deep and total penetration of successive Administrations by foreign agents. The information they acquired was continuously made available to, among others, Colonel Qathafi. Successive governments of President Mitterrand were also penetrated, again at the highest levels.

Although there is a widely held belief that Qathafi masterminded the attack and multiple kidnappings of the OPEC oil ministers in Vienna in 1975, the truth I have discovered reveals that a quite different Head of State was responsible.

Major international airlines that paid millions of dollars of protection money to a Palestinian terror group; a Lockerbie disaster that could and should have been averted; a White House obsession that, contrary to United

States law, was preoccupied with the murder of a fellow Head of State; the reason for the massacre of thousands of Palestinians in the camps of Sabra and Chatila; the reality of the Israeli-Palestinian issue – these and other revelations, which represented for me a personal road to Damascus, lay waiting.

One of the first truths to be established was one of the most basic. Ilich Ramirez Sanchez, birthplace Caracas, date of birth October 12th, 1949. By 1975, before his 26th birthday, he had become the world's most wanted man. Where do you go from there? So much left-over life to kill.

For a man with such a high profile of activity it seemed to me to be unlikely that Carlos would have permanent residence in any of the countries where he was on the 'most wanted' list. If that judgement was correct then I could eliminate a substantial part of the planet. Great Britain. France. Holland. West Germany. Austria. Switzerland. The list grew ever longer. Italy. The United States. Much of the Middle East. A substantial part of Latin America but, curiously, not his native Venezuela. I spoke to contacts in a variety of secret services. The trouble was they all offered a different hiding place. Libya was a strong contender because of his alleged links with Colonel Qathafi. South Yemen was another favourite because of his alleged links with the Popular Front for the Liberation of Palestine, the PFLP. Some secret agents assured me that he was in Iraq, living in a sumptuous villa in Baghdad. Others agreed about the villa but placed it in Saudi Arabia, or Algeria, or Iran. Many, indeed most, were certain that he was dead, that he had become an embarrassment to his masters. They took the view that the KGB had succeeded where every security service in the West had failed, it had eliminated Carlos.

I was sure that Carlos was still alive, that all his obituaries were premature. In November 1984, more than one year after I had begun, I got lucky. A contact in the French Security Service, the Direction de la Surveillance du Territoire (DST) introduced me to a Lebanese

Palestinian, Ibrahim Ahmed Hussein, in Paris.

Over dinner in a restaurant on the Boulevard Saint Germain he asked me a multitude of questions, to establish to his own satisfaction exactly why I was looking for Carlos. Eventually he said, 'You will have to go to Milan.'

My journey had begun.

PART ONE

1

PASS THE PARCEL

Flying to Milan during the winter is like buying a ticket in a lottery. Sometimes you land there, sometimes the winter fogs decide that your plane will come down in Turin or Bologna or anywhere. This time the fog stayed away. We were only forty-five minutes late.

My instructions were simple. Make a phone call and ask for Danielli. One hour and an alarming car drive later Danielli's wife was pouring coffee for two in their apartment.

By the time that the coffee had become a full course Italian dinner our conversation had moved on to Carlos and his links with Brigate Rosse, the Red Brigades. In view of the fact that Carlos has in the last fifteen years been linked with virtually every known terrorist group, freedom fighting organization, revolutionary cell and guerrilla group I expressed some scepticism. 'How can you be sure of those links?' I asked.

Danielli responded quietly. The softness of his tone gave a curious validity to his words. 'Because I was – am – a member of Brigate Rosse and Carlos has sat at this table.'

I had heard similar claims before.

'Can you lead me to Carlos?'

'Yes.'

'When?'

'As soon as you can travel to Paris.'

'But I've just come from Paris.'

'Then you must return. That's if you want to get to Carlos.'

I waited in Milan for a few days while Danielli attempted to make contact with his friend in Paris.

'I've spoken to Gustavo. There's a problem.'

'I thought there might be.'

Danielli mistook my ruefulness for cynicism.

'It's not what you think. Gustavo's genuine. He just doesn't happen to speak English. And from what you've told me you don't speak Portuguese or French.'

'No, I'm still learning English. Gustavo is Portuguese then?'

'Brazilian. The French granted him political asylum some years ago. He lives in Paris.'

'Where he then met Carlos?' I asked.

Danielli leaned across the table. 'Some questions are better left unasked.'

'Why is he prepared to help me?'

'He wanted to know about you. I told him to go out and buy your last book. He's spent the last three days reading it. He phoned this morning. Now he will help you.'

It was agreed that I would re-contact Danielli in January, by which time, he assured me, Gustavo 'will have overcome the language problem'.

During the first week of January 1985 Danielli telephoned to say that 'our friend is ready for you now'. It was arranged that I would be met at Charles de Gaulle airport.

'How will I know him?' I asked.

'When you have come through Customs. Just wait.'

The following day found me doing just that. A man in his mid-thirties approached me.

'Mr David?'

'Yes.'

'Gustavo sent me to meet you.'

Without any more conversation he picked up my suitcase and made for the exit. As we drove in a battered estate car through Paris I remembered Danielli's advice that some questions were better not asked. By the time we had reached somewhere in the 10th Arrondissement,

I had established that my driver's name was Louis and he preferred Gauloises.

Somebody, presumably Gustavo, had arranged for me to stay at a small discreet pension. The enigmatic Louis told me that he would return that evening at eight o'clock, then departed.

In my room I studied a street map of Paris. Perhaps the location of the pension would offer some clues as to the relationship of Gustavo with Carlos. The man I was hunting had been very active in Paris in the mid 1970s but my marked-up map showed that the attacks he had carried out and his various safe houses had all been on the other side of the Seine. The one fact of potential significance was that his close colleague of that period, Michel Moukharbel, had lived in the 10th Arrondissement before Carlos murdered him in June 1975.

To describe where I was staying as a pension proved on investigation to be flattering. They didn't even serve breakfast. Rooms could be rented by the hour.

Wandering the area that afternoon I was struck by its cosmopolitan nature. Algerian restaurants. Turkish cafés. Sweat shops peopled by Arabs and Indians. Chinese and Sikhs buying obscure vegetables. The late Michel Moukharbel's residence was across the road from the hospital St Louis. A few doors down was a police station, two doors more an undertaker. Every modern facility that a man at war with society might need.

That evening I dined with Gustavo and René at the Café de Trocadero. Gustavo looked like an elderly jockey – a few inches over five feet tall, mid to late forties, dark skin, small moustache, well-cut suit, no tie. Despite his name, René did not look French. An Interpol poster would have described him as of Middle Eastern appearance. They spoke to each other in a mixture of Portuguese and Spanish. René spoke to me in excellent English that had elements of a curious accent I couldn't place. He said that his colleague wished to know my views on the Palestinian issue.

It was not the easiest of questions to respond to.

5

In the 1960s, the 1970s even, there would have been little difficulty. At that time, like many non-Jews in Europe, I was strongly sympathetic to the Israeli position. I saw a small country surrounded on all sides by hostility, its very existence threatened. I had been appalled and outraged by the massacre at the Munich Olympic Games. I had applauded the Israeli forces who had snatched to safety the passengers from the Air France plane at Entebbe. I had holidayed on a moshav in the Israeli-occupied Sinai desert in 1978, toured Eilat, Jerusalem and Tel Aviv.

Now, after the Israeli invasion of Lebanon in 1982, and particularly in the light of the massacres at Sabra and Chatila, I had been forced to reconsider easily formed opinions. I explained to my dinner companions that I could no longer give easy quick answers to the question of Palestine, that the hunt I had embarked upon was not just for one man but an attempt to discover for myself the truth of this issue. If they were to ask me the same questions when my research was finished I would have a view, an opinion based upon whatever reality I had personally discovered. Until then . . .

Gustavo told me that he wanted me to discover that truth. The first thing I had to do was to go to Algiers. There I would meet someone who could put me in touch with the man I was looking for.

In March 1985 I was on a plane from London to Algiers. My dinner companions in Paris had asked me if I was prepared to pay for René to fly from Paris and I had been happy to agree. I wondered if the whole thing was a con to give René a few days at my expense in Algiers. A few hours would give the answer. It had been arranged that René would meet me at Algerian passport control.

Having collected my suitcase, I approached the queue by the Customs desk. There was no sign of René. As I stood there mentally cursing my naïveté, René appeared out of a small office. He motioned for me to join him.

'Your passport.'

I handed it to him and he went back into the office. A few minutes later he reappeared, picked up my case and we walked out of the airport. As I walked a few paces behind him I glanced in my passport. There was no entry stamp.

As René drove us from the airport the thought occurred that I could vanish without trace in this country. There would be nothing to indicate I had ever been there.

In Algiers there seemed to be an excessive amount of troop movement. Combat vehicles, troop carriers, military jeeps, checkpoints. René's observation that there were no more soldiers in the streets than usual was hardly reassuring.

René had already booked us both into the Hotel El Djazair. That afternoon we had a visitor. After much kissing and handshaking René introduced me to his friend.

'He is happy to help you. He understands who you are and what you want to do.'

I thanked the man for whatever assistance he was planning to give me.

After more conversation in French we stood up. We all shook hands and he left the hotel.

'What happens now, René?'

'It is all arranged.'

'What?'

'For you to meet the man you want to talk to.'

There was no-one sitting near us in the coffee lounge.

'You mean Carlos?'

'Yes.'

'What, here in Algiers?'

René laughed. 'No, of course not. He's not welcome here since Boumedienne died.'

'Where then?'

'Are you happy to go to Beirut?'

'Well I wouldn't say happy was the word but I'm prepared to go to hell if that's where he is.'

'No need for that. Just Beirut.'

My bemusement clearly showed. René asked me what was the matter.

7

'The man we just met. He's prepared to help me. Without asking me a single question?'

'He asked many questions. I gave him the answers, also he and Gustavo are old friends.'

'But then why did I have to come to Algiers?'

'He wanted to see you for himself.'

Later that day René elaborated. By his standards he became positively loquacious. Having met me in René's company the nameless one now knew precisely what I looked like. There would be no danger of Carlos being duped by someone else. He would have photographs of me. Somewhere, sometime since I had arrived in Algiers I had been photographed.

Back in London, I began to prepare for my trip to Beirut. I consulted a number of friends who knew the ground rules in the Lebanon. Their first responses were disturbingly uniform. 'Don't go.' They ticked off the risks. Arrest, kidnapping and death were the three most popular arguments used in various attempts to dissuade me. Then there was the problem of getting there. To fly direct into Beirut was high risk unless I was being met and driven into the city by someone I trusted. To enter the country from the south, from Israel, and then drive to Beirut was considered even more hazardous. To fly to Syria, then drive from Damascus, was at that time not only extremely difficult to set up but also highly dangerous. That left the ferries from Cyprus. Assuming the ferry was operating, there was always the chance of it being blown out of the water. If Carlos was indeed in Beirut he had chosen one of the safest places on earth in which to hide. Providing he could cope with the anarchy that prevailed, it was unlikely that any police or security forces would come looking for him there.

René had told me to expect a phone call from someone in Beirut called Samir. 'He will look after you.' When it came it caught me unprepared. It was nearly two o'clock in the morning.

'Mr David?'

8

'Yes. Who's this?'

'Samir. I will be meeting you at the airport. Please write down this number and phone me when you have arranged your flight. I suggest you fly next week.'

'Samir. I don't know if I can arrange a visa that quickly.'

'You do not need one. I will arrange all of that at this end.'

And he was gone.

It was early May, 1985. Middle East Airlines would be happy to convey me the following week. I requested that my name should not appear on the passenger manifest, confined my packing to one walk-on case and carefully monitored all available news of the current madness in Lebanon.

'Welcome to Beirut, Mr David.'

Samir, a handsome-looking man in his mid to late thirties, found me almost as soon as I entered the terminal building.

'Am I that easy to recognize as a stranger?'

He laughed. Laughter came easily to this man, as I would discover. He nodded approvingly when I told him that I was carrying my entire luggage and took my case from me. The airport, like any on earth, was a seething mass of humanity – with one essential difference. It looked like the Beirut Gun Club were holding their annual convention in the terminal. Samir took the passport I offered him. Later, when I looked at it, there was no indication that I had entered the country. Again the thought struck me – if I vanished, who would know? Perhaps more importantly, who would care?

The BMW that Samir drove was only a few years old. I was less impressed with the fact that, having motioned me into the back seat and then installed himself in the driver's seat, he casually locked us both in. He was pressing the horn before the car was in first gear. As we moved off he shouted,

'We will talk when we are home. But for now, please keep your head down.'

He handed me a copy of a Lebanese newspaper and for the entire trip, a journey occasionally interrupted by security checkpoints, I closely studied a totally incomprehensible Arabic text. He drove with an urgency that I deeply appreciated. The weather was cool but by the time we had arrived at his high-rise apartment in West Beirut I was soaked in my own sweat. When Samir's wife handed me a cup of coffee it was only with considerable effort that I managed to stop my hand shaking and spilling the contents on an immaculate white rug.

Samir explained that this was to be my home while I was in Beirut. Later, when we were alone having yet more coffee at a nearby hotel, the Beau Rivage, I attempted to persuade him to accept some form of payment. He refused.

'You are writing a book on Lebanon, on the Palestinians, is that correct?'

'Yes.'

'And also on Sabra and Chatila.'

'That will be part of it, yes.'

'Good. Tonight I will take you to Carlos.'

'Is he here in Beirut?'

'No, first we make a drive.'

And make a drive we did. Out along the Corniche with a tranquil Mediterranean on one side and awesome devastation on the other. Point counterpoint. Small vans dispensing mobile coffee; refugees living in the shattered ruins of the US Embassy. Security controls checking for bombs, street sellers hustling duty-free cigarettes. Lovers strolling, arms interlocked so that hers reached over his shoulder and idly played with the barrel of the gun he was carrying.

We stayed on the coast road until we were close to Jounieh then swung inland. It was growing dark. It became impossible for me to track where we were or where we were going. I was aware that we were climbing and heading in the general direction of the Bekaa, home of the Iranian Fundamentalists, a realization that did my pulse rate no good at all. Eventually we stopped in what appeared to be a small village. At the door of a white-washed house were three men dressed in green denims, all armed. To my relief, Samir obviously knew them. After a moment we were shown in. If I had been walking any closer to Samir I would have been walking up his back. We entered a large living room. Dark, heavily carved Italian-style furniture sat beneath ornate paintings that were not to Western tastes, garish, poor draughtsmanship, lacking any subtlety. There were about eight men in the room. Some sprawled on couches, others leaned on walls. From the cigarette smoke that hung in the air they might have been there for days. As we entered one of their number stood, then moved forwards with his hand extended. The others were staring at me.

'My name is Carlos.'

We shook hands.

'I'm David Yallop.'

'Yes, I know.'

He turned to the others and spoke in Arabic. They left the room, still staring at me. Carlos motioned me to an armchair and we both sat down.

'No problems in Beirut?'

'Apart from the war, no, none at all.'

'You must forgive me, if sometimes I do not find the right word. My English is . . .' he groped for a word, 'rusty.'

A manservant came in with a tray of coffee and glasses of water. Carlos smiled and then, as if to show off his knowledge of me, remarked:

'I know you don't drink alcohol but I understand you like café Arabi.'

'Did your people also tell you why I have been looking for you?'

'Of course. After thinking it over for some time I decided to help you. You know of course that many many lies have been written about me. I think it is time for truth to be told. Without all the bullshit.'

His accent was curious, Spanish yet not Spanish, elements of other cultures. Soft spoken, occasionally rising to a higher register. Particularly when he became animated. There was no evidence on the face of any plastic surgery. He looked very much like an older version of the photos in my briefcase – photos taken before he was known to the world in general – except that now he had a thick heavy moustache. He had also put on weight. I judged him to be about fifteen stone. He still had a full head of hair, much lighter than I had imagined. His brown eyes stared at me as we talked. Sometimes they were full of life, at other moments expressionless. He could pass in a London or Paris street without attracting a second glance. He frequently had. For five minutes, possibly ten, we chatted in a desultory manner. It was very Arabic. Many times in the future when I would find myself talking to somebody in the Middle East – Arafat in Tunisia or Qathafi in Tripoli or a Palestinian refugee in a camp – I would recall those first ten minutes. There is a ritual quality to such meetings. Pleasantries are exchanged. Compliments paid. The small change of such relationships carefully counted. Coffees are sipped, positions weighed and attitudes gently explored in this social foreplay. Eventually . . .

'I assume you have many questions.'

'Yes, a great many.'

'In your case, apart from your files, you have a tape recorder?'

'Yes. It's not on though.'

'Of course not. You are not a foolish man. I am afraid I cannot allow you to record our conversation. But make whatever notes you wish.'

Again he displayed his knowledge of me.

'You can write in shorthand. It will be easy for you.'

'I understand that. You do however leave me with a problem. I'm going to need proof that you are Carlos.'

'What I will tell you about myself could not come from anyone else.'

'I'm glad to hear that but it still leaves me with the same problem. I don't want to leave myself vulnerable.

The last interview that Abu Nidal gave was denounced by the Israelis as a hoax.'

He roared with laughter. 'Any truth that does not suit the Israelis is denounced. You know that. They claim to be the chosen people. They also claim a monopoly on truth. I am sorry, Mr Yallop. No tapes and no photographs.'

'Fair enough, but I must have some form of definitive proof. In the past when you have claimed responsibility for a particular action you have sometimes put your fingerprints on a letter. That will do for me. No-one will call your fingerprints a hoax.'

Again he laughed.

'I will make a deal with you. You want me to tell my life story?'

'Yes.'

'I think we will need more than one meeting. On our last meeting I will give you my fingerprints.'

He leaned forward across the small coffee table that was between us and continued:

'If I give them to you before our last meeting – please do not be offended – I have no way of knowing who might appear with you.'

'That's fine.'

'Good. Some more coffee?'

While he was out of the room I took the opportunity to look around. There were no books in evidence, in fact nothing to indicate that the house was a permanent residence for Carlos. Just another of the many safe houses that he had known in his life. On a table at the other end of the room were some photos. I crossed quickly to look at them. Staring back at me were images of myself, including my passport photograph. I had reseated myself by the time he reappeared.

'I sleep little and usually not well. That means we can talk for many hours. Now would you like to begin?'

That first meeting, lasting until dawn, was followed by a second in the Lebanon in September 1985. Again I was driven north of Beirut, and again we talked throughout the night. I attempted as far as possible to progress my questions in a chronological manner, but inevitably we both digressed. For the sake of clarity what follows has been placed in a chronological sequence. It also includes material that I had researched prior to these meetings.

At that first meeting Carlos observed:

'I am prepared to place my story, such as it is, in your hands. I do not intend to hide anything from you but you must understand that you may ask me questions that I cannot answer for a number of reasons.'

I asked him why he was prepared to trust me. He leaned back in his chair and smiled.

'To place my story in your hands is not much. You are placing your life in mine.'

2

HIS STORY

Ilich Ramirez Sanchez was born in Venezuela on October 12th 1949.

It is supremely apt and fitting that a man who has become known worldwide solely through acts of violence should have been born at that time and place.

His birthday is the anniversary of the 'discovery' of Venezuela by Columbus. A discovery that led to the wholesale slaughter and enslavement of the indigenous Indians by the Spanish. Invasion may be a more accurate term. Within one hundred years the population of what was to become Latin America and the Caribbean was reduced from 100 million to 10 million. October 12th is now a national holiday in Venezuela.

Ilich was born into a family that he described as belonging to 'the petite bourgeoisie'. Whatever its precise sociological label it certainly by First World definitions contained some unusual elements.

Both parents are Venezuelans from the town of Michelena in the State of Tachira. The area, which is close to the Colombian border, forms part of the Andes. Traditional characteristics of the people from this region include a deep religiosity, the prudence normally associated with people from the mountains, and some other more unusual traits. It is for example an area that has given the country many of its dictators. His mother, Elba Maria, grew up in a highly politicized environment. Her grandfather led groups of guerrillas against a succession of Venezuelan rulers. In 1899 his group fought their way virtually from the Colombian border to Caracas and seized power. Later, after another coup had placed the Vice President in power, the grandfather again led a number of attacks on the ruling junta. In one of these he attempted to assassinate the Governor of Tachira, was caught and imprisoned in chains for seven years.

Ilich's father, Jose Altagracia Ramirez Navas, was, at the time of his son's birth, a very successful lawyer. Indeed, Ilich proudly told me that in thirty-four years of law practice his father never lost a case. His professional success has brought by Latin American standards considerable wealth, not the millions that the media have talked of, but enough to ensure a good living standard. Possibly journalists have been tempted to describe him as a millionaire because it gave them an immediate alliteration with Marxist as well as providing an apparent contradiction.

In Venezuelan society the family are described as middle-class; what distinguishes them from the working-class is the father's profession. In the case of Jose, it was a profession that was second choice. He had originally planned to become a priest.

As a young man he was convinced that his vocation was to become a Roman Catholic priest. He joined a seminary in Caracas and studied for five years but the comparisons he made between the relatively comfortable existence in the seminary and the squalor and poverty that abounded, not only in the capital but throughout the entire country, inevitably produced a range of inner conflicts and questions that his superior was unable to answer. In 1939 he was expelled.

Deciding to study law, he moved to the Colombian capital, Bogotá. While attending the Free University he became attracted to one of Latin America's great revolutionaries, the lawyer turned politician Jorge Eliecer Gaitan. Recalling this period of his life he observed:

'I became his disciple, his personal friend and an enthusiastic activist in the Gaitan movement. I believe that Gaitan was the greatest leader of the non-Marxist left in Latin America.'

After two years at the Free University and a third at the Javeriana he returned to Caracas and graduated with his law degree from the Central University in 1943. He began practising law in San Cristobal near his birthplace and spent most of his free time studying the teachings of Lenin. The devout Catholic youth destined for the priesthood had by now become a brilliant lawyer committed to the far left. He considers Lenin to be 'the most important occurrence in the twentieth century until man walked on the moon'.

His commitment to Lenin does not extend however to the Communist Party. 'Neither my children nor myself have ever been activists of the Venezuelan Communist Party. Neither have any of them ever been members.

'My independently minded character has led me to behave in relation to our Venezuelan politics through a personal analysis of events as they take place.'

Jose is very prone to talk in this manner, it is one of his characteristics that his eldest son undoubtedly inherited.

The father's 'personal analysis of events' led him in the early 1940s to assist in the foundation of a new political party, the Accion Democratica, headed by Romulo Betancourt. In October 1945 a combination of the military and Accion Democratica overthrew President Medina Angarita. During the short period of de facto government that followed, Jose objected strongly and actively against what he saw as a continuation of corrupt government. In May 1946 his fellow founder members decided enough was enough and he was imprisoned. Being imprisoned by hateful dictatorial right-wing tyrants is perhaps to be expected if you are of the far left persuasion in Latin America; to be imprisoned by the left-wing party you have helped to create is not unique but a shade more unexpected. When Jose Ramirez was told that he would be tried by a Military Court he protested. Demanding to be charged under the correct procedure and tried by a Civil Court, he spent over two hundred hours on hunger strike. The government released him.

Disenchanted by the actions of his former colleague Betancourt, now ruling the country largely by personal decree, Jose returned not only to his legal practice but to his study of the Russian revolution. His admiration of Lenin's philosophies led him to a deep appreciation of the work of Gustavo and Eduardo Machado, two key figures in the history of the Venezuelan Communist Party. These two men, apart from deeply influencing the father, were destined to play an unwittingly significant part in the Carlos story.

In 1948 he married Elba Maria Sanchez, an attractive young woman from his home town. The same year his friend Jorge Eliecer Gaitan was murdered in Bogotá. Gaitan had been walking with a group of his youthful supporters to a political meeting when the attack occurred. Among those supporters was a young Cuban called Fidel Castro. The murder plunged Colombia into a crisis from which much of the anarchy, violence and lawlessness that has bedevilled the country over the past forty-odd years can be directly traced.

There was a widespread protest by the ordinary people of Colombia at Gaitan's murder. When the army attempted to subdue the crowds with extreme violence the protest erupted into extreme violence on all sides. Mob rule prevailed in Bogotá for a number of days. If the Colombian Communists had seized the opportunity, supreme power was theirs for the taking; instead its leaders became a potential government not in exile but in hiding as the violence spread. The uprising in the capital became known as 'Bogotazo'. It left the city in ruins and led directly to a vicious five-year civil war that brought with it the deaths of hundreds of thousands of people and evil repression.

Life in Venezuela in 1948 was also full of turmoil. In November of that year another coup took place. Betancourt and his colleagues were ousted and replaced by a military junta headed by Delgado Chalbaud. Within two years Chalbaud would be murdered to be replaced by a pig-faced dictator called Perez Jimenez.

Venezuela was at that time a country in which half the adult population was totally illiterate. A country without television that relied on the heavily censored press and radio for its information. A country of such extreme poverty that for many the only way to survive was to sell your body. It was estimated that in Caracas alone there were four thousand brothels, but this excludes the prostitution that was practised in the city's nightclubs, cabarets and bars. Abandoned children were estimated as numbering half a million. These were the have nots. The haves, as always, had it rather better. Within a few years Christian Dior and Yves St Laurent opened boutiques in the capital. Venezuela earned the reputation of being one of the world's greatest consumers of imported Scotch whisky and champagne. There were more Cadillacs than Fords in the wealthy San Bernardino section of the city. Elegant restaurants, bars and nightclubs appeared in the smart Sabana Grande section of Caracas. When the students at the newly opened University protested at such obvious contradictions Perez Jimenez promptly closed it down.

This was the climate of Latin American violence, injustice, exploitation and corruption into which Ilich Ramirez Sanchez was born.

As the young boy developed, his features closely resembled his attractive mother, Elba. The dark hair and brown eyes are two very noticeable similarities. His youthful views and attitudes, however, were very much shaped by his father's perceptions of the world.

The birth of Ilich was followed by a second son, Lenin, in 1951, a daughter, Natasha, who died aged three months in 1955, and finally a third son in September 1958.

Jose remarked that he wanted a three-syllable Russian name for the new-born. The nine-year-old Ilich responded.

'You shouldn't have to look for long. We'll call him Vladimir. Then the full name of the greatest man in history will be complete.'

The two eldest boys already enjoyed an environment

as unusual as the names they carried. Although they lived in a modest part of Caracas they did not attend local primary schools, instead the father paid for teachers who were also personal friends to educate the boys at home. They never went out alone, they were always accompanied by one or both parents. When looking at the subsequent career of their first born it would be difficult to plead lack of parental guidance, care or love in mitigation.

Despite the closeness of their relationship with their children, by the time of the birth of Vladimir the parents were having serious marital difficulties. Divorce for the devoutly Catholic Elba was difficult to contemplate, so a curious form of separation began. As is clearly indicated by the use of private tutors, Jose Altagracia Ramirez was unimpressed by the standard of education that was then available in Venezuela. Elba expressed a desire to travel. The parents evolved an answer that satisfied them both.

On October 25th, 1958, Elba and the three children flew to Kingston, Jamaica. After a short stay they moved on to Mexico City. It was the start of a nomadic existence. Five months were spent in Mexico, followed by six months in the West Indies. Then Caracas for a few months. Then a year, this time complete with father, in Bogotá. There was also an extended stay in Miami where Jose became so enraptured with the American way of life that he entered into negotiations to buy a home, presumably one with separate bedrooms.

A Protestant school in Jamaica; Professor Llinas Vegas in Bogotá; a private school in Mexico City. It certainly made for variety. The constant upheavals inevitably disrupted any friendships that the children would form. They relied on each other more and more. Ilich and Lenin became inseparable and both over-indulged the much younger Vlad. Lenin recalled:

'We loved him like a toy. We both pampered him. Even though he's a grown man now, he still gets that treatment from the family.'

While the negotiations to buy a home in Florida were in

progress the value of the Venezuelan currency collapsed. Currency restrictions concerning the export of capital brought the family back first to the West Indies and then to Venezuela. They returned on February 23rd, 1961. The Caribbean safari was over.

In 1958, when Elba Sanchez and her children had left Venezuela, they left a country which had recently deposed the dictator Perez Jimenez. They left a country where opposition parties had been outlawed. Strict press censorship applied. The imprisonment, torture and murder of political opponents were a regular occurrence. Labour syndicates and peasants' unions were abolished and democracy was buried six feet down.

In 1961, when the family returned, the country was ruled by the democratically elected Accion Democratica, the party that Jose had helped to form in the 1940s. It was also the party that had imprisoned him when he began objecting to their concept of democracy. President Romulo Betancourt favoured a multi-class party: a government that reflected a wide body of opinion but not too wide a body. By 1961, the groups that were acceptable to Betancourt included political parties that broadly shared the aims of the President: the business community, particularly the economic elite, the armed forces, and the Church.

Among those excluded were students, the Communist Party and the unorganized masses; they had no official channels either to exercise power or to affect policy. Most of the benefits from the increasing oil revenues were channelled to peasant groups and labour associations that met with Presidential approval, to the military and to the already wealthy industrialists.

Power was centralized in Caracas; local decision-making was null and void. Betancourt frequently suspended all guarantees of personal and civil liberties. He censored or closed newspapers that were critical of the Government or showed any sympathy towards an ever-growing guerrilla movement. He closed the University, ordered the arrest of political opponents, had parties declared illegal and their members arrested, and outlawed the freedom of groups to assemble and demonstrate. Illegal imprisonment, torture and the murder of political opponents were now carried out by a new national police force, Direccion General de Policia, known as Digepol. This was the democracy to which Elba and her children returned.

At first Ilich and Lenin attended a private school in the San Bernardino area in Caracas, the Colegio Americano. After they had completed their first year of secondary education there, Jose moved them in early 1962 to a state school, the Liceo Fermin Toro. Fermin Toro is co-educational and teaches up to University entrance level. Against the background of national unrest and armed guerrilla movements it also functioned as a fertile breeding ground for young revolutionaries.

During these years the parents were reconciled and the family lived in an old part of the city called El Silencio. Even then it was a poor run-down area. Their apartment, number seven in Block One of a huge estate, is very reminiscent of the soul-less council estates that litter Europe. The building looks down on to O'Leary Square. In the 1960s the square was regularly transformed into a battleground. The students would meet there to express their support for the guerrilla movements and chant anti-government slogans. With equal regularity the police and the army would arrive and attack the crowds with batons and tear gas. The Ramirez family had a grandstand view of the proceedings. Based upon what Ilich Ramirez Sanchez told me it was far more likely that he would be in the square below rather than the balcony above.

'I got my first combat experience in Venezuela. I took a very active part in the confrontations between students and the police forces. I remember well the Molotov cocktails, the guns. Setting fire to cars. Stone throwing at the troops. Our school was in the centre of the city. I took part in many demonstrations. In fact I was one of the leaders. Again and again we paralysed the city. I got my training for all this at Fermin Toro. Sometimes we operated with the guerrillas. We would draw the police attacks to us so that the guerrillas could mount an operation.

'It was during these years [1963 to 1966] that I had my first real contact with the poor who would come rushing down from the barrios, the squalid shanty towns that encircled Caracas. From those days I identified with the poorest of our people. The first real attack that I took part in was on the offices of Pan Am. We threw a petrol bomb. Later our group split into two, some went to the mountains to join Douglas Bravo and the other guerrillas, others, including me, stayed in the city for our training courses. I became chief of our group at school. I became head of the Communist Youth movement at Fermin Toro.'

In 1966 Ilich and Lenin successfully passed their final examinations at Fermin Toro and qualified for the University of Caracas. If Fermin Toro was a hotbed of unrest then the University was a furnace. Jose Ramirez saw very clearly what lay ahead if his sons stayed in Caracas. Ilich recalled, 'My father was afraid. Not for himself but for me. He was very disturbed at my activities. That I was head of the Communist Youth movement. That I controlled over two hundred students. I had many arguments with him over politics. He wanted to get me as far away from the rebels in Venezuela as he could. He decided to send the family to London.'

As Carlos began to tell me how, in mid August 1966, he had flown to London with his mother and brothers, I pointed out to him that we had not covered his trips to Cuba and the training that he had received there.

'The reason that we have not covered them is because they did not happen. I have never been to Cuba.'

I protested that this aspect of his career had been written and commented upon for many years, that TV programmes, literally hundreds of newspaper articles, a number of books – all had recounted how, in 1966, the Venezuelan Communist Party had sent him to Havana for special training.

'And you? You believe all this?'

'Are you telling me that this whole aspect of your Cuba training is false? That it's disinformation?'

'I'm telling you it is bullshit. In January 1966 I was at school, working hard. My finals for the University entrance exam were only a few months away. The idea that I took off in mid-term to attend this conference is absurd.'

'And these subsequent visits to Cuba for training?'

'I've told you already. I have never been to Cuba. Ever.'

'You were preoccupied in 1966, preparing for your exams?'

'Yes.'

'Yet you still found time to take an active part in the street demonstrations. The Molotov cocktails. Setting fire to cars. You also became head of the Communist Youth movement at Fermin Toro.'

'Finding an hour here, thirty minutes there. That is one thing. How long am I supposed to have been in Cuba?'

'None of the accounts specifies how long, but for that kind of training it would be months rather than days. The most detailed of these accounts places the training *after* you had left Fermin Toro late in 1966.'

'After I left the school I have already told you where I went. I went to London with my family.'

Mentally I put the issue of his alleged Cuban training in a pending file and moved on. The mood had grown tense during our interchanges about the training in Havana. It lightened considerably as Carlos recalled life in London during the swinging sixties.

Travelling to a foreign country was not a novel experience for the family: but nothing had prepared them for London. The music of The Beatles, The Stones, The Kinks and Procul Harum was far removed from the Latin American rhythms of Caracas. The miniskirted women, the espresso bars, the boutiques, the street buzz were just a few of the new and exciting things waiting to be discovered.

By early September Elba Sanchez had the three boys back in school. Ilich and Lenin were sent to Stafford House, a sixth-form crammer that also specializes in English courses for foreign students. For the first term the two youths concentrated on English, then broadened their studies to include O Level work on English, Physics, Mathematics and Chemistry. Recalling these studies Carlos observed with a smile:

'This is the period of course when I was not only studying all day at Stafford House in Kensington but according to what you have read I was also attending training courses in Cuba.'

Having passed their O Levels in June 1967, they transferred to another crammer, the Earls Court Tutorial College in Redcliffe Square, to study for A Levels. Their lives and their life styles in this period are again full of the everyday. Far from KGB training to transform him into a one-man army, the first time he touched a gun was courtesy of a pistol club in Chelsea. He asserted that he and Lenin joined the club in 1966. I asked him if the irony of receiving weapon training from the English had ever occurred to him. His head was nodding quickly as I asked the question.

'Indeed, many times. If the East had chosen to mount a disinformation campaign about me instead of the West, just think of the fun they could have had with little things like that. I can imagine it. "He was trained by the British Secret Service at an elite school for killers in the heart of London. When he first went there he could not hit the target. When he had completed his training he was a crack marksman, ready to kill for his British masters."'

Back in Venezuela in 1967, the Central University in Caracas was subjected to an invasion from the armed forces. Douglas Bravo and his fellow guerrillas were still mounting attacks from their mountain hideouts but for Ilich, now fully engrossed in London life, it was another world, another time.

The on-off marriage of Jose and Elba moved back into a positive phase in late 1967 when the father joined the family in London. Over the Christmas celebrations in their Earls Court apartment the family discussed future plans for the three boys. The Sorbonne in Paris was one of a number of possibilities. The father was impressed when they visited the University, but was less impressed with the price of property in Paris, and that idea was abandoned. Early 1968 saw them back at the crammer studying with the future unresolved.

Before their departure from Caracas, Ilich and Lenin had sat an entrance examination for the Patrice Lumumba University in Moscow and applied for a grant. Scholarships were normally awarded only to Party members. Neither Jose Navas nor his sons were or ever would become members. To the father, being an admirer of Marx and Lenin was quite different from joining the Communist Party, particularly after Khrushchev's speech to the 20th Party Congress revealed some of the true monstrosity of Stalin. However, he had maintained good relations with two founding members of the Venezuelan Communist Party, Gustavo and Eduardo Machado.

The VCP agreed to sponsor scholarships to Patrice Lumumba University for the two boys. While the official applications were being made Ilich and Lenin dropped their A Level studies and began taking Russian language lessons.

Elba Sanchez located a seventy-year-old nun, Alexia Haxel, who gave Russian lessons in Holland Park.

Miss Haxel was undoubtedly reasonable when it came to fees, but in view of the fact that she had emigrated from Russia soon after the overthrow of the Tsar the language that she taught the two boys was of little use to them in the modern world. When they arrived in Moscow in September 1968 and began to show off their expertise in the native language eyebrows were raised and much laughter was heard. Two Latin Americans with the unlikely Christian names of Ilich and Lenin speaking in pre-revolutionary Russian were considered a wonderful joke. Girls would approach Lenin just to ask him his name; when he responded they would roar with laughter.

To judge from the writings and statements made by a wide variety of self declared 'experts on terrorism' very little academic work was done at the University. It has been referred to as 'School for Terrorism', 'Killer College' and other similarly colourful labels. It has been described as a processing plant in which Third World students were trained for the future world revolution. The truth was more prosaic.

The University was founded in 1961, the same year that its namesake, the first Prime Minister/of the Congo, was murdered by the CIA. At the time the Ramirez brothers attended there was a teaching staff of approximately 1,200 lecturers; nearly eighty per cent of the staff held Master or PhD degrees. For many years it was the Soviet Union's principal contribution to education in the Third World. Two thirds of the 6,000 or so student intake came largely from Asia, Africa and Latin America, the other third being Soviet students. The staff–student ratio of one to five compared favourably with many Western universities. Unlike many of its Western counterparts it was well funded. To ensure that all students had an adequate grasp of Russian they followed a preparatory language course throughout their first academic year. The bias was towards the sciences and many students subsequently went on to take higher degrees. Students from more than ninety countries were selected through Soviet friendship societies overseas, irrespective of their political backgrounds. Membership of the Communist Party was not a pre-requisite.

Education at the University was strictly disciplined with tightly defined steps and regular examinations. Student committees imposed severe punishments for fighting and drunkenness. Physical education was compulsory for all. The rector, Professor Vladimir Stanis, did not see it as part of the University's function to produce committed communists although he considered that 'it would be nice if they did become communists'.

Nevertheless, there was of course a heavy KGB presence within the University. All Heads of Academic and Student Departments were members of the KGB. Overseas students were billeted on the campus, three to a room, the third student always a Russian. Upon arrival each student was discreetly evaluated by a member of the KGB, and those who were considered to have 'potential' were activated straight away. The rest were merely monitored, usually by that third room member. Periodic reports were made and the students also continually 'reassessed'.

Into this curious world in the autumn of 1968 came the Ramirez brothers – not from Third World poverty and backwardness but from swinging London. Unlike many of their new peer group Ilich and Lenin had no first-hand experiences of the refugee camps of the Middle East. They had never known the hunger or deprivation that had been the lot of their colleagues from Africa, nor had they experienced the sort of life under totalitarian rule that their new-found friends from the Warsaw Pact countries knew all too well.

Not only were many of those friends highly motivated, they were also inclined to take life in general very seriously and to obey University edicts unquestioningly. The Latin American contingent, or at least part of it, had a quite different outlook. While most of the Latins were prepared to work hard, they were certainly equally prepared to argue, disagree and disrupt. Ilich in particular was drawn to this alternative method of study.

'My father had always taught us to question our teachers if we felt that any of the opinions expressed were . . . what is the word – dubious. We did a lot of questioning in Moscow.'

'They must have considered you highly disruptive.'

'They considered some of us, me included, a pain.'

We were rapidly approaching another minefield in our conversation. Rather than interrupt the flow I took a temporary detour.

'Your father is also a man who taught you that Marx and Lenin were two of the greatest influences in the history of the human race. Here you were in late 1968 in the Soviet Union. Did it seem in any way to be a historic homecoming?'

'Not as significant as that but we were indeed eager to discover the reality. To see first-hand the Soviet way of life. We had read much about it, had learned much from our father. Now we had an opportunity actually to experience the Communist way of life.'

'How did the reality compare with the theory?'

'Very badly. Life in Russia, certainly in Moscow between 1968 and 1970, had very little to do with the teachings of Lenin. I am not talking about the ordinary people. I mean the authorities. They were completely rigid. In Moscow I discovered for the first time what that saying about toeing the party line really means. "You will attend a meeting tonight of the Venezuelan Communist Party. You will attend a meeting on Saturday afternoon of the Association of Latin American Student Associations. You will not leave the city without permission." And so on . . .'

'And what was your response to these instructions?'

'Listen, I was nineteen years of age when I went to Russia. Moscow was full of beautiful young women, all looking for fun. What do you think my response was? Given a choice between discussing the Venezuelan party line on guerrilla actions and having a good time with some music, a woman and a bottle of vodka, the political discussion came very low in my priorities.'

It became apparent as we talked that for both Ilich and Lenin the Swinging Sixties truly began not in London but in Moscow. Liberated from the family home, they became like children let loose in a sweet factory. Both were studying for engineering degrees. They worked hard but played harder. When the Venezuelan Communist Party, the VCP, sent instructions that none of the students they had sponsored should socialize with Cubans, Mexicans, Colombians or Panamanians, the Ramirez brothers and a number of their fellow countrymen put two fingers in the air and went out of their way to make friendships with people from those countries.

When the VCP stated that the official line was to advocate political change by peaceful means through the domestic ballot box the students split. Some went to the right of that position and wanted the democracy to start right there within the group, others went to the left and supported the Venezuelan guerrilla Douglas Bravo and his followers who continued to reject the possibility of change by peaceful means and were still fighting the Government from their mountain camps. Secretly Ilich began to organize a pro-Bravo cell within the group that espoused the democratic path.

The definitions 'right wing' and 'democratic path' are, like any other labels, flexible, depending on individual interpretation. What the right-wingers within the student groupings were aiming for was not the sort of democracy found in the USA or Great Britain. This was a group that would have had nothing in common with the cut and thrust of Western parliamentary debate. They espoused strict unquestioning conformity to a pre-ordained position. A conservative position. While continuing his studies and his carousing, Ilich and the other rebels, numbering some twenty-five, infiltrated this group to monitor and report back to the pro-Douglas Bravo guerrilla sympathizers. Student politics. In this instance, the undergraduate games were destined to have extremely far reaching consequences.

Despite the fact that the Ramirez parents divorced during this period, the curious half-marriage continued. Senor Ramirez Navas still maintained the monthly payments to his wife, and still took a deep interest in his three sons. For both parents their children were perfect creations.

While the majority of students at Patrice Lumumba University managed on monthly Soviet grants of ninety roubles (at that time approximately ninety pounds), the Ramirez boys regularly received additional cheques for two to three hundred dollars from their father which they generously spent on a dolce vita life style not just for themselves but for all their friends. When the authorities frowned and the VCP remonstrated, Jose ignored the danger signs, brushed their objections to one side and continued sending money to his sons.

In March 1969, the University authorities booked two hundred students for demonstrating and rioting outside a foreign embassy. Among them was Ilich who was also accused of an 'Act of hooliganism. Damage to private property.'

It all started when some thirty Iranian students were advised by their embassy that their passports would not be renewed. A number of them had their old ones seized. To all intents and purposes they had been stripped of their citizenship by the Shah's officials and abandoned in Moscow. A demonstration was planned and organized at an emergency student meeting and on March 11th over two hundred students clashed with the Russian police and the KGB outside the Iranian Embassy. By Western standards of the period – this was the time of the riots of '68, anti-Vietnam crusades and the murder of Martin Luther King – the confrontation was mild. No-one was shot. No-one was beaten senseless. By Moscow standards of the time it was hot stuff. Tramcars packed with students were stopped before they reached the Embassy area and many, including Lenin, were unceremoniously pulled off and rounded up. Ilich, with his pink complexion and fur hat, was mistaken for a local resident and allowed to go. As he hurried towards the centre of the demonstration there was a great deal of scuffling. When a fellow student was grabbed by the police a large bottle of black ink fell out of his bag on to the snow. Before anyone could stop him Ilich picked it up and hurled it. His target was the Iranian Embassy. He ruefully recalled the moment.

'I missed the embassy. The bottle of ink went straight through a window of a private residence.'

Ilich was lifted by the arms right off the ground by security police and thrown in the back of a police van with other arrested students. He had bruises on his upper arms for several weeks. The security police eventually released the students with a severe warning which was repeated by the University authorities.

'Of course many of those who have written about me have said that my arrest at that demonstration was just a little game played by the KGB. That it was all part of a clever disinformation exercise.'

'Was it?'

He shook his head slowly, there was a faint smile on his face, then, standing up over me for a moment, he turned and walked a few paces across the room. His head was still shaking from side to side when, turning to face me again, he continued.

'I do not know where they get this crap from. The Shah's people withdrew the right to return to their own country of thirty students. Without that action there would not have been the meetings and the demonstration. The Shah was on the payroll of the CIA not the KGB. Does anyone seriously believe that the KGB deliberately organized this demonstration, then arrested hundreds of students just to give me some kind of cover story?'

'Judging from what I've read a great many people appear to believe exactly that. As you know many of those who have written about you insist that you are a KGB agent. Just as they insist that before going to Russia you were trained by the KGB in Cuba.'

'And you. What do you believe?'

'I believe that you want to convince me that you are not and never have been either a Cuban or a Russian agent. Before you ask me if you have succeeded I'll tell you that it's too soon. I'm not given to rushing to judgement.'

For a moment he considered this and then smiled again.

By the end of their first academic year Ilich and Lenin had successfully completed their general course in preparatory Russian and were attending lectures for their degree courses. Both clearly felt it was time for light relief.

'We caught the Moscow to Copenhagen express and

from there travelled to Amsterdam. Lenny had his guitar and I had a lot of fun.'

Then, as now, Amsterdam had much to offer its visitors. Some were attracted by the Van Goghs or the Rijksmuseum, others by the canals that interlace the city. Ilich and his brother were in search of other diversions.

'Sex, drugs and rock'n'roll. I remember the night we arrived going into the Paradiso to hear the music. I cannot sing a note. Lenny is the one with the voice and he plays the guitar really well. Someone gave me a joint to smoke. I do not remember much about the rest of the evening, except that we slept in Dam Square. We looked worse than the characters in Rembrandt's Night Watch. The next night I went window shopping in the red light district.'

'Did you buy anything?'

He laughed. 'Those girls do not give credit.'

Eventually the brothers caught a ferry to England and rejoined their mother and their younger brother Vladimir for a summer holiday spent quietly in England. In the light of the pace at which they were living in Moscow the two eldest boys probably needed all the rest they could get. Returning to the fray for the autumn term they redoubled their efforts, outside the lecture rooms. Ilich met a Cuban woman named Sonia Marina Oriola and began an affair. There were also the vodka and guitar parties, and the intrigue of University politics. In the late autumn the divisions between the opposing sections of the Venezuelan Communists attending the University became open hostilities. The secret cell that Ilich had created to infiltrate the conservative element opposed to Douglas Bravo and his guerrillas was discovered. The Ramirez brothers were ordered to follow the party line, but they were disinclined to take orders, particularly from fellow Venezuelans. Ilich considered they needed some parental advice, not from the sweet and charming Elba, but from their father many thousands of miles away in Caracas. He went to the medical department complaining of severe stomach pains and, in view of his well known predilection for alcohol, the examining doctor concluded that he was suffering from a stomach ulcer. When Ilich asked that he be allowed to return to his London home so that his mother could supervise his treatment the request was granted. Having spent Christmas with his mother in London he flew to Caracas to see Senor Navas.

'I did have stomach pains, that is quite true, but I exaggerated the pain. I needed to talk to my father. The University authorities did not want a foreign student becoming critically ill so they were happy for me to go home to London. They didn't know that I then planned to fly to Caracas.'

'Your father has been quoted as saying you spent some time in a London hospital. It has been stated that no London hospital has any record of treating you between July 1969 and February 1970. It has been suggested that during this period you might have been receiving training at the DGI camp at Matanzas in Cuba or in the Middle East, or that you might have stayed in London involved in intelligence work.'

'That is more bullshit. I spent the summer of sixty-nine with the rest of the family in London. In September Lenny and I went back to Patrice Lumumba. In October and November the row with the VCP happened. In December the University let me go back to London for treatment. It is true that I never had any hospital treatment. That was my invention to keep the University happy and also my father. I spent Christmas with my mother and Vlad in London, then flew to Venezuela. I spent about a week with my father then flew back to London in early January. I stayed with my mother and Vlad again, just lying about, having a good time, chasing some English girls. In about the middle of February I returned to Moscow and the University.'

He had paused several times during this recital, staring into the middle distance as he attempted to recall a sequence of events that had occurred some fifteen years previously.

'Those days you spent with your father in Caracas. Tell me about them.'

'I told him about experiences at Patrice Lumumba. About the demonstration outside the Iranian Embassy. The trouble I was having at the University with the authorities and with the members of the VCP, how so many of them had betrayed the guerrilla movement. How they had become conservative – a crowd of bourgeois. About the arguments because Lenny and I refused to attend meetings of the Venezuelan Communist Youth in Moscow. I asked him if he was with me or the VCP.'

'How did he respond?'

Carlos smiled as he recalled that reunion with his father.

'He responded exactly as I knew he would. My father has never failed me. He said, "I am with you my love." Then he hugged me and kissed me. He was sad that I had come to hate the Soviet version of Communism but his attitude was "You have seen it first-hand and reached the same conclusions as I have reached here in Venezuela".'

Back in Moscow in mid February Ilich, secure in the knowledge of his father's support, became even more active in his confrontations with the VCP, with his tutors and with officialdom in general. He was also busy off-campus with Sonia. In early spring he was advised that he had been officially censured by the VCP in Moscow which had informed Caracas of the problems they were having with him. At about the same time, Sonia told him that she was pregnant.

Supremely indifferent to these difficulties, Ilich continued to arrange meetings of his now not so secret cell of Venezuelans. Prior to their discovery they had formulated a secret plan to go to the Middle East in the summer vacation of 1970 for training in guerrilla warfare. They would return in time for the winter term. After completing their degree courses they would fly to Venezuela and join Douglas Bravo and the other guerrillas still fighting in the mountains. They would inherit Che Guevara's legacy and lead the revolution to its ultimate and inevitable triumph. It must have seemed a very exciting prospect, particularly after the third bottle of vodka. Ilich, because he was the driving force behind the idea and also multi-lingual, was chosen to go first and prepare the way for his colleagues. He had already made some useful contacts among the Palestinian students on campus, particularly with a member of the Popular Front for the Liberation of Palestine, the PFLP, an organization headed by George Habash and Wadi Haddad.

The fact that by spring 1970 Ilich was confronted with an array of obstacles entirely of his own making did not deter him. With a mixture of self-assured bravado and arrogance topped up with a good dash of Latin American machismo, the over-indulged and self-indulgent twenty-year-old considered the world was his oyster, with beluga caviar to follow.

In late June the VCP in Caracas responded to the complaints from the orthodox element among the Venezuelan students and withdrew their sponsorship of both Ilich and Lenin. This inevitably led to the withdrawal of their registration and a few days later they were summoned to the office of the University Dean. After a seemingly endless list of offences had been read out the brothers were advised that they had both been expelled. Fifteen years later, as Carlos recounted that event, the bitterness was still discernible. Again his responses anticipated my questions.

'Of course, if you have read all those lies written about me you will know that they say that my expulsion was all part of this clever KGB disinformation nonsense.'

I nodded but remained silent, hoping that the silence would provoke him into developing the theme.

'Lenny was very upset about being expelled. He blamed me. He was very keen to get his university degree. He planned to go back to Venezuela as an engineer, not a guerrilla. I wanted to help the revolution in our country. I told him, before you can build the new, you have to tear down the old.'

'Many have written that you received such training in the Soviet Union.'

'Are these the same people who have also written

about all this training I am supposed to have received in Cuba?'

'Yes. They talk of training in Moscow and also allege that you were trained at special camps at Odessa, at Baku, at Simferopol and at Tashkent. The identity of the training camp varies depending on the identity of the author.'

'More fantasy.'

'Did you have any contact with Voennaya Kafedra?'

'No, I had no contact with them.' He paused just for a moment, staring at me with unblinking eyes. 'I did not realize you spoke Russian.'

'I don't. Just know the odd word.'

'The name of the Military Section attached to Patrice Lumumba are very odd words to know.'

He stared at his heavy gold wrist watch, then spoke rapidly in unintelligible Russian. I looked at him uncomprehendingly. Carlos smiled.

'If I had been given training in Moscow or anywhere else in the Soviet Union why would I go to the Middle East to get training from the Palestinians? Remember our plan was to return to Venezuela when we had been trained. The Soviets were strongly opposed to Douglas Bravo and the guerrillas. That is the reason we needed to go to the Middle East.'

'But in the event you never did go back to Venezuela.'

'That is because of the expulsions. When that happened my plan to come back to Moscow and collect the others for training was destroyed. I could not return to the University. Also events that occurred in Jordan set me on another path and when I eventually returned to Europe I discovered that my group in Patrice Lumumba had disbanded.'

'What happened to Sonia?'

'She was expelled. She returned to Havana and our child, a little girl, was born there.'

'Have you ever seen her since you left Patrice Lumumba?'

'No. For a while we wrote to each other. I sent parcels

37

for our daughter through the Cuban Embassy. Then nothing. She would not even tell me the name of our daughter. Perhaps after everything that has happened it is for the best.'

It was obvious that Sonia was not a passing affair for Carlos. Some fifteen years later she appeared to have become a romanticized figure, the perfect woman.

The bitterness that Carlos still harboured about his expulsion centred on his relationship with this woman. In his eyes the love of his life had been destroyed not by his own actions at the University but because of tiresome factional squabbling and the intransigent Soviet authorities. His anti-Soviet activities, his dissolute life, his many absences from tutorials – none of these was a relevant factor for Carlos.

'The PFLP man in Moscow. What was his name?'

'I do not remember. He was just a student.'

'Was it Mohammed Boudia?'

He looked at me in astonishment.

'I never met Mohammed Boudia, not in Moscow or Paris. He was murdered by the Mossad before I began operations in Paris.'

'Yes, I'm aware of that. It's just those writers again. It's been stated that Boudia recruited you in Moscow.'

Carlos spoke deliberately, as if talking to a small child.

'No-one recruited me in Moscow. I took a letter of introduction from a young member of the Popular Front to Ghassan Kanafani in Beirut. The letter explained about the plans of my secret group to get training then join the guerrillas of Douglas Bravo. Boudia had nothing to do with this.'

Before we moved on to discuss his experiences in the Middle East there was something I wanted to know.

'Just now when you spoke to me in Russian. I've no idea what you were saying to me.'

He stood up and stretched.

'I wanted to see if perhaps you are fluent in Russian.'

I nodded and smiled. 'So what did you say?'

'Oh just something like "I think you are an agent of

38

the KGB and in five minutes you will be taken outside and shot".'

I stopped smiling. I stopped making notes. Carlos sat down again. On the table between us was a basket brimming with packs of cigarettes. He took a pack of Marlboro, opened it and offered one to me. I had not smoked for nearly two years but I automatically reached out and took one which he lit for me. I felt a long way from home.

When he spoke his voice was reassuring.

'It is all right. I just wanted to see how you would react.'

'It's a good job I don't speak Russian.'

'It is.'

3

BLACK SEPTEMBER

When Ilich Ramirez Sanchez flew into Beirut in early July 1970 he flew into the cauldron that we call 'the problem of the Middle East'. It is a 'problem' that has caused the deaths of hundreds of thousands, a problem with a multitude of 'solutions', the solutions varying with whichever interested party is proposing them. The problem is that one man's country is another man's homeland. The problem has two names – Israel and Palestine.

Many of the first-generation Israelis came from the ghettoes of Europe, displacing the Palestinians and forcing hundreds of thousands of them into ghettoes. In modern parlance these ghettoes have been renamed – refugee camps. Where there had been a Jewish diaspora there took place an Arab diaspora. The words of the Israeli national anthem begin 'Our hope is not yet lost to return to the land of our fathers'. These same words are now written on many walls in the Palestinian camps. Moral law stemming from the barbarity of the Holocaust has replaced international law derived from civilized nations.

The Arabs of Palestine refused to accept the establishment of a Jewish state in part of Palestine because they considered it illegal and because most of the manifestos of Zionism indicated an intention to create a 'Greater Israel' that would incorporate a large part of the Arab world, 'From the Nile to the Euphrates'.

The Jews of Israel refuse to countenance a Palestinian state in part of Israel because many of the

Palestinian manifestos assert that the entire country should revert to Arab control.

The paradoxes are everywhere. Yasser Arafat has survived over fifty attempts on his life; many if not the majority of these attempts on the Chairman of the Palestine Liberation Organisation have been perpetrated by fellow Arabs who consider Arafat a dangerous moderate and his organization a betrayal of the Palestinian cause.

When the government of Israel had as its Prime Minister Menachem Begin, it described the PLO as a 'syndicate of murderers'. Yitzhak Shamir has described Arafat as a man with 'bottomless hate in his heart', who would try, given the opportunity, to finish the job started by Adolf Hitler. On countless occasions both Begin and Shamir have justified their refusal to talk to the PLO on the grounds that 'it is a terrorist organization'.

On the 10th of April, 1948, the Palestinian village of Deir Yassin, near Jerusalem, was destroyed. Its inhabitants, 260 men, women and children, were slaughtered; some were shot, some hacked to death. The attack was a combined operation by two Jewish groups, the Irgun, whose Commander in Chief was Menachem Begin, and the Stern Gang, one of whose leaders was Yitzhak Shamir. In 1980 Begin was awarded the Nobel Peace Prize. In 1983, when Begin resigned from office, he was succeeded as Prime Minister of Israel by Yitzhak Shamir. History is written by winners.

Somewhere outside I heard the sound of a dog barking. I glanced at my watch. It was nearly one-thirty in the morning. I had been talking to Carlos for more than five hours. I offered a silent prayer of thanks for his insomnia.

'Did you tell your family that you were going to the Middle East?'

Carlos poured yet more coffee into the small cups as he considered the question.

'Lenin knew of course. He was with me in Moscow while I made the arrangements.'

41

'I planned to ask you about those. What route did you take?'

'If I remember correctly I bought a cheap student ticket to East Berlin, changed flights at Schönefeld and flew to Beirut. After the trouble I had had at the University there was no other way. The Soviets certainly would not have let me fly direct to Beirut! They strongly disapproved of guerrillas. Palestinians, Venezuelans, Cubans – any kind. They considered them all terrorists!'

'Did you tell your parents where you were going?'

'My mother was told. Not my father. He would have caught the next plane to London if he had known what I was planning. He was told I was going touring through Europe for a while before I came back to London.'

'What were your first impressions of Beirut?'

'I was only there for a day. I contacted Ghassan Kanafani at the offices of the Popular Front. I gave him the letter I had brought from Moscow. The following day I took a letter from Ghassan to Bassam Abu Sharif who was running the Front's press office in Amman. He arranged for me to attend a summer camp just north of Amman. "Summer camp" was of course a cover.'

'For a training camp?'

'Yes. I arrived there in late July.'

'At the exact time that you were at that camp north of Amman, virtually the entire Baader-Meinhof group was also at a training camp in the same area. Did you meet them?'

'No. I heard they were there. They caused so much trouble it would have been difficult not to hear they were out there, but you must know they went out through the PLO. My contacts were with the Popular Front.'

'A case of different group, different camps. Surely all the various groups within the Palestinian movement were in close contact with each other and to a degree interlocked. Joint actions?'

Carlos started to explain the complex relationships that existed within the Palestinian world. Yes, of course men like Habash and Haddad had regular contacts with

Arafat, Abu Iyad, Abu Jihad and other members of Al Fatah, but much less contact than for example exists between rival political parties in Western democracies. As for the various guerrilla actions, again and again Carlos saw many examples that indicated the right hand had no idea what the left was doing. He was not alone in observing this phenomenon. General Moshe Dayan once memorably observed: 'The day that I see a group of Arabs forming an orderly, disciplined queue at a bus stop is the day for Israel to start worrying.'

'Tell me about the training you were given at the camp.'

'At the first camp I was with a group of mixed nationalities as well as a number of Arabs. After about ten days the camp was closed. Things were getting hotter in Jordan. The camp was considered a security risk and the last thing the Front wanted was for a group of foreigners to be caught or killed by the Jordanians. We had been given some preparatory training with small arms but I wanted to be fully trained. I had not come all the way from Moscow just to fire a Kalashnikov, collect a kaffiyeh and catch a plane home. My mission was to get professional training and discover the reality of the Palestinian revolution. I wanted to learn about the various organizations and then decide if my group in Patrice Lumumba should join me.'

Thus in early August Carlos had a further meeting with Bassam Abu Sharif. It was agreed that he would be allowed to join 'a real fedayeen camp'. He also officially joined the PFLP and was taken to a regular camp between the towns of Ajlun and Jerash in the Gilead mountains in northern Jordan.

During his training at this camp Dr George Habash, one of the leaders of the PFLP, paid a visit before leaving for a trip to North Korea. A Venezuelan who had joined the Popular Front and was training in Jordan was unusual. Habash engaged him in conversation. Carlos talked to him of his home country and his family. When Habash expressed admiration for Castro and Cuba, Carlos told him of his Cuban 'wife' Sonia. For Carlos the meeting left a deep and lasting impression.

George Habash is a man whom it is easy to remember. He was born in Lydda, Palestine, in 1925, the son of a wealthy grain merchant. The family's religion was Greek Orthodox. Habash was studying medicine at the American University in Beirut when the British withdrew from Palestine in May 1948. Within months his family were refugees in Jordan and his birthplace had been renamed Lod in Israel. The memories of what he saw and heard during those times were seared deep into his soul.

Having graduated in the early 1950s, Dr Habash established a clinic for the poor in Amman. One of his co-founders was another Greek Orthodox Palestinian, Dr Wadi Haddad. By vocation both men were committed to the sanctity of life. By the time that Carlos met George Habash in Jordan both doctors had embraced what for them was now the paramount vocation – death.

In the intervening years Greek Orthodoxy had been replaced by Marxism, the stethoscope by the Kalashnikov and the Habash-created Arab Nationalist Movement by the PFLP. There had been a time when Habash and his colleagues had pinned their hopes of liberating Palestine on the rise of Gamal Abdul Nasser, particularly after he annexed the Suez Canal and provoked the war of 1956. The following year Hussein of Jordan was nearly overthrown by Nasserite supporters, among them Habash and Haddad. They dreamed not merely of regaining Palestine but of a socialist Arabia. When the King successfully crushed that particular revolution Dr Habash was obliged to move his clinic to Damascus. When the Baath socialists came to power in Syria with a somewhat different philosophy of revolution Habash was forced to move again, this time back to Beirut. In 1968 he was arrested by the Syrians and accused of plotting the overthrow of the Baath regime. His arrest came after the PFLP had blown up the trans-Arabia pipeline. Six months later Wadi Haddad organized and led a brilliant and daring escape for his friend when with four of their colleagues disguised as military policemen he sprung Habash from a maximum security prison. It was a dramatic and early success for the PFLP which had been formed a year earlier.

Within that one year the PFLP had acquired over three thousand active members and many hundreds of thousands of ordinary Palestinians who sympathized with its Marxist-Leninist ideologies. To George Habash, Yasser Arafat was 'a fat bourgeois who is taking money from Arab countries which stinks of American oil'. The enemy had become 'Israel, plus Zionism, plus Imperialism, plus all reactionary powers'. The battleground had become 'worldwide'. It was a daunting agenda.

King Hussein was one of the 'reactionary powers' as far as the far left of the Palestinian movements was concerned. By early 1970 the King's rule over Jordan was being inexorably replaced with anarchy.

Jordan had always had among its population many hundreds of thousands of indigenous Palestinians. After Israel's declaration of independence in the late 1940s that number had swollen to more than a million. Now, some twenty years later, the displaced represented for Jordan's rulers a serious threat to stability.

The PFLP publicly called for Hussein's overthrow – a case of the non-paying guest wishing to evict the owner of the hotel. Nayef Hawatmeḥ's Popular Democratic Front – even further to the left than Habash's PFLP – also saw the removal of King Hussein as a vital step on the road to their revolutionary Garden of Eden. Within Jordan the various fedayeen groups encroached ever further on the state's prerogatives. A large part of Jordan became virtually a state within a state. The fedayeen created its own police force and initiated frequent armed confrontations with the Jordanian army; their own radio station went on air nationally; they set up road blocks and hijacked vehicles; money was extorted from local businessmen and traders; some of Hawatmeh's supporters broadcast Marxist propaganda from the minarets, others took to sexually assaulting and raping local women. The fedayeen swaggered around Amman and other cities like modern-day cowboys, armed to the teeth. The Israelis were pouring agents provocateurs into the country from the West Bank, some were Arabs who had been bribed or blackmailed, others were Mossad/CIA agents. Their purpose was to raise the temperature even higher, to provoke the King into letting his army loose to destroy the entire PLO.

In June there was serious fighting between the fedayeen and the Jordanian army. Arafat and the King worked desperately to defuse the situation. Neither leader wanted a major confrontation. Somehow the situation was prevented from deteriorating to all-out war. Again in June governments of the West expressed outrage at a Palestinian attempt on the King's life. The reality was that the King's car had been fired upon, though he was not in it at the time. The 'attempt' had been rigged up by some of his most senior officers, who then rushed to the Palace to tell him of the 'murder' attempt and his good fortune. The plan was to push the King over the brink and provoke him into declaring war on the Palestinians. When the King demurred the United States intervened.

The Israelis, particularly Defence Minister Moshe Dayan and his advisers, were by mid 1970 growing desperate. Despite a military superiority that gave them the status of Goliath against the Palestinian David, Dayan and his colleagues were discovering a fundamental military truth: guerrilla actions and infiltrations cannot be crushed by air strikes. For over a year Jordan had been hit hard and continuously as part of a two-stage strategy. The Israelis had believed that they could bomb the fedayeen out of existence. They also believed that the constant attacks, during which there were many civilian deaths and appalling damage, would provoke the King into unleashing his army against the Palestinians. By June 1970 it was clear to the Israeli military that the strategy had failed on both counts. The options they considered included a full-scale invasion of Jordan. This was ruled out on political grounds. The constant air attacks had pushed Western patience near to the limit. A major invasion might well end with irresistible international pressure on Israel to withdraw to its pre-1967 borders, which for Israel was unthinkable.

With King Hussein letting it be known that he had no intention of giving the order for civil war in his country and that, despite the many abuses by the fedayeen, ultimately he did not consider them a serious threat to the throne, the Israelis played their American card. There was a series of top secret discussions between Moshe Dayan and the Secretariat of State. Also involved in these discussions were senior officials of the US State Department.

King Hussein had been a CIA asset since 1957, the year after the Suez war. Since that time he had been paid three hundred and fifty million dollars every year by the CIA. In return the King provided intelligence information, allowed American intelligence agencies to operate freely in Jordan and distributed part of his twice-yearly payments from the agency to Jordanian government officials who also furnished intelligence information and co-operated with the CIA.

The Secretariat of State took a policy decision.

In July 1970 the second part of that year's CIA payment to the King was withheld. In early August the King received one month's payment instead of the six months that was now overdue. He telephoned the American Ambassador.

'Why do you only pay one month?'

'Your Majesty, you should know that the United States only backs the winning horse.'

Containing his anger, the King considered his options. He concluded that the United States considered Jordan a two-horse race – the King and Arafat. He also concluded that if he did not move against the Palestinians, the Americans were planning to replace him with one of his generals and carnage would follow. There was also the problem of some 12,000 Iraqi soldiers currently based in Jordan. Intelligence reports indicated that there was a secret agreement between the PLO and the Iraqi regime in Baghdad. In the event of full-scale war the Jordanian intelligence had warned the King that the Iraqi army would fight alongside the Palestinians.

In June 1970, when the Jordanian army were indiscriminately executing Palestinian fedayeen, the PFLP seized the Amman Intercontinental Hotel, complete with staff and thirty-nine foreign guests. George Habash threatened to blow up the hotel with the hostages inside unless the killings in the Palestinian camps stopped. The King intervened and yet another incident that threatened to provoke civil war was defused. But Jordan was becoming increasingly like a forest fire. No sooner were the flames created by Habash extinguished, than those created by his colleague Haddad erupted.

If Dr George Habash gave his organization the intellectual rationale, his fellow doctor Wadi Haddad was the man who by his activities gave Habash a world stage for his oratory.

The son of a teacher, Haddad was born in Safad in Galilee just before the Second World War. At nine years of age, he became a refugee with the creation of Israel in 1948. His childhood experiences, as he watched the effectiveness of Jewish terror tactics, had left a lasting effect. He devoutly believed that if terror could give the Jews Israel then comparable terror could give the Arabs Palestine.

George Habash mixed terror tactics with political philosophy. For his fellow classmate at the American University Medical School in Beirut undiluted terror stripped of rhetoric was the path to their joint goal. Throughout his life Haddad shunned personal publicity. He was content for his work in many fields to speak for him.

For Wadi Haddad the battleground was indeed worldwide – aerial hijackings, airport attacks, bomb explosions in European capitals. If person or property had an Israeli connection it was deemed a legitimate target. Apart from striking at what they perceived to be the enemy, the PFLP sought and achieved by such actions the second of its main aims, publicity. George Habash put it succinctly, 'When we set fire to a store in London, those few flames are worth the burning down of two kibbutzim.'

In this war without frontiers publicity was vital. The Israelis had given countless demonstrations that in this area as in many others they had a marked superiority. The Israeli lobby in the United States and indeed throughout the world had proved long before 1970 to be a formidable machine. Its point of view and its arguments prevailed, invariably unquestioned.

Now, through the activities of the PFLP, a different point of view and a different argument were being heard. Inevitably it was against a backdrop of violence involving actions that were deemed terrorism. Inevitably the effects were more frequently examined than the causes, but through the growing publicity that the PFLP was attracting a great many people were beginning to consider, possibly for the first time in their lives, the Palestinian problem.

Mossad had already tried to kill both Habash and Haddad many times. A few days before Ilich Ramirez flew into Beirut an Israeli commando squad paid a midnight visit to the city. If they had succeeded in their objective it is doubtful that the world at large would ever have heard of Carlos. Their aim was to murder Wadi Haddad.

During the early hours of 11th July 1970 Haddad was entertaining Leila Khaled, an important member of his guerrilla squads. His wife Samia and their eight-year-old son Hani were sleeping peacefully in the next room. At 2.14 am six Soviet-made Katyusha anti-tank rockets were fired automatically by an electronic timing device from a rented room directly across Muhiedden Elchayat Street. They smashed into Haddad's third-floor flat in the Katarji block. Two of the rockets malfunctioned but the other four exploded with sounds that were heard all over Beirut. It was astonishing that no-one was killed. Haddad and Khaled suffered superficial injuries, his wife and son staggered from the bedroom cut and burned and were rushed to hospital. The casualty doctor declined to treat them unless paid in advance, then Haddad appeared and the reciprocal agreement that exists within the medical profession was honoured.

Habash's visit to the guerrilla camp took place on the first of September. Two days later he left for his meeting in Pyongyang with senior members of the North Korean government. For Habash it was one of countless journeys made over many years in an attempt to put the issue of a Palestinian homeland on to the international agenda. Within days of his departure Wadi Haddad, acting independently of Habash, ensured that the entire world became aware of the Palestinian issue. His actions were also to engulf Jordan in a bloody civil war which came perilously close to provoking a superpower confrontation.

By September 1970, intermittent fighting between the Jordanian army and the Palestinian guerrillas had been taking place in the capital for a number of days. The United States, through the CIA, turned the screw even tighter by yet again advancing to the King only one month's payment.

Baghdad radio announced that the Iraqi government would order its 12,000 troops stationed in Jordan to take up arms against the Jordanian army unless it ceased its operations against the Palestinian guerrillas. Arafat, who like the King was desperately attempting to control the uncontrollable, nevertheless believed that if it came to a showdown the Iraqi troops would prove to be the decisive element and would ensure the defeat of the Jordanian army. The King had clearly reached the same conclusion – he decided to invest a substantial part of the September CIA payment.

At the Mufraq air base in Jordan a secret and unscheduled flight from Baghdad arrived with the Iraqi Defence Minister, Hardan al-Tikriti, on board. He disembarked carrying two very large empty suitcases. Two hours later he left, again carrying his own suitcases. It was obvious to those watching that the cases were now very heavy. During the subsequent events that occurred in Jordan the Iraqi troops, whose headquarters were in Mufraq, at no time made any attempt to leave barracks. The Iraqi card had been removed from the table. It was promptly replaced by what George Habash called 'the joker in the pack', the PFLP.

The plans that Wadi Haddad had been making with Leila Khaled in Beirut, which were so rudely interrupted by the Israeli attempt to kill him, had reached fruition.

In a concerted act of air piracy unprecedented in the history of civil aviation the commercial airways suddenly became more dangerous than any place on earth. The day that anarchy took control of the pilot's cabin was September 6th, 1970.

11.50 am. An American Boeing 707 of TWA carrying 145 passengers and 10 crew from Frankfurt to New York is hijacked over Belgium and forced to fly to the Middle East where it lands at a desert airstrip in Jordan called Dawson's Field. The airfield is under the absolute control of the PFLP.

1.14 pm. A Swissair DC-8 airliner flying from Zurich to New York with 143 passengers and 12 crew is hijacked over central France. Again the pilot, flying at gunpoint, changes course and lands at Dawson's Field.

1.50 pm. Two hijackers attempt to seize an El Al Boeing 707 flying from Tel Aviv to New York via Amsterdam. In this instance the hijack fails because the team that Haddad sent functioned at less than half strength. There should have been five of them on the plane, but the insistence of three passengers who claimed to be Senegalese that their first class seats should be located near the pilot's cabin aroused the suspicions of an El Al official at Schiphol airport. Their tickets were returned and they were advised to try another airline. They made no attempt to contact the two other members of the team, Leila Khaled and Patrick Arguello, in the passenger lounge as Haddad had instructed them to do. Undeterred, the two proceeded with the attempted hijack. When the plane was flying over the east coast of England they rose from their seats. Arguello grabbed an air hostess and, holding a gun to her head, demanded that the security door to the flight deck be unlocked. The captain refused to obey Arguello's orders and hell broke out. Before any semblance of order was restored an Israeli steward had been seriously wounded with a shot to the stomach, Arguello had been beaten then shot, a grenade with the pin removed rolled the length of the aisle but failed to explode, and Leila Khaled had been overpowered. The plane made an emergency landing at Heathrow. A physical tug of war over Leila Khaled broke out between the Israeli security team on the plane and the British police. Eventually the police team won and Khaled was taken to Ealing police station.

4.00 pm. The three other members of Khaled's team who had been turned away by El Al at Amsterdam took the advice to 'try another airline'. A Pan American 747 Jumbo Jet flying from Amsterdam to New York is seized. The three 'Senegalese' cannot divert the plane to Dawson's Field because their leader, Khaled, is the only member of their team with the navigational instructions supplied by Haddad. They order the pilot to fly to Beirut where the aircraft manages to land safely with the fuel supply almost exhausted. The following day the three Palestinian hijackers take the plane and its 18 crew and 158 passengers to Cairo. Three minutes after they have ordered the last passengers and crew from the plane the hijackers also jump clear as the first of their pre-set time bombs explodes.

The PFLP, who had accepted full responsibility for all the hijacks, stated that the Jumbo Jet had been destroyed as a protest against Egypt's acceptance of the Middle East cease-fire agreement. They also announced that the hijacks had been carried out because they were opposed to the peace talks and that the singling out of the American airliners was a symbolic blow against 'an American plot to liquidate the Palestinian cause by supplying arms to Israel'. The PFLP said that the Swissair plane and its passengers would be held until the Swiss government released the three Arabs serving twelve-year prison sentences for their part in an attack on an El Al plane at Zurich airport in February 1969. The British government were warned to 'think well' about the treatment of Leila Khaled. Wadi Haddad was a man who looked after his own.

Meanwhile, at a desert airstrip some 40 miles north of Amman, an extraordinary scenario was developing. Over 300 passengers had spent the night on two planes as prisoners of PFLP guerrillas who were dug in around the planes with mortars, machine guns and bazookas. Although the area was ringed at a distance by armoured-car units of the Jordanian army, the Jordanians were powerless to effect a rescue because the guerrillas, having planted hundreds of sticks of gelignite in each plane, were threatening to blow them up with everyone on board if the Jordanian army attempted anything. The guerrillas renamed Dawson's Field 'Revolution Airfield'.

In temperatures of over 190 degrees Fahrenheit, the passengers were obliged to sit and sweat it out. They were let out periodically to exercise and the children on board were allowed to play in the shade of the planes' wings. Later, all the women and children on board, with the exception of Israeli citizens, and all the elderly and infirm were taken in a convoy of buses to Amman and accommodated at the Intercontinental Hotel. The released passengers, about one hundred in number and including Jewish women and children of non-Israeli nationalities, said they had been well treated by the guerrillas who had behaved with kindness and courtesy. They described the PFLP members as 'very determined men'.

To indicate just how determined they were, the PFLP in Amman issued a statement which said that until its demands were met it would hold as hostages those passengers who were of American, British, Israeli, Swiss and West German nationalities.

The PFLP spokesman was Ghassan Kanafani, the man whom Carlos had first contacted upon his arrival in the Middle East.

Apart from the demand for the freedom of the three PFLP members held by the Swiss they also wanted the British government to release Leila Khaled and return Patrick Arguello's body within 72 hours. Kanafani also demanded the immediate release by the West German government of three Arabs imprisoned in West Germany following the attack on an El Al bus at Munich airport in February 1970.

Diplomatic activity between the respective governments became frenetic as world condemnation of the PFLP attacks mounted. Outbreaks of fighting between the Jordanian army and the Palestinian guerrillas occurred in Amman. Out at Dawson's Field, the guerrillas allowed a large number of foreign correspondents to conduct a press conference with the passengers still being held. At the United Nations Secretary General U. Thant issued a statement:

> These criminal acts of hijacking planes, of detaining passengers and crew, of blowing up aircraft, and of the detention of passengers in transit, are most deplorable and must be condemned. However understandable and even justifiable some of the grievances of the perpetrators may be, their acts are savage and inhuman. It is high time that the international community, through the appropriate agencies and organizations, adopted prompt and effective measures to put a stop to this return to the law of the jungle.

The following day, to indicate how unimpressed they were with a Secretary General who paid lip service to the cause as he condemned the effect, the PFLP went into action again. Haddad was determined that his point of view would prevail and that his demands would be met. A British VC-10 airliner with 105 passengers and 10 crew was hijacked over the Persian Gulf. After refuelling at Beirut, with the Lebanese army forced outside the airport by the local PFLP, the plane joined the two others at Dawson's Field.

The implications of this latest hijack were not lost on the British government. In its bid for Leila Khaled's release the PFLP had upped the stakes to a frightening level. Since Wadi Haddad seemed able to pluck airliners from the sky with the ease of a man picking ripe fruit, the British government responded with alacrity. British airlines BOAC and BEA announced that all flights to and through Beirut would be cancelled until the Lebanese government demonstrated that they and not the PFLP had full control of Beirut airport. In London the most elaborate peacetime security measures ever undertaken were set up at Heathrow Airport. Armed police, metal detectors, special checks on hand luggage, body searches – these and other security checks that are now a regular feature of air travel came into being during this time. Similar precautions were also established at other West European airports.

Prime Minister Edward Heath began a series of crisis Cabinet meetings, as did many other governments with a stake in the planes and the people held at Dawson's Field.

Whilst Western governments entered into secret negotiations with the PFLP through Red Cross contacts, the Israeli government adopted a hard-line approach and demanded the extradition of Leila Khaled to Israel.

Against the background of an increasingly deteriorating situation in Jordan, members of the PFLP continued to control events at the airfield. Ghassan Kanafani and another contact of Carlos's, Bassam Abu Sharif, were among the Popular Front Members who liaised with Red Cross officials to ensure relief supplies of food and medicine reached the hostages. On September 11th they and their colleagues organized the safe removal of all the hostages from the blistering heat, but the relief was short-lived for the hundred shocked and exhausted passengers and crew. While the three airliners were blown up with the news media in full attendance, the hostages were spread between Amman and North Jordan. For many what followed as the country plunged into civil war was by far the worst part of the nightmare. By September 29th, when the last of the hostages were released, the civil war that had been raging since September 17th was almost over.

Many of the hostages had personally observed the realities of that war. They had been safe-housed in buildings that had come under continuous shellfire from the Jordanian army. The released passengers talked of 'murderous shelling by the Jordanians', of how some of the guerrillas who had actually been guarding them were killed by shellfire. They also talked at great length of being treated with 'great humanity' by the guerrillas, of how their guards had shared their food with the captives. Rabbi Abraham Harari-Raful observed, 'The guerrillas treated us like friends and hugged and kissed us goodbye when we were handed over to the Red Cross.'

All of the PFLP's principal demands were met. Leila Khaled and the guerrillas held by the Swiss and West German governments returned to great acclaim in Beirut in early October. In the interim period Jordan had become a killing field. Estimates of exactly how many died varied widely and wildly. Yasser Arafat talked in the midst of the war of 'a sea of blood and twenty thousand killed and wounded'. Other Palestinian groups put the figure as high as thirty thousand. The actual figure would seem to be in the region of three thousand, most of them innocent civilians.

During the course of the war Iraq ignored constant appeals from the guerrillas to come to their aid, thus illustrating the wisdom of the investment King Hussein had made with the two suitcases of dollars to Iraq's Defence Minister.

When the beleaguered Palestinians appealed to Syria's Hafiz al-Asad his response to their requests for unlimited help was less than wholehearted. At that moment he was locked in a bitter struggle for absolute power within Syria. Having sent a consignment of small arms over the border, Asad telephoned Hardan al-Tikriti in Baghdad. The suitcase-carrier declined to commit the 12,000 Iraqi soldiers based in Jordan to fight alongside the embattled Palestinians. On the 18th of September Syrian armour crossed the Jordanian border and seized the town of Irbid. Asad was later to claim that he was reluctant to engage his forces in a full-scale war against the Jordanians whom he did not regard as Syria's enemy. His purpose was to help the guerrillas establish a safe haven in northern Jordan and to ensure that the massacre stopped. To achieve that aim it was vital to send in Syrian air cover. This Asad refused to do, thus leaving his brigades dangerously vulnerable to counter-attack. There were, however, two other factors: the United States and Israel.

President Nixon and his National Security Adviser, Henry Kissinger, saw Syria's intervention in the civil war as part of the Soviet Union's grand design for the region. In reality they could not have been further from the truth, but then reality has not featured heavily in the career of either man. King Hussein called on his American friends for help and advised Nixon that if the United States would not assist his hard-pressed army he would do the unthinkable and ask Israel for assistance against the Syrians. To plan to depart from the Arab consensus was an extraordinary step for the King to take, and the United States quickly responded to his cry for help. Within twenty-four hours Kissinger and Yitzhak Rabin, Israel's ambassador in Washington, had formulated a plan for Israel to launch air and armoured attacks against Syrian forces. Washington put airborne forces on full alert and the American Sixth Fleet headed at full steam for the eastern Mediterranean.

Wadi Haddad's hijackers had now brought the world to the edge of Armageddon. If Syria sustained an attack from both Israel and the United States, the special relationship that then existed between Syria and the Soviet Union would rapidly ensure a superpower confrontation. With Israel massing her troops along the Golan Heights and Syria's armed divisions getting a pounding on the ground from the Jordanian 40th Armoured Division and from the air by the Jordanian Air Force, the situation stood balanced on a knife edge. Then Asad cut his losses and ordered the remnants of his armoured brigades to retreat. He had no intention of taking on Jordan aided by Israel and the United States. The Syrian defeat took place on September 23rd. The Palestinians continued to fight on alone.

In some respects the war was a grim replay of the barbarity that followed the declaration of the State of Israel in 1947. Then the Arabs, fighting with Lee Enfield rifles dating from the First World War, and dangerously old hand grenades and home-made bombs, took on Jews fighting with tanks, planes and automatic weapons.

Now, in 1970, there were some 32,000 fedayeen armed with 6,000 guns. Opposing them, with the full range of modern sophisticated weaponry, were the entire Jordanian armed forces. This time Arabs were fighting Arabs. The outcome without intervention was inevitable. The Palestinians were quite literally slaughtered.

Their dead lay unburied in the streets of Amman. In the refugee camps of Jebel Wahdat and Jebel Hussein situated in the capital the scene beggared description. Civilians bled to death. Medical attention was minimal. Much the same could be seen further north where among the beleaguered fedayeen was a Venezuelan named Ilich Ramirez Sanchez. Meanwhile, Israel was being acclaimed for its symbolic support of Jordan by Nixon and Kissinger. The long-term significance of the fact that yet again Washington's helpful junior partner in the Middle East had assisted in keeping the peace was lost on men still fighting the war.

Carlos vividly recalled this period. 'Early in September the camp was closed. All the experienced fighters, the best men, were needed for the war. I found myself left with the youngsters, with the injured. I was furious. I did not know anything about the hijacks that Wadi Haddad was planning, but everyone in the camp knew it was only a matter of time before there was a full-scale war in Jordan. I was still in the early stages of training but I felt that the best way to train was to fight.

'I complained many times to the officer in charge of the camp. After a while I was sent with a small group of fighters to guard an underground store of ammunition outside a small village. By now the war had started. There was very heavy fighting in and around many of the towns. At Irbid, Jerash, Zarqa and many other places. Many of our fighters were killed. Our camp commander gave orders that we should stand and fight to the death to protect this vital arms base. Many other groups withdrew but ours stayed. Towards the end of September we were transferred to a new training camp in the mountains near the forest of Jerash. Our base was between the Gaza camp and the town of Burma.

'The war was supposed to be over by now but it was not. During this time I was wounded in the leg. In between bursts of fighting we carried on training, there were about sixty of us. I finished my training in November. I came first in the examinations and in everything we were tested on.'

In November, Carlos recounted, he was moved yet again, to another camp in northern Jordan. There an important meeting of all PLO leaders took place. At this time Carlos had another meeting with George Habash. Notwithstanding the fact that by the actions of the PFLP the wrath not only of Jordan but of much of the international community had fallen upon the Palestinian heads, Habash was unrepentant. He still firmly believed that the way forward was to overthrow a number of Arab regimes, beginning with King Hussein's. After the Wadi Haddad hijackings, the PFLP had been suspended from membership of the central committee of the PLO. When it became obvious that civil war was inevitable, the Popular Front had been readmitted, so that it was a united Palestinian army of guerrillas under the overall command of Yasser Arafat that was torn to shreds. Now, during what was in effect a phoney peace, the recriminations erupted again. What had saved the remnants of the Palestinian guerrillas from total annihilation was not the posturing of Israel and the United States but the authority of Egypt's President Nasser. Having unleashed his army, King Hussein was determined to destroy the Palestinian forces within his country. Slaughter of a massive nature was inevitable until President Nasser advised the King that if he could not control Jordan's army, then he, Nasser, would, with his own. Having imposed a peace of sorts, Nasser, the father figure of Arab politics, died on the 28th of September. The fragile peace was again in danger of withering. It was against this background that Habash, Arafat and the other Palestinian leaders met at the camp where Carlos was based, in November.

Apart from blaming each other for the civil war, there was much else for these men to consider. There was a new President in Egypt, Anwar Sadat. In Damascus General Hafiz al-Asad orchestrated a coup and seized power; in his case he declared that it was not a coup, merely 'a Corrective Movement'. The effect was much the same. His principal rivals were put into prison, where they remain to this day. In Jordan itself the future of the Palestinians, which had never been particularly promising, now looked as bleak as the mountain range where they had gathered.

Relatively oblivious to these momentous events, the young man from Caracas was finding his own personal reality.

'In those days, when I was alongside 201 Fatah command, I was with some of the very best fighters in the entire PLO. By this time it was winter. There were heavy falls of snow. We had no winter clothes, no tents, little food. I remember waking up and my body being covered with lice. On New Year's Eve I did a continuous guard duty of twelve hours.

'About this time the Popular Front adopted a new fighting tactic. Small guerrilla groups were operating from bases high in the mountains. I thought this was a very bad idea. Small groups of seven men are vulnerable. You can get picked off one at a time, there are not enough of you to mount a counter attack. I complained bitterly to our political leader. He agreed with me, but he could not convince the other leaders at their weekly meetings.

'Our first base under this new fighting tactic was a cave. This is how I first came to meet the Bedouin people and to learn a little about their way of life. Their women were very special. They had a certain je ne sais quoi.

'In the middle of January my brother Lenin sent a Telex for me to the editor of "Al Hadaf" in Damascus. It was sent on to my camp. My father was planning to visit the family in London. He still believed I was travelling in Europe. The family were anxious for me to get back to London before he started asking questions. I talked about the problem to George Habash and he agreed I should go. To reduce my risks, he arranged for me to be given a PLO ID card. Any Front fighters who were caught by the Jordanians were subjected to instant execution. I travelled to Beirut at the end of January and from there flew to Amsterdam. In London I discovered that my group in Moscow had vanished but by then I was committed to the Palestinian cause. Their struggle had become mine. I was no longer someone who held just an abstract belief about the value of international revolution. I had found my destiny.'

He paused, remembering. Recalling perhaps a lost idealism. Then he broke the mood with laughter.

'What have you remembered?'

'How I found my destiny and "lost" my passport. I did not want to pass through Customs in England with a Venezuelan passport covered with Middle East stamps so I went to the Venezuelan Embassy in Amsterdam, told them I had lost it and got a new one.'

'Which also presumably helped you overcome any awkward questions from your father?'

He smiled again.

'Exactly.'

4

THE PLAYBOY OF
KNIGHTSBRIDGE

Ramirez returned to a new London address. During his absence his mother Elba and his brothers had moved to Walpole Street, Chelsea. Waiting there to see him with the rest of the family was his father. As far as Jose was concerned his son had been touring Europe since his dismissal in July 1970 from the Patrice Lumumba University. Inevitably, after the initial excitement of his return had subsided, his future became the subject of discussion with his parents. They began to plan with their eldest son how he should pick up the pieces of his academic education. Their youngest son, Vladimir, was happily settled at St Marylebone Grammar School. His activities included playing in a Jewish football team in the Maccabi League, where he was known as Isaac Ramirez. Lenin was working hard at the London School of Economics studying for a degree in engineering. Ilich told his father that he had decided not to continue his study of the Sciences. At Moscow, when his education was rudely interrupted he had been reading Mathematics and Chemistry. Father and son went to Paris, where Ilich was offered a place in the Law Faculty at the Sorbonne, despite the fact that at that time he could not speak a word of French. They explored possible accommodation in the area around the University and, finding nothing to their liking, returned to London.

'Did you make any contact at that time with the Popular Front in Paris?'

'No, that did not come until much later, after I had

met Wadi Haddad. In early 1971, my first thoughts were to keep my father happy and continue with education.'

Ilich registered for a course in International Economics at the LSE. He might well have found his destiny but at that time he was prepared to defer to his father's wishes, at least to a point. It was an exercise in pragmatism, his father was still keeping the entire family. Soon after Senor Navas had returned to Venezuela in the late spring of 1971 Ilich again became preoccupied with events in the Middle East. Attending parties at the Venezuelan Embassy with his mother and enjoying himself on the diplomatic circuit in London were very pleasant, but the twenty-one-year-old now knew there was more to life than what he regarded as the vacuous cocktail chatter of the Latin American community of West London.

With Senor Navas safely back in Caracas, Ilich began consulting flight schedules. In July, travelling via Paris, he flew to Beirut.

From the mid to late 1940s Lebanon, already beset with the problem of how to share power between its Christian and Muslim factions, had continuously failed to cope with another problem, the Palestinians. Between 150,000 and 200,000 had fled into Lebanon from their homeland by 1950. Many had been placed by United Nations officials in special camps on the outskirts of Tyre, Beirut, Tripoli or the old army barracks near Baalbek. Conditions were appalling but the Lebanese authorities took comfort in the fact that the camps would only be used for a short time, until Israel had been defeated and these unwelcome and unwanted visitors could return home.

The weeks of patient waiting became decades of despair. The majority of Palestinians were classified as non-citizens. No rights, only privileges. The privilege to take a poorly paid job on a building site. The privilege to live in a camp like Chatila with thirty thousand others. The privilege of being subjected to random and constant arrest, interrogation and imprisonment without trial. There were so many privileges if you were a Palestinian living in

Lebanon. The Lebanese talk with great pride of how their country was the 'Riviera of the Middle East', of how one can 'ski in the mountains in the morning and swim in the Mediterranean in the afternoon'. It is difficult to meet a Lebanese who has actually performed this alluring double pursuit. It is impossible to meet a Palestinian who has.

To the Christian Maronites these dispossessed people represented a threat. To the Lebanese Muslims they represented the key which would open the door to absolute control of their country. The ordinary Palestinian people were caught between these two positions. Added to the ordinary people was a dangerous element – the fedayeen. Although few in number at first, after the 1967 war and Black September in Jordan they increased the Palestinian population in Lebanon to a figure approaching four hundred thousand.

By 1971 Lebanon had been grappling with the refugee problem for twenty-five years. It had also begun to bear the brunt of Israeli 'reprisals'. Every raiding party sent from Southern Lebanon into Israel ensured yet again a disproportionate response, and when the Israelis dropped bombs and fired rockets into Lebanese villages the fatalities were just as likely to be Lebanese as Palestinian. The Lebanese forces were weak and divided and unable or unwilling to exert authority. When Black September forced large numbers of the fedayeen into Lebanon the clashes took on a regular pattern. When Israel alleged that the Palestinians had again created a state within a state, for many there was a powerful feeling of déjà vu.

For the Palestinian leadership a moral catch 22 began to present itself. Failure to fight Israel on all or any front would be to admit they would never return to their homeland and their dreams of an independent Palestinian state would remain just that. Yet to fight this enemy would ensure deadly retaliation not merely on their own people but also on their host country.

Lebanon's problems did not stop with retaliation strikes. In the early 1970s the Israelis went further. They began what they called pre-emptive raids. These involved killing and wounding people and destroying their homes on the basis that they might be your enemy.

When Ilich Ramirez Sanchez returned to Beirut in July 1971, the Palestinian numbers in Lebanon were increasing by large numbers on a daily basis, as refugees fled from Jordan.

With Nasser gone there was no longer a restraining hand on either the fedayeen or King Hussein's forces. By April 1971 fighting was particularly bitter in the area where Ramirez had been based in the previous year. By July the areas of Jerash and Ajlun were awash with blood. This was the last stand for the fedayeen in Jordan. Many, rather than face capture, which would be followed by certain torture then execution by the Jordanians, chose to kill their entire families, then themselves. Others crossed the River Jordan and surrendered to the Israelis rather than put their lives at the mercy of the Jordanians.

The Jordanian Prime Minister, Wasfi Tal, exulted at the defeat of the Palestinians, but he was to pay a high price for his denunciation of the Palestinian leadership. Initially that price was exacted politically.

On July 19th Iraq closed its border with Jordan and demanded the recall of the Jordanian Ambassador to Iraq and the expulsion of Jordan from the Arab League. The following day Colonel Qathafi of Libya urged armed intervention by the Arab countries against Jordan 'to save the Palestinian guerrillas'. President Sadat of Egypt, in a speech on July 23rd, described King Hussein as 'the butcher of the Palestinian resistance movement', said that he would 'pay dearly for his crimes' and alleged that the United States was behind him. Syria closed its border with Jordan on July 25th in protest against the 'liquidation' of the guerrillas and Algeria broke off relations with Jordan on July 29th for the same reason.

Not one Arab country came to the aid of the Palestinians while they were slaughtered. Of the force of 2,500, all that remained from over thirty thousand of the previous year, all but 200 were either killed or captured. Many more had already moved into Lebanon after Black

September. King Hussein's army of over sixty thousand men, with its nine infantry brigades and two armoured brigades, together with his air force of F-104 and Hawker Hunter fighters had not merely annihilated the fedayeen, who were armed only with Kalashnikovs, they had ensured that their problem with the militant Palestinians simply did not exist any more. Now that problem had been inherited by Lebanon and by many other countries.

If Lebanon was destined to bear the after-effects of the Jordanian civil war then assuredly they would not suffer alone. Out of that carnage more carnage would directly flow. When the moderates within the PLO movement – and Arafat and those close to him *are* moderates – spawned a terrorist organization called Black September, it made the work of men like Wadi Haddad so much easier. I do not know what Haddad's reaction was when he first learned that Fatah had created its own rival terror group, but I suspect he must have laughed and muttered in Arabic 'the more the merrier'.

Back in Beirut, Ilich Ramirez met Bassam Abu Sharif and discussed what had happened in Jordan after his departure. He also met again George Habash, who subsequently introduced him to Wadi Haddad.

Haddad took to the young Venezuelan at once. Apart from the fact that Ramirez was a committed fully trained member of the Popular Front, he also offered, by dint of his nationality, a huge bonus. As a non-Arab he could get through a Customs checkpoint in Europe much more easily and set up in London or Paris without attracting suspicion.

'I became aware that the Front had a major financial problem. It was at that time almost without funds. Haddad discussed this problem with me at great length. Then he proposed a solution. In the first week of September I returned to London and began work.'

'What kind of work?'

'To assist in kidnapping a wealthy member of a hostile state. Holding him hostage for a large ransom.'

'Are we talking about wealthy Arabs or wealthy Jews?'

'Arabs.'

'Presumably "hostile state" is defined as a country that is not whole-heartedly supporting the Palestinian cause?'

'Precisely.'

'Did you come back from Beirut via Paris on a false passport?'

'Yes.'

'Supplied, of course, by the Popular Front?'

'Yes. I cannot remember which one I used. There have been so many since that time.'

'Tell me about this kidnap in Europe.'

'I cannot give you the details, other than to tell you it was abandoned.'

'Why was that?'

'Haddad decided to move on to the next operation.'

'Which was?'

'The assassination of the Jordanian Ambassador, Zaid Rifai. This was due to take place in London in November. Before then I had been keeping watch on Rifai's movements to establish a pattern. Other members of the Front came and joined me in London. I organized a safe house for them.'

'Where?'

'In West London. Not far from the Jordanian Embassy in Phillimore Gardens.'

'While all this was going on what did your mother and brothers think you were doing?'

'Studying at the LSE.'

'You were telling me about the assassination of Zaid Rifai.'

'We were delayed waiting for guns to be brought into the country.'

'Where were they coming from?'

'From France.'

'Diplomatic bags?'

He shook his head. 'We had no need to use that method into Britain. It was always easy to get anything into your country. There were so many ways. Ferries from France was always the easiest. On this occasion there was an unexpected development. Before we got the guns Black September launched an attack against Rifai. They wounded him but the Ambassador survived.'

'Are you telling me that before they launched that attack you had no knowledge of their plans?'

'None at all. They were under Abu Iyad. We were under Haddad.'

'No dialogue? No co-operation? No joint planning?'

'None at all.'

It was my turn to shake my head, in disbelief. He saw my expression.

'Look at that time, if Haddad could have killed Arafat or Iyad or any of the other Fatah leaders he would have. Fatah blamed the Front for the war in Jordan.'

'How were you planning to kill the Ambassador?'

'Go to his private house when we would know he was there. Force our way in at gunpoint and shoot him.'

'How did Black September carry out their attack?'

'If I remember correctly they stood in the middle of a road in Kensington and sprayed his car with a sub-machine gun.'

'Did the police catch them?'

'No. They caught me instead. But I talked my way out of it and they let me go.'

'How had the British police become aware of your involvement with the Palestinians?'

'Someone in the Black September group gave my real name and address to the British police. That's what the Special Branch officers told me when they interrogated me.'

'Do you believe that?'

'Yes, I do. Some time later a contact in French intelligence confirmed it.'

'Did you have good contacts in French intelligence?'

'Yes. Not at the time of the attempt on Rifai, but later, yes.'

'What about contacts with other intelligence agencies?'

'One of the main reasons I am still alive is because I have many contacts in many countries.'

'I'm talking specifically about contacts with Western intelligence. Perhaps without identifying individuals you could tell me some of the countries?'

He shrugged. 'France, Germany, Italy, the United States. There are others.'

'What about Eastern Bloc countries?'

'East Germany, Yugoslavia, Romania, Hungary, Czechoslovakia.'

'The Soviet Union?'

'Not with those bastards. All I have ever had from them is trouble.'

Making notes rapidly I brought him back to the first bombshell he had dropped during this part of the interview – the fact that he had planned to kill the Jordanian Ambassador, had subsequently been betrayed by a rival Palestinian group, had been interviewed by Special Branch and then allowed to go on his way.

He was very precise about the details. He even recalled the exact date of his arrest. December 22nd, 1971, just eight days after the attack on Rifai by Black September. At 7.30 pm armed members of the police force raided a house in Earls Court Square in which they found Lenin. Having searched the house they ordered Lenin to accompany them to the family home at 12 Walpole Street, Chelsea. Clearly Lenin was extra insurance against any potential violent resistance from Ilich. Drawing their guns, they entered the house through the basement. It was now nearly ten o'clock in the evening, therefore the search and questioning at the Earls Court Square house that belonged to Venezuelan friends had been extensive. The fact that the police knew where Lenin lived indicates that he, like his brother, had probably been under surveillance. According to Carlos, three groups of officers in seven cars made the raid on the Chelsea home. By police standards of the time, this was a major exercise.

In the basement, the police began to fan out and search. They discovered Carlos upstairs watching television. Having shown their search warrant, they went through the house systematically while two of their number closely questioned Carlos. They found nothing. All incriminating evidence, according to Carlos, was deposited at a safe house. Eventually they thanked the family and left. Carlos told me that he was followed continuously, day and night, for about a week until the police lost interest in him and gave up. During the search he had been questioned by officers fluent in Spanish about his political activities, his trips abroad, how he lived and what he did.

On the mantelpiece in the living room in the Chelsea flat the Special Branch officers stumbled on one piece of carelessness. They discovered a false Italian passport, complete with false name but with Carlos's photo in it. Carlos passed off the discovery by telling the police officers that it belonged to a friend. This they accepted and Ramirez went free.

Before we left this part of his life Carlos gave me another jolt. He explained how the Black September attack on the Jordanian Ambassador on December 15th had been the second in a series of planned attacks on Jordanian subjects. The objective was to obtain what they considered revenge for the massacre they had suffered at the hands of the Jordanian forces, to hit at those close to the King. The first attack was carried out in Cairo. The target was the man who had exulted at the carnage in the Palestinian refugee camps and rejoiced at the annihilation of the fedayeen in Jerash and Ajlun, Prime Minister Wasfi Tal.

On November 28th Wasfi Tal was shot down as he entered the Sheraton Hotel in Cairo. Four Palestinians were immediately arrested and charged with his killing. An organization previously unknown claimed responsibility – its name was Black September. The four arrested expressed jubilation at the killing of Tal and their leader, Mansur Sulayman Khalifah, declared that the group had been after him for six months.

Khalifah claimed to have drunk the blood of Tal after he had been shot, an act that was confirmed by witnesses.

Much of the world was shocked at such barbarity and a new terror group had made its entrance on the international stage. This, briefly, is the generally accepted account. Carlos had a different story.

'Yes, Black September planned to carry out the killing. They also planned that the attack in London should happen the same day. Obviously their plans for the London attack were delayed by a few weeks. As for the attack in Cairo, Wasfi Tal was dead before Black September began firing. He was killed by his own security guard acting on behalf of elements in the Palace in Amman, President Sadat and the CIA.'

When I asked him why such a grouping wished the Prime Minister of Jordan dead, Carlos replied, 'Tal was about to sign an agreement with the PLO that would let them return to Jordan.'

'But not five minutes before he'd been celebrating the destruction of the fedayeen in Jordan.'

'Indeed he had, but in the Arab world you draw your enemy to you, that way he is less dangerous.'

'How can you prove that the Prime Minister was murdered by his own people and not by the Black September group who were firing at him?'

'Ask the Egyptians to give you the Coroner's report.'

'Just like that?'

'Sure. If the report confirms it was Black September what have they got to lose?'

'Why would the Egyptians and the Americans be a party to this assassination?'

'Sadat was already conspiring with Kissinger. It would not fit with the plans of those two to see the PLO re-established as a political force in Jordan. They wanted to see it destroyed, not re-established.'

'I wouldn't argue with that conclusion but even so . . .'

He cut across me and, pointing a finger directly at me, repeated, 'Get the Coroner's report.'

I was curious why this particular death in a story with so many deaths should be of importance to Carlos, but then a great deal about this man merely served further to arouse my curiosity rather than satisfy it.

Wadi Haddad was a very careful man. He kept detailed meticulous records because he believed that to defeat Israel he needed an intelligence system that was superior to Mossad. Israeli intelligence had succeeded in the past in infiltrating every Palestinian group and would often succeed in the future, but they never managed to infiltrate the Middle East centre of operations of Haddad's group. Ilich Ramirez Sanchez told me that when he advised Haddad, through PFLP contacts in Paris, of the police raid on his Walpole Street home, Haddad took a policy decision: Ramirez must be frozen, put on ice, indefinitely. In that manner Haddad would perhaps be able to identify exactly how the British Special Branch had become aware of him. In the meantime he represented too great a risk to be of use. Operations such as those engaged in by Haddad were too costly, too dangerous to be placed in greater jeopardy by one over-enthusiastic Venezuelan. The pragmatic doctor, quietly moving between his bases in Aden, Baghdad and Beirut, was not prepared to have any of his various operations or his people put in greater danger than already existed. Ramirez was expendable. He was told to keep in touch while Haddad and Black September competed for the headlines.

Thus it was not until the summer of 1973 that Ilich Ramirez Sanchez again caught a flight to Beirut.

In 1972 both sides in the Israel–Palestine issue decided that henceforth there would be no frontiers, no civilians; 'no-go areas' were words that were expunged from the lexicon.

In February Haddad's section of the PFLP hijacked a Lufthansa Jumbo Jet and diverted it to Aden. Among the 170 passengers was Joseph Kennedy, son of Robert Kennedy. A five million dollar ransom was demanded and paid – Haddad's finances were no longer a problem. Also in February Mohammed Boudia, the head of Wadi Haddad's European cell, led his Paris-based group on a rampage throughout the continent. They blew up oil tanks in Holland, murdered five Jordanians in West Germany, damaged an oil pipeline in Hamburg and in the same city blew up a factory with industrial contracts with Israel. A Black September unit hijacked a Sabena Boeing 707 and forced it to land at Lod Airport in Israel where the group demanded the release of 371 Arab prisoners. An Israeli squad attacked the plane, killing two of the hijackers and a female passenger.

In May Wadi Haddad, using his non-Arab contacts, demonstrated to the world in general, and to the rival Black September organization in particular, precisely how to create terror at Lod Airport. Among the arrivals on an Air France flight from Paris and Rome were three Japanese who pulled out sub-machine guns and hand grenades and began firing into the crowded concourse. The final casualty figures were twenty-seven killed and sixty-nine injured. Two of the Japanese committed suicide; the third, Kozo Okamoto, was overpowered and subsequently sentenced to life imprisonment. Again Israel retaliated with attacks on bases in South Lebanon, again the innocent died. At Lod the Japanese had killed, among others, pilgrims from Peru. In South Lebanon, the Israelis killed, among others, Lebanese women and children.

The carnage continued. The figures of the dead and wounded climbed ever higher, but what of Ilich Ramirez Sanchez, the man who is believed to have masterminded at least some if not all of these attacks?

'In February 1972 I was fully occupied helping my mother move to a new apartment. We left the Walpole Street house and moved to Phillimore Court on Kensington High Street. In September I took work teaching Spanish in Mayfair and began a course at the London School of Economics, studying for a degree in International Economics. Apart from that I went on holidays with the rest of the family. The summer holidays were in Spain.'

'That doesn't seem much to keep a young man fully occupied.'

Again there was that laugh. 'I was fully occupied having

74

a ball. Don't forget it was what they called Swinging London.'

'How did you manage for money? You were the eldest son. Didn't the family expect you to get full-time work?'

'Not at that time. I was still a student. Maybe not studying as much as I should have, but I studied. As for money, we were looked after by my father. He gave the family a monthly allowance that was more than enough. Apart from the activities that I have mentioned there were parties that I used to go to with Lenny and functions that I took my mother to. She liked me to escort her.'

'You must be aware that among the many actions in which you are supposed to have taken part there is the Munich Olympic Games attack in September 1972?'

'That is just another of the fantasies. I have told you. In September 1972 I was teaching Spanish at the Langham Secretarial College in Park Lane, attending the LSE, helping my mother around the home and having a lot of fun.'

'Life had proved less amusing for some of your Palestinian friends.'

'Who are you talking about?'

'I was thinking particularly of Ghassan Kanafani and Bassam Abu Sharif.'

'Indeed, Ghassan and his niece died in Beirut when the Israelis planted a bomb in his car. Bassam was badly injured when he opened a parcel bomb. A little present from Tel Aviv. What about them?'

'Those attacks on your friends took place in July 1972. When you heard about them did it make you reconsider your position?'

'In what way?'

'These were the first two men you had met on your first trip to the Middle East. Now one was dead, the other very badly injured. When those attacks occurred you were safely in London. Didn't life in London seem preferable to fighting someone else's war in the Middle East?'

He paused a long time before responding. It was the longest period of silence between us thus far.

'The time for me in London in 1972 and the following year was a strange period. In some ways unreal. In part I still felt a boy, obliged to be obedient to the wishes of his family. But the other part of me carried the cause of the Palestinians deep inside. I told you earlier I had found my destiny, it was with these people and their cause. When I heard of the death of a friend it made me more determined to help in their struggle which had become mine.'

'Did you discuss any of these feelings with anyone at the time?'

'Sometimes. If I trusted someone I would talk a little about the Middle East and the situation there. At that time of course it seemed that most people in London were pro-Israeli and anti-Palestinian. Now, I believe, things are different.'

While Ramirez went about his everyday life in London the war that knew no frontiers continued. Beirut was far from being the only city that the war came to on a personal basis. PLO officials were killed in Algiers, Tunis, Paris and Rome. Israelis died in Madrid and London. After the Munich attack by Black September, Prime Minister Golda Meir approved the unleashing of a specialist killer squad to avenge the eleven Israeli deaths that had occurred at Munich. It rampaged throughout the world until one of its sections murdered Ahmed Bouchiki in Lillehammer on July 21st, 1973. The Mossad assassins had believed the man to be Ali Hassan Salameh, whom they considered to be one of the chief planners of the Munich massacre. Ahmed Bouchiki was a Moroccan waiter – another innocent victim in a war without end.

During this period the only guns fired by Ilich Ramirez Sanchez were those he aimed at the targets in a pistol and rifle club in West London.

It was also during this period that he met a Colombian woman who was to become more than just someone with whom he could discuss the situation in the Middle East. Maria Nydia Romero de Tobon was as close to the young Venezuelan as anyone got. When she met him in late

1972 in London he was Ilich Ramirez Sanchez. Within a year she was one of the few who knew of the secret metamorphosis that transformed him into Carlos.

Nydia's grandfather had been one of the founding members of the Colombian Liberal party and a close friend of a man who had deeply influenced Ilich's father – the revolutionary Jorge Eliecer Gaitan. Her father was a successful businessman in Bogotá, her husband a professor of law at two universities and a political writer of repute. Nydia, like her husband Romero Buj, was politically to the far left, but she managed to combine her politics with a fondness for bourgeois life.

Educated at Colombia National University, she graduated in law and political science. Between 1965 and 1971 she gained a reputation fighting for justice and labour law reform in the courts of Bogotà. By the early 1970s her marriage was over in all but name. It had produced three sons. Deciding to continue her studies in Europe, she brought the youngest child, Alphonso, with her. Like Ilich, she explored the possibility of studying at the Sorbonne in Paris before deciding on London.

In 1972, Nydia was employed teaching Spanish at a school in Walton upon Thames. She was also involved in a number of part-time jobs for Colombian concerns, particularly the cultural section of the Colombian Centre in London. It was here, according to Carlos, that they met. At that time they were two Latin Americans drifting in a foreign city. They made a curious couple. The plump twenty-three-year-old Ramirez with his middle-aged dress-style of blazers and flannels. Nydia the diminutive thirty-nine-year-old, alternately serious student of world politics, then scatter-brained hedonist. More brother and elder sister than young lovers. Both proclaimed an attachment to Maoism but both preferred to spend an evening singing the songs of their home countries at parties where Lenin and his friends entertained with guitars, drums, maracas and flute. It was all a long way from the cause that had enabled Ramirez to find his destiny. While he chatted late into the night with Nydia, exploring revolutionary theories, men and women were dying in many places. On February 21st, 1973, for example, they were dying in the skies over the Sinai Desert and in their homes in South Lebanon. The lowest estimated total of the people killed on that day is one hundred and sixty-six.

While attempting to land at Cairo airport a Libyan Boeing 727 passenger plane wandered fifty miles off course over the Sinai Desert. It was shot down by Israeli fighter jets, resulting in the loss of 106 lives. General Moshe Dayan placed the blame squarely on the shoulders of the dead pilot, Jacques Bourges, and concluded that there was no need for an inquiry and no question of paying compensation. He and Prime Minister Golda Meir justified their pilots' actions with the observation 'They were only obeying orders'. Twenty-four hours later, after they had had an opportunity to consider world reaction, it was announced that Israel was now prepared to consider paying compensation.

At virtually the same time as her fighter planes were shooting down a defenceless commercial aircraft, Israel's army invaded South Lebanon to attack guerrilla bases. Claiming that the bases had been training camps for the Black September members and the Japanese kamikaze responsible for the Munich and Lod Airport attacks, the Israelis stated they had killed 'sixty terrorists'. Among the buildings attacked were a clinic and a United Nations food depot. Among those killed was a teenage trainee nurse.

Within one week Black September retaliated, not against an Israeli target but an international one. Storming a diplomatic reception in Sudan, they seized a number of the party guests as hostages and demanded the release from various prisons around the world of a curious assortment of people. They wanted Robert Kennedy's assassin, Sirhan Sirhan, freed from a Californian prison, the release of sixty Palestinian guerrillas held in Jordanian gaols and the Baader-Meinhof leaders freed from West German prisons. When the Black September group realized that they were not holding the West German Ambassador to the Sudan, the names of the Baader-Meinhof group were removed from the list of demands. In the event none of their demands was met and, after killing the American Ambassador, Cleo Noel, his chargé d'affaires, Curtis Moore, and Belgian envoy, Gut Eid, the eight-man squad surrendered to the Sudanese army.

The killings continued on both sides, but in this deadly game of kill or be killed the odds always favoured the Israelis. The Israeli intelligence targeted for destruction the man they contended was now the leader of Black September in Europe, Mohammed Boudia. They were wrong: Boudia was a key member of the Haddad Group. By the middle of 1973 Boudia had access to an extraordinary array of international elements. Boudia, aided by Wadi Haddad and his senior colleagues, built up a network of Palestinian contacts throughout Europe, on both sides of the Iron Curtain. But that was only the start. Of far greater significance were the other revolutionaries with whom Mohammed Boudia established contacts. Some came via Wadi Haddad and the training camps in the Middle East. Others came from a personal recommendation here, a murmured approval there. What Boudia established has been given many names: 'The Terror Network', 'The Carlos Connection', even 'Russia's Ultimate Secret Weapon'. There has been talk of 'Inner Circles' and 'Outer Circles', of 'Marxist Terror Groups' and various other examples of journalistic hyperbole. The reader would again and again be left with the conviction that a crack regiment of killer anarchists controlled by the Kremlin was on the rampage. It was never that but to Boudia it certainly had its uses.

There were Basques, Bretons, Corsicans, Irish. There were the Red Brigades of Italy. Baader-Meinhof and the Second of June Movement of West Germany. The Japanese Red Army and the Turkish People's Movement. Some fought for independence in their respective countries. Others fought to assert a political position. Some believed in an international revolution and were appalled at the nationalism of the Palestinians. Many if not all believed that 'only violence can change the world' yet at the same time they disagreed about the nature of exactly what kind of change they wanted. To believe as some self-appointed terror experts do that overseeing this array of anarchy was Moscow and the Soviet Union flies in the face of the factual evidence.

Wadi Haddad at no time in his life displayed the slightest interest in international worldwide revolution. He had one target and one alone. Israel. It is abundantly clear that from time to time the Haddad group worked on a quid pro quo basis but in his eyes and in the eyes of men like Boudia there had to be an end result that assisted the Palestinian struggle to regain their homeland. Thus if the Japanese Red Army wanted to be trained in the Middle East, to assist them in their own struggle, it was arranged. They then balanced the books by slaughtering innocent people at Lod Airport, with guns supplied by Boudia.

Boudia was able to take these various international elements, many of them contradictory, and use them to his own ends. Assistance from French extremists might mean giving them some small arms. Stolen identity cards from the Red Brigades might be exchanged for a Kalashnikov. Hand grenades stolen by the Germans would be exchanged for information on a potential target. Close examination establishes not 'Russia's ultimate secret weapon', more an international swap shop.

Throughout the late spring and the early summer of 1973, the Israelis quietly hunted Boudia throughout Paris. In June they caught up with him.

Boudia spent the night of June 27th with one of his mistresses at an apartment in rue Boinod in the 18th Arrondissement. He left soon after dawn, driving to another of his safe houses located in rue des Fosses-Saint-Bernard. Just before 11.00 am Boudia emerged, unlocked his car and got in. As he leaned forward to insert the ignition key the land mine under his seat exploded.

The death of Mohammed Boudia caused a dramatic change in the life of Carlos. He told me: 'If the Israelis had never killed Boudia, Haddad may well have left me doing nothing in London for ever.

'In July 1973, I flew again to Beirut. After spending time with various members of the Popular Front I had another meeting with Wadi Haddad. I told him that I wanted to work full time to help his struggle. He accepted this.

'I wrote to my father telling him that I had now finished my studies, that I planned to travel to learn more languages and that of course I would visit my home in London whenever I could. In late September, just before the October War, I returned to Europe.

'I was no longer just a university student giving part of his time to other work. From now on I was committed to devoting all of my time, all of my energies and all of whatever talent I possessed to my work. This was the beginning of the true Carlos.'

5

COMMANDO BOUDIA

By the time we had reached 'the beginning of the true Carlos' I was well into my second interview with him. It was now September 1985. Since our first meeting I had attempted to assimilate some of the implications arising from the first interview and prepare for the second. It was obvious that even if Carlos was prepared to talk through the night again, which he was, there would still be a need for a third and final interview.

During this second meeting, again near Baalbek, but at a different location, our discussion provided a perfect example of the gulf between what Carlos asserted was 'the reality' and, if he were to be believed, the extraordinary myths that have been woven around him.

'According to what I have read, when Mohammed Boudia was killed, you took over control of his entire European operation.'

He was smoking a large cigar. He took it from his mouth and carefully studied the ash as if seeking a response from the burning leaves.

'Do you believe everything you read?'

'Of course not.'

'Do you believe I took over Boudia's group?'

'I have an open mind on that. I'd add that if you did, Wadi Haddad was a very naïve man, and whatever else he was, naïveté does not appear to have been one of his characteristics.'

He nodded approvingly.

'Good. Why would he have been naïve to put me in charge?'

'I'm supposed to be asking you the questions.'

'Please.' He gestured, inviting me to continue.

'At the time of Boudia's death in June 1973, you were virtually an unknown element. Your planned attack on the Jordanian Ambassador had been pre-empted by Black September. Experience in the field of battle in Jordan is, I would have thought, no guarantee that a man can effectively function in actions that are planned to take place in large cities. Particularly the kind of actions that Haddad wanted.'

He had been nodding throughout my comments. It seemed for a moment like being the only pupil in a master class.

'And that is why Haddad put Michel Moukharbel in charge after the Israelis murdered Boudia,' he said.

'Had Moukharbel been Boudia's number two?'

'Yes. Haddad told me that before I would even be accepted as a full member of the Moukharbel group I had to prove myself both to him and to the others.'

'And how did Haddad propose you should do that?'

'By assassinating Joseph Edward Sieff.'

He said it so calmly. I have seen men show far greater concern when ordering a meal, yet here we sat discussing the planned murder of the President of the Marks and Spencer retail chain who was also, as Carlos was quick to point out, one of the leading Zionists in Great Britain. Before moving on to discuss this attack, the comments he had previously made gave rise, as so many of his comments did, to further questions.

In January 1973 a Palestinian commando unit, usually believed to be under the overall control of Mohammed Boudia, had attempted to attack Schönau Castle in Austria, the transit camp for Jews leaving Russia.

On September 28th the same year, two Palestinians seized a number of Jewish hostages on the train travelling from Bratislava in Czechoslovakia to the Austrian border town of Marchegg. In little more than twenty-four hours Bruno Kreisky's government capitulated and the Schönau camp was closed.

For the Palestinians it was an impressive victory. No blood had been shed and they had achieved a propaganda coup of enormous magnitude. The two Palestinians had called themselves 'The Eagles of Palestinian Revolution', a previously unknown group. It was generally accepted that the name masked the true identity of the group responsible. No-one subsequently claimed responsibility for the operation but a number of writers asserted that it was a Popular Front operation, controlled by Boudia until his death, and then by Carlos.

His remarks to me concerning how he came to work with the Paris-based group appeared to rule out any involvement by him. I began to question him on these events. Yet again his responses entirely contradicted all that had been written.

'What date was the Schönau operation?' he asked me.

'It began early on the morning of September 28th, 1973.'

'I did not return from Beirut until late September.'

'How late?'

He shrugged.

'About the 25th. Look, I have already told you my first job was to prove myself and that was the attack on Sieff.'

'Was the Schönau operation controlled by Moukharbel in Paris?'

'No. I think Moukharbel might have safe-housed them in Paris, but no more than that.'

'Then who was behind the Schönau attack?'

'The Syrians.'

'The Syrians!'

'The two men were members of Al Saiqa. The group that had tried and failed in January were also members of Al Saiqa, not Popular Front.'

'That first attempt has been attributed to Black September and also to Boudia. Later, when that unit was put on trial, the Austrians alleged they were members of Al Saiqa but . . .'

'They were members of Al Saiqa, so were the comrades who succeeded. The plan worked to perfection.'

'Yes, I know. The camp was closed.'

'That was only part of it. It got worldwide publicity. There were protests from Israel's friends and it distracted Golda Meir at just the right time. She first flew into a rage. Then she flew to Vienna.'

He chuckled at his own humour.

'Imagine. The Arabs are about to launch the October War on Israel and they trick the Prime Minister into flying to Austria to rant at Kreisky. Just a few days before the War and two Syrian Palestinians manage singlehandedly to distract the entire Israel nation.'

I almost regretted puncturing his good humour.

'But the Arabs still lost the war.'

'No! The Egyptians and the Americans stole certain victory from the Arabs.'

It was an interesting debating position but time pressed.

'You were about to tell me of your first attack, against Joseph Edward Sieff.'

'All Moukharbel would give me was an old gun and five bullets. He said that the French security raid on the Turks in Paris had left them without any more weapons.'

I asked Carlos to elaborate.

'The THKO [Turkish People's Liberation Army] were planning a major operation. Michel Moukharbel had given them a whole range of weapons – grenades, guns, radio transmitters, receivers. All he would give me in Paris was an old Beretta and five bullets.'

'What was the attack that the Turks were planning?'

'They were going to assassinate Henry Kissinger.'

'Why?'

'You're joking.'

'Not at all. In 1973 a group of men planning to kill the Secretary of State of the United States might have a variety of motives. Whether they were justified is of course another question altogether.'

'Kissinger and Sadat were the main reasons that the Arabs did not win the war. After the war Kissinger got busy involving himself in the peace negotiations. Whatever else was going to come out of those talks there certainly was not going to be anything to benefit the Arabs.'

'And was that the reason why they planned to kill him?'

'That was our reason for helping them. They wanted to wipe out the American domination of their country. *That* was their reason.'

Henry Kissinger flew to Europe to attend peace talks on the Middle East. The Turkish group had been advised that Kissinger was planning to come to Paris and then Geneva. They planned to launch a machine gun and grenade attack on him in one of those cities. Unknown to the group, they had been infiltrated. French Intelligence were aware of the Turkish plans.

On December 20th, 1973 a French DST team raided a villa at Villiers-sur-Marne on the outskirts of Paris. They arrested ten members of THKO and seized a vast array of equipment and arms.

At the time of the French raid Carlos was in London, stalking Haddad's chosen target, Edward Sieff.

The Sieff family had a long history of commitment not merely to Israel but to Zionism. Edward Sieff was Vice President of the Zionist Federation of Great Britain. Over many decades his family had donated many millions of pounds to the Zionist cause.

Carlos concluded what had been a fairly lengthy dissertation on the Sieff family with the observation, 'You must understand. I am not and never have been anti-Semitic. Anti-Zionist, yes. Anti-Jew, never.'

'I thought you might be going to say that some of your best friends are Jews.'

He tapped his aquiline nose. 'Many times in my life people have thought that I was Jewish.'

The irony clearly escaped him.

'Where were you staying in London at this time?'

'I had the use of three places. The family home at Phillimore Court, Nydia's flat and Angela's.'

Angela was Maria Angeles Otaola Baranca, a young Basque woman who had abbreviated her name to Angela

Otaola after coming to England in the early 1970s. The slim dark-haired Angela had a lively sense of humour. She had come to England to improve her command of the language and to sample some of the swinging capital. The Venezuelan was more than equal to satisfying both needs. Carlos told me that they had met only shortly before he made the attack on Sieff. Their friendship had soon developed into a love affair. Angela lived in Hereford Road, West London, in a small flat that served the Venezuelan in a variety of ways.

'My family were out of London at that time so I had full use of Phillimore Court. The Beretta and the bullets I kept at Angela's. The week after Christmas '73 I was ready. Because I had so little ammunition I had not been able to test the gun. I had kept my eye in with some target practice at my shooting club. I drove in the family car to North London where Sieff lived. I knew the odds were against me. No back-up man as driver. No hand grenades. Just one gun and five bullets.'

'You also had the element of surprise against an unarmed man.'

'Surprise yes, but I did not know whether he was armed or had armed guards. I had previously kept watch on the house and did not see any security, but there might have been guards in the house. At this time the British police often gave armed protection to Zionists. I rang Sieff's doorbell just before seven in the evening. The street was quiet. His servant opened the door, I pointed the gun at him and said, "Take me to your master." At the top of the stairs a woman opened a door, then seeing me quickly slammed it. I had to act quickly. Sieff was in the bathroom. The servant knocked on the door. When Sieff unlocked it I pushed the servant away as the door opened. With my gun almost touching Sieff's face I fired. The shot hit him just below the nose. I tried to fire two more shots but the damn bullets would not fire. Three shots would have killed him for sure. I thought I heard someone talking on a phone. I had to get out of there. I ran back down the stairs and out of the house. I had left my car parked directly outside. I drove into Regent's Park and stopped the car. I had worn a coat with a hood on it for the attack so I took it off and threw it into the back of the car. Then I drove home.'

'Back to Phillimore Court?'

'No, first I went to Angela's to hide the gun. Then I went to Phillimore Court.'

'How did you feel during the attack?'

'My mind was racing. I was very nervous. Once I had stopped the car outside Sieff's house there was no more time for feelings, only action. I moved very fast. It was all over in a minute. Afterwards I felt angry.'

'Angry?'

'Yes. If Moukharbel had given me the things I had asked for then there is no doubt that Sieff would have died. You know he survived?'

'Yes. It was called a miraculous survival. Apparently his teeth deflected the bullet.'

Carlos almost snorted. 'It was incredible that he survived, even though I could only get one shot off.'

From apparently nowhere Carlos produced a gun. It lay in the palm of his hand pointing towards me.

'This is a Makarov. If I had had one of these on that evening Sieff would be dead now.'

'He is. He died in 1982.'

His response to this news was extraordinary. For a man who knew so much about Edward Sieff it was curious that news of his death was a revelation. His face wreathed in smiles. He placed the gun on the table between us and leapt to his feet calling out in Arabic. He moved to the door and, opening it, continued to call out and chatter excitedly. An Arab servant appeared and then vanished again. The group of men that had been present when I had arrived began to appear. Throughout this my eyes were being drawn to the gun on the table.

Carlos was apparently telling his associates of the news I had given him. The manservant reappeared carrying a tray with glasses and a bottle of Dom Perignon. By now the room was crowded. The bottle was opened and the glasses filled. Carlos proposed a toast and the assembled company drank to whatever the man had said. One turned and stared at me. I was still sitting exactly where I had been before this had begun. The man took a step towards me and spoke with a very heavy Arab accent.

'Why you no drink?'

I felt an enormous surge of anger. Taking off my glasses and placing them next to the Makarov I stood up. With an effort I controlled myself as I spoke.

'Firstly, I don't drink, and secondly I have no desire to join your private party.'

While he was attempting to make sense of that Carlos swung around to the man. He muttered something in Arabic and his companion, still staring hard at me, moved back to the group.

'He does not drink. You heard him.'

Then Carlos said to me, 'I will not be long. You have brought me such good news. I have to celebrate. One less Zionist is always cause for celebration.'

'Your gun. You've forgotten your gun.'

He nodded and took it from the table. He pulled back the jacket of his grey suit and I saw for the first time the shoulder harness that he was wearing. In a moment harness and gun vanished and the jacket was rebuttoned around an ample stomach.

Eventually Carlos cleared the room and sat down again.

'I'm sorry for interrupting our conversation. I had to share the good news with my comrades. You know I planned another attack on Sieff, in January 1974. I had by then got what I needed from Michel Moukharbel – the correct guns and many other things – but Sieff and his family had gone to Bermuda. By the time he returned I was busy with new operations.'

'Obviously Haddad's response to the attack on Edward Sieff was, from your point of view, a good one?'

'He was very pleased. The Popular Front in Beirut claimed the credit for the attack, which had been agreed.

It was useful, it kept attention away from what I and others were doing on behalf of Wadi Haddad.'

'On behalf of Wadi Haddad.' It certainly was not on behalf of Dr George Habash's section of the Popular Front. Habash had broken with Haddad in 1972. The continuous hijackings, particularly when the end game was money, did not fit with Habash's revolutionary philosophy. The violence and the concept of terror that Haddad was now applying caused a permanent break between the two former doctors of medicine. It is significant that Carlos stayed with the Haddad group: the corruption of his youthful revolutionary ideas was now well on the way to completion. The issues, aims and aspirations would grow ever murkier.

'What did you do next?'

'Among the things I brought back from Paris in January 1974 were some radio transmitters and a quantity of plastic explosives.'

'Had you been trained to use plastic?'

'Yes, in the Middle East. These were just plastic grenades.'

'Had your mother and brothers returned from their Christmas holidays by now?'

'Yes, but I kept the weapons and the other things at one of my secret houses.'

'When you talk of secret houses, what exactly do you mean?'

'Angela's or Nydia's. Later there were of course other secret houses. Officially, when I was in London, I lived with my mother.'

'How much did these two women know of your activities?'

'They knew some. Nydia more than Angela. In fact Nydia was a good member of our group. I took her to Paris before the attack on Sieff and introduced her to Moukharbel. She agreed to give us whatever help we asked for. It is useful to have a number of women in a foreign city.'

'Yes, Mohammed Boudia believed that too.'

He nodded in agreement.

'The next target was the Israeli Zionist Bank in the City of London. The Bank Hapoalim. This was towards the end of January 1974.'

'Who had selected the target?'

'I had suggested it. Wadi Haddad approved. He informed Michel who informed me. I simply put one of the plastic grenades into a parcel, opened the doors and threw it in the direction of the cashier's desk, but the door came back and hit my arm as I was about to throw the package, deflecting my aim. The bomb slipped along the floor before exploding. No-one was killed but part of the bank was destroyed. There was very good coverage in the newspapers and on television.'

An actor responding to the reviews of his latest performance.

'Weren't you concerned about getting caught in the middle of the City in broad daylight?'

'No. I move quickly on an operation.' (He patted his stomach.) 'I was thinner then, and fitter. Also, I had the car parked outside the bank. In the car I had the radio transmitter. After the attack, when I was driving back to Kensington, I listened on the police frequencies. I knew everything they were doing.'

'You had now committed two attacks. On both of them you were seen. A description of you was issued which matched your appearance perfectly at the time. Did that worry you?'

'Not at all. The police said they were looking for an Arab. Look, in 1971 when they interrogated me at my home in Chelsea, they found a false passport and did nothing. Now they were looking for an Arab. It was obvious that the police had made no connection between their interrogation of me in 1971 and the attacks on Sieff and the Bank.'

'How would you have felt if any of the bank employees had been seriously injured or killed?'

He shrugged. 'If someone works in a Zionist bank, that is a risk they must take.'

'Just like that?'

'Yes. The war against the Zionist should not be confined to Israel. Israel is largely sustained by the Zionists who would not dream of living there. It is how they get rid of their guilt.'

Having demonstrated that guilt did not feature heavily in his own emotions, Carlos continued his story. He told me that in early February he flew to Beirut. Michel Moukharbel joined him out there and they discussed with Haddad their next battle campaigns.

Also joining them in the Lebanon were members of the Japanese Red Army. They had just successfully attacked the Shell oil refineries in Singapore. Wadi Haddad believed that it added to Western paranoia if operations such as this, during which the Japanese blew up 15 oil storage tanks, were claimed as joint attacks by the PFLP and the JRA. The reality, Carlos explained, was that the Japanese had not functioned as a separate fighting entity since early 1972. From then on they were controlled by Haddad's section of the Popular Front. The more nationalities that were at his disposal, the easier it became for Haddad to plan more and more international attacks.

Moukharbel was given his next targets – three strongly pro-Israel newspaper offices in Paris. This time the attacks would be claimed in the new name for the Paris group, Commando Boudia.

Moukharbel augmented the team for these attacks with men and women already living in Paris. All were from the far left and the group included disaffected Corsicans, Algerians and French who, without the nationalistic aspirations of their comrades, still felt deeply enough about the Middle East problem to take the law into their own hands.

The targets were the monthly magazine *L'Arche,* the weekly *Minute* and the daily newspaper *L'Aurore.* The French colleagues who were assisting in the multiple attack asked if ORTF, a television and radio station, could be added to the list. Moukharbel agreed.

For Carlos the pace was quickening. Like a juggler who begins with the easy task of keeping two objects in the air and then adds more and more, the degree of skill required grew ever greater. It was apparent from his remarks that by March 1974, when he and Moukharbel returned from their briefings in Aden and Beirut, Carlos considered he had earned the right to be head of the Paris operation.

It was equally apparent that Haddad, Moukharbel and others disagreed. One botched assassination followed by an inept bomb attack on a bank did not, in the eyes of Wadi Haddad, put Carlos in the first division of violent action. This was an element of his relationship with Moukharbel that was to prove a constant cause of friction, with ultimately fatal results.

Bucking for leadership was just one of the things that preoccupied Carlos. There was the problem of planning the multiple bombing in Paris, the problem of getting guns and explosives into Paris, the same problem of getting them into London, the problem of keeping a growing number of mistresses relatively happy. Then, in April, Carlos told me, he had another problem to handle. His father had arrived in London from Caracas. Tipped off by his mother, he dutifully telephoned the Phillimore Court apartment and affected great surprise when he discovered his father was there.

He immediately flew to London and for fifteen days played the role of the obedient son. I questioned him closely about this. He assured me that the first time his father was made aware of the truth was in July 1975, by which time the entire world knew. His brother Lenin and his mother Elba were aware that he had gone to the Middle East after his expulsion from Patrice Lumumba University, but they knew nothing else.

With his father safely on the plane back to Venezuela, Carlos hurried back to his other problems in Paris.

In July a Japanese member of the Haddad group, Takamoto Takahashi, brought a vast array of weapons through French Customs. Moukharbel and Carlos got to work. Arms were moved to Geneva. Yet more arms

93

were stored at La Galerie Lignel, an art gallery in the very exclusive rue de Verneuil. The gallery was owned by Jean-Charles Lignel, a Frenchman born in Algiers, son of a wealthy and politically powerful family largely based in Lyons. Unknown to him, the manager was a member of Commando Boudia. Like Carlos, he has been given many a name and many a nationality. His real name is Antonio Expedito Carvalho Pereira; his nationality, Brazilian.

The plan for the multiple bombing in Paris began to take shape. The various elements were drawn together. Moukharbel decreed that the attacks should take place on August 3rd, 1974.

Just a few days before the planned attack Commando Boudia was presented with another problem. On the evening of July 26th, another Japanese member of Haddad's group arrived at Orly Airport from Beirut. The first mistake that the man who would later be known as Suzuki Furuya had made was to fly direct from Beirut to Paris. For many years Haddad had made it a strict rule that no-one ever went directly from Beirut to their final destination. Anyone, let alone an individual bent on the kind of activities in which the Popular Front indulged, was liable to be extensively searched and questioned coming from Beirut. Furuya was either very stupid or arrogant or both.

A Japanese traveller arriving from Beirut with only hand luggage was demonstrably inviting interrogation. He duly got it. Opening the executive black and chrome briefcase to the Customs officer he displayed an Aladdin's cave. The man's real name was Yoshiaki Yamada, the subsequent confusion concerning his true identity undoubtedly rose from what was in his small black case. There was an American passport that stated he was Furuya, and a Taiwanese passport that assured the reader the bearer's name was Suzuki. There was a third false passport, this time Japanese, that declared that he was Furuya again. Digging deeper, the Customs officer found a false compartment concealing 10,000 dollars. Like the passports, they were counterfeit. Yamada was also carrying in the case a number of coded messages written on rice paper, one of which, subsequently decoded by the Japanese Ambassador to Paris, read: 'Little Miss Full Moon. I am ill with desire for you. Let me embrace your beautiful body again. Your love slave, Suzuki'!

Yamada's arrest was kept secret for a number of days. French security established that 'Little Miss Full Moon' was a salesgirl called Mariko Yamamoto who worked in the Japanese shop in Avenue L'Opéra. She was not only a salesgirl, she was also a member of the Japanese Red Army, her principal function being to act as letterbox for members of the Red Army wishing to contact other elements of Haddad's Paris section.

The DST kept watch on her workplace and her apartment. Within a week ten members of the Red Army had been arrested. Two were subsequently released, having convinced the French security officers that they believed the people who had been holding meetings in their homes were art students.

The French authorities asked the other eight where they would like to go. The leader of the Red Army in Paris, Takamoto, who earlier that month had brought through French Customs enough arms and ammunition to start a small war, said that although his final destination would be Poland, he would like to be flown to Amsterdam. Within a few weeks accommodating Takamoto's wishes would prove to be highly embarrassing for French security.

The DST announced that they had arrested every single Paris-based member of the Red Army. This must have come as particularly pleasing news to the twenty-three Red Army members hidden in Paris by Moukharbel and Carlos. Throughout this entire episode, French security continued to remain ignorant of any links between the Japanese Red Army and the Popular Front, who meanwhile were engaged in the count-down to their multiple bombing.

It has been written that the cars they used for this operation were stolen. I asked Carlos about this.

'The four cars were hired from a Paris hire car

company. We hired two Estafettes and two Renaults. I hired them myself using a false Italian driving licence. I paid with a blank postal cheque.'

'And how do you transform a Renault or an Estafette into a bomb?'

'All you require is a bottle of camping gas, a kilo of explosive and an alarm clock. If the gas bottle is open just before you leave the car it will fill the car, which of course you will have carefully sealed. At the required moment – in the case of the operation we are discussing, that was two am – the alarm will ignite the explosive, and bang! We had chosen the time carefully to ensure that all the workers in the buildings would have gone. We did not want to kill any of the workers.'

'You felt differently at the time of the bank bombing in London.'

'I did not. Moukharbel did. The timing in Paris was his decision.'

'Did you agree with it?'

'Yes. To place four car bombs outside such buildings in the heart of Paris during working hours, particularly the State Television, which is well guarded, would have been very dangerous for us.'

'It might also be extremely unhealthy for any pedestrians.'

'The one we parked outside the TV station failed to blow up. The alarm clock stopped. The other three were completely successful. The impact of that attack was a very big one.'

'Yes, I'm sure it was, but you could have killed passersby.'

'And what could the Israelis have killed when they blew up Mohammed Boudia at eleven in the morning?'

We moved on to discuss the problems that the arrest of the careless Japanese courier, Yamada, posed. Commando Boudia were determined to get him released. Wadi Haddad sent word that the release of Yamada was to be given maximum priority. He also gave the green light for two attacks that Moukharbel had suggested in

West Germany, one on a factory in Mannheim, the other on the Israeli Government Travel Office in Frankfurt. Both attacks were carried out at night-time during the last week of August by members of the German Revolutionary cells acting in liaison with Commando Boudia in Paris.

Carlos, meanwhile, was considering the problem of freeing Yamada. He was to lead the operation, as he had the multiple car bombing. The student of terror was graduating rapidly, but no matter how proficient he became at terrifying, killing or maiming he would never lead Commando Boudia while Moukharbel was alive. And since it was another rigid rule of Haddad's that no group leader ever took part in an operation, it was more than likely, given the increasing risks Carlos was obliged to take, that he would never live long enough to obtain promotion to group leader.

The two men considered various solutions to the problem of Yamada. It was decided that they should attack a French embassy in Europe, hold the ambassador hostage and demand the release of Yamada. In the event of the French government proving obdurate it was agreed that a second operation should be planned.

'We studied a number of embassies. We also surveyed various ambassadorial residences and followed the ambassadors to learn their movements. This was going on throughout August. We finally decided upon the French Ambassador at The Hague.'

'What were some of the others that you considered?'

'The French embassies in England, Italy and Germany were three I remember, there were several others.'

'What made you decide on The Hague?'

'If we needed to bring additional pressure on the French government it was essential that any secondary action should take place in Paris, to achieve maximum impact. Getting back quickly from London might present a problem, and the government in England might be stubborn. They might also close the airports and ports. The Italians might go raving mad and storm the French Embassy in

Rome and cause a bloodbath. The Germans would be on the alert after the bombings at the end of August. The Dutch have always been a reasonable people and, since there had not at that time been any major operation in Holland, it would take them completely by surprise.'

He had ticked off the various countries like someone in a supermarket checking that they had bought all their provisions for the weekend. The Japanese Red Army chose three of their number to carry out the actual attack, leaving Carlos free if there was a need for secondary action. At this point a further complication arose. Yet again it concerned the Japanese and false passports.

On August the 15th, a number of Japanese of Korean nationality launched an assassination attempt on South Korea's President Park. At first their guns malfunctioned. By the time they began to fire, President Park had ducked behind a large table on the rostrum and his wife received the bullets intended for him. She was dead on arrival at hospital.

The assassination squad was arrested and police investigators discovered that they were using false passports. One of the Red Army members that Moukharbel and Carlos were hiding in Paris was using an identical false passport supplied by Wadi Haddad. DST action in Paris alerted Moukharbel. With the exception of the three Japanese commandos who were to take part in the Embassy attack he quickly moved the remainder to Zurich. This transference to Switzerland took place on September 3rd, 1974.

On Thursday Carlos, the Brazilian Antonio Pereira and two of the Japanese hit squad travelled by train from Paris. Pereira travelled separately carrying the M26 grenades and the weapons that were to be used during the Embassy attack. Neither French nor Dutch Customs detected the weapons and, late the same day, the entire group met at a hotel in Amsterdam. Among them, courtesy of the French government, was Takamoto.

On Friday, leaving Pereira to look after two of the Japanese team, Carlos and Takamoto, the Japanese leader, drove in a car hired by Pereira to the French Embassy at The Hague. They monitored the arrival of the French Ambassador, Jacques Senard, and his subsequent departure at lunchtime. The plan was for Takamoto to return to Amsterdam, collect the other members of his team and the armaments and return immediately to the French Embassy. They would then be in place to launch the attack any time after one-thirty when the Ambassador returned from lunch. He would be arrested at gunpoint, marched into his own Embassy and negotiations with both Dutch and French governments could begin.

The plan relied on very precise timing. It was crucial that the Japanese hit team should be in place well before the Ambassador's return. Initial reconnaissance had established that the French Embassy was very close to the United States Embassy. This presented a problem that concerned Carlos and the Japanese: the French might or might not have armed guards at their Embassy, the Americans most certainly would.

Speed would be their greatest weapon, that and the element of surprise. Observation indicated no unusual activity within the environs of the French Embassy.

It was at this point in his story that Carlos revealed the first hitch in the plan.

'At one o'clock I was waiting outside the French Embassy. At half past four I was still there waiting.'

'What had happened to the Japanese?'

'They got lost. Then the hire car broke down.'

'What about the Brazilian, Antonio Pereira?'

'During the afternoon I telephoned him from a call box many times. He was out.'

No link man. This ensured that Carlos, the overall commando leader of this particular operation, was left dangerously exposed.

'By half past four in the afternoon the American Embassy guards were taking an interest in me. I had to move away from the area.'

Shortly after Carlos had moved away to escape the attention of the American guards, the Japanese finally arrived. Finding Carlos gone they promptly went into action. The ambassador's chauffeur was hauled from his car at gunpoint and marched towards the Embassy doors. At exactly that moment a police car chanced to be passing. Within moments a gun battle developed at the entrance to the Embassy. The shots brought Carlos hurrying back to the scene.

'I heard police sirens. People were running towards the Embassy. As I approached I heard gunfire from inside the building. Then a policewoman was carried out. I stayed around, mingling with the crowd until the police cleared the entire area. Then I got back on the phone and tried to talk to our Japanese comrades inside the Embassy, but by then the police had cut all the lines.'

When the hit squad had burst into the Embassy the Ambassador, Count Jacques Senard, was in the middle of a meeting with executives of the French oil company Total, consequently the Japanese found that they had eleven hostages. Three hours after the siege had begun they told the Dutch police what they wanted in exchange for the eleven lives they held in the palms of their hands. They demanded that their colleague Yamada be released from prison and brought to the Embassy. They also demanded that a Boeing plane with two pilots and a full tank of fuel should be put at their disposal at Amsterdam's Schiphol airport. Later in the evening they made a further demand – one million dollars, cash.

The Japanese Red Army members added a chilling postscript: 'If at three o'clock in the morning our demands are not met, the hostages will be executed at regular intervals. Every physical approach to the building will be considered as an aggressive act.'

Inside the Embassy the three Japanese confined themselves and their eleven hostages in the Ambassador's office on the fourth floor. Within hours the room of just 25 square metres smelt like a sewer. Their captors refused to let anyone leave the room or to allow chemical toilets to be sent into the building. A wastepaper basket served as a communal toilet. During the initial shoot-out one of the Japanese team had been hit in the arm. As the hours ticked by and the room became increasingly foul, his wound turned septic. While they waited for the Dutch and French governments to respond to their demands the Japanese passed the time in a variety of ways which included using a portrait of the late President Pompidou for target practice and firing a shot between the legs of Ambassador Senard.

Senard demonstrated extraordinary savoir faire throughout the entire ordeal. He displayed not only an elegant composure and great courage, but considerable style. To help pass the time he tore embassy stationery into small pieces and made them into an improvized pack of playing cards. He then proceeded to set a wide range of bridge problems to the gathering, much to the bemusement of his three Japanese guests who appeared to be long on a philosophy of death and rather short on a philosophy of life.

At first the Japanese commandos had indicated they planned to fly to Paris, where undoubtedly further demands intended to embarrass the French government would be made. The French pre-empted that strategy by rushing through the necessary legal paperwork enabling them to remove Yamada from French soil. Escorted by twenty-four members of the Brigade Anti-Commando, a counter insurgency unit with a killer reputation, he was flown to Amsterdam on an air force Mystère 20. Also on the plane was the Director of the Police Judicière of Paris, Jean Ducret.

At Schiphol Yamada was put into direct radio telephone link with his colleagues inside the Embassy. In him the Japanese clearly had their own version of the very cool Ambassador Senard. Yamada was told by his French guards that if anyone inside the Embassy was shot he would certainly be killed. He calmly related this information to the hit team, constantly referring to himself in the third person. His colleagues were equally calm and asked for his opinion as to where they should first shoot the Ambassador. Hand, arm, leg or foot?

The French, insisting that the Mystère jet was French territory, refused to hand over Yamada to the Dutch. In Paris the Minister of the Interior, Michel Poniatowski, a man with a reputation for bombastic intransigence, was discovering that the Dutch were disinclined to be impressed with a French Minister who was clearly playing to an electoral gallery. His prime concern was to be seen taking a hard line. The Dutch considered the top priority to be to prevent any loss of life. Suddenly the eleven hostages, Yamada and his three colleagues were a political issue between the two nations.

With the Japanese Ambassador negotiating on behalf of the Dutch government with three of his country-men, it became three nations. With the nearby American Embassy serving as a forward command post for the Dutch, it became four.

The French refused to agree to the demand for two French pilots. They wanted all the hostages released before they would yield up Yamada. It was unaccept-able to the Japanese hit team.

The Dutch made a counter offer at ten o'clock on Saturday morning. They would put a KLM plane and Dutch pilots at the disposal of the Red Army. In return they insisted that no hostages and no weapons were to leave the country. This was also unacceptable to the Japanese.

By Saturday evening, with the Embassy siege into its second day, another player in this deadly game was con-templating taking the field. His name was Carlos: his venue, Paris.

'On Saturday evening I started thinking about the sec-ondary operation to support the Japanese. There were two problems. I had to warn them not to leave the Embassy during the night, no matter what proposals were made to them. It would be far too dangerous. I smelt a trap.'

'And what was the second problem?'

'I needed bombs and weapons to carry out the second action.'

'Surely you had access to the enormous quantity that

102

the Japanese had brought into France in July?'

'No. I was unable to make contact with the various people who controlled the safe houses. It was the weekend.'

'But you've told me that before the operation in The Hague you had considered the likelihood of the need for a second action?'

'I know, but no details had been worked out. Then on Sunday morning the Dutch President indicated that there were very serious disagreements between his government and the French. He said that the French would take the responsibility for all that happened, he also indicated that diplomatic relations between his country and France were under a very severe strain because of the Embassy situation.'

'The comment about the French having to take responsibility. What did you understand by that?'

'That the French wanted to storm the Embassy with their Brigade anti-Commando. They were keeping their prisoner on the plane. They were refusing to send a Boeing 707 to Holland to fly our comrades to the Middle East. It all pointed that way. They were getting ready for a bloodbath. Moukharbel and I could not understand why the Japanese did not start killing their hostages.'

'Is that what you would have done if you had been inside that Embassy that weekend?'

'Of course.'

'But the French threatened to kill Yamada if the Japanese had killed any of their hostages.'

'I am aware of that, but they would not have dared to kill him in cold blood. There would have been an international uproar.'

'Do I understand you? It is perfectly all right for the Japanese to kill their prisoners but unacceptable for the French to do the same?'

'No, no, no. What I am saying is that the French would not have dared to because how many bombs would follow such an action? How many French citizens would die because they had killed one Japanese? Not in the course of storming the Embassy, but in cold blood.'

'When did you decide on the second operation?'

'At two o'clock on Sunday afternoon. It was obvious that the Embassy operation was going to fail. It was equally obvious that another "Munich" was going to happen. A massacre at the Embassy.'

'So to prevent that you decided there should be a massacre in Paris?'

'Yes. And it had to be done immediately. I would like to have got a machine gun and some plastic bombs but as I have said that was impossible at the weekend. All we had was my own gun and two hand grenades.'

'What about Moukharbel?'

'He never carried arms. I decided that the operation should be carried out Algerian style. Sudden terror. Two hand grenades in a café in the middle of Paris. Moukharbel persuaded me to throw just one.'

'To limit the injuries?'

'To ensure I had a second for another attack if it was needed.'

'And the café you decided to attack was Le Drugstore?'

'Yes.'

In the mid 1970s Le Drugstore was one of *the* places to go on a Sunday afternoon. A complex of shops with an excess of chrome and glass, it was considered trendy and very chic by its predominantly young regular clientele.

Shortly after 5 pm Le Drugstore was doing excellent business. The café on the first floor was crowded. The tables were full, with an overflow leaning on the brass balustrade that ran around the area, looking down on the crowd below queuing at the news kiosk, window shopping.

Entering the Drugstore from Boulevard St Germain, Carlos mixed with the crowd. Moments later he climbed the stairs to the first floor and, approaching the brass rail, pulled the pin from an M26 hand grenade, then hurled it into the crowd below. In the four seconds before it exploded he was down the stairs and back on the street.

An M26 hand grenade has what its accompanying technical literature describes as 'a casualty zone of fifty feet'.

It was indeed as Carlos described it to me, 'an attack Algerian style'. Terror from nowhere.

The sound as the grenade exploded in the confined space was deafening. Metal and steel fragments and shattered glass flew in every direction. Two died, more than thirty were injured.

The French pop singer Jean-Jacques Debout narrowly escaped injury. A few minutes before the attack he had entered the Drugstore to buy cigarettes. Seeing a long queue, he decided to try another kiosk. He strolled out of the shopping complex moments before the grenade exploded.

'A young child covered in blood ran outside and fell onto the pavement. I followed him to offer help. Another small child had a hand blown off. There were bodies strewn all over the place. At the foot of the stairs. Under the tables, and yet more looking as though they were cut in two lying on the devastated counters. Everywhere blood and fragments of glass.'

Various survivors gave the police descriptions of the unknown assailant. 'A young man, twenty-five to thirty years old. Long hair. Well dressed. European type.' The police added a remarkable observation of their own. 'The description clearly indicates that this is not a fanatic.'

When Carlos had reached the point in his account where he had vanished into Boulevard St Germain, I felt compelled to interrupt him.

'From various remarks that you have made to me I form the impression that you are very fond of children?'

'Yes, that is so. I like other people's children very much. One of my own children is somewhere in Cuba. I miss her a lot.'

'One? You have others?'

'Yes,' he replied. 'But no questions on that subject.'

'Yet, despite this great fondness for children you brought suffering to a number of them that afternoon in Paris. How do you justify that? How do you feel about that?'

'This was war. In war sometimes such things happen. You know that. It does not make them right or wrong. They just happen. What is the difference between an Israeli pilot dropping bombs on a school in Lebanon and what I did in the Drugstore?'

'I think there might be a number of differences but the one that particularly concerns me is that you chose that specific target on that day and, having chosen it, you saw your victims virtually face to face. What went through your mind in those moments on the first floor of the Drugstore before you threw that grenade?'

He considered the question and its implications for a moment then, with a partial shrug, palms extended upwards, said, 'At moments like that, you do not think, you act.'

'And afterwards?'

'Afterwards we contacted the Press agencies, stating that the attack had been carried out by the Japanese Red Army to resolve the situation at The Hague. To press home the point Moukharbel left a number of empty grenade boxes in certain locations in Paris to persuade the Government we had many weapons. Then we told them where the boxes were and said, "Next time a cinema."'

'And would you have been prepared to throw that last grenade into a crowded cinema?'

'Of course. There is no point in making empty threats.'

'But what of the innocent people? Ordinary people without power or influence?'

He pointed a finger at me. 'Understand this, Mr Yallop. These ordinary people have great power. Much influence. It manifests in what is called public opinion. They may not care about the Palestinians. They certainly do not care about some members of the Red Army. But throw a grenade among them and they care very much.'

'Eventually both the Dutch and the French governments capitulated. Did that end of the affair justify the means used to attain it?'

'Of course.'

I had been searching for a point of connection. Trying to find a position that was common to both of us with regard to this entire episode. I had failed to find it.

Carlos's subsequent comments indicated that the path to a 'successful conclusion' was not quite so straight. Roundly abusing the French government of the time, led by Prime Minister Chirac, he accused them of cynical suppression of the truth. Having decided to do a deal, Carlos said, Chirac and his colleagues went to great lengths to ensure that the French public did not link the events at the Drugstore with those at The Hague.

When the Chief Police Commissioner of Paris, Jean Paolini, was asked about the telephone threats and a possible connection with events at The Hague, he said, 'There is nothing to suggest that a link be made between these two events.'

To Carlos this could only mean that the French government was prepared to play God with the lives of ordinary Parisians – which is, of course, something that he was already doing. He had dropped the safety pin from the M26 hand grenade at the Drugstore and within hours French security had identified it. In view of the fact that they had seized a quantity of these grenades the previous December when raiding the villa where the Turkish People's Liberation Army were based, it would have been self-evident that whoever had thrown the grenade was part of a much larger organization than fringe activism. By September 1974, French Intelligence had established that the grenades were part of a large batch stolen from an American base in West Germany. After the siege at the French Embassy was over, further identical M26 grenades, left by the Japanese Red Army, were also found. The links were irrefutable. The French government again suppressed this information.

The French public were not the only ones to be ill-informed. If Moukharbel's intelligence-gathering had been even half way efficient, he and Carlos would have learned that, at the time they launched the attack at The Hague, the French authorities were planning to expel Yamada from France within a few weeks. All he could be charged with was issuing false documents and carrying counterfeit money. Having squeezed as much information out of him as they could, the French had decided to get him out of the country to avoid precisely the kind of attacks that were launched to secure his freedom. Even by Carlos's rationale both attacks were unnecessary.

At almost precisely the same time as the Commissioner of the Paris police was reassuring the French public, his Government, fully aware of the implications of the attack on the Drugstore, had bowed to the request from the Red Army team in the Embassy and despatched a Boeing 707 to Holland. They had also agreed to the demand that all the documents discovered in Yamada's case should be handed over. They were, of course, photocopied, but they would enable the Red Army to discover just how much of their Paris operation had been penetrated.

On the two further demands, one million dollars cash and the desire of the Red Army to take some of their hostages on the Boeing for release once they had landed at a safe haven, the French remained obdurate. Yamada would only be handed over in exchange for all the hostages and the French were not prepared to pay a cent.

The negotiations continued into Tuesday. The Dutch government haggled the amount down to $300,000. Yamada checked it to ensure that it was not counterfeit and, speaking in perfect French for the first time since his arrest, remarked, 'I know all about counterfeit money.'

The hostages were finally exchanged for Yamada on Tuesday and a volunteer crew of three flew out of Holland with the Red Army members, including Yamada. They planned to join Wadi Haddad in South Yemen, but the plane was refused permission to land. Eventually the Syrians accepted the plane and confiscated the $300,000: heroic actions for the Palestinian cause were acceptable, common criminality was not. The money was handed over to the French

Ambassador and eventually found its way back to Holland.[1]

An ironic postscript to the kidnapping was added by one of the Dutch team appointed by Prime Minister Den Uyl. 'The negotiations with the French were more difficult than with the Japanese.'

According to Carlos one of the direct results of the attacks at The Hague and in Paris in September 1974 was to eliminate from Moukharbel's resources the ability to call upon Red Army members who had embraced the Palestinian cause. Their numbers had never been great, thirty activists at the most. After The Hague they became marked men and women. The anonymity of the Oriental features that had once worked so effectively for Haddad became a liability.

Even Latin American elements of Moukharbel's organization began to feel the effect of increased French vigilance. Several Brazilians were expelled, but the security forces never got their hands on the prize catch, Antonio Expedito Carvalho Pereira. Carlos refused to be drawn about this man. When I asked him for details he laughed.

'I will just tell you that Antonio Pereira vanished. If you want to know how then ask the DST. I think perhaps they will be too embarrassed to tell you.'

Recalling the general situation in Europe at that time Carlos remarked, 'It was hard. Very hard. The work that we were doing needed many qualities. Men had to be brave. They had to be fit. They needed many skills and a great deal of experience. The organization in Paris needed to be improved. I made many recommendations to the Old Man [Wadi Haddad].'

'Such as?'

'Such as the need for highly trained soldiers. For greater efficiency. More money and weapons.'

---

[1] The French government returned only $200,000 to the Dutch. They kept the remaining $100,000, insisting that this was to cover handling costs.

Apart from visiting Haddad in South Yemen during the autumn of 1974 Carlos spent the closing months of that year in London and Paris. There were the many friends and acquaintances who knew nothing of his dangerous other life. In London there was an adoring mother, Elba Maria, and his two brothers Vladimir and Lenin, who knew a little. There was Angela Otaola who knew more. There was Nydia who knew a lot. There was the diplomatic circuit that Carlos dropped in and out of with ease, which knew nothing at all.

Mohammed Boudia's exploits both in and out of the boudoir had created a legend that obviously impressed and influenced Carlos. His attempts to emulate the Algerian in all fields of activity lacked Boudia's certain style but the young Venezuelan certainly scored high for endeavour and enthusiasm. None of the women in his life had come to Europe seeking revolutionary adventure. Their various Grand European Tours were designed to acquire further education whilst pursuing the maximum amount of fun. For a number of them Carlos represented an opportunity for interesting diversion – from teaching Spanish in darkest Surrey and studying for a degree in social administration at the London School of Economics for Nydia Tobon; from work as assistant manager at Bistro 17 in West London for Angela Otaola.

In Paris, Boudia would certainly have approved of both the quantity and the quality of the women that his would-be successor kept entertained. There was the refined young lady from Colombia, Amparo Silva Masmela. Amparo's demure exterior masked a young woman in her early twenties who loved not wisely but too often. Sometimes brunette, sometimes blonde, she changed her men as frequently as her hair style but the tenacious Carlos held a special place in her affections. Arriving in Paris late in 1974 to study political economics, she initially resided with the Sisters of the Assumption at a hostel in the 16th Arrondissement. After meeting Carlos her lifestyle changed dramatically. She obtained employment in the correspondence department of Lloyds

Bank on the Boulevard des Capucines and took out a lease on an apartment at 11 rue Amélie, a few doors down from the local police station and convenient for the Air France terminal at Les Invalides. Under the bed that she frequently shared with Carlos were enough plastic explosives, hand grenades and automatic weapons to start a small war.

Over in number nine rue Toullier there was the Venezuelan, Nancy Sanchez, who studied anthropology at the Sorbonne by day and vied with her flat mate, yet another Venezuelan, Maria Teresa Lara, for Carlos's favours and attentions during the nights. Both knew a lot about the reality behind this happy-go-lucky wealthy businessman from Peru called Carlos Martinez.

The rue Toullier flat in the Latin Quarter was very typical of the area. Student friends dropped in to take a bath or share a bottle of red wine while they put the world to rights. There were frequent parties and plenty of music and casual relationships. It was obviously an atmosphere that appealed to the hedonist in Carlos. In terms of a safe house it would be the last place on earth to choose. There was little privacy and the constant possibility of police visits in response to complaints about noisy parties.

Other visitors to the rue Toullier flat were fellow Venezuelan students Albaida Salazar and Leyma Gonzales Duque, Cuban boyfriends from the Embassy and the South African-born Angela Armstrong. Within months this mini United Nations would have cause to regret ever having met Carlos.

Laced into this potentially lethal mix of a part-social, part-business milieu were the other darker elements of this man. There was his superior, Michel Moukharbel, pulling the various strands of Haddad's European cell together. Through Moukharbel Carlos developed contacts with other people/organizations that owed allegiance at least in part to Haddad and through him to the Palestinian cause, or rather Haddad's vision of that cause.

These contacts included Cuban Intelligence. I was particularly interested in the Cubans.

'You must be aware that those who insist that you are or were a KGB agent point to your involvement with Cuban Intelligence in Paris. They argue that the Cuban DGI is controlled by the KGB.'

'The Cubans are even more inefficient than the Palestinians. I met these Cubans at Nancy's flat. They were chasing the women. Look, it was obvious to me that they were Cuban Intelligence. The only thing I wanted from them was news of Sonia and my daughter. They could not even get that for me. I have never worked with or for the Cubans.'

'You must be aware that after the rue Toullier affair France expelled a number of Cuban diplomats?'

He nodded.

'Poniatowski had to do something. The Cubans were a perfect . . .'

He groped for a word.

'Scapegoat?'

'Exactly. They were perfect scapegoats. What happened at the rue Toullier was a big scandal for the French. Throwing out a few Cubans was perfect. It distracted from the stupidity of the DST.'

'Before rue Toullier, what kind of relationship did you have with the DST?'

He stared at me intently.

'Relationship?'

'Was there an understanding?'

For a moment there was no response, then he smiled and nodded.

'Can you elaborate?'

'This is very dangerous ground. For both of us.'

'I realize that, but to strip away the lies and the myths that surround you it's important that you tell me as much as you can.'

'Some things are better left unsaid.'

'Am I to assume that today in September 1985 that relationship with French Intelligence continues?'

'It continues.'

'When did it begin?'

'In 1973. After Michel Moukharbel took command of Commando Boudia. Now I must ask you to question me on other matters.'

It was like glimpsing into a room that contains alluring decor, or chancing for a moment upon a secret garden. Carlos reminded me that early during our first meeting he had told me that there might be subjects that he could not discuss, areas too delicate.

I understood very precisely his reluctance. Looking at him I felt that he was probably already regretting what he had confirmed for me about his 'understanding' with the DST.

'I understand your reluctance. I hope you understand that this is an aspect of your life that is of great interest to me.'

His teeth gleamed as he smiled and inhaled at the same time. They were a good set of teeth.

'And not only to you. Look, I enjoy life. Sooner or later it will end. I would rather that it was later.'

'What are we discussing? Is it your insurance policy?'

'Insurance policy, what is that?'

How very appropriate that the man generally regarded as 'the world's most wanted' should affect not to understand the concept of insurance.

'Your guarantee in some way or other that protects your life.'

'Yes.'

'Would I be correct in concluding that you have similar understandings with other countries?'

'Yes.'

He held up a warning hand.

'Now, please, Mr Yallop. No more.'

I felt that certain areas of his mind were marked 'Trespassers will be shot'. I nodded accepting that fact. We returned to the closing months of 1974.

In December 1974, Colonel Ramon Trabal, the Uruguayan military attaché to Britain and France, was murdered, shot in broad daylight in Paris. It is one of an enormous number of killings and attacks with which the name of Carlos has been linked. After the rue Toullier affair there were reports that evidence linking Carlos with this attack was found at one of his safe houses.

'That would be notes made by Moukharbel. He made notes on everything. We had nothing to do with Trabal's death. After rue Toullier and again after Vienna I was of course held responsible for everything that happened in the world. Most of it is bullshit but it helped me for years.'

'In what way?'

'The more they blamed me for, the bigger they made me. The bigger they made me, the less they came looking for me.'

'Who are "they"?'

'The first "they" is the media – Press, television, writers – people like you. The second "they" are the intelligence agencies.'

It was a situation which, as I explored it with Carlos, evidently held for him ironic elements. He contended that much of the fantasy that has been written about him came in the first instance from certain Western secret services. He specifically identified the CIA and MI6.

In his view they had seized upon him as a propaganda weapon in the Cold War. Again and again they had asserted that he was controlled by Moscow and that the KGB pulled the strings on a vast array of international groups.

Carlos had clearly had many years to consider this phenomenon. It was, he insisted, 'a disinformation service that was and continues to be global'.

Without having spent many hours with this man one might have concluded that this was either the view of a paranoid or an attempt at a whitewash. I have met in my life many people suffering from delusions and paranoia. Carlos did not fit the pattern. As for whitewash, he was extraordinarily frank when recounting the various deeds for which he did accept responsibility. I reserved judgement and turned back to late 1974. If he had not been involved in the murder of Colonel Trabal, what had he been doing at that time?

'Preparing a rocket attack on an El Al plane.'

'A commercial passenger plane?'

'Of course.'

'Again the potential damage and loss of life of ordinary people. How would that assist the Palestinian cause?'

'You should ask that question of the Iraqis. They ordered the attack, but it was part of their rejectionist front policy.'

Briefly Carlos drew a picture of the political situation in the closing months of 1974. In October, at the Rabat Summit, Arab leaders approved two main resolutions. The first recognized the PLO as the only legitimate representative of the Palestinian people, which in effect conferred on the Arafat-led organization the status of a Palestinian government in exile. The second resolution committed King Hussein of Jordan to hand over the West Bank, when it was liberated, to the PLO. It was an important victory for the doves within the Palestinian movement and clearly signposted the ultimate objective: a deal with Israel that would result in a Palestinian state being established in the West Bank and the Gaza Strip. In return the Palestinians would cede the rest of the disputed territory and officially recognize Israel.

Others saw it as no victory for doves or anyone else – they were bitterly opposed to this development. Some of their number, Secretary of State Kissinger and Israel's leaders, were predictable, others less so. Among this latter category were several Arab nations and consequently those Palestinian factions which they either controlled or influenced.

In November Yasser Arafat spoke at the United Nations in New York. He talked of his desires for his people: '. . . we are prepared to settle for a little homeland of our own, in order to have peace with Israel, until the day when the Israelis decide of their own free will to join with us in the creation of a Democratic State of our dreams.'

He ended his speech with two lines that have continued to haunt not only the United Nations but all who address themselves to this issue.

'I have come bearing an olive branch and a freedom fighter's gun. Do not let the olive branch fall from my hand.'

Among those Arab countries which were deeply hostile to any Palestinian initiative towards a peaceful solution with Israel was Iraq. Its ruling Baath party saw the destruction of Israel as the solution, and talked freely of pushing all the Jews into the sea. Whatever their public posturing, Iraq's leaders viewed the events at Rabat and New York with alarm. If Arafat's Fatah, which dominated the PLO, made a reality of their dream for a little homeland and a democratic state, the Middle East domino theory came into play – create one truly democratic Arab state and the oppressed Arab people living under dictatorships or monarchist rulers will start demanding more of the same.

Six days after Arafat's speech the rejectionists moved to change the climate of political opinion. The Popular Democratic Front (PDF), a breakaway element of the Popular Front headed by Nayef Hawatmeh, launched a terror attack in Israel. Their target was an apartment block at Beit Shean. Four Israeli civilians were killed. The PDF announced that it had carried out the attack to demonstrate that, although Arafat still held an olive branch, he also held a gun.

The fact that the Iraqi-financed PDF was controlled by a man called Nayef Hawatmeh and not by a man called Arafat was ignored by Israel and her supporters. To them this action confirmed yet again the truth of the remarks made by Israel's ambassador to the UN when, in response to Arafat's speech, he condemned the UN for inviting Arafat to speak. To Ambassador Tekoah, the PLO was nothing but 'a murder organization' and the UN had 'capitulated' to it.

Also ignored was the fact that not only Hawatmeh's organization, but also the Popular Front and Ahmed

Jibril's offshoot, the PFLP (GC), had broken with the PLO a month before the Rabat Summit because of the PLO's 'moderation'. Over the years these more extreme Palestinian groups have proved themselves time and again to be Israel's best allies.

Thus it was that Iraq instructed Wadi Haddad to destroy the Arafat peace initiative further with an attack on an El Al passenger plane. The instruction had been passed to Moukharbel in the late summer of 1974.

The Iraqi regime had wanted the attack to take place just before the Rabat Summit, thereby effectively sabotaging the conference resolutions on the Palestinian issue. The arrest of Yamada and the events at The Hague and the Drugstore had delayed full preparation, but Carlos had not entirely neglected the operation.

'I considered Heathrow and a number of airports on the Continent. Iraq had already supplied us with RPG 7s [portable rocket launchers]. Because our main base was in France, Moukharbel decided that the operation should take place at Orly airport. I submitted my plan, which was first considered by Michel and then by Wadi Haddad. Every detail of the attack had to be approved by the Old Man.'

Haddad duly approved the plan and the attack was due to take place in December, when an industrial dispute leading to a strike at Orly caused a postponement.

In January the plan was reactivated. Two members of the hit squad that Haddad had sent to France in December left one of Moukharbel's safe houses in the 10th Arrondissement in Paris on Monday 13th.

Their driver was Johannes Weinrich, who three days earlier (using false papers indicating he was Klaus Muller) had hired the white Peugeot 504 car from Hertz at Les Invalides air terminal.

Following behind in a blue Simca 110 came Carlos.

Near Orly airport Weinrich transferred to the Simca and he and Carlos drove to a rendezvous point near the cemetery at Thiasis, a few miles from the airport. The hit team of two Lebanese Palestinians drove to the airport and proceeded to park their car virtually on the runway. Employees of Swissair and Alitalia watched first with curiosity and then with growing horror and astonishment as one man emerged from the car brandishing a gun while his colleague, carrying an RPG 7 rocket launcher, calmly walked to a small terrace and, leaning the bazooka on a rail, pointed it in the direction of an El Al Boeing 707 which was taxiing down the runway. The plane, carrying 136 passengers and a crew of seven, was bound for Montreal and New York. The gunman made an adjustment to the rocket launcher and fired. His aim was too high and the rocket sailed over the Boeing and hit a Yugoslavian DC9. Hearing the explosion, the El Al pilot ignored the order to stop from the control tower and violently accelerated. The gunman had by now reloaded and moved to near the Peugeot car. He fired again, the tremendous recoil from the rocket launcher throwing him backwards. The RPG 7 smashed into the Peugeot's windscreen as the second rocket found not the El Al plane but an administrative block. The first rocket had hit an empty plane, but metal splinters caused minor injuries to a policeman, a Yugoslav steward and a luggage handler. The second rocket injured no-one.

With one of the Palestinians knocking the remnants of the windscreen out, the other drove off at high speed to the rendezvous point. The transfer was observed by a country police officer who happened to be passing by on his bike. As the Simca roared off in the direction of Paris, the curious policeman propped his bicycle against a wall and approached the abandoned Peugeot.

In the back seat he discovered the RPG 7 rocket launcher and two rockets. Back at the airport, police discovered a Tokarev 7.62 gun on the tarmac. The chapter of mishaps for Carlos and his team continued when a Croatian exile group claimed the 'attack' on the Yugoslavian DC9.

French security was further bemused when, later on Sunday, Carlos telephoned Reuters Agency in Paris and claimed responsibility for the attack in the name of

Mohammed Boudia Commando. Still later, the France Presse Agency in Beirut received a telephone call claiming the attack had been carried out by Black September. The caller stated that the attack had been carried out in retaliation for a recent rocket attack on the PLO offices in Beirut. Subsequently another caller denied that Black September was responsible. While Commissioner Jean Herranz, who ran the Middle East desk at the DST, became increasingly bewildered, Michel Moukharbel conducted a post mortem. It was, Carlos told me, a rigid rule of Haddad's that a full post mortem be carried out after every attack – to ensure that everything had gone to plan, and to see if any lessons could be learned. Carlos indicated that, not surprisingly, this particular post mortem was lengthy and heated. His own view of the fiasco was more philosophical than Moukharbel's. Talking of the gunman he said,

'He fired twice and missed the plane. Call it error, human weakness. He had been well trained in South Yemen and was regarded as a man of courage who had been tested in the field of battle. Sometimes these things happen. If I recall correctly he was distracted just at the point of firing.'

I refrained from asking if he was distracted twice.

'Whose idea was it to go back and try again just one week later?'

'Michel's. He insisted that we had to try again. It was not just an idea. It was an order.'

If anywhere in France was going to be well guarded so soon after such an attack it would surely be the place that had been attacked.

In the days that followed the attack the French press was full of a range of reactions.

The operation had not been without some success for the Iraqi regime. Israel's Minister of Information, Aharon Yariv, declared: 'This attack should be yet another warning to those countries that receive terrorists on to their land. It confirms yet again the significance of the olive branch that Arafat brandished at the United Nations.'

Yariv went on to denounce the meeting between a member of the French Government and Yasser Arafat only a few weeks earlier. He called the attack at Orly 'the consequences of this political gesture'. The fact that the PLO had already condemned the attack, calling it 'a criminal operation which represents a plot against the Palestinian people', was predictably ignored by Yariv.

While members of the Yugoslavian Embassy were discussing with the French government the grave implications of a Croatian group of freedom fighters based in Paris, Moukharbel got down to planning a second attempt.

The men he commanded for this operation, whatever else their deficiencies, were not lacking in bravado. Wiser heads would have counselled waiting for many weeks if not months before returning to Orly. The same day that the abortive attack had taken place, after the Moukharbel post mortem, Carlos and the Palestinian bazooka 'expert' were back at the airport.

As the existing security at Orly was reinforced with an additional seven hundred and fifty men, the majority heavily armed and steel-helmeted members of the much hated CRS, the Republic Security Companies, Carlos and his companion calmly wandered around the airport observing the security measures and making notes.

They arrived at the conclusion that the best place to launch the second rocket attack was from the observation balcony. It offered an uninterrupted view of departing and arriving planes. But to launch an attack from the balcony posed certain difficulties.

'The team would not be able to escape after hitting their target unless they took hostages. There was also the very real possibility that many people would be killed and we wished to avoid that.'

'But people on the El Al plane that you were planning to hit would also have been killed.'

'The answer to that is simple – never fly El Al. Our concern was not for those passengers. They represented people who by flying on Israel's airline were making a

1. The classroom nonentity: Ilich Ramirez Sanchez
at sixteen years of age.

2. Fermin Toro school, Caracas.

3. Political discussion Venezuelan-style in the 1960s.

4-6. The myths talk of a multi-millionaire Marxist father and a family that lived in luxury, the reality is in sharp contrast: *above left* Jose Altagracia Ramirez Navas; *above right* the family lived in this block of flats in Caracas; *below* the 'fabulous family ranch' in San Cristobal: Senor Navas lives in a shack behind this building.

7. The playboy of Knightsbridge with his mother, Elba Maria Sanchez, and a family friend at a diplomatic reception in London in February 1973.

8-9. *Above* Dawson's Field, 1970. The myth says Carlos was there. He wasn't, but Bassam Abu Sharif (*below*, with the author) was.

10-11. More myth in the making: the Olympic Games at Munich were shattered by a Palestinian attack that many have stated was planned by Carlos. It wasn't. The man responsible, Abu Iyad, is seen below.

بيانات خاصّة بالسائق

INDICATIONS RELATIVES AU CONDUCTEUR
INFORMATION REGARDING THE DRIVER

(1) Nom:
    Name:
(2) Prénoms:
    Christian names:
(3) Lieu de naissance:
    Birth place:
(4) Date de naissance:
    Date of birth:
(5) Domicile:
    Address:

(١) الاسم
(٢) اللَّقب
(٣) محل الميلاد
(٤) تاريخ الميلاد ١٩٤٧
(٥) السكن

12-14. January 1974 - enter reality: Edward Sieff (*above left*) the day after the attack on him. *Above right* One of the many false documents used by Ramirez, in this instance a counterfeit Kuwaiti driving licence. *Below* The London family home on High Street Kensington from where Ramirez set out on the night he shot Sieff.

15-17. The pace quickens: *left* the offices of *Minute* newspaper in Paris after Carlos bombed them; *below left* a very courageous man, Ambassador Count Jacques Senard during the French Embassy siege in The Hague; *below right* part-time art-dealer, full-time terrorist, Antonio Expedito Carvalho Pereira.

statement of support for the country we are at war with. My concern was for ordinary members of the French public and also our men. Do not forget they too would be in danger.'

Yet again I was experiencing difficulty in relating to Carlos. I take the view that all human life is precious and sacred. In North Lebanon I was confronted with a man who operated on a sliding scale of values with regard to the human race. There is nothing unique in this attitude, many have it and in the Israeli-Palestinian conflict those with such values, or lack of values, are not confined to one side or the other.

'We went back again to Orly on Friday. This time we had a full rehearsal, without arms.'

'What was the basic plan for the attack?'

'It was simple. The attack was planned for Sunday. This time their Algerian leader would be with them. I was to accompany the three men from Paris with the weapons. We would then carry out a final check on the observation balcony. They would then go into the toilets and assemble the bazooka. They would return to the balcony and fire just once at the El Al plane as it started to leave the boarding area. The marksman was told to fire just one shot from 25 metres to make sure he hit the correct target. We did not want any more planes being hit accidentally.'

On Sunday there would of course be an even greater number of people at Orly. Families with their children indulging in the curious pastime of watching arriving and departing planes. It was an aspect of which Carlos was fully aware.

'I did not want to do the operation on Sunday. Apart from the many sightseers, Sunday schedules are subject to sudden change. I also felt that we needed more time to observe the police and security forces. Michel Moukharbel insisted that we must carry out the attack on that Sunday. The three commandos agreed with him.'

On Sunday the 19th of January the convoy ride from Paris to Orly was repeated. Carlos led the way driving the Simca. The hit team were in another hire car, a

Citroën. At the wheel was the German who had hired all the cars, Johannes Weinrich.

Once at Orly, Carlos accompanied the three commandos onto the balcony. Establishing that everything on the observation balcony was normal, the four came back down again, collected the parts of the rocket launcher from the cars, plus guns and hand grenades, then, with the exception of Carlos, paid a further 2 franc admission charge to return to the balcony.

As Carlos and Weinrich drove out of the airport car park the hit team were discovering a problem that had not occurred to them during the various reconnaissance trips. The toilets were all in use. Not only that, but there was a queue.

By the time the hit squad had finally got into a toilet, assembled and armed the rocket launcher and emerged, the El Al jet was taxiing for take off. Because they had left the RPG 7 in the back of the abandoned Peugeot on the previous Monday they had been forced to mount this second attack with an inferior rocket launcher, an RPG 2, a much smaller version with an appropriately shorter range. Emerging onto the balcony, the hit man saw that the plane was already 250 metres away. There was no possibility of hitting it. Nevertheless, to the astonishment of a watching CRS guard, the bazooka was raised to a firing position. The guard, oblivious to the crowded observation platform, opened fire with a sustained burst from a sub-machine gun. One of the hit squad started throwing hand grenades. The madness of the Middle East had again arrived at Orly.

What followed was pandemonium and terror in equal measure – a running gunfight between three Palestinians and an increasing number of the CRS through the departure lounge; passengers, sightseers and airline staff all trapped in the midst of a small war. Twenty people were injured including one of the Palestinians and a member of the CRS.

Sticking to the original plan, the hit team began to grab hostages and push them into the toilets on the second floor. When the initial panic subsided the three held ten hostages, including a pregnant woman and her five-year-old daughter.

They were destined to be held for seventeen hours, most of which they were forced by their captors to spend standing up. Negotiations began with notes being passed under the washroom door. One of these told the French security forces that the three men were members of Commando Boudia.

Michel Poniatowski, the Minister who had been so anxious to take the hardest of lines at the time of the Embassy siege at The Hague, arrived to take personal command of the security forces. Actual negotiations were conducted by a very brave Egyptian Ambassador, whose own life during the early stages was very much at risk. He, just as much as Israel, represented the enemy to these men of the rejectionist front.

In the middle of the night, with negotiations at a stalemate, the men surrounding the toilets suddenly heard a burst of firing from within. Fearing carnage, the Egyptian Ambassador anxiously attempted to establish the cause. The hit team declined to enlighten him. It transpired that, contrary to fears, they had not shot some of the hostages, but merely indulged in shooting into the ceiling to keep the French alert. Eventually the three men exchanged their ten hostages for an Air France plane and a crew of three. Destination unknown.

Throughout the all-night negotiations Carlos and Moukharbel were waiting in Paris. They were attempting to monitor the situation which, in view of the fact that there was a virtual black-out of news imposed by the Government, was difficult. If Poniatowski had maintained his initial hard line and refused to do a deal Carlos was ready with his guns and hand grenades to create more terror in the capital.

The errors and mistakes made by Carlos and the team he supervised continued to dog the Orly operation until the very end. When he dumped the hired cars he neglected to remove the hire forms and a parking ticket. It was a little more evidence to assist Herranz and his colleagues at the DST, a little more cause for acrimony in the deteriorating relationship of Moukharbel and Carlos.

Carlos was reluctant to discuss their relationship in any great depth but his various comments on the subject established several things. He felt by early 1975 that he rather than Moukharbel should be Haddad's top man in Europe. He further believed that Moukharbel was inclined to act impulsively, thereby putting the lives of Haddad's European team at risk. To judge from his remarks in 1985, the twenty-five-year-old Venezuelan was bucking hard for the job held by the thirty-four-year-old Lebanese. It was a situation so predictable and normal in the conventional business world as to be a cliché. But theirs was not the normal business world. The profit and loss in their line of work were alternative words for alive or dead.

The aftermath of the second botched attack at Orly was not confined to a testy post mortem between Carlos and Moukharbel. Many others were arriving independently at their own conclusions. Among the first to condemn the Orly attack was virtually the entire Arab world. As a consequence the three-man hit team and the three-man Air France crew experienced the greatest difficulty in finding a country that would accept the plane. Once airborne, the hit team had told the pilot to head for Beirut. When the Lebanese refused to let the plane land, it headed for Damascus, where the Syrians were equally hostile. At Baghdad, the home of the government that had actually demanded the two attacks, the plane was allowed to refuel, then ordered back into the skies. To have accepted the hit team without demur, with the eyes of the political world upon them, was considered by the Iraqi regime far too compromising. Kuwait, Saudi Arabia, Egypt, even South Yemen – all refused to let the Air France plane land. The legendary Flying Dutchman appeared to have acquired a twentieth-century equivalent, a Flying French jet liner doomed continuously to circumnavigate the globe. But jet liners need constant refuelling – with the plane again desperately low on fuel, the French Ambassador in Baghdad appealed to the Iraqi government to put an end to what had now become a seventeen-hour nightmare flight. The appeal got the Iraqis off the hook. Now, while continuing to condemn the Orly attacks, they could be shown to be acting with great compassion. The Air France Boeing was allowed to land. The three-man hit team was immediately arrested and taken away by the police. Nothing more was ever heard of them. I asked Carlos what had happened to them after the plane had landed. Yet again there was that lopsided smile.

'They stayed for a few days in Baghdad as guests of the Iraqi government. Within the week they were flown to South Yemen to rejoin Wadi Haddad.'

The official Iraqi government response for the benefit of international opinion was somewhat different. The plane had 'been allowed to land for humanitarian reasons and out of consideration for Franco-Iraqi relations'.

The real bonus for the Iraqis was not long in coming. Having roundly condemned the attacks, the French press laid the responsibility for controlling not only those who had perpetrated them but the global behaviour of some four million Palestinians at Yasser Arafat's doorstep, a theme that was taken up by the Israeli government and a number of other countries. Quite how Arafat was supposed to control the entire Palestinian population and act as judge, jury and executioner was not explained. President Sadat, while also castigating Arafat, claimed that the attacks were aimed at sabotaging his impending visit to France.

All of this took place against a background of acrimonious peace talks that had been dragging on since the October War of 1973. The mood of the times can be best judged by the comments of Kissinger, who expressed the opinion that if the Arab oil nations applied oil sanctions again, the United States could not rule out the use of force. It was a view which confirmed that nineteenth-century gunboat diplomacy was alive and well in the White House.

Apart from the injuries and terror that the two attacks had caused, Carlos and his hit team reaped a rich harvest in propaganda for their Iraqi paymasters. Carlos observed, 'The fact that the actual attacks, in terms of the objectives desired, were a total failure was quickly forgotten. The Iraqis were delighted with the outcome. Many of the political gains that the PLO had achieved at Rabat and New York were wiped out overnight.'

Only *Le Monde* carried, on the 23rd of January, one of the most significant aspects of the Orly affair. Its reporters had interviewed the three-man crew of the Boeing when it returned safely to Orly. The pilot, Captain Jean Vignau, said, 'The terrorists used the strongest terms to condemn Mr Arafat and Egypt, where they refused to land when Arab airports were closing one after another.'

In March 1975 Moukharbel and Carlos began to plan the next operation ordered by Wadi Haddad. Like a number of Haddad's operations in the past and others that lay in the future, this was a fund-raising operation. The location was London, the target the Ambassador in Britain for the United Arab Emirates, Mohammed Mahdi al-Tajir.

For Wadi Haddad, al-Tajir represented a classic example of the elite ruling Arab class who, while continuing to indulge every fanciful whim, remained indifferent to the plight of the homeless Palestinians. The Ambassador also had money. Buckets of it. Extremely large buckets. For a lad who had learned his English at Preston Grammar School and had begun his working life as a clerk in the British broking firm of Gray Mackenzie in Bahrain, al-Tajir had, through the patronage of Sheik Rashid bin Said, the ruler of Dubai, done rather well for himself. His major source of wealth stemmed from the discovery of oil in the sheikdom in 1966. Al-Tajir was granted a half per cent commission on all sales. By the time of his diplomatic appointment to Britain in 1972 he was already considered one of the world's richest men. The estimates fluctuated widely, from £2 billion to £10 billion. The Ambassador made no attempt to hide his wealth, rather he flaunted it. He bought a string of stately homes in southern England. Art experts frequently declared that he had amassed the biggest collection of gold and silver works of art in the world. When questioned about the extent of his wealth in the same year that Wadi Haddad took a personal interest in him, al-Tajir replied, 'One billion, two billion, I am worth much more than that. On this telephone I can get any amount of money I want.'

I asked Carlos how much Haddad had considered al-Tajir should pick up the phone and ask for, once they had kidnapped him.

'Fifty million dollars.'

After the Orly débâcle, Haddad left nothing to chance. The instructions that he gave Moukharbel were detailed and precise. To ensure maximum security two new safe houses were to be acquired. With regard to arms, Carlos already had in London in the spring of 1975 more than adequate resources, which were safehoused at Nydia's Knightsbridge flat and Angela's Bayswater address. They included hand grenades, a collection of hand guns that included a Browning, a Beretta, a Mauser automatic, a Browning pistol, a Czech Vzor automatic complete with silencer, plastic explosives, sticks of gelignite, a gas gun to render the potential victim temporarily unconscious, and for good measure a couple of rubber truncheons. Haddad was determined that there would be no repetition of that September weekend in Paris, when through inept planning Carlos had been reduced to two hand grenades.

To safehouse the hit team Carlos leased a bedsit in Chesterton Road in the Notting Hill area of West London. He signed the lease on April 7th. At the same time, posing as an Ecuadorian called Anton Bouvier and with Nydia posing as his 'French wife, Françoise', he took out a lease on 14 Comeragh Mews, also in West London. I was loath to interrupt his account of this particular operation, but at the mention of the name

Anton Bouvier, I had no alternative. All who have written at any length about Carlos inevitably get to Anton Bouvier. He is invariably described as a senior officer of the KGB responsible for training Carlos in Cuba in 1966. He is then described as Carlos's KGB control, the man who ran him. The various accounts assert that Bouvier was constantly by Carlos's side in Paris and London in the early to mid 1970s. As already recorded earlier, Carlos had dismissed the stories of his Cuban training in their entirety. Now the name Bouvier had come from his lips.

He was again adamant that he had never received training in Cuba, from Bouvier or anyone else. As for Bouvier – tapping his chest he said, 'I am Anton Bouvier. Just as I have been a great many other people.'

There was no arguing with that. He had indeed been a multitude, each with his own individual passport and identification papers. His identities included Hector Hugo Dupont, an American from New York; Cenon Clarke, an American from New York; Hector Hugo Dupont, an Anglo-Frenchman, and yet another American, Glenn Gebhard. He was also Adolfo Bernal from Chile, and Carlos Martinez Torres, an economist from Peru. He answered to the names Johnny and Salim and at least six others. He was the veritable man for all seasons and all situations, yet the Bouvier identity was special. Around this identity a tale of Russian intrigue had been woven. I asked Carlos why he had felt the need to create Bouvier.

'When I took the lease on the Chesterton Road place I used the name and passport of Adolfo Bernal of Chile. Is he supposed to be another KGB officer? When Nydia and I took a lease on Comeragh Mews, we pretended to be Mr and Mrs Bouvier and I used one of my Ecuadorian passports. It was no big thing. If something went wrong and we had to get out of London in a hurry then the British would be hunting for a Chilean and two Ecuadorians who did not exist. You do not think I was going to sign those leases in the name of Ilich Ramirez Sanchez, do you?'

At the Chesterton Road address Carlos converted a small closet into a darkroom. The Comeragh Mews house was entirely self-contained and had for this particular operation one very large advantage. The ground floor had formerly been a stables; newly converted, it was now a drive-in garage. Useful if you're planning to kidnap an ambassador – the by then unconscious al-Tajir would be driven straight in and removed from the car behind closed doors. He would be carried up the internal stairs to a bedroom where he was to be photographed. The photos would then be developed at Chesterton Road. This would confirm for al-Tajir's embassy that they were indeed holding him. They would be threatened that he would be murdered if any contact was made with the British police. The fifty million dollars was to be paid into a numbered Swiss bank account where it would immediately be transferred to an account in Aden. Confirmation that the money had arrived in South Yemen would ensure that al-Tajir was blindfolded, driven around London for an hour to disorientate him, then dumped, unhurt, in Kensington Gardens, which, apart from being close to his official residence and his Embassy, was also close to the two safe houses.

As the two safe houses were leased, the hit team assembled in London. Moukharbel and Carlos headed the team, although Moukharbel would as usual, under instructions from Wadi Haddad, take no part in the snatch. Carlos headed the active unit, which included among its members four Germans, Hans-Joachim Klein, Wilfried Böse, Brigitte Kuhlmann and a member of the Revolutionary Cells who was an excellent photographer. Nydia was on hand to cover domestic arrangements and to ensure that al-Tajir was well fed.

The logistics and the planning were excellent but the kidnap never took place.

'The arrangement was that a member of the diplomatic staff in the Iraqi Embassy would supply us with information concerning al-Tajir's movements. It never came. I kept the whole team in London for nearly three weeks.

During that time we carried out surveillance on al-Tajir's embassy and his home. We saw him once, with two of his bodyguards. It was essential to build up a pattern of his movements. Either the Iraqis lost their nerve or simply changed their minds. Very frustrating.'

Except for al-Tajir.

'One of the safe houses you were using throughout this period was Angela Otaola's flat in Bayswater?'

'Yes, I have already told you that.'

'What you haven't referred to is the fact that by April 1975 Angela had acquired a new boyfriend who was living with her.'

'Barry Woodhams?'

'Yes. When you assembled with Moukharbel the various elements of this operation in London, to leave guns, bombs and God knows what else in the home of a woman you trusted is understandable, but to leave them there after you discovered she had moved in her new boyfriend. Why?'

He shrugged and smiled.

'Why not? I had met Barry a few times with Angela before they lived together. He seemed OK. There was no reason for him to go and open a suitcase that I just happened to keep there.'

Woodhams had in fact known Angela before she had met Carlos. They had been neighbours in nearby Garway Road in early 1972. The two men had a number of things in common, not least their interest in guns, left-wing politics and an eye for an attractive woman. They were also both a long way from their native lands.

Woodhams, two years older than Carlos, spent his early life in what was then Northern Rhodesia, where his father was a civil servant. Before being sent to England for a grammar school education at the age of fourteen, Barry Woodhams had accompanied his father on numerous hunting expeditions and developed considerable expertise with both rifles and shotguns. Unlike a great many White Rhodesians of the period, his political interests were well to the left.

At the time Carlos met him, Woodhams was working as a bio-chemist at London University. Previously he had worked at the Government's secret and highly controversial research establishment at Porton Down in Wiltshire.

Perhaps it was the shock of discovering that Angela had a new live-in boyfriend that caused Carlos to confuse his own nationality when he was introduced to Barry Woodhams. He said he was Carlos Martinez from Chile. Angela made no comment, though he had introduced himself to her as Carlos Martinez from Peru. With such a dazzling array of names and nationalities the odds on such a mistake inevitably increased.

Carlos accepted that he had been supplanted as Angela's lover, but instead of packing his incriminating bag and stealing quietly into the night, he chose instead to befriend Woodhams. They would talk long into the night, too long for Angela, who frequently gave up and went to bed alone. He would regale them with stories of his flash nights out in clubs such as Churchill's in Bond Street and of his highstakes poker schools. Carlos gave them both the benefit of his views on a whole range of subjects, ranging from the ineptness of the political left in Great Britain through the best shooting position for rifle work, to the ease with which airport security could be breached. This was only a few months after Carlos had given the entire world two demonstrations on this subject at Orly. He retained a key to the room where his case was kept and often Angela and Barry would come home to find him waiting for them, fresh in from Paris with some duty free brandy and cigarettes for them. The three of them would go out to nearby restaurants or to Angelo's, a late night drinking club that was popular not only with the local foreigners but also off duty detectives from the nearby Paddington Green police station.

Such men are instantly recognizable.

'Did you realize that Angelo's would have more than its fair share of plain clothes police?'

'Sure.'

'And that didn't worry you? Didn't stop you using the place?'

'Not at all.'

'And you never felt any misgivings about leaving a suitcase full of guns, false passports, hand grenades and the other tools of your trade at Angela's flat?'

'No, I gave her Nydia's phone number. In case anything ever happened to me. I told her to phone and Nydia would come and collect.'

'Just a thought. Did you discuss any of these arrangements with Moukharbel?'

'No, why should I?'

'Because he was your boss. Head of Operations for Haddad in Europe.'

'Sure. But these things were none of his business.'

Among the other items which Carlos kept in that suitcase were writings which indicate that although the Al-Tajir kidnap was aborted there were many others to be planned, and yet more to be considered. Possible targets were discussed and death lists drawn up. Much of this was only provisional – all operations had to be referred to Wadi Haddad in Aden – but although the various targets never went beyond the elementary planning and suggestion stage, they make sombre reading.

The provisional death lists that Carlos drew up were not confined to Zionists or even ordinary Jews. Non-Jews were also on these lists and even some Arabs.

Thus the lists were not just obscenely but absurdly long. There were hundreds of names: the President of the Afars and the Issas; President Sadat's wife; Sheik Yamani. Their names were alongside those of Vera Lynn, John Osborne and his then wife Jill Bennett, Yehudi Menuhin, Lord Drogheda. The list of over five hundred was a veritable Who's Who of celebrities. Many were entirely unconnected in any way with the Israel-Palestine issue, they were on the death list solely because they were well known figures. To kill such a person undoubtedly accords the killer and his cause what Andy Warhol called 'fifteen minutes of fame'. To kill a few of them would up the ante to decades of notoriety. The extraordinary size of the list moves it into the realms of fantasy.

There were other much more seriously considered targets. These included plans to kidnap a large group of diplomats during an Embassy function in West Germany. In the event that holding this group hostage did not produce the desired results – the freeing of the Baader-Meinhof group that were then in prison in West Germany – then six of the hostages would be shot and a Volkswagen bus fully loaded with explosives would be detonated by a second commando group in the underground car park of the Chase Bank in Frankfurt. If that did not secure the release of the Baader-Meinhof prisoners a third commando unit would detonate 20 kilograms of explosives in a major hotel in Hamburg. The initial attack on the diplomatic group would occur when a particular country was celebrating its National Day and had invited all the other Ambassadors based in Germany to join in the celebrations. It was quite apparent from what Carlos said to me that this series of outrages had gone some considerable way from idle doodlings on paper.

'The plans for this series of operations were discussed in great detail in February 1975. The discussions took place in Paris. Michel and I discussed these matters with a number of our German comrades.'

'Had you received approval from Wadi Haddad?'

'For the original idea, yes. It would obviously require many details to be worked out. It was agreed that there should be further meetings then the final plans were to be submitted to the Old Man.'

'You were obviously prepared to kill a great many people in this series of operations?'

'Yes.'

'Merely to obtain the freedom for about half a dozen who, you have told me, you were very unimpressed with during the summer of 1970 in Jordan.'

'By 1975 these people had become very important to Haddad. We had very good relations with our German friends. They worked well on behalf of the Palestinians.

They wanted Ulrike Meinhof, Andreas Baader and the others free and Haddad saw great value in that.'

'Propaganda value?'

'Of course, but also it would give him more Europeans to help in the struggle. After the Red Army affair in France Haddad considered he needed Europeans to replace our Japanese comrades.'

'But the plan was never put into operation. Why was that?'

'Because of what happened at rue Toullier.'

We had reached what was a crucial period in the life of this man. After rue Toullier he would be out of the shadows for the rest of his life. No longer unknown but clearly identified and wanted very badly by a great many people and a great many intelligence agencies.

By the end of 1975 two events, the rue Toullier affair and the Vienna operation, ensured that Ilich Ramirez Sanchez would become the world's most wanted man.

In early June 1975, Carlos was in Paris awaiting the return of Moukharbel from Beirut. The head of the European section had been in the Middle East to attend a series of forward planning meetings with Haddad and other senior members of the organization. Among the areas discussed were the plans for the series of attacks planned in West Germany. These were now off the drawing board and well advanced. On starting his return to Paris, Moukharbel made a mistake that was ultimately to prove fatal. Ignoring the strict directive from Haddad that no member of the organization should ever travel directly from Beirut to their final point of destination, he booked to fly direct to Orly. The intelligence agencies of the world were fully aware by 1975 that Beirut was one of the key centres for the kind of activities in which Haddad and others indulged. In the light of the Orly attacks only a few months before, the attacks on the Drugstore and the French Embassy at The Hague, and the triple car bombs in Paris, all of which had occurred within the past twelve months, it was an act of madness to fly direct to France. Inevitably he was questioned at passport control in Beirut a little more closely than was usual. His carry-on case was searched and gave further proof of just how careless Haddad's top man in Europe had become. Documents detailing his planning discussions were found after an extensive search of his bags. This search was only carried out because in his carry-on case the passport officer discovered several more passports. It was a re-run of the Yamada affair.

Moukharbel was arrested and held for questioning. Lebanese Intelligence had been created and trained by the French. They combined all the aspects of their Gallic training with a number of Arab refinements. These included their own versions of physical and psychological torture. On the third day of his ordeal at the hands of the Lebanese, Moukharbel noted a new face in the room, a civilian who said little and smoked sweet-scented tobacco in a pipe. From the interchanges between this man and his Lebanese captors, Moukharbel became convinced that the stranger, an American, was a senior CIA officer.

Moukharbel later insisted that he did not break. Lebanese Intelligence said 'he sang like a canary'. Exactly who was telling the truth can be gauged from subsequent events. Moukharbel was then put in the first available plane to Orly and Lebanese Intelligence advised the DST in Paris of the date and time of his arrival.

At Orly airport a very worried and frightened Michel Moukharbel passed through Customs without trouble. The intelligence officers in Beirut had returned to him before his departure the false passports and the incriminating documents, having first discreetly copied and photographed them. A cat-and-mouse game had then been put into operation. The mouse was self-evident, the cat's name was Jean Herranz, the Commissioner in charge of Division B2 of the DST, the section that dealt with Middle East terrorism. As Moukharbel queued to buy a bus ticket for the journey to central Paris, two plain clothes DST officers quietly joined the queue. It was June 13th. Michel Moukharbel had fourteen days to live.

The DST had been hunting the Commando Boudia group for almost a year and had made error after error during their investigation. Now they were tailing the head of the Commando and were totally ignorant of that fact. Their own errors were now compounded by Lebanese Intelligence, who, instead of rushing copies of the documents discovered in Moukharbel's luggage to Paris by personal courier, merely filed them. Moukharbel had not sung, he had not even offered the faintest of tunes to his interrogators. Precisely what he said remains a mystery but in view of what happened after he arrived in France there is no doubt whatever that he succeeded in keeping secret his role as head of Haddad's European operations. Obviously the Lebanese advised their French counterparts that Moukharbel was worth watching, hence the tail, but they remained oblivious of the fact that this small, unassuming man with his pencil moustache and the air and manner of a tired waiter was responsible for much of the death and carnage that had occurred in France and other parts of Europe over the previous five years.

The DST officers watched as Moukharbel entered his apartment block at 25 Avenue Claude Vellefaux. Ordering coffee at a nearby café that commands a view of the entrance to the block of flats, they sat and waited. Inside his apartment Moukharbel considered the situation.

He wanted to phone Carlos and warn him. Equally, he wanted to phone a contact in Venice so that Wadi Haddad could be advised. Phoning from the apartment was unthinkable, even phoning from a café was dangerous. He might have been followed from the airport. He concluded that it was best to sit tight and do absolutely nothing for a couple of days. If he had been followed the DST would soon tire of the game and call their men back to base.

Carlos was at this point blissfully untroubled. As far as he was concerned, although Moukharbel had been due back from the Middle East nearly a week earlier, visits to Beirut or Aden had a way of becoming extended, particularly in the chaotic, badly organized, unpunctual world of Palestinian politics.

Besides, there were also such pleasant diversions.

At the rue Toullier apartment Maria Lara had moved out. The fact that Carlos was conducting affairs with both her and her flat mate Nancy Sanchez had, even in the swinging, laid-back Latin Quarter, inevitably begun to generate a certain atmosphere. The dual relationships continued, but at separate venues, an almost British arrangement. Maria's place at the flat had been taken by Albaida Salazar. The late night parties, the wine and the music continued without remit. A short car ride away at their 'home' in rue Amélie, Amparo Masmela continued to offer diversion from the rue Toullier scene.

In London there was always the faithful Nydia, still living in the charming mews residence as Mrs Bouvier. Carlos had kept the lease running in the expectation that the plan to kidnap Ambassador Al-Tajir would soon reach fulfilment. Less than half a mile away were Angela and Barry and his suitcase. Just down the road, safehoused in the Chesterton Road flat awaiting the kidnap operation, was the German Wilfried Böse.

On Sunday, the fifteenth of June, Carlos's seemingly well ordered world began to collapse. It happened simultaneously in London and Paris.

On that morning, Barry Woodhams began to redecorate the four-roomed Bayswater flat he shared with Angela. He began by pulling a chest of drawers away from the fireplace and found lying underneath a passport in the name of Adolfo Bernal. Next to it on the floor was a Kuwaiti driving licence. The details were in Arabic, the name of the owner was in fact Bernard Muller. In both Ramirez's photograph stared back at him.

Woodhams stared across the sitting room at the black leather case. The zipper was padlocked. He wanted to know more. The cheap padlock presented no problem. The first thing he found was a 7.36 mm Czech Vzor automatic pistol; the barrel was threaded to take the silencer that lay next to it. There was a spare magazine and fifteen rounds. Underneath there were a number of sealed packages. Further exploration would leave evidence that he had been into the case which had been left for 'safe keeping'. Barry Woodhams carefully replaced the items and pondered.

He resolved to tell Angela of his discoveries, then have a word with Carlos the next time he was over from Paris. The odd thing was, when he did tell Angela, she didn't seem to be at all surprised.

By his actions, or lack of them, that Sunday, Woodhams unwittingly had a profound effect on a number of events and on a number of people's lives. A visit to Paddington Green Police Station that day, a clandestine Special Branch operation. We are all on borrowed time, some more than others.

On the other side of the Channel, the oblivious centre of Woodhams' attention on that day was about to get a surprise visitor. Carlos was having lunch with two of his mistresses, Nancy and Maria.

'Michel had been back from the Lebanon for a couple of days when he appeared during lunch at the rue Toullier flat. I greeted him warmly and gave him some wine, but he seemed very nervous, very preoccupied. There was obviously something wrong. At first he would not talk about it. He had a suitcase with him and he wanted me to take it to his flat in Claude Vellefaux. I remember he wanted me to give it to him at six that evening.'

'What time did he come to see you?'

'Oh, two, two-thirty. It was the normal routine for him to make contact with me through the girls at rue Toullier.'

'This was the first contact you had with him since he had gone to Beirut?'

'Yes. I was eager to discuss what had been agreed in Beirut and Aden. But he did not want to talk about it at that time.'

'Would that be because of the presence of the women?'

There was a look of genuine surprise on his face. 'No, of course not. Michel just kept on insisting that he had another meeting that afternoon and that he did not want to carry his suitcase around town. So he wanted me as a favour to take it to his place later.'

'What was your response?'

'I refused. I had better things to do than be his porter.'

'What was there in that case that so worried Moukharbel?'

'That is what I wanted to know. Then he opened it and showed me some of the documents he was carrying. They came from Wadi Haddad. They were plans covering future operations and details of how arms and money would be sent to Europe. There were details covering the operations we were planning in West Germany and details of the plans for the assassination of Natan [Asher Ben Natan, Israeli Ambassador to France]. Michel should not have been carrying such documents around the streets of Paris. When he told me that he had also brought all these documents from Beirut and that he had been arrested and interrogated at Beirut airport I was furious.'

'How should he have brought them to France?'

'In a diplomatic pouch. That was the normal way.'

'Which countries offered that facility?'

Carlos shrugged. 'Iraq. Yemen. Saudi Arabia. Kuwait. Syria. There were plenty who were sympathetic.'

'Did he tell you what had happened during his interrogation in Beirut?'

'Not then. He said he would tell me all about that when I brought the case to him. He insisted that the Lebanese had got nothing out of him.'

'Did you believe him?'

'I did not know what to believe. I was convinced that they had only let him go to see who he would lead them to. I insisted that he immediately make contact with the centre and advise them what had happened.'

'What is the centre?'

'Wadi Haddad's headquarters. There were three at that time. One in Beirut, one in Aden, one in Baghdad.'

'After what he had told you, did you agree to bring the suitcase to him that evening?'

'Of course. I did not want him loose in Paris carrying such documents.'

Unknown to either Moukharbel or Carlos, the DST officers had followed a very preoccupied Moukharbel across Paris to the Latin Quarter. The Lebanese had been correct in assuming that there might have been a watch kept on him since his return to France. His mistake had been in assuming that after two days of inactivity the DST had tired of the game. Though still wholly ignorant of Moukharbel's importance, they remained curious.

Now equally anxious, Carlos had emerged from 9 rue Toullier carrying the suitcase and checking out the street. The DST duty officer took a series of long range photographs with a zoom lens. One of them shows a pensive but unaware Carlos.

Commissioner Jean Herranz studied the reports coming in from his men. They did not make sense. Nothing that he had yet learned indicated that Moukharbel had links with any known organization. The visit that the Lebanese had made to rue Toullier meant nothing. There were no known activists in that area. Aware that he was operating on a very limited budget, Herranz confined the DST's continuing interest in Moukharbel to placing a watch on the Claude Vellefaux apartment block.

Not realizing that they had yet to feature in Herranz's first division of 'most wanted', Moukharbel and Carlos were becoming increasingly paranoid.

By the evening of the 15th of June contact had finally been made with Wadi Haddad. It was a tortuous procedure. The link was a member of the Popular Front based in Venice who phoned a contact in Beirut who then phoned Haddad in Aden. When the man in Venice eventually re-contacted Moukharbel there was a frenzy of activity. Haddad had read the situation well.

'The Old Man decided that the entire organization in Paris should be temporarily disbanded. Everyone with a direct contact to us was immediately sent to another country. Scattered throughout Europe. The guns, grenades and all materials were moved immediately from rue Toullier. Haddad assumed that Moukharbel had been followed there. We took the stuff to rue Amélie making very sure that we were not followed. Contact with Moukharbel was kept to a minimum. I had to go with him to a safe deposit bank in Paris to retrieve some important documents concerning our plans.'

At midnight on the 15th of June Carlos telephoned Nydia. He advised her of Moukharbel's arrest and interrogation in Beirut. In view of the fact that Lebanese intelligence had examined Moukharbel's address book, it was obvious that all contacts recorded in it were now vulnerable. These included the charming house of Mr and Mrs Bouvier in Comeragh Mews. Mr Bouvier, in the shape of Carlos, was in Paris but Mrs Bouvier (Nydia Tobon) was still living in the house. Despite the fact that it was so late, Carlos insisted that Nydia should immediately contact Wilfried Böse, who was still safehoused at the Chesterton Road address. Apart from Churchill's Hotel Moukharbel had also stayed at the Chesterton Road safe house in late April and early May – that too was now vulnerable.

A clear indication that pressure was beginning to tell on Carlos can be seen from his insistence that Nydia should leave one exposed safe house only to move into another which, if Moukharbel had been persuaded to talk, was equally at risk.

Early on the morning of 16th June Carlos phoned again from Paris. This time, he told me, he spoke to Böse and Nydia at the Chesterton Road bedsitter. He told Böse to come to Paris and arranged to meet him at the Gare du Nord at 11.00 am on the 17th. As he recalled these events ten years later it was easy to see the rising anxiety that had gripped him in late June 1975.

Having met Böse and outlined the situation to him, Carlos promised to create new false passports for Böse and Moukharbel. Böse's would be in the name of Axel Claudius. A further indication of how increasing panic was affecting judgement can be gauged from the fact that Moukharbel insisted that Böse stay with him while the false passports were being created. Thus Böse was moved from a London safe house that at that time held no interest for either the British or the French security forces to a Paris safe house that was under surveillance by the DST. On the 21st of June both Carlos and Moukharbel telephoned Nydia. Moukharbel, ill at ease and frightened, wanted to come to London. It was agreed that Nydia would look after him. Carlos took his boss to Les Invalides air terminal in Paris. It was the last time he would see him until the evening of the 27th of June.

Nydia waited for several hours at the air terminal in West Kensington but Moukharbel never appeared – he had vanished. When Carlos learned this from Nydia his paranoia increased. In fact, Moukharbel was being held by British security for extensive questioning. If there had been anything like efficient liaison between British and French intelligence, the obvious strategy would have been to allow Moukharbel into England and follow him, but, as will become clear, there was no liaison, efficient or otherwise, between the two countries on this affair until it was far too late to be of any real use.

On June 23rd Carlos telephoned Nydia again. There was still no sign of Moukharbel. By now sound judgement had completely deserted him: he asked Nydia Tobon to travel to Paris. Instead of following Haddad's dictum of dispersing the Paris cell he was in effect summoning key members of the unit into a minefield.

With the DST blundering around Paris, not knowing what they were looking for, and members of the Popular Front arriving by virtually every boat and plane seeking the head of Haddad's European cell, who had apparently vanished into thin air, the situation had all the elements of a Keystone Cops farce, but it was to be comedy with a very bitter twist.

Michel Moukharbel had been bounced back by British security and subsequently arrested by the DST on June 23rd. Ignorant of this fact, Carlos met Böse the following day and gave him the new false passports for himself and Moukharbel. He then left to meet Nydia. The main topic of conversation was the still-missing Moukharbel. Carlos dismissed Nydia's entreaties that he should return to London with her, despite Haddad's order to leave, despite the writing on the wall saying in large letters that it was a time to cut and run. Carlos told me, 'I felt I had to stay in Paris and take care of everything.'

Carlos had felt for over a year that it should be he and not Moukharbel who headed the European cell of Wadi Haddad. Now, at least on a temporary basis and in the worst possible manner, he had become the number one man. His subsequent actions merely compounded the series of errors. Instead of sending Böse immediately out of the country, he allowed him to stay at Moukharbel's flat. A few hours after Carlos had a further meeting with Nydia Tobon on June 25th, Wilfried Böse was arrested by the DST at the flat of Michel Moukharbel. Carlos was unaware of this development, but the fact that Böse subsequently failed to turn up for a meeting at a café on St Germain des Prés should have set more alarm bells ringing. Still Carlos declined to leave the country. His ineptness as self-appointed leader was only matched by the incompetence of the DST. Böse gave them a cock and bull story that the reason he was carrying false passports and false ID was because he was investigating the arrest and false imprisonment of trade unionists and left-wing dissidents in Franco's Spain. The DST naïvely accepted this explanation and on the 26th of June handed Böse over to the German police at the Saargemund frontier post, thereby performing on behalf of Carlos one of the tasks he should have effected for himself, the removal of Wilfried Böse from Paris. With two men now having vanished, Carlos took this opportunity to phone Angela Otaola in London to apologize for his inability to attend her birthday party that evening.

On the morning of Friday, 27th June there was a considerable amount of activity in the small rue Toullier flat. Nancy Sanchez, who was returning to Venezuela that evening to continue her studies, was planning her farewell party. One of her main rivals, Maria Lara, had by happy coincidence already left Paris bound for an Algerian holiday. At least Nancy would have Carlos to herself on this last day.

They happened to meet their friend Angela Armstrong at the nearby post office in rue Cujas and invited her to join their early evening drinks party. Angela was busy and was later to thank providence that she didn't make it to that party. She was also to conclude after subsequent events that Nancy looked completely demoralized and drained at the time of their chance encounter as if 'she had learned the truth about Carlos'. Angela Armstrong is not the first to discover that hindsight has twenty twenty vision.

The post office was hot, sticky and crowded. It was end of term at the nearby Sorbonne, school was out and eager to get on holiday. Carlos, understandably preoccupied, became irritated with the delays. He tried Haddad's contact in Venice, no reply. He tried Nydia, now back in London, no reply. Nancy, meanwhile, had more luck contacting her family in Caracas. Angela was another advising friends and family of travel arrangements, in her case for her young daughter, who was flying unaccompanied the following morning to England for a summer holiday. Departures were, it seemed, scheduled for everyone but the one man who should have been on the first plane out.

I asked Carlos what had possessed him to stay in Paris when everything was urging him to make a quick getaway. He shrugged and opened his hands in a helpless manner.

'I was confused and uncertain. I felt the need to talk to the Old Man, but I could not make contact.'

That indecision was to prove lethal for a number of people.

While Carlos and Nancy Sanchez were organizing the party at the rue Toullier apartment, Michel Moukharbel was facing his fourth day of continuous interrogation at DST headquarters.

Despite the fears and apprehensions that he had expressed before his arrest, he was holding up remarkably well. Moukharbel had a resilience, an inner strength, based upon many years of struggle in his attempts to assist the Palestinian cause. His mentor and best friend, Mohammed Boudia, had found in Moukharbel a man as resourceful as himself. Together they had planned and perpetrated much on behalf of their comrades in the Middle East. Whatever weaknesses, real or imagined, Carlos saw in his boss, they were not on display to Commissioner Jean Herranz.

Moukharbel produced papers that showed he was a merchant engaged in buying and selling Persian and Kurdish carpets, hence his need for frequent trips to the Middle East. As for the various papers and passports on which Herranz had received a very vague report from his colleagues in Beirut, Moukharbel stated that he had found them in the street in Beirut. It was obvious, he said, that they would be of interest to the DST and he had planned to bring them to DST headquarters as soon as he had returned from Beirut. As a Lebanese citizen he knew full well the incompetence of his own country's security forces. He had wanted to make sure that they came into the hands of a really efficient security service. Now, because he had acted in a public-spirited manner, he was being treated like one of these damn terrorists that made these such dangerous times to live in.

As for Wilfried Böse, he was a German lawyer, a good one, but he was prone to adopt any liberal cause. It would be typical of him to be concerned about the oppressed trade unionists in Spain.

This was the basis of his responses to the interminable questions of Herranz and his colleagues. By the afternoon of the 27th of June Herranz was convinced that Moukharbel was telling him the truth. There was just one thing that troubled him. What had happened to the documents after Moukharbel had returned to Paris on the 13th of June? He certainly hadn't brought them in to the DST.

That, Moukharbel told them, was because of the treatment he had received at the hands of the Lebanese security men. He was not anxious to get more of the same from the French. The documents? He had given them to a friend for safekeeping.

At this point Herranz sprang one of those little surprises that are so beloved of all police officers. He produced a photograph of Carlos, standing outside his rue Toullier apartment, Moukharbel's briefcase in his hand. Standing next to him was Moukharbel.

Confronted with this, Moukharbel had little alternative to agreeing that yes, this was the friend with whom he had left the case. In answers to their further questions he told them that the man was Carlos Martinez, a Peruvian, son of wealthy parents, a playboy, a joker. Certainly not a man to be mixed up with anything unsavoury. Just a friend that could be trusted to look after a briefcase while he, Moukharbel, decided what to do with its contents. Moukharbel offered to contact Maria Lara, 'the girlfriend of the playboy. She will put me in touch with him.'

It all seemed very reasonable to Herranz. If Moukharbel would accompany them to the apartment of this woman, make contact with this man Carlos, formally identify his briefcase and its contents, then that would be the end of the affair. Moukharbel would be free to go, having earned the thanks of the DST for his attempts to assist them in their fight against terrorism.

If the DST had released Moukharbel, thereby permitting him to contact Carlos and advise him of the story he had told the DST, he would undoubtedly have pulled off this extraordinary bluff. But Herranz was eager to examine the contents of this by now famous briefcase and felt the sooner it was in his hands the better. He had been hunting the Mohammed Boudia group for a long time and considered the contents of this briefcase might just give him a few clues. What luck that of all the people who could have picked it up in a dusty Beirut street it should be this insignificant Lebanese, who despite his ordeal in Beirut had brought the case and its contents to Paris.

Moukharbel, knowing that Maria Lara had already gone on holiday, evidently assumed that, wherever Carlos was, he would not be in rue Toullier.

Having attended a goodbye party for a retiring colleague, Chief Commissioner Herranz selected two of his officers, Divisional Inspector Raymond Doubs and Inspector Jean Donatini, to accompany Moukharbel and himself on their visit to rue Toullier. They drove across the Seine and along the Boulevard St Germain into the heart of the Left Bank. It was one of the hottest evenings of the year, and through open windows and café doors came the sounds of Paris enjoying the heatwave.

In the apartment of 9 rue Toullier, the party – such as it had been – was almost over by eight-thirty. Nancy had already left for the airport. At 8.45 there were only five people left. The men from the DST, having already rung the bell of the wrong flat and disturbed a dinner party, knocked on the apartment door. Precisely what took place then has remained shrouded in half truths and speculation. This is what Carlos told me.

'One of them knocked on the door and opened it. It was not locked. Two men entered, saying "Police". They were Herranz and his assistant Doubs. They came in and said they were looking for Maria Lara. I told them she had gone off to the south on holiday about a week before.

'I invited them to sit down and have a drink. The mood when they came in was relaxed and I made sure it stayed that way. I had been drinking since early afternoon, but that was not a problem. I can take plenty of drink. Herranz asked to see our passports. We gave them to him. Mine was of course the Peruvian one in the name of Carlos Andreas Martinez Torres. Herranz made notes and did most of the talking. He started asking me questions about Michel Moukharbel. "Did I know this Lebanese guy? What was my connection with him?" I told him that the name did not mean anything to me and Herranz smiled and said, "Well, Michel knows you. He gave us this address."'

This was of course not true, the DST had stumbled on the rue Toullier address by following Moukharbel, but Carlos had no way of knowing that as he talked to

Herranz. It was the first of a number of deadly gambits that Herranz played.

'The Commissioner took out a photograph showing me and Michel. It had been taken near the rue Toullier apartment. It had never occurred to me that they might be watching the place. I needed to forestall them, so I began to ask them questions. "What's the problem you have with this Lebanese? Is it something to do with drugs or terrorism? These are terrible times we live in." That sort of thing. I asked them for ID too. What they showed me confirmed they were DST. It was about then that I decided to have a shave.'

The surprise that showed on my face provoked laughter in Carlos.

'I thought that if I acted and behaved in a natural, normal manner, the Inspector might well think, he is just an ordinary businessman, so I had a shave, poured some more drinks. When the police had first come in I had been in my shirtsleeves. After I finished shaving I casually put on my jacket. No-one took any notice. I had a gun in the jacket, a Tokarev, with a full clip. The party, such as it had been, was more or less over at this stage. I remember asking Herranz where this Michel was, and when Officer Doubs said, "He's in one of our cars outside," I suggested they should bring him up. That would soon resolve whether or not I knew this man.

'My suggestion obviously surprised them. Herranz and Doubs moved a small distance away and had a discussion in low voices. Eventually Herranz told his colleague to bring Michel up. He was gone some time.'

Carlos paused and sipped the drink that was on the table between us. He stared thoughtfully at the wall opposite. For a moment he was no longer in a lime-washed villa in Baalbek, with a distant dog barking in the new day's first light; he was again in Paris on Friday 27th June 1975. The time about nine-thirty.

'I realized that I was trapped, so I quietly prepared for battle. I had another drink and gave one to Herranz. Ten, maybe fifteen minutes later, Officer Doubs, Inspector

Donatini and Michel all entered. Herranz and I had been sitting chatting. We got up when they all came in. Michel had changed dramatically. He looked totally defeated. It seemed to me that he had been tortured both physically and psychologically. Just a broken shadow. Herranz pointed at Michel and asked me if I knew him. I said that I had never seen him before in my life. Then Herranz asked Michel the same question. Michel lifted his right arm very slowly and when he spoke his voice croaked. "This is the man I gave the suitcase to." As he said that he pointed at me. For me this was the moment to act.

'I got out my gun. I shot Donatini first because he was trying to get his gun out. He had a big reputation for being quick with a gun. I was quicker. I got him on the left temple. Then I shot Doubs between the eyes. I spun to shoot Herranz. One of the women, Albaida, got in my firing line. I pulled her to one side and got Herranz high in the throat. Michel was now the only one standing. He was crouched to one side, his hands over his face. His fear angered me. He had made no attempt to come to my aid. He was responsible for betraying me. I moved to him, stood directly in front of him, and shot him between the eyes. I grabbed my case, and before leaving the room I shot Michel again as he lay on the floor, this time in the left temple.

'As I ran out of the front door of the apartment, instead of going over the connecting bridge to the front of number nine, I jumped down into the courtyard of number eleven. I had three shots left in the magazine and a spare clip. I tucked my gun in the back of my jeans and went out on to the street through the front door of number eleven. Luck was with me. The rue Toullier area was having a power cut and the street lights were off. I knew the police cars would be to my right. As I came out onto the street I turned left, walking calmly. As I reached the end of the street I heard shooting. I did not look back. From the time I had got my gun out to the time I was walking down the street, six seconds.'

As Carlos escaped into the darkness, the acrid smell

of cordite still permeated the small living room. The shocked partygoers began to stir. Of the four men who had been shot, three were beyond help, only the badly wounded Herranz was still breathing. He was rushed to the Cochin Hospital and survived to face embarrassing questions from his superiors and scathing attacks from the French media.

When Carlos had leapt not only to safety but also to instant world-wide notoriety, the shade of a previous occupant of number eleven rue Toullier, through which the man with the racing heart and the still warm gun escaped into the night, should surely have been permitted a moment in which his prophetic words were acknowledged. During the early years of this century, Rainer Maria Rilke had taken up residence in a shabby rented room at number eleven. Observing his surroundings he wrote, 'So this is where people come to live; I would have thought it is a city to die in . . . The street began to give off smells from all sides. It smelled as far as I could distinguish, of iodoform, the grease of pommes frites, fear.'[1]

Although Commissioner Herranz survived, there was indeed a fourth death in that room – Ilich Ramirez Sanchez. Never again could he use his real name, or make open contact with his family or friends. From now on the safe houses, the false papers, the multiple identities would become the rule rather than the exception. Run, Carlos, run.

'After Herranz had shown you a photo of you and Moukharbel together why did you continue to insist that you had never seen him before in your life?'

'Yes, that was a mistake.'

'Does it seem to you now, ten years later, that shooting the DST officers and Michel were also mistakes?'

'Of course not. It was either them or me.'

'I can see how you would have come to that belief at the time. But those police officers were not carrying guns. Moukharbel had not betrayed you. If he had the

[1] *The Notebooks of Malte Laurids Brigge*, Picador 1988

DST would not have strolled into that apartment and sat drinking with you for over half an hour. They were grossly incompetent, but there's no evidence to suggest that any of them had suicidal tendencies.'

Carlos removed the horn-rimmed glasses he had been wearing and stared with those dark unblinking brown eyes directly at me. Then his gaze dropped and he rubbed his chin thoughtfully with his right hand.

'Who is it that says the DST were not armed?'

'There was ferocious criticism throughout the French press because Herranz and his colleagues had gone to the rue Toullier unarmed. The French government of the day admitted this was a serious error of judgement.'

He spread his arms expansively before me. His gesture stating that he considered I had proved his point.

'Imagine how much greater the uproar would have been if the French government had admitted that the three agents were indeed armed and that I had outgunned them. As for Michel, these men would not have been in the rue Toullier except for the many mistakes that Michel had made.'

'It seems to me that you shot him not because of betrayal but because he did not come to your aid during the gun battle.'

'That is right.'

'But he was not armed.'

'He could have grabbed one of them. He just stood there. The Old Man's number one in Paris. Shivering in the corner of the room.'

I felt that observation was particularly significant. Ten years after the event, the anger that Carlos felt about someone, anyone, other than he, being head of Haddad's Paris operation was clearly on display. All the wrongs, real or imagined. All the slights. The contempt that the young have for the old. The arrogance and vanity. The lack of acknowledgement for work well done, for tasks well performed. Somewhere from that time of idealism which had sent him on a voyage of discovery into the Middle East in the summer of 1970, somewhere since then, metamorphosis. The young man who had dreamed of joining Douglas Bravo and the guerrillas in the mountains ranged around Caracas had journeyed instead to the European capitals to wound, frighten, maim and kill, and by the summer of 1975 had discovered like many before him that once embarked on a nightmare journey such as his the only path forward is covered with ever more blood. Thus in a grubby, nondescript, two-room apartment in the Latin Quarter three men had their lives snuffed out and a fourth survived by a miracle, merely because the irritation in Carlos erupted into murderous resentment.

'He could have grabbed one of them. He just stood there. The Old Man's number one in Paris. Shivering in the corner of the room.'

Having driven Nancy Sanchez to Charles de Gaulle airport, Dr Jose Luis Gonzalez Duque returned to the rue Toullier apartment to collect his wife Leyma and Albaida Salazar and take them to dinner. He walked into number nine to discover three dead men on the floor and his wife and Albaida under arrest. The French police promptly arrested the doctor for good measure. All three were entirely innocent, but that night and in the days and nights that followed even casual acquaintanceship with this man called Carlos Martinez guaranteed immediate arrest, imprisonment and intensive interrogation by the shell-shocked DST.

Carlos, walking as quickly as he dare, hurried along St Germain towards the safe haven of Amparo Silva Masmela's apartment in rue Amélie. To judge from the account he gave me, having reached that particular sanctuary his behaviour became increasingly erratic. He gave no thought to moving the large store of weapons in the apartment, no consideration to salvaging what he could of Commando Boudia. He appears to have been largely motivated into attempts to justify the carnage and destruction that he had singlehandedly wrought on Haddad's Paris operation. He repeatedly left the rue Amélie flat during the late evening to phone Nydia in London. When he finally made contact with her he instructed her to burn a variety of incriminating documents. Others, including the passport of Anton Bouvier, were to be posted to a variety of friends for safekeeping. He told her that he had killed Moukharbel because of his betrayal. Returning to the rue Amélie safe house he sat down and began to write a series of letters.

Two of these were to Angela Otaola in London. He told her that he had killed Moukharbel, 'sent him to a better life, for being a traitor'. If of course Moukharbel had betrayed his colleague, then not only would the DST have arrived at rue Toullier armed and in large numbers, they would also have known of the safe house in rue Amélie, where Carlos sat writing his letters of self-justification.

On the morning of June 28th, with the entire French press giving the first details of the rue Toullier murders, Carlos strolled from the apartment to the nearby air terminal. There, sitting with her young daughter, was Angela Armstrong.

'Carlos! Carlos!' she called out across the crowded terminal hall. It was another hot, sticky day and even chatting with someone of whom she was not particularly fond gave welcome diversion from the interminable queue. She had already been waiting nearly forty-five minutes to book her daughter's flight. With the entire French police force, as well as the DST and the SDECE (the French external intelligence service) seeking him and monitoring all exits out of France, Carlos had chosen this moment to stroll around the air terminal concourse, like a man taking his weekend promenade.

Responding to her shouted greeting, Carlos casually moved over to join her. He put his arm around her shoulder, something he had never done before. After exchanging greetings with eight-year-old Nina, he guided Angela a short distance away from the queue.

'I have got problems.'

'Is it Peru? Are you trying to get a ticket for a flight there?'

'Have you heard the news?'

He began speaking rapidly in Spanish. Too rapidly.

'Carlos you'll have to slow down or speak in English.'

He chose English. 'I have just shot two men, and the Arab bastard who betrayed me. I kill all those who betray me. Luis and his wife are OK [a reference to the arrested Dr Jose Luis Gonzalez Duque and his wife]. Write to Nancy. Tell her to stay in Venezuela. She will be all right there. It is a nuisance, we will have to make the papers again. I am going to the Middle East now. Goodbye.'

With a calm, cool wave, Carlos, preoccupied with the problems of acquiring a new passport, ambled towards the exit.

Rejoining the queue, Angela was totally bemused by the strange encounter. He hadn't seemed drunk. Having safely seen her young daughter off, Angela made for the exit. At the nearby Metro her eye was caught by a large newspaper billboard emblazoned with just three words: 'FUSILLADE RUE TOULLIER'.

Even by his own standards, his own unique mix of arrogance, stupidity and indifference, it had indeed been an extraordinary performance. What had possessed him to walk into what should have been for him one of the most dangerous places in the world that morning?

'What better way to check out how efficiently French security was functioning?'

'They had your photograph?'

'Yes they did, but this was Saturday morning and this was France. There is no way the DST or anyone else in France can function as efficiently as your questions imply. There is no way for that matter that any country on earth could function that efficiently. In the long term, yes. In the short term – totally ineffective.'

There are two popular theories about how Carlos escaped from Paris during that hot summer of 1975. Both link his escape with his Cuban acquaintances in Paris. One theory has Carlos, assisted by Cuban DGI agents, being passed on to Algerian diplomats, who in turn drove him to Lyons, then on to Marseilles. With the police watching all airports, this theory propounds that Carlos was put on a fruit boat to Algiers. The second theory again has the Cuban secret service playing a vital part: Carlos is equipped with a Cuban diplomatic passport then driven through Europe to East Germany where he safely boards a plane to the Middle East.

I put both theories to the man sitting across the coffee table. He nodded continuously as I outlined them. When I had finished I asked what the truth of this particular moment was. His response was as surprising as anything he said to me that night.

'I caught a plane to London. I used my own genuine Venezuelan passport. I stayed in London nearly a month.'

If walking around the Paris air terminal a few hours after the rue Toullier shootings was an act of madness, then to catch a plane to London indicates terminal insanity and a lunatic disregard for personal safety and freedom. If caught in France the guillotine awaited him. If caught in London a very long prison sentence, followed, if still living, by extradition to France to stand trial.

It was true that in London there were Nydia and Angela Otaola and Barry Woodhams, but how long would any of these continue to offer him sanctuary when the connection was made?

The running had begun. For the rest of his life he would never be able to walk out on to the street without checking. Never be able to act on impulse. Never know if the moment of betrayal had come. No wonder he sleeps so badly. I asked him what possessed him to fly directly into such danger. He was non-committal. I asked him if he could prove that he had flown to London. He removed his glasses and stretched in the white leather couch.

'If you are as good as they say you are, you will get your own proof.'

As for why he had come to London,

'I needed somewhere safe while I made contact with the Old Man and developed a plan of action. Organized new papers. That Saturday, French security were hunting a Peruvian named Carlos Andreas Martinez Torres. They had never heard of a Venezuelan called Ilich Ramirez Sanchez. With luck they never would.'

'And the Cuban connection?'

'I have told you before. There was no Cuban connection, unless the fact that a few members of the Cuban Embassy were brought to the rue Toullier apartment by their girlfriends is a connection. That was just some nonsense from the French government.'

'To use the Cubans as scapegoats?'

'Exactly.'

Having checked out the various flight times to London, Carlos returned to the rue Amélie apartment of Amparo Masmela. Yet again if he had really believed that Moukharbel had betrayed him it is inconceivable that he would have left either the weapons store or Amparo in the flat. He packed an overnight bag – additional clothes would be purchased in London – took some spare clips of ammunition from the weapon store for his Tokarev automatic, put the gun back in his pocket and kissed Amparo goodbye.

At the same time, Wilfried Böse was appearing in front of a judge in Saarbrucken charged with carrying false identity papers. An indication of just how disorganized the DST in Paris were can be gauged by the fact that no-one thought to contact the Germans and advise them of events. A quick response would have ensured that at least one important member of Moukharbel's group remained safely under lock and key. Böse repeated his story about needing false papers because he had been asked to investigate the plight of left-wing dissidents in Spain. He was set free and promptly vanished. He had two more appointments with Fate, one in Vienna, the final one at Entebbe.

The efficiency of German counter-intelligence also left something to be desired. In March a key member of Commando Boudia, Johannes Weinrich, had been arrested in Frankfurt. The incriminating details that he and Carlos had left in the hired car after the Orly débâcle had finally caught up with him. After preliminary questioning had failed to elicit any information from Weinrich he was allowed to remain untroubled in his cell until October, at which time he complained of a urinary infection, was granted bail and disappeared.

While the German authorities were busy releasing one person who, if he had so chosen, could have given the French vital accurate information on Carlos, and ignoring another, a third who; if she had wanted to, could have advised the French police of virtually his precise location that Saturday remained silent. Angela Armstrong, having digested the garbled accounts in the French press, now knew the frightening accuracy of the remarks that Carlos had casually uttered at the air terminal. Carlos does appear to have had the luck of the devil himself in his choice of friends and acquaintances. A man who opens a case containing guns and false passports and then locks it up resolving to have a word with the owner next time he's in town. A woman who, confronted with the fact that she has just conversed with a triple murderer, does not go directly to the police but instead worries and frets about what she should do and finally decides to fly to London for the weekend. It was ironic that in her attempt to distance herself from Carlos and his activities Angela Armstrong should elect to go to the same city that he was heading for.

The French media, meanwhile, were beginning to have a field day with the story. The newspaper *Libération* appeared to view the affair as the terrorist equivalent of a European football match. Their headline two days after the killings read, 'MATCH. CARLOS 3 – D.S.T. 0'. There was media speculation that 'L'Affaire rue Toullier' was connected with the Baader-Meinhof group, with Turkish dissidents, with South American elements, with ETA, with the Japanese Red Army, with the Italian Red Brigade, with Breton separatists. Like Carlos, it was a story that was destined to run and run.

When it became obvious that Herranz and his colleagues had gone unarmed to rue Toullier, the condemnation was devastating. A curious osmosis took place.

Having built Carlos up as the key figure and leader of this strangely amorphous international terror organization, the French press, radio and television then castigated the DST for viewing Carlos as someone of total insignificance. The truth lay neatly in the middle.

On Monday, 30th June, Angela Armstrong flew back to Paris. She left her daughter Nina in the care of the child's godparents, 'just for a few days'. The few days were destined to become many months.

She returned to her secretarial work at the Collège de France, still unsure about what course of action to take. The French police resolved the problem for her. She was arrested on Wednesday, 2nd July and was charged with being an accomplice and in contact with Carlos and others who, as agents of a foreign power, were acting in a manner to harm France diplomatically and militarily.

Conviction of such an offence carried a sentence of twenty years' imprisonment. Angela was eventually released on bail after twenty-five days in custody and advised that she was free to do anything except leave France. The case against her was subsequently quietly filed away.

On Tuesday the 1st of July, twenty-four hours before Angela Armstrong experienced a very nasty shock in Paris, Barry Woodhams had a similar moment in London. Browsing through his *Guardian* newspaper, his eye was caught by a small item about the shootings. The article said that French police were hunting a man called Carlos Martinez.

Woodhams brooded about the item during his day's work at London University. Returning to the Bayswater flat, he began to remove the contents from Carlos's suitcase and examine them. As he did, he laid them out on the carpet.

There were, of course, the items that he had discovered previously: the Czech automatic and the ammunition, the Chilean passport, the Kuwaiti driving licence, the silencer, the Vzor. There were also some slabs of plastic explosive, some sticks of gelignite, some stamps for forging British entry visas and a Browning 9 mm gun. There was also a green metal box which was locked. Failing to open it, Woodhams could only guess at its contents.

He lit another cigarette and pondered. He didn't trust the police. Never had done. If he went to them with the bag how could he explain the partial discoveries he had made in mid June? He decided instead to contact the *Guardian* newspaper.

By the time that Wednesday's edition of the paper was out on the streets with its front page scoop, 'ARMS CACHE FOUND IN FLAT', both Woodhams and Angela Otaola were in Paddington Green police station where they were 'continuing to help police with their enquiries'. The *Guardian* article had concluded with the information that the cache of arms had been kept behind a bookcase in the flat. On the shelves of the bookcase, among the other paperbacks, was a copy of Frederick Forsyth's novel *The Day of the Jackal*. It didn't matter that the book belonged to Barry Woodhams, now the press had a label, a highly commercial one, to pin on the mysterious Carlos. There were guns, there were killings, there was international intrigue, there were pretty girls involved in London and Paris, and now there was a label. The fictional would-be assassin of General de Gaulle had sprung from Forsyth's pages and acquired flesh and blood. He was very much alive. So was the story and the myth. Within hours the world's press ran the screaming headline, 'THE JACKAL ON THE RUN'.

Not to be outdone, the French police were making dramatic discoveries of their own. A stub in a cheque book found on Moukharbel eventually led them to rue Amélie, to Amparo Silva Masmela, and to her apartment that should have had a letter pinned to the door addressed to the DST, containing a note headed, 'Everything That You've Ever Wanted To Know About Commando Boudia'.

Moukharbel and Carlos were undoubtedly a very formidable team, not merely in planning and perpetrating acts of terror, but also, from Wadi Haddad's perspective, in perpetrating acts of breathtaking stupidity. The avoidable arrest at Beirut airport, and Moukharbel's wanton carelessness in carrying incriminating documents so openly, were actions that led directly to the arrest of the head of Paris operations. Carlos, by panicking before, during and after the events at rue Toullier, singlehandedly destroyed the entire infrastructure of Commando Boudia. His failure to leave Paris before that fateful Friday evening, the shooting not only of his boss but three members of the DST, his failure to remove the incriminating evidence stored at rue Amélie, his failure to remove the incriminating evidence at Angela Otaola's Bayswater flat as soon as Barry Woodhams came on the scene, the letters he wrote to Angela directly after the multiple murders, his appearance at the air terminal and his conversation with Angela Armstrong – the list of errors and fatal mistakes grew ever longer.

Among the items that the French police found at Amparo Masmela's flat were the following: 2 Skorpion machine-pistols, 10 pistols, 15 sticks of dynamite, 6 kilos of plastic explosive, 3 bombs ready-primed, 33 clips of ammunition, 30 electric detonators, 28 M26 hand grenades, a large quantity of forging equipment and identity documents and passport stamps from many countries, a large quantity of blank false Ecuadorian passports and false passports all bearing photos of Carlos that indicated he was a citizen of the United States, Peru, Chile and a number of other countries.

The M26 hand grenades were part of a large consignment stolen by the Baader-Meinhof group from a United States military base in West Germany. They linked Commando Boudia directly with the Japanese Red Army action at the French Embassy in The Hague. They also directly linked the cell with the attack on the Drugstore and with a Red Army group that had been based at La Porte Maillot. The electric detonators linked the cell directly with the Turkish activists who had been discovered and expelled from France in December 1973 when, according to what Carlos told me, they were planning to assassinate the United States Secretary of State, Henry Kissinger.

The French police also found in the apartment a range of documents indicating that the cell had drawn up a French death list which included leading politicians ranging from the far right to the far left. The list also included many French personalities. They found plans for the assassination of the Israeli Ambassador in Paris. Finally the police found Moukharbel's diary. With Boswellian diligence Moukharbel had noted the various operations, the costs incurred and the dates planning meetings took place.

When the various discoveries were made public, they were greeted with cynical scepticism by much of the French media, which simply refused to believe that the men who ran Commando Boudia could be so inept as to leave such incriminating evidence waiting to be discovered.

Each new discovery served not to reduce the mysterious Carlos in stature, but to increase his reputation. Virtually overnight he was elevated from being an anonymous, overweight, stupid, machismo Latin American to a real-life James Bond. One could choose a variety of masters for this man who was suddenly being sighted in twenty different cities at the same time. He worked for Mossad, for the Arabs, for the CIA, for Chile, for Russia. He was a man, as his many false passports indicated, from everywhere who had apparently vanished into nowhere.

The myth was developing fast. The collection of exotic women helped. Each discovery, courtesy of his ineptness, helped. And his new name, The Jackal, certainly helped.

If Carlos had indeed escaped to London, as he assured me he had, then he certainly believed in making life difficult not only for others but also for himself. The British police and then MI5 were still interrogating Barry Woodhams and Angela Otaola when Carlos's next helpful contribution to their enquiries arrived. Just in case the police missed it, Carlos had obligingly written two letters.

Dear Angela, as you know things were very serious here and I've taken off. I did not ring you because

I had to tear up your postcard. I'm sending you this letter in duplicate, to the bistro and your house, because if anything happens to me and I've got the address wrong, one of them will reach you. Don't ring my girlfriend yet. I'm going on a trip for an undetermined time. But I hope I won't be long in returning. As for the 'Chiquitin', I've sent him to a better life for his treachery.

Kisses, Carlos.

Spanish-speaking members of the Special Branch immediately translated 'Chiquitin' as 'our little one', a clear ironic reference to the late Michel Moukharbel. But who, they asked Angela, was the girlfriend?

The petrified Basque remembered a phone number that Carlos had given her, 'Just in case you ever need to get hold of me quickly.' She had kept it in a jar of glass marbles in the flat. The number was Nydia Tobon's.

On Monday the 30th of June, a day before Barry Woodhams read the newspaper report that prompted him to break open the lock on Carlos's bag for the second time, there were two alleged sightings of the Venezuelan close to the Bayswater flat where the arms cache was stored. At lunchtime the owner of the launderette on the ground floor below Angela's flat was convinced that he saw Carlos 'hanging around outside the block of flats. He made me suspicious, so I kept an eye on him. I saw him go down the alley to Angela's flat several times. I never spoke to him, but I'm sure it was him.'

According to the owner of Angelo's, the nearby drinking club that Carlos had used in the past, 'Carlos popped in for a few minutes before closing time. He was alone and looked nervous.' When these sightings became front-page news, the police declined to comment. If the sightings were accurate, then clearly Carlos – having made a noose for himself – was doing all he could to get it around his neck. Within two days he lost any potential use of both Angela Otaola's flat and Nydia Tobon's. Nydia, incriminated in the letters written by

Carlos to Angela, was arrested. She protested her innocence and told the police that she had believed Carlos was working for foreign exiles, which in view of the fact that there are millions of Palestinians scattered throughout the world had a certain plausibility.

Confronted with Angela Otaola's allegation that she was the woman who, acting on instructions from Carlos, had the previous year collected a metal case from the Basque, she was in more difficult waters.

The metal case in question had been found in the larger case safehoused at Angela's. Its contents have never been revealed. I have established that it contained the Beretta gun with which Carlos attempted to murder Edward Sieff, a gas gun, two Russian grenades, an M26 grenade identical to that thrown in the Drugstore in Paris, and a couple of rubber truncheons.

Life became even more difficult for Nydia Tobon when she was confronted with the passport belonging to a certain Anton Bouvier. She had obeyed the instructions Carlos told me he had given her and posted it to a friend, fellow Colombian Anna Pugsley. Unfortunately for Nydia, she had incorrectly addressed the envelope. The Post Office had opened the package and, finding an Ecuadorian passport inside, had forwarded it to the Ecuadorian Embassy. They soon realized it was a forgery and contacted Scotland Yard.

As police investigations continued, Scotland Yard stated that they had located two safe houses used by Carlos in London. They never revealed the addresses, which were in fact the Comeragh Mews residence that was due to serve as temporary accommodation for a certain Arab Ambassador and the flat at 23 Chesterton Road.

On the 2nd July, Scotland Yard had established the true identity of Carlos, that he was in fact the Venezuelan, Ilich Ramirez Sanchez. Undeterred, much of the world's press continued to call him Carlos the Jackal, and to speculate about his true nationality.

In the second week of July there were further press reports of an alleged sighting of Carlos, this time in the Knightsbridge area by an unidentified 'friend of the Ramirez family'. At first Scotland Yard denied the sighting, then a few days later confirmed that they accepted it as accurate. In either event, false or true, Carlos was not caught by the British police. If, as he insisted to me, he had indeed flown from Paris to London the day after the rue Toullier shootings and then spent a month in London, the British police force and security services are guilty of the most appalling negligence. The evidence available to me at the time of my second interview with Carlos was ambiguous. Three different people in three different places asserting that they had seen him might appear to be proof positive but many a person in a variety of countries was equally insistent that they had seen Carlos at exactly this time. Surely British security could not be so incompetent?

Not only the British, but also the security forces of France, Germany, Holland, Belgium and Italy were insisting that, at the time of this third alleged sighting in West London, Carlos was now travelling on a false Chilean passport, number 035857, in the name of Hector Hugo Dupont. Dupont – now there is a good old Chilean name. Further, the security sections of these countries gave a strong indication to the world's press that they believed Carlos had already reached safe refuge in Beirut.

By this time Barry Woodhams had been released without being charged, but his girlfriend Angela Otaola was less fortunate. She was charged with three counts of possessing arms. It finished her relationship with Woodhams, whom, rather than Carlos, she considered responsible for her problems. Later that year she was sentenced to one year's imprisonment. Upon her release she was deported back to Spain.

Nydia Tobon was also sentenced to one year's imprisonment after being found guilty of receiving a stolen blank Italian identity card, one of a batch originally stolen by the Red Brigades. She too was deported after serving her sentence. Nydia received her LSE degree while in prison. Perhaps encouraged by this, she fought her deportation order, insisting that she had been treated cruelly by British justice. My research at the time of my second interview with Carlos strongly indicated that she had in fact been extremely fortunate not to have faced far more serious charges and a much longer term of imprisonment.

In France, whether looking for scapegoats or not, the government duly discovered a few. Poniatowski called a press conference at which he announced the expulsion of three Cuban diplomats whom he accused of being members of the DGI (the Direccion General de Inteligencia), which they almost certainly were. They were further accused of 'having had several meetings with Carlos', which again they certainly did, at the rue Toullier parties. He did not produce a shred of evidence to suggest that these meetings had any sinister significance. This being 1975, when a popular view of the world was to believe that the Soviet Union masterminded every single act of terrorism perpetrated on the planet, Poniatowski was very anxious to drag the Soviets into the affair if he could.

It was rumoured at the time that he had been prevented from naming the Soviet Union by President Giscard d'Estaing, who was about to make a visit to Moscow and had no desire to make waves for his hosts on the eve of his trip. Again no evidence was offered to support the innuendo. Poniatowski may conceivably have been influenced in his judgement and his remarks by the fact that his own name appeared on a 'death list' found in the rue Amélie apartment.

The Minister stated at the time he revealed the expulsion of the three Cubans 'certain foreign intelligences are giving aid to international terrorist organizations'.

In Paris the authorities were still busily engaged either imprisoning or deporting friends and acquaintances of Carlos. Amparo Silva Masmela went to prison, Albaida Salazar and Leyma Duque were deported to Venezuela. Maria Teresa Lara decided to prolong her holiday in Algiers. Of the man who had singlehandedly brought about all this there was not a trace.

The week following Poniatowski's comments, the Soviet Union responded. It is to date the only public statement they have ever made about the world's most wanted man. Their response entitled 'Who profits from the Carlos Affair?' was broadcast on Moscow Radio in a French language transmission on the 16th July.

The French press has been giving a lot of coverage to the so-called Carlos Affair. Our listeners are well acquainted with the case and there is no need to go into details. However, an ordinary act of gangsterism is being presented by Poniatowski as an international conspiracy, in which certain foreign states are supposed to be participating. This is an unmistakable allusion to the socialist countries and obviously the Soviet Union.

In its statement on the Carlos Affair, the Communist group in the French National Assembly has stressed that the twist given to it bears eloquent witness to the tendency of certain circles in France to worsen relations with the socialist countries and to present the French Communists as secret accomplices of this terrorist group.

It is quite obvious that those who attribute to the Carlos Affair a dimension of international conspiracy supposedly supported by the socialist countries had precisely this aim in mind . . . At a time when peaceful coexistence between the countries of East and West is becoming the norm and when there has been a radical turn to detente in progress, there are still men in France who would like to put a brake on this progress, and return to the cold war period. In pursuance of this aim, no methods are banned. Suffice it to recall the provocative but unsuccessful machinations of publishing anti-Soviet articles in the *Quotidien de Paris*.

Today it is the Carlos Affair; it is safe to predict that the outcome of this affair will be just as scandalous.

As Carlos sat across the coffee table from me, he had

dismissed the stories that he was a KGB agent, a creature controlled by the men who resided in the large stone building in Dzerzhinsky Square. The French turned up the heat another few notches by trying to bring public pressure on the British government of the day. They denounced a Cuban diplomat based in London, Angel Dalmau, stating that he had been in regular contact with Nydia Tobon. Then, in an apparent attempt to get the British to expel not only Dalmau but other members of the Cuban Embassy they observed, 'It has been noted in Paris that there have been a number of unusual and recent departures from London of several members of the DGI, the Cuban Secret Service.'

Publicly, the British Foreign Office declined to comment and took no action. Privately they were outraged and in their own off-the-record briefings stated that there was no truth in the allegations about Dalmau or any other member of the Cuban Embassy.

'Where did you go when you left London?'

'I left London towards the end of July and flew to Algiers. I stayed in the capital for a few weeks then flew to Aden.'

'Your reunion with Wadi Haddad. Was that a difficult meeting?'

He smiled again.

'That is what I like about the English language. It has a beautiful ability to understate. Difficult.'

Laughter welled up from within him.

'Yes, it was difficult.'

I waited quietly for him to continue.

'The Old Man interrogated me for hours. Questions, then more questions, just like you. Why had I not left Paris earlier? Why did I shoot Michel? Why did I go to London? Why did I not follow the agreed escape route?'

'Which was?'

'To Algiers and then the near East.'

'In view of the fact that you later led the Vienna operation you were obviously able to give him satisfactory answers?'

'Not at all. He told me that I was finished. That I would never again be part of the Popular Front.'

'He clearly changed his mind.'

He nodded.

'What caused him to reconsider?'

His response revealed one of the many obscenities in the story of Ilich Ramirez Sanchez.

'After rue Toullier the stories that were written about me made me famous. Carlos the Jackal became known throughout the world. When these writers began to give me credit for all these operations that were nothing to do with me that just made me more famous.'

It had been said quietly. No hint of arrogance, yet his use of the word 'credit' appalled me. Credit? For the murders of the innocent Peruvian pilgrims at Lod? For the massacre at Rome in which over thirty people were roasted to death? If these acts be held to be creditworthy anywhere in the world, then surely the world has gone mad.

'And these stories, totally without any foundation in fact, impressed Wadi Haddad?'

'Firstly, they amused him. He knew the truth, as did other Palestinians. Look, Lod Airport was planned by Wadi Haddad. The attack at the Munich Olympic Games was planned by Abu Iyad. I was not involved in any way at all in those.'

'And it amused him when the British, the French, the Italians, the Americans, the Germans and the rest of them said you were responsible?'

'Oh yes, very much. You must understand that an important part of Wadi Haddad's philosophy was a belief in the use of terror. He had learned that lesson from the British and the Jews. He had personally seen how effective the use of terror tactics could be when they had been used against the Palestinians.'

'Did he feel that the fact that you had been built up by the media into the world's super terrorist could be turned to advantage?'

'Yes, he did. That is why he changed his mind about

throwing me out of the Popular Front.'

'And how did you feel about the way the media had built you up?'

'I was very pleased. Delighted. It saved my neck with the Old Man and the bigger they made me the less police would come looking for me. I became the world's most wanted man, whom very few really wanted to search for.'

He told of how, during his month in London after the killings in Paris, he had gone regularly to various newsagents, particularly shops in the Soho area that specialize in foreign periodicals, how he had eagerly scanned all the papers and magazines for articles about himself, how he had torn them out, collected them. Then he would proudly produce them in Aden to Wadi Haddad. He recalled very well an article in *The Times* headed 'Is the Jackal a Moscow-trained terrorist who has broken out of control?' That had particularly pleased him. He assured me he had no love for the Soviets after his expulsion from Patrice Lumumba University. In his eyes, if the West wanted to lay responsibility for Carlos at the door of the KGB it was an unexpected bonus. Super terrorist. Super KGB agent. Super bogey man. The more the merrier. He now had his own fifteen minutes of fame which might, with luck, run the full hour.

Wadi Haddad saw the enormous potential in the myth that had been created by a combination of cleverly placed pieces of disinformation dropped by security agencies into the laps of unquestioning writers and commentators.

'The attack on OPEC and the kidnapping of the oil ministers in Vienna. Whose idea was that?'

Carlos seemed almost surprised by my question.

'Qathafi, of course.'

The Libyan Head of State, Mu'Ammar Qathafi, has been held responsible by much of the world, not only for the attack on the OPEC headquarters in Vienna in December 1975, but a great many other outrages, but there has always been a significant lack of conclusive proof. Now the man who led that attack was supplying it.

This revelation came in the latter stages of my second interview with Carlos. He gave details of not only the OPEC attack but also his subsequent activities. It was obvious, however, that there would have to be a third and final interview before this man's extraordinary life story could be brought up to date. He agreed to see me again in October. We had for the second time talked through the night. These interviews had about them their own ebbs and flows of energy. Periods of apparent fatigue and tiredness were followed by rapid excitement and high mental activity. Carlos had, for example, become highly animated when discussing the events leading up to the killing of Moukharbel and the DST officers, then, when asked for details of his subsequent stay in London, he had appeared almost bored and languid. It was as if the adrenalin only pumped in him when he recalled violent actions.

After some further conversation about his activities in the ten years since the OPEC attack he stretched and stood up, his action signalling to me that we would go no further on this occasion.

'Until October.'

A moment later he had left the room. As I bent down to collect my files and pages and pages of notes Samir entered the room.

'It was good?'

'Yes, Samir. Thank you very much. It was good. Shukran.'

6

APPOINTMENT IN BEIRUT

As I prepared for my third and final trip to Beirut I frequently found myself offering a silent prayer of thanks to my late mother. I had much to thank her for, not least the gift she had given me beyond the grave – the right to hold an Irish passport. Although London-born, I was able to claim dual nationality because Una Nora had been born in Cork. This, as well as the two British passports I hold, gave me comfort as I planned this final flight. To my knowledge, up to that time only one Irishman, Aidan Walsh, had been abducted in West Beirut. Walsh, the deputy director of United Nations Relief and Works Agency, UNRWA, had been snatched on May 15th, 1985, not long after my first trip to the city. He was released the following day, as soon as his kidnappers established his identity.

There were no Arabs imprisoned in Ireland whose release could be demanded for mine and I had already realized from earlier trips that many Arabs strongly identified with that particular element of Irish society which seeks unification with Ulster. To such straws do men who travel hopefully cling. A talisman that would ward off all the evils of Beirut.

There were other more tangible reasons to feel buoyant, other factors that convinced me this would be third time very lucky – I had pulled it off, succeeded beyond even my most optimistic expectations. I had set out to find the world's most wanted man and, if possible, interview him. Now, after this third interview, and after a minimal period of further investigation and research,

I would be able to sit down and write the book that I had first conceived in late 1983. With luck it would be written and published during 1986.

In early October, just a few days before I was due to take my flight, the news coming out of Beirut made my blood run cold. Four Soviet diplomats had been kidnapped in the city. Within forty-eight hours one of them, Consular Attaché Arkady Katkov, had been murdered and his body dumped on a rubbish tip near the ruins of the sports stadium. Of his three friends and colleagues, there was no word. Both the kidnappings and the killing had been claimed by the Islamic Liberation Organization, which threatened to kill the remaining Soviet hostages if Moscow failed to stop Syrian forces fighting Sunni Muslim militiamen in the northern Lebanese city of Tripoli.

If 'they' were prepared to kidnap and kill Soviet diplomats then it was open season on anyone. Because of the deep relationships that existed between the Soviet Union and a number of countries in the region, particularly Syria, and also because of a global perception that you did not mess around with the USSR, it had long been received wisdom that not only her diplomats, but her ordinary citizens, could leave mother Russia and travel unimpeded around the world. Many who clung to the theory that the Soviets were responsible ultimately for virtually all acts of terrorism also considered that this was the telling factor.

I considered yet again the country that I was about to visit. Just mentally recounting a few of the events that had taken place during that year alone should have been sufficient reason to start unpacking my bags.

First, there were the kidnappings for which 'they' were responsible. Exactly who 'they' were varied – in 1985 in Lebanon those names included Islamic Jihad, Armed Struggle Cells, Arab Commando Cells, the Islamic Liberation Organization, The Revolutionary Organization of Socialist Muslims and the Vengeance Party. There were Sunni Muslims who could make you vanish, Shiite Muslims who could arrange your disappearance. You could be snatched by the Armed Revolutionary Brigades. The list was seemingly infinite. So was the number of victims they claimed. Hundreds upon hundreds of Lebanese who were considered so un-newsworthy by the Western media that neither the event nor their names were ever published.

The kidnapping of the Swiss Chargé d'Affaires in West Beirut on January the 3rd, followed by the American Roman Catholic priest Lawrence Jenco on the 8th had got the year off to what passed for Lebanese normality. There had been a Dutch priest who was first kidnapped, then horribly tortured to death, American journalist Terry Anderson, French Vice-Consul Marcel Fontaine, British journalist Alec Collett. Teachers, doctors, professors of agriculture, Iranian photographers, Canadian relief workers, Red Cross workers – no-one was safe, no-one immune. What foolishness to seek such immunity. What stupidity to look for protection from an Irish passport.

Second, there were the private wars. On March 1st thirty-six Americans working with the United Nations Interim Force in Lebanon, UNIFIL, were evacuated from Southern Lebanon. Observers said their departure emphasized the increasing anti-American feeling in Lebanon and the danger of becoming kidnap victims or targets for attacks by militant Shiite groups. There is no doubt in my mind that the real reason they were moved out was revealed to the world precisely one week later. A car bomb exploded in the Shiite Beirut suburb of Bir Al-Abed. At least eighty people were blown up, a further two hundred were seriously injured. Virtually all of them were civilian, by anyone's definition. Within one hour of the attack survivors hung a large banner on what was left of one of the bomb-blasted buildings, it proclaimed 'Made In The USA'. Their conclusion was faultless: the man who had conceived the attack was the head of the CIA, William Casey. Through this act he hoped to obtain revenge for three earlier bombing atrocities on American installations in Beirut. With the aid of Saudi Arabian money and Lebanese personnel, Casey had targeted for destruction the fundamentalist Muslim leader Sheik Mohamed Fadlallah. The head of the CIA believed that Fadlallah was behind the attacks not only on the American Marine HQ in Beirut but also the French battalion headquarters, two attacks that took three hundred lives. The car-bomb outside Fadlallah's home in March 1985 was planned to send him to join those three hundred. Fadlallah was uninjured.

Southern Lebanon was occupied by Israeli troops and their collaborators, the South Lebanon Army. The crack Seventh Armoured Brigade was demonstrating that it was not all it was cracked up to be. During early 1985 there were continuous reports of Israeli Army indiscipline, ranging from the torture to the killing of civilians. Israeli Shin Beth agents appeared to be fully occupied creating a private fiefdom in the South. As Lebanese citizens continued to fight a bitter and increasingly efficient war of resistance against the occupying Israelis, the country that continuingly boasted of being the only democracy in the Middle East resorted to ever more undemocratic methods.

Predictably when the Israeli army began to pull back another little private war erupted. This one was between Christians and Muslims.

By the time of my first trip to Lebanon in 1985 Western reporters and TV crews were rapidly vacating Lebanon, particularly West Beirut. Fear. Of being the next to be snatched from the streets of the capital or, in the South, of joining in the grave those reporters already killed by Israeli forces.

By April, too, Sunni was fighting Shia in the streets of Beirut. The sound of firing in the streets of West Beirut became a constant feature of what passed for everyday life in the city.

Yet more private wars – the Palestinian refugees in the camps of Sabra, Chatila and Bourj al-Barajneh became locked in a vicious battle with the Amal Shia Muslim movement. The three camps were in a state of constant siege. Any who dared to run the gauntlet, to obtain food, water, medicine, were shot.

To the north of Beirut, by the early autumn, yet another little private war was raging in the area around the city of Tripoli. This one was being fought out between the Syrian-backed Lebanese factions and Sunni militia.

During the year a considerable number of planes were hijacked and forced to fly to Beirut. Some of them were already scheduled to fly to that city – it was almost as if Beirut had become the only city known to hijackers in the mid 1980s, just as Havana was the one word revolutionaries could utter in the 1960s.

The most notable hijack, one that had the media scurrying back to the city from which they had fled, was the TWA Boeing 727 taken over by Lebanese Shiites on June 14th. One passenger was eventually murdered and tossed on the tarmac at Beirut: Robert Stetham, a United States Navy diver, found guilty of carrying an American passport. Eventually all the other passengers, having initially been taken from the plane and hidden in Beirut, were released unharmed.

What happened that year is simple to recount; why is not. Neither is it, thank God, a story I am seeking to tell. Millions of words over many years have been written about the tragedy of Lebanon, to explain its history, the warring countries, the hostile factions. Whenever I am asked to explain exactly who is on whose side, my response is always the same: 'Do you want to know the line-up before or after coffee?'

I brooded for a few days, during which I tried in vain to get a phone call through to Samir. Finally, in the middle of the night, the phone rang and I heard his voice, faintly but unmistakably, on the line.

'Mr David. How are you?'

'I'm very well, Samir. More to the point, how are you and your family?'

'Everybody is well, thank you. It is a good time for you to visit. Everything is quiet.'

Samir's view of what represented 'quiet' had always differed somewhat from my own.

'Are you sure?'

'Yes, there will be no problems. When will you come?'

I advised him of my flight details, carefully repeating the time the flight was due in Beirut. He was my real insurance, not an Irish passport. As long as Samir was there to meet me at the arrival barrier, I felt everything would be fine. My personal guardian angel.

As I climbed into Samir's very battered car I was not particularly reassured to find him handing me a Druze cap to wear.

Samir told me that, as on my previous trips, he had arranged for me to stay with a relation in West Beirut. A safe house in a high-rise block close to the sea.

When we were alone, Samir told me of the arrangements. He would return later that day to drive me north-east and I would meet for the third and final time the man who had caused me to come back to the madness of Lebanon, a beautiful country where the ugliest things happen. As before, when he was about to leave, Samir recited a litany of survival.

'Please, Mr David, do not go out alone. Better not to go out at all. If you need anything, ask my brother Bashir. He will be happy to get it for you.'

I reassured him that, without him to accompany me, I had not the slightest desire to leave the apartment.

Left to my own devices I began to make my final preparations for the interview with Carlos. The fear that had consumed me on the drive from the airport had by now turned to excitement, the adrenalin was pumping. In twenty-four hours it would all be over.

Some hours later, my preparations completed, I stepped out onto the small balcony that led directly from the room. It was getting dark. To my right, just a short distance away, I could see the Mediterranean. Below me and to my left, the dusk was beginning to fill in the bomb craters, to smooth away the bullet- and shell-pockmarked buildings. Darkness making whole again for a few hours a city that was torn apart. Samir would be coming for me soon. I watched a pack of wild dogs, a variety of colours, shapes and sizes, scavenging in the street. Presumably they had been family pets once, although that was hard to imagine. I had never seen anyone stroke a dog in this city, not even a Christian.

I cannot remember how long the noise behind me in the flat had been going on, I just recall suddenly being aware of it. At first I thought it was a family argument and decided it would be more discreet to stay out on the balcony, then I became aware of a tone in the noise. The Arabic had been incomprehensible. The grief was familiar. Grief speaks in only one language.

I hurried into the living room. Bashir, his wife and a number of men and women I had never seen before were there. The men were crying openly, without making the slightest attempt to hide their grief. The women were sobbing and wailing. A number of people were proclaiming. It was obvious that some dreadful calamity had happened. I wanted to offer some comfort, some sympathy. Bashir saw me and walked over. Putting my arm around him, I steered him into the small bedroom. Still crying, he sat on the edge of the bed. My Arabic was as non-existent as his English. We both had a few words of the other's language but those few words were never going to be adequate for a moment like this.

He chattered in Arabic while I leafed through my Arabic phrase book. Fine for ordering a coffee. For thanking someone for their kindness. Then, suddenly, the need to find an appropriate phrase became meaningless.

'Mr David. Samir is dead.'

Slowly, grotesquely, with the aid of the phrase book and fragments of English, French, Spanish and Italian, I got the story.

Samir had been on his way to collect me when, near Chatila, his car had been hit by a rocket-propelled grenade. He had driven slap into yet another little private war, this one between the Amal militia and the Palestinians. This man who knew not only Beirut but the entire country as well as he knew the secret corners of his very soul, this man who knew very exactly the line-up, had driven directly into a battle. What had possessed him to take such a dangerous route? Samir the survivor. The man who calmly handed me a variety of passes every time we met at the airport. Passes that ensured we went through countless checkpoints without hindrance. The man who had calmly driven me twice out of Beirut in the darkness, first towards Jounieh, then inland, climbing ever higher in the direction of Baalbek, which was at that time one of the most dangerous regions in the world for a pair of strangers, had now come to his end in broad daylight in the middle of his home town. It was unreal.

Later, I insisted on going with Bashir and his family to visit Samir's wife and children. Samir had already proudly told me during our long night drives of his family, of how his wife, who was fluent in English, had taught him the language.

I was by this time experiencing a profound guilt. If Samir had not been coming for me he would not have been on that road outside the gates to the Chatila Palestinian refugee camp. I felt responsible. I still feel responsible. The family are Lebanese Christians, and perhaps it was that spiritual bond which made this meeting a little easier. A family whose faith had its roots in Greek Catholicism and the Englishman with the Irish passport who still retained deep within him his Roman Catholic childhood. Gifts from the past, dusted down and pressed into service.

Incredibly, Samir's wife showed greater concern for my own situation than her own. Even the most secretive of men talk in bed and she was aware of why I was in Beirut and of whom I was due to meet. Perhaps the distraction of my dilemma helped her keep at bay for a little while some of the realities of her own appalling loss. I don't know, but then I have frequently been astonished at the strength that some can display when confronting the most dreadful. She felt 'that the man you have come to see' would make contact when Samir failed to appear with me. It was agreed that I would stay at Bashir's apartment and wait.

After a week I decided it was pointless. Samir was in his grave and I felt terribly alone and vulnerable. I had not left the flat once. Perhaps it was the confinement that was affecting me. Life and death were still going on in the city, but I was no part of it. High in the sky, detached from it all. It gave me just the slightest glimmer of a hostage's existence. There had been no word from Carlos and I concluded that, when Samir and I had failed to arrive, rather than make contact, as Samir's wife had naïvely assumed and I clutching at straws had accepted, he had wisely vanished from the safe house where we were due to meet. Vanishing ensured he remained the world's most wanted man. To have remained and made contact when a man as trustworthy as Samir failed to show might well, in Carlos's mind, put his continuing freedom at risk. I recalled his remarks when I had asked him for his fingerprints and he had eventually agreed to give them to me at our final meeting.

'If I give them to you sooner than our last meeting, and please do not be offended, I have no way of knowing who you might appear with.'

With Samir dead there was no way on earth I could appear at the door of Carlos until he re-established contact. Samir's wife insisted on some of the female members of the family accompanying me to the airport.

'No-one will dare to drag you from the car if you are with us.'

Slight protection or not, I was acutely aware that I needed all the help I could get.

As I stepped from the car at the international airport I suddenly realized that I was soaked in perspiration and that my clothes were sodden. I said my goodbyes and thrust the Druze cap into the widow's hands.

'Samir gave this to me. Please take it.'

She seemed for a moment as if she was going to break down, then, clutching the cap with both hands, she kissed it.

'I'll see you again. Soon.'

'Inshaa-allaah.'

Inshaa-allaah indeed. It was to be more than three years before we met again.

PART TWO

7

'CARLOS IS DEAD'

During the last week of October 1985 the *Daily Express* ran a double-page centre-spread. Its headline was 'The world's ten most wanted criminals'. The sub-heading stated 'TOP OF THE LIST – CARLOS THE JACKAL'. There, staring from the newspaper, was that face yet again. It mattered little that virtually all the biographical details given were, based on my own research, inaccurate. What did matter was that my hunt for this man had led to Samir's death. What also mattered was that I had to re-establish contact with him again.

How could I track down the Nameless One in Algiers again, or René or Gustavo? Could I fly to Charles de Gaulle airport and wander around looking for a driver called Louis? It was equally likely that the phone number I had been given for Danielli in Milan was merely a public call box in a café. Whether it was or not it gave me the man I was seeking. With considerable relief I heard his soft, almost feminine voice on the line.

Since the early 1970s my telephone lines have occasionally been tapped. One of the advantages in talking on the phone to someone like Danielli is that a man who has been in the Brigate Rosse and survived has developed a number of useful techniques. These included the ability to conduct elliptical telephone conversations.

'Hello. I've been meaning to call you for some time. Just rang to say how much I enjoyed our evening together. I told you the pasta would be better than any you could get in Italy.'

He chuckled and obviously recalled our meal together and the compliment I had paid his wife.

'For London it was excellent, David. And how is everything?'

'I've been mountain climbing. Set myself a target of three peaks. Got to the top of the first two then ran out of guides.'

'Such strenuous activity for a man of your age.'

We continued in this vein for a while. If anyone was listening they might well have deduced that I was a keep fit fanatic. Eventually I said,

'I'll be going back to that restaurant next Wednesday evening, Danielli. I'll give your compliments to the chef.'

We agreed to stay in touch and said our goodbyes. I stared at the phone and, not for the first time in my life, concluded that there must be an easier way of getting through it. Then I picked up the telephone again and booked a flight to Milan for the following Wednesday.

I had planned to phone Danielli on arrival, but there was no need. He had been at the airport in time for the previous flight. He opened the boot of his car and threw in my case. Later, after dinner, when we were alone, I told him some of the events since our last meeting. He said little, nodded a great deal and asked the occasional question. He was particularly interested in the circumstances surrounding the death of Samir. I told him all I knew, but he still appeared uneasy.

'And this man's death, you are sure it was just a random event? Just an unfortunate accident?'

'Men, women and children are dying every day in Lebanon. The country's awash in blood. Do you think there might be something more to it then?'

He shrugged. 'It's possible. Perhaps someone wanted to prevent that third meeting with Carlos.'

'Then why didn't they come after me?'

'There would have been no need. Once your friend Samir was killed how would you get to Carlos?'

How indeed? It was my anxiety to find an answer to that question that had brought me back to Milan and

Danielli, and that is precisely what I told him. Putting that issue to one side for a while, he began to question me very closely about what Carlos had told me regarding his links and contacts with Brigate Rosse, the Red Brigades. Eventually he was satisfied.

'Why all the questions?'

'I wanted to be absolutely sure that the man you have interviewed was Carlos.'

That jolted me. Having talked away two entire nights with Carlos I had no doubt about his authenticity. The wealth of detail, the minutiae of the man's life as he revealed it to me, had totally convinced me that this was indeed Ilich Ramirez Sanchez. With or without his fingerprints, there was no doubt in my mind that he was the genuine article. To my relief, when I shared some of that detail with Danielli, any doubts that he might have had were put to rest.

That still left me with the problem of re-establishing contact. Danielli was optimistic. It was only a matter of explaining the situation to Gustavo in Paris for the links via Algiers to the Lebanon to be reactivated. It would take a little time but it would be done.

In January 1986, Danielli brought me bad news. It transpired that the man in Algiers, the one I had dubbed The Nameless One, had been unable to make contact. He had tried, and Danielli told me he had tried very hard, but Carlos had vanished. Danielli reassured me.

'He was always doing that back in the old days. He'd never settle anywhere for long. After what happened in Beirut he would be very cautious. Remember he was trained by Wadi Haddad. Don't worry, they'll keep trying. Sooner or later they will renew contact.'

The following month, February 1986, the news was far worse. Carlos was dead.

It was first reported in the Israeli newspaper *Davar*. It was picked up by the international press and the story sped around the world. If it was accurate it certainly presented me with a definitive reason why Danielli's friends could find no trace of the man. *If* it was accurate.

My research had already established that reports of his death had been appearing in a variety of newspapers and magazines for more than ten years. The earliest had appeared in the French press in December 1975, bang in the middle of the OPEC operation in Vienna led by Carlos. I had established that the French government of the time had, through its intelligence agencies, deliberately run a disinformation exercise. In the midst of the Vienna attack, with the entire world's media speculating about the identity of the perpetrators, and in many instances guessing correctly that Carlos was involved, French newspapers had advised their readers that it could not be Carlos because he had been murdered 'by his Middle East masters' after the rue Toullier killings in 1975. The lies were to ensure that the French government was not placed in the potentially embarrassing and politically disastrous position of applying to the Austrians for extradition of Carlos to France. To have put him on public trial and have the extraordinary incompetence of the DST made a matter of official public record was not a prospect that appealed to the government in Paris. The implications of the long prison sentence that would undoubtedly be handed out after a débâcle of a trial appealed even less to the French government. With Carlos in prison, his friends would be bound to come for him. They would bring terror to France until he was released. By the time that the identity of Carlos as the leader of the OPEC attack had been established beyond all doubt Carlos had vanished in Algeria.

The report in *Davar* was disturbingly different. It had a source, a good one. His identity was not revealed in the article, he was merely referred to as 'one of the heads of the intelligence community who retired recently'. If a former head of Mossad was going on the record, albeit without identification, then I took the view that the report should be treated seriously.

Experience has long taught me to place little reliance on secondary accounts, particularly those carried in newspapers. Having with a little difficulty acquired a copy of

Davar, I then, with considerably more difficulty, had the original text in Hebrew translated. It was a series of three long articles, consisting very largely of a diatribe against Palestinians in general and certain individuals in particular. There was much about Abu Nidal, George Habash, Wadi Haddad and Abu Ibrahim. All men that Israel considers terrorists and Palestinians consider heroic freedom fighters. What had caught the attention of the world's press was not the history of Carlos contained within the articles, which I was relieved to see contained a variety of easily proved errors, but the opening paragraphs, the hooker to the series.

We will not be surprised if it is discovered that Carlos is buried beneath the sands of the Libyan desert, said one of the heads of the Intelligence community who retired recently. He knew too much. Thus it appears they killed him. His up-to-date knowledge of the plans of the Arab leaders and their security systems in international terror appeared to them too dangerous. All the time that Carlos was efficient they bought his services. After a new generation of professional terrorists had arisen they had no need of lone wolves. Thus it appears they killed him.

It was long on speculation and rhetoric, short on fact. What worried me was trying to answer the question, why? Why now? Why had an Israeli intelligence chief, retired or not, broken the traditional silence of his profession and gone public with a story that he must have known would receive international attention? Why now, in February 1986?

I ran certain events through my mind. October 1985, my third and final meeting with Carlos is prevented by the death of Samir; January 1986, the Algerian who had direct contact with Carlos cannot trace him; February 1986, Carlos is declared dead by a senior Israeli intelligence chief. I sit with the unique information obtained from Carlos over nearly twenty hours of interviewing, which in the light of this report now has even greater importance. So what should I do? The answer that leapt predictably to mind was that the book should be written as fast as possible and then published. But suppose, I asked myself, just suppose you have been set up? Intelligence agencies around the world are very clever at playing Western writers. What if that third meeting had been prevented because it had to be? It seemed an impossible scenario. Why on earth would anyone go to so much trouble? Who would go to so much trouble? If they indeed had then obviously a third interview at which the man I am talking to gives me a set of his fingerprints could not take place. The fingerprints of Ilich Ramirez Sanchez were on file, held by Venezuelan Intelligence, Interpol, Special Branch in Great Britain, the CIA in Washington and a number of European intelligence agencies. If it were a set-up, then whoever was responsible might well have worked on the basis that I would somehow obtain a copy of the genuine fingerprints.

A perverse intuition kept telling me that Carlos was still alive. I felt that, if I could establish the identity of this mysterious retired head of intelligence, it might help me resolve the dilemma. I comforted myself with the thought that the men from Mossad have been known to be wrong from time to time and that this *Davar* report might well be one of those occasions.

Only a few weeks before, on February 4th, 1986, Israeli fighter jets had forced a Libyan civilian plane to land in Israel. Acting on information from Mossad, the Israeli Government, particularly its Foreign Minister, Yitzhak Shamir, had been convinced that Abu Nidal was on the plane, returning from a conference in Libya to his base in Damascus. Shamir had also been convinced that George Habash was on the plane. It was an act that many nations denounced as 'air piracy'. Forcing down, after interception, an unarmed passenger plane from international air space might well have been justified in some eyes if Abu Nidal had been on board. He was not, and neither was Habash.

If Mossad could be wrong about the whereabouts of Abu Nidal and Habash, they could equally be wrong about the whereabouts of Carlos, dead or alive. If it was a disinformation ploy, whoever was responsible would now be sitting back and waiting for me to write the book and publish. The longer that time went by the more likely they were to deduce they had been rumbled and then the more dangerous and precarious would become my own situation. Consequently, when I next met Danielli, I was very alert for the slightest suggestion from him that I should not bother with obtaining a third interview but should publish and be damned.

'David, our friends are still looking.'

'What do you make of this Israeli story that he's dead?'

He laughed. 'Carlos has been "dead" many times. We all have to die some time, of course, perhaps this time the story is accurate. What are you going to do?'

'I'm going to keep looking for Carlos.'

He nodded, almost approvingly.

'And if he is dead?'

'I want to see the body.'

'If the Israeli report is correct the Libyans are never going to confirm it. If they did, it would be a complete admission of their involvement with Carlos.'

'Human nature, Danielli, is a curious thing. The temptation to talk, to boast that you were the one who killed the famous Carlos will be very strong.'

'Not as strong as the fear that if you do talk, if you do boast, you might end up joining Carlos. David, it could take you years to get at the truth.'

'So do you think I should call it a day? Sit down and write the book now?'

I had asked the question as casually as I could. His response might well affect many things, particularly our relationship.

'Do you think your work is finished? That your research is completed?'

'No, there's more to be done. Much more.'

'Then you obviously must continue. I'll give you all the help I can. So will my friends in Paris and their contact in Algiers. If Carlos is still alive we will find him.'

Finding him began to look increasingly unlikely. Contacts in a number of countries gave me the same response when I told them I was looking for Carlos. 'He's dead isn't he?'

It began to appear that I was chasing a ghost.

During the spring of 1986 a number of events occurred that radically affected the directions in which I moved.

In Beirut on March 28th British teachers Philip Padfield and Leigh Douglas were kidnapped in West Beirut.

On April 11th, Brian Keenan was kidnapped. Keenan, like myself, held dual nationality, an Irish passport and a British one.

On April 16th the Revolutionary Organization of Socialist Muslims announced in Beirut that it had executed British journalist Alec Collett. Poor Collett, his only 'crime' had been to show the wrong passport at the wrong checkpoint.

On April 17th British journalist John McCarthy was kidnapped on the airport road south of Beirut city. The same day the bodies of the British teachers Philip Padfield and Leigh Douglas, and the American librarian Peter Kilburn, were found shot dead.

Any remaining illusions about a passport offering protection were eliminated. If you were white then to be out on the streets of West Beirut had become a suicidal act. Even more evil was thrown into the stew on April 17th when, using his pregnant girlfriend as an unwitting donkey, Nezar Hindawi, a Jordanian Palestinian, attempted to place a bomb on an El Al flight from London to Tel Aviv. This time the finger was pointed not at Libya but at Syria. Later in the year, after Hindawi had been found guilty and sentenced to forty-five years' imprisonment, Britain broke off diplomatic relations with Syria.

For a man hunting Carlos life was becoming daily more

difficult. There were no diplomatic relations with Libya, Iran and Syria. Lebanon was a country to visit only if one was tired of life. A wave of anti-American and anti-British feeling swept through dozens of countries, particularly the Middle East. It seemed by the summer of 1986 I was overdue for at least one lucky break. Within one week I got two.

At a party I met a member of the Austrian diplomatic service. Karl is short, plump, with a pair of small glasses perched on the end of his nose. We discussed books and he asked me what I was currently working on. I gave him my standard answer, 'Oh, it's a book about the Middle East.'

He courteously replied, 'Well, if there is anything that I can do to assist your research I will be happy to help.'

I was in like Quinn.

'Just two things. I'd like an Austrian passport and I'd like to interview Bruno Kreisky.'

He considered the carpet for a moment, then said, 'The passport I cannot help you with, but I think I can get you to Dr Kreisky.'

We were joined by other party guests and the subject of conversation was changed. Before I left we exchanged telephone numbers and he promised to get back to me.

Two days later there was another shaft of sunlight.

I had finally established the identity of the retired intelligence head who claimed that Carlos was dead. It was a name that sent bells ringing in my head: General Yehoshua Saguy, former Director of Israeli military intelligence. Somewhere in the mass of information I had acquired during this investigation I had read that name. I began working my way through countless files and dozens of books.

At this point the telephone rang. It was Karl at the Austrian Embassy.

'Dr Kreisky will be delighted to talk with you.'

I arranged to fly to Vienna in November to spend an evening with the former Chancellor of Austria. I pulled out the file I had put together on Kreisky and studied it. He had been Head of State at the time of the attack on Schönau Castle in 1973, an attack allegedly masterminded by Carlos. Subsequently, due to his position at the head of the Government in 1975, he was also the man who had been forced to negotiate with Carlos during the attack on OPEC. There was an even more compelling reason for me to meet him. I saw Dr Kreisky as the man who could unlock the door to Mu'Ammar Qathafi's inner sanctum in Libya. I was anxious to talk to the Colonel. I began to prepare my questions for Dr Kreisky.

Aware that he spoke fluent English, I travelled alone to Vienna. Because this city was the scene of one of the most sensational attacks involving Carlos, I deliberately arrived several days before the appointed time. Wandering the tourist-free streets, particularly those near what in 1975 had been the headquarters of OPEC, I was struck by the lasting impression that the film *The Third Man* had made upon me. Try as I might, my eyes could not focus on the colours but continued to see the city in black and white. I even found the film playing at a small cinema and thought that this was a splendid coincidence until I was told, 'Oh they've been showing that film for years.' Eleven years earlier the city had been the background to a drama, starring a plump Venezuelan who had held the lives of some of the world's most influential men in the palm of his hand.

During long and dangerous negotiations with the Austrian police Carlos had remarked, 'I command Kreisky and everybody else here. I decide who shall go and who will stay.' Then later, 'Tell Kreisky that I know all the tricks. He should not try any.'

Carlos considered that he controlled not only the fates of some seventy hostages within the building but the entire country of Austria and that the man who actually did, Chancellor Kreisky, was subordinate to his every whim.

Within minutes of arriving at Kreisky's home in a quiet suburb of the city I began to regret not bringing an interpreter with me. The house was shuttered and dark. Eventually my continual ringing brought a security guard, not from inside but from nearby bushes. As he approached I could see that he was pointing a gun directly at me, which meant our subsequent conversation, conducted in appalling German and equally appalling English, was rather stilted. It was at this point that Dr Kreisky's car arrived. In a moment the residence was flooded with light and the bustle of life, including a number of armed security guards. They had all, it seemed, been observing me in the darkness. One in particular seemed highly reluctant to leave me with the former Chancellor. When we were alone I commented on the unusual amount of security. Unusual that is for a man who, having resigned the Chancellorship in 1983, was semi-retired from political life. Having first apologized for his late arrival – he had stopped his chauffeur so that they could render assistance at a traffic accident – he explained.

'The security forces are over-reacting I'm afraid. They have some evidence of a conspiracy to kill me.'

It appeared that someone had been conducting lengthy surveillance from a roof top overlooking Kreisky's garden. Whoever it had been was a heavy smoker, of Arab cigarettes. It was a highly appropriate beginning to our conversation. During his long political career Dr Kreisky had incurred the wrath not only of Abu Nidal but also of a succession of Israeli leaders. It was a career that was unique in many respects. How many Heads of State who have been imprisoned by the Nazis and condemned by the Israelis are also Jewish?

Bruno Kreisky, a militant socialist from his early teens, was arrested by the fascist Dolfuss dictatorship in Vienna in 1935 and charged with treason. He defended himself with great courage against a regime that had outlawed the Socialist movement. Possibly because his performance in court was the subject of international press comment, his sentence was comparatively light, one year's imprisonment. On March 14th, 1938, the day after the Nazis annexed Austria in the 'Anschluss', he was arrested again, this time by the Gestapo. After being kept in prison for a number of months, he was expelled from the country. It was perhaps this forced removal from his native land that later in his life helped him to relate to and understand the aspirations of the Palestinian people. A Jew who realized that the Palestinians had also suffered from a diaspora.

Of his pre-war imprisonment he said to me, 'The only thing I learned was how to get on with people I dislike.'

During his thirteen years as Austria's leader he had ample opportunity to demonstrate that he had remembered the lesson.

Of President Reagan and President Chernenko he observed, 'It is extraordinary to me that two such ignorant men could in theory be leaders of two great world powers. It was only in theory, of course. Both men were merely figureheads, but even as figureheads they displayed breathtaking stupidity. I met them both. I was left unimpressed.'

Of Israeli Prime Minister Golda Meir, he said:

'She came rushing into my office and started banging the desk. She appeared to be demanding something. It was difficult to tell exactly what because of all the noise she was making. It transpired that she was ordering me to re-open Schönau Castle as a transit camp for the Jewish refugees from the USSR. I refused but assured her that Austria would continue to accept the refugees. I think it was at that point she called my action anti-Semitic. It was then that I started banging the desk. I remember saying, "There are three Jews in this room." The Israeli Ambassador, Yitchak Patish, and the Austrian Minister of the Interior, Rosch, were also present.

'It was the first time since she had entered my office that she was silent. My closest relatives were liquidated by Hitler. Fourteen of them in Auschwitz. This was a matter of public record, as was my own imprisonment then expulsion by the Gestapo. I had known Golda Meir for some years. It was inconceivable that she could know nothing of my personal history. Schönau stayed closed, but we continued to accept Soviet Jews, as I had promised

Mrs Meir we would. Over twenty thousand the year after the attack on Schönau. Interestingly, the majority of Jews who managed to get out of the Soviet Union refused to go to Israel; in increasing numbers they preferred the USA, Canada, Western Europe, anywhere but Israel.'

It became clear, as our conversation progressed, that Kreisky, the agnostic Jew, was most emphatically an anti-Zionist. He also had a keen awareness of some of the ironies of modern history.

'Israel is a consequence of Hitler. Without Hitler there would have been a colony of people who would have liked to have lived in Palestine, but they would never have been a success and they would never have achieved nationhood. Hitler created Israel.'

He was equally convinced that Israel had destroyed the moral basis on which it had been built by its 'policy of war' and its 'policy of semi-fascism'.

'One does not have to look any further than the policies of Begin and Shamir to discover this policy of semi-fascism. They practise it against the Palestinians under their control.

'The position of the Palestinians in Israel and the occupied territories is apartheid. They have no rights, economically they are displaced, politically they are displaced. Their lives are totally controlled by the Israeli army. Fascism is not confined to Hitler's treatment of the Jews. Fascism is brutal force. Israel is always boasting that it is the only democratic country in the Middle East. What a libel of all that democracy truly represents! Israel, as long as men like Begin and Shamir dominate it, will remain a fascist state.'

Were a non-Jew to make this observation, there would be immediate denunciation and allegations of anti-Semitism. When a Jew makes it, all that varies is the allegation, it becomes the charge that the speaker is a self-hating Jew. Dr Bruno Kreisky seemed to be far removed from this curious and dubious category. He had stopped practising his faith when a young man, and I could not detect any bitterness towards Judaism. He had seen at first hand, in pre-war Austria, some of the worst excesses of nationalism and in his mind, when he considered the State of Israel, those same excesses had emerged again. He mourned the passing of the men and women who had created that State.

'How can men like Begin and Shamir assume power? There was no room at the top for such people forty years ago. It drew its strength very largely from those with a European heritage. Then, because of the collective failure of both Jews and Arabs to resolve their differences peacefully, various countries in the Arab world turned against their Jewish minorities. They were very ably assisted in this by the Jews already in Israel, who applied every conceivable pressure on these Arab Jews to leave their own countries and take up residence in Israel. And so they came, Jews from Iraq, from Morocco, from Tunisia, from the entire Arab world. These are people who have never lived under democracy. They are ready supporters of the Begins and Shamirs of Israel.'

Not only, in Bruno Kreisky's opinion, did the Jews who left their Arab homelands form a potentially receptive audience to Israeli right-wing rhetoric, they also represented powerful evidence that strikes at the very core of Israel's existence.

'The philosophy upon which the State of Israel is built is that all Jews emigrated from Palestine. That simply is not true, neither is it true that they all descended from the tribes of Israel. The Jews are not a race. They are not exclusively from Palestine. Judaism as a religion spread to many countries. Jews came from the Caucasus, from Libya. There are huge tribes of Negro Jews, thirty, forty thousand people. In Ethiopia there are over fifty thousand Jews whose language is not even Semitic. Unlike mainstream Jewry, they have monks and nuns, their allegiance is to the Bible, not rabbinical law. Under Israel's Law of Return, these Ethiopians are of the same race as the Russian, Polish and American Jews. Such a versatile law.'

Our conversation moved back to the events that had

provoked Golda Meir to visit Vienna and bang the Chancellor's desk.

Carlos had insisted to me that he had not been involved in any way in the 1973 attack on Schönau Castle. I was intrigued to know if the former Chancellor had any information on this matter.

'Golda Meir was not alone in condemning your decision to close Schönau Castle. Excluding the Arab world I think it would be fair to say that you got a largely hostile Press reaction?'

'That's correct. Imagine what that Press reaction would have been if I had not negotiated with those Palestinians, if we had gone in with guns blazing. I'd been in Munich just a year earlier for the Olympic Games. I was there when the massacre at Furstenfeldbruck airport took place. Those events were very much in my mind when I considered how to respond to the train attack in 1973. I have no doubt whatsoever, I never have had, that if I had refused to negotiate then at least six people – the two Arabs and their four hostages – would have died. The total might have been much higher. One cannot be generous with other people's lives. It had been obvious to my government for many months that Schönau was a potential 'super Munich'. I'm sure you know that this attempt in September 1973 was not the first by the Palestinians. We had already taken the decision to close the camp *before* the September attack. Closing it saved at the minimum six lives. We closed it yet continued freely to accept all refugees – never forget that is what happened. At no time either before, during or after Schönau did Austria close its borders to refugees, Jewish or Gentile. Well, you tell me who wins?'

'It seems to me that both the Israelis and the Arabs won. The Arabs were able to claim a propaganda victory. The Israelis continued to receive Russian Jews via Austria.'

'Exactly. The art of compromise has yet to be learned in Israel. There will not be a lasting peace in the region until it is.'

'Golda Meir later wrote that she was appalled by the

comment you made to her, "You and I come from two different worlds." [1]

'What I actually said, and I am sure you will be able to find it quoted at the time, was, "We come from two different worlds, you from a world of war, I from a world of peace." I have never believed that terror can be stopped by counter-terror. Golda Meir did.'

'Were you ever able to establish exactly who was behind the hijacking of the train and the kidnapping of the refugees?'

'Yes, the same group who had tried to attack the Castle in January 1973. A Syrian group.'

'Al Saiqa?'

'Yes, that's the name.'

It was one on the board for Carlos. His version of those particular events had now been confirmed by a source that was not only independent but highly authoritative. Further confirmation followed dramatically.

'I also learned from the Egyptians that the attack was planned in Damascus and that its real purpose was to distract the Israelis while the Syrians and the Egyptians made their final preparations for the Yom Kippur War.'

'In view of the fact that it convulsed Israel and caused Prime Minister Meir to come to Vienna, it would appear that those two Palestinians succeeded.'

'Most certainly. There is perhaps also a small ironic postscript to this affair. Some time later, when I visited Israel, Golda Meir praised me during the course of one of her speeches for all that I had done for the Russian Jews.'

'Was Carlos involved in any way in this 1973 attack?'

'Carlos? Not at all. Just Syrian Palestinians. Carlos was not a problem here in Austria until the OPEC attack.'

I asked Dr Kreisky to identify the source of the plan to attack and kidnap the OPEC ministers. Who exactly was behind the operation and what had their aims been?

'I believe there was only one aim behind the attack.

[1] *My Life,* Golda Meir, Weidenfeld & Nicolson, 1975

Carlos wanted money. Lots of it. There was no political aim that either I or my intelligence officers could ever establish.'

'I'm sure you're aware that virtually every commentator who has written about this affair points the finger at Mu'Ammar Qathafi?'

'Yes, I am very aware of that. I'm equally aware that the accusation is nonsense. Neither Qathafi, nor for that matter any Libyan, had a hand in the OPEC attack.'

'Are you sure?'

'I am certain. Because these allegations began to circulate very soon after the attack, they were very carefully examined by Austrian Security. They did not stand up to that examination. It has served a number of countries to blame Qathafi. Ask them for the evidence. We did. I'm still waiting for it. In 1982 I invited Colonel Qathafi to this country. To this city. I knew full well before I gave him that invitation that I would be subjected to considerable international criticism. If there had been a shred, a single shred of evidence that either he or any of his fellow countrymen had been involved in the OPEC attack I would never have allowed him into this city, this selfsame city where that attack took place and men were murdered.'

The former Chancellor of Austria's logic was unassailable. What disturbed me and disturbed me very greatly was the knowledge that Carlos had insisted to me that the man who had conceived the idea for the OPEC attack was Qathafi.

'THE MOST DANGEROUS MAN IN THE WORLD'

Although he was no longer Austria's leader when I interviewed him, I was acutely aware that Kreisky had very good relations with a number of Arab leaders. One of my reasons for wanting to meet him had been to enlist his help in getting to Colonel Qathafi. Dr Kreisky promised to do what he could.

Back in London, when the tapes of my interview with him had been transcribed, I was struck by the extraordinary frankness of the man. He might well look like an elderly koala bear but he was a bear with very trenchant views. He was also a man who, even in the autumn of his life, retained that same courage he had demonstrated against the Dolfuss regime and the Gestapo. In the early 1980s Abu Nidal had threatened to kill him. In the mid 1980s Dr Kreisky had calmly sat down with the most senior members of the Abu Nidal group and discussed politics. Dr Kreisky was the first man to alert me to what I was later to establish beyond any doubt. Mossad has for many years penetrated the Abu Nidal group and on a number of occasions Mossad agents, posing as loyal members of Nidal's group, have actually formulated policy. I had also asked Dr Kreisky where he thought Carlos might be. To my relief he did not express the view that the man I was hunting was dead.

'I think he's in the Middle East. Probably in the Mediterranean.'

Well, he certainly had been when I talked to him.

While I waited for the good doctor to weave some

magic with the Libyans I studied closely the file I had compiled on Colonel Qathafi, the man whom President Reagan has called 'the most dangerous man in the world'. On another occasion (April 9th, 1986), the United States President described the leader of Libya as 'the Mad Dog of the Middle East'.

Over the years other Heads of State have weighed in with their opinions of Qathafi. 'A vicious criminal, one hundred per cent sick and possessed of a demon' was how President Sadat of Egypt saw him, while President Numeiry of Sudan observed, 'He has a split personality – both evil.'

Not what one would call a good press.

When the twenty-seven-year-old Captain Mu'Ammar Abumeniar el Qathafi, with the assistance of just eleven brother officers, deposed King Idris and seized power in Libya on September 1st 1969, press, radio and television throughout the world responded with 'Captain who?' The heads of at least four Western countries were, if they troubled to consult their various intelligence agencies, in a position to give a fairly informed response to that question. Within a decade every intelligence agency on either side of the Iron Curtain supplemented that existing information with thousands of reports and millions of words on the junior officer who had become in the eyes of President Reagan the most dangerous man in the world. What exactly had Qathafi done to justify such an extraordinary title?

When Qathafi was born in a Bedouin tent twenty miles south of the Libyan city of Sitre during the spring of 1942, the North African campaign of the Second World War was approaching its most decisive battle. In October of that year the British Eighth Army, led by General Montgomery, defeated the Axis forces led by Field Marshal Rommel. The end of Libya as an Italian colony was in sight. For the Libyan people that day could not come too soon.

The Italians, who saw Libya as their 'fourth shore', had begun their inordinately cruel and oppressive colonization of Libya in 1911. During the First World War, Libyan resistance leaders threw in their lot with the Turks and the Germans and fought against the British and Italians. They paid an appalling price for having joined those who ultimately proved to be the losers.

When the Italian fascist dictator Benito Mussolini came to power in 1922 he promptly set about the domination not merely of the Libyan coastal cities that Italy already controlled but of the entire country. He declared, 'Civilization, in fact, is what Italy is creating on the fourth shore of our sea. Western civilization in general, and fascist civilization in particular.'

Libya's historical archives are full of material covering Mussolini's 'civilization' of their country, including film footage that details the bombing of civilians, the rape and subsequent disembowelling of Libyan women, the destruction of mosques, the burning of the Koran, mass public executions of resistance fighters. Those who were not hanged, to encourage the others, were forced into aeroplanes, then thrown out while the planes were in mid-air. Between ten and twenty thousand Libyans were executed every year. Nomads such as the Bedouin were force-marched into concentration camps, where they died in their tens of thousands. A two-hundred-mile barbed wire fence, built by the occupying forces, was erected along the border with Egypt to stop Libyans escaping. Qathafi's maternal grandfather was murdered and many hundreds of his tribe were forced to seek sanctuary in neighbouring Chad.

At the end of the war in 1945 Libya ranked as one of the poorest and most under-privileged countries on earth. Over ninety-three per cent of the population was illiterate. There were just four Libyan graduates in the entire country.

As at the end of the First World War, the winners sat down to divide the spoils. The French established themselves in the southern province. The United States gained five bases including what virtually amounted to a self-contained city, the Wheelus airbase to the east of Tripoli.

The British acquired military bases in Tobruk and El Adem. Over 100,000 Italian 'settlers' stayed, many still occupying key positions in what remained of the Libyan infrastructure and insisting that they owned most of the land. Banking was dominated by foreign companies, with Barclays the unchallenged leader. There was an elderly weak monarch, King Idris, who surrounded himself with corrupt ministers and advisers.

It can be clearly seen just how successfully the winners divided the spoils. A UN General Assembly vote in 1949 declared the country 'an independent sovereign state' and, again through the National Assembly, Idris was placed gently on the throne in December 1951. The reality of who controlled what as outlined above gives an unusual interpretation to 'independence'.

Abdul Hamid Bakoush, who was later to become Prime Minister, gave a concise description of that reality. 'Libya was just a tray of sand in 1951. It had an income of £3 million a year, and that came from Britain and the United States in rent for the bases on Libyan territory.'

Within seven months of the enthronement of King Idris, a corrupt Arab king had been deposed by a group of young army officers. The king was Farouk of Egypt. Among the officers responsible for his overthrow was an impassioned colonel, Gamal Abdul Nasser.

At the primary school in Sitre, the newly enrolled Qathafi listened enraptured to Nasser broadcasting on the Voice of Cairo wavelength. Daily he read the accounts carried in Egyptian newspapers of the deeds of Nasser and his brother officers. Many years later he could still quote verbatim huge extracts from the speeches of Nasser. The ten-year-old Qathafi began to study the reality of his own country and he began to dream.

In 1958 oil was discovered in Libya. The poor backward agricultural country whose prospects for economic development had been bleak should have been transformed. It was not. What was transformed were the bank balances of the Libyan royal family and its ministers and advisers. The poor got poorer and the rich got Cadillacs.

In the following ten years Libya began to resemble the Klondike gold rush. Oil men came in droves. By 1969 over ninety per cent of Libyan oil was being produced by thirty-eight foreign companies. From time to time the King complained about the low royalties and, after great shows of reluctance, the oil companies increased the Libyan share of this new-found wealth. By 1969 Libya was supplying a quarter of Western Europe's oil. It was of high quality, with very little sulphur, a factor of increasing importance as the West finally began to worry a little about pollution. It was close to Europe, the right side of the Suez Canal, which had been closed since the 1967 war. With Nigeria in the early throes of the Biafra War, Libyan oil was not only the closest, it was the cheapest. The oil companies refused to acknowledge this reality and declined to increase the price they were paying the Libyans. The large majority of oil experts concluded that Libya was being plundered and that it was only a matter of time before the Libyans themselves came to the same conclusion. By 1969 the country's oil revenue was slightly in excess of four hundred million pounds per annum, but the oil companies were making billions of pounds profit. On September 1st of that year, came the dawn.

Mu'Ammar Qathafi's name first entered Libyan security files in November 1959. A report circulated to all police stations in and near Sitre described the seventeen-year-old as 'a dangerous student . . . a young man with non-conforming ideas and probably a trouble-maker'. What particularly concerned Libyan security were Qathafi's 'disturbing activities of a political nature'. These activities were hardly the earth-shattering stuff of revolution. Qathafi was inclined to gather fellow students around him and offer a critical analysis on the current state of Libyan affairs.

The security file on Qathafi grew slightly larger in October 1961 when he organized a demonstration protesting against Syria's decision to break away from the United Arab Republic. The demonstration could be considered a success from all sides, the students eventually dispersed after a great deal of marching and shouting, there were forty-two arrests and Qathafi was expelled from Sebha Central School.

After his expulsion from Sebha Central and a further period of schooling in Tripoli and Misurata, Qathafi enrolled at the Royal Libyan Military Academy in Benghazi in 1963.

The fact that Qathafi was not only allowed to join the Academy but was accepted into the Cyrenaican Defence Force, the elite group that guarded and protected the King, would indicate extraordinary lapses both by the police and the Libyan security services. They were only the first of many.

The young officer cadets were trained by British personnel. The CO, Colonel Lough, remembers Qathafi as 'our most backward cadet . . . he was probably not as stupid as I thought at the time. Part of his problem was that he would not learn English. I didn't like him and he made life difficult for my officers and men because he went out of his way to be rude to them.'

In 1966 the British granted Qathafi permission to attend a four-month training course in England. He received extensive training on a 'troop leader' course in Dorset. His subsequent comments indicate that he was not impressed with swinging London, a city that a young Venezuelan named Ilich Ramirez Sanchez would be exploring later the same year. Carlos most certainly had a great deal more fun in the capital than the austere, devout Muslim. An indication of just how austere can be gauged from the fact that among the rules that applied in his secret revolutionary cell were, no drinking, no chasing women and no card playing.

By 1969 there were nearly as many people in Libya who were plotting to overthrow the King as there were oil men. There was the plot that included the chief of staff of the army, Abdul Aziz al Shehli. There was the plot that included a Libyan army colonel, not Qathafi, who had the backing of the Iraqi government. There was the plot that included the former Prime Minister,

Abdul Hamid Bakoush, by then comfortably ensconced as Libyan Ambassador to France. Many believed that the elderly King was sick of the wheeling and dealing that swirled around his throne and wanted to abdicate. The trouble was that, with everyone extremely busy plotting, no-one had time to listen to the King.

Despite US State Department denials, after Qathafi's emergence as the new ruler in September, that they had no prior knowledge of this particular plot, there is significant evidence that the United States administration had very substantial early warnings. Some of that evidence comes from former Prime Minister Bakoush.

'I heard about Qathafi's coup attempt two months before it took place. I knew the names of five or six of the men concerned. I went to the American Embassy in Paris to have a chat about it. I talked in particular to the CIA station chief there. This was almost two months before the coup and I told them all about it. I also went to see Idris in Turkey and told him. He refused to go back to Libya.'

The former Prime Minister insists that he was not the sole source for the Americans. 'The Americans had contacts with Qathafi through their embassy in Tripoli. They encouraged him to take over. There were dozens of CIA operatives in Libya at the time and they knew what was going on.'

Bakoush believes that the Americans were dominated by the thought that if, for example, the plot involving senior officers had succeeded then they might form close links with Nasser so that such people would not be under the control of the United States.

'So they discovered this group of ignorant young officers, unknown to everyone, led by Qathafi. They seemed weak, inspired largely by personal ambition and could in US opinion be controlled.'

The official State Department explanation, given to a Senate inquiry, flatly contradicts the allegations of American connivance in the coup; indeed, it complains that there was a local intelligence failure.

'The US Embassy in Tripoli had not anticipated the Libyan coup. The young military officers [who plotted the coup] were not known to US government officials. The US government therefore did not anticipate the radical changes which were to follow.'

Like many a State Department explanation, it is contradicted by the facts.

Whatever prior knowledge they had of the planned coup, President Nixon and Secretary of State Kissinger gave a great deal more than tacit support to ensure that Qathafi remained in power. Kissinger had a number of option studies drawn up. These included an assessment by the Defense Department and another by the CIA. Extracts from these studies have been made available to me by CIA sources. The Defense Department assessment included an evaluation of the Libyan Army's potential ability. It concluded that an invasion of Libya by two Marine divisions would be more than sufficient to bring down Qathafi and his colleagues and also to secure the oil fields against possible sabotage.

The CIA was even more bullish. It considered that the Marines were unnecessary and that it would be a simple matter to bring down Qathafi and replace him with a leader more favourably disposed towards the United States. This report draws on material originally derived from the former Prime Minister Bakoush and therefore demonstrably makes the State Department's official position untenable.

Consideration was then given by Nixon and Kissinger as to whether action to topple Qathafi, covert or otherwise, could be justified. A scenario was considered in which the recently deposed Libyan government would be secretly instructed by the US government to request America's help 'to oust a usurper'.

The Defense Department study, anticipating this possibility, recommended the utilization of Wheelus base for any potential invasion and suggested that, if Britain were involved, the RAF station at El Adem could also be brought into play.

President Nixon, one of the world's original cold warriors, ably assisted by the like-minded Kissinger, concluded that Mu'Ammar Qathafi held two aces – Libyan oil and his intense dislike of Godless Communism. If the President sent in the Marines and the new regime were overthrown, there was no guarantee that whoever replaced it would be as hostile towards Moscow as this devout Muslim. The President decided that Libya's new leader was a man 'he could do business with' and the plan to invade Libya was filed.

Libya's new young leaders, meanwhile, were getting down to business without consulting either the President or his Secretary of State.

The coup itself had been virtually bloodless. One man had been killed and eleven injured. As coups go, the treatment of the old regime was a model of benevolence. No-one was executed, some who were imprisoned lived in a style difficult to find in many an hotel. Bakoush, for example, said, 'I was treated very well. I had television, radio, books, good food. Friends could come and see me.'

Others were not given exactly four star treatment. The number three in the Libyan Army under King Idris, Colonel Aziz Shenib, was incarcerated in Tripoli's largest prison for criminals, before he was released and given a number of ambassadorial posts.

Within days Qathafi, Jalloud, his closest colleague, and the ten other junior officers had turned their minds to weightier problems.

Qathafi was convinced that what he called a 'second Pig's Bay' operation was going to be mounted. This one, unlike President Kennedy's attempt to invade Cuba, would be a very professional exercise. He believed that the foreign bases in Libya would be used and that the Anglo-American operation would also involve the American Sixth Fleet and the Royal Navy. It was almost as if Qathafi had been present in the White House as Nixon and Kissinger deliberated. He promptly suspended all training flights from both British and American bases.

Then he went further. The British were ordered out of their bases and the Americans out of theirs. During his negotiations with British Ambassador Donald Maitland, Qathafi said, 'Libya's freedom will be incomplete so long as a single foreign soldier remains in our land. Britain no longer rules an Empire on which the sun never sets, and Libya is no longer the puppet state it had been when the defence agreement was signed in 1953.'

Both Britain and the United States meekly obliged, and within months of taking over Qathafi had removed all foreign forces from Libyan soil. Italians had their properties sequestered, as did the handful of Jews living in Libya. The veil was abolished and women emancipated. All rents were reduced by thirty per cent and a minimum daily wage of one pound was introduced. Two months after taking over, the new regime nationalized all foreign banks.

In what was to prove a rare act of self-aggrandisement, Qathafi promoted himself from Captain to Colonel. On the first day of the coup, when Nasser sent his emissary Mohammed Heikel to meet the new leaders, the wily Egyptian newspaper editor was horrified at Qathafi's naïveté, sincerity and intensity. Qathafi said to him, 'We have carried out this revolution. Now it is for Nasser to tell us what to do.'

While Nasser considered how to keep his excitable protégé relatively calm, particularly with regard to his dreams of immediate Arab unity throughout the entire Middle East, Qathafi and his colleagues demonstrated that they had a full agenda. Having dealt with the British, the American, the Italian and Jewish residents, he turned his attention to Libya's oil. For the first three months or so, it had continued to flow out of the country, undisturbed by events. Now, having disposed of the foreign military bases and foreign banking, he concentrated on loosening the foreigners' hold on Libya's liquid assets.

An indication of how complete the Libyan rout of not only the independents but the seven multi-nationals was can be gauged from the following fact. In the year that

King Idris was removed from power Libya's oil revenues were £400 million. Two years later they were £2,000 million. The implications and effects of this victory were far-reaching. Where Libya led, the rest of OPEC soon followed. The balance of power on this particular battlefield had shifted.

As Qathafi predictably won friends among the other Middle Eastern oil-producing countries, there were also less predictable elements who demonstrated their approval of the new regime.

In January 1970, two members of Qathafi's secret cell who had both played important roles in the coup decided it was time for a counter-revolution. Colonels Adam Hawaz and Musa Ahmed had become alarmed at Qathafi's unquestioning devotion to Nasser and all he represented. Before their plans to topple Qathafi could be implemented, the CIA and Egyptian Intelligence passed information to Qathafi on their activities and they were arrested. Qathafi, ignoring the fact that one of his sources had been the CIA, accused the plotters of wanting 'imperialism' to return to power in Libya. He used this argument as further justification of his demand that all foreign bases should be evacuated.

In June 1970, yet another plot was unmasked. This one involved a member of the Idris Royal Family, Prince Abdullah al Abid, who with five thousand mercenaries was planning to invade Libya from Chad. Again Qathafi was tipped off, this time by French Intelligence. There are also allegations that the CIA again played a key role, but I have been unable to acquire any firm evidence of this. Ironically, a month after some of the plotters had been arrested, the regime announced that one of them had 'confessed' that the five thousand recruits were to be 'armed by the CIA'.

Then, in March 1971, an attempt to place King Idris's former counsellor on the Libyan throne was thwarted by a combination of British and Italian Intelligence. Certainly, in the first few years after he came to power, Qathafi had many friends in the unlikeliest of high places. He had also acquired a formidable number of enemies. To offend such a powerful lobby as the oil cartel guaranteed lasting enmity. To offend the Israeli lobby on a global basis ensured for the Libyan leader that he would become for ever the ultimate bogey man.

From his very early days in power Qathafi has displayed an unremitting hostility to Israel. He has identified completely with the Palestinian cause and called for all-out war against the State of Israel. For Qathafi, there have been no half measures, no fudged compromises. Qathafi's solution to the Palestinian problem was simple – 'We push all the Jews into the sea.' His bemusement which turned to anger at King Hussein's slaughter of the Palestinians during the Black September of 1970 prompted an equally dramatic answer to the problem which he offered to President Nasser.

'You should set up a gallows in the public square and hang King Hussein.'

At the Cairo conference of 22nd September 1970, called by President Nasser in an attempt to end the bloodshed in Jordan, the following interchanges were recorded by Mohammed Heikel.

King Faisal of Saudi Arabia: 'I agree with Your Excellency [President Nasser] that all this [the fighting in Jordan] appears to be a plan to liquidate the resistance movement.'

Qathafi: 'I don't agree with the efforts you are making. I think we should send armed forces to Amman, armed forces from Iraq and Syria.'

Faisal: 'You want to send our armies to fight in Jordan. It is not practicable.'

Nasser: 'I think we should be patient.'

Faisal: 'I think that if we send our armies anywhere we should send them to fight the Jews.'

Qathafi: 'What Hussein is doing is worse than the Jews. It's only a difference in the names.'

Nasser: 'The difficulty is that if we send our troops to Jordan this will only result in the liquidation of the rest of the Palestinians. I would like you to hear the contents of a message that I received this morning from the Soviet Union. They are asking us to exercise the utmost restraint because the international situation is becoming extremely delicate and any miscalculation might result in the Arabs losing all the reputation which they have recovered over the past three years.'

Faisal: 'I don't think you should call an Arab King a madman who should be taken to an asylum.'

Qathafi: 'But all his family are mad. It's a matter of record.' (A reference to the mental illnesses of Hussein's father and brother.)

Faisal: 'Well perhaps all of us are mad.'

Nasser: 'Sometimes, when you see what is going on in the Arab world, Your Majesty, I think this may be so. I suggest we appoint a doctor to examine us regularly and find out who is crazy.'

Of that trio of Arab leaders only Qathafi is still alive today. Over the past twenty-one years there have been many who without the benefit of a doctor's report have declared Mu'Ammar Qathafi 'crazy'.

My own interest in Mu'Ammar Qathafi lay in the fact that he is linked again and again with Carlos. It is alleged that Carlos received his initial training in Libya and that he subsequently set forth at his master's orders to implement a unique kind of foreign policy – to kill, maim, frighten and terrorize.

It is asserted as an indisputable 'fact' that Qathafi financed and masterminded the Carlos-led attack on OPEC in 1975. Carlos stated this categorically to me. Now, after what had happened in Beirut in October 1985, it had become imperative to establish the truth surrounding that affair.

Once Carlos had been linked by writers and governments to Qathafi in January 1976, the dam broke. He became allegedly associated with the Libyan leader continuously. Just two months later, in March 1976, the Egyptians, who had been the first to accuse Qathafi of planning the OPEC attack, declared that Carlos was in charge of Libya, with Qathafi functioning merely as token leader.

As I began to prepare a list of questions to put to the Libyan leader, I recalled something that Bruno Kreisky had said to me, an observation based on a relationship he had developed with Qathafi over ten meetings with him. Indeed, Bruno Kreisky could, if he was inclined, rightly claim to know Qathafi better than anyone else in the West.

'I'm sure you will discover that a vast number of the allegations that are made about "Qathafi the terrorist" are just disinformation. The irony is that above all else Qathafi fears the terrorist. He is on his guard against an attack from the extremists within the Palestinian movement.'

In January 1987 I received a phone call from Dr Kreisky. There was a problem with regard to my trip to Libya. In the light of all that had gone before in this enterprise I would have been very surprised if there had not been a problem. It centred on the United States attack on Libya the previous April, an attack that had been carried out with the help of the British. It seemed Qathafi had agreed to the interview, but what worried not him but his advisers was the fact that I would be entering Libya on a British passport. Feelings in Libya were still running high about the attack. Again my mother's heritage came to the rescue.

'Any problems if I'm travelling on an Irish passport, Doctor?'

'No, none at all.'

The fact that Britain did not have diplomatic relations with Libya necessitated a stop *en route* to acquire a visa. I chose Malta: there were one or two people I wanted to interview on the island, including Prime Minister Mifsud Bonnici. In late February I was on a plane heading for Luqa airport.

I was apprehensive. My anxieties had increased when, walking into my dressing room shortly before leaving home, I discovered Anna, my wife, quietly unpicking the American Stars and Stripes from a casual jacket I

213

was about to pack. The coat was a legacy from the Los Angeles Olympic Games of 1984. Her action and my own perception of it underlined the fact this was a journey to hostile territory.

Once in Malta, having arranged to interview Mifsud Bonnici on my way back home from Libya, I took a taxi out to the Libyan Embassy (or, as the Libyans prefer to call them, 'People's Bureaus') to obtain my visa. I had booked a flight from Luqa to Tripoli the following day.

The Bureau was shuttered and locked. Repeated ringing finally produced a security guard, who only spoke Maltese. Fortunately Joe, my taxi driver, was fluent in both tongues.

'He says the Embassy is closed.'

'Yes, I can see that, Joe. Would you ask him what time the consular section reopens.'

'He says it won't be reopening. Not until tomorrow at nine in the morning.'

Well, there would still be time to make the flight. The following day Joe appeared at my hotel at eight-thirty and we drove again to the Libyan Embassy. It was still locked and shuttered. Again much ringing produced the same security man.

'He says the Embassy is closed.'

'I think we're getting in a rut, Joe. Yesterday he said it would be open at nine this morning. It is now nine.'

'He says it's closed today because it's a Saint's Holiday.'

'But they're Muslims. What are they doing celebrating a Catholic Saint's Day?'

'He says they do it out of respect for Malta.'

The following day we tried. Again the Embassy was closed.

'He says it's Friday.'

'Would you tell him I'm extremely grateful for the information, which in view of the fact that I've been in Malta so long and have lost all sense of time, comes as a great shock.'

They both appeared to enjoy that.

'He says the Libyans never work on Friday.'

'Would you ask him whether they come in on Saturday mornings please.'

'He says, sometimes they do, sometimes they don't.'

On Saturday Joe and I, by now old friends, were back at the Libyan Embassy. To my intense relief the doors were open. The beaming security guard was waiting on the steps. He proudly waved his arm in the direction of the open doors, obviously wishing to take the full credit for this extraordinary feat. Leaving Joe to reminisce with the security guard, I went into the Embassy.

'We have no instructions either from Vienna or Tripoli about you. I suggest you return to London.'

I told the Consul what he could do with that suggestion. I also told him what I thought about his opening hours and finished with advising him that since I had been invited to Libya by Colonel Qathafi, perhaps he should pick up the phone to the Colonel and have me checked out. I saw him blanch at this suggestion. He phoned Tripoli – not Qathafi, but the Ministry for Foreign Affairs. They confirmed that I was expected; indeed, they had expected me several days before. I thought I was finally getting somewhere, but petty bureaucracy is the same in any language and petty bureaucrats do not like being bested. He threw an ace on the table.

'I will need three photographs.'

'This is my Reader's Ticket for the British Museum. Will that do?'

Impassively the Consul studied the ticket, which had a photograph of me on it. He reached for a large pair of scissors, then, cutting the ticket in half, stapled the photo to the visa application. A flurry of stamping and seven Maltese pounds later I had my visa.

I was the only European on the plane. Apprehension seized me again. I was heading towards a city that just ten months previously had been bombed by American F-111 planes. Some of those planes had taken off from my country. Many had been killed. Many had been injured. If American tourists would not come to Britain because they feared Libyan reprisal attacks, what was I doing flying to Libya?

I was escorted into the arrivals hall by the security man who expressed surprise that there was not a Government car waiting and told me he would phone the Ministry of Foreign Affairs. Nearly two hours later the men from the Ministry arrived in a very battered Pontiac that would have been considered a collector's item in Britain.

It became obvious on the journey that these Government officials had no knowledge either of me or of what Bruno Kreisky had arranged through their Vienna Bureau. They took me to the Hotel Al Wahat, had a few words with the man on reception, then disappeared.

About four or five hundred yards from the hotel was the Mediterranean: the previous year the American planes had come hurtling towards Tripoli from that direction, leaving death, injury, destruction and terror; the President's response to the 'irrefutable evidence' he claimed to have of Libyan terrorism.

Within a year of moving into the White House President Ronald Reagan had developed one particular obsession that would remain with him through his two terms of office – Colonel Mu'Ammar Qathafi.

By early 1986 the President saw an opportunity to resolve once and for all the problems that he believed Qathafi represented. Qathafi had declared that Libya's territorial waters in the region of the Gulf of Sidra would be extended beyond the internationally recognized twelve-mile limit. He drew a 'line of death' that in some areas extended one hundred and twenty miles off the coast of Libya.

As early as August 1981 the Reagan administration had responded to Qathafi's 'line of death'. On August 19th, two US Navy F-14 fighters on dawn patrol more than thirty miles inside the territorial waters claimed by the Libyan leader saw Libyan Air Force jets approaching. Two of them were shot down. The 'non-provocative US Naval exercise' was subsequently concluded.

In early March 1986, the US Sixth Fleet returned to the

area in an operation called Prairie Fire. The commander of the Sixth Fleet, if not given a free hand, was certainly given a full one. His brief included the following: 'If there is a single US casualty you will, with Presidential approval, bomb five military targets . . . If Qathafi takes aggressive action, again, after Presidential approval you will bomb Libya inland, striking oil-pumping facilities and other economic targets.'

The 'naval exercises' began on March 23rd and finished on March 26th. In those three days American Intelligence calculated that seventy-two Libyans had been killed. Libyan authorities stated that over two hundred Libyans had been killed. There were no American casualties.

In West Berlin on April 5th there was a bomb explosion in the nightclub, La Belle Disco. One American serviceman and a Turkish woman were killed.

The CIA advised the President that telephone intercepts both before and after the nightclub attack established 'irrefutably' that Libya was responsible.

During the early hours of April 15th, President Reagan launched an air attack on Tripoli and Benghazi. Over thirty Air Force and Navy bombers struck the two cities at two in the morning. A number of these planes had taken off from Britain. My subsequent research will show that the attack in reality had only one target – Qathafi himself. Forty-one civilians were killed and another two hundred and twenty-six injured. Mu'Ammar Qathafi was unharmed.

Afterwards Reagan cited on national television the 'irrefutable' evidence of Libyan involvement in the Berlin bombing. He summarized three of the intercepted messages and said the action he had ordered was in 'self defence'.

'Today,' he said from the Oval Office, 'we have done what we had to do. If necessary, we shall do it again.'

My own investigation established to my satisfaction that if indeed Reagan believed that by bombing Libyan cities and attempting to kill Qathafi he was exacting revenge for the La Belle Disco attack, he was badly misinformed. He bombed the wrong country and tried to kill the wrong leader.

The bombings were not, the President told us, anything else but a 'measured response'. I was anxious to see the effects of this measured response, but it was obvious that that could only be allowed with Ministry minders. Well, I would do without the minders. Before seeking out the areas where the bombs had fallen, I wandered around the rest of the city.

The first image that struck me forcibly was the sight of school children. School starts early in Libya, and by lunchtime these youngsters, many of them no more than four or five years old, were on their way home, moving through busy streets in the city, unescorted and happy. These little children, many with suitcases and satchels almost as big as they were, showed not the slightest trepidation as they wandered through the capital city. Many came over and chattered to me in Arabic, my strange white face clearly arousing their curiosity. It was unimaginable in freedom-loving Britain or democratic America that children so young would be allowed to wander about unaccompanied in a comparable major city.

In due course I located a considerable number of the wrecked and bomb-damaged buildings. It was obvious that after the dead, dying and injured had been removed, these buildings had been deliberately left untouched. I had been told that Qathafi's own home had been left as the Americans left it.

In view of British and American assertions that only military targets had been hit, I was curious to see these targets. Without exception those that I found unaided by Ministry minders were either obvious civilian dwellings or foreign Embassies. Another irony was that the French Government had refused to allow the F-111s that took off from England to over-fly French air space, and the French Embassy in Tripoli sustained virtually a direct hit.

This part of the President's 'measured response' had clearly lost its tape measure. These domestic dwellings and embassies were on what would have represented final target runs for the American planes on their way to attack their real target, Qathafi's private residence in the heart of the giant Babal-Aziziya barracks. Tracking these bombed buildings at ground level, it was apparent that a number of the planes had dropped their bombs just moments too soon.

Although interviewing survivors of the bombings was not possible on this trip, I was intrigued to see if the Ministry would give me access to the damaged buildings. As I have already noted, I had privately examined a number and photographed them. I wanted to see if an official tour covered all that I had found for myself. It did.

I have already referred to my conviction that the April bombings of Tripoli and Benghazi had only one aim – to kill Qathafi. I will in due course give my reasons for holding that opinion, but if any sceptic could stand in the ruins of Qathafi's home and not come to the conclusion that the whole affair was simply a Presidential contract taken out on the Libyan leader's life I would be very surprised.

The barracks, shaped like a huge pear, is over six miles in length. I went all over it. There are tennis courts, football pitches and gardens, as well as many barrack rooms and several communications centres, one containing a bunker-like complex and the entire infrastructure that can be found on similar bases in the West. More unusually, it has a detached two-storey house. This, until the night of April 15th, 1986, was where Qathafi lived with his wife and children.

The only building in this entire vast complex that was damaged was Qathafi's home. Even the famous Bedouin tent where the Libyan leader frequently entertained official guests was not damaged, although it is close to the home. In the courtyard there was the wreckage of an F-111 plane that was found some fifteen kilometres away and carefully brought and placed on what had been Qathafi's doorstep.

With equal care a book of remembrance has been placed

in the reception area. Scores of foreign diplomats had recorded their signatures in it. Broken furniture, children's toys, plastic and cheap, originating from Malta, brought childhood memories of the London Blitz flooding back.

Eventually I was joined at the hotel by Professor Abdullah from Tripoli University, who advised me that he would be acting as my interpreter. His English was excellent and we spent the remainder of the day quietly talking as we waited to be beckoned. I was curious as to exactly where the interview was going to take place; so, it appeared, was the Professor. It could be in Tripoli, possibly Sitre, perhaps Benghazi or Sebha, maybe a car ride away, maybe a plane trip. It seemed that we were indeed about to visit the court of the moving target. Bruno Kreisky had told me of his first meeting with Qathafi and of how, having been flown deep into the Libyan desert, he was kept waiting in the sun for over an hour. He subsequently remonstrated with Qathafi, who was initially surprised at the complaint, then apologized. An hour for a Head of State, nine days for an author, the scale seemed about right.

From time to time during the day the Professor would excuse himself and go to a phone. At about five-thirty he indicated that we should take a drive in his car. A short while later we drove into the Aziziya barracks. If Qathafi was somewhere inside, then the security for a man in mortal fear of his life left much to be desired. A solitary guard in an observation tower waved us towards the main administration block. At the reception area a junior officer chatted to Professor Abdullah for a few minutes, then showed us into a large waiting room. The furnishings were comparable to those I had seen in Qathafi's home – cheap Italianate furniture, curtains that would have looked comfortable in a third-rate motel. The whole effect was the antithesis of ostentation. A tray of coffee later we were escorted down a long corridor and led into a room that was identical to the first. For a moment I thought we were back in that room but the view of the Aziziya barracks from the windows was different. Over a second coffee I mentally ran through my game plan. At a given point in the interview I planned to talk to Qathafi about my search for Carlos. I had no intention of revealing my meetings north of Beirut. To have done so to the man whom the intelligence agencies of many countries had inextricably linked with the Venezuelan might open up situations beyond my control, including, perhaps, my ability to leave Libya. With British diplomatic representation reduced to a junior located near the dustbins of the Italian Embassy, there would be little that my Government could do for me, even assuming they wanted to, which was not an assumption I made. As for the Irish, I felt sure that once they discovered my dual nationality they would merely bounce the ball back to Whitehall. There were also other problems. If I indicated through my questions that I accepted the alleged link as factual, this might terminate the interview. It seemed to me that what was required was a little poker.

The Professor and I were moved again, this time to a smaller version of the previous two rooms. As we entered my interpreter smiled. 'Ah, so we are going to talk to him in Tripoli,' he said.

Evidently the preamble could have led us anywhere, including to a car and a plane and a flight to Sebha. Now the Professor indicated that we were close to the Libyan leader. A few moments later we were even closer. We were shown into a small office. There, working at his desk like a clerk catching up with his bookwork, was Colonel Qathafi. He rose. I was introduced and we shook hands. As he motioned for me to sit my interpreter suddenly spoke.

'And how is our good friend Kreisky?'

Qathafi's voice had been so soft that I had not heard him. I moved my tape recorder close to the Libyan leader and the Professor and, recovering my composure, began.

At first we discussed the subject that goes to the very heart of this work, that has occupied me for so many years – the Palestinian issue.

'Colonel Qathafi. There is a body of opinion to which I have been exposed in many countries. It believes that certain Arab countries feel their personal interests are best served by prolonging the Palestinian issue rather than resolutely attempting to resolve it. Are there such Arab countries?'

'Yes, of course. In the Gulf, Saudi Arabia, Jordan and others their leaders hold such views. And in doing so they display something like an ignorance and a short-sightedness in their analysis because prolonging the occupation of Arab lands constitutes a danger to Arab lands as a whole. It will enable the Zionist entity to become very dangerous to the Arab nations. It will be a danger to the Arabs whether they belong to the right or the left because they too will become involved in a struggle for their very existence. The Zionists will try to dominate and they will attempt to dominate all of the Arab world irrespective of whether a particular Arab country leans to the left or the right. Any who attempt to castrate the liberation of Palestine in this manner risk elimination from that very Zionist entity they have sought to sustain.'

'Why has the oil weapon not been used to resolve the Palestinian issue?'

'Most of the oil is not under Arab free will. It is in areas which are dominated by American interests. Although I'm sure that the people of the peninsula are not told of this domination. The Saudis, for example, are not free with regard to the Palestinian issue. Maybe they are emotionally with the Palestinian issue, but practically they are under the domination of companies like Aramco.'

I was curious to discover if the years had mellowed him at all. Whether he could now envisage an accommodation with Israel. I asked him if there were any circumstances under which he would seek a political solution. His response could have been one uttered during the heady days of September 1969.

'It is not possible, it is not possible. There can only

be one solution. That is for the Jews, the Israelis, to leave Palestine and go back to their countries. Therefore war is the only solution.'

I turned to a subject that had left a deep impression upon me when it happened: the Libyan Embassy siege and the killing of Police Officer Yvonne Fletcher. I asked him if he regretted the death of this young woman.

'Yes, of course I do.'

'Many people in Britain felt at the time, and still feel today, a deep anger that her murderer left the country unpunished.'

'He was executed.'

'When?'

'Some time ago. You would have to ask the Committees for the details.'

Throughout the interview so far Mu'Ammar Qathafi had been relaxed and calm. Serene is perhaps an odd word to use to describe the West's biggest bogey man, but serene he certainly had been. My next question raised the temperature dramatically.

'In 1978 President Carter passed an executive order banning assassinations. My research, which I ought to add has been going on continuously for over three years, indicates that President Reagan, in conjunction with the CIA and other US government agencies, approved plans to bring about your overthrow. Violently, if that appeared to be the only way. By violently, I mean your death. The evidence establishes that these plans date back to 1981. My research further indicates that you have been aware of the Reagan 1981 approval for a very long time and that your sources are Russian Intelligence. Is my information correct?'

The serenity and the tranquillity vanished as Professor Abdullah finished his translation. Qathafi smashed the palm of his hand down on a copy of my last book, which was on his desk.

'First of all, you must be provided with the plans and the evidence concerning the assassination attempts that Reagan has made against me. The details should be included in this book you are writing.'

Qathafi reached into a drawer in his desk, rummaged for a moment, then produced a file. This was followed by four or five video cassettes. Betamax system, Sony make L-500. Qathafi gesticulated at me with one of the tapes.

'And after all these conspiracies failed they attacked my house directly. You have seen the house?'

'Yes, I have. The fact that it's the only building in this entire complex that was hit adds powerful weight to the view that the main purpose of the attack was to kill you.'

'When the planes bombed, the *first* building to be hit either in Benghazi or Tripoli was my home. The *first* building.'

'What are those video tapes, Colonel?'

'These were made by the CIA and other people in the Reagan administration. Made to convince Reagan to eliminate me. Made to be shown to intelligence, the foreign minister, foreign affairs, the White House. The CIA wrote a book entitled "Death to Gadaffi". G, A, D, A, F, F, I. They cannot even spell my name correctly. They made a film entitled "The Kidnapping of the President". Then another entitled "The Flying Wolf"; its purpose was to show how I could be attacked.'

I was aware that part of the CIA campaign since the early days of Reagan's presidency had been to wage a psychological war against the Libyan leader, to get him off balance and induce acute paranoia. At that moment during the interview I began to wonder if they had succeeded beyond their wildest expectations. There was little time for reflection. Qathafi was motoring in high gear.

'They wrote another book, "The Provocateur". Its purpose was to recruit someone, an agent, during one of my foreign trips. The plan was to attack me when I visited France, and they asked me about the letters of my name because they wanted to design a set, a machine which could be activated. After the book was published. Such a machine was in fact designed to be used against me, to kill me. Explosives were placed under my car on another occasion. Another attempt was made by placing explosives in furniture and chairs. We caught them. We still have the furniture. You can take pictures of it.'

Qathafi picked up one of the video cassettes. 'This one was made by the CIA in 1981. Reagan's advisers told the CIA, "Keep it short, the President has a low attention span." The film lasts fifteen minutes.'

'You seem to be remarkably well informed on these aspects. Am I right that the source of your information is your Russian friends?'

Qathafi laughed. 'We have many sources. Many friends.'

'Are these sources, these friends, similar to those that were close to President Mitterrand for a number of years?'

He stopped laughing.

'How do you know that?'

'From one of *my* friends.'

He nodded, but in that area I could not draw him any further. The 'friend' to whom I had referred was a member of French Intelligence. He had told me that they had discovered a Libyan spy, or rather a Libyan-paid spy, in Mitterrand's cabinet, a man who for years had been making highly sensitive information available to his paymasters in Tripoli.

A military aide entered the room. I thought for a moment that the interview was going to be terminated before I had got to the main item on my agenda. Qathafi waved him away. I had opened up the flood gates and there was more to come.

'Reagan's intelligence agencies used every means to persuade their President that I had to be eliminated. They invented my "killer squads" in 1981. Even before Reagan had become President they had made secret reports on me that concluded "the only way Qathafi can be removed from power is by assassination".'

He opened up the file on his desk and, turning over a few pages, continued.

'Reagan seems to like flowers.'

'I beg your pardon?'

'His people give their reports these childish names. "Flower" is the code word they use for their operations against me. "Tulip" is the code word for the plots and plans against me that involve using traitors and Egyptians. "Rose" is the code word for their plans for military attacks against me including joint actions with the Egyptians. Mubarak is their partner. The nightclub in Berlin – the President knows, as I know, who was responsible. It was not Qathafi. It was not Libya.'

'Was it Asad? Was it Syria?'

For a moment I thought he was going to confirm my own view, but he wasn't going to be drawn any further on that issue. He looked at the file again.

'Afterwards they came here to kill me and killed instead many men, women and children. Still they continued with their plotting. More lies that they planted in the American press about me. This time they had a new code word for their plans.'

He referred to the file, then spoke a word of English – Veil.

'And yet it is me, not Reagan, who is called "terrorist".'

Before we left this area Qathafi for good measure also talked about 'Operation Ramadan', a 1985 United States/Egyptian conspiracy involving American B52 bombers and Egyptian ground forces. Objective: Kill Qathafi.

What struck me with great force, even more than the information he was revealing to me, was that he had it in the first place. If this material were accurate, and on that evening in Tripoli I had no way of establishing that, its implications were sensational. The CIA had been penetrated, as had the State Department, the Defense Department, the whole caboodle. I was aware that a significant number of the CIA's top analysts had been convinced for a long time that somewhere in their midst, or working on the staffs of the various oversight committees that monitored the CIA, was a Soviet spy. I had always assumed that this was Cold War paranoia – until I talked to Qathafi.

'President Reagan has called you "The Most Danger-ous Man in the World". What's your reaction to that?'

Qathafi gestured towards the pile of videos and the file and smiled. 'Perhaps he finds the ideas in my Green Book dangerous?'

We talked not only of what Qathafi saw as President Reagan's obsession but of other men's obsessions. Of President Kennedy and his attempts to have Fidel Castro murdered. Of Prime Minister Anthony Eden and his instructions that Nasser should be murdered. Then we moved on to Carlos. I had briefed Professor Abdullah on this during our conversations at the hotel. I indicated to him that now was the appropriate time to explain my rationale to Qathafi.

Briefly, it was an outline of my view that a book looking at the Palestinian issue would reach a wider audience if that issue was examined within a specific framework, of how I had concluded that as the issue of terrorism was a global concern, it offered an excellent frame in which to set the story. Carlos, the world's most wanted man, had acquired his notoriety while working on behalf of the Palestinians. Eventually the Professor said to me that Qathafi understood and agreed that my approach could be a very effective one. I took a deep breath.

'I'm looking for Carlos.'

Qathafi studied me for a moment then, half turning, gazed out of a small window across the barracks. His eyes seemed to look dreamily into the middle distance. Still holding that position, he responded.

'Does he exist?'

It had been a long day and a long evening. I felt it was going to be an even longer night. Qathafi continued to gaze out of the window as he replied.

'Carlos never comes here.'

'Well, I would like to go to where he is.'

'That would be best, but we do not know where he is. Does he exist?'

It was a hell of a question, particularly coming from a man who, according to the former Military Head of

227

Mossad, had had Carlos killed and buried in the Libyan sands.

I delicately went through some of the information that I had accumulated, including conversations conducted on my behalf with Carlos's father.

'Then you know him before us.'

I persevered. 'I think that it might be within your power, Colonel, to find a path for me that leads to this man.'

'But he has disappeared for a long time, we have not heard about him. None talk about him.'

I went at it every way I could. He seemed more than convinced of the merits of why I needed to find and talk to Carlos.

'We would very much like to see Carlos in this country.'

'Why?'

'We would like to put him on trial. He murdered a Libyan in Vienna.'

'You regard him as a criminal?'

'Yes, I do. Just a common criminal. When the plane with the oil ministers landed in Tripoli, I wanted Carlos and his gang arrested. My security told me that if our people attempted to storm the plane everyone would be killed. If that had happened I'm sure that you can imagine the headlines in the West. "Qathafi murders oil ministers." We had to let them go back to Algiers.'

'Who was behind the OPEC attack, Colonel?'

'Wadi Haddad, but he is dead.'

'Yes, but who was behind Wadi Haddad? Which country? Which Arab leader?'

'I think for the answer to that question you must look closely at the relationships of Wadi Haddad.'

Back at Al Wahat hotel I considered some of the implications of the interview. If Mu'Ammar Qathafi's statements to me about the Reagan administration were accurate, and his insistence that he had no knowledge of the whereabouts of Carlos, alive or dead, was also true, then I was presented with a wonderful paradox. Was he telling me the truth about Reagan and lying about Carlos? Only time and a great deal more work would give me the answer.

Returning to London, there was little time to consider the implications of my various interviews in Malta or Libya. The files in my suitcases were replaced with a number of others and a day later I was on another plane, to Caracas in Venezuela, which, notwithstanding the seventeen different cities or countries that other writers have confidently identified, is the birthplace of Carlos.

9

'DON'T STOP AT THE TRAFFIC LIGHTS'

During the previous December I had succeeded in establishing where Carlos's father, Jose Altagracia Ramirez Navas, lived. This was a man that every writer on Carlos has described as 'a millionaire revolutionary Marxist'. The man I had talked to through two nights in Lebanon had recalled a humbler environment than that of a millionaire's son. After the death of Samir in Beirut, conversation with Senor Navas was vital, and original research in Latin America essential.

Unfortunately, the father took a different view. With the aid of a Spanish interpreter, I contacted Ramirez Navas by telephone. No mention was made of my meetings in Lebanon with his son, but the central thrust of this book was explained to him. He refused to grant me an interview. He was sent a Spanish edition of my last book with a full covering letter, but there was no response. In January, again through my interpreter, Maria, we telephoned the father, again we were told that the family would not co-operate with me. I had sent Maria ahead of me to Venezuela in early March. Now I was on my way to join her and to discover, I hoped, some irrefutable truths about Carlos. With luck they should throw some light on the questions that incessantly haunted me about the validity of the man I had met.

Arriving in Caracas on March 22nd, I learned from Maria that luck, as far as I was concerned, was in rather short supply.

A few days before my arrival a student in urgent need

of a toilet had relieved himself against the side of a parked car. A policeman nearby caught sight of the student and, instead of remonstrating with the young man or booking him for a minor offence, drew his gun and shot him dead. Hearing this, I made a mental note to check on the location of toilets when out researching. Student rioting throughout the city had followed and the Government had adopted a siege mentality. Within days of my arrival it was announced that no-one under the age of twenty-one could leave Caracas and travel to what Venezuelans call the interior, namely anywhere outside Caracas, or abroad, unless they had in their possession a special permit from the Government. The army were everywhere, every road out of Caracas had a series of road blocks manned by armed security and soldiers. For Carlos it would have seemed just like old times.

It was against this backdrop that Maria had been attempting to set up on my behalf a series of interviews, including meetings with President Jaime Lusinchi and the Minister of the Interior. Everything had been progressing smoothly until one trigger-happy police officer had sent the country into tumult. Now the last thing on earth any Government official wanted to do was to talk to me about the political disturbances of the 1950s and 1960s. With the President blaming the riots not on the students but on 'subversive elements that include drug smugglers', neither Lusinchi nor his Ministers wanted to take a nostalgic walk down memory lane towards the civil war that had rocked their country.

Driving into Caracas from the airport, Maria, busily briefing me on the situation, automatically stopped at a set of traffic signals. A friend of hers who was with us began to shout excitedly in Spanish. Maria revved up and roared through the red lights. Her friend had pointed out that no-one stops after dark at red lights in Caracas, for fear of robbery. Indeed, it is a valid defence in the local courts.

I reflected on the contrast with the country I had just left. No soldiers on the streets, no road blocks, just the occasional policeman on traffic duty, a capital that one could wander all over at any time of the night. At that moment Tripoli seemed positively appealing.

Base camp was the Hotel Avila in the San Bernardino district, close to where Ilich and Lenin had initially been schooled after the family returned to the country in 1961. Apart from the national unrest that continued throughout my trip, there were other things that would have been familiar to a returning Carlos. Caracas is situated in a large valley; the more money you have the lower in the valley you live. High around the walls of the valley at night are thousands of small lights winking and gleaming at dusk. It is as if the entire valley is perpetually celebrating Christmas. The daylight reveals the reality and the source of the lights: the barrios, shanty after shanty where the poor struggle to get through their lives. I had always thought the Nob Hill concept predicated living high above the tumult and the heat. Not so in Caracas. When the torrential rains come, the barrios are the first to be washed away. Accompanied by a rather tense Maria, I wandered around some of these shanty towns during my stay. Bits of tattered dirty cloth took the place of glass over the holes that passed for windows. Human excrement was tipped into a stream. There was refuse everywhere. Twenty-two carat squalor only a few yards from where a ceremonial guard in the cathedral mounts permanent watch over the remains of the country's liberator, Simon Bolivar.

In one such area we were approached by some locals. They were seeking help, their television set had broken down. I am completely technophobic but, not wishing to appear unhelpful, I offered to take a look.

Pushing the free-range chickens and barking mongrels to one side they showed us into a dark living room. The man of the hut proudly pointed to his new TV. It had been 'liberated' during the recent riots. Notwithstanding my total technical ignorance, I soon established what the fault was and why he could not get a picture. The machine he had acquired was a computer monitor. We had some difficulty in explaining to him exactly what the function of a computer screen is, but he seemed eventually to get the point and, thanking me profusely for making my expertise available to him, insisted we have a cup of tea, which, in view of his circumstances and the fact that in Venezuela a bottle of milk is six times more expensive than a litre of petrol, was a gracious gesture.

The day after my arrival, with the temperature climbing to 95 degrees, I discussed tactics with Maria. First, she gave me a brief run-down, from the President through to his Cabinet, on who was sleeping with whom. The men hold the power, the women the appointments books, and from initial observation, the female posterior and thighs rule above everything in Caracas. Presumably the dresses slashed to the top of the thigh are to ensure some form of ventilation for the impossibly tight fittings.

Leaving Maria to re-establish contact with Carlos's father, I decided to play what I hoped was the one ace I had brought with me – the phone number of a Colonel in Military Intelligence. A friend in German Intelligence had assured me that the Colonel was an honest man and that his integrity was beyond question. I sincerely hoped that his assessment was accurate in view of what I wanted to talk to him about. One point in the Colonel's favour was that he could, if my information was correct, speak reasonable English. I had no desire to involve Maria in this particular gambit. I called the number and, by doggedly repeating the Colonel's name while I mutilated the Spanish language, got through to him. I mentioned the name of our mutual friend.

'Ah, yes. He phoned me and told me about you. I have of course read your books. They are excellent. Excellent.'

I was flattered.

'Be careful what you say on this phone. The hotel switchboard is bugged and my phone is bugged.'

I was bemused. 'How can you be sure, Colonel?'

'Because I put the bugs in.'

'On your own phone?'

'Yes. For security.'

I have long held the view that intelligence agents occupy a different world from the rest of us. The Colonel was living proof. He was also remarkably informed.

'I hope the two-hour delay to your flight yesterday did not seriously inconvenience you.'

I was tempted to ask him what I had had for breakfast but stopped myself, just in case he told me. We arranged a meeting at the hotel at a time when I would be alone.

I wandered in the hotel grounds, waiting for Maria to rejoin me, looking at exotic tropical flowers coloured so brilliantly that it almost hurt the eyes to consider them. Whatever perfume they had was wasted upon me. T. S. Eliot, writing on Kipling, observed, 'The first condition of understanding a foreign country is to smell it.' If so, I was labouring under some difficulty. For some reason, as yet undiscovered by the doctors, I lost the use of my senses of smell and taste a few years ago. Now in a country where I was rendered virtually mute because of my ignorance of their language, I was heavily reliant on a young woman who for a variety of reasons could only be told bits of the story.

'Maria. Caracas – what does it smell of?'

'Smell?'

She took a deep sniff to double-check.

'Gasoline and ripe fruit.'

The news from the patriarch of the Ramirez family was not good. He refused to grant me an interview unless his son Lenin approved. In the absence of the number one son, fully occupied with bringing his own version of havoc to the world, Lenin was running the show. A strange inversion of roles – son becomes father, and father becomes son.

Later the same day we telephoned Lenin. He confirmed that after my letter and books had arrived they had had a family conference. They had decided not to co-operate. Lenin, 'out of courtesy', agreed to meet me. It became apparent, as I listened to Maria, that Lenin and his father were playing a Latin American version of piggy in the middle: putting the onus on each other to ensure that I was left stranded. Lenin had grudgingly agreed to meet me, if I cared to drive to Valencia in three days' time. It was a mere one hundred and fifty kilometres away through the road blocks. Later, as if to underline the point that I was a long way from home, the Government announced that they were cutting the entire water supply to the capital for a minimum of seventy-two hours. This, with the temperature in the high nineties, was obviously the perfect time to do maintenance work on the city's water pipes. I went to the hotel bar and bought two dozen bottles of the only available water, Es Bernardo Agua de Mesa. Agua Minerale. It was, of course, fizzy water.

A couple of days later, having showered, shaved and cleaned my teeth in Bernard's best bubbly, we set out to conduct my first interview. Maria was puzzled at my insistence on buying all the local papers. Papers that I could not read. That was true, but I was looking for a particular item that, Spanish or not, I would fully understand – the arrest of a particular man, someone who had been the main item on the menu during my dinner with the Colonel. The man's name is Stefano Delle Chiaie.

In August 1980, a bomb hidden in a suitcase exploded at Bologna railway station in Italy. It was a Saturday, the first day of the national holiday, and the station was crowded. The explosion killed 85 people and injured over two hundred more. The men who had committed this appalling act had never been caught.

I had investigated this atrocity, as well as a number of others, while researching *In God's Name*. In 1982 the investigating magistrate in Bologna, Aldo Gentile, issued an international warrant for the arrest of five men wanted in connection with the bombing. He told reporters, 'The man who was carrying the suitcase is among these five.' Top of the list was Stefano Delle Chiaie, a neo-Fascist and member of the illegal Italian Masonic Lodge P2. It was and still is my belief that it had been members of this Masonic Lodge who had conspired and murdered Pope John Paul the First. My research had also established that

P2 were also responsible for many other crimes, including the Bologna outrage. That same research indicated Delle Chiaie's deep involvement.

While I was in Malta, a Member of Parliament, discussing my last book with me, had talked of Stefano Delle Chiaie. His name had entered our conversation when I mentioned that I was on my way to Caracas. The MP had asked if I intended to interview Delle Chiaie who was, he said, living in the Venezuelan capital in the Chacaito district using the name of Alfredo di Mauro. It was said casually, as if it was not of any great moment, and then our conversation moved back to a discussion of the Pope's murder.

I was aware that the Maltese MP was a man with a wide range of contacts in Italy. His suggestion that I should interview Delle Chiaie, a man who featured high on Interpol's 'Most Wanted' list, was not an outlandish one: though on the run, Delle Chiaie had given several interviews. I did not want to talk to him, but I thought the magistrate in Bologna might like to.

At an appropriate moment during dinner with the Colonel I asked him if the name Stefano Delle Chiaie held any meaning for him. Like all good intelligence men, and I came to realize that the Colonel was very good indeed, he gave the minimum away.

'Yes, I know of him. Why?'

'I'm told that he is living here in this city. In view of the fact that he is the prime suspect for the Bologna bombing I thought you might like to arrest him and ship him out to Italy.'

'Caracas is very big. Where would one look for such a man?'

I told him the suburb and the false name. He nodded, lit an extremely large cigar, then looked at me.

'He is already under surveillance.'

'Oh come on, Colonel. No need to be that ungracious.'

'I assure you.'

'Then why hasn't he been arrested, or is he here as the guest of the Minister of the Interior?'

'He will be arrested within the week.'

'Within the week?'

'Yes.'

Now two days had gone by and I was feeling uncomfortable. There was no sign of his arrest in the papers. Meanwhile, there was an interview to think about: Eduardo Machado.

As I sat talking to Eduardo Machado in his home, I was aware that this plump eighty-five-year-old man with a full head of snow white hair represented a living piece of Latin American history. My main objective in talking to him was to establish some of the truth about Carlos's early life and about the path that had led to the Patrice Lumumba University in Moscow. Despite his age Eduardo displayed great energy and lucidity in my conversations with him. His recall of his extraordinary life appeared total. With his late brother Gustavo he had waged a continuous struggle on behalf of the working class from the early years of the twentieth century. It was a fight that had led in many directions, often including arrest and imprisonment.

Listening to Eduardo recalling long-forgotten battles gave direct insights to the world into which Ilich Ramirez came in the late 1940s. Carlos's father, a contemporary of the Machado brothers and for many years a close friend, had been influenced by the same struggle, the same aspirations.

Eduardo Machado also gave me factual details concerning the Patrice Lumumba period of Carlos's life, including his behaviour at the University and the facts surrounding his expulsion. Although this information contradicted much that has been written about Carlos, my overwhelming emotion at the end of my final interview with Machado was one of relief. There had been one or two areas where his story conflicted with what Carlos had told me, but basically there was nothing to sharpen the anxiety that had been with me since the aborted third meeting in Lebanon. The small but vital part of the portrait of Ilich Ramirez Sanchez that Machado had been able to paint for me was very largely consistent with what Ramirez himself had told me. The hunt for the full reality and the man continued.

The following day, in a coffee bar in Valencia, Lenin Ramirez Sanchez and I came out for the first round. The fact that he had resolved that under no circumstances would the Ramirez family co-operate did not, of course, endear him to me, but there was more to it than that. My quest to establish the irrefutable truth of his brother's life failed to impress him. He readily accepted that much that has been written about his brother was a mixture of error, lies and disinformation, but it did not bother him. For a man who had in theory been schooled in left-wing politics from an early age, his inability to see anything in historic terms was remarkable. If there had ever been any revolutionary flame burning in him, it had been snuffed out a long time before we met.

Despite himself, Lenin began to open up a little. What provoked him was my outline of some of the specific lies that had been written about Carlos, lies that concerned truths that I knew would be within the compass of his own personal knowledge. We talked of his brother's alleged links to the KGB. The most important single piece of information that I obtained was the fact that Carlos was still alive. From time to time he sent postcards to the family. As Lenin wryly observed, 'He sends the cards quite openly. He feels that by doing it that way he is saving the Venezuelan Secret Service the trouble of opening his letters then having to reseal them.'

It was reassuring to hear him speak in present tenses. The cards undoubtedly would come from somewhere other than where Carlos was staying. Brussels was one such city that Lenin mentioned. It became clear that Carlos had written recently: certainly long after the Mossad-inspired story of his death.

By the end of the evening he had agreed to give me limited help. He would answer any questions of fact concerning both himself and his brother. In return I promised that I would not attempt to interview his father.

It was a trade – that I could live with. We arranged to meet at my Caracas hotel the following day.

Next day, an hour after the agreed time, there was still no sign of Lenin.

On Sunday morning events took an upward turn. In view of the fact that I was planning to interview Douglas Bravo that evening, I was surprised to hear Maria's voice on the phone before midday.

'Several of the papers are writing about you.'

'What do they say, Maria?'

'They're quoting from your last book about this man who was arrested yesterday in Caracas. His name's Stefano Delle Chiaie.'

One of the facts that shone out like a lighthouse beacon from my interviews with Douglas Bravo was that if Carlos desired to get involved in a guerrilla war, his wanderings around the Middle East merely served to distract him from the war being waged in his own backyard.

Venezuela in the 1960s offered everything a young revolutionary could be seeking. If the country threw up a Fidel Castro or a Che Guevara during those years, then it was Douglas Bravo, though he would be the very last man to accept such a comparison. Unlike Castro and Guevara, Douglas Bravo had not marched triumphantly into the capital city: there are many reasons for that, not least the interminable wrangling between factions of the Venezuelan Communist Party, the lack of logistical support and the quality of the government's war machine.

When I met him in Caracas he was in his mid-fifties but looked twenty years younger. He had a full head of hair and the body of a dancer – trim, carrying very little extra weight. His long period of survival in the most hostile of mountain conditions had left other marks. He is one of the most self-contained, introspective men I have ever met. It was difficult to believe that this quietly spoken man had for nearly two decades been at the top of his country's most-wanted list with a fortune of Bolivars on his head. I also talked to his wife Argelia, who had been an active part of the guerrilla movement. Despite being subjected to continuous electrical torture for many hours, she had refused to reveal her husband's secret base location. Both had retained their left-wing beliefs. Both were aware that duplicity and deceit exist on either side of the Iron Curtain.

Bravo had taken to the mountains with a small group in 1961. Caught and imprisoned in 1961, he escaped the same year and continued to wage a guerrilla war, against overwhelming odds, until 1974. He continued to live clandestinely until 1979. Nearly twenty years, most of them in a country living under a state of siege in all but name.

This was the man who had fired the imagination of Ilich Ramirez Sanchez, the man who without knowing it had propelled the young student on a path that it became clear Bravo most certainly disapproved of, and it was obvious why a man like Bravo would disapprove: it is one thing to take on professional soldiers, quite another to throw hand grenades into crowded Parisian cafés.

Unlike Carlos, Douglas Bravo believes that revolution, like charity, begins at home. As he outlined some of the realities that existed in Venezuela, it was easy to see why.

Much has been heard in recent years of 'Los Desaparecidos', 'The Disappeared' of Argentina and Chile. Little is heard of the thousands who have disappeared in democracy-loving Venezuela, of the tens of thousands who are held without trial, often for years. The use of torture was and still is widespread. To read the annual State Department report on human rights practices and compare it with the reality that has existed in Venezuela for decades is to realize that the report should be on sale on the fiction shelves of bookshops. The day I conducted my first interview with Douglas Bravo, over fifty thousand protestors had taken to the streets. The catalyst had been the murder of the young student. The cause and the underlying reasons were much the same ones that had, in the 1960s, compelled Bravo to conduct his mountain guerrilla war. A war on which the Venezuelan Communist Party had dutifully followed the Moscow line. They condemned Bravo's action, refused to give any support and insisted that the correct way was to follow the legal path. In many Western eyes such guerrilla wars are ultimately controlled by Moscow: to accept any other explanation than a universal Communist conspiracy is to be confronted with some uncomfortable questions. Blame the Reds, it's always easier.

Although Douglas Bravo has not to his knowledge ever met Carlos, they have communicated. The details that Bravo shared with me confirmed yet again the veracity of my interviews in North Lebanon; unfortunately they did not take me any closer to my quarry. Their last exchange of letters had been in 1981.

A couple of days after I had concluded my interviews with Bravo, I kept an appointment with one of the men who a decade or so earlier had been hunting him – the Colonel.

In the light of the events of the previous weekend, it was not surprising that the Colonel gave every impression of being a man at peace with the world.

'You see. I promised you, within the week.'

'Yes, just as I was beginning to wonder about you.'

'And what were you beginning to wonder?'

'Whether you were on Delle Chiaie's payroll. Surely some of your colleagues must have been. I hear he's been living here for over three years. I realize this country moves at a different pace from Europe, but three years, Colonel. Under surveillance all the time, was he?'

The Colonel at least had the grace to laugh, but he left the question of possible corruption among Venezuelan Intelligence unanswered.

'I suppose there will now be one of those long interminable battles before he's extradited to Italy?'

He checked his watch.

'He will be arriving on board an Air Force plane at the Ciampino military airport in Rome in a few hours. Reason for expulsion, using a false passport. It avoids a

241

public airing in this country of the Bologna affair and other matters.'

'I'm impressed. I wish I could get that kind of service in this country.'

'I would like to thank you for your help. I am most grateful.'

'Colonel, I tell you most sincerely, it was a pleasure. Let me get you another beer.'

When I returned to the table with the drinks there was a pale yellow folder where I had been sitting. I looked questioningly at the Colonel.

'I thought that information might be of some use to you.'

I opened the folder. It contained a complete photographic set of the fingerprints of Ilich Ramirez Sanchez. It also contained details of his immigration records, listing every arrival and departure from Venezuela that Ramirez had made, and copies of a number of foreign intelligence agency reports.

At our first meeting I had told the Colonel of the investigation I was conducting, of my hunt for facts to enable me to strip away the myths that surrounded Carlos. I had made no requests, he had merely read my mind, or perhaps he had that bugged as well as my hotel phone.

'It's my turn to thank you.'

'It's nothing. What was it you said? It's a pleasure. Now, can I be of any further help?'

I gave him a shopping list. I kept it small but each item was to me vital. He quietly noted my requests, then asked me, 'Do you know where he is now?'

'No.'

'How long will you continue to look for him?'

'Until I find him, Colonel.'

Lenin Ramirez continued to be unpredictable. He failed to show up for the rearranged appointment. He failed to respond to telephone messages left with his secretary. He was becoming as elusive as his elder brother. I wondered if it was a family trait, this ability to vanish into thin air.

An appointment was made for Thursday, the 2nd of April. Again it was agreed that we would talk at the hotel. Late in the morning of the appointed day I received a call from Lenin. He couldn't make the hotel, but suggested lunch. At the eleventh hour he had moved the meeting place from the privacy available at the Hotel Avila to the atmosphere of a crowded popular restaurant, and just to add to the fun he was bringing his wife along. When I told Maria of the new arrangements she gave an impressive display of swearing in Spanish which appeared to last for several minutes without a single repetition. Leaving her to make contact with Nydia Tobon, whom we had located in Colombia, I joined Mr and Mrs Ramirez for a working lunch.

We were well into round five by now; Lenin opened with an impressive flurry. I had switched on my tape recorder and had asked him the first question.

'I do not want that tape recorder to pick up my voice.'

'Then tell me, Lenin, how do you propose I interview you?'

'Switch it on when you are talking. Switch it off when I'm talking.'

I began at the beginning with questions about date and place of birth and slowly, sometimes through gritted teeth, moved forwards.

Little pieces of the puzzle began to fall into place. The man in North Lebanon was scoring a perfect answer paper. The dates and places of the early youthful travels around the Caribbean, the over-indulged, over-protected childhood. 'The first time we had to make our own beds was when we came to London in 1966.'

I did not, of course, indicate to Lenin, or indeed to anyone else in Venezuela, that I had already interviewed Carlos twice in 1985. There was one other definitive source that I could draw on, thus masking my own work. Carlos had been interviewed by the Syrian-born poet Assem el-Jundi in 1979, the series of three interviews originally appearing in the Arabic magazine *Al Watan Al Arabi*, published in Paris. Where the interviews had taken place was not revealed, but my own research strongly suggested a location near Beirut. These interviews, along with a large body of other material I had gathered together, formed part of the basis for some of my own questions to Carlos. Inevitably, and not surprisingly, they had produced similar answers to the statements he had made to el-Jundi.

Now Lenin disputed some of the statements attributed by the Syrian writer to his brother. Without knowing it he was also taking issue with what Carlos had said to me.

Lenin vehemently denied that his brother had been a political activist during their time at the Fermin Toro school in Caracas. The fire-bombing of the Pan Am offices, the youthful assistance to Douglas Bravo's guerrillas – none of this, Lenin insisted, had happened. It was an interesting conflict of evidence but not, in my mind, significant. Carlos would not be the first person or the last to put a dramatic gloss either on events or their own involvement in them.

As the lunch progressed, Lenin's resistance to my questions became markedly reduced. The tape began to run unhindered by stops and starts. He ridiculed the suggestion made by many that Carlos had been trained by the Cubans or the KGB. He was adamant that, up to 1973, the year he had last seen his brother, Carlos had never been to Cuba.

In an interview lasting nearly five hours he had, without knowing it, confirmed much and also added to my knowledge of Ilich Ramirez Sanchez. There were a large number of gaps, caused, he stated, by loss of memory. It was arranged that I would let him have the questions dealing with these areas and he promised to let me have full replies before I returned to London.

Nydia Tobon, erstwhile comrade, mistress, lover, banker, safe-house organizer (depending on which paper you read) of Carlos, proved at first as unco-operative as Lenin Ramirez. Eventually she reluctantly agreed to talk to me if I came to Bogotá. A few days later Maria flew with me to the Colombian capital.

If Nydia Tobon had been a key element in the PFLP's European infrastructure in the early 1970s then one need look no further for a reason why the Palestinians are still without a homeland. Talking to her was to confront mental disorganization at Olympic level. With Nydia at the heart of their planning it is inexplicable to me how Carlos and Michel Moukharbel and the others avoided arrest for a week, let alone years.

It is possible that the constant repetition of 'I don't know' and 'I'm not sure' and 'I can't remember' was all part of a brilliant acting performance but I do not think so. I had reached the state where often I knew a great deal more than the person I was interviewing and it presented a grave risk of leading the witness, one that I guarded against at all times. Painfully, slowly, I was obliged to point out the errors of fact to Nydia. It is, of course, entirely possible that she had chosen to blot out of her memory certain events or transpose them with others. She was clearly very fearful of compromising either herself, Carlos or anyone else.

Gradually the real reason for her display of convoluted thinking emerged. There was within her a deep bitterness about her arrest and imprisonment in London. She blamed Carlos. She blamed Moukharbel. She blamed the British police. She blamed the British judicial system. The one person who remained without blame was Nydia Tobon.

Having worked our way through as much personal therapy as time allowed, the situation improved and the information began to flow. She began to paint a fascinating picture of her relationship with the Moukharbel group. As she did so several shocks were delivered to me. Her story too began to contradict some of the statements made to me by Carlos. Just little things at first, then, without being aware of it, Nydia threw a very large spanner into the works that I had been constructing since 1983.

'Tell me about Anton Bouvier,' I said.

I was expecting her perhaps to smile and then to say

that Bouvier and Carlos were one and the same man. So much for my expectations.

'I met him for the first time in April 1975. Moukharbel asked me to go with him to the air terminal because another comrade was about to arrive.'

'The air terminal in Cromwell Road?'

'Yes. I had to guess which of the passengers it might be. I couldn't pick anyone out. Eventually the least likely man joined us. He looked about forty years old. A respectable professor. He was even carrying an umbrella and briefcase.'

'Can you describe him?'

'He had a strange resemblance to Carlos. A round face, thin lips, dark glasses, full head of hair, dark.'

'This was Anton Bouvier?'

'Yes.'

'Where had he come from?'

'France.'

'And after he arrived in London, what then?'

'André left for Paris and Carlos returned to London.'

'From where?'

'From Paris.'

'What nationality was this Anton Bouvier?'

'From Ecuador.'

'Definitely?'

'Yes.'

'His Ecuadorian passport was a false one. Where was he really from?'

'As far as I know he was Ecuadorian.'

'Did you ever see Carlos and Bouvier together?'

'Yes, on a number of occasions.'

Based on what Carlos had told me, this was of course a physical impossibility. He had insisted that he was Bouvier. Now, according to the woman who had safehoused Bouvier, posed as his wife to obtain the lease on a new safe house in Comeragh Mews, gone shopping with the man, talked with him, Bouvier had a life force of his own. Either Nydia Tobon was lying to me or Carlos had lied as we talked through the Lebanese nights. I was also very aware of a third, awful possibility.

Nydia could be telling the truth, while Carlos had been obliged to commit himself one way or the other under my questioning when he didn't really know, or was unsure. If that interpretation were the correct one, it raised the question: was the man I had interviewed an impostor? Colombian ashes in my mouth.

It transpired that barely a month after she had met him, Bouvier vanished into thin air. A month later, in June 1975, came the murders at rue Toullier to be followed quickly by Nydia Tobon's arrest and imprisonment. She claimed that she had not heard from Carlos after her arrest.

I went back and forth over the three-year period of their relationship from October 1972 to June 1975, pulling out from her mind half-forgotten incidents and fragments that she had simply chosen to forget. Before we finished many hours later she threw me another spanner. It concerned the escape that Carlos had made from Paris after he had sent three men prematurely to their graves. He had insisted to me that, contrary to the widely held view, he had not escaped from France to Algiers, but had, astonishingly, gone to London. Nydia talked of him getting out of France via the European mainland. I asked her if it was possible that he had gone to London. She was adamant. 'He would not have gone to London without contacting me. He never came to London.'

I had learned quite a lot from talking to Nydia, but if she was correct about Bouvier and London post rue Toullier I was confronted with a truly extraordinary situation. If Carlos had lied to me about those things, whatever the reason, then it merely underlined the wisdom of checking every fact, every detail that he had given to me. But why lie about these matters when he had, as my subsequent research was establishing, told the truth on so much else?

Before we parted Nydia gave me a copy of a book she had written entitled *Carlos, Terrorist or Guerrilla?* She told me I could use any of it I wished.

I handed the book to Maria on the plane back to Caracas.

'Maria, I'd like you to translate this please.'

'All of it?'

'Every full stop, every comma.'

'Anything in particular that you're looking for?'

'Oh just some little scraps of truth, lass.'

In Caracas, it came as no surprise that the expected sheaf of answers to the outstanding questions I had asked Lenin had not appeared. I called him. Three days and many phone calls later contact was renewed.

'Yes. Sorry about that, David. Been busy. I will let you have them before you leave. When are you going, by the way?'

I told him. It was only a few days away. I went to Fermin Toro school and wandered around the empty classrooms. Once upon a time an overweight boy named Ilich had sat in these rooms. Now the tatty rundown school, reminiscent of many in the deprived cities of the world, gave nothing away.

It was clear that I needed to do a lot more of my own digging in this country. Before catching a plane home there was one more interview. Every political figure that I had wanted to talk to had become dramatically unavailable after the recent riots and demonstration, but a member of Carlos Andres Perez's political team was prepared to meet me. At the time of my visit the country was beginning to look towards the Presidential election of 1988. Perez was the nearest thing to a racing certainty that I have ever seen in politics. The man running the press campaign for the potential President was Pastor Heydra. I didn't want to talk to Pastor about the chances of his boss; I just wanted him to recall a classmate at Fermin Toro.

'Oh yes, I remember him. We were in the same class at Fermin Toro.'

'What was he like as a young lad?'

'The fool of the class. At the time I was the leader of the Communist Youth and I was also general secretary of the Students Union. Part of my job was to assess the qualities of all the other students.'

'And your assessment of Ilich?'

'An idiot. I have never for one moment believed all the myths that have been written about him because he was such a fool.'

The image of the young guerrilla – leader of the Communist Youth, link man with Bravo's guerrillas, thorn in the side of the ruling regime – was suddenly subject to total demolition. It was done calmly, without rancour.

'He was a very shy person, introverted, everybody would make fun of him. Girls? He was scared and shy of girls.'

He talked of the armed guerrilla struggle and of how the students became emotionally involved in what they saw as an epic fight, an heroic cause. Pastor Heydra insisted that it was he, not Ilich, who became head of the Communist Youth in the school. As for the fire-bombing of the Pan Am building:

'It didn't happen. There were pickets, demonstrations, marches. But fire-bombing Pan Am? That's ridiculous. Ilich would go to these demonstrations, but he always hung back. He would never get involved in anything. The most passive militant I have ever seen. The only job I entrusted to him was to hand out leaflets, even then he usually left them in the toilet.'

Even allowing for the need that Carlos may have had to colour his youthful activities, if others could confirm what Pastor Heydra was telling me, then what Carlos had told me was pure fantasy.

By Heydra's account, the young Carlos was a non-entity. He took very little part in political activity in a school where political activity ran rife. He took no part in sports, had no close friends other than his brother Lenin. He had read a great deal on the background and history of Communism, but in Pastor's opinion the only motivation this had given the young Ilich Ramirez Sanchez was to 'participate at an intellectual level', an armchair revolutionary.

By the time I boarded the plane for London in April 1987 – needless to say without the promised answers from Lenin Ramirez – my earlier suspicions were beginning to harden. Previous doubts were starting to crystallize. I was long past the point where there were more questions than answers. This had become a journey through a wilderness of mirrors that often dissolved to become a walk through Alice's looking glass.

Was Anton Bouvier a separate entity from Carlos? And if he was, had one met the other in Cuba in the mid 1960s and trained him? If Carlos had indeed come to London after committing triple murder in Paris how could I prove it? 'If you're as good as they say you are, you'll find the evidence,' he had said to me.

The prep schools that Carlos claimed to have attended in West London had long closed their doors. Where were their records? Where were their former teachers? Where was the pistol club that Carlos had told me he joined? The club where he had claimed he first held a gun and received his first lessons in the use of arms. If the prep school records could be found and the pistol club located then that would drive a coach and four through the alleged KGB training in Cuba and Moscow. If.

Carlos confirmed that he had not received hospital treatment in London during the winter of 1969/70. In this at least his version was consistent with what had been written by others but were they right? How do you access such hospital records if you are not a doctor?

Carlos had talked of the plot to assassinate Secretary of State Henry Kissinger in Paris during December 1973 and of how the planned attack was prevented at the eleventh hour by a raid by a French DST team on a villa on the outskirts of Paris and the arrest of ten members of the Turkish THKO organization. The raid and the arrests were documented. What the Turkish unit had been planning had never been revealed. Perhaps my friend in French Military Intelligence could confirm the Carlos allegation? So many questions, some big, some small. All crucial. Experience has taught me that the small questions and answers often hold the key to far bigger parts of the puzzle.

I had thought that, when I had made my third visit to Beirut in October 1985, work on this book was all but completed.

Now, seventeen months later, I was beginning to realize that it had only just begun.

10

A GOVERNMENT IN EXILE

After my return from Latin America to find the roots, I concluded that it was time to examine some of the branches, particularly the Palestinian branch of this man's tree. There was an obvious need to talk to Yasser Arafat, to George Habash, Abu Iyad, Abu Jihad, Bassam Abu Sharif. What better place to begin than with the captain, Arafat? Leader of a government in exile.

Dr Bruno Kreisky yet again kindly interceded on my behalf and in April 1987 advised me that I would shortly be receiving an invitation from Arafat. Precisely which country I would be talking to the leader of the PLO in remained a mystery.

It could be Tunisia, it could be Iraq, it could be Algeria, it might be Egypt, perhaps Jordan. The reason for this studied vagueness was explained to me by the then Palestinian equivalent of Ambassador to Austria, Daoud Barakat. 'The Israelis have been trying to kill him for many years. He is obliged to be frequently on the move and to keep those movements secret.'

Over the past twenty years the Israelis have indeed made a number of attempts to kill the Palestinian leader. A conservative estimate would be fifty. They have also made frequent attempts to kill every other Palestinian on my interview list. The private war that knows no frontiers continues to this day.

I told the Palestinians in Vienna that, given adequate notice, I was fully prepared to travel anywhere in the world to talk to Arafat. In turn they advised me that I could not be given adequate notice. 'You will just have to be ready to go anywhere at any time.'

During the early summer of 1987 Nydia Tobon threw me another spanner. In Bogota she had insisted that Carlos and Anton Bouvier were two different people. Since my return Maria had been fully occupied translating Tobon's book on Carlos. At this stage she didn't know of my concern about Bouvier's identity, but she had of course been present, translating, when I spoke to Nydia. Now, as she worked her way through Nydia's somewhat deathless prose, she came across something that puzzled her.

'It's about this business of Bouvier.'

'What about it?'

'When we talked to her in Bogota she said that Bouvier and Carlos were two different people.'

'So?'

'So, in her book she states categorically that they are one and the same. That Carlos is or was Bouvier.'

If, as has been observed, hell is other people, I hope Nydia Tobon has to spend at least part of eternity with Lenin Sanchez. One of them, based on what she had written, had sent me chasing a non-existent shadow, the other had me continually checking the post for a non-existent list of answers to the questions I had left him.

By mid-summer Lenin Ramirez, based on the frequent phone calls to Venezuela and his permanent presence in his bathroom, was demonstrating a critical bowel condition. I decided that the agreement we had made – his co-operation with questions, my promise not to interview his father – was null and void. Unable to leave London, where I continually awaited Yasser Arafat's pleasure, I briefed Maria and put her on a plane to Caracas.

Eventually my perseverance produced the dividend of an enigmatic suggestion from Faisal Aweidah, the man in charge of the PLO legation.

'I think you should be in Tunisia at the beginning of October.'

A few days later this became firmer. 'Arafat will see

you in Tunis on Sunday the 4th of October.'

I travelled via Milan, an unusual route, for two reasons. I had agreed to take part in a television debate on the death of Pope John Paul the First, and I wanted to talk to Danielli. I had been trying to contact Danielli for months without success and I hoped that on this particular Friday he would be watching TV.

The flight out to Milan on the Thursday was possibly the most enjoyable that I have ever experienced. It was not because of the in-flight service, just the reading material I had brought along. A contact in Washington had couriered me an early release copy of Bob Woodward's latest book, *Veil: The Secret Wars of the C.I.A. 1981–1987*. Since returning from Latin America I had been attempting to establish the veracity of what Colonel Qathafi had said to me. I was especially preoccupied with the Colonel's information concerning the large range of conspiracies he had alleged President Reagan and two White House administrations had perpetrated against Libya in general and Qathafi in particular. Now, based on the writings of Bob Woodward, I had startling confirmation of what I had been seeking.

Woodward's sources, most notably the then Head of the CIA, William Casey, present the other side of the coin, the United States side. Every single aspect that Qathafi had talked to me about was verified – Reagan's near pathological obsession with the Libyan leader, the disinformation exercises, the lies, the deadly games that the President and his Cabinet played. And the names of those games – Rose, Tulip, Veil – all of them known and named by Qathafi. All of them known to the Colonel virtually from their inception. The implications of this are quite extraordinary. How did Qathafi learn this information? The conclusion is irrefutable. Throughout the entire eight years of Reagan's Presidency the most secret inner sanctums of the White House, of the CIA, of the State Department had been penetrated. Many could gain by such penetration but who could effect it? Surely not

Libyan Intelligence? Surely Soviet Intelligence? When did the penetration begin? When did it end? Has it indeed ended?

Shortly after returning to my Milan hotel room from the television studios, the phone rang.

'David?'

'Yes.'

'Outside the Cathedral in fifteen minutes?'

'Yes.'

My hotel was only a few minutes' walk from Milan Cathedral. I waited, idly watching the still-active night life. Exactly fifteen minutes after the phone call Danielli pulled up in his car, allowed me to get in, then roared away. After Danielli had stopped in a quiet side street he turned and smiled.

I said, 'I had assumed you had vanished like Carlos.'

'No, I don't have the use of that apartment any more.'

It transpired that, contrary to my belief, it had not been Danielli's home. Just somewhere he had borrowed when we had first met, like his charming 'wife'. Precautions against the possibility that I might be something other than an author seeking truth. The phone number he had given me was not for the apartment but for another address that he had the use of. As both were now redundant he saw no risk in revealing these facts to me. A careful man, Danielli. He had some revelations for me. All bad.

'Gustavo and René are no longer in Paris.'

'When did they leave?'

'Soon after telling me that the man you met in Algiers was dead.'

'How did he die, Danielli?'

'Not from old age. You're becoming a fairly dangerous man to know, David.'

One violent death might be a tragic accident, but two and a further two men vanishing was, in my mind, pushing the laws of coincidence to their outer limits. One by one the links in the chain that had originally led me to Carlos had been cut and neatly removed. I was aware that if these events were more than just mere coincidence then Danielli stood next in line.

The news that Danielli had given me put me into a quiet despair. Hoping against hope, I had remained confident that he and his friends in Paris and Algiers would come through, would succeed in putting me back in contact with Carlos. Now it was quite clear that that route was closed.

'Danielli, I think it might be for the best if we do not meet or talk again after tonight. You have your own life to lead and I'd feel a lot happier if you eventually died of old age.'

'I'm prepared to try and help some more.'

'I'm sure you are, but it's better that you don't.'

For a moment he hesitated; perhaps he was going to argue the point. Then he nodded in acceptance.

'Let me drive you back to your hotel.'

'No, I'll walk. It's a warm night.'

We shook hands and I got out of the car.

'What will you do now, David?'

I stared at him for a moment. Wondering about him.

'I'll keep looking until I find the bastard. Take care of yourself.'

'You too. Ciao.'

A moment later he was gone.

In London Faisal Aweidah had told me that I would be met at Tunis Airport. I wasn't. He had also advised me that I would be seeing Arafat the same day. I didn't.

At my hotel I got busy on the telephone. I phoned London; Faisal Aweidah was not in.

I tried Vienna, Paris and a number of other cities. Wherever else the PLO leaders were that Saturday night, they were definitely not at their desks.

The following day, after a further series of phone calls, I made contact with Khalid, a young member of the PLO who numbered among his talents one that was particularly useful to me – he spoke excellent English.

Over numerous coffees in the hotel I explained to Khalid, a member of Arafat's personal staff, exactly what I was doing in Tunisia. He listened intently, made a number of phone calls, then advised me that a car would collect me at 7.00 pm that evening for my interview with the PLO chairman. He departed. I waited patiently. The car did not come.

After three days, with Khalid's assistance I first went to interview one of the founder members of Al-Fatah, Salah Khalaf, better known under his *nom de guerre,* Abu Iyad.

Born in Jaffa in 1933, the son of a grocer, Khalaf had first met Arafat in Cairo in 1951, just three years after his own family had been forced to leave Palestine.

In the early 1950s, having obtained degrees in philosophy and literature at the Dar al-Ulum college in Cairo, Abu Iyad abandoned what contemporaries told me was a potentially brilliant academic career. He chose instead to return to his family now living in Gaza to work as a schoolteacher under appalling conditions in the refugee camps. At night he underwent training with a commando unit attached to the Egyptian army.

In March 1968 he took part in the battle of Karameh. It was as a result of what happened at Karameh that the PLO became a force to be reckoned with. It was not, however, the battle of Karameh, or even the multiple hijacking that ended at Dawson's Field that riveted the non-Arab world's attention on the Palestinians. Stemming directly out of the slaughter in Jordan came an organization whose very name is a synonym for terror – Black September – linked for ever with the horror that the Munich Olympic Games of 1972 became.

Now, in October 1987, I sat down to talk to the man who had, as the executive in charge of Fatah and PLO security and intelligence services, assumed responsibility for the planning and organization of that Black September operation.

Khalid explained to Abu Iyad the overall framework of the book I was writing.

'Would you like to interview one of the men who took part in the Munich operation?'

'Yes, I would.'

'He is not in Tunisia, but in three days I can arrange it. He is one of the three that survived. His name is Samir.'

'Am I right in thinking that Black September functioned for just three years?'

'Yes, from 1971 to 1974. Three, maybe three and a half years.'

Lighting yet another cigarette (he smoked an entire pack during this interview) Abu Iyad explained to me that 'much that has been written about Black September, like much that has been written on the Israeli/Palestinian issue over the years, does not stand up to close examination'. In the light of my own research I felt that that was a masterly understatement. I moved on to another creation of Abu Iyad's: Sabri al-Banna, or, to give him the *nom de guerre* by which he is known throughout the world, Abu Nidal.

Abu Iyad's relationship with the only man who is in serious competition with Carlos for the title of the world's most wanted man began late in 1967 at the time of the Six Day War.

'I met him in Amman at that time. Before then he had been working in the building industry in Jedda. He joined a secret cell of the Iraqi Baath party while working for Aramco. What a combination! When the Saudi intelligence discovered that, he was dismissed. The Saudis then imprisoned and tortured him before finally expelling him. That together with the war brought him to us in Amman.'

'Is it correct to say that you became his patron?'

'Between 1967 and the early 1970s this would be accurate. But when it became obvious that he was no longer under the control of Fatah but of the Iraqi secret service I withdrew my support.'

'I think that the break between Abu Nidal and Fatah came in March 1974?'

'That was when we made it official, but in reality the break had happened the year before. In September 1973

Nidal sent a group to Paris on behalf of Iraq. They took a dozen or so of the Saudis as hostage. The world said Black September was responsible, it wasn't. It was a terrorist action by Nidal for Iraq.'

'What was the purpose?'

'Two purposes. One, to damage the PLO politically. Two, to frighten Saudi Arabia.'

It was an interesting echo of what Carlos had said to me about the two attacks at Orly in 1975. Then the Iraqi regime had used Carlos to halt the political initiatives of Arafat.

'In April 1980, just seven years after you withdrew your support for Abu Nidal and stopped giving him the benefit of your patronage, he tried to kill you. Your car in Belgrade was blown up. After that attempt on your life, what were your thoughts about your earlier support for Abu Nidal?'

Abu Iyad listened carefully as Khalid translated, then burst into loud laughter. Perhaps sometimes life's ironies do cross linguistic barriers.

'Oh, that was not the first attempt he made on me. He had made many attempts before, about twenty. And since Belgrade, possibly another ten.'

He began laughing again.

'For a man who has survived some thirty attempts on his life by Abu Nidal's men you seem to treat him very lightly.'

'So many operations. So many failures. We catch his people every time.'

'And then a trial and execution?'

'Certainly not. Just a minute.'

Abu Iyad picked up a phone and spoke rapidly into it. A moment later one of his bodyguards hurried into the room, a man in his mid-twenties, dressed in khaki fatigues, Kalashnikov in his hand. Abu Iyad began to talk to him. The man responded. There were a number of interchanges, then Abu Iyad dismissed the man and indicated that Khalid should translate.

'Abu Iyad asked him how he came to be protecting

his, Abu Iyad's, life. The guard said he was sent by Abu Nidal to kill Abu Iyad.'

I had heard in the Arab world many times the philosophy of drawing one's enemy close but this struck me as an extreme example.

Abu Iyad continued, 'This is my response to Abu Nidal.'

'You use them all as bodyguards?'

'Most of them. Under close supervision of course.'

Of course.

Our discussion moved to how Abu Nidal's organization had been penetrated for many years by Mossad. Penetrated to such a degree that Abu Iyad, the head of PLO intelligence and counter-intelligence, with all that that implies, told me of his conviction that frequently the targets selected by Abu Nidal have been chosen by Mossad, and when not by Israeli Intelligence then often by Nidal's Iraqi and subsequently Syrian masters. He cited an example of Mossad targeting: Arafat's PLO representative in London, Said Hammami.

'At the time of Said Hammami's murder in January 1978 he was in the middle of very secret negotiations with members of the Israeli government. Perhaps not so much negotiations as a continuous dialogue. His message to the Israelis can be reduced to this: "We undertake to recognize Israel at the end of public and official negotiations that lead to the creation of a Palestinian mini-state in the West Bank and Gaza." Now, remember Hammami had been given this brief at the end of 1973. Since that date we have been prepared to give the Israelis what they have always demanded.'

'Presumably this dialogue of Hammami's had to be secret because so many in the various Palestinian movements would have violently objected. They were still seeking a return to the 1947 borders.'

'That's correct. Arafat would have needed time to sell the idea to our people. That job would of course be much easier if he could be confident of Israeli support.'

'So for four to five years Said Hammami worked on

this secret agenda. Who did he talk to?'

'Principally Uri Avneri, who in turn talked to Prime Minister Rabin. We gave them the bottom line we have always understood they wanted.'

'Why didn't they take it?'

'Rabin had to sell it to himself and then his people, just as much as Arafat did to ours. It would obviously take time. By January 1978 we felt we had made some progress. Then Said Hammami was murdered. His murder was followed by a further twenty between 1978 and 1983. All of these men were hand-picked, many of them before their deaths had been having the same dialogue, not only with the Israelis but with a number of governments. All were killed by Abu Nidal's organization.'

'But there's no Mossad penetration needed for that. Nidal is opposed to dialogue just as much as Israel's hawks are.'

'A long time before Said's murder he was warned by British Special Branch that he was on Mossad's hit list. They told him their information came from the CIA. Said was also told by British Security that the British government had warned the Israeli Embassy that all known Mossad agents would be kicked out of Britain if the Israelis started getting the guns out.'

The implication was clear: prevented by the British from doing the job themselves, Mossad had whistled up Abu Nidal.

Abu Iyad told me how Mossad had first penetrated an organization that in theory not only Israel but the United States and many other countries are seeking to destroy.

'By 1976 the Abu Nidal group had been penetrated by Mossad. It had also been penetrated by the CIA. The initial plan to plant agents within his group was created by the CIA and the Moroccan Intelligence service. I'm sure that you are already aware that certain parts of the CIA have a special relationship with Mossad. Those elements advised Mossad of the joint Moroccan/CIA plan to infiltrate.'

'What was the Moroccan interest in this?'

'Their intelligence has close links with the CIA. King Hassan has been a CIA asset for many many years. From the very beginning of his operations Abu Nidal has always recruited from Morocco and other North African countries. In 1981 I was handed by Moroccan Intelligence a list of nineteen people who were Abu Nidal group members based in Spain. They had been given the list by Mossad.'

'Who, presumably, if they had so desired, could have eliminated the entire Nidal group based in Spain.'

'Of course. Last year [1986] I saw Abu Nidal in Algeria. The first time I have seen him for fourteen years.'

'Had he changed?'

'Yes, for the worse. I discussed with him the list of his nineteen members in Spain. A list that I had because of Mossad's infiltration of his organization.'

'What was his response?'

'He said, "If Abu Nidal did not exist then Mossad would have created Abu Nidal to do such acts. They need Abu Nidal. Any Abu Nidal."'

'In 1975, Fatah tried Abu Nidal in absentia and he was sentenced to death. The fact that he could attend your PNC last year in Algeria would indicate that that trial and sentence were just window dressing. Has the PLO now become like Mossad? Does it too have a need for Abu Nidal?'

'The decision to commute the death sentence on him was not mine. Others argued that by letting him live we could continue to obtain information on the real enemy.'

'At an appalling price. Rome and Vienna airports. The Egypt Air hijack. I find it difficult to understand how you could break bread with such a man.'

'Do you also find it difficult to understand why both the CIA and Mossad continue to let Abu Nidal perform such operations when their agents who have penetrated his organization could kill him any day they wanted to?'

'Yes, I do.'

'In February 1986 Yitzhak Shamir said, "Israel will get Abu Nidal." Perhaps Shamir will tell you why Israel has yet to "get" him. Apart from the many other services that Abu Nidal has performed on behalf of Israel they owe Nidal a tremendous debt for giving them the pretext to invade Lebanon in 1982.'

'His group's attempt to murder Ambassador Argov in London?'

'Precisely. There is no doubt whatsoever in my mind that Mossad knew of the plan before it was put into action. They could have stopped Nidal's people in London before the shooting of Argov. They didn't.'

'Are you saying that the attempt on Argov was a Mossad plan?'

'No, not at all. But they could have stopped it.'

'Who was behind that operation?'

'Iraq.'

It was not the answer I had expected. Abu Iyad then outlined an extraordinary scenario. Iraq's long war with Iran was going badly by 1982. Early gains had been lost. Casualties in a war against an enemy that believed martyrdom and heaven awaited death on the battlefield were mounting ever higher. Morale was low. For the first time, a decisive Iranian victory was no longer impossible. There were calls in Teheran for an advance on Baghdad. In the previous year Saddam Hussein had survived five assassination attempts. Many hundreds of officers and soldiers were arrested after an abortive coup attempt. Iran had rejected an offer for cease fire in November 1981. Then there was the factor that represented Saddam Hussein's greatest fear – attack on his Western front by Iran's ally and Iraq's enemy for many years, Syria.

It is an indisputable fact that Israel's leaders, particularly Defence Minister Sharon, had been preparing, indeed were fully prepared, to invade Lebanon for many months. What was lacking was a pretext, an incident that would be serious enough to be acceptable to the Reagan Administration in general and Secretary of State

Alexander Haig in particular. On Thursday 3rd of June, 1982, there was an incident – the attempted assassination of Shlomo Argov outside the Dorchester Hotel in London by members of Abu Nidal.

Apart from the intelligence information available to Abu Iyad, my own research had convinced me that from 1973 until the end of 1982, Abu Nidal and his organization were answerable to Saddam Hussein. At the end of 1982 he switched his allegiances to Syria and President Asad, but in June 1982 he was still under the protection of and receiving support from Hussein. By provoking the Israeli invasion of Lebanon Nidal singlehandedly eliminated any danger of a Syrian invasion of Iraq. Israel's attack on Lebanon began within twenty-four hours of the wounding of Ambassador Argov. One of Israel's first acts was to neutralize the Syrian war machine. They destroyed the entire Syrian air defence system in the Lebanon and shot down nearly one hundred Syrian warplanes. Saddam Hussein could forget about the threat on his Western front and concentrate on his war with Iran. Significantly, Saddam Hussein offered the Iranians yet another cease fire, on the grounds that they should join forces against their common enemy, Israel. The offer was rejected by the Iranians, but if Abu Iyad's analysis was correct, then Hussein had removed one very powerful enemy from the battlefield by unleashing Abu Nidal in London. He had also triggered the carnage that was to occur in Lebanon, a war in which thousands died, a war that culminated in an obscenity called Sabra and Chatila.

After discussing Abu Nidal, a man who believes that Israel would have created him if he did not already exist, I began to question Abu Iyad about Carlos, a man created by many. His view of the Carlos of the 70s and the 80s was identical to the opinion of former classmate Pastor Heydra when considering the Carlos of the 60s.

'Carlos is an empty drum.'

'Can you elaborate on that?'

18. An extraordinary photograph of Carlos, secretly taken by the French DST only days before he murdered three men and seriously wounded a fourth.

19-22. *Above left* Photograph from a false Peruvian passport bearing the name that would be for ever linked with him - Carlos Andres Martinez Torres. *Above right* Anton Bouvier, a man of many parts, but was he Carlos? *Below left* Michel Moukharbel. *Below right* 'Where people come to die', 9 rue Toullier the morning after.

23-6. Safe houses, unsafe contents: *above left* 11 rue Amélie; *above right* Barry Woodhams examining the contents of a Carlos suitcase; *below left* Wilfried Böse; *below right* what the DST found under Amparo Silva Masmela's bed.

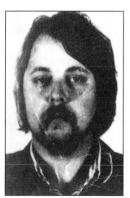

27-9. Some of the ladies of the chorus: *clockwise from top left* Nydia Maria Tobon; Nancy Sanchez; Angela Otaola, posing shortly before her arrest.

30-31. 'One cannot be generous with other people's lives': Chancellor Bruno Kreisky (*above*). *Below* Three of the many who were destined to be victims of the world's most audacious kidnap: (*from left to right*) Dr Valentin Hernandez Acosta, Dr Jamshid Amouzegar, Sheikh Ahmed Zaki Yamani.

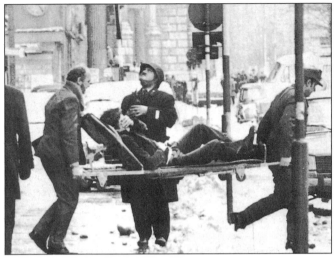

32-4. 'We came together, we will all leave or die together': Hans Joachim Klein is carried from OPEC headquarters on a stretcher. Gabriele Tiedemann, a murderous cold-blooded bitch. Khalid, gun in hand, escorts a group of hostages.

35. Carlos, complete with Che Guevara beret, in total and absolute control.

36. The master of ceremonies directing the opening moments of act two: Austrian officials stand powerless as Tiedemann (*far left*) emerges from the bus and Khalid (*far right*) climbs onto the plane.

37. Carlos at Algiers airport, $20 million richer.

'He has nothing to say. He has nothing to do with our struggle apart from one or two operations.'

'Have you met him?'

'Yes, a number of times in Beirut and then once in Germany.'

'Do you know where he is now?'

The sixty-four thousand dollar question. It got an unexpected answer.

'Now he is staying in Romania. At the moment he is there.'

Coming from the executive who ran the PLO intelligence services this had to be taken very seriously, especially as Abu Iyad's intelligence infrastructure had been in part set up by the KGB.

We discussed Carlos at considerable length. In the light of Abu Iyad's Russian connections of many years, particularly with their intelligence agencies, his opinion on one aspect of the man that has virtually become holy writ was particularly relevant.

'Carlos has no connection with the KGB, he never has had a connection with them. He is not even a leftist, just someone pretending to be of the left.'

Several days later I interviewed Abu Iyad again. During the course of a long, wide-ranging session I discussed yet again the man whom I was hunting.

'How do you rate the intelligence you have that tells you Carlos is in Romania?'

'High. First-class.'

'I need to get to him.'

'I believe that will be difficult and probably it's impossible for you to meet like that, person to person, just like that. You will have to meet him through the Romanian government. My advice is to go through the Romanian government.'

'I have no contacts there. An official approach would be met, I am quite sure, with an official denial.'

The small, chubby chain-smoker sitting across the desk from me smiled.

'Yes, I'm sure it would be.'

'Can you unlock that door for me, Abu Iyad?'

'I will try, but it will take a little time. Also Abu Nidal, I will try there too, but not yet. We will keep in continuous contact and I will arrange it.'

Further interviews with Abu Daoud and George Habash followed this second meeting with Abu Iyad. From both I learnt first-hand a great deal about the Black September and Popular Front operations, Wadi Haddad and a certain Venezuelan. Interestingly, Dr George Habash's assessment of Carlos sharply contradicted the view held by Abu Iyad.

'He was a good fighter. An excellent fighter. I admired very much his ability to face the difficult life of a fighter in Jordan.'

Habash told me that he had not seen Carlos for eight years but promised he would have enquiries made. We talked at length about his own life and struggles. Habash is a sick man, a botched operation has left him partially paralysed, but his brain remains sharp and his memory lucid. I knew from my research that Carlos held Habash in very high regard. If the Doctor could reach out and locate him there was every likelihood that Carlos would respond positively. A further interview with Habash was arranged: this would take place in the city where he lived when not on what seemed almost continuous trips – Damascus.

By the time I had been in Tunisia for a week I had achieved a considerable number of my objectives. Apart from two long interviews with Abu Iyad and a shorter one with Dr George Habash, there were two other interviews that I had not expected on this trip. Both were remarkable in many ways, not least because the two men in question had never been interviewed before. Abu Iyad's hand had reached out and plucked them from their respective hiding places. One was a man that Israel would dearly like to lay her hands on. The other an individual that the head of Vienna police, Dr Werner Liebhardt, would have arrested on sight.

The *noms de guerre* were Samir and Khalid. The first

had been a member of the Black September group responsible for the Munich Olympic Games attack of September 1972. The second had been Carlos's number two during the OPEC attack in Vienna in December 1975. Both talked freely of their involvement in these two operations, clearing away much of the myth that surrounds both attacks.

At no time did I indicate to Khalid that I had met Carlos; in many respects their separate versions of the OPEC attack were identical, but there were significant differences. The most important one was the name of the man who had first conceived the idea for the attack on OPEC and the kidnapping of the oil ministers. Carlos had asserted it was Qathafi. Khalid had a different name. As he quietly explained the situation and circumstances that existed he also produced a very powerful motive for the attack. If Khalid was right, and his evidence was very persuasive, then the man responsible lived not in Tripoli but in a different Arab capital.

After talking to Khalid I wandered around various Palestinian enclaves with my mind in a whirl. If Khalid was indeed right then Carlos was wrong. Either he had deliberately misinformed me or he did not know who had masterminded the OPEC attack. If he did not know there was surely only one logical explanation. He was an impostor, someone's double agent. Who would go to such inordinate lengths to lead me down a false path? And why? Yet again I asked myself why Carlos had given me those interviews. I felt sure this was the key to the whole thing. Now one week late I was finally going to meet the man who perhaps somewhere in the darkest corners of his soul knew the truth.

Carlos had made one particular allegation among the many that he had tossed at me through two long summer nights. If that allegation could eventually be substantiated, then I was about to meet a man who, even by what often passes for standards in the Middle East, was guilty of such acts that to describe them as evil would be to reduce them to banality. That central allegation was that the chairman of the PLO, Yasser Arafat, had conspired in the murders of thousands of Palestinians in Beirut at the Sabra and Chatila camps in the late summer of 1982.

The fact that I finally got to meet Arafat was not thanks to anyone on his own personal team of assistants. It was pure chance. A meeting with Basel Aql, an influential Palestinian based in London.

Basel assured me that he would intercede immediately on my behalf, that I would definitely see Arafat that very night. At eleven in the evening I gave up and went to bed. At twelve the phone woke me up. It was Basel. They were coming to get me. The interview would take place as soon as I arrived.

I was driven to the Tunis suburb of Menzah. Apart from armed guards there were some thirty to forty Palestinians sitting and standing around a modest white-washed villa, idly chatting.

The villa was ablaze with light and activity. I was shown downstairs past rooms where a large range of transmitting and receiving equipment was also working the night shift. No sooner was I in a very large well furnished basement room than the Old Man, as his close colleagues call him, came bounding into the room and shook my hand. Firm handshake, wet smile and equally rheumy eyes. The familiar olive green uniform with the white checked keffiyeh on his head and the equally familiar holster with its pistol on his hip. What looks like designer stubble on TV is in reality a conventional beard.

We sat directly opposite each other in comfortable armchairs and I began to question the man whose death would be cause for the champagne to flow in the streets of Israel. My mind was still very full of the allegations that Carlos had made to me. To confront Arafat on that central issue was not a real proposition but I decided to throw a curver.

'I want to go back into Beirut, specifically to the Sabra and Chatila camps, to talk to some of the survivors of the massacre. I also want to go to South Lebanon. I'm aware of the dangers, particularly because of the colour of my skin. Can you assist me?'

'South Lebanon is not a problem. We can arrange for you to go via Cyprus. That we can manage.'

'What about Beirut and the Sabra and Chatila camps?'

'Beirut no. I strongly advise against it.'

'What about Red Crescent [the Palestinian Red Cross], could I go in as one of their doctors?'

'I wouldn't advise it. Look at what is going on in Beirut. The city is now a slaughterhouse. When we were there, there were no kidnappings, no embassy sieges, no hostage taking and the foreign committee was safe. We organized two evacuations for the Americans, one through the mountains, the other by sea. But now, if you were to attempt Beirut and the camps, I think you would vanish within hours.'

Arafat was not telling me anything I did not already know. I had been curious to see if there was any reaction at the mention of Sabra and Chatila.

Whenever the opportunity presented itself during this research I would bring up the question of the hostages – Terry Anderson, Terry Waite, John McCarthy, Brian Keenan and the many other missing people who had indeed 'vanished within hours'. Qathafi had been interesting on this: his information was that Terry Waite might well be a man controlled by British or American intelligence. He said that a transmitting device had been discovered on Waite after his abduction. It begged the question of how Qathafi knew what had been discovered *after* the kidnap. I had duly asked it and the Colonel, somewhat lamely I thought, said, 'It's what I've been told.' I had urged him to intervene, argued that if he secured the release of some or any of the hostages it could do his image in the West nothing but good. I knew his influence in Lebanon was limited but felt every effort, no matter how small, should be made to get these men out of hell. He had promised to do what he could. Now with Arafat I again brought up the issue of the hostages.

'Do you think that Terry Waite is still alive?'

'Yes.'

'Where do you think he is being held?'

'In Lebanon. He is in what they call the higher section, the Bekaa, sometimes he and the others are moved to the Southern section, South Beirut.'

'And the others?'

'They are also in the same area.'

'Why are they being held? There have been no demands.'

'Yes, they have made demands.'

'Not publicly?'

'No, but secretly.'

'Money?'

'No, not money. Part of a package, an Iranian deal, more weapons, trade.'

I returned again to the subject that, with regard to Yasser Arafat, concerned me above all others.

'It is my understanding that there is within the PLO a report on the massacres at Sabra and Chatila. Either a report or an analysis carried out by your organization. I have the Israeli report, I have also researched information from a number of other sources. I would like a copy of your report.'

'Maybe we can give it to you. It has not yet been accepted widely enough within the PLO, therefore our files on this are not open, but I will try to let some of these files be made available to you.'

It was such a curious response. This was October 1987, five years after mass killings that had such shocking implications – world reaction included over four hundred thousand Israelis taking to the streets of Tel Aviv to demand an official inquiry. Prime Minister Menachem Begin was forced to retreat from his 'Goyim kill goyim and then blame the Jews' position and bow to the demand. Subsequently, in February 1983, the Commission of Inquiry, known as the Kahan Commission, having considered some evidence in public, some in secret, published part of its findings while other conclusions remained secret.

Some observers considered the report a whitewash of Israel's alleged involvement, others saw it as a vindication of Israel's involvement. Whatever its flaws, at least some attempt had been made by Israel to arrive at the truth. Why then such reticence by the Palestinian leadership to do the same? Was it possible that Carlos had spoken the truth when he made his appalling allegations to me?

Without revealing my inner concerns I made it clear to Arafat why access to the PLO report was vital. I drew a parallel with the massacre of the Palestinians that had occurred at Deir Yassin in 1948. A massacre that many in Israel do not care to remember. A massacre of which new generations in the West are not even aware.

Those who do not remember history are condemned to relive it. The Jews know that. Was it a lesson that the Arabs have yet to learn?

I remarked to Arafat that for many in the West, thanks to the efficiency of Israeli propaganda, to say Palestinian is to say terrorist. A full exposure of events like those that occurred at Sabra and Chatila would offer an alternative synonym: victim.

Yasser Arafat may have kept me waiting to talk to him but now he certainly gave time generously. We talked through that Saturday night until dawn.

It was a wide-ranging conversation: the origins of the Israel–Palestine conflict; the oil weapon; the wealth of the PLO; terrorism; hostage-taking.

Later in this interview I returned again to the Sabra and Chatila massacres. We discussed what degree of complicity, if any, existed between the Israeli forces then occupying Beirut and the actual perpetrators.

'You must read what Elie Houbeika has said. He gave an interview to an Arab magazine. He was the head of the groups who participated in the massacres. Later he escaped from East Beirut. Now he is working with the Syrians. He was the "hero" of this massacre because he controlled the group from the Phalangists who participated.'

'I intend to interview Houbeika.'

'The Syrians will never allow it. He is under their control.'

It was a moment to ask about Carlos. Yasser Arafat, like Abu Iyad and other Palestinians except Habash, was not impressed by Carlos.

'What was your reaction to the OPEC attack led by Carlos?'

'Astonishment. This was not in any way a Palestinian operation.'

'Did you approve of it?'

'Not at all. For me it had no Palestinian political objective or target. It was carried out for quite different reasons.'

'Which were?'

'Money.'

'But Carlos was part of the Popular Front at the time of that attack.'

'No, no. No, not at all. He had relationships, understandings, with some Arab intelligence services by then, but not with us.'

'Have you any idea where he is now?'

'No. It is many years since I have seen him in Beirut.'

'Wadi Haddad is considered by many observers to have been the mastermind behind the OPEC attack.'

'No, no. Of that I am sure. I met him before his death. I asked him many questions about that attack. He said to me that he had not arranged it.'

Yasser Arafat is a man whose political obituary has been written many times. Like those in Israel who have tried repeatedly to kill him, political observers have consistently underrated his powers of survival. Over the past thirty years he has made many mistakes. Sometimes his cards have been played badly. Sometimes he has held no cards at all. His achievements, however, have been truly extraordinary. He has somehow held together the various political factions that comprise the PLO, even bringing the recalcitrant Popular Front and its leader, Dr George Habash, back into the fold. He has wheeled and dealed his way through the convoluted politics of the

Middle East, feeling at times – as he ruefully observed to his biographer, Alan Hart – that he was the only client in a brothel. His balancing act has been far from perfect, indeed on occasions he has fallen completely off the highwire, but somehow there has always been a safety net.

The fact that now, over forty years after the State of Israel became a reality, the issue of the Palestinians is still the key to lasting peace in the Middle East, the fact that his people's aspirations have not been consigned to the dusty shelves of history, is his greatest achievement. This is the precise reason why the Israelis are still fighting tooth and nail to avoid a direct dialogue with Arafat and his PLO colleagues. Former Prime Minister Shamir declares that Arafat and his colleagues are terrorists. Perhaps they are. Or perhaps more significantly they were. It should not be a debarment to peace talks. After all, Shamir and his predecessor, Menachem Begin, were also terrorists. Men with a great deal of blood on their hands. Men still officially wanted by Interpol for acts of terrorism. But as I have already observed, history is written by winners.

Subsequently in Tunis I interviewed Abu Iyad again, also Abu Jihad. The only one on the list that remained unticked was Bassam Abu Sharif, still in temporary exile in Algiers. He was important in my hunt for Carlos. He had certainly known him well when the Venezuelan had first come out to the Middle East, and internal evidence in the *Al Watan Al Arabi* interviews with Carlos carried out in late 1979 suggested that Abu Sharif had been present when Carlos had talked to the writer.

I decided that he would have to wait until another time and flew back to London.

11

HERE, THERE AND EVERYWHERE

Sometimes, life is very well written. An example of this occurred soon after I had returned from the Middle East. My son had a friend over one Saturday. When the boy's father came to collect him, I recalled an untranslated letter I had received from the Austrian Minister of the Interior, Dr Karl Blecha, concerning the OPEC attack. I knew that the boy's mother was multi-lingual.

'Tony, could you ask Susan to translate this for me please. It's German.'

'No problem. I'll do it for you now. I speak German.'

Tony promptly read out the letter in English then remarked,

'The OPEC attack. That was Carlos, wasn't it?'

'Yes.'

'He was in my night school class when I was learning Russian.'

'When was that?'

'Early 1970s.'

'Where did you go for these lessons?'

'Red Lion Square.'

Extraordinary – after years of costly research, thousands of miles of travel digging up facts and establishing truths, I get this from the father of my son's closest friend. The immediate importance was that this Russian course definitely placed him in Central London for an entire year. This at a time when, depending on which writer one selected, Carlos was engaged in a variety of activities in a variety of countries.

Reflecting on the pure happenstance that had brought this unlikely source of information to me, I wondered if I should perhaps abandon all of my global research, strap a loud-hailer to my car and tour the streets of London.

After some protracted research I managed to establish that Ilich Ramirez Sanchez had indeed enrolled at the Central London Polytechnic in September 1972. He had also applied for and had been given a State aided grant.

It got better. Tony's wife Susan had maintained a close friendship with one of the Russian teachers at the Poly, Lorissa Kovalyova. When I interviewed Lorissa I discovered that she had taught at the Patrice Lumumba University in Moscow at precisely the same time as Lenin and Ilich were attending the University. She had a very clear recollection of both young men and also of the circumstances surrounding their expulsion.

In April 1988, another man whose help I had enlisted in my hunt for Carlos died a violent death, though his killing was unconnected with the assistance he was giving me.

During the early hours of April 16th, that private war between Israel and a wide spectrum of Palestinian activists came to the villa of Khalil al-Wazzir, better known by his *nom de guerre*, Abu Jihad. Over seventy bullets were fired into his body before his killers vanished.

No-one has ever claimed responsibility. No-one needed to do so. His death had 'made in Israel' written all over it. No-one doubted that the men who left behind them in the Tunisian villa a blood-spattered room, where a few months earlier I had sat talking to Abu Jihad, had been sent by the Israeli Cabinet. In the days following Jihad's death certain members of that Cabinet could not refrain from gloating to certain reporters, off the record of course. It was revealed that indeed Shamir's government had ordered the killing, that a combined operation involving Mossad, Military Intelligence, a thirty-strong commando unit, high speed boats, Air Force and Naval personnel and a Boeing 707 had ensured that Jihad, Arafat's joint number two with Abu Iyad, was eliminated.

The media pointed to the fact that Jihad was the key

Palestinian controller of the Intifada and that this was the prime reason why he was killed.

The Intifada – the uprising of the Palestinian communities living in the West Bank and in the Gaza Strip – had erupted on December 9th, 1987. Four Palestinians were killed that day and a further seven injured when an Israeli truck collided with two van-loads of Palestinian workers returning from Israel. There had been far worse incidents in the past since Israel occupied these territories after the 1967 war, but this particular one provoked a spontaneous uprising. The Intifada took both the occupying Israelis and the PLO completely by surprise. Since then the former have struggled to repress it, the latter to control it, and Jihad was the man at the head of that control. This was not, however, the reason why Abu Jihad died.

Other commentators gave as the explanation for his death the fact that Jihad, as the PLO's Military Commander, had scored some significant successes recently, most notably when a Palestinian hang-glider came over the border from Lebanon and killed six Israeli soldiers, injuring a further twelve before the lone Palestinian was shot. In reality, Jihad had had nothing to do with this particular attack. It was, as Israeli Intelligence well knew, the work of Ahmed Jibril. Neither this, nor the actual Jihad-inspired attacks on Israeli targets were the reason why he died.

When the *Washington Post* headlined its front page story on Jihad's death with 'High Backing Seen for Assassination', it was absolutely correct but in view of the fact that it merely detailed the Israeli Cabinet decision to unleash its forces against Jihad, the *Post* had got hold of only part of the story.

The 'High Backing' also included the President of Tunisia, Ben Ali, and the United States government, specifically the State Department.

By 1987, Abu Jihad had despaired of ever seeing a settlement of the Palestinian issue through a peaceful process of negotiation. This man, one of the original co-founders of Al Fatah, had seen and heard it all. For a long time it had been abundantly clear to Jihad that the Palestinians would never see even a fragment of their lands returned to them unless the United States policies of decades underwent a radical sea change. With the extraordinary power of the Israeli lobby in America completely mesmerizing successive Presidents, Jihad concluded that it would require a very dramatic event to make the White House change the direction it had been following for forty years. He began to consider exactly what form that dramatic event should take.

His first idea was to have the Saudi Arabian King assassinated. The murder of King Fahd, ruler of the pro-Western, pro-United States Saudi Arabia, would certainly concentrate the minds of America's leaders. He was dissuaded from this course of action by colleagues to whom I have spoken. They do not include Yasser Arafat, who was excluded from these deliberations.

When Jihad received intelligence that Secretary of State George Shultz planned to embark on a series of trips to the Middle East to advance his own proposals for peace, Abu Jihad concluded that, in Shultz, he had the ideal alternative target. The murder of the second most powerful political figure in the United States while visiting Israel would most certainly cause a powerful concentration of minds throughout the world.

Jihad contacted and then met Abu Nidal. The thinking behind the multiple hijack that ended on Dawson's Field in Jordan and the attack on the Israeli athletes during the Munich Olympic Games was reactivated. The philosophy that says, if you will only take us seriously when we hurt or destroy your vested interests, then stand by for action was re-born.

Jihad had re-met Nidal several years before. While in Tripoli attempting to bring about reconciliation between the continuously arguing and estranged Palestinian groups, Habash, Abu Mõusa et al, Jihad had attended a meeting with Qathafi and some of the warring factions. During the meeting Qathafi, like a conjurer with a hat and a white rabbit, brought Abu Nidal into the room. In view of the fact that the PLO had years before cut off all contact with Nidal and sentenced him to death in absentia, Jihad railed at Qathafi and left the meeting. It was, however, the beginning of new contact with Nidal, contact that continued.

In Algiers, during late 1987, Jihad and Nidal conferred, agreed and planned. On March 4th, 1988, a car loaded with TNT explosives and a pre-set timing device was parked less than three hundred yards from the hotel in Jerusalem where Secretary of State Shultz was staying. The plan was for the bomb to activate when Shultz left his hotel. Two hours before his departure the car was 'discovered' by Israeli police.

Whether Israeli Intelligence knew of the attempt before the event is a moot point. I have been assured that they did, but I have no definite proof of that. Through their long-standing infiltration of the Abu Nidal Organization, Mossad soon established that the man behind the attempt on Shultz was Abu Jihad. Four days after the attempt had been thwarted the Israeli Cabinet met. The ten-man Inner Cabinet, with only its Labour members – Peres, Weitzman and Navon – objecting, took the decision to assassinate Jihad. Because of the minority objections, Prime Minister Shamir took out insurance: details of what Israel was planning were laid before the Reagan Administration and a green light requested. The State Department sanctioned the killing, with one condition. Secretary of State Shultz was planning a further trip to Israel in early April; the Israelis were told by their American allies that Abu Jihad's death could not occur until Shultz was safely out of the region. By the end of the first week in April 1988 Shultz had been and gone and the Israelis had their green light.

On the night of April 15th, the American Cemetery close to the embassy was ablaze with light and activity. Normally in total darkness with a maximum of two Military Police patrolling, on this particular evening it was manned by thirty Military Police and a marine back-up.

278

As part of the joint American/Israeli operation it had been agreed that the cemetery would serve as a fall-back position if the Israeli unit ran into heavy opposition. Later reports stated that part of the Israeli operation was a back-up squad of their own who had been given the task of jamming the telephones in the area. Mossad may perhaps be surprised to learn that this unit failed in their task. The telephones continued to work. Despite the fact that a neighbour to Jihad phoned the police at least twice, first to report intruders, second to report hearing and seeing gun-fire in Jihad's garden, the Tunisian police declined to send a car out. The firing that the woman had witnessed was the killing of Jihad's gardener and an elderly servant, not, as the press reported, Jihad's bodyguard. By a curious coincidence on that evening virtually all members of the Tunisian police force had been taking part in a large exercise between nine in the evening and midnight. At midnight they had all been stood down and appear to have been on a mass collective meal break. The killing of Jihad took place at one-thirty in the morning. The Israeli unit were wearing Tunisian National Guard uniforms.

The assassination of Jihad was not quite the flawless operation that the myth gives one to expect from the Israelis. The telephone jamming had failed and without Tunisian complicity so would have the entire operation.

In their panic, the killers ignored the top secret files on Abu Jihad's desk, files that were far more valuable than the taking of one man's life, for they contained a wealth of detail on the entire infrastructure of Palestinian resistance on the West Bank and in the Gaza Strip. They also detailed forward planning on the Intifada. One of the killers dropped his earpiece in the moments after the shooting. This, with other elements, confirmed that the killing squad were in continuous radio contact with the Boeing flying just outside Tunisian air space. In the plane were, among others, Major General Ehud Barak, deputy to the Israeli Commander-in-Chief; Dan Shomron, Chief of Staff; Air Force Commander Avihu

Bin-Nun, and the Head of Military Intelligence, Amnon Shahak.

In the journey back to the Tunisian beach and the waiting rubber dinghies, one of the retreating units took a wrong turning and ripped the bottom out of the vehicle. Again, without Tunisian connivance, the entire unit could so easily have been caught.

Shamir was later to state that the first he knew of Jihad's death was when he heard it on the radio. He neglected to add that the radio in question was the radio-link from the Boeing to the Prime Minister's office. He also neglected to say that when the unit returned he waded out into the sea to greet them and rejoice. Perhaps for a few moments he was reliving his earlier days when he had no need for younger men to do his killing for him.

This, based on my research, is how the democratic nations of Israel and the United States, aided and abetted by Tunisia, disposed of the problem of Abu Jihad.

With Abu Jihad dead, help from his PLO colleague Abu Iyad became even more important in my hunt. In June, after some prompting from a London-based friend of Iyad's, he finally came through. The friend advised me that it was now confirmed that Carlos was living in Romania under the direct protection of President Ceauşescu. That was the good news. The bad news was that Iyad, having spoken to Carlos, had learned that he was forbidden by Ceauşescu to talk to any foreigners. My response was immediate.

'I don't see a problem. Ask Abu Iyad to get me a Romanian passport and papers.'

That, it transpired, was impossible. Through the intermediary I was advised that Abu Iyad would contact Carlos again in a few weeks and persuade him to come to Algiers, where I could meet him. The suggested meeting place was interesting, not least because it recalled my meeting with the man with no name, yet another of the unfortunates in a growing list of people who, since I had begun this particular investigation in 1983, could now only be spoken of in the past tense.

Algiers.

Perhaps then the man I had met in Lebanon had after all been the genuine article. Since those two meetings my view of his authenticity had swung first one way and then the other. A piece of evidence would be obtained that appeared to give firm proof that it had indeed been Carlos, then later a further piece would point to a set-up.

In June the mutual friend returned from a trip to Tunisia and a series of meetings with the inner circle of the PLO. He had not forgotten my manhunt.

'I'm afraid I've got bad news.'

'Yes?'

'When I spoke to Abu Iyad from London in June, I was of course discreet on the telephone. He was equally discreet. When I reminded him of your need to talk to Carlos I did not mention that name on the phone.'

'Very wise, unless you want Special Branch to pay a visit.'

'Abu Iyad thought I was talking about Abu Nidal.'

'So Nidal's in Romania and we do not know where Carlos is?'

'Precisely.'

Abu Nidal was on my list, if only because I believed he might, if so inclined, throw some light on exactly where one overweight Venezuelan was. Again I wondered how to get my hands on a Romanian passport and papers. The mutual friend assured me there was no need for that.

'I understand that Abu Nidal will be going to the Middle East in the near future. When he is there it will be much easier to arrange.'

In July I pointed Maria back to Venezuela to conduct further research while I flew to Germany. I had established contact with Gabriele Tiedemann, one of the Carlos group that had attacked the OPEC headquarters in Vienna. She had not been too difficult to find. After Vienna, Tiedemann had not rested on her dubious laurels. The successful kidnap of an Austrian industrialist, released after a large ransom had been paid, was followed by a less than successful attempt at shooting her way through a Swiss border post. In the middle of 1988 she was approaching the end of a fourteen-year prison sentence for attempted murder.

There are two Tiedemanns. One a cold-blooded bitch of a woman who can kill as casually as you or I would reach for a biscuit; the other is an amalgam of the Virgin Mary and Little Nell. Innocence personified. When we corresponded she was going through one of her Little Nell phases – something that professional criminals describe as 'working your ticket'. My interest in her was not confined to her own account of the OPEC attack; I was far more interested in her relationship with Carlos. I hoped that the time she had spent in his company might assist me in solving the puzzle about the authenticity of the man with whom I had talked two nights away.

Her tremulous letters to me established that she had a marked disinclination to recall the past. My thoughts turned to a man who over the years had become as close to her as anyone living: Pastor Heinrich Albertz.

There were two other men I was anxious to talk to in West Germany. They sat very neatly at either end of the political spectrum. One was an enemy of the State, the other a protector of it. They knew each other well yet had never met.

Peter Jurgen Boock, second-generation member of the notorious Red Army Faction (RAF), was a protégé of its founder members, Andreas Baader, Gudrun Ensslin and Ulrike Meinhof. In May 1984, Boock was sentenced for his alleged involvement in a number of Red Army actions which included the murder of Jurgen Ponto; an attempted rocket launcher attack on the Federal Prosecutor's office in Karlsruhe; and the kidnapping and murder of Hanns-Martin Schleyer. The judgement was three terms of life imprisonment, plus fifteen years.

My research had established that it was highly likely that Boock and Carlos knew each other very well. The evidence was only circumstantial, but it was persuasive.

The speciality of Christian Lochte, President of the BKA, the office for the Protection of the Constitution in Hamburg, was counter-intelligence. He was the second man I wanted to see. Research indicated that, for a man occupying such a position, Lochte held some very unusual views. He thought that the police computers of Germany knew far too much, that at least a third of the files held on the Hamburg computers of the State Security police should be deleted. He also believed that many of the men and women serving long prison sentences could be released immediately without any threat to society. For me he had come highly recommended from contacts in Italian and French security.

After breakfasting, I was about to leave my hotel in Bremen with my interpreter when we received a phone call from Pastor Albertz. A close friend of his had died during the night. Conscious of the fact that I had flown to Bremen specifically to talk to him, Pastor Albertz said he would still see me but would prefer our meeting to take place later in the year. Having agreed to the postponement George (my interpreter) and I drove to Hamburg.

Against considerable odds, I had persuaded the prison authorities to let me into their maximum security prison in Hamburg, but before meeting Peter Boock, I talked at length to Christian Lochte. Tall, tanned, blond-haired, he looked more like a recently retired member of the West German Olympic team than a man charged with guarding the country's constitution. To ensure survival against any potential terrorist attack Lochte, like Boock, functions in offices that closely resemble a maximum security prison. My interview with him was fascinating and far-ranging – the La Belle Disco bombing that had triggered the bombing of Libya by the United States; the author Claire Sterling and her influence on the thinking of men like the late William Casey, former head of the CIA; Mossad's ability at successfully peddling disinformation; the Munich Olympic Games massacre; the OPEC attack, and, inevitably, Carlos. Christian Lochte confirmed many of the conclusions I had reached. In other areas he was able to give me new and vital information. The one area that he could throw no light on at all was the Venezuelan. Lochte asked a question I was growing accustomed to hearing.

'Nobody knows where he is. Is he still alive?'

'Yes, I'm sure he is.'

'Is he an old age pensioner?'

The idea of the world's most wanted man drawing his old age pension was surreal and slightly premature. At the time I was talking to Lochte, Carlos was still in his thirties.

If Christian Lochte could not offer me any fresh information or insights into Ilich Ramirez Sanchez, Peter Boock more than compensated. My hunch had been right. During the 1970s Peter Boock had formed a close friendship with Wadi Haddad, the man who controlled Carlos after his emergence from the ranks of the Palestinian guerrillas in 1971 until Haddad's own death in 1978 – a crucial period in the Carlos story. Boock was with Haddad in South Yemen and Iraq before the OPEC attack. He was also with him for long periods after that operation. Inevitably he had met Carlos and got to know him well.

Of Peter Boock himself? An unnaturally thin man. The legacy of years of drug abuse. The very long hair indicated a man in his thirties caught in a time warp of fashion. Highly intelligent; despite his long imprisonment sharply aware of the political realities of Europe and the Middle East. Due to his favoured position at Haddad's side he had been privy to the most secret details concerning a number of the Haddad operations. Without knowing it, Peter Boock confirmed chapter and verse what Khalid, Carlos's second in command for the OPEC attack, had told me in the Middle East. The satisfaction gained in having that account confirmed from a second primary source was balanced by the dismay I felt. Both men contradicted what Carlos had told me. Either Carlos had deliberately lied to me about the OPEC affair or he was indeed an impostor.

In all I interviewed Peter Boock three times in his maximum security residence, each interview pulling out more details, more facts. On some areas he flatly refused to answer my questions on the grounds that he did not wish to incriminate others. Most tantalizingly of all in this regard was the matter of Anton Bouvier, the man that the pundits would have as Carlos's KGB case officer. It was obvious from his reaction when I showed him Bouvier's photograph that he knew the man. Indeed, he said as much. He also knew his real name, but no matter how I went at it, he would not give it to me. He said that 'Bouvier' was a Palestinian whom he had met 'only in the Middle East'. Whatever else, it was clear that Bouvier and Carlos were two different men, contrary to what 'Carlos' had insisted to me. Boock also maintained that Carlos was never a KGB agent, an opinion that contradicted the pundits – by this stage of my investigation that contradiction hardly came as a surprise – but agreed with what 'Carlos' had said to me. It was a mare's nest.

By this stage, mid 1988, I had a certain sympathy with Pontius Pilate when he asked, 'What is truth?' I began to wonder if this entire investigation was allegorical, and that what was being actually demonstrated to me under the surface was a sub-text – something along the lines of 'the journey is the experience' or 'definitive truth does not exist'. I had a very long cold shower, gave myself a good talking to, forgot about *Heart of Darkness,* and got on with the research.

Information was beginning to flow in. From Venezuela, from Germany, from Brazil. The Colonel in Caracas was turning up trumps, including his contacts in the STASI, East Germany's secret service. When I finally got to interview Pastor Albertz in Bremen in October I learned nothing about Carlos but a great deal about Gabriele Tiedemann. In London I located and interviewed Cheryl Drew, the barrister who had defended Nydia Tobon after her arrest in July 1975. In the same city, after some magical words of reassurance from the Venezuelan Ambassador, Francisco Kerdal-Vegas, a great many Latin American doors were opened to me. In November I flew again to Algiers, and this time the authorities decided to record my visit in my passport.

There were a number of reasons for this trip. I had been tipped off in the middle of the year that at their National Congress the Palestinians intended to declare an Independent Palestinian State, that within that declaration the Palestinian leadership would for the first time, by its acceptance of specific Security Council Resolutions, recognize the right of existence of Israel. By now aspirations for the Palestinian leadership had shrunk to the West Bank, the Gaza Strip and Jerusalem. To understand the enormous significance of this it is essential to study a map of the area showing Palestine and Israel as conceived by the United Nations partition recommendation of 29 November 1947. The demands enshrined in the declaration that I heard made in Algiers are in truth pathetically small when compared with that map. Yet still the killings continued.

Apart from talking at length to Yasser Arafat and Abu Iyad in Algiers, I finally caught up with Bassam Abu Sharif. Unfortunately, he confined our conversation to the political implications of the Palestinian declaration. 'We must talk of Carlos on another occasion,' he remarked. Pinning this particular other occasion to a precise date proved an impossibility.

Among others that I talked to on this trip was a clown by the name of Abu Abbas. Abbas had sprung to international attention after the hijacking of the Italian cruise ship *Achille Lauro*. During the hijack, one passenger, a sick elderly man confined to a wheelchair, had been murdered and his body tossed overboard. The man's name was Leon Klinghoffer, his 'crime' was that he was a Jew. Although not taking an active part in the hijack, Abbas had masterminded it for his Syrian masters.

The hijack had come at a crucial moment for the PLO. Two members of its Executive Committee were due in London as part of a joint Jordanian/Palestinian delegation for talks with Foreign Secretary Geoffrey Howe. This meeting was the brainchild of Prime Minister Margaret Thatcher. For the Palestinians it was a major political breakthrough – if the promised land lay through a door in the White House, many believed that Mrs Thatcher held the key. In Damascus President Asad and his intelligence chiefs were deeply concerned. A negotiated settlement to the issue of Palestinian independence that excluded Syrian involvement was not on Asad's agenda. It never has been. It never will be. Abu Abbas, who is based in Damascus and is controlled by Syrian intelligence, not the PLO, was given certain instructions. Orders would be a more exact description. He was also given money and arms.

The London talks were due to start in mid October 1985. On the 7th of October, the *Achille Lauro* was hijacked. The London talks were cancelled soon after, for very specious reasons, and Leon Klinghoffer was murdered. Abu Abbas had served his Syrian controllers well. I wanted to talk to him at some length, and probe the Syrian connection to this affair, but things turned out differently. Perhaps the heat was to blame. Then again, perhaps it was the appalling Algerian version of Montezuma's revenge that I was fighting. I'm afraid my objectivity went out of the window.

'If I could turn now to the *Achille Lauro*.'

'What about it?'

'I'd like a full account of precisely why that boat was hijacked at that time. I would also like to know why Leon Klinghoffer was murdered.'

'Who says he was murdered?'

'Of course he was.'

'Not at all. Perhaps he jumped over the side for a swim and his wheelchair weighed him down.'

'You bastard.'

'What?'

'I said, you bastard. You son of a bitch.'

'Where are you going?'

'Outside. I don't want to stay in the same room as you.'

'What about the interview?'

'Fuck the interview.'

*　　*　　*

Back in London I found confirmation of an arrangement for which I had been waiting a long time. Colonel Qathafi had granted my request for a second interview.

There was also another man in Tripoli who was on my list. During my conversations with Abu Iyad in Algiers he had told me that Abu Nidal was on the move. In June Abu Iyad had predicted Nidal would be moving soon out of Romania and back to the Middle East. In November he was able to confirm that, having first gone to Damascus, Nidal had then flown to Tripoli. If he stayed put for a while there was every chance of talking to him.

I had also discussed at some length the elusive Carlos. Abu Iyad was genuinely puzzled. 'As I told you when we first met my information was that he was in Bucharest. It was only when I attempted to make personal contact with him that I discovered the intelligence was incorrect. It came from very good sources. Carlos certainly had been in Romania but where he is now no-one can tell me.'

In November 1988, another interview took place with Nydia Tobon, this time in Paris. She was adamant that Anton Bouvier and Carlos were two separate people. She cited instances of seeing them together, of her shopping expeditions to the local supermarket with Bouvier, their conversations both with and without Carlos.

So why had she asserted in her book that they were one and the same?

'I wanted to confuse the British.'

During the same month I prepared for an extensive trip – via Malta to Libya to talk to Nidal and Qathafi, then back to Malta, and after further interviews on the George Cross Island, on to Beirut. The situation in Lebanon was still dangerously unstable; anarchy still prevailed. There had been very little hard news on the many hostages, but in a telephone conversation with Samir's widow she had quietly observed that, if I came to Beirut, 'I will put you in contact with someone who can help you.' Enough had been said before this remark to make it clear to me that the 'help' could lead me to Carlos. It was only a straw, but this far into the hunt to locate Carlos, I was clutching at anything. After Beirut I planned to go to Israel, the West Bank and the Gaza Strip. A trip to see a little of the reality of Israel and the Palestinians was central to this investigation and long overdue.

The Libyan Embassy shuffle in Valletta duly performed, this time without incident, I flew on to Tripoli. Having waited about a week before my first meeting with the Colonel, I assumed there would be a comparable delay on this second occasion. I promptly contacted the man whose name and phone number Abu Iyad had given me, Mustafa Murad, deputy head of the Fatah Revolutionary Council, better known as the Abu Nidal group. I was expected. The interview with Nidal would take place the following morning.

Abu Iyad had told me that the interview would probably take place at a training camp in the Asswani region of Tripoli, where several hundred followers of Sabra al-Banna, Nidal's actual name, were based. I slept badly that night.

The following morning a battered car collected me from the pre-arranged meeting place, an entrance to a park near my hotel. We drove to a Western suburb of the city; precisely where, I could not identify. It was not an area I had visited during my first trip. The building I entered was as neglected as the car that had brought me to it. We went downstairs to the basement. What is it with these Palestinians? Perhaps a fear of bomb attack? The majority of the main players that I had talked to had shown a predilection for subterranean dwelling.

Nidal is not a physically imposing man. If he was pointed out in the street and you were told he was a retired nightwatchman, I think you would accept it without comment. Small of stature, for a man who is just a few months younger than I am (fifty-one years of age at that time) he was in appalling physical condition, overweight by a good thirty pounds, face bloated, bald, a chain-smoker. There was one other highly disturbing feature. He was drunk.

The room was as shabby as the exterior of the house. He rose unsteadily to his feet to greet me from behind a desk. Then, waving me into a nearby chair, he slumped back into his own. It was ten o'clock in the morning. On a small table nearby there were various bottles of spirits. During the course of the next two hours Abu Nidal did severe damage to a couple of bottles of Chivas Regal and a couple of bottles of brandy.

For a man who was drunk Abu Nidal was surprisingly lucid. We began in typical Arab fashion. The last thing you open with is what you really want to talk about.

'And how is my good friend Salah Khalaf?'

He caught me unprepared with that opening. Abu Iyad is invariably referred to, even by those close to him, by his *nom de guerre*. What really stopped me in my tracks was the reference to 'my good friend'. The reader may recall, during my account of my first interview with Abu Iyad, the small matter of Nidal trying to kill him in Belgrade by blowing up his car. Iyad had gone on to tell me that Nidal had made about thirty attempts on his life. If Nidal considered Iyad his 'good friend', the mind boggles at what he might do to an individual he considered his enemy.

Through Nidal's interpreter, whose command of English left a good deal to be desired, I indicated with a certain malicious intent that 'Salah is in excellent health'. The information appeared to please Nidal.

In the light of the implications of the Palestinian National Congress resolutions that had been passed in Algiers the previous month and Abu Nidal's implacable hostility to any talk of compromise, his reactions to what had occurred in Algiers were predictable.

'Arafat is a traitor to the Palestinian cause. Those who surround him and support him are also traitors.'

'Land for peace does not appeal to you?'

'My family was the richest in Palestine. My father was the richest man. He owned over six thousand acres. His lands reached from south of Jaffa to the Gaza Strip. All that land. All that land was confiscated by the Jews. You tell me. How much of my own land should I accept from the thieving Israeli government in return for giving them this peace? Where our orchards were, immigrant Jews now live. The home that I grew up in is now a district court for the Israeli Army. What should I accept in return for giving these people peace? The ground floor?'

'So no compromise?'

He slammed his hand on the desk.

'None.'

'Since 1973 your organization has carried out, by my calculation, over one hundred attacks around the world. Is my figure accurate?'

'Yes.'

'These attacks have resulted in the deaths of many hundreds of people and the destruction of a vast amount of property including embassies, planes, airports and synagogues. It's fifteen years since you began these activities. You haven't even recovered one room of the house you grew up in. What does that tell you about your tactics?'

The interpreter struggled with that one. I was not sure if his difficulties were linguistic or diplomatic. Eventually he got the question over to Nidal.

'It tells me that my enemy is powerful and has very powerful friends, particularly the Americans and the British and the PLO.'

'Will there therefore be more attacks? More operations?'

'Yes. But for the present I am content to watch Arafat destroy himself with this so-called moderation and peace process.'

'Are Syria and Iraq also content just to sit and watch?'

He laughed. 'No, they wish to have more operations as soon as possible. For the time being they will have to look to others for that.'

'So the West should expect some action in the near future?'

'Yes, they should.'

At this stage of my interview with Abu Nidal, there were just the three of us in the room. It seemed an opportune moment to explore an area that might have been much more dangerous with others from his organization present.

'Many have talked to me about Mossad penetration of your organization.'

He wagged a finger at me as he responded. 'Every organization can be penetrated. The only one that I have ever known of that was not penetrated was Wadi Haddad's.'

'Yes, I accept that. What concerns me is whether you have been manipulated by Mossad as well as penetrated. Who in the Abu Nidal organization decides the specific targets? Are they always targets that you and you alone have decided upon?'

'Of course not. This is a democratic organization. Others make suggestions, come up with ideas.'

The idea that Abu Nidal is a democrat struck me as so obscene that I had to pause, sip another café Arabi and compose myself.

'The attack on Israeli Ambassador Argov in London. Can you tell me where the idea for that came from?'

He shook his head.

'Did it come from Baghdad?'

He stopped shaking his head.

'Salah should be more careful.'

I was walking on eggshells and knew it, but if I'd been wrong, why not an outright denial?

'The attacks on Rome and Vienna airports. Who came up with those targets?'

'Members of this organization.'

'In January 1978, I am told you attended a meeting in Baghdad. My information is that also present at that meeting were Wadi Haddad and Carlos.'

'I had many meetings with them. I had good relations then with the Popular Front.'

'This was a very special meeting. The meeting had been called by very senior members of the KGB. The Soviet Union had become deeply alarmed at the presence of Sadat in Jerusalem.'

'Yes.'

'I am told that the KGB offered the three of you vast amounts of money and vast amounts of arms.'

'Who has told you these things?'

'A number of people. Are they accurate?'

'Yes they're accurate.'

I knew why the offer had been made but I wanted to hear it coming out of the mouth of one of the three men to whom it had been made. I was gambling that, by this time, Nidal might just have had enough alcohol to be indiscreet.

'Why did they make such an offer?'

'To help the struggle against Israel. To stop any other leader in the Arab world going down the path that Sadat had walked.'

'And what was to happen to any Arab leader who followed Sadat?'

He drew a finger across his throat.

'Assassination?'

He nodded.

'What was the reaction of Carlos?'

He smiled as he inwardly recalled a moment in Baghdad.

'He got up, said he would have nothing to do with the idea and left the meeting.'

'But you accepted the idea?'

'Yes, I did, but Wadi Haddad did not, he was a dying man, but tell me, since then, how many Arab leaders have reached an accommodation with Israel?'

'None.'

He nodded, smiling.

'And Carlos. Where is he now?'

'I've no idea. He has not been heard of for a long time. Perhaps he is dead.'

'Like you're supposed to be dead, according to Mossad anyway.'

'No, Mossad know better than that.'

'Yes, I think they do.'

We discussed many other subjects during which he again demonstrated that unnerving ability to throw me

293

from my line of thought, not least with this casual interchange near the end of our meeting.

'Where do you live?' he asked me.

'In London.'

'Oh, I know London well. I have been there several times.'

I could not draw him on details of that extraordinary statement. Eventually, declining the vast array of salads, meats and food that were brought in, I thanked him for the time he had given me and left. Drinking copious cups of coffee with the man to keep my ever constricting throat reasonably loose was bad enough. I wouldn't break bread with him if we were the last two left on this planet.

Returning to my hotel, my mind was full of the implications of this interview and what it had produced. There had been powerful confirmation of what were by any criteria truly sensational facts, yet I felt far from elated. Depressed would have been a more accurate description. Depressed at the amorality of men like Abu Nidal, depressed because I had been optimistically confident that Nidal would be able to answer the one question for which above all others I sought the answer: where was Carlos?

For the next two days I quietly prepared for my second interview with the Colonel. Then the men from the Ministry advised me that the interview would take place that evening. About an hour later I phoned my wife, Anna, in London. She had been desperate to reach me for several days. Numerous messages had simply not been given to me. While gardening, her father had fallen from a ladder and sustained a fractured skull. He was dying in a Wellington hospital.

Anna was planning to fly to New Zealand the following day. I could hear her fighting back the tears as she told me to stay in the Middle East until my work was done. Arrangements had been made for friends to look after our two children. Reassuring her as adequately as one can via an international phone call, I told her to cancel the arrangements and said that somehow I would get home before she flew out. Suddenly Qathafi, Carlos and the rest of it seemed very unimportant.

My wife left for her home country the day after my return from Tripoli. With her departure came news that her father had died. In the few days before I took our children to join her, there was much to do: apart from the packing, there was the small matter of obtaining from the New Zealand High Commission as a matter of extreme urgency individual passports for my children. My mind was full of the tragedy that had come from nowhere, but there was one aspect of my work that required immediate and urgent attention. It concerned an awareness of another potential tragedy. It concerned a situation of which I had become aware when talking to Abu Nidal. I had information that I wished to give at the earliest opportunity to our security forces.

I contacted Brian Crozier, cold warrior par excellence. I was aware not only through my own research but also through an interview with Crozier that he had had for many years a special relationship with MI6 and also the CIA. I told Crozier that, notwithstanding the various pressures of my personal life, we had to talk before I caught a plane to New Zealand. I also advised him that he should arrange for someone from MI6 to be present at that meeting.

Two days later I visited Crozier's office in Piccadilly. Waiting for me with him was a diminutive man from MI6. I will call him Frank.

For some time I had been attempting to obtain access to police and security files on Carlos. Part of those attempts had been to offer Crozier, and therefore the British security services, the opportunity to put through my interview specific questions to Abu Nidal and also to Colonel Qathafi. I now had some answers for Crozier and his friends, but my other information was far more urgent.

Before this meeting I had typed up an eight-page debriefing document. It covered a variety of subjects – the *Achille Lauro* hijack and the culpability of the Syrian regime; serious leaks from within the CIA relating to the Israeli attack on the PLO headquarters in Tunisia; evidence obtained directly from Qathafi of how successive Reagan administrations had been penetrated by Soviet espionage. I detailed how this penetration included the State Department and the CIA. The debriefing document also shared with its readers the fact that Russian intelligence had been fully aware *before* the United States attacks on Libya in April 1986 of what was going to occur, and that on this occasion they had *not* shared that intelligence with Qathafi.

The document also addressed itself to the various questions I had asked on behalf of Crozier and his associates. But the reason, above all others, why I had been insistent on this meeting was not part of any brief. It concerned my conviction that in the near future there would be a significant terrorist attack on an American target. In the debriefing document I wrote of 'Abu Nidal being put under considerable pressure from both the Syrians and the Iraqis to resume terror tactics', of 'both countries deeply desired the failure of Arafat's attempts to arrive at a solution on the Palestinian issue through moderation'. For good measure I also mentioned Mossad's 'extraordinary degree of penetration of the Abu Nidal organization'.

Having given Crozier and the MI6 agent a copy of this report, I elaborated on it. I emphasized that there would soon be an attack on an American target and that this attack would emanate from Damascus. To my astonishment the MI6 agent was far more interested in Nidal's drinking and eating habits. He wanted to know what food had been served. I told him. When he also wanted to know the full details of where I had met Nidal I could hardly believe my ears. I had not interrupted an emotionally fraught week for this. I am very, very aware of police and security procedures when it comes to establishing veracity. Investigations around the world over twenty-five years have taught me much. If he wanted to know exactly where I had been, he had but to run a check through recent flight departures or simply ask to look at my various passports.

Nonplussed, I got on with my travel preparations. Two weeks later, while I was in New Zealand, the news I had dreaded to hear reached me. Pan Am Flight 103 flying from London to New York had blown up over the small town of Lockerbie in Scotland. All the 259 passengers and crew were killed. Eleven inhabitants of Lockerbie died in the hell that rained from the sky. It was revealed that this disaster had taken place despite nine security bulletins warning of a terrorist outrage. One of these bulletins even described a radio cassette player containing a bomb that had been found in a car used by a member of the Popular Front for the Liberation of Palestine. It was just such a device that blew up Flight 103. It was also revealed that there had been an anonymous phone call in early December to the US Embassy in Helsinki. The caller had stated that a bomb would be placed on a Pan Am flight between Frankfurt and the United States in December. Pan Am's Flight 103 had originated in Frankfurt. The Federal Aviation Administration had conveyed this warning in a bulletin which was circulated to US embassies worldwide on December 9th. It was only disclosed to embassy staff in Moscow.

Within hours of the outrage, long before any forensic evidence could remotely justify it, the finger of accusation was being publicly pointed at a breakaway Palestinian organization. The Popular Front for the Liberation of Palestine – General Command, the PFLP-GC. The group is under the absolute control of the Syrian regime. Its leader is Ahmed Jibril, a Syrian ex-army officer. Its headquarters are in Damascus. It is, and always has been, bitterly opposed to any PLO attempts at reaching an accommodation with Israel.

Raw intelligence such as the kind I gave to British security is rare enough. Seldom, if ever, do all pieces of the jigsaw come from one source, from one carrier. I had just spent several hours with Abu Nidal, a man who is 'most wanted' by many. The pieces of the puzzle that I brought away from that meeting, together with the other pieces already in the possession of security forces, should have been more than enough to prevent the Lockerbie disaster. Doubtless 'Frank', when he retires from MI6, will be duly honoured for his services to this country. A knighthood perhaps?

There is a postscript to this affair. When I contacted Brian Crozier after the Lockerbie disaster he observed, 'At least you pointed them in the right direction.' He did not comment on the fact that I had pointed 'them' before the event. He confirmed that the array of information I had provided had been passed on to the CIA. He told me later that 'they consider you have been influenced by the propaganda you have been exposed to'. Coming from a man who has spent most of his lifetime peddling propaganda, I found that particularly rich. Coming from the CIA and MI6 who, by refusing to be similarly 'influenced', had ensured the Lockerbie disaster would become a reality, I found that obscene.

In mid January 1989 I began to pick up the pieces of the aborted Middle East trip. Waiting for Qathafi was something I was getting used to. It could take many months to rearrange that interview. A phone call to Beirut gave me an alternative game plan – Samir's widow and children were going to visit relations in the town of Tyre in South Lebanon. They would be there throughout February. South Lebanon was still bandit country but, compared with the evil of Beirut, it was almost an alluring prospect. Almost. If I could persuade the Israeli government to let me enter Lebanon from Israel it would offer a relatively safe journey to Tyre.

The Israeli embassy in London advised me that permission to enter South Lebanon from Israel had, after considerable initial reluctance, been granted by the government.

A few days before I was due to fly out I received an invitation to lunch. It came from Basel Aql, the charming

Palestinian whose intervention had brought the waiting for Arafat in Tunis to a merciful end. As part of an initiative to get the Palestinian position across to the general public Basel was planning to invite a number of media people for lunch. When deep into research I avoid reporters as much as possible: I was about to decline politely the invitation when he mentioned the name of the man who would be there to talk to reporters. I accepted the invitation immediately. The man in question was Bassam Abu Sharif, Yasser Arafat's favourite stalking horse.

Given the right opportunity, and assuming he *would* talk, I was convinced that Bassam could solve the puzzle which by now had become almost an obsession with me. Was the man I had met twice in North Lebanon the real Carlos? Lunch surrounded by reporters was far from the right opportunity, but perhaps there might be an appropriate moment.

Bassam Abu Sharif was here for secret talks with Foreign Office officials. The very positive elements flowing from the Algerian declaration were, it seemed, beginning if not to bear fruit, at least to give an indication of ripening seeds.

Peter Snow of the BBC and several American Bureau chiefs were at the lunch. The conversation about peace prospects flowed freely. At the end of an excellent but frustrating meal I seized an opportunity. Sharif was about to leave to return to the Foreign Office. His Special Branch minders were waiting outside. I inveigled him into a momentarily empty drawing room. Quickly I told him of my two encounters with Carlos, of my subsequent growing suspicions. He listened carefully, then asked me a question.

'Where exactly did these meetings take place?'

'Difficult to be precise. I was taken north of Beirut, almost to Jounieh, then we turned inland towards the Baalbek for some time, fifty minutes or so.'

'Then the man you have spoken to is not Carlos.'

I just stared at him.

'I know where Carlos is and I know he has not moved from that place for five years.'

'Where is he, Bassam?'

He smiled, then, responding to the urgings of Basel, left with the Special Branch bodyguard.

I felt like a drowning man who had suddenly been thrown by a huge wave towards the sanctuary of the shore, only to be swept with equal suddenness back out to sea.

12

AMONG GOD'S CHOSEN, AND LESSER MORTALS

During my first few days in Israel, as I was setting up interviews and establishing contacts there was ample time to reflect on the roots of 'the problem', the 'issue', that has been at the heart of the search for peace within the region. As I wandered in Tel Aviv and Jerusalem my mind went back in time. To understand the present, we must be aware of the past.

One of the results of the 1914–18 War was the collapse of the Ottoman Empire which for more than four hundred years had been the dominant power in the Eastern Mediterranean, much of North Africa and the Balkans. This collapse produced the potential for the creation of specific individual nations in many Arab countries. This opportunity for change had been preceded some forty years earlier by the birth of two ideologies that were to grow into monstrous versions of Tweedle Dee and Tweedle Dum, definitive examples of an irresistible force and an immovable object – Zionism and Arab Nationalism. Both aspired to give practical expression to the deeply felt national and religious aspirations of the Jewish and Arab peoples. The Jewish movement hoped to achieve this by establishing a Jewish country in what was the homeland of the Palestinians. The Arab movement sought to create an Arab consciousness and pride so that its peoples would rise up and overthrow the hated Turkish rule.

In 1878 the first Zionist colony, Petah Tikva, was established in Palestine north of Jaffa. At that time there were just twenty-four thousand Jews in the entire country and close on half a million Palestinian Arabs.

While the Arabs petitioned their Turkish rulers against Zionist mass immigration, to which the Ottoman authorities responded with a wide range of restrictive laws, the ingenuity of the Zionist leaders enabled them to step up their policy of buying land at prices vastly in excess of the going market value – in this fashion men like the German millionaire Baron Maurice de Hirsch and the French millionaire Baron Edmond de Rothschild managed, with great diligence, to circumvent the laws. By 1914 the Jewish population of Palestine had reached eighty thousand.

One of the alliances forged during the First World War was between Britain and those Arabs who sought to overthrow Ottoman rule. Sharif Hussein of Mecca, for example, hoped, by siding with Britain and the Western Allies against Constantinople, to win unity and independence for the Arabs. Hussein concluded an agreement with Sir Henry McMahon, the British High Commissioner of Egypt, that in the eyes of the Arabs ensured any post-war settlement would recognize the independence of a united Arab state comprising the Arab provinces of the Ottoman Empire, including Palestine. Hussein and his followers were unaware that, in May 1916, Britain, France and Russia had reached a secret agreement that most of Palestine was to be internationalized.

If the Arabs were unaware of this perfidy, the Zionists most certainly were aware. In little more than one year from the signing of that secret accord they made an astonishing breakthrough in their attempts to make their dreams and plans a reality. It took the shape of another secret agreement, this time contained in a letter from Arthur James Balfour, British Secretary of State for Foreign Affairs, to Baron Lionel Walter de Rothschild, a British Zionist. The letter has become known as the Balfour Declaration. On November 2nd, 1917, it was published with the approval of the British Cabinet and the United States. The crucial part reads:

His Majesty's Government view with favour the establishment in Palestine of a National Home for the Jewish people, and will use their best endeavours to facilitate the achievement of this object, it being clearly understood that nothing shall be done which may prejudice the civil and religious rights of existing non-Jewish communities in Palestine, or the rights and political status enjoyed by Jews in any country.

The declaration contained two promises, one to the Zionists, one to the Palestinians, that are clearly contradictory. The answer to this conundrum can be found in establishing what exactly were the intentions of the British government. Quite simply, they had no intention of honouring their promise to the Palestinians. British policy was never openly stated but it can be found within a memorandum that Balfour wrote on the 11th of August 1919:

In Palestine we do not propose even going through the form of consulting the wishes of the present inhabitants of the country . . . The four great powers are committed to Zionism. And Zionism, be it right or wrong, good or bad, is rooted in age-long traditions, in present needs, in future hopes, of far profounder import than the desires and prejudices of the seven hundred thousand Arabs who now inhabit that ancient land.

By the time that was written the Ottoman Empire had collapsed in disarray and the whole of Palestine had been occupied for eleven months by Allied Forces under the command of General Allenby.

Successive British governments, while adhering to the Balfour line in public, were in private capable of demonstrating other points of view. A letter from William Ormsby Gore, Secretary of State for the Colonies, to Prime Minister Neville Chamberlain on the 9th of January 1938 in part reads:

The Arabs are treacherous and untrustworthy; the Jews greedy and, when freed from persecution, aggressive . . . I am convinced that the Arabs cannot be trusted to govern the Jews any more than the Jews can be trusted to govern the Arabs.

During the following week, on the 14th of January 1938, the Head of Eastern Affairs at the Foreign Office, George William Rendel, writing to Ormsby Gore, observed that '. . . all the information which has reached the Foreign Office goes to show that the Arabs would infinitely rather remain indefinitely under British Mandate than see a Jewish State set up in any part of Palestine.' The seeds of the Middle East problem were now well planted, and they would produce bitter fruit.

After the Nazi persecutions of the 30s and 40s the trickle of Jewish immigrants became a flood. The blood of six million Jews murdered by the Third Reich served to fertilize those seeds into full flower.

During my first week of this particular trip to Israel, I visited the Yad Vashem memorial on the hills west of Jerusalem. This memorial functions at a number of levels. At one it commemorates the Holocaust. At a second it states that out of that Holocaust Israel was born. At a third, by the selection of material on display, it declares that all who oppose the State of Israel are also Nazis. The Third Reich, its leaders and followers, are not alone in the dock at Yad Vashem. The Israelis have also placed the British alongside them. Photographs of SS officers and their concentration camp victims are under the same roof as photographs of British paratroopers turning away survivors of that Holocaust from the shores of Palestine. Also in that dock are Arabs, photographs of the Grand Mufti Haj Amin being greeted in Germany by Heinrich Himmler. Nearby, the Mufti's words urging the German government to prevent the Jews of Europe going to Palestine. It is indeed an indisputable fact that the Grand Mufti threw in his lot with the Third Reich. He considered the British perfidious and believed that

Palestine could only be saved for his Arab people if the British were defeated by Germany and her allies. The historical indictment within Yad Vashem is not, however, complete. There has been selective editing. Missing from the collection is any record of Jewish collaboration and attempted collaboration with the Third Reich. Missing, for example, is any reference to Avraham Stern, leader of a group of Jewish terrorists known as 'The Stern Gang'. Also missing is any reference to a Stern Gang member since 1939, who became the Gang's operations commander in 1942, the former Prime Minister of Israel, Yitzhak Shamir. These men should also be in the dock at Yad Vashem. Not because of their acts against the occupying British (including the killing of Lord Moyne, the British Minister Resident for the Middle East, on the 6th of November 1944, and the murder of Count Folk Bernadotte, the UN Special Mediator on Palestine, on the 17th of September 1948), they should be there for another far more obscene reason – Avraham Stern and his organization sought an accommodation with Hitler and the Third Reich regime. They regarded Hitler merely as the latest in a long line of historic persecutors. The enemy, the real enemy in their eyes, was the occupying power in Palestine, the British.

In September 1940 the Stern group drew up an agreement with an Italian agent in Jerusalem through which Mussolini would recognize a Zionist state in return for Stern group collaboration with the Italian Army when it invaded Palestine. As it became apparent to Stern and his colleagues that the chances of an Italian invasion might be delayed, they turned to the Third Reich. When the Second World War ended a copy of the Stern proposal for an alliance between his movement and the Third Reich was discovered in the files of the German Embassy in Turkey. This is no forgery, clever or otherwise, the document is accepted by historians as genuine. It is dated January 11th, 1941. At this time the Stern Gang still laid claim to the title, the National Military Organization, or Irgun Zvai Leumi. Irgun, the original Jewish terrorist organization. It begins to become reminiscent of the splintering of various Palestinian factions in the late 1960s and early 1970s. Within three years of the formulation of this document the break between the Stern Gang and Irgun would be complete, with a man rising to take charge of the Irgun killer squads named Menachem Begin, future Prime Minister and Nobel Peace Prize winner. All that lay in the future; in January 1941 Stern and his followers saw themselves as the true National Military Organization, the NMO:

> '*Proposal of the National Military Organization (Irgun Zvai Leumi) Concerning the Solution of the Jewish Question in Europe and the Participation of the NMO in the War on the side of Germany*'
>
> *The evacuation of the Jewish masses from Europe is a precondition for solving the Jewish question; but this can only be made possible and complete through the settlement of these masses in the home of the Jewish people, Palestine, and through the establishment of a Jewish state in its historical boundaries . . .*
>
> *The NMO, which is well acquainted with the goodwill of the German Reich government and its authorities towards Zionist activity inside Germany and towards Zionist emigration plans, is of the opinion that:*
>
> *1 Common interests could exist between the establishment of a New Order in Europe in conformity with the German concept, and the true national aspirations of the Jewish people as they are embodied by the NMO.*
> *2 Cooperation between the new Germany and a renewed volkishnational Hebrium would be possible and*
> *3 The establishment of the historical Jewish state on a national and totalitarian basis, and bound by a treaty with the German Reich, would be in the interest of a maintained and strengthened future German position of power in the Near East.*

Proceeding from these considerations, the NMO in Palestine, under the condition the above-mentioned national aspirations of the Israeli freedom movement are recognized on the side of the German Reich, offers to actively take part in the war on Germany's side.

This offer by the NMO . . . would be connected to the military training and organizing of Jewish manpower in Europe, under the leadership and command of the NMO. These military units would take part in the fight to conquer Palestine, should such a front be decided upon.

The indirect participation of the Israeli freedom movement in the New Order in Europe, already in the preparatory stage, would be linked with a positive-radical solution of the European Jewish problem in conformity with the above-mentioned national aspirations of the Jewish people. This would extraordinarily strengthen the moral basis of the New Order in the eyes of all humanity.[1]

When Menachem Begin became Prime Minister of Israel in 1977, appointing Shamir as Foreign Minister, he honoured Stern by having postage stamps issued with his portrait.

The Zionists have achieved their 'national home for the Jewish people in Palestine'. The Arabs have achieved independence in Iraq, in Syria, in Yemen, in the Federation of South Arabia, in many countries. Just how much independence is highly debatable. Many have gained much. The Palestinians have lost every inch of land that was once theirs.

By 1947 the British no longer had the will to attempt to resolve a problem that was largely of their own making. The British Mandate to control Palestine had resulted in an uncontrollable situation. They referred the problem

---

[1] I am indebted to the Jewish author, Lenni Brenner, who located this document, and quoted it in his book *Zionism in the age of the Dictators*

to the United Nations for a solution. The result was the creation of a separate Jewish state (Israel) while other parts of Palestine were incorporated into what had been known as TransJordan, or in the case of the small Gaza Strip, into Egypt. Palestine ceased to exist except in the hearts and minds of men. A succession of wars between Israel and the Arabs in 1948, 1956 and 1967 – each won by Israel – resulted in all the land that had once been Palestine falling under the total and absolute control of Israel. By 1970, the twenty-four thousand Jews of 1878 had grown to a figure of nearly three million. Under that absolute Israeli control were one and a half million Palestinians. A further one million Palestinians had been forced from their homelands. Massacres such as Deir Yassin led to the first mass exodus in 1948. A second exodus had occurred after the 1967 war.

Propaganda notwithstanding, the Palestinians still living in Israel, the Gaza Strip and on the West Bank in 1970 posed little threat to the occupying forces. It was the Palestinians and their allies beyond their absolute control who gave concern to successive Israeli governments.

From 1948 to their crushing defeat of 1967 the Arab world had been unable to decide whether the struggle to recover Palestine did or did not take precedence over the revolutionary aims enshrined in their respective national ideologies. The 1967 war dramatically clarified their collective thinking. The recovery not of Palestine but of national lands lost in the war became the primary objective for certain Arab countries. Self interest is a powerful motivation. Doubtless the fact that a number of Arab nations had also lost substantial territories played a significant part in this re-evaluation.

Egypt lost the entire Sinai peninsula with its oilfields and the Palestinian Gaza Strip on the coast adjoining Israel, which she had administered since the 1948 war. The Israeli army established defences along the East bank of the Suez Canal and subsequently destroyed by artillery and air attack the Egyptian oil refineries at Suez and the other Egyptian towns along the West Bank of the Canal.

Syria lost the Golan Heights into which it had previously built its crucial Southern defence system. The Israeli forces only halted at Kuneitra after superpower intervention. All that stood between them and Damascus was some fifty miles of level plain.

Jordan lost the West Bank of the Jordan river and, most devastatingly for the entire Arab world, this loss included Jerusalem. As a consequence it lost virtually all its important tourist industry. Jordan was also forced to absorb a further 350,000 Palestinian refugees from the West Bank.

Israel's victory on all fronts produced complete disillusionment and despair among the Arabs, who had been confident that the Soviet military hardware acquired by both Syria and Egypt would ensure at the very least that no further land would be lost. But an abundance of sophisticated weaponry, combined with an inability to use it, does not produce victory.

The losers were prepared to make important concessions. The winners, not for the first or the last time, showed a complete inability to demonstrate in their victory a shred of magnanimity. Having been manoeuvred into fighting a war they knew they could not win, President Nasser of Egypt and King Hussein of Jordan subsequently demonstrated that a lack of courage and resolve can lose a peace just as easily as a war. In exchange for recovering their lost territories both leaders were prepared to recognize Israel, recognize its right to exist in peace, recognize its right to use the Suez Canal and the Strait of Tiran and to bury the claims of the Palestinian people. Their particular hopes and aspirations were covered in United Nations Resolution 242 with the affirmation of the necessity 'for achieving a just settlement of the refugee problem'. Palestine and its people had been reduced to just two words, 'refugee problem'.

It was readily apparent to the Palestinians, not only in Israel and the occupied territories but throughout the world, that there might be some value in the saying 'the Lord helps those who help themselves'.

Out of that recognition a wide spectrum of Palestinian groups deduced that the Western powers' main concern, possibly sole concern, was how to prevent Israel and the Arab world engaging in another war that might seriously disrupt oil supplies, thus creating a price spiral and a global economic crisis. Over 55 per cent of the world's oil came from this region. Even more significant, over 62 per cent of the world's proven oil reserves was also in this same area. Compared with the potential crisis which could develop from that situation the Palestinian issue was to many Western observers just a minor irritant.

It is universally accepted that one man's terrorist is another man's freedom fighter. The Palestine Liberation Organization, the PLO, is regarded by Israel as a terrorist organization. It is a definition that has been widely accepted not only by the majority of Israelis but by many in the wider world since its inception in 1964. The fact that successive Israeli leaders owed their own rise to power in no small measure to acts that many would also consider to be terrorism is rarely cause for comment. In the Middle East language as well as land are vulnerable to theft.

The PLO is in fact not one organization headed by one man, Yasser Arafat, but a number of organizations each with its own leadership. The PLO is merely the umbrella under which several groups shelter. When the Palestinians obtain their own homeland and country there is no danger of a single-party state. The problem for the potential voter will be that he or she will be spoiled for choice.

The PLO rightly claims to represent all Palestinian people. It is recognized as such by many countries throughout the world, but in my father's house there are many rooms. And when Ilich Ramirez Sanchez arrived in Lebanon in the middle of 1970 there were a number of choices for a young man who sought guerrilla training and knowledge of the Palestinian movements. The fedayeen, Palestinian commandos, could be found under many titles and names.

There was Al Fatah, the biggest and most influential of the organizations that make up the PLO – its leader, Yasser Arafat; its politics, middle of the road.

There was the Popular Front for the Liberation of Palestine (PFLP). The leaders: Dr George Habash and Dr Wadi Haddad. Politics: Marxism/Maoism.

There was also the Popular Democratic Front for the Liberation of Palestine (PDFLP) led by Nayef Hawatmeh. Politics: Communist. And there was the PFLP (General Command) led by Ahmed Jibril. Politics: middle of the road.

There were many other groups whose aims ranged from the sweetly conciliatory to the rabidly confrontational. It was a very broad church.

The exact size and numbers of any of these groups has always been very difficult to ascertain with any precise degree of accuracy. Various bodies in the western world, the Israeli lobby in the USA, for example, have invariably overestimated and distorted the size and capacity of all of the Palestinian groups while, paradoxically, Israel's leaders have frequently dismissed them as being of little consequence. Some of Israel's leaders have gone even further: Golda Meir, then Prime Minister, observed during an interview with Alan Hart, 'the Palestinians do not exist'.[1]

Between the end of the 1967 war and 1970, the Palestinians who 'did not exist' killed at least 150 Israeli soldiers and wounded a further 600 during a large number of guerrilla actions. Many of these died during Al Fatah's 'popular war of liberation' fought in the West Bank and Gaza. But if the suffering inflicted by the Palestinians was high, the price that their commandos and their ordinary citizens paid was higher still. Between September 1967 and early January 1968 many hundreds of Fatah commandos were killed and more than one thousand of their fighters captured. As in many wars those who paid the highest price were

[1] BBC *Panorama*, 9th August 1971

the non-combatants. Within the occupied territories of the West Bank and Gaza there were curfews, cordons, constant house-to-house searches, detentions without trial, deportations, neighbourhood or collective punishment, including the closure of shops, schools and offices. Houses were destroyed on the grounds that the owners had given or were suspected to have given shelter to Fatah activists. The number of homes destroyed varied from the figure given by Moshe Dayan of 516 to the figure given by *The Times* of 7,000. There was torture on a widespread scale. There was also active collusion between Israel and West Germany: moral blackmail on the Germans because of the Holocaust resulted in Mossad being given biographical details and photographs of every Palestinian student studying in Germany. Many went back to fight in this 'popular war'; of five hundred who were trained in Algeria before returning to the West Bank and Gaza more than four hundred and fifty were eliminated with the help of the data obtained from West Germany.

Confronted with a situation in which the ordinary Palestinian citizen in the occupied territories was being subjected to the harassment recorded above it comes as no surprise to learn that in the eyes of that ordinary citizen the 'popular' war was very unpopular indeed. Having seen the Arab armies soundly defeated by one of the most highly trained and best equipped forces on earth, the butcher in Gaza City and the baker in Ramallah concluded that there was no future in supporting a war in which their side was represented by a few hundred men. They also believed that the only hope for peace and a lasting settlement was one in which Israel would be recognized as part of a deal involving the Israelis withdrawing to the pre-1967 war frontiers and the establishment of an independent Palestine on the West Bank and in Gaza. For many Palestinians this belief entailed a profound sacrifice it meant accepting that they would never again return to their lands and homes in what was now Israel – but it was a belief based on the realities. As such, these ordinary people showed themselves years ahead of the thinking of those who claimed to be their leaders and light years ahead of the thinking of every leader that Israel has yet had.

By early 1968 the Fatah remnants had regrouped in Jordan. To avoid the risk of fatal confrontations with the Jordanian army they operated without fixed bases, a cave here, a safe house there. The units were small and highly mobile. At this time Arafat and his colleagues had less than four hundred fedayeen under their command. Syria was not prepared to act as a launch pad for these hit-and-run attacks. Lebanon was ruled out for a variety of highly valid reasons. Within a few years Fatah and other Palestinian groups would forget each and every one of those reasons.

The decision therefore to use Jordan as their launch pad for attacks into Israel ensured that Al Fatah would place King Hussein under constant threat of massive Israeli retaliation. The threat of this would have deterred many another Arab country, but Jordan was different: apart from the 350,000 Palestinian refugees that the country had absorbed after the 1967 war, there were 1.8 million indigenous Palestinians, many serving in the Jordanian forces, some as senior officers. The situation placed the King of Jordan on a tightrope. In an effort to remove himself from such a precarious position, King Hussein announced in February 1968 that he was 'taking firm and forceful steps' to deal with the fedayeen. Jordan would regard the use of its soil as a launch pad for Palestinian groups into Israel as an 'unparalleled crime'. It was a clear signal to Israel, which responded within one month by invading Jordan.

On the 18th of March several Israeli children were wounded when their school bus hit a mine. A doctor travelling with them was killed. The Israelis announced that it was the thirty-seventh act of murder and sabotage carried out by the Palestinians based in Jordan and that these attacks had killed six and wounded forty-four. Retaliation, or to use another word Israel has stolen from the language, 'reprisal', was inevitable. Newspapers and radio stations openly declared that there would soon be an attack 'on terrorist bases in Jordan'. For the Israelis to make their intentions so public was to send a clear signal back to King Hussein. 'We are coming in to destroy Fatah. Stay out of the way or you will get hurt.' Prior to the invasion Moshe Dayan told reporters that the fighting would be over within a few hours and he would 'parade captured terrorist leaders in Jerusalem'.

It is a well established fact of war that a guerrilla army cannot win if it stands and fights using conventional battle tactics. Success can only be achieved through hit and run. In this instance Fatah decided to stay and fight – the build-up to this particular action had attracted worldwide attention, to hit and run would be interpreted by many as yet another Arab defeat. Arafat and his colleagues considered it was time to stand and die. The place designated for this last stand was a refugee camp near the small town of Karameh, which means 'dignity'.

On the evening of March 20th Arafat addressed his fighters. They numbered 297. Many were young boys. Arafat was later to recount that moment to Alan Hart.[1]

> One of the child fighters asked me if they could defeat the Israelis. I tried to laugh but really I wanted to cry. I answered: 'No, my brave one, we cannot defeat them. We are less than 300 and they will be many thousands who are equipped with the latest American tanks and other weapons. We cannot defeat them but we can teach them a lesson. The Arab nation is watching us. We must shoulder our responsibility like men, with courage and dignity. We must plant the notion of steadfastness in this nation. We must shatter the myth of the invincible army.'

The following morning, having invaded Jordan, the Israelis launched a full-scale attack on Karameh with infantry, armour, artillery and planes. Helicopters landed

---

[1] *Arafat – Terrorist or Peacemaker*, Sidgwick & Jackson, 1987.

paratroopers to the rear of the town. Military intelligence had advised them that the entire Fatah leadership was in the town. Contrary to what Dayan had told reporters before the invasion, the purpose was not subsequently to parade those leaders through the streets of Jerusalem. The plan was to eliminate the entire three hundred in Karameh. At first it seemed to the Israelis that they had entered a ghost town. Loudspeaker demands that the inhabitants come out with their hands up into the square in front of the mosque reverberated down empty alleyways. Suddenly, from nowhere, the men and children of Fatah threw themselves on the Israeli tanks. Some climbed onto the tanks and put grenades inside them. Others with dynamite strapped to their bodies hurled themselves at the tanks. Then the unbelievable happened – Israeli soldiers leapt from the tanks that had been hit and ran for cover and their lives. Inevitably they regrouped and recovered from the shock. Their over-whelming superiority of numbers and fire power began to take effect. By eleven in the morning, after six hours of fighting, a third of Fatah guerrillas were dead. It was at this point that the Jordanians joined the battle, after watching the fighting for some hours. Their intervention was crucial. Late in the day the Israelis withdrew. They left eighteen wrecked tanks behind, their casualties were twenty-eight dead and ninety wounded. In a land where an Israeli life is often thought to be worth that of one hundred Arabs it was a humiliating defeat. Fatah's losses were ninety-three killed and 'many' wounded. Jordan's losses were put at 128 killed and wounded. The fact that the Israelis had inflicted such heavy losses but had still turned and run for home merely compounded their defeat.

Just how important that Arab success was in a small Arab town can be gauged by subsequent events. There is no doubt that defeat for Arafat and his fedayeen at Karameh would have ensured that the Palestinian cause was lost.

Victory made the fedayeen heroes of the Arab world. An invincible army, like many an invincible army before, had been beaten. It did not compensate for the defeats that the Arabs had suffered in 1948, 1956 and 1967 but its effect on the average Arab throughout the world was as powerful as Entebbe was for the average Jew in 1976.

The benefits for Fatah were immediately obvious. At the end of the fighting their numbers were reduced to just over two hundred. Within three days they had over five thousand volunteers. Over the next eighteen months a further 25,000 joined Fatah to fight. Also within days of the battles, cars and trucks began to arrive at Fatah's new headquarters at Salt. They contained blankets, clothes and food from Palestinian communities around the world. Money began to pour in. As those Palestinians who had been scattered around the globe since the creation of the State of Israel started to digest the implications of this battle they began to feel hope, then they began to organize. Palestinian schools, clinics, hospitals and orphanages were established. An infrastructure was built. An exiled people dared to dream.

Some days after my arrival I spent a considerable number of hours in part of Israel's Public Relations industry. From Major Moshe Fogel at the Army Press Centre, which is itself part of the Government Press Centre, I was given a full briefing. What this bright, highly intelligent man (I was to meet many Israeli officers in the days ahead, all equally bright and intelligent) gave me, was the Israeli Army position as of February 1989. Nothing in the intervening period of time has come to hand to indicate that there have been any radical shifts in that position.

To summarize it, the Palestinians in the occupied territories, namely the West Bank and Gaza, are not wholeheartedly behind the PLO; there are splits and divisions, and in the main the Palestinians are 'happy living under occupation'.

'The dilemma that we face with the Intifada is that the Israeli Army regard it as a security problem, one to be resolved internally one way or the other. The Palestinians regard what is going on in those territories as only part of a greater problem. I am talking of Palestinians scattered throughout the world as well as some of those living under occupation. They are looking for the Independent State of Palestine and they are seeking a State that will be of slightly larger dimensions than the occupied territories.'

The Major produced maps and photographs taken by aerial reconnaissance and pointed out to me the ridge of mountains running down Israel that cuts Jerusalem from Tel Aviv. The mountain range, argued Moshe Fogel, provided a perfect fall-back position if you were attacked from the West Bank or anywhere along Israel's border with Jordan.

If, however, Israel were to secede any of that territory, give up the West Bank, it would be giving away that plain with its vitally strategic positions. Therefore, in the view of the Israeli Army, 'We can never give up the West Bank.' The Major stressed he was talking from a military viewpoint. 'What the political viewpoint is will depend on which politician you talk to.'

The day after talking to Major Fogel I headed north to the Israeli border with Lebanon. The journey illustrated the relative smallness of this country. A drive from Tel Aviv of under two hours in a taxi for less than one hundred dollars, and there was the border. But though small, much of the country on that ride north was devoid of people.

The following morning I was due to go through the Israeli border post and customs into Lebanon at 8 am. I crossed over one hour earlier. Before I met up with United Nations personnel I had a private visit to make, to Samir's widow in Tyre. During my last telephone conversation with her she had indicated that after we met I would have to journey to a town called Chebaa in a remote part of South Lebanon near the Syrian border. Armed with this knowledge, when earlier in the previous week I contacted the United Nations officer in South Lebanon, Timor Goksell, I had requested permission to enter that area. It was one in which the Norwegian troops attached to the United Nations peace keeping forces were deployed. To my relief Goksell had raised no objections.

Waiting in the morning sun for any vehicle heading north from the Israeli border control, I stood chatting to the duty officer in charge. Nearby were parked a number of large lorries packed with citrus fruit. Their presence puzzled me. They were facing north towards an Arab country. I gestured in the direction of the lorries.

'Doing some trade with Lebanon?'

He gave a wry smile.

'Not Lebanon. Saudi Arabia and some of the Gulf States.'

'But they have a total trade boycott with Israel.'

'Sure they do. The lorries are waiting for clearance that there are loading facilities at Naqoura. The fruit is taken there then loaded on to boats that take it to Beirut. There it's re-boxed, given 'produce of Lebanon' labels, and shipped to the Arabs.'

'So much for a total trade boycott.'

He eyed me keenly.

'Are you a newspaper reporter?'

'No, I'm not.'

'Good.'

Hitching a lift to Tyre proved an interesting exercise. The first stage, through South Lebanon, presented no problem, for it was controlled by the Israelis and their surrogate forces, the South Lebanese Army (SLA). Having been dropped near the UNIFIL (the United Nations Interim Force in Lebanon) base at Naqoura I continued to head north. I was now in a zone where UNIFIL held a mandate, but heading towards bandit country. Three lifts later, including one from a member of the Fiji Battalion, I arrived at Tyre. Following the instructions that Samir's widow had given me I eventually found a café. Its clientele appeared to be exclusively members of the Amal militia, who viewed the appearance of a white-faced European with considerable interest. I was just hoping to God that this was the café that I had been intended to go to. Establishing that I was talking to the owner, I repeated in parrot-like fashion the sentence I had been told to utter in Arabic. The owner gave no indication that I was welcome and merely pointed to an empty table. I sat drinking coffee, attempting to become invisible. To my relief, the door soon opened and one of Samir's sons entered.

A short while later I was drinking more coffee in friendlier surroundings, though the widow's Tyre-based male relations did give me the occasional curious stare.

It had been more than three years since I said goodbye to Samir's wife at Beirut airport. At that time I had lost Carlos and she had lost something far more important. Since then I had often felt an enveloping deep guilt. If I had not been in Beirut that day, if Samir had not been hurrying home to take me on that final drive . . . if. There had been no hint of reproach then, there was none now. We talked of the everyday things, of how her children were, of how my family was. I told her a little of my feelings, and if not of my guilt then of how in some way I felt responsible. She merely smiled and said, 'Inshaa-Allaah' – such an all-encompassing word.

I wanted to stay much longer but was aware that I had already missed an assignation with the UNIFIL staff at the Israeli border. Now I would have to try and catch them at Naqoura. I explained the problem, which, like so many I had given this family, was quickly solved. A relation would drive me back south to the UNIFIL headquarters. Samir's widow gave me a letter which would serve as an introduction to the mukhtar, or headman, of Chebaa. She told me the name of the man I needed to talk to in the town and advised me it would be easier if this introduction were organized by the mukhtar. 'The man that the mukhtar will introduce you to will tell you where Carlos is,' she said.

Just like that. After an additional hunt of so many years the answer I was seeking was waiting for me in a town in South Lebanon. It seemed so simple.

Clutching my small travelling bag, I hurried towards the UNIFIL headquarters in search of Timor Goksell. Waiting by the roadside were a group of about a dozen reporters and TV cameramen. It was not a happy moment. It got worse.

'You David Yallop?'

'Yes.'

'We waited for you on the border. What happened?'

'Taxi was late.'

'But you've just come from the north.'

'Where are you all off to then?'

'Same place as you, the Norwegian-controlled area.'

'Why?'

'Oh come on, same reason you want to go there. To find out about Chebaa.'

Since the previous week, when I had quietly arranged a journey for one to this remote mountain town close to Mount Hermon, it had suddenly become the object of intensive international media interest. Preoccupied with my own interviews and research, this sudden focus on Chebaa had passed me by.

On the 11th of March 1978 a commando raid for which the PLO subsequently claimed responsibility took place near Tel Aviv. The Israelis put their casualties at thirty-seven dead and seventy-six wounded. The Israeli response was to invade Lebanon the same week and occupy the entire region south of the Litani river, with the exception of the city of Tyre and the immediate surrounding area. Within four days the United Nations Security Council had adopted Resolution 425. It called for strict respect for the territorial integrity, sovereignty and political independence of Lebanon within its internationally recognized boundaries. It also called for Israel to cease its military action immediately and to withdraw its forces from Lebanese territory. In the light of a request from the Government of Lebanon the United Nations also established an interim force for Southern Lebanon composed of personnel drawn from Member States.

The terms of reference for this United Nations force were to confirm the withdrawal of Israeli forces, to restore international peace and security and to assist the Lebanese Government in ensuring the return of its effective control of the area. Now, eleven years later, these forces, who had initially only been mandated for six months, were still attempting to perform an impossible task.

Hamstrung by guidelines that include the non-use of force except in self defence and also non-intervention in the internal affairs of Lebanon, they had, after the full-scale Israeli invasion of 1982, been given the further task of providing protection and humanitarian assistance to the local population.

In the previous month the Israeli-controlled SLA and the GSS had begun a series of deportations in the area where the Norwegian forces operated. Many civilians, the majority of them women and children, some of them mentally retarded, had been forcibly removed from their homes. They were forbidden to take with them any personal possessions, were transported out of South Lebanon and, having been ordered never to return to their villages or towns, were dumped on the roadside. The reason given was that they were relatives of, or supporters of, Lebanese resistance groups.

The town of Chebaa came in for particular attention. It had long resisted Israel's plan to open a recruiting office for the SLA in the heart of the village. In the early hours of January the 25th, dawn raids by the GSS forcibly removed thirty-seven inhabitants, again mainly women and children. The Norwegian UNIFIL forces were powerless to intervene. All they could do was to report what had occurred to the United Nations headquarters in New York.

The expulsions from Chebaa continued. By the weekend before I went into Lebanon the number for just Chebaa had reached seventy. The Norwegians, under the terms of the UN mandate, could do nothing except listen to the screams of Lebanese women and children pleading for them to stop the expulsions. At a meeting with Israeli officers to discuss the situation, the Norwegian CO, Colonel Jan-Erik Karlsen, had erupted.

'I'm not ready to reach any agreement with the IDF [the Israeli Defence Force]. In World War Two my fellow countrymen sacrificed their lives in the struggle against the Nazis who were trying to expel Jews from Norway. Nowadays in South Lebanon you behave exactly like the Nazis did.'

It was this that had brought the media streaming in to Lebanon, but no-one was allowed out of Chebaa, and no-one was allowed in. This was the town I now had to get into. If Samir's widow were right, there was a man in there who knew where Carlos was.

We left Tyre, the city that Alexander had built, a city with its Roman columns and its shattered 1960s concrete, and, courtesy of the Italian Air Force, clattered across South Lebanon. The area from the Litani river to the Israeli border is typically hilly lowland crisscrossed by fairly steep valleys. As we flew towards the eastern border with Syria it became more mountainous. Mount Hermon, rising to over 2,800 metres, began to dominate the skyline. The area of operations for UNIFIL battalions and their back-up is without railways or airports. The road network is extensive but in poor condition. Over half a million people live here, a fifth of that number in the Tyre region, the rest scattered across the country, their only tangible protection from anarchy being just under six thousand United Nations troops drawn from countries as diverse as Fiji, Finland, Ireland, Ghana and Norway. We landed close to the Norwegian battalion headquarters at Ebl el-Saqi.

'Colonel, I would like to go into Chebaa.'

'You are aware that the town is completely cut off by the SLA and the GSS?'

'Yes, I am. I was hoping you might be able to overcome that problem.'

He laughed.

'You would have to go into the town inside an APC [Armoured Personnel Carrier] and you would have to wear a uniform.'

'I would regard that as an honour.'

'You're very gracious. I will take you and your friends in soon after dawn tomorrow.'

I hadn't bargained on my 'friends' coming along for the ride but at least another hurdle had been cleared.

Shortly after our arrival at Ebl el-Saqi we met the elders of the town. It was soon apparent that the Norwegians had formed an excellent rapport with the local people, one that had been strengthened by Colonel Karlsen's decision to have his men living throughout the region rather than in barracks.

They get up early in the Norwegian army. By six in the morning we had showered, breakfasted and been given Norwegian forces uniforms. A short while later, bouncing about inside three APCs, we were on our way. There was only one real moment of tension – when we stopped at the SLA post outside Chebaa. The SLA were told we were taking in vital medical supplies for the sick, which indeed we were. Before starting out I had asked one of the Norwegian officers what would happen if the SLA insisted on searching the vehicles.

'We will refuse.'

'And if they insist?'

'We will resist them.'

As the delay at the checkpoint continued the men inside my APC very calmly began to clip magazines of ammunition into their guns and flick off the safety catches. The sole representative of the world's press in my particular vehicle lay stretched out opposite where the soldiers and I were sitting. Fast asleep, snoring off too much Norwegian hospitality. If there were going to be a shoot-out the opening paragraphs of his filed despatch might want a little in terms of accuracy. After about twenty minutes the driver engaged gear and a short while later we entered Chebaa.

The Mukhtar, Sheik Rashid Abu Zahoui, received us in his home. Ninety years of age, he sat bolt upright in a full lotus position on the carpeted floor, his mind as sharp as the mountain air of his town. He was also disarmingly honest.

'What justification do they give for sealing off the town? In what way do they claim the action is legal?' I asked.

'They state that they wish to stop us smuggling.'

'Are there in fact people in this town who engage in smuggling?'

'Yes, of course. It is one of our main sources of income.'

'How long for?'

'Since before I was born. Long before then.'

'What do you smuggle?'

'The iron or the smoke [cigarettes] from Beirut and from the Bekaa. We smuggle them up the mountain and into Syria by pack mule.'

'So this is the reason why the town is under siege?'

'No, it's the reason they are now giving. The real reason is our refusal to have a recruiting post in the town for the SLA. In early December an Israeli general came here. His name was Seb Sakrin. He told me, "I want a recruiting post in this town." I refused, just as some years ago I refused to let the Palestinians have a recruiting post, just as even earlier I had refused the Syrians. I have also refused to let any of them carry guns in this town. Only UNIFIL or Lebanese army sent by my government in Beirut are allowed to carry weapons here.'

It became apparent that this elderly man saw his town as part of Lebanon, no more, no less. Close to the town to the north, the Bekaa valley begins, a Hezbollah strong-hold. On the other side of the mountain range is Syria. To the south, Israel. The Mukhtar and his people, largely Sunni Muslims, only gave allegiance to their country's duly elected government. In early 1989 that was something that was still likely to change overnight.

When the others trooped outside to gather eyewitness accounts from people who had witnessed the dawn raid by over one hundred GSS men, I grabbed the local man who had been interpreting for the Mukhtar.

'I have a letter for the Mukhtar. Would you give it to him please and translate his response?'

The man nodded and handed the letter that Samir's widow had given me to the Mukhtar. He stared at the envelope for a moment, then, pulling out an antique pair of spectacles, opened it and read it. I was relieved to note that he was nodding as he read. A moment later he handed it back to the interpreter and a conversation between them followed.

'The Mukhtar says, the man you wish to talk to is not here.'

'Why not? Was he taken by the GSS?'

'No, he is outside Lebanon.'

'Where?'

'In Gaza.'

As I attempted to digest that, the Mukhtar spoke again. The interpreter nodded.

'The Mukhtar says that you should go to Gaza City. To Marna House. Alya Shawa will find him for you.'

'Are you sure he is in Gaza? How long will he be there for?'

Again words passed between the two men.

'Yes, the Mukhtar is certain he is there. He will be in Gaza City until the end of the month.'

I spoke directly to the elderly man.

'Shukran jazeelan Mukhtar.'

He grinned and, clasping my hand between his, said something. I looked enquiringly at the interpreter.

'Be careful of the Israelis.'

I hurried out to catch up with the others before they became curious.

I was sure that Samir's widow would not have sent me on a wild hopeless chase across Lebanon, but always the answer I was seeking was just out of reach, just around the next corner. I needed a little time alone to work this one out.

Some days later, back in Israel, I was still trying to make sense of the fact that a man who should have been in Chebaa was in the Gaza Strip. It was when I interviewed Uri Lubrani that unwittingly I obtained a possible explanation.

Lubrani knows more about Lebanon than most. He is adviser to the Israeli government on their northern neighbour. During the course of our discussion I raised the subject of Chebaa, then still under siege. By way of apology for the actions of the SLA and its leader Major General Antoine Lahd, Uri Lubrani told me how he had raised the matter of Chebaa with Lahd.

'I asked him why the hell he had thrown an eighty-year-old man, young children and the rest of these people out of Chebaa. Lahd said to me, "You know in ordinary times if there were these demonstrations and riots in Chebaa, these people would not be alive. With Amal and Hezbollah they would not be alive. You must appreciate that. These people are members of certain families. If a member of that family misbehaves then the entire family must understand that something happens to them."'

'Mr Lubrani, what Lahd has done is unjustifiable by any legal or civilized criteria. Among the expulsions are young mentally retarded children.'

'I . . . I don't know. I haven't seen them. I don't know.'

'As we talk now, today in Tel Aviv, that town is still sealed off. The only reason that life-sustaining medicines are getting in is because of the Norwegians.'

'I know, I know, but you know this town is a focal point for smuggling to Syria and to us.'

'What do they bring to you? I know they take iron to Syria, what do they bring here, tobacco?'

'What about drugs?'

'Indeed, what about drugs? Cocaine? Heroin?'

'You name it. I mean, I hope not hard ones, but certainly hashish, cocaine. So Lahd tells me, "How do you expect me, bearing in mind your own set of values, to manage here? If I were dealing with this problem in the Lebanese way the problem would be soon eliminated. Look me in the eye and tell me you won't shout to high heaven and I'll deal with it." But we say no.'

'Not the best of allies for Israel?'

'That's putting it very mildly.'

After the Israeli invasion of Lebanon in 1982 and their subsequent partial withdrawal, the forces brought back not only their dead and wounded, many returned with 'the habit'. The habit varied, as it had with the Americans in Vietnam; for some it was hash, for others opium. Addictions require feeding. For many years Lebanon has been the biggest producer of hashish in the Middle East. For many years the Syrian Army has guarded the fields in the Bekaa valley while the farmers harvested their highly lucrative cash crops, the dark green bushes of marijuana, the poppies that yield opium. The invasion of 1982 opened up a new market, Israel.

Listening to members of Israel's drug squads talking it soon became obvious why a man in Chebaa or indeed any other part of Lebanon might take the risk of travelling south and across the border.

A kilo of heroin of good unadulterated quality fetches at its source in the Bekaa approximately four thousand pounds. When it reaches Beirut its price has doubled; by the time it reaches Chebaa and the surrounding area and the so-called Israeli security zone the kilo is worth twenty-two thousand pounds. Get it across the Israeli border and the price has doubled again to over forty thousand pounds. Two hours' drive to Tel Aviv and the price is now sixty to seventy thousand pounds. Not content with the already guaranteed huge margins, the drug cartels of Tel Aviv frequently doctor the heroin, adding grape sugar, soda and other elements to the high grade Lebanese product. This increases each kilo by between fifty and one hundred per cent. A 'fix' is then sold in the streets of Tel Aviv, or Jaffa, or Jerusalem, for approximately one hundred pounds. What began as a kilo worth four thousand pounds has now become worth six hundred thousand pounds.

I had no way of knowing if the man I had gone looking for in Chebaa was involved in this trade, but I had established that there were clearly illegal points of entry into Israel, so-called 'green points', that were being used repeatedly. With courage, cunning and luck a man could get into Israel without troubling the tranquillity of the Israeli customs.

On Friday, February 10th I had another meeting with

Major Moshe Fogel and told him that I wanted to go into the Gaza Strip. With the Intifada still raging he was not very enthusiastic at the prospect of yet another foreign writer getting some first-hand experience of the Palestinian uprising. Knowing that the Israelis frequently seal off the entire Strip I had decided to go by the official route to ensure I actually got in. Eventually it was arranged for the following week. With the weekend approaching the Major told me that under no circumstances could I enter the area until Tuesday the 14th. It was arranged that I would go to the Israeli checkpoint on the morning of the 14th where I would be met. Satisfied, I travelled to Jerusalem and promptly made arrangements through Palestinian contacts to go in with an interpreter that weekend. I was determined that a conducted tour of the Gaza with the Israelis should not be my only experience of this region.

It was pouring with rain when Mahmoud and I caught a taxi van from Jerusalem. The other ten occupants were all residents of Gaza City. With luck the Israeli border guards would not be too curious about one battered van. I told Mahmoud that if I got pulled off the van he should make no effort to accompany me, but should wait for one hour in Omar Mukhtar Square, then return to the Colony Hotel in Jerusalem. As we neared the checkpoint the Arabs sitting either side of me put out their cigarettes.

The Arab driver dutifully stopped at the checkpoint. An Israeli soldier stared for a moment at the driver's papers, then gestured for him to continue. No count, no search.

My destination, the Marna House, was in fact a small hotel and Alya Shawa its owner. When contacting her on the previous evening from Jerusalem, I had merely booked two rooms and offered no explanation as to why I was coming to Gaza City. The taxi van disgorged its entire contents in the main square where the stalls were doing a lively business despite the downpour. While Mahmoud attempted to extract a taxi from the chaos of what I later realized was a virtually perpetual traffic jam, I stood trying to come to terms with what was going on around me. Donkeys and carts attempted to weave through what looked like a rally meeting point for every battered taxi and car in the Middle East. Vendors extolled a range of cheap ware from aerosol sprays and cheap trinkets to fresh oranges and potatoes. From the doorway of Rajab M. Kalaph, Great Factory for Rattan and Cane Furniture, an elderly man caught my eye and, oblivious of the traffic, began to weave towards me.

'British reporter?'

My God, was my nationality that obvious?

'No. British author.'

'Do you know David Hirst of the *Guardian*?'

'By reputation, yes.'

'A good friend of mine. Have you come to write about Gaza?'

'Yes.'

'Good. I'll see you in the Press Office. In one hour. My name is Hassan Abu Sha'ban.'

A moment later he was gone. By now Mahmoud had returned with a taxi.

'Mahmoud, do you know where the Press Office might be?'

'Of course.'

'Fine, first the Marna House.'

A short while later I introduced myself to Alya. Redoubtable is the word that immediately comes to mind when recalling this woman of indeterminate age. She could be anything between thirty-five and fifty-five, she was that kind of woman. Alone in her office I told her of my conversation in Chebaa and the name of the man who, according to the Mukhtar, was in Gaza. Her eyes glazed and she frowned.

'I do not know him.'

'Are you sure? Sheik Rashid Abu Zahoui seemed confident you could find him for me.'

Perhaps it was the mention of the Sheik's name. Alya picked up the phone on her desk, dialled a number and a conversation in Arabic took place. I watched her

329

carefully, to my relief she was smiling. Replacing the phone, she swung her chair back to me and said,

'He has gone to the West Bank.'

This was cause for smiling?

'Just for a few days. He will return to Gaza on Monday evening.'

'Right, in that case, Alya, we would like to stay until Tuesday morning, please. Is that a problem?'

'Not at all, I have no other guests at the moment. Some are due later, but there is plenty of room. I will tell Mahmoud where to contact your friend on Monday evening.'

'I am very grateful.'

'It is us that should be grateful. If you have come to write about what is going on here, we are in your debt. Where will you begin?'

'I have an appointment at the Press Office with Hassan Abu Sha'ban.'

'Ah, the schoolteacher. He's a good man.'

I was beginning to see why the Sheik had given me her name. The identity and the whereabouts of the man from Chebaa had thrown her for a moment, but only a moment. I concluded, after many conversations with her, that she probably had a mental file on everyone in the city.

At the Press Office Hassan was working. We sat drinking sweet tea and casually chatting about simple everyday events in this city, events like his brother's arrest and imprisonment.

'He's a lawyer. The Israelis arrested him. No trial. Kept him in prison for six months. Then they took him to Ketziot prison in the Negev desert. They forced him to kneel on the sand. He was handcuffed from behind. His head was pushed down between his knees. Then they pushed a plastic pipe up his nose to force him to raise his head. Every time he raised his head they smashed him on the skull with sticks and told him to keep his head down.'

'What was his alleged offence?'

'He has yet to be told.'

330

'This week the State Department published its annual report, a global survey on human rights practices for 1988. Among the statements it made about Israel was that torture and other cruel, inhuman or degrading treatment were clearly prohibited by Israeli law.'

'My brother will be greatly comforted to learn that. Doubtless this report also says that people do not disappear here?'

'Yes, it does.'

'This newspaper I have just bought.'

'What about it?'

'*Al-Fajr*. It was founded in 1972 by Yusef Nasr; he edited the paper until 1974. He was kidnapped by Shin Bet. Vanished. Never been seen since. There are many vanish like that. On some occasions when they have done with them they return the body. Hassan Abdul Halim, a journalist. Vanished for a month, then his body was found near Ramallah. Must go, I have children to teach. Perhaps we'll meet later.'

Mahmoud quietly gestured to me. While I had been talking to the schoolteacher an attractive young woman had entered. Having no need to assist me with the schoolteacher, who spoke English fluently, Mahmoud had been quietly talking to the young woman. He suggested I should do the same.

'Is she a journalist?'

We were, after all, in a Press Office, and I was not sure if he wanted me to give her an interview or conduct one. I was still preoccupied with my own concerns and my desire to maintain a low profile. I checked myself and felt deeply ashamed. Total strangers were taking me on instant trust. I might well have been something other than I claimed to be, might well have been a member of Shin Bet posing as a reporter, a device that Israel's secret service was using increasingly to obtain information, to compromise Palestinians and ultimately to arrest and imprison them.

'No, she's not a journalist but her husband is, he's in prison.'

'Would you explain who I am and what I'm doing here. A book that in part deals with the Palestinian/Israeli issue.'

The young woman came and sat down. Another tray of sweet tea appeared.

'Tell me about your husband.'

'He was arrested on the 28th of February, 1987. He was held for six months in the Russian compound in Jerusalem and many other prisons on the West Bank. It was difficult to find exactly where he was being held. As soon as we did and tried to visit him, they would move him.'

'Was he charged with any offence during those six months?'

'No, after six months he was brought here to Gaza and sentenced to two and a half years by a Military Court on the 7th September 1987.'

'She's remarkably precise about dates.'

'She says she has had much time to remember them.'

'What was her husband's alleged crime?'

'Incitement and distributing leaflets and membership of Fatah organization.'

'Was he a member of Fatah?'

'That's what they accused him of being.'

'Yes, but was he a member?'

'No, that was the accusation. No evidence was ever produced at the Military Court to substantiate the charge. In fact he is a journalist.'

'Where is he now?'

'Central prison, here. Gaza.'

'And his name?'

'Tawfik Mohammed Abu Khusa.'

'How long had they been married at the time of his arrest?'

'Four months.'

'Just four months?'

'I was lucky. I had four months after our wedding. Some husbands are arrested immediately after their wedding party. Others are arrested during their wedding

332

ceremonies. Zaid al Aide, for example, he was arrested during his wedding and put under administrative detention for six months. He was released last September.'

'No trial?'

'No trial, with administrative detention there is no trial.'

'What were the grounds for arresting this Zaid?'

'He was accused of being responsible for the Intifada in the Tal Essultan area. That's near the border with Egypt.'

'And this accusation did not lead to a subsequent trial?'

'No, that is normal here.'

Words like 'normal' or 'basic human rights' mean different things in different places. In Gaza and the West Bank I was to discover they held no meaning that I could grasp, hold on to, and identify.

There were other words too that had new definitions. The Israeli government has promulgated a huge number of Military Orders, to ensure that it governs the Occupied Territories as it wants to. Many of these Military Orders contravene Article 64 of the Geneva Convention. Article 64 limits the authority of an occupying power from significantly altering existing laws in an occupied area. Many of these contraventions constitute profound violations of fundamental human rights. Military Order No. 424 defines a 'child' as a person who has not completed its twelfth year; a 'juvenile' as one who is aged between twelve but not yet fourteen, and a 'youth' as someone aged between fourteen and sixteen years. The military courts, ignoring their own laws, have redefined even those criteria, for them anyone aged over fourteen is an 'adult'.

Under Military Order No. 62 the phrase 'Hostile Terrorist Activities' is defined: this empowers the military authorities and intelligence agencies to arrest any resident of the occupied territories, *regardless of age,* who is suspected of engaging in such activities, these include: writing slogans on walls, singing nationalist songs, possessing nationalistic literature, raising a flag, making the 'V' for victory sign, displaying the colours of the Palestinian flag, and wearing a necklace or any jewellery designed in the shape of Palestine.

In 1987, confronted by growing international criticism, the Israeli government set up a special judicial commission of inquiry, headed by former Israeli Supreme Court President Landau. This inquiry confirmed that the GSS, or Shin Bet, Israel's secret security police, had for many years illegally used physical and psychological pressure to compel confessions from persons suspected of Hostile Terrorist Activities. Among the methods used on what were defined as children, juveniles, youths and adults were the following.

The 'chair' method, which is the blindfolding or hooding of the prisoner with hands manacled behind in such a position that the individual can neither stand nor sit, this produces severe cramp and temporary paralysis; 'hooding', in which the head and shoulders of the prisoner are covered with heavy cloth sacks, frequently soaked with water, urine or excrement; burning the flesh with cigarettes or scalding water; hanging suspended from the ceiling by the wrists; placement for long periods of time in extremely small, metal cubicles; standing for hours or even days with arms extended; forced hot then cold showers; deprivation of sleep; electrical shock; deprivation of adequate food, bathroom or toilet facilities, warm clothing and medical treatment. Prisoners were also subjected to a range of beatings from truncheons, wires, fists, kickings and karate.

The Commission also established that for many years Shin Bet had indulged in perjury on a routine basis to obtain convictions. The Landau Commission, in a secret annex to its report, recommended that limited and clearly delineated 'physical and psychological pressure', which it again secretly defined, should be allowed to be applied in appropriate circumstances. The Commission also exonerated the Military Courts for accepting sixteen years of perjured testimony and further recommended that no-one be prosecuted for sixteen years of practising the torture and brutality that the Commission had established as irrefutable fact.

On November 8th 1987 the Israeli government voted to accept the Landau Commission recommendations. Thus, in a country that is constantly telling the world that it is the only democracy in the Middle East, torture and inhuman brutal behaviour became, after a democratic vote, legalized. Now, fifteen months later, I was discovering the post-Landau Commission quality of life in the occupied territories.

What hit me again and again throughout these interviews was the calmness of the speakers. Only the schoolteacher had exhibited any anger, and then only mildly. The others, as they talked to me, displayed such calm. They spoke quietly. Inhuman, brutal experiences had not brutalized them. They were gentle. They were soft. These characteristics showed themselves repeatedly, not just during this first morning, but in every minute of my time in the Gaza Strip. There can be no doubt that the Intifada has also released deep anger. We have all seen the stone-throwing, tyre-burning demonstrations; what I was privileged to see was another side of the uprising, and this side, unlike the street demonstrations, will ultimately prove irresistible.

When I had talked to the Israeli undercover drug agents and the military about the problem of drugs and their illegal entry, several very significant facts had emerged. The first, the huge profits involved, has already been referred to. Another dealt with the actual size of the problem in Israel. No-one would be quoted on the record, but it was quite clear we were talking about many thousands, not hundreds, of addicts. There was another potentially much more serious aspect to this situation, which when I stumbled on it persuaded me that perhaps I now had the explanation as to why the man I had sought in Chebaa had gone walkabout through Israel and into both the West Bank and Gaza. Drugs were not only traded for money, they also changed hands for weapons

335

– Israeli weapons. Senior members of the Israeli Defence Force admitted that what I had learned was true. It was, understandably, a development that deeply concerned them.

Talking to a member of the banned Hamas organization in Gaza I asked him about this.

'Sure, it happens. It's another aspect of our war, our fight against Israel. If their soldiers want to poison their bodies, we encourage them. We trade drugs with them. Not for money. For weapons.'

'Can you give me an example?'

'In October 1987, four people belonging to Islamic Jihad were killed here. On that occasion the Israeli forces found some of these weapons, about fourteen M16 rifles and Ouzis.'

'Where was this?'

'In Gaza, Shuja'iyah. The Israeli press said they had been stolen from military stores. They had not. They were traded for drugs.'

'Do you foresee the day when weapons like that, weapons obtained from the Israeli Army, are brought out of their hiding places and used against the Israelis?'

He shrugged.

'It rests with Israel. Despite all they have done to us, still our leaders talk of peace and insist the weapons are not brought out, but Arafat cannot live for ever and when he has gone, we shall see.'

At two in the afternoon on Saturday I visited an Arab hospital. I had been continuously interviewing since early morning. Nothing in my life had prepared me for what I was experiencing, for what I was hearing, or for what I was seeing.

At the hospital I went into a ward. The brass plaque on the wall informed me that the ward was dedicated to the memory of George Horsh Schofield and his wife of Oaklands, Greenfield, Yorkshire, by their son, Captain G. A. Schofield, in November 1917. The contents of the ward appeared to be dedicated to something quite different.

It was small, just five beds. Four were occupied. It was visiting time. Groups of families were gathered around the patients. Memories of how precious that hour of love and affection is were etched in my mind. I was reluctant to intrude. Mahmoud explained and, without exception, the families invited me to join their various groups.

'This young man, Mahmoud. Would you ask him how he came to be here please.'

'His name is Said Sadani. He is nineteen years of age. Last Thursday he was shot in the leg by an Israeli soldier in the Al Taraj quarter in Gaza. A plastic bullet.'

'Was there a demonstration prior to this shooting?'

'In this quarter we have Israeli checkpoints. There was a demonstration. Tyre burning, the road blocked. He was passing the area. He had nothing to do with the event. A military jeep drove past him towards the road block, then stopped. Two of the soldiers fired bullets in the air. The third stayed in the jeep. He turned around, saw Said looking at him and fired at him.'

'Had he taken part in any demonstrations before this occurred last Thursday?'

'Yes, he has taken part in a number. Also he was arrested on 28th July last year, held under administrative detention in Ansar Three[1] for five months and released on 27th December.'

'No charges? No trial?'

'No and no reasons. This is the regular method.'

'And now less than two months later, he's in hospital. Would you ask him about conditions in Ansar Three.'

'The conditions were bad. For example, he and the others were frequently forced to stand in the sun for three hours at a time. The food was very bad. Frequently they were also locked in their cells for long periods. In August the soldiers tried to force the administrative detainees to work for the army. They refused and told the guards that under administrative detention they could not be forced

---

[1] Ansar Three is the name by which most Palestinians refer to the Ketziot Prison in the Negev desert.

to work. The soldiers then started to force the prisoners back into their cells. One of the guards began physically to attack the prisoners, from this a mini-demonstration began. The prison director-general, his name is Semar, ordered the prisoners to the tents instead of cells. It was very hot, no water, some of them refused and asked to be returned to their cells. Among those who made this request was Assad Shawa. Semar said, "If you don't go into the tent I'll have you shot." Assad said, "You can shoot me, I'm not going into the tent." The director-general told one of his officers, Captain Tsemah, to fire. He did. Shot Assad in the chest and killed him.'

'Can you put a date on that?'

'August 16th, 1988.'

'Captain Tsemah was moved to another prison to avoid any clashes in the future. The prison administration appointed a commission of inquiry to investigate the shooting. Not a real committee to establish the truth, just a mock one. Among those who witnessed the killing was Abdullah Yaghi. As a senior prisoner to the guards, one of the prisoners' leaders, he was responsible. When he was giving evidence to the commission he stated how he had seen the Israeli captain shoot Assad Shawa. As a result of that evidence Abdullah's detention has been extended by a further five months. He has been told by the Israelis, you will only be let out when you change your affidavit about the shooting. He refused. He is still in Ansar Three.'

In the next bed was a thirteen-year-old boy, Hassen Abu Hamdi. His legs were heavily bandaged.

'Has he been shot too?'

'No. He was taking part in a demonstration. There were road blocks, tyre burning. The soldiers came and talked to him in Hebrew. He didn't understand what they were saying. Not a word. They talked and talked. Still he did not understand, so they picked him up and placed him inside the burning tyres. Then the soldiers drove off. He couldn't get out of the tyres. His legs started to burn. Passersby rescued him and brought him here. This was on the 3rd of January. He's been hospitalized since then.'

In the next bed was an eighteen-year-old, Mahmoud Abu El Kheir. He looked dreadfully ill. I was inclined to pass by quietly but his mother gestured me to a seat next to her.

'He has been beaten very badly by the army in the stomach.'

'What did they beat him with?'

'Batons and their boots. As a result he has lost the use of one kidney. The surgeons want to take it out but he refused to have the operation. He is from the Beach Camp. There was a demonstration there the day that Arafat was talking in Geneva.'

'It is of course forbidden to hold any demonstrations in favour of the PLO?'

'Of course.'

'Yet the Israelis are incessantly telling the world that Arafat and the rest of the PLO command very little support among the people living here?'

'The only way they can give that lie any credibility is to ban all pro-PLO demonstrations.'

In the next bed was fifteen-year-old Mahmoud Ahmed Elayyan from the Sabra quarter of Gaza town. He had also been shot in the leg on the previous Thursday. In his case the bullet was still in his left thigh. The doctors had warned the family that if they operated the leg might be permanently paralysed. The alternative was to leave the bullet in his thigh. On that Thursday a General Strike had been called by the leaders of the Intifada, to commemorate its fifteenth month. Mahmoud had been part of one of the many demonstrations that took place that day. We talked to his parents, who were totally exhausted. We soon found out why.

'They say that last night the soldiers came to their quarter. They entered many houses and beat the people living in them, men, women, children. They smashed all the furniture. Then the Army forced everyone in the neighbourhood aged from fifteen to forty out into the rain. This raid began at midnight or just before.'

'It rained throughout the night. How long were they forced to stand there?'

'The beatings finished about two in the morning. Then they were forced at gunpoint out into the rain. They had to stand there until five in the morning. I should point out, David, what they are telling you is not unusual. It happens on a very regular basis. The mother is saying that she and the other women were forced to take down Palestinian flags from the streets and clean away the slogans.'

'Approximately how many Israeli military took part in this operation?'

'About two hundred soldiers and twenty military vehicles. She also says that the entire area is now, as we speak, under curfew. No-one allowed in or out. There are about one hundred and fifty soldiers there spraying the area with hot water and coloured water.'

'They took a risk breaking curfew to see their son.'

'Yes, if they had been seen, they would have been shot.'

As at the Press Office, so in this small ward. Quietly spoken stories given by remarkably calm people. To hear these accounts given in such a manner, so carefully, so thoughtfully, left a lasting impression. In Israel both before and after this time in Gaza I observed an arrogance and a belligerence that stalked the land. In the Gaza Strip and the West Bank I witnessed a very unusual humility. In Israel there had been continual talk of a 'final solution' that called for even more murderous violence and ultimately forced removal of all Palestinians from the West Bank and the Gaza Strip. In Gaza itself the inhabitants had a different solution. Peace and a just settlement that safeguarded both Jew and Arab. Who then are the terrorists?

From the hospital we drove to another part of the town, to an address we had been given earlier in the day.

Accompanying us on this journey was Amin, who knew the family I now wished to talk to. It was as well that he was with us. The family were initially very reluctant to talk to me. After Amin had persuaded them to see me the reason for their reluctance was soon established.

The father of the family, Shaban Hassan Dalul, had been a farmer. Had being the operative word. In 1948 the land that he, his father, and his family had farmed for generations, growing wheat and barley, had been occupied by Israelis. No sale. No purchase. Just taken. Now he made a living as a middleman, buying and selling citrus fruit. Fifty-eight years of age, he well remembered life under the British Mandate. He and his wife had had eleven children. Had is again the operative word. One son, Rashad, twenty years of age, was currently in an Israeli prison, where he had spent most of the past five years, the majority of that time on a series of administrative detentions. No charges. No trial.

Another of his sons, Mousbah Shaaban Hassan Dalul, was dead at eighteen years of age. In mid December Israeli soldiers and security forces came to the house at eleven at night, demanding to see Mousbah. He was not there and the father, aware that Mousbah was a sympathizer of the militant Islamic Jihad, attempted to deflect the Army by stating that his son worked in Israel and only made visits home infrequently. The Army took the father to Military Headquarters and, after further interrogation, forced him to stand in the pouring rain throughout the night. In the morning they threw him out onto the street. Returning home, he advised Mousbah of what had taken place and told him to go directly to the security forces to see exactly what they wanted with him. Mousbah became very frightened and chose instead to go and live with friends some two kilometres away. On the 29th of December the Army and Israeli security forces mounted a major operation at midnight seeking Mousbah and the friends who had given him shelter. All that the father subsequently learned was that Mousbah and one of the four young men with him, Sami, had been repeatedly shot after security forces had surrounded their hideout. Mousbah's body had been taken to Tel Aviv and an autopsy performed. The Army then returned the body, ordered the family to restrict the funeral service to a maximum of ten people and also insisted that the burial took place at half past eleven at night and that it be confined to a twenty-minute service. By way of explanation when they had brought the body and given these orders, an Israeli officer had said to the father,

'This is your son. He is dead.'

Subsequently the father had attempted to find out what exactly the circumstances were that had brought about his son's death. The military authorities in Gaza had refused to answer his questions and told him that if he persisted he would be arrested and imprisoned.

Immediately after the funeral, when the family returned to their home, the Army and the security forces had appeared, wrecked the home and threatened the family. The Israeli officer in charge of this operation told the parents,

'If you attempt to do anything about your son's case we are ready to kill another twenty of you.'

It had been this threat that had made the family reluctant to talk to me. Subsequently Amin had persuaded them that this conspiracy of silence had to be broken.

It was dusk when we left the home of Shaban Hassan Dalul. By the car I paused for a moment deep in thought. Amin was staring at me.

'Amin. It's nearly curfew time. We should all be in our homes.'

'Yes.'

'The other family that lost a son when Mousbah was killed, Sami's family.'

'Yes.'

'I would like to interview them. Now. Is that possible?' He smiled.

'I was hoping you would make that request.'

Amin clearly knew what had occurred, but with characteristic Arab restraint, wanted me to make the running, ask the questions, seek the truth.

'Before we go to their home I will show you where they were killed.'

Some of the roads that we attempted to drive on were impassable, flooded by the recent incessant rains to depths of several feet. The word road conjures up a false image: these were earthen gaps between the refugee camps and the shanty slums, awash with the detritus of human displacement and forced removal. On the outskirts of Gaza town, in Zeitun area, we began to drive across farmland planted with cabbages. We stopped by a shack. Nearby a number of bedouin were permanently camped: nomads with nowhere to wander in an area that is the most densely populated on earth.

The shack consisted of a couple of storage rooms, used at some time in the past as a collection point for the crops. They were now empty. On the 29th of December, five young men had been sleeping in one and an elderly woman, the mother of two of them, in the other.

'What happened?'

'Let them tell you.'

A short drive later and we were in the home of the Erheim family. Apart from Amin, Mahmoud and myself, a group of young men were gathered in the bitterly cold room. There was also one other person, the mother, Mrs Erheim. During the late evening of December 29th, she had taken food to the shack for the five men. Her husband had died of a heart attack in 1973; previously one of her sons, Mahar, had, they calmly told me, 'been murdered by the Israelis in 1969'. On the night that she took the food, another son, Sami, had died. A third, Hani, was currently being held in Gaza Central Prison. A fourth, Mashadi, was living abroad. Two more, Nidal and Yasser, were among the group I was now talking to. I was curious to know why they were hiding out in the shack. Yasser explained.

'Since the Intifada began in December 1987, Sami, Hani and myself have been regularly taken from this house out into the citrus fields and beaten repeatedly by the Army. As a result of these fierce beatings we have all been hospitalized.'

'Where?'

'The Al Shifa hospital, it's near the Beach Camp. Hani received the fiercest beatings.'

'Why Hani?'

'Hani is a religious man. He is regarded as an Islamic Jihad leader. When he was discharged by the hospital they came and took him out into the fields and beat him badly again. He was again in Al Shifa hospital. The soldiers came into the hospital and beat him again. Four times the beatings he received in the fields were so bad he was hospitalized. During three of his stays in the hospital the army came, also the Shin Bet, and beat him repeatedly.'

Yasser showed me medical records and documents that confirmed that Hani had suffered a wide variety of injuries and had indeed been hospitalized. He also showed me medical records concerning the injuries that he and Sami had sustained. Apart from any other consideration the evidence both oral and documentary gave a powerful reason why they would choose to sleep in a shack rather than risk being dragged from their beds for another beating in a dark field far removed from any curious reporters or television crews.

It also became clear as they responded to my questions that the Erheim family had not been specifically targeted by the Israeli forces.

'These beatings are not unusual; many, many of the men and boys in Gaza suffer these. Regularly.'

'These beatings, are they with batons?'

'With batons, clubs, with their boots, with the butts of rifles. Many tens of soldiers and security forces storm the houses and take the men and the boys into the citrus fields and beat them. They beat them so fiercely so that many times when the soldiers were beating me, my brothers and cousins, the clubs of the soldiers met each other, the clubs and the batons, like a race, to beat as fast as possible.'

'Did you and the others attempt to resist?'

'We were handcuffed in the back. We were also gagged and blindfolded.'

At half past ten at night on December 29th Israeli soldiers and security forces had come again to the Erheim home. Finding the home unoccupied the forces continued their search. At the first relative's home they stormed into, they had again drawn a blank. At a second, belonging to family cousins, they had dragged out the male relations and beaten them, then they had closed in on the shack in the cabbage field. As Yasser observed, 'The soldiers already knew these places.' The forces were led by an Israeli captain well known to the local Palestinians, who uses the false name of Abu Salim, an Iraqi Jew. As I was to establish during my visit to Gaza, the use of false Arab names is a device commonly used by Shin Bet. It was now between eleven and twelve at night. A helicopter was used in this operation and additional army forces were also brought to the cabbage field.

'Abu Salim operated a siren. It was the signal to start firing. The soldiers immediately opened fire. Firing into the hut.'

'Before the firing began, were you asked to surrender, Nidal?'

'No. We don't have any sort of weapons. We had no pistols. We had no guns. When the firing started Sami and Mousbah ran outside. The firing just continued. My mother had been asleep in the other room. She began to scream and cry. Abu Salim came in and grabbed me by the hair and said I had to identify the man who had been killed. I was blindfolded and dragged along the ground for a short distance, then I was stood up and the blindfold removed. I saw by the military car, not one man, but two. The bodies of my brother Sami and Mousbah Dalul. I was shocked and could not speak. Abu Salim began to beat me and said I had to talk fast and identify the two persons killed. Sami and Mousbah were wearing only trousers. From their heads to their feet they were bleeding. The soldiers had taken off their clothes except for the trousers.'

'Do you have any idea how many shots had been fired?'

Yasser stood up and moved to a small chest of drawers, opening it he took out a tin and handed it to me. Inside I counted fifty-eight bullets.

'I collected these from inside the hut and just outside on the next day. The number of bullets that entered their bodies, only the Israelis could tell you that. Nidal says at the beginning the shooting was fast, intensive, later on it was sporadic, then it became intensive again. I think the sporadic firing was from pistols and that Sami and Mousbah were shot not by the Army but by the security service. I would estimate from what Nidal has told me that at least eighty bullets were fired that night in the area.'

I turned back to Nidal.

'What happened after you had identified Sami and Mousbah?'

'I was taken back to the door of the hut, handcuffed and blindfolded. Then I heard three or four more shots and my brother Hani screaming and shouting. I thought they had killed him and began shouting. Then the soldiers started beating me with batons and kicking me. I was knocked to the ground and then the kicking started again. I began to bleed a lot from the nose and face. Then I was taken back to the military car, the bodies of Sami and Mousbah were on the same vehicle, it was a big jeep.'

'How long, from beginning to end, was this whole attack?'

'I cannot be certain. I would say about twenty minutes.'

'And where was your mother?'

'Mother remained in the hut. She had been beaten very badly by the soldiers.'

I looked at the mother. She had not uttered a word since I had entered the room, had not moved. When I had arrived Yasser and Nidal explained that she had not spoken since the morning after the attack. Before that night, they told me, she had been a healthy, vigorous woman. The beating that this seventy-four-year-old woman had suffered had induced a trauma so profound that to all appearances she had been left virtually catatonic. From her condition and the fragmented words she had spoken the following morning to Yasser he had established what had happened to her during the attack. Since that time, she had not uttered a word. I asked her sons what the doctors had said about their mother's condition.

'The doctors don't have a treatment for her case. She can't talk and will not be able to talk and she is very weak.'

'And what do the doctors say is exactly wrong with her?'

'They say she is unconscious, she can't talk, can't remember anything, unconscious.'

An ordinary word to describe an extraordinary condition and also an inaccurate one. Whatever else Mrs Erheim was, she was not unconscious in the normal meaning of that word. Her eyes followed me, her thin arms fluttered occasionally. Several times during that evening and again the following morning when I returned to continue these interviews I asked if it would not be better to talk in another room, away from the mother, away from those pale blue eyes. Her sons assured me that it was best to have her with us. God only knows what she made of our conversations, of how much she comprehended, but before I had finished the second interview on the Sunday morning, Mrs Erheim did give me a partial answer to that mystery.

More details of this appalling story unfolded. If what was said to me was a true factual account of what had taken place in that field during the night of December 29th, then truly awful crimes had been committed by Israeli Army personnel and security forces. Two young innocent men had been coldly murdered, a third, Nidal, shot in the leg *after* his capture and arrest; an elderly woman had been beaten so badly that she now existed in a twilight world. And there was indeed powerful evidence to support the belief that this was indeed true.

On Sunday morning when we returned to the breeze block, windowless hovel that the Erheims called home, the journey on what constitutes an ordinary working day in Gaza town presented graphic visual images of this land that the Israeli government are so desperate to hold on to.

The continuous heavy rain, on a town without any apparent drainage system, had turned the roads into a Middle East version of the Everglades swamps of Florida. The car at times became a motor boat as it swung from side to side seeking drier terrain. The squalor, degradation and poverty on all sides made the barrios of Caracas seem positively desirable. Donkey-drawn carts scrabbled for a foothold, chickens by the dozen struggled to find dry ground. Small children urinated into free-running filthy water, several feet deep, that contained open sewerage; children who despite the biting cold were splashing through this filth virtually naked. What desperation was there in the Palestinians to desire ownership of this place? What desperation in the Israelis to deny them?

On the journey from the hut to Gaza prison the vehicle containing the five young men in their various states of life had stopped. Farid, though handcuffed and hooded, could hear and understand the conversation that took place in Hebrew. He had worked in Israel for some time and, if not fluent, could speak and understand a considerable amount of the native language.

'One soldier said, "We must hurry to save him. Get him to the hospital." The other soldier said to him, "We have no need to hurry, let him die." The military vehicle stayed there for a while. The soldiers smoked. After a while they checked on Sami again. One of the soldiers said, "Good. He's dead. Now we can move on."'

The grim account went mercilessly on and on. Of the beatings the survivors suffered in the prisons of Ansar Two and Gaza Central. Of Hani's interrogation, forced to stand while blood continued to pour from the bullet wounds in his legs. Of cruelty piled on cruelty. Near the end of this numbing account I observed to Nidal that it was an extraordinary story.

'No, no, it's a very ordinary story. These things happen here to many people.'

If it had been difficult for me to sit listening and

348

questioning throughout this 'ordinary story', the telling had not been easy for these young men. Nidal, particularly, cried openly as he spoke. He recounted how, gripped by the hair, his face had been repeatedly pushed close to the dead Mousbah by the security forces who demanded again and again that he identify the dead youth. Close enough to count at least seven bullet holes in his dead friend's head and face.

The most compelling piece of evidence that confirmed their accounts came near the end of the second interview, although in truth it had already occurred to me long before. What had puzzled me was the presence of Nidal and Farid in the Erheim home. If these were dangerous criminals, then what were they doing here talking to me?

Nidal had been released after eighteen days. After the first night of beatings and interrogation there had been no further questioning. No charges had been brought against him.

It was the same for Farid: released after eighteen days; no charges.

Hani was still being held at the time of my interviews with the others in early February 1989; he had not been charged with any alleged crime.

Near the end of this second interview my eyes were drawn again to Mrs Erheim. She had sat without uttering a single word for nearly seven hours. Now, as I looked at her she was speaking, but not with her mouth. There were no words, just tears running down wrinkled and lined skin.

The Israeli Army conclusion on what had taken place was that Mousbah and Sami had been 'shot while resisting arrest'. Exactly how they were resisting arrest as two unarmed youths in a hut surrounded by over one hundred members of the military and an unidentified number of armed members of the Shin Bet has yet to be revealed by the Israeli Army. Also waiting to be revealed is how so many shots were fired into the heads of these young men at close range. The Gaza Strip, like the West Bank and the other territories that Israel occupies by force, are areas where the Israeli Military is not merely judge and jury, it is also executioner.

Talking later that morning to members of the Gaza Bar Association about the state of the law, or lack of it, in these areas was a revealing exercise.

In the military courts all judges are serving Israeli officers, some of them without any legal qualifications. The concept of legal precedent, in which a trial judge is bound to follow, regarding to the law, decisions previously given, often does not apply in Gaza and the West Bank. Judges are far more likely to regard as persuasive their own previous decisions. Israel, which has yet to ratify the Covenant on International Civil and Political Rights, does not consider itself legally bound by its terms of reference. Neither do the military courts consider themselves bound by the Universal Declaration of Human Rights or the Fourth Geneva Convention Relative to the Protection of Civilian Persons in Time of War. The Israeli officers who sit in judgement on the Palestinians brought before them are, quite literally, a law unto themselves. Without the vestige of a Court of Appeal.

The Intifada, or uprising, began in December 1987. One year later there had been 432 deaths; 46,000 injured people; 33 Palestinians expelled; 5,000 subjected to administrative detention, no charges, no trial, a minimum of six months' imprisonment; at least 2,000 curfew days; more than 1,000 olive and fruit trees uprooted; 560 buildings, the majority of them homes, demolished. All West Bank schools were closed in the spring of 1988 and had not been allowed to re-open by the end of that year; schools throughout the Gaza Strip had all been forcibly closed for long periods; Press offices and newspapers had been closed; there had been more than 150 prolonged sieges of towns, villages and refugee camps. The attrition just went on and on.

On the Sunday afternoon in Gaza I was given what was for a European male a rare opportunity, to talk without Arab male chaperons, excluding Mahmoud my interpreter, to a group of women in one of the refugee camps. Women have always occupied a very special position in Arab society, but for this group the Intifada had dramatically changed that position.

The members of the Palestinian women's movement whom I met that day displayed a militancy that I had not, apart from the members of Hamas that I met, found within their men. As two world wars had freed millions of women from the kitchen and the bedroom, so these women had found new interests, new areas of activity. They told me how they collected buckets of stones for the young boys and men to throw at the Army, how they in turn had suffered severe beatings, and in some cases imprisonment and even death, how they had formed support groups for each other and for families where men had been killed or imprisoned. They told me of the cottage industries that had sprung up, small factories, garment making, potters, and of their aspiration that the entire Palestinian race should become and should live as one huge extended family. Through the Intifada they had clearly found freedoms that exhilarated them. It was difficult to imagine them reverting to their previous docile role when the Palestinian people are finally given a homeland.

As one of them remarked to me, 'We have found our role, we are equal to the men.'

She spoke with difficulty, still recovering from a beating that had culminated in a fractured jaw from the butt of a rifle.

What I was hearing and seeing was leaving a mark upon me. Mentally the effect was like being subjected to sustained and continuous beating. I had come to this place to seek a man who, if Samir's widow was right, could tell me where Carlos was. Instead I was discovering, first-hand, truths of far greater import. None of these truths justified throwing a hand grenade into a crowded Paris café on a Sunday afternoon, but they were perhaps beginning to give some insights into the mind of the man who had thrown it. If the young Venezuelan had heard of or witnessed similar acts of inhumanity in that far-off Jordanian suffering of 1970 then perhaps for him there was an acceptable rationale that propelled him on to the home of Edward Sieff and from there to lasting notoriety. If you brutalize a man do not be surprised if he then acts in a brutal manner.

One aspect of what the Palestinian women talked to me about seemed to be so unlikely, so incredible, I felt compelled to explore it further. Back at the Marna House I explained my need to Alya Shawa. She listened, then reached for her phone. After a brief conversation, she turned to me.

'I have the person who can answer your questions. Would you like to talk to him this evening?'

'Yes, Alya, I would, and thank you.'

'Don't be silly, I've already told you, it is we that should be thanking you.'

Later that day I sat down with a man who needed no interpreter, Dr Haider Abed El Shafi, born in the town of Gaza in 1919. His description of the Gaza town that he had grown up in bore no relation to the present. Then it had been a medium-size agricultural town with a population that largely tilled the grounds of the Gaza district, an area that went north of Ashdod and east to Beersheba. At that time the Jews owned less than 3 per cent of the land and represented less than 10 per cent of the population. When the Green Line was established by the United Nations after the Second World War, in one fell swoop the means of livelihood for the majority of the population of the town was lost. Now, as I observed to the Doctor, it looked like an animated Bosch painting of hell.

Eventually I turned our conversation to the subject that had so concerned me during my meeting with the Palestinian women earlier that day.

'Dr El Shafi. This afternoon a number of Palestinian women insisted to me that they had suffered involuntary abortions through inhaling tear-gas fired and thrown by Israeli forces. Is there any validity to those claims?'

'There is great validity. Our doctors began to receive

more cases of abortions. It was first noticed at Al Shifa hospital, then at more and more hospitals and clinics, especially those that specialize in the field of gynaecology and obstetrics.'

'Can you put an approximate date on when you began to notice this increase?'

'Yes, it was nearly one month after the beginning of the Intifada, at the beginning of January 1988. Confronted with what seemed an inexplicably high rate of abortions the doctors began to investigate. First, they established that there had been a twenty to thirty per cent increase in the number of cases of involuntary abortions or miscarriages compared with the same period for the previous year. Second, they noticed that many of the cases were coming from the refugee camps. Third, they established most of these women had been subjected to a tear-gas attack. The fourth observation that the doctors made was that most of these women had suffered some psychological disturbance.'

'Can you give some examples of how the psychological disturbances were triggered?'

'Either their homes had been entered by soldiers and wrecked, or their children had been taken by the soldiers to the jails during the night, or they were confronted by shooting inside the camps.

'These observations continued throughout the entire period when the soldiers were using the tear-gas weapon most frequently, namely the end of December 1987 through to March 1988.'

'I understand that the Israeli government has denied that there was any increase in these figures and has asserted that they are the same as those for the previous relative period.'

'As Chairman of the Arab Medical Council I say to you that the Israeli government is very welcome to examine our findings, also the evidence upon which those findings are based.'

'Do I understand you correctly? They've issued a denial without studying the evidence?'

'You understand me perfectly.'

'And what about your efforts to establish the composition of this tear-gas in order to prepare an effective antidote?'

'Our first problem was that we only had access to empty cases, empty bullets. Second, we had no laboratories either in Gaza or the West Bank to analyse the effects of this type of gas. We asked the Commander of the Israeli Civil Administration for details. He said that it was a matter for the security forces. We asked them, they ignored the request for information repeatedly. Eventually they said that this was classified information and they were not allowed to give us the details.'

'How many cases in the Gaza Strip have there been?'

'That fall within the categories we have been discussing? Between ninety and one hundred and five. For the West Bank figures you would need to talk to my colleagues there.'

'It's fifteen months since the Intifada began. Have you now been able to get from the Israelis the chemical composition of the tear-gas?'

'No, they still maintain it is a military secret. I remember on January the tenth last year we obtained, after a demonstration, an empty tear-gas case. It had its manufacture date on it. "January 1988. Made in the USA."'

'And fired January 1988. Gaza.'

'Yes. Fired before the end of the second week of January.'

'Have you tried to bring pressure through the American Medical Association for the suppliers in the States to reveal what this gas is exactly made of?'

'Indeed we have. Many Americans have visited. I particularly recall a black Senator who came last February. We and these people did all we could to make the implications public. We never got the information, but the public pressure brought about a change of tactics by the Israeli forces. First we had been subjected to indiscriminate shooting of live ammunition. After public outcry that eased a little and for a while tear-gas became the main weapon; after further international criticism they began to concentrate on breaking the limbs of the people. I remember, during March and April last year, nearly five hundred cases were subjected to fracture and a range of double fractures. You may recall Mr Rabin was particularly keen on that policy. At the end of April it became difficult for me to monitor any Israeli policy changes.'

'Why was that?'

'I was arrested on the 29th of April and put under administrative detention for six months. No reason of course was given.'

'Did they think perhaps that you were making too much fuss about their policy changes?'

The Doctor roared with laughter.

'Well, they certainly considered my continuous complaints about the effect of tear-gas to be irritating. I had also had meetings in Israel with many Israelis, especially from the Peace Now movements, from the leftist parties, meetings with academics. These people were deeply affected by what they had seen in our hospitals. The injuries, especially the injuries suffered by the children: most of those injured are below fifteen years of age, nearly half of those killed have been below fifteen years of age. Some of these injured children have been taken from the hospitals and beaten and injured further. Injured children taken from the reception areas, from first aid, sometimes from the operation room, sometimes from surgical wards. Al Shifa is again one such hospital where I have witnessed these things. There are others.'

'Have they ever taken anybody from the operating table?'

'Yes.'

'From the operating table itself?'

'Yes.'

'Have you had cases where people have been returned to hospital with additional injuries?'

'Yes.'

'Is there anything that is sacred or sacrosanct, Doctor? If an occupying force is going to violate an operating theatre, is there anything that is beyond the pale?'

'It would appear not. Babies have been beaten. Some of course have died in their mothers' arms. Pregnant women in the last month of their term. I have photographs you are welcome to have, severe bruising all over the abdomen. Age is no protection. A woman of eighty-five, partially paralysed for many years with disease, severely beaten on the ribs and the abdomen. In that case the military spokesman subsequently stated that the woman had attacked the soldiers when they came to arrest her nephew. This is a woman who for many years has only been able to cross the room with the greatest difficulty.'

Later I asked Dr El Shafi how he saw the future.

'I am optimistic. I feel that we are going to attain peace. Not soon. The way of peace is not easy, it is difficult, more difficult than the way of war, but I feel that we have started our way of peace. It is a matter of patience, a matter of time, and the Palestinians are very patient. I sincerely hope that we do not reach a point where everything is spoilt and radicalism prevails. I want a just and a durable peace settlement in the Middle East, one which embraces Palestinian rights and Israeli rights.'

A taxi-drive took us to the home of the Tarazi family in Gaza 15 District.

The pleasantly furnished living room was dominated by a single photograph of one family member – nineteen-year-old Khader Elias Tarazi, the first Christian Palestinian to die since the eruption of the Intifada.

On the 8th of February 1988 his mother had sent Khader to the fresh market in front of the Greek Church. While shopping for the family's groceries a demonstration broke out nearby. By the time the soldiers arrived, Khader had made his purchases and, carrying his two bags on his bicycle, attempted to cross the road. As the youths who had actually taken part in the street-demonstration scattered, members of the Israeli army grabbed Khader and immediately began smashing his body and head with their truncheons. Other shoppers attempted to stop them, shouting that Khader had not been part of the demonstration. Ignoring the protests the soldiers continued to beat Khader; they broke a leg, they broke an arm, but still the beating continued. Eventually the nine who were attacking him, urged on by three more sitting in the jeep watching, threw the injured young man across the front of the jeep. He was spreadeagled across the bonnet and his hands handcuffed to a crush bar at the front of the vehicle. They drove down the main road in this fashion, occasionally braking hard then racing off with the youth still handcuffed to the front of the vehicle. During the drive he sustained further injuries, to his skull and to his spinal cord. His back was broken. His face continually battered against the bonnet.

At the Military Prison in Gaza the Israeli doctor refused to give him any medication or to attend to his injuries and stated that because Khader was in a very serious condition he did not want the responsibility of dealing with the case without the necessary paperwork.

The unconscious body of Khader was then transported to Ansar Two prison, there it was thrown in one of the tents already occupied by some thirty to forty prisoners. When they saw the condition of Khader they began to protest. They screamed that he must be taken immediately to a hospital, that a doctor must be summoned. The entire tent was punished for this. They were ordered to strip naked and stand outside their tent. It was February. Almost a year to the day later, despite a leather coat, T-shirts and jumpers, my bones ached with the cold of the Gaza Strip. At eleven at night Khader was taken to Soroka Hospital in Beer Sheva. He was dead on arrival. He had in fact died in the tent.

When Khader had not returned home by mid-afternoon his mother went out looking for him. When eventually eyewitnesses of what had occurred outside the Greek Church spoke to Mrs Nawal Tarazi, she was sure that they were wrong. It must be some other lad that the soldiers have taken away, she thought. Yet the eyewitnesses were sure it was her son. Arriving at Ansar Two, the Israeli officers initially insisted that they had no prisoner of that name. Eventually they said, well, yes, but he must have been very sick when you sent him out shopping on his bicycle, so sick in fact that he is now dead. She stayed outside the prison until six in the evening, unaware that inside its walls thirty-five men were standing naked in the cold while the life of her son ebbed away behind them.

For three days they refused to give her any information. 'They' included the Military Governor of Gaza Town. After three days the Military Governor spoke to a member of the Tarazi family, an engineer. 'Tell your relatives that their son is dead.' Thus Hazem, the engineer, came to the family with news of their son.

Khader's body had by now been transferred again, this time to Abu Kabeer hospital. Officially it was for a post mortem. Mrs Tarazi stated to me categorically that at this time many of the organs of the body were illegally removed. She also stated that this had been confirmed by a medical examination before the funeral. The Israeli authorities then insisted that Khader be buried at midnight, just as they had insisted on midnight burials for Mousbah and Sami and many others. This time, however, they were dealing with a devout Catholic family who were equally insistent on a Christian service at a Christian hour. Their point of view, their wishes, finally prevailed. If any official inquiry has ever been held into the circumstances of Khader's death the Tarazi family has no knowledge of it. Indeed the family made a written application for such an inquiry. They demanded that the soldiers who had murdered their son be identified and brought to trial. The ruling military ignored their requests and demands and the family were told that if they continued to ask for an inquiry, they would be courting further trouble. They continued to ask for an enquiry. Some seven months after Khader's death the soldiers and Shin Bet paid a midnight visit to the Tarazi family. On the night of the 12th of July 1988 they entered the house and began beating Kamal, the older brother. When Mr Tarazi attempted to stop them he too sustained a beating. Dragging the by-now unconscious Kamal from his bed the military left. Kamal has since July 1988 been held without trial in Ansar Three prison.

At the United Nations Relief and Works Agency, UNRWA, United Nations personnel showed me a range of weapons they had collected. The gun that sprayed out fifteen rubber bullets at a time, indiscriminately. Tear-gas canisters that bounced erratically after firing. They empty their contents in ten minutes; the effects, as Dr El Shafi had already testified, lasted considerably longer. Huge stones, not thrown by Palestinian children, they would not have been able to lift these. They had been dropped from Israeli helicopters or hurled by heavy machinery. A fibre glass truncheon, weighing about three kilos, M16 bullets, dum dum bullets, plastic, rubber. The litany of violence and its attendant hand props seemed endless.

On Monday evening I sat in the Marna House. In a nearby room I could hear the chatter of some new arrivals but I was in no mood for exchanging either visiting cards or pleasantries. One way or another I have been interviewing people for more than twenty-five years, people that have ranged from Cardinals to crooks, Heads of State to heads of Mafia families, mass charmers, mass murderers. I have been confronted by great good and great evil. I have been driven, sometimes relentlessly, in pursuit of justice. Justice for a fat, funny film star, for a simple-minded teenager, for a naïve New Zealand farmer. I have seen inhumanity wearing its many clothes and adopting its many roles. I lack the cynical protective shell so beloved by journalists and reporters, particularly foreign correspondents. 'Anybody here been raped who speaks English' is not a line that will ever come out of my mouth.

Nothing in my life had prepared me for these last three days in the Gaza Strip. No wonder experienced, life-hardened politicians have gone there and to the West Bank and, having seen, reacted. I wondered how they would have reacted if they had also heard.

'I have spoken to your friend. He is waiting for you.'

It was Mahmoud. I stared at him blankly.

'The man you spoke about to Mrs Shawa.'

Did he mean the Doctor? I'd already interviewed him. Did Amin have someone else for me to talk to?

Mahmoud and I continued to stare at each other for a moment. Then came the light. The elusive man from Chebaa. The reason I had come to this place. I got up and walked towards the front door.

'David. What about your tapes, your recorder, your notes?'

'I somehow feel, Mahmoud, that this man will prefer to talk off the record.'

Mahmoud would make an excellent diplomat. He knew so little about me yet never asked a single question. In truth he had for three days spent every waking moment asking questions on my behalf. He had been asked by a mutual friend to do a job, perform a service, and he had done it with a quiet effectiveness. Not once through the interminable hours of interviews had he expressed surprise or shown any emotion. I asked him about that.

'I come from the West Bank. There it is the same as Gaza.'

I had found that difficult to believe and had quietly decided to establish the veracity of that for myself, using a different interpreter.

We drove through the curfew-quiet streets of Gaza town. Our driver recounted an incident that he had witnessed early that day. A foreign journalist, internationally known, had come into Gaza to do a quick story. His car had been stoned. The outraged reporter had begun shouting that all Palestinians are animals. Mahmoud asked the driver a question in Arabic. Getting the reply he nodded and smiled. I looked at him enquiringly.

'The reporter was driving an Israeli hire car. Israeli number plate. Dumb bastard.'

The man from Chebaa showed us into his living room. Having no desire to put yet another individual into the hands of Shin Bet, I will call him Omar. I never asked him what impelled him to make such perilous journeys from his home town in Southern Lebanon through the heart of Israel to the occupied territories. I could hazard a guess but then again I just might be guessing incorrectly. I showed him the letter that Samir's widow had given me for the Mukhtar. He read it silently, then, nodding, asked us to join him for coffee.

We talked for a while of everyday things, although 'everyday things' takes on an unusual meaning in a place like Gaza. We also talked of Samir and his family. A careful man this, he was running his own private inventory on my knowledge of his relations. Throughout all this Mahmoud translated without once asking me what the hell we were doing in that apartment.

'He says that he knows what information you are seeking,' Mahmoud said eventually.

'Can he be of help?'

I did not need to have the reply translated. One word from it was enough.

'Damascus. He says the man you are looking for is in Damascus.'

'Whereabouts in the city?'

'That he does not know. But he is certain that he is there. He has lived there for many years.'

'How many years?'

Omar shrugged, mentally calculating.

'At least five years, maybe more, perhaps seven.'

I remembered what Bassam Abu Sharif had said to me in London, just a few days before I had flown to Israel. 'I know where Carlos is and I know that he has not moved from that place for five years.'

So far, so good – if accurate.

'Do you know exactly where in Damascus Carlos is living?'

Omar smiled as he listened to Mahmoud translating.

'No, he has always taken very good care that no-one knows such things.'

'Can you help me to get to him?'

'It's possible, but it will take time.'

It was agreed that we would maintain contact through Samir's widow. There was another part of the puzzle that I was desperately anxious to solve.

'This Carlos who lives in Damascus. Is he the man I have already met in the Lebanon?'

Mahmoud translated. There was clearly bewilderment in Omar's reaction. They talked back and forth for a moment and as they did so the realization of my own stupidity pushed adrenalin through my body, wiping out all trace of fatigue.

'He says that the man in Damascus is Ramirez. Is Carlos. Although he uses many other names he is certain of that.'

I was suddenly aware that I was walking on very thin ice.

'Other names? Can he remember any of them?'

'Ahmed. Mohamed. Michel. There are others.'

'And he is safehoused and protected by the Syrians?'

Omar smiled and nodded.

'At the very highest level.'

'President Asad?'

'Yes.'

There were many other questions that I wanted to ask but my earlier blunder had seriously unnerved me.

'I'm very grateful, Omar. Shukran. Hatha shay kuweis. Shukran jazeelan.'

Omar offered us more coffee, but I declined and stood up. I wanted to get back to the hotel.

Alone in my room I quietly cursed my own stupidity. I could blame fatigue. I could point the finger at the trauma of the past three days and nights, but it was still a very dumb thing to have done.

At this stage of the investigation I was convinced that whoever the man was whom I had twice met and talked with through the night, he was not Ilich Ramirez Sanchez. Samir had been the final link in the hunt that had led to that man. Now a relation or close friend of Samir's was stating categorically that Ramirez, the real Carlos, was in Damascus. It pushed the laws of coincidence beyond breaking point. Samir may well have been in on the operation, may well have known that the man I talked to north of Beirut was an impostor. To alert Omar to the truth that I had so painfully worked out for myself over the years of investigation would be perhaps to alert this man in Damascus. In either event I now finally had a city where, if Omar was right, Ramirez or the impostor was living and had lived for five years or more. That at least fitted with Bassam's comments, but before I went charging into the Syrian capital I wanted to be sure.

In the morning I dróve with Amin and Mahmoud to the border. Mahmoud took the taxi on to Jerusalem. Amin stood a short distance from the border post waiting to watch me keep my appointment with the Israeli army.

My guide back into the Gaza Strip was an army captain called Richard, a young man in his early to mid-twenties. He greeted me with a pure BBC English accent. It transpired that he had been brought up less than a mile from where I live in London. For the past three days I had been exposed to the reality of Gaza as seen by a number of Palestinians and as I had personally found it. Now I was to get a flavour of what constituted reality in the same region for the Israeli army.

The Israeli army view of the Intifada, as expounded by Richard and various other army officers I met in Gaza that day, was equally revealing: 'The Intifada has died down. It lacks popular support. The people are clamouring to work in Israel.'

To judge from not only Richard but his brother officers, order had now been fully achieved. I stood outside the Yellow Mosque in the centre of Jabalia listening to a major declaring that this had been where the Intifada had originally erupted. That it had been at that time 'the hottest place in the entire occupied territories, now everything is under control'.

Near the end of my time with the Israeli Defence Forces Richard apologized for the 'lack of action. You didn't even get one stone thrown at you. Usually people are able to say, "I got stoned in the Gaza."'

Clearly much had changed since the beginning of the Intifada. At that time the Western world had been shocked and horrified at the television pictures that showed soldiers breaking the arms and legs of handcuffed Palestinians. The Israeli government had been subjected to international criticism. Some of it had come from their own servants; from Israeli Ambassadors around the world cables and phone calls came in: 'Get those television crews out of the Gaza and West Bank. Control those reporters.' Not only the press but visiting politicians were frequently prevented from going into the territories. By the time I was there the IDF had got its act together. Smooth, trouble-free tours ensured that the visitor listened to assurances that all was now well, everything was under control. And if the odd occasional disturbance did break out, well, every Palestinian death was independently investigated, orders to fire were strictly observed. No-one, I was told, ever fired other than at the legs. They painted such a tranquil picture for me. Of course it bore no relation to what I had discovered. Nor did it bear any relation to what had actually occurred in the Gaza Strip during the time I was there. (At the back of this book the reader will find a factual record of the reality of the Gaza Strip covering the period of Friday February 10th to Monday February 13th, 1989.)

It may be recalled that when I had questioned my interpreter Mahmoud about the fact that he had shown no emotion as horror had been piled on horror during the Gaza interviews his response had been, 'I come from the West Bank. There it is just the same as Gaza.' I went to discover if that was true. After just four days I knew the answer.

It began in Bethlehem, where I went to meet a new interpreter, Zaid. There was a three-day strike in progress. Palestinians were protesting about Israeli taxes. Waiting outside the Palestinian Press Office, I leaned against a wall. A few street stalls nearby were selling café Arabi and food. An army jeep pulled up and the Arabs at the stalls quietly carried on with their snacks. Swinging a long truncheon one soldier advanced on a particular stall, while his colleagues in the jeep slouched, watching. The soldier began to smash one teenager with his truncheon. He hit him several times on the body, the blows he aimed at the teenager's head were fended off. Thinking that perhaps the press card I was carrying might finally be of some use I put down my case and, advancing towards the two, began to take photographs. The soldiers in the jeep shouted to their colleague. He advanced towards me, a sweating animal on heat. I expected a preliminary verbal exchange and was caught by surprise when, without a word, he snatched my camera, opened the back and pulled out the film, then threw the camera back at me. He hurried back to the jeep and a moment later they roared away down the narrow street. I was immediately surrounded by Palestinians. They wanted to buy me coffee, to offer me cigarettes. They were pathetically effusive with gratitude. Zaid had by now emerged from the Press Office.

'We had better go before they come back for you. I will take you to my home.'

Home for Zaid was the refugee camp of Dheisheh, where ten thousand people live on one kilometre of land. Zaid had been born there. There was a heavy concentration of army at the main gate but Zaid knew other ways into this place.

Our first call was to the home of Ibrahim Ahmad Hussein Odeh. He was not at home. He will never be at home again. His mother had been born in a village some thirty kilometres south of Bethlehem, in 1927; she had been forcibly removed by the Israelis in 1953. Since then Dheisheh refugee camp has been her home. On the 9th of May 1988, at 10.30 am, Israeli soldiers with bulldozers were demolishing several homes in the camp, part of their policy of collective punishment. A demonstration broke out. Ibrahim, fully occupied within his home, was helping his wife with the cleaning and the polishing. From an upstairs room his attention was drawn to the activity taking place some two hundred yards away. In the downstairs living room he stood continuing to watch from behind the closed window. He called his wife, telling her what was going on outside. She came and stood next to him and he placed his arm around her. A soldier on the top of the bulldozer turned into direct eyeline with the couple. He picked up his rifle, took aim and fired. With his arm still around his wife's shoulders, Ibrahim's brains exploded all over the living room. The soldier continued to fire directly through the closed windows. I counted nine separate bullet entries in the glass, in the walls, in the ceiling. The furniture in the room was covered in dried blood stains. On the ceiling there was dry matter and a hank of human hair blowing gently. I asked his mother why it had been left there. 'It's all that's left of him,' she said. Zaid told me that Ibrahim had been killed with a dum dum bullet. It was academic really. When a man's brains are blown all over his living room, the kind of bullet used is of little interest to the victim. Ibrahim was thirty-four years of age, the father of eight children, the youngest born three months after his murder. His eldest was thirteen when his father was slaughtered. The Israeli soldier and his comrades returned to their other demolition work. No-one from the military came to the house of Ibrahim that day.

The following day, after the funeral, the family returned to their home. As is the Arab custom at a time of mourning, the Koran was played on a tape cassette. If death could not bring the soldiers the Koran could. They smashed their way into the house, demolished the cassette recorder and started to break up the furniture. They said they were searching for some young Palestinians. They ordered the family to remain indoors. As the soldiers were leaving Ibrahim's three-year-old daughter began crying and shouting at the soldiers. 'You killed my father. You are bad men.' One of the men hit her around the face.

Three days after Ibrahim died the Israelis returned. This time there were members of the civil administration, members of military police and members of Shin Bet. They had come to apologize. 'We are very sorry. It was a mistake. No order for the soldiers to fire was given.' One of the Israeli officers turned to the grieving mother of Ibrahim. 'Never mind, perhaps some time in the future you can have another son.' At the time Mrs Hanneh Odeh was sixty-one years of age.

Like a number of the men I had interviewed in Gaza, my interpreter, Zaid, had been imprisoned by Israel. As we moved around Dheisheh refugee camp he talked a little of his experiences inside the notorious Ansar Three prison.

'It's a zoo. In fact, you would not treat animals like we were treated. These Jews are obsessed with prison numbers. You are given your number in Hebrew. If you forget it you're punished. Mine was 698. Beatings were regularly carried out. No cigarettes. No letters. Disgusting food that you force down to survive. Temperatures so high, forty, sometimes forty-five degrees in the Negev desert, that if you want hot water you put a bowl of cold water outside your tent in the morning and by lunchtime it's hot.'

Again and again in the Gaza Strip I had heard of the Israeli prison governor of Ansar Three, Colonel Semar. Zaid recounted how, after the Palestinian prisoners refused to work, claiming they were political prisoners, Semar came and shouted at them.

'Who is the man among you? Come on, who is the man?'

One of the Palestinians stepped forward and said, 'We are all men.' Semar got out his gun and shot him. Pour encourager les autres. Again Semar asked,

'Who now is the man among you?'

Another Palestinian stepped forward and said, 'We are all men.' Again, moments later he was shot dead by the prison governor. A riot ensued. A further forty prisoners were shot, some with live ammunition, some with rubber bullets. At least two were seriously injured. The prison was sealed for twenty days. No-one could get in or out. After the murders the surviving prisoners went on a general strike including a hunger strike. They refused to come out of their tents for three days. 'No-one talked. There was only the voice of the desert storms. The rain and the wind.'

Each day, when I had finished confronting this reality, I would return to the Colony Hotel in Jerusalem, return to a comfortable room, to hot water, to clean sheets and excellent food. Return to this other world. As I ate alone I would listen to tourists complaining loudly how their sight-seeing tours had been curtailed because of the Intifada. While an Arab waiter tended to her every need one elderly matron loudly proclaimed to the entire restaurant,

'These damn Palestinians. I don't know why the Israelis don't send them all back to their homes.'

The following morning I went back again to Beit Sahour and the home of the Saada family. On October 30th, 1988, this family of Roman Catholics attended mass while outside the army was waiting for the congregation to emerge from Church. When a demonstration against this intrusion into a religious activity erupted, the soldiers began to fire indiscriminately. Nineteen-year-old Iyad Bishara Abu Saada was hit by a plastic bullet in the abdomen. Rising to his feet, he made his way to the stone-throwers, took three stones, threw them at the soldiers, then collapsed and died. The plastic bullet had severed a main artery. The grim game of hide and seek with Iyad's body began. The Israelis, Mrs Saada insisted, wanted to snatch the body and get it to a hospital so that organs for use as transplants could be taken from it.

Mrs Saada was specific, naming hospitals, both Arab and Israeli, where she alleged this appalling practice goes on. She talked of specific cases, identifying particular dead youths, where, she insisted, subsequent autopsies had confirmed the removal of a variety of organs. She talked of Israeli doctors, accompanied by soldiers, making offers of large amounts of money to grieving parents. Even in an area awash with inhumanity it seemed to be an incredible accusation. Arab doctors, both in Gaza and the West Bank, confirmed to me that it did indeed happen but, unlike the Saada family, they would not go on record.

An indication of the validity of the family's testimony

on this can, perhaps, be gauged from another of their allegations. They insisted that there were plain-clothes Israeli hit teams, both men and women, operating secretly in the occupied territories. The hit teams, the Saada family asserted, dressed as Palestinians, infiltrated towns, villages and refugee camps, took part in demonstrations against Israeli soldiers, then turned on others in the crowd and either arrested them or simply murdered them in cold blood. These murders, the family contended, took place not only at open demonstrations but inside people's homes. She named two of the killer squads, insisted that they operated under the code names of Cherry and Samson – Duvdevan and Shimson. Later I talked to IDF officers about this allegation. They dismissed it as a fantasy. In mid 1991 what those officers had dismissed as fantasy was established as fact. Among those confirming the veracity of this story were some of the selfsame army officers who had earlier dismissed it. Killer Israeli squads do indeed roam through the West Bank and Gaza, just as Shin Bet agents pose as Western journalists. Stealing organs from dead Arab bodies no longer seems such a fantastic allegation.

Iyad's friends eluded the searchers. He was buried the same day he died after a service at the same church where only a few hours earlier he had attended Holy Mass. Four days later, with the family still in mourning, the army paid a visit. They tear-gassed both the home and the house next door. In one were the mourning men, in the other the women. At least thirteen canisters of tear-gas were thrown and fired into these two crowded dwellings. Clearly discernible telltale marks on the marble exterior walls and other areas showed the places where some of these canisters had impacted.

On Saturday 2nd of April 1988, twenty-three-year-old Salim Khalef Al Shaer washed, shaved and dressed, then walked down into the nearby city of Bethlehem. It was Saturday morning. There was bound to be a demonstration against the Israeli forces, there always was on Saturday. He arrived in the old vegetable market shortly before ten. The demonstration had already started, and, picking up a few stones, Salim joined in. Moments later a burst of firing was directed at him. Bullets splattered around nearby doorways. One round splattered his face. According to eyewitnesses the firing came from soldiers standing just fifteen metres from Salim. Again the grim game of chase the corpse was enacted. His friends rushed his body directly to a nearby mosque. His family were sent for and a funeral service performed immediately.

When the funeral entourage came out of the mosque bearing Salim's body the army were waiting for them. As the procession made its way to the graves near Rahill it was subjected to an aerial attack. Helicopters dropped tear-gas canisters and large stones directly on the mourners. The two helicopters continued to make low swoops as Salim was buried. Salim was in his grave within ninety minutes of walking out of his home.

Subsequently the IDF stated categorically that Salim had been about to throw a Molotov cocktail at the soldiers. Unfortunately for the IDF, an ABC TV team were filming the demonstration and their film irrefutably established that Salim neither held nor threw a Molotov cocktail.

His family had just finished recounting the above details to me. Coffee was being poured as I studied a number of photographs of the funeral procession. The large stones and the plumes of white tear-gas were clearly visible as they descended. I was just about to reach out for my coffee when a window shattered, then another. Suddenly the room was full of tear-gas. In moments everyone began to cough, to choke, our eyes, mouths and nostrils streaming. The effect on my senses was quite literally stunning. There was a tremendous burning sensation in my nose, in the back of my throat and in my chest. The most extraordinary thing was the behaviour of everyone else in that small, clean, simply furnished living room.

We were all suffering from the effects of the attack, yet the prime, indeed it seemed the sole, concern of this family was to assist the stranger from London who, moments before, had with his questions reduced several members of the family to tears as they had recalled the last two hours in the life of Salim. A wet towel was thrown over my head and I was bundled outside. Totally disorientated, I knelt on the ground coughing and vomiting. I couldn't taste the tear-gas, of course, for once my inability to taste or smell was an asset, but my nervous system went into overdrive. My heart began to palpitate wildly. I suffered a severe attack of tachycardia. Eventually, as the physical reactions began to subside, I was able to get to my feet. I was bemused, there was no sign of any soldiers. Then I realized that we were at the back of the house and the attack had come from the front. Mousa, my interpreter on this occasion, told me that the army had driven off to another area. He said the family were anxious about me, wanted me to get away before the army came back, in case 'you get into trouble'. That well-meant, kind thought triggered me into anger.

'Get into trouble, Mousa? What for? For not obliging the bastards by choking to death?'

I had been in that house for nearly two hours when this attack was made. No-one had entered. No-one had departed. No suspicious movement. On our way to the Shaer home we had encountered on a nearby road a small line of stones, not even a beginner's road block. Our driver had swerved around them and continued without reducing the car's speed. During my interview with the family, Mousa had on one occasion drawn my attention to an Israeli army unit working in the area. The unit were firing tear-gas canisters directly into houses some distance away. I could see no children with or without stones. I could see no Palestinians or civilians at all. I had passed a comment on the mindlessness of the unit's actions and returned to sit on a couch and continue the interview.

A short while later I, along with the others in that room, was on the receiving end of that mindlessness.

When I had partially recovered, I wanted to go to find the local Israeli commander, wanted to tell him

371

in simple English what I thought about the behaviour of this unit. Mousa begged me not to.

'If you do that what will they do? So maybe they offer you the big apology. Maybe they don't. It won't matter. When you've gone the army will come back here and make this family suffer. Write what has happened in your book. It's a small thing here. Such small things happen every day.'

'Won't that cause trouble for this family too?'

'If you complain today, while you are here, that will cause trouble. If you complain in the future in your book it will not matter either to the family or to the army.'

'All right, Mousa, I'll do as you ask. One thing though. I can't do this myself. I'm the wrong race and the wrong sex. You must ask the father. If any of the women who were in there are pregnant they must go immediately to a doctor for a full examination.'

He did not ask why I had made such a bizarre request. He already knew. He just nodded.

I conducted both on the West Bank and in Gaza many more interviews than the few I have commented on here. There is just one more that I wish to put on permanent record.

In July 1988, the army imposed another curfew on the town of Beit Sahour. On Sunday, 17th July, after eleven days, the army lifted the curfew. It had been imposed after an act that was considered by the military to be mass civil disobedience. The citizens of the town had returned over one thousand identity cards to the Israeli authorities. There were no processions, no demonstrations, just a mass return of Israeli identity cards. On Monday, July 18th, with the curfew lifted, there were visits to friends to make, there was shopping to be done. At five in the evening Mrs Hillal sent her seventeen-year-old son Edmund into the town centre to buy some fresh bread and with him went his fifteen-year-old brother John.

So soon after the curfew had been lifted, the town was peaceful and quiet, people preoccupied with the everyday. The two youths were within sight of the bakery as they walked along Al Nasser Street holding hands. They began to pass the Shanin building, an empty five-storey office block that had been requisitioned by the Israeli Defence Forces. A permanent squad of never less than four soldiers manned an observation post on the flat roof. Suddenly John's hand was wrenched from his brother's and he heard an explosion of sound. His brother lay on the floor, his head crushed under a large slab of rock. John looked up to see soldiers laughing down at him. He screamed at them.

'You sons of dogs. You have killed my brother.'

An ambulance was called by John but his brother had indeed been killed instantly.

This time, at least, there was an Israeli government inquiry. The family told me that the inquiry had concluded that the stone slab – so heavy that it took three men to lift it from the dead body – had blown over the edge of the roof at the precise and exact moment that the two boys were walking underneath. Having blown from the roof, it hit a boy that eyewitnesses asserted to me was at least three metres from the building. These same eyewitnesses were also categoric about the weather – there was no wind.

Again the Palestinians and the Israelis played hide and seek with the corpse. Again the family were forced to have a midnight funeral service.

Subsequently Defence Minister Yitzhak Rabin came. Not to talk to the family but to stand where Edmund had been crushed to death and stare at the roof.

This family of Edmund's are Israelis. With, in theory, the full might and protection of Israeli law and Israeli democracy to comfort them. They are of course also Palestinians. Their son died on the 18th of July 1988. When I interviewed them in the middle of February 1989 they were still waiting for that law and that democracy to be accorded to them. There were at least four soldiers on the roof when Edmund's life was crushed from him, yet at the time of writing none of them has to my knowledge been charged with any crime.

On this trip I had planned not just to discover some of the Palestinian reality but to examine at first-hand, through interviews, the Israeli government point of view on the Intifada and on Palestinian aspirations for their own independent country. I had wanted to speak to Prime Minister Shamir, Foreign Minister Arens and Defence Minister Rabin. While I was in Gaza and the West Bank all three men very obligingly made public comments that rendered the need to interview them totally redundant.

First Arens:

'The IDF is conducting its struggle against the Intifada in an honourable manner. It is a humane army, acting with great patience.'

Then Rabin, talking specifically of the condemnations that had been made of Israel in the State Department's report on human rights:

'Israel has nothing to hide from because we are not ashamed of what we are doing.'

Finally, Prime Minister Shamir:

'There will never be a Palestinian State. There is no power on earth that can force us to accept it.'

With leaders like the three just quoted – and the Cabinet contains others like Ariel Sharon who frequently advocates the forcible removal of all Palestinians from the West Bank and the Gaza Strip – there is awful inevitability about the future unless a miracle occurs and a sense of justice for all in the area prevails.

The writing is on the wall. It has been there now for many years. Others too have read it and attempted to pull Israel back from a self-inflicted disaster. Among them Israeli citizens. Among them survivors of Hitler's Holocaust, that time of darkness which Prime Minister Menachem Begin and others have sought to hide behind and use – and this is surely the greatest obscenity – to justify their actions. A great evil perpetrated against the Jews during the Second World War does not, cannot, justify other evils perpetrated by Jews on the Palestinian race.

Yes, the writing on the wall has been read by many

in Israel. There is the Peace Now movement. After the massacres of Sabra and Chatila in September 1982 they organized a protest demonstration. More than 400,000 Israelis marched through the streets of Tel Aviv. After the Intifada erupted in December 1987 thousands of them were out again on the streets of Israel, including a group of Holocaust survivors bearing a placard that read 'To remember also means not to act like Nazis'. In January 1988 nearly 100,000 Peace Now supporters again took to the streets of Tel Aviv, this time to denounce Rabin's policies in the occupied territories.

A minority, but a growing minority, of serving soldiers and officers in the IDF are going public with their condemnations of their government's intransigence on the Palestinian issue. There is the Democratic Movement of Women in Israel. The movement Yesh Gevul, 'There is a Limit', which talks of Israeli 'occupation and brutal repression by IDF forces and moral and political deprivation', and this from an organization of IDF reservists. There is the Israeli Council for Israeli-Palestinian Peace. The Doctors Against the Occupation. These organizations and the people they represent are the soul and the conscience of Israel, but the men of arrogance still hold power in the Knesset. Yesterday's men riding Second World War buses with destination boards that state 'Armageddon'.

On the 17th of February I returned to London. My mind was still spinning with the implications of what I had heard and seen during the past few weeks.

13

WAITING FOR QATHAFI

After my second trip to Libya had been aborted because
of my father-in-law's death, I had feared a long delay before that particular door would be opened again,
but when I returned from Israel cables from the Libyan
government were waiting for me. I was welcome to return
as soon as I wished.

I had a different hotel and a different minder for this
third visit to Libya.

I picked up the first indications that my next interview
with Colonel Qathafi was not going to happen overnight
the day after my arrival on March 2nd. I was in Tripoli, the
Colonel was in Benghazi.

While I waited, I polished and refined the questions
I had prepared for him in London. I also had time to
consider some of the implications of my recent trips and
interviews, particularly my conversation in Gaza with
Omar. Carlos, according to him, was in Damascus. He
had offered to assist in establishing a precise location but
I felt that his assistance might be a long time coming, if
at all. I had to be absolutely certain in my own mind
that Carlos was indeed living in the Syrian capital before I even attempted to get into a country which, like
Libya, had no diplomatic relations with Britain. There
was always the gambit of the Irish passport to bring into
play but I still wanted to be one hundred per cent sure.

As a possible permanent location for the man whom I
was hunting I could think of nothing in the mountain of
information that I had acquired on Ramirez that contradicted this idea and there were clues that might well

confirm it. As I wrestled with the problem and listened to Bashir, the man from the ministry, daily saying to me, 'Maybe tomorrow,' I attempted to put this waiting time to some use.

I paid a further two visits to the Aziziya Barracks, to the partially demolished former home of Qathafi. The Reagan-ruined building was much as I remembered it, still serving as a reminder of the President's attempt to kill 'the most dangerous man in the world'. There was more graffiti on the walls than at the time of my first visit. 'Swedish Libyan Friendship Organization. Murder 12.1.89.' 'Australian MPs Condemn this Action of US Aggression. 14.1.89.' 'Down Down USA.' and much more besides. Those gestures of solidarity were written on the walls of what had been the living room.

In the days that followed I began to explore the city again. The other wrecked dwellings were also unchanged from my previous visits.

I had made some interesting contacts in Tripoli and two in particular gave me significant help. The first was a feisty little man, Amin Doughan, publisher of a Beiruti newspaper. The second perhaps should remain unidentified. He was a former member of Asad's government in Syria who had argued with the President, resigned his Cabinet post and was still alive. Let's call him Patrick. With Amin I discussed Lebanon in general and Beirut in particular, then with both Patrick and Amin I took a chance. I talked of Carlos, the book I was writing and the various endless strands that I was attempting to draw together. As my friendship with both men flowered I eventually talked to them of my need to find Ramirez and of my meetings in Northern Lebanon with the man who would be Carlos. I was very aware that this was not without a variety of risks.

The day after my disclosures to them Amin phoned my room and invited me to join him and Patrick for coffee. Over dinner with an old friend the previous evening, Patrick had talked of my hunt for Carlos. I began to twitch. Both men had promised to keep my confidence.

Then Patrick told me who he had been talking to – a senior member of Libyan Intelligence, with special responsibility for Syrian affairs. He had listened to Patrick without comment then said,

'Tell him that Carlos is in Damascus.'

I had not indicated to either Amin or Patrick that Damascus had already been put in the frame by a man from Chebaa. This, from such a source, was powerful confirmation. I was desperate to talk to the Libyan Intelligence Chief and Patrick interceded on my behalf. Unfortunately his efforts were unsuccessful. The Libyan declined to meet me, but he did add a further observation.

'Tell him I am certain of my information. Carlos has been in Damascus for a number of years.'

Suddenly the fact that I had been in Libya nearly two weeks waiting to talk to Qathafi was just a minor irritation. I felt certain that I had finally succeeded. A global hunt was now reduced to just one city.

The following day, with my Irish passport in my pocket and Bashir by my side, I went to the Syrian Embassy in Tripoli and applied for a visa.

As I continued to wait for Qathafi I turned over and over in my mind the confirmation I had been given concerning the whereabouts of Carlos.

Beyond any doubt Libyan Intelligence was stating that Carlos, the real Carlos, was living in Damascus and had been resident there for a number of years. The man from Chebaa, Omar, had said exactly the same thing. I was convinced that the man I had met twice in North Lebanon in 1985 was an impostor. Not just a run of the mill fantasist but obviously a member of some country's secret service – a professional and a very good one. He had not just been briefed, he had been trained. Who had trained him? Why had they trained him? Why had I been targeted? How could it be that Samir could and did lead me to this impostor who sat waiting for me, and yet his close friend or perhaps even a relation could point correctly to where the real Carlos actually lived?

Whoever had briefed and trained the man I had met

had been good, very good, but not quite good enough. My request for the man's fingerprints had presented them with an insoluble problem. I wanted to take his fingerprints myself. I made that clear to him. No chance of slipping a set belonging to the real man. They had to abort the third interview in such a manner that I would be convinced that Samir's death was a million-to-one chance. They waited until I was actually in Beirut, about to make that third trip, then killed the witting or unwitting Samir. They must have reasoned that, armed with two long, sensational interviews, I would rush to print.

Why go to such lengths? To such extraordinary efforts? Who gains? Long before this third trip to Libya I knew the answer to that one. The riddle of Samir and his friend in Chebaa gnawed away at me. One led to a fake, the other apparently to the genuine article. There was a man within the PLO who could, if he were inclined, remove any lingering doubt about the actual location of the real Carlos. I got busy on the phone.

The man I wanted to talk to was of course Bassam Abu Sharif. I was one hundred per cent sure that he knew where Carlos was. Five previous attempts had failed to extract the information from him, but I was confident that this time I could make him an offer he would find irresistible – it was already packed in my suitcase. Something I had picked up in Jerusalem. Something for Abu Iyad. Well, perhaps they wouldn't mind sharing my gift.

Telephone calls to London established that Anna had contacted Bassam Abu Sharif. He was in Tunis and would be delighted to talk to me. I patted my gift from Jerusalem and said a silent prayer.

During my fourth week of waiting I announced to the ever-faithful Bashir that I planned to fly to Tunis for a few days and would then return. I was acutely aware that Bassam is a man who stays nowhere very long. Bashir went into a huddle with his superiors at the ministry and then came back beaming from ear to ear.

'We have had a meeting about you going.'

'Yes.'

'You cannot go. The Leader is expecting to see you.'

'And what will happen if I go to the airport?'

'You will not be allowed to go outside.'

Towards the end of my fourth week my patience was finally rewarded. I had long before then concluded that what I had been confronted with here was not Qathafi's rudeness but Libyan bureaucratic foul-up. The men from the ministry had expected me to come at the end of the month. None had thought to advise me of the interminable conference in Benghazi. None had thought to suggest that I came at the end of March rather than the beginning. Having been presented with me, instead of telling the Colonel, they had kept me dangling until his return to the capital. On Sunday 26th of March the waiting was over. A few days before, I also finally obtained a visa from the Syrians. There was one major problem, it was only valid for a month. Assuming that I did get on a plane to Damascus, and that assumption would only begin to become a reality if Bassam would give the vital corroboration, there was a great deal to do before I went hunting in Damascus. I put that problem temporarily aside. Bashir, Salah, my interpreter on this occasion, and I drove to the Aziziya barracks.

It was our second journey of the day to the barracks. We had gone in response to a summons 'from the Leader's office'. The routine was identical to that of my first interview with Qathafi. Courteously received, into first waiting room, coffee served. After an Algerian Delegation came and went, followed by a Latin American Delegation that also arrived and departed, we were shown through into the second waiting room.

With the secretary leading the way we walked not into the office where I had been previously but out into the open. After a short distance we approached a Bedouin tent. The light was fading, a brazier of wood was burning near the entrance, where Qathafi was waiting to greet me, wearing long flowing robes. It was reminiscent of a scene from *Lawrence of Arabia*.

Having exchanged greetings he motioned me into the tent.

'It is two years since we last met,' he said.

We chatted, among other things about the death of my father-in-law, while a Libyan television crew filmed and local press took photographs. When I observed that I would refrain from questioning him until they had left he made an almost imperceptible gesture of the hand and they departed. We drank fresh orange juice as I turned to the main agenda. The world had moved on in a variety of ways since our first meeting and I was especially interested to learn Qathafi's views on some of the changes that had taken place. I asked him for his response to the new stance of the PLO: its recognition of Israel's right to exist and acceptance that they had permanently lost most of their homeland; the statements that Arafat had made indicating that the Palestinians would settle for the mini-state of the West Bank and the Gaza Strip.

'As for Yasser Arafat, the policies he now follows will not actually lead to the proper conclusion. Those policies will have another result. They will lead to war. The Israeli position will be uncovered. The Palestinian side has offered everything that they have. Everything that they own. Eventually the Israelis will be in the cage of accusation. Inevitably world opinion will change. It will side with the Palestinians. Slowly the Zionists will be seen to be like the Nazi criminals. New Nazis. Their policies will be uncovered in front of the world. Then, when Israeli intransigence on these issues is there for all to see, even their present friends, there will be war.'

When it became apparent to Qathafi that I had recently been into the occupied territories conducting extensive interviews, our roles reversed. He was clearly eager for first-hand information and questioned me at some length on the conditions on the West Bank and in the Gaza Strip and on the morale of the Palestinians. He confirmed that he was still giving financial aid to the Intifada. Some time before he was killed in Tunis by an Israeli task force, Abu Jihad had extracted from

Qathafi the promise of four million dollars a month to finance the uprising. When Qathafi revealed to me that during the previous week he and President Asad had agreed to cut off all financial assistance to the PLO, it left the interesting problem of exactly how one could continue to finance the uprising. I asked the Colonel about this. He smiled and quietly observed, 'There are other ways, apart from the PLO, to ensure that the people in the territories get help.'

We talked of the secret attempts being made by President Bush to arrive at an understanding with Libya and of how Qathafi had rejected them. He wants open negotiation or none. Other countries have also taken part in these secret dialogues to bring about a rapprochement between Libya and the United States. They include France, Egypt and Saudi Arabia.

Again I raised the issue of the hostages being held in Lebanon and Qathafi promised to exert what pressure he could on Iran. Moving to what was for the Colonel a far more personal area I questioned him again about the 1986 bombing of Tripoli and Benghazi.

'We were expecting the attack that night, but I was not expecting that it would be concentrated over my domicile and against my family, my children. In reality that was not expected, therefore I was at home with my family, expecting that the attack would be made over military objectives. We were ready, but I was surprised that the attack was concentrated over my bedroom, over my children's bedrooms.'

'But you were expecting the attack that night?'

'Yes.'

'Did your intelligence information come from those same sources that we have already talked about? Those "many friends" who kept you informed over the years of the various Reagan Administration conspiracies to destroy you?'

'From those sources and from others.'

'Could you be specific?'

'The Saudis contacted me through a person before

382

the bombing night and they affirmed that the Americans would effect the bombing.'

'The Saudis?'

'Yes, the Saudis. Because the Saudis had failed to persuade the Americans not to carry out the attack. They asked me not to effect the counterpart Libyan attack against the European countries. The Saudis argued that to do so would merely strengthen any European alliance with America. To hold back a Libyan counter attack would weaken such an alliance and bring Europe closer to us. Therefore we restricted our attack to the reconnaissance station of the Sixth Fleet at Lampedusa. The counter attacks against Crete and Sicily were cancelled.'

'And this was because of Saudi intervention?'

'Yes.'

'I understand from the Maltese Prime Minister that air traffic control at Luqa also warned you of the F-111s that were entering your air space?'

'Yes, that is correct.'

'I also understand that either King Hassan of Morocco or a member of his government telephoned you shortly before the attack.'

'Yes.'

'And that this particular telephone call was to reassure you that there would not be an attack.'

'I did not personally speak to the Moroccans. Others in Tripoli did. Why do you ask of the Moroccans?'

'Because, Colonel, their King is a CIA asset, as I am sure you already know, and I have been told from an American source that his CIA controller asked him, shortly before the attack, to phone you to reassure you. But the real purpose of that telephone call was to enable the Americans to get an electronic fix, a precise one, on your exact physical location.'

'I don't believe that Hassan would involve himself in this way.'

'But a member of his staff or government?'

'Oh, that is more than possible.'

When I judged the moment to be right, I talked of a certain Venezuelan. I reminded him of our earlier conversation about Carlos and then I elaborated, told him of my meetings in Lebanon in 1985 and took him briefly through my hunt since that time. He followed my discourse closely, and when I had indicated to Salah that I had finished, Colonel Qathafi responded immediately. This time there was no dreamy look into middle distance.

'Carlos is still alive? Is he still alive, Carlos?'

'You tell me, Colonel.'

'I will tell you about the information I have about Carlos. Until now I believe that it is an invisible person. Like Abu Nidal. I don't believe there is a real personality called Abu Nidal, nor one called Carlos. This is a joke or an insinuation played by many parts. And even if once there had existed such personalities, I believe they have died.

'If Abu Nidal, a man, a personality by that name, ever existed, he is now dead. In the past we heard that this man had heart disease and lived with special apparatus to organize the rhythm of his heart. The Abu Nidal Organization is like similar organizations in the Arab world which hide the death of their leaders in order to continue to dominate their followers. They maintain that Ali the Imam, the apostle of the Prophet, the Imam of the Shiites, is alive. He is dead, but the Shiites continually state that he is still alive. The Christians believe that Christ is still alive and will one day be among them again. Abu Nidal's organization has the same tradition. Anyone could of course say, "I am Abu Nidal." The same is true of Carlos. I do not believe he is a real personality. If there ever was such a person then he has long been dead. He has even by reputation been inactive for quite a few years. It seems that he has disappeared already. These personalities appear when the atmosphere, the times, are appropriate.'

'When this "personality" came here in December 1975 with a planeload of oil ministers, when this "phantom" arrived at your main airport with among others your own oil minister, Ezzedin Ali Mabruk, did you meet him at that time? Or indeed at any other time?'

'Never. Is he the real Carlos? The man who kidnapped the OPEC ministers?'

'Yes.'

'This means that there is then a real personality called Carlos.'

'Your colleague Major Jalloud spent several hours talking to him.'

'Indeed, he was at the airport and he did talk to the hijackers. But who among us knows who is Carlos among them? It was probably not Carlos. One who was pretending perhaps to be Carlos. You yourself have met such a person. One who is not. Who is a false Carlos.'

'It has been said and written many times that you were the man behind the OPEC attack. That the plan was yours. That you subsequently paid Carlos several million dollars. That your own embassy, the Libyan Embassy in Vienna, supplied the guns and grenades.'

'This is not true. There is no evidence. It has not been proved.'

'No, but it has been alleged.'

'Anyone could allege.'

'It has also been alleged that your Oil Minister was in fact the person who gave Carlos the layout of the Conference room. What is your response to that?'

'During this event a Libyan was assassinated. How do you think we could deal with an assassin when the first victim is a Libyan? They came to our airport. They refused to surrender. They surrendered in Algeria.'

'Did Major Jalloud attempt to persuade them to get out of the plane? To abandon the operation?'

'Yes. He attempted to negotiate the release of the prisoners. They refused.'

'To the Colonel's knowledge, is Carlos in Libya?'

'He has never come to Libya, neither the false one nor the real one.'

'Other than on that one occasion.'

'If he came to Libya, we would put him on trial and

385

sit in judgement on him for assassinating our Libyan representative and for kidnapping our Minister.'

I asked the Colonel if I could interview Jalloud and also two other men who I believed could throw light on Carlos and his present whereabouts, Sayeed Qadhaf Al Dam and Ahmed Qadhaf Al Dam. He agreed at once. When I indicated that I had no further questions we stood and then walked slowly out of the tent. Salah hurried in front of us. The guards had turned the fire out of the brazier onto the ground and added additional wood. The flames burned brightly in the pitch black night, bright enough I would have thought for anyone to avoid them easily. Salah, head held erect, marched straight through the flames. Rather than leaping out, he seemed instead to pause for a moment in deep thought. His trousers caught fire and Qathafi, walking beside me, instinctively nudged me and pointed, then laughed. I called out.

'Salah. Your trousers! They're on fire!'

The interpreter did not turn, just continued to stride away into the black night, his progress marked by his blazing trousers. Qathafi heaved with laughter, shook my hand and moved off. Suddenly, as if from nowhere, a bodyguard encircled him, then he was gone.

Qathafi had demonstrably lied to me about Nidal. I wondered if there were other things about which he had been economical with the truth.

For the next four days I found myself bogged down again by Libyan bureaucracy. It was now the end of March. I checked out of my open prison by the Mediterranean and caught a flight to Tunis.

14

TUNISIAN INTERLUDE

As I walked into Bassam's office just outside Tunis, as well as my ever-present black case I was carrying two gifts. The first, a bottle of whisky, Bassam accepted with an almost perfunctory 'thank you'. The second gift, inside an ordinary white plastic bag, provoked a quite different reaction, one that I had anticipated. I handed him the bag.

'It's earth, Bassam. I dug it from the ground in Jerusalem.'

He kissed the bag then cried. He ran some of the earth through his fingers. A Palestinian, finally in direct touch with a fragment of his heritage. I had selected this small symbolic gift well, Bassam was born in the village of Kufra Akam in the Jerusalem area in 1946.

In the two months since our last meeting I had given a great deal of thought to the problem of getting Bassam Abu Sharif to share with me the true whereabouts of Carlos. Now, sitting alone with him late on a sunny morning, I tried a different approach. I began not by asking him about the man from Caracas, but about the man from Jerusalem – about himself.

He had journeyed far, from a bourgeois environment – his father was manager of the Arab bank – to become eventually one of the PLO's most radical and influential minds. His parents were not, unlike so many others, expelled from their homeland. Initially it was his father's profession that caused the family to move, opening new bank branches in Amman. Bassam's education was at a French college in Jordan run by the De la Salle brothers, and from there he went to the American University in Beirut where he gained BSc in chemistry. Further studies were in economics, administration, sociology, psychology, philosophy.

'I was not looking for more degrees. I wanted education and these were the years of establishing my own evaluation of things, political, social – it was a period of formation.'

Like so many others in the region, even as a young boy he had been moved by the emergence of Nasser, but his political awareness came gradually.

'My actual political formation started at the university. One was in contact with and exposed to the entire political spectrum.'

With his family's relative wealth he could easily have become a dilettante, using the Palestinian revolutionary movement as a plaything. Others had done so. He lived on campus in Beirut but his interests took him increasingly into the world inhabited by the majority of Palestinians, the camps. That exposure inevitably moved him to more radical activities. Twice he was expelled from Lebanon. Moving further to the left, he joined Habash's Popular Front, where for a number of years he worked with Ghassan Kanafani on the Popular Front's newspaper.

We talked of a person's roots and the importance of them.

'It's tough. Very, very tough. You can't imagine how tough it is to . . . when one gets alone with himself, and probably that would last ten minutes in the midst of our work, there are always ten minutes when a person talks to himself and he feels very lonely. Away from my children, my wife, my family, but that does not mean I don't have roots. I feel that I have roots, and probably this is one of the points that make me more enthusiastic to carry on this work, in order to get back to these roots.'

He plunged his hand into the bag I had given him and pulled out a handful of earth.

'My roots are there. In Jerusalem. I know it very well. It's clear in my head all the time. My land, cousins are there, nephews are there, the nice days I used to have. By the way, I was never stopped from returning. Even when I was a university student, all my summer vacations were spent there. Old Jerusalem and the family and the nice places of Jerusalem or Ramallah or in the village, ploughing with the people, or going in the early morning with the sheep – these were lovely moments for me. The roots are there and I feel that I belong there. I feel that I will not be in a position of stability or equilibrium until I get there. I do not belong here in Tunisia, or in Algeria, or any of the other places in the world where I have rested my head. There is no peace. I was practically kicked out of Damascus. We were in Beirut, we had to go out from Beirut. We were in Amman, we had to go out from Amman. Until we have our own State this situation will continue.'

I have never in my entire time during this investigation seen a shred of evidence that indicates Bassam ever picked up the Kalashnikov. Like Kanafani, his weapons were words, as they and others attempted to combat what they saw as the lies and distortions of the Israeli propaganda machine. In July 1972 Kanafani was assassinated by Mossad; a car bomb in Beirut killed not only him but also his young niece. Three weeks later Bassam was the target. A book sent in the post exploded when he opened it. The bomb left him permanently blinded in one eye and mutilated in one hand. Seventeen years later, as he talked of his hopes for a lasting and just peace with Israel, the shrapnel from that parcel bomb still caused him acute pain.

We talked of many things on that day in Tunis. Near the end I reminded him of our earlier conversations and of my need to locate and talk to Carlos. He looked at me again with that smile.

'In that case, David, you must go to Damascus.'

I had it. Three times over and in spades. I had been right about the *Al Watan* interviews, Bassam had been present when Carlos had talked to the writer. He talked at length about the Venezuelan, suggested a particular course of action that I should follow in Damascus, and several times counselled great caution.

'You must be very, very careful. It will be dangerous for you. If they know you are aware that he is living in Damascus, protected by them, you will be at great risk.'

Coming from a man whose face and body will bear to the end of his days the attempt the Israelis made upon his life, these were words of advice to weigh very carefully.

The day after Bassam had confirmed, without knowing it, what I had already learned from Omar in Gaza Town and from Libyan Intelligence in Tripoli, I spent six hours talking to Abu Iyad. It was a different location from our previous meeting and the number of his bodyguards had been heavily increased due to changes that the PLO had made to protect what remained of its original leadership since the killing of Abu Jihad.

I discussed Carlos and Iyad filled in some gaps and confirmed other aspects of the Venezuelan's life, particularly from the mid 1970s until the present time. Perhaps he had known all along, or perhaps the Intelligence information had recently come into his hands, but during this meeting he too identified Damascus as the city where Carlos was living. He was unaware of my meeting with Bassam on the previous day, yet his advice concerning my planned trip to the Syrian capital was, in some respects, identical. Like Bassam, he urged the greatest caution.

We talked of my recent interview with Qathafi, of how he had expressed the view that both Carlos and Abu Nidal were, if they had ever lived, dead. Iyad roared with laughter.

'He joked with you.'

'Yes. Strange sense of humour, particularly as Abu Nidal lives in the same city.'

Iyad laughed again and nodded.

'How was your meeting with Abu Nidal?'

'Very interesting, especially in view of the fact that he was drunk.'

'Providing he did not have a gun as well as a bottle in his hands, a good way to see him.'

We discussed Nidal in great depth, including once again the fact that he had been so badly penetrated by Mossad. Abu Iyad revealed on this occasion that the Tunisians and Moroccans who had successfully entered the ranks of the Nidal Organization had been jointly trained by the CIA and Mossad.

He was delighted with the bag of Jerusalem earth that I gave him and immediately arranged for it to be placed in a glass jar in his office.

'Every time I look at it, I will remember Jerusalem.'

At the end of our time together he walked out with me into the courtyard of his villa. Through Khalid he again prevailed upon me to take the greatest care in Damascus.

'In some places, some countries, I could arrange your protection, but in Syria and the Bekaa it is not possible.'

As we stood chatting in the late afternoon sun his bodyguards, though keeping a distance, were heavily in evidence.

'Still using Nidal's assassins to protect yourself, Abu Iyad?'

He shook with laughter at Khalid's translation.

'It's my personal reply to Nidal. While they are around me, there is no problem. Remember what I have said about the Syrians.'

In January 1991 Abu Iyad was murdered in Tunis. His killer was a member of the Abu Nidal Organization, but the man who had ordered his death was the man who actually controls the Abu Nidal group, President Saddam Hussein of Iraq. But that lay in the future as, in April 1989, I prepared to leave Tunisia. There was much to be done. Too much time had already been invested, too many labyrinths explored, to risk going into Damascus without the maximum preparation. If I got lucky, very lucky, there was perhaps the chance of one meeting with Carlos. In view of what had happened in North Lebanon, unresolved elements had to be resolved before I embarked on that journey.

During the summer of 1989, as I began the tortuous process of obtaining from the Syrian government another visa, I continued to dig, continued the hunt. Not for the man, I knew beyond reasonable doubt exactly where he was, but for the true story of that man. The research continued, indeed it continued long after I went to Syria, but as the summer began to move inexorably into autumn it was clear that I had much of this man's reality, much of the truth. It was time to take stock. To carefully consider and to clarify precisely what I had learned of the life of Ilich Ramirez Sanchez.

15

THE TRUTH – PART ONE

The reality? The truth? Well, whichever country or countries had chosen and trained the man whom I had interviewed twice in North Lebanon, they had done a great deal of homework. Their selection of the specific agent had been first-class. His memory for detail, often small items casually tossed in, his ability to run the gamut of moods and emotions, indicated a talent to embrace the quintessential elements of another man's personality that was remarkable. A truly huge loss to the acting profession. To avoid possible confusion I will from here on refer to that man as Carlos Two. Whoever he was, whoever he works for, he is not Ilich Ramirez Sanchez, alias Carlos.

What was particularly impressive was how Carlos Two avoided so many pitfalls, particularly the danger of taking on board much of the large amount of lies and disinformation that surrounds the real man. His briefings had clearly been based on the most accurate intelligence ever assembled.

One or more of the intelligence agencies of this world had gone to inordinate trouble. By the summer of 1989 I had cut the list of Carlos Two's potential masters down to just two. I was close to working out who had done it; I knew for certain why.

'THE FOOL OF THE CLASS'
Ramirez was indeed born in Venezuela. To be more precise, in the Razetti Clinic in the El Recreo district of Caracas at 5.30 in the morning on October 12th, 1949. Carlos Two had described the family that he claimed

membership of as 'petite bourgeoisie'. That description, which flatly contradicted what every single writer has confidently asserted, also transpired to be accurate. The vast ranch, the millionaire Marxist father, are merely the beginnings of the myth.

Jose Altagracia Ramirez Navas was indeed a successful lawyer, wealthy by Latin American standards, where the majority of the population live on less than two hundred dollars a month, but never in the millionaire category. The history of Carlos's parents, his early life including his Caribbean travels, all checked out. Confirmation came from Ramirez's father, his brother Lenin and from the official records that I acquired, including immigration files, intelligence files, visa and passport records.

The marital strains, the private tutors, the return to Venezuela on February 23rd, 1961 and the initial attendance of Ilich and Lenin Ramirez at the private Liceo America, were also entirely accurate. It was at that point that the agent or, more likely, his masters made their first mistake.

Significantly, it was an error that appears on the official records: 'Liceo America until 1962 then entry to Liceo Fermin Toro.' The father and Venezuelan contemporaries confirmed that the two boys transferred to a state school called Liceo de Neuva Esparta and stayed there for approximately six months before transferring to Fermin Toro. It is highly unlikely that Ramirez would have forgotten this six-month academic sojourn: their father had pulled his two eldest sons out of Neuva Esparta in the middle of the academic year because as a Marxist-Leninist he took deep exception to the school giving religious instruction.

For Senor Navas this was not unusual behaviour. On the day that Ilich was born the father had stopped smoking, 'for the sake of my child's health'. In the years that followed his highly successful legal practice became increasingly secondary to his preoccupation with his children. Of the time that his sons spent at Fermin Toro he ruefully observed, 'If I had understood the degree of militancy that existed in Fermin Toro I would never have sent them there.'

Senor Navas chaperoned the boys to and from school. He engaged in arguments with their teachers if he perceived an injustice. The father has recounted a number of such episodes to me. They contribute to a portrait of a man who cared very deeply for his children. A man who clearly devoted many years exclusively to their growth and development.

To ensure that his sons were correctly instructed on Instrucción Civica, Ramirez Navas wrote a small book which he then used to teach his sons 'Social, Moral and Civic Formation'. It is well written, the concepts are clear and a child in his early teens would be able to understand the explanations offered. The book was subsequently printed privately, as Ramirez Navas hoped it would be officially adopted as a recommended textbook. It never was, and copies of it lie gathering dust and slowly falling apart in his very humble dwelling. In view of the fact that it had first been published at the insistence of Ilich it was curious that neither the book nor the reason for its existence had been mentioned by Carlos Two in North Lebanon.

The next brick that fell from the carefully constructed edifice was bigger. It concerned Carlos Two's claims about his revolutionary activities during his Fermin Toro years.

If one believed his remarks about 'combat experience', the 'Molotov cocktails and the guns' and his 'petrol bombing of Pan Am's Caracas offices' at a mere fourteen years of age, Carlos Two had graduated with an honours degree in anarchism. The truth was more prosaic.

All of the activities that Carlos Two described to me, with the exception of the firebombing of Pan Am, did indeed happen in the years 1963 to 1966 when Ramirez attended Fermin Toro. The trouble is he was never a part of them.

Even Carlos Two's description of where the family lived at that time on O'Leary Square was incorrect.

Far from having 'a grandstand view from their balcony of the riots in the square below', the Ramirez family lived at the back of the block.

In his account of the Pan Am bombing, Carlos Two had walked into an interesting bear-trap. Extensive research established that no such attack ever occurred. Further research established that the source for this particular claim was the real Carlos. Obviously by the time Ilich Ramirez Sanchez 'claimed' responsibility for this non-existent attack, during an interview he gave to the Syrian writer, El-Jundi, he was beginning to believe his own publicity. Beginning to believe the myth.

Among the people Maria and I located in Venezuela was Anita Castellanos, school nurse at Fermin Toro since 1943. She remembered Ilich and Lenin very well.

'They were very, very quiet and always together. The father is the main reason that I remember them. Every day he would come to the school with them, and every day collect them. He was the only parent that showed such a keen interest in the progress of children at Fermin Toro.'

For good measure she also observed that in her opinion Lenin was much brighter academically than his elder brother. An observation that I subsequently confirmed as accurate when I obtained their entire school records.

The myth of the revolutionary activities of young Ilich during the years 1963 to 1966 was born out of a deliberate disinformation exercise conducted both by the British Secret Service and the CIA. It began after the events of rue Toullier in 1975, and was confirmed in newspaper stories and books. It continues to the present day. So powerful had the myth become that it clearly fooled whoever was controlling the agent I had interviewed in 1985, but his controllers should not feel too badly about those errors; by then the myth had also fooled a President of the USA, his Secretary of State and his head of CIA, even though, as Paul Valéry has observed, 'What has been believed by everyone at all times and in all places has every chance of being wrong.'

Certain elements of personality are developed early in life. Ilich and his brothers were not exceptions to this rule. Ilich was the quiet, thoughtful, gentle, courteous member of the Ramirez Family. He was also timid. Contemporaries at Fermin Toro confirmed this view. Carlos Rios told me, 'The two brothers were always together, always carrying books under their arms. They sat in class one behind the other. They seemed to have no friends other than each other. Both were very quiet. I have no memory of them getting involved with girls.'

And socially?

'We would go to lots of parties. The custom was to take a bottle of Cacique rum or to pay ten Bolivars. We would dance to Salsa music, Joe Cuba, Ray Barretop, Pacheco y su charanga, Justo Betancourt. This was before the influence of US music began to be felt. If the Ramirez boys came it would be Lenin who made an impact. He'd play guitar and sing. Ilich did neither of these things. You would find him leaning against a wall, not joining in.'

As recorded in an earlier chapter, another classmate, Pastor Heydra, completely demolished the image of Carlos the young guerrilla, the hyperactive revolutionary. Heydra had painted a damning picture of an inadequate youth:

'Ilich was the fool of the class. An idiot. He was a very shy person, introverted, everybody would make fun of him. He was scared and very shy of girls.'

For Ilich Ramirez Sanchez there had been no guerrilla actions, no Pan Am bombings and no leadership of the Young Communist Party.

On the 3rd of February 1965 elections for the student union were held. The winners for List One, a combination of the Venezuelan Communist Party and MIR, Movimineto Izquierda Revolucionaria, were Pastor Heydra, Amilcar Gomez and Eduardo Rotte. Neither of the Ramirez boys stood for election, despite Carlos Two's claims. Another example of Carlos the man fantasizing about Ilich the youth. One of the school songs of the time proclaims:

God rules in the sky
Christians rule on earth
and in the centre of Caracas
the Fermintorianos rule.

If they did it was without any notable assistance from
Ilich Ramirez Sanchez. By 1965 there was a great deal
of student unrest. Demonstrations against United States
involvement in Vietnam. Demonstrations supporting
Douglas Bravo and the other guerrillas waging civil war,
against President Leoni, against the police, against rising
prices, 'la lucha de la locha por la leche', the struggle of
a dime for milk. During that year the school director
was changed, enter Senor Modesto Toutesant, exit a
large number of student activists. The Ramirez brothers
were untouched by this purge.

The Communist Party was banned in 1962; it remained a prohibited organization until years after Ilich
had left Venezuela. Pastor Heydra explained that he and
his fellow activists organized the students into cells
and that putting it at its very highest Ilich could never
be described as more than a 'passive sympathizer'.

As for the alleged Cuban adventures of Ilich Ramirez,
adventures that would become much loved by many
writers – his attendance at the famous Tri-Continental
conference in Havana during January 1966; his subsequent training later that year by both Cuban Intelligence
and the KGB; his 'invasions' of Venezuela – Heydra was
in danger of choking on his own laughter when I put these
elements of the Carlos myth to him.

His derision was well-founded. School records confirm
that at the time of the Tri-Continental conference,
Fermin Toro students had returned to school after
a brief Christmas holiday and that neither Ilich nor
Lenin missed a day's schooling between then and
the beginning of the summer holidays in July 1966.
It should be noted that there were no diplomatic
relations between Venezuela and Cuba at the time
and the period is marked with great hostility between

the two countries. There were no flights from Caracas to Havana.

'I HAVE BEEN VERY HAPPY IN LONDON'

At this stage yet another small brick comes out of the edifice constructed for my benefit. The man who would be Carlos had told me that because of his role in the forefront of agitation in Caracas his father had sent all three sons and Mrs Ramirez to London. 'He wanted to get me as far away from the rebels in Venezuela as he could.' Senor Navas and Lenin both told me that the decision to continue the education of all three boys in London had been taken because Navas, an admirer of much in the Old World, believed that they would greatly benefit from exposure to the educational systems there. There was talk of trying the Sorbonne in Paris, the Patrice Lumumba University in Moscow, preparing for a University in the United States. Eventually it was agreed to apply for places at Patrice Lumumba University for the two eldest sons and that while they explored the potential of the Sorbonne and continued their education in London, Vladimir the youngest would be placed for his secondary education in Marylebone Grammar School. Ever a cautious man, Ramirez Navas made enquiries about a good crammer in London for Ilich and Lenin. The one that received the best recommendation was Stafford House. The two boys were duly accepted as part of the new September intake.

On August 4th, 1966, passports on behalf of Ilich and Lenin were issued. Their parents' marriage was about to enter another 'off' period. On August 17th Senor Navas said goodbye to his wife Elba and their three sons at Maiquetia airport outside Caracas; they arrived in London the following day.

Long before I had embarked on this investigation Stafford House Tutorial College had vanished from its original location in Kensington. I traced it to Canterbury, where it still had the same Principal from the time when the Ramirez brothers had attended the school. Buried away in its archives were the files on Ilich and Lenin.

If I could confirm Ilich's attendance in 1966, then his alleged KGB training in Cuba in the same year would be exposed as a series of lies.

Their applications, duly signed by both boys and their father, contained only one error. Precisely the same one as their Venezuelan school records – no mention of their six-month stay at Neuva Esparta. If some intelligence agency was preparing a disinformation exercise, they would undoubtedly access as many official records as they could: errors such as the omission of this particular school by the man who attempted to convince me he was indeed Carlos would be inevitable.

Carlos Two had named the courses taken by the real Carlos correctly. For the first two terms, English, then additional courses in Physics, Mathematics and Chemistry.

Apart from the dubious privilege of having, at least in part, educated the world's most wanted man, Stafford House has a fascinating list of former students. They include the present Sultan of Brunei, the brother of former Greek Prime Minister Papandreou, about twenty members of the Al Thani Royal Family of Qatar, the Hon. Anne Waldegrave, sister of Government Minister William Waldegrave, Sheridan Morley, and a lady named Carol Thatcher, daughter of former Prime Minister Margaret Thatcher. In the light of subsequent events the school reports of Ilich Ramirez are particularly interesting.

'He is not yet as clever as he thinks or imagines. He talks far too loudly and too long.' That was for Autumn 1966. At the end of the Spring term his English teacher was equally caustic. 'It would help if he realized that he knows a little less than he thinks he does.'

During the years that lay ahead Ilich Ramirez Sanchez was to give countless demonstrations that he had yet to learn that fundamental lesson of life.

I also eventually found the pistol club where, for the first time in his life, Carlos had held a gun. He and Lenin joined the Royal Kensington Rifle Club in 1966. The reality is somewhat less grand than the imposing title, a collection of dilapidated buildings and sheds on a railway cutting near the Cromwell Road. Some of the current members, without ever for one moment relating Ilich Ramirez to Carlos, remembered the two quietly spoken, conservatively dressed Venezuelan teenagers. Notwithstanding its location, the Club is run very correctly: there is a three-month probationary period, references are taken and checked, the current President of the Club, which has a membership of two hundred and seventy, is a former Mayor of Kensington and Chelsea.

Among other pleasant distractions that occupied both brothers, Lenin confirmed their joint fascination with the entire gamut of what had become 'Swinging London'. It is obvious that, freed from the constant watchful eyes of their father, both of the elder boys, not supervised by an over-indulgent mother, began fully to enjoy life. To add to the more obvious escape routes from learning English verbs such as the pop music and the mini-skirted girls and the rifle club where Ilich, according to his brother, constantly demonstrated a below average ability to hit the target, they joined a judo club. In Caracas Ilich Sanchez had shown a marked disinclination to get involved in sporting activities, whether it be swimming, volleyball, soccer or basketball. It was a feature of his personality that resurfaced in London. Lenin told me:

'I went for about two years. I like it as sport. Illy dropped out after about a year.'

The A-level course and the circumstances of how they came to go to the Patrice Lumumba University in Moscow were confirmed to me by Lenin, his father and Gustavo Machado who had arranged their sponsorship and grant. During this time their mother, when not looking after the three boys, appears to have been more than fully occupied in constantly moving home. Initially they had stayed for a few days on arrival in London at a bed and breakfast in Gloucester Terrace, then a leased apartment at 20b Weatherby Mansions in Earls Court, then 70 Chandos Court near Buckingham Gate. By the time the two eldest had gone to Patrice Lumumba University, the family address was 12 Walpole Street in Chelsea, virtually next door to the Duke of York's Headquarters, an ideal location for a young man soon destined to learn some of the ways of military life in Jordan.

The reason for the constant shuffling of addresses in West London throws an interesting light on the Ramirez family's finances. Within a few years many writers would be perpetuating the myth of the millionaire Marxist father. The truth is that the family ran a tight financial ship. Elba, constantly searching for better value for money, found the succession of apartments recorded above. Employing a maid in Caracas at about twenty Bolivars a week, about five dollars, was not a particular strain on the family exchequer; living in London was a quite different proposition. The Ramirez family's nine-year stay in England cost Senor Ramirez Navas $139,534.88 in total, $1,162.79 per month. Hardly millionaire class.

'NO GUNS BUT PLENTY OF VODKA'
The account given to me by Carlos Two of his 'period at Patrice Lumumba University' left me, despite the rising anger that I felt towards this man, full of admiration. Again and again that account checked out. Lenin, his father, fellow students who had been at Patrice Lumumba University at that time, intelligence records – all of these sources and others that I do not wish to identify confirmed the extraordinary accuracy of Carlos Two's account. I was becoming convinced that the impostor was a KGB agent. 'How else,' I asked myself, 'could they have so accurately put that period of Ramirez's life together?'

Swinging London was indeed merely the hors d'oeuvres for the Ramirez brothers. Swinging Moscow was the main course. As Lenin observed to me, 'No guns, but plenty of vodka.' The political intrigues with the various Venezuelan factions, the recalcitrant behaviour, all checked out. But as I dug deeper there were errors and omissions, some perhaps explicable, some certainly inexcusable.

When I had met the man who claimed to be Carlos I had talked to him about this first significant separation from *both* parents. In part his response was, 'Well it was for less than a year. Lenny and I went to Moscow in the autumn of 1968. We came back to London and joined Vlad and my mother for the summer holidays of 1969. We had only been apart for about nine months.'

From both Lenin and his father I confirmed that Elba Sanchez had flown to Moscow to spend Christmas 1968 with her two eldest sons. Senor Ramirez Navas had flown from Caracas to London to spend the same period of time with their youngest son Vladimir.

The Cuban lover, Sonia Marina Oriola, checked out. She was a mature student doing a post-graduate language course at Lomosov University in Moscow. Twice divorced when she met Ilich, their relationship had indeed resulted in a pregnancy, a fact that caused her own expulsion from her University.

Carlos Two made no mention of the fact that both he and Lenin were active in the black market. With their student grant plus the regular banker's drafts from their father, they bought luxury goods in the hard currency shops, 'Beryozka'. When returning from their trips to London, Lenin told me, they would 'bring into the Soviet Union jeans, Japanese watches and a variety of items, these too were traded on the black market'.

The account I had been given of the demonstration outside the Iranian embassy, including 'I missed the embassy. The bottle of ink went straight through a window of a private residence', had neglected to add the reason. It was not because of Ilich's poor aim: Lenin told me, 'The Russian police were deliberately guarding the wrong building to draw off the demonstrators. Illy and I were very impressed with the police tactics.'

These were perhaps small insignificant matters. Two other elements in the story I had been told through two long Middle East nights were not. I had questioned this font of so much knowledge closely about his problem with an ulcer. I had particularly pressed him as to whether he had been hospitalized in London. I'd even quoted the author Colin Smith, who had written that no London hospital has any record of treating a young Venezuelan for a stomach ulcer between July 1969 and February 1970. The ulcer in itself was not important, but Smith, building on his assertion, had speculated that this 'missing' period in the young man's life covered trips to the Middle East or Cuba for KGB training, or a trip to London to carry out KGB intelligence work. The account given to me by the impostor proved to be entirely accurate, except that it omitted one significant detail.

Official records held in Caracas confirm that Ramirez returned to London via Paris on January 3rd on Air France flight 216, arriving Orly on January 4th at 10.35 am. French records confirm that he flew from Orly at 1200 hours. British records confirm that he arrived Heathrow at 12.55. What was missing in the account I had been given was the fact that after chronically over-indulging himself for the rest of the month in London Ramirez experienced acute abdominal pain for three days. He was then examined by his doctor, Dr Amorosco-Ceneño, in the early hours of February 2nd, 1970. The doctor immediately arranged for his emergency admission to the Westminster Hospital, which he entered at three in the morning. The subsequent diagnosis was a peptic ulcer, which in view of the fact that the medical records state that Ramirez admitted drinking two bottles of whisky a week is hardly surprising. He was discharged on February 10th.

The reality of the reason for the long flight to see his father is also fascinating in the light of the myths of KGB involvement that have swirled around Ramirez. He wanted out of Patrice Lumumba University. He had not gone home just to talk about his problems with the fellow students, he was completely disillusioned with the reality of the Communist system that he had experienced first-hand in Moscow. It took, Senor Ramirez Navas confirmed to me, all his powers of persuasion to extract from Ilich a promise that he would return and complete his University course.

There was also a fatal flaw in the story I had been told concerning the expulsion of Ilich Ramirez from Patrice Lumumba University, a flaw that would not have been there if that agent had been briefed by the KGB.

According to him, there were only two expulsions, his own and Lenin's. Patrice Lumumba University records confirmed what Lenin Ramirez has told me. Twenty Venezuelan students were expelled at that time. The predominant reason was the same in all cases, the Venezuelan Communist Party had withdrawn their sponsorship. Every single member of the Douglas Bravo group of sympathizers was summarily dismissed. The man who had demanded these mass expulsions was a Venezuelan hard-line Communist, Eduardo Mancera, Secretary of International Relations. He felt that those 'relations' were not being assisted by the twenty rebels.

Lorissa Kovalyova, a teacher at the University during the period spent there by the Ramirez brothers, confirmed to me that, 'The reasons they were expelled were not solely to do with their lack of progress academically, that particularly applies to Lenin. The reasons were also political.'

She also confirmed what fellow Venezuelan students had told me. Ilich did not go on any KGB terrorist courses. 'He did not even get to fire a gun at the Polygon.'

Polygon is Russian for firing range. Near every University in the Soviet Union there was a Polygon and military training facilities. These were primarily for Russian students; national service was compulsory in the Soviet Union for two years, starting at eighteen years of age. Soviet undergraduates were obliged to spend three months a year on their local University training ground. This was organized by the military department, Voennaya Kafedra, the words that had caused Carlos Two to threaten to have me murdered. That agent had clearly been fluent in the Russian language, just as many a member of Mossad or the Syrian Intelligence is.

The final piece of evidence for this part of the puzzle did not come to hand until mid 1992. The KGB file on Ilich Ramirez Sanchez.

Taken in isolation the information in the file would have to be regarded and considered with the deepest scepticism if only on the basis of Soviet Union self interest. Taken in conjunction with all the other evidence recorded in this chapter from a very wide range of sources it powerfully confirms the fact that Ramirez was not and never has been a KGB agent.

The Ramirez KGB file reveals that, like any other student at Patrice Lumumba University, the Venezuelan was considered for potential recruitment. The Personnel Department suggested in writing that Ramirez should be employed, but when the KGB Departmental Head reviewed the case history, particularly his 'appalling record as a student', he personally rejected the recommendation.

The file also reveals that Ramirez made several attempts in the 1980s to gain access to the Soviet Union, travelling on false passports. 'Despite his pompous and arrogant appearance and his posturing as a foreign diplomat', he was consistently refused entry.

TRAINING DAYS IN JORDAN

Bassam Abu Sharif confirmed to me that the account I had been given covering the period from July 21st 1970 to the end of January 1971 was, based on his own recollections, completely correct. Others within the PFLP who confirmed those details included the leader of that organization, Dr George Habash. The opinion that Habash held of Ramirez, that 'he was a good fighter', was based on this period, on the bloody events of Black September. Carlos Two's low opinion of the Baader-Meinhof members was shared by every Palestinian to whom I talked; others who had been with Carlos in Jordan in the summer of 1970 held an equally low opinion of him. While acknowledging his commitment to their cause, they also recollected what a pain he was. In an echo of those school reports from Stafford House, he was remembered as someone 'who was always running off at the mouth, thought he knew it all, wanted always to argue about tactics'.

Tactics were not the only aspects that provoked criticism from Ilich. Former members of those training camps recalled he was highly critical of the Palestinians confining their revolutionary aspirations to a homeland for their people and restricting their potential target to Israel. To Ilich Ramirez Sanchez, a man who at that stage of his life dreamed of world revolution, this was parochial thinking. What happened in Europe and Latin America was, in his mind, just as important. During this time Ramirez made his first contacts with a wide variety of Secret Services. Peter Boock, a protégé of the founding members of Baader-Meinhof, explained to me,

'It wasn't anything special at that time for so many secret services to be involved with Palestinian affairs. For example, the Iraqi secret service may have been responsible for the purchase of weapons, the Syrians for procuring cars and transport, the Saudi Arabians for the money to finance these activities. This was all done through their respective secret services, covert operations. There was not a single camp in Jordan where you could not find at least three or four representatives of these countries.'

On subsequent trips to the Middle East, trips that took Carlos to Beirut, Baghdad and Aden, he enlarged on these contacts, formed friendships across the international spectrum of what he saw as a global revolution, members of the IRA, the Red Brigades, ETA, the Turks and other movements. It was this absolute genius for forming potential liaisons that would keep Ramirez ahead in the killing game. That, and the organizational ability of Wadi Haddad. It was Haddad, not Moscow, who created what others have called the terror network; once Carlos became an active member of the Haddad group all of those contacts were available to him.

THE PLAYBOY OF KNIGHTSBRIDGE

Research in Holland, Latin America and London established very precisely the veracity of what Carlos Two had told me about his return from the Middle East. Having arrived in Amsterdam from Beirut on February 1st, 1971, the real Ilich booked into a small hotel. He then burned his passport and reported its 'loss' to the Dutch police. On the 3rd of February he applied to the Venezuelan Consul, Brigadier General Enrique La Cruz Parilli, for a new passport which was duly issued. He also telephoned to his mother's London home, which was now 12 Walpole Street, pleading that as well as the 'lost' passport, he was without money. Lenin was despatched to Amsterdam with funds. This enabled Ilich to be fully briefed by his brother on the state of play in the Ramirez household. He was particularly anxious about his waiting father's state of mind. Was he in for a roasting?

Such an interesting contradiction. On the one hand the twenty-one-year-old felt confident enough to argue vehemently with seasoned Palestinian guerrillas about tactics; on the other, having acquitted himself well through the dark days of Black September in Jordan, he comes scurrying home when Lenin's telex alerts him to the fact that Daddy is paying a visit to London.

The family conferences about Ilich's future were confirmed by Senor Ramirez Navas who also recalled the change of academic direction that Ilich was planning, away from Mathematics and Chemistry towards either Law or Economics. The trip to Paris to consider the Sorbonne also checked out but my own research threw up a further contradiction in the tale.

I had asked Carlos Two if he had contacted the Popular Front while he was in Paris. He had told me that he had not and that indeed his preoccupation at that time was to keep his father happy and 'to continue with education'.

During that stay in Paris the real Ilich did make contact, not with the Popular Front, but with members of Douglas Bravo's organization, who in turn communicated with Bravo. The former Venezuelan guerrilla leader had a very clear memory of this episode.

'First of all he expressed his wish to come and join the guerrillas in Venezuela, but at the same time he was now linked with the Palestinians. Subsequently he realized that it was not possible for him to come here. The situation had changed and because we are internationalists in that respect it did not matter where he took up the cause of the revolution. We lost direct touch with him.'

If I had been talking to the real Carlos this moment in his life would have been talked about. Douglas Bravo and his movement were the entire motivation for the Middle East training.

Carlos Two's comments concerning his registering for a degree course at the London School of Economics seemed for a long time to be yet another error. One probably based on statements made by his father to the press in 1975. There was no record of Ilich Ramirez Sanchez ever attending the LSE. Had son lied to father? Eventually I established the truth. The University of London, not the LSE, confirmed that Ramirez had indeed registered as an external student for the BSc (Economics) degree, but he did so for the term beginning September 1972 – a year later than stated.

Ramirez was indeed 'happy to continue his education' but on his own terms and in his own time. Lenin confirmed that in the period early 1971 to the autumn of 1972 his elder brother did attend a variety of lectures at the LSE, but 'it was all very casual, informal, if you came to a lecture, fine, if you did not, well no-one seemed to get excited about your absence'. Part of the mind of Ilich Ramirez concerned itself with deferring to his father's wishes but he also had other preoccupations. A close friend of Elba Sanchez, Nelly Arteaga, recalled a moment that perfectly illustrates this.

Nelly had first met some members of the Ramirez family through her brother, José Antonio, another Venezuelan who studied at Patrice Lumumba University. Unlike the Ramirez brothers, Jose Antonio had gone on to obtain a first class degree. In November 1970 José Antonio had introduced his sister to Elba and her two youngest sons. The friendship between the two women became a close one. Nelly was able to cast considerable light on what the father, Senor Navas, knew of his eldest son's activities in the Middle East at this time. In January 1971, with Ilich still far away in Jordan, she paid one of her frequent visits to the Walpole Street apartment.

'Elba said to me, "Look what I've got here, el viejo. The old man."

'Dr Ramirez had made a sudden, surprise visit to England. Nobody had expected him. I said to Elba, "Has he come to see the children?" She said, "I'll tell you what the problem is. We haven't heard from Ilich for two or three months. The whole family is very worried."

'Several weeks later I was in the apartment, talking to Dr Ramirez. We were alone, talking about politics. All of a sudden he started crying. Sobbing like a baby. I asked him what troubled him. He said, "I have no news of Ilich, maybe he is dead. Perhaps they have killed him. I just don't know."

'I asked him to explain himself. He said, "We think that he is in the Middle East training to be a guerrillero."

'We talked some more on this subject. I thought that the old man was merely being hysterical. Over-anxious about his eldest son. How could it be that this lad was in the Middle East? Soon after Ilich did indeed appear and I dismissed his father's outburst as the worrying of an over-anxious father. In early February 1971 I met Ilich for the first time. During my first conversation with him, I recalled how anxious both of his parents had been over his absence.

'"Where have you been, Ilich? Your father has been going half mad worrying about you."'

His response?

'I've been in the Middle East, learning how to kill Jews.'

At the time Nelly dismissed the remark as childish bravado. Soon afterwards she was married to a Jewish furrier, Lionel Isaacs. The witnesses were Ilich and Lenin Ramirez Sanchez. The wedding breakfast took place at the Ramirez apartment. Four years later senior Scotland Yard officers paid the Isaacs a visit; they wanted to know all about their friendship with the Ramirez family, particularly Ilich. They told the Isaacs of a death list compiled by Ilich: among the names on it, they said, was Lionel Isaacs.

That was still in the future as he went about the business of being a dutiful son. A son much admired and commented on not only by Nelly Isaacs but by many whom I interviewed who knew the family well during this period. Venezuelan Embassy staff such as Deborah Herrara, Alicia Aguereverre, Josefina Spiro. Social friends such as Maria Mena, Carlotta Wigglesworth. There are many more. There is a constant theme running through their various recollections.

Based on many accounts from differing vantage points all three Ramirez boys were dutiful sons. Polite and attentive to guests. Caring about their mother to an extra-ordinary degree. They accompanied her whenever she went shopping, shared out the domestic chores, something that appears to have been unique among young Venezuelan males of the period. Vladimir, possibly because he came to England at a relatively youthful age, became the most anglicized of the three. His clothes were more in keeping with the fashions of the time, Ilich and Lenin dressed more conservatively, youthful middle-aged men. Ilich controlled the family's budget and would remonstrate with his brothers if he considered they were being profligate, yet he was more than capable in the art of self-indulgence – an expensive silk dressing gown, an expensive box of Havana cigars – he was already showing the Hilton hotel mentality.

During the summer holidays, however, Ilich put his dark blue blazers and his three-piece suits back in the wardrobe, put on his jeans, packed a small bag and caught a plane to Beirut. The 'nice well mannered boy' was going back to get some more training.

Bassam Abu Sharif confirmed meeting Carlos again in mid 1971. George Habash also confirmed that at that time he renewed his acquaintanceship with the young Venezuelan and also introduced him to Wadi Haddad. In July 1971 the Jordanian Army was still busily engaged in killing Palestinian fedayeen but, according to the man I had met in North Lebanon and indeed the actual Carlos in his El-Jundi interview, Wadi Haddad had other plans in mind for the Venezuelan. Plans that would certainly not feature on any University of London degree course. They involved filling the coffers of the Popular Front through a series of kidnappings. The potential victims, who were to be held until an agreed ransom had been paid, were wealthy Arabs resident in London.

Hard as I have tried, no evidence has come to light of any such activity in London during the latter part of 1971. The very nature of such operations in which the petrified target would be only too thankful that his life had been spared mitigates against such evidence ever becoming available but the circumstantial evidence indicates that such operations, if they occurred, were part of a continuing secret agenda for Wadi Haddad. Members of Haddad's section of the Popular Front have confirmed to me that such activities did take place during the 1970s but they dismissed any involvement by Carlos before December 1973.

There is no doubt that Haddad did indeed have such a secret agenda and that it was put into action on a number of occasions. Examples such as the Lufthansa hijack and subsequent ransom payment of five million dollars have been recorded in an earlier chapter. Haddad also indulged in massive extortion, including blackmailing the State airline companies of certain countries to take out 'insurance' running into millions of dollars per year.

The offer was simple: pay or your planes will be hijacked and destroyed.

Carlos Two had, in North Lebanon, gone on to recount Haddad's plans for him not merely to kidnap but to murder. He had claimed the target was the Jordanian Ambassador, Zaid Rifai. Concerning his own involvement, members of the Popular Front scornfully dismissed his statements.

'You must understand, Mr David, Wadi Haddad's evaluation of Carlos concluded that, very largely, he was a fool. Someone to be used perhaps, but only under tight control. He would never have given Carlos anything important to carry out as early as 1971. Maybe he met a couple of our people at the airport, that would be it, no more. This Carlos, so much air.'

As previously recounted, before Haddad's group could effect their attack on the Jordanian Ambassador, they were pre-empted by Black September, the PLO's in-house terrorist group, who succeeded in wounding Ambassador Zaid Rifai.

A senior police officer who at the time of this attack was a member of the Arab Squad of the Special Branch talked to me at length of the subsequent police investigation. The police soon established the identity of the leader of the Black September killer squad, Khelfa Sahel, who had obligingly left a string of clues all over West London. The police alerted all departure points from the country with a full description. Due to appalling incompetence by the police and customs officers manning the Folkestone departure point, Sahel was able to escape on a ferry to France. He made his way to Paris. Special Branch traced him to the French capital and a warrant for his arrest was issued. He was promptly pulled in by members of the DST. Two Special Branch officers immediately flew to Paris and requested that they be allowed to interview Sahel. Permission was denied. The French authorities, not for the first time and certainly not for the last, then set about colluding with a terrorist organization to ensure that an individual wanted for a very serious crime should escape.

The two Special Branch officers had an artist's impression of Sahel, a good one. They managed to view him through the cell peephole. It was their man. Double confirmation came when it was established that the fingerprints on the sub-machine gun used in the attempt on the Ambassador and those of the man being held in a Paris police cell matched. Suddenly the issue became 'diplomatic'. There were long telephone conversations between members of the French government and the British Foreign Office. The two Special Branch members sat doggedly in the Paris police station awaiting developments. Eventually they were advised that Sahel had been taken to Marseilles where he had been put on a boat to the Algerian port of Skida. These events, recorded here publicly for the first time, give a graphic illustration that perfidy occurs on both sides of the English Channel.

Information made available to me from DST sources completely confirms the accuracy of the above account, with one very ironic addition. The French were anxious to placate the British police; as a sop they gave them the name of a man in London who they assured their British colleagues was the real ringleader of the attack on Ambassador Rifai. The name had been fed to them by Mohammed Boudia, the name given was that of a man whom Boudia had never met but his contacts told him was 'a pain in the arse. Someone we would be better without.' The name was Ilich Ramirez Sanchez.

Irony now became farce.

On December 22nd, 1971, just eight days after the attempt to murder the Jordanian Ambassador, armed Special Branch officers carried out the raids and subsequent interrogation of Ramirez that are recorded in an earlier chapter. Lenin Ramirez confirmed very precisely to me all of the details. They exactly matched those I had been previously given by Carlos Two. Ilich Ramirez did indeed talk his way out of this situation, including explaining away the false Italian passport that he had carelessly left on the mantelpiece. He was free to continue his dreams of world revolution. Dreams that would eventually become a reality of murder and mayhem.

There was a curious postscript to this episode. I was advised by senior serving members of Special Branch that there is no record on file of this armed raid. I was offered from police sources an explanation for this omission from Special Branch files by a senior officer.

'The problem is that at the time you're talking about [December 1971] there was no centralized computer system. If that raid was carried out by officers based at Chelsea, they may never have sent details of the operation to the Yard.'

Perhaps, or did someone remove that particular cock-up from the files after the rue Toullier shootings?

Carlos Two had asserted that as a result of that visit from Special Branch officers, he was put on ice by Wadi Haddad, but it was not quite like that.

Abu Nidal's response was derisory: 'Put on ice? You make him sound like a key member of Wadi Haddad's group. Listen, Haddad did not even consider Carlos had any use until late 1973.'

Abu Iyad confirmed this view. 'It is simply fantastic these stories of Carlos here, Carlos there, Carlos almost everywhere. It was not until the end of 1973 that Carlos was allocated his first operation and then he botched it. Carlos began as an irrelevance to our fight, he remained one. Sure, he had his uses, but to say he was "put on ice in 1971" makes him into someone important. If it is important to the Palestinian strugle to have an inept troublemaker then Carlos was important.'

A Front member and close colleague of Haddad added, 'When Haddad learned that Paris had passed the name Ramirez to the DST, I remember him saying to me, "You see, I told you the Venezuelan would be useful." "Put on ice"? No, Wadi Haddad chose to ignore Carlos. He had more important things to concern himself with.'

If Carlos Two had wholly misrepresented the role of his alter ego in Haddad's greater vision of the future –

based in no small measure on the statements contained in the El-Jundi interview by the real Carlos – he scored very highly on the facts of an operation which is not mentioned at all in that interview – the killing of Wasfi Tal. Carlos Two had alleged that the Jordanian Prime Minister, although targeted by Black September, was in fact murdered by his own Jordanian security guards. I never could get my hands on the Coroner's report on Tal, but in the light of other information it became superfluous.

The Godfather of Black September, the man who decided the targets, planned the operations and picked the death teams, was Abu Iyad.

'Yes, that is totally correct. At the moment that my men raised their guns outside the Sheraton Hotel in Cairo, Wasfi Tal's bodyguards opened fire, not at our people, but at Tal, the man they were supposed to be protecting. At first we believed that we were responsible, but later, through my contacts in Jordan's secret service, I established the truth. I was also informed that the widow of Wasfi Tal was eventually told what had really happened. What concerned me more than who had actually killed the man was the fact that our security had been infiltrated. The Jordanians knew what was going to happen and when it was going to happen. As for Sadat's prior knowledge and CIA complicity, you must draw your own conclusions. I would merely say to you that if the Jordanian secret service had prior knowledge, and they did, then the CIA also had prior knowledge; the Jordanian secret service and the CIA have been playmates for many many years.'

The claims made by Carlos Two concerning his activities in London between December 1971 and the summer of 1973 were highly accurate. There would come a time when his name would be linked with a number of the atrocities that occurred around the world during this period. The facts show that there is no link. He was no more involved, for example, in the massacre at Lod Airport in May 1972 or the Munich Olympic Games attack that took place in September 1972, than I was.

Many members of the Venezuelan circuit living in London confirmed his continuing presence in the city throughout this time, even including the fact that he spent his summer holidays with the other members of the Ramirez family in July and August 1972. Records prove that he and his family moved from 12 Walpole Street to Flat 4, Phillimore Court – first floor, two bedrooms, twenty pounds per week – signing a three-year lease in February. He attended many official embassy functions and continued his sessions at the Royal Kensington Rifle Club. He also registered as an external student for a BSc Economics degree at the University of London. In September 1972 he started work as a Spanish teacher at the Langham Secretarial College in Park Lane, and in October he met Nydia Tobon for the first time at the Colombian Centre in Earls Court Square.

There was also an interesting additional activity, one that the real Carlos would surely have included in his account of that period, the renewing of his contact with a former teacher, particularly as the real Carlos had insisted on being in her class.

The real Carlos might be excused for neglecting to mention that he had become a member and frequent visitor of the Playboy Club and Churchills – a night-spot where the group known as the Princess Margaret set could be frequently seen – such decadent behaviour might conflict with a revolutionary image. But to forget that in September 1972 he applied for and was given a government grant to attend the Central Polytechnic for a variety of courses was less likely, particularly as the Russian language class he insisted on joining was run by a lady who was the last teacher he said goodbye to at Patrice Lumumba University – Lorissa Kovalyova. At that time he had offered a one-line explanation to her for his expulsion from the University.

'Girls. Then more girls.'

Now he had come back, if not to haunt her then at least to cause the maximum disruption during her lessons. In view of the fact that Lorissa was teaching

Russian for beginners she was puzzled as to why Ramirez, after having in his own fashion completed the one-year preparatory course in Russian at Patrice Lumumba University, should wish to start again on the bottom rung of the linguistic ladder. Head of the Russian section at the Central Polytechnic, Mr Bondaryenko, told her that the Venezuelan had been particularly anxious to attend her lessons. She agreed, then asked Ramirez why.

'He told me that he wanted a better understanding of spoken Russian. During the course of the year's work he would constantly distract the attention of the rest of the class. When we would have group discussions he would begin to argue about "the revolution". This was supposed to be a period of conversational Russian and Ilich would continually turn it into a political discussion. He attempted to persuade his classmates that the Russians had yet to experience the revolution, that they were bourgeois and that they, the class, should form a group with him, travel to the Soviet Union and start a revolution.'

'And what was your response to that?'

'I would take him out into the corridor during the break and tell him that he must not disrupt the class in that manner. His response was to suggest that we should both go back to the Soviet Union and start the revolution.'

'Just the two of you?'

'Yes.'

'Was he serious?'

'I don't know. He seemed to be but he might well have just been playing the fool.'

Shades of Fermin Toro and Stafford House.

The reason he chose this particular teacher? I think it becomes apparent from another section of one of my interviews with this charming but perhaps slightly naïve woman.

'Sometimes when I would take him out into the corridor to remonstrate with him he would suggest that we saw each other socially. He wanted to take me out for drinks, for meals, wanted to come back to my home. I do have a recollection of having a drink with him on one occasion, but no more than that.'

Thus every Monday evening from September 1972 to June 1973 Ilich Ramirez Sanchez is very precisely placed: Central Polytechnic, Red Lion Square, London. Lorissa was also able to confirm seeing Ramirez during the day at Central as he attended other course work.

Perhaps if he had chatted less and listened more at Central, the LSE and the University of London, he might have achieved a better result when he sat part one of his degree examination in June 1973. He scraped a pass in Economics, 46 – it must have been a male teacher – and failed in his other four subjects, including Russian, where he could only manage 23.

So full of contradictions this man. He mouths on about starting a revolution in the Soviet Union. Talks to Lorissa of his campaign plan. 'First we must organize a massed group, one that is really reliable. Then after that, movement.' Yet he makes no mention of his training in Jordan with the Popular Front. On the other hand he continues to talk among the Venezuelan set of his hatred of Jews and his love of Arabs.

The real Carlos claimed in the interview he gave El-Jundi that during this period, although he did nothing on behalf of the Popular Front, he was engaged in other 'revolutionary activities'. Ironically Carlos Two in the version he gave me was much nearer the truth. Between 1971 and mid 1973 there is not a shred of evidence that the real Carlos engaged in Europe in anything more revolutionary than attempting to persuade his Russian teacher and her class to join him in taking on the Soviet Union. He was for the entire period no more than an armchair revolutionary, a playboy of Knightsbridge. The evidence is overwhelming that in terms of terrorist activities Carlos remained a virgin until December 1973.

Having failed to get his Russian teacher and his English pupils at the Langham Secretarial College into bed might deter some men, but not Mr Machismo. October 12th, 1972 was his twenty-third birthday. It found Carlos at the

Colombian Centre in Earls Court at a modest party that was being given, not for his benefit, but to celebrate Race Day. Also there alone was a Colombian woman, Nydia Tobon.

If Nydia is to be believed, Ramirez also failed in his sexual aspirations towards her, but in many respects he had found a soul mate. Two Latin Americans living in a foreign city, both espoused beliefs that were far left, both equally enjoyed the capitalistic decadent way of life, both would have indignantly denied that last observation. They spent their first night at the Colombian Centre talking until dawn, then Nydia drove him back to his mother's flat at Phillimore Court.

As indicated in earlier chapters Nydia Tobon has a highly selective memory. The reason for that became clear to me during my years of investigation when she finally admitted to Maria, one of my researchers, that she is in love with the man who materially assisted in her spending a period of time in an English prison. There is obviously unfinished business between her and Ilich Ramirez.

His line in chat to her leaves something to be desired. In 1973, when the Watergate scandal was beginning to break, he remarked,

'I want to see socialism triumph all over the world. We are being governed by the CIA, by thugs such as Truman, Johnson, Nixon. In the name of what? Of democratic principles!'

Having delivered himself of a few hundred yards of his ideas for a world revolution, Ilich Ramirez would then return to the comfortable apartment in Phillimore Court, an apartment paid for by his father. Prior to retiring he would slip into his silk dressing gown, pour a large Napoleon brandy and light an expensive Havana cigar, all, like the rent, paid for by his father.

Unusually for Ramirez, during the first few months of his friendship with Nydia he managed to refrain from talking about his training in the Middle East. There were the inevitable pro-Arab and anti-Jewish remarks but no inkling of any secretly cherished aspirations to take an active role in the Palestinian struggle. There is of course an excellent reason for that. Until the middle of 1973 he did not feature in Haddad's plans. It is crystal clear that he never would have. Wadi Haddad only moved Ramirez onto the list of possible players because of a specific Mossad operation.

Ramirez continued to study in his own half-hearted way, continued to enjoy the social round with Elba. On February the 5th they attended an Embassy reception given by the Venezuelan air attaché. He asked the official photographer to take a shot of his little group, mother and a couple of friends. Typically, he never paid for the photograph. There he stands with that lopsided grin, so unbeloved by the girls he kept trying to target. Given the fact that he constantly drooled from over-salivating, he was very resistible.

In the real world of the Arab-Israeli conflict, life and death went on. Ramirez, from all contemporary accounts, remained unmoved by the shooting down of the Libyan airliner by Israeli fighter jets on February 21st, untouched by the Black September attack on a diplomatic reception in the Sudan on March 1st, and uncaring of the IRA explosions at the Old Bailey and Whitehall on March 8th. As spring moved into early summer he had other preoccupations, as Nydia Tobon told me.

'I continued going out with Ilich. We would go to the Serpentine, to Hyde Park, to the Festival Hall, he particularly liked the music of Tchaikovsky. We would go to little pubs on the Fulham Road, cafés in Soho and Bayswater. During this time [the first half of 1973] I met his mother on a number of occasions and also his brothers. Lenin would frequently come to parties with us and entertain. He's a very good musician and singer. Unlike Ilich who has a voice like a frog and cannot play a note.'

Nydia herself had by now begun a two-year degree course at the LSE arranged by Ilich. While the Venezuelan would-be revolutionary struggled with work for his Economics degree, the Colombian left-winger got down to grappling with 'Social Planning in Developing Countries'.

They were perhaps destined to open an exclusive private school for foreign students in Kensington until Mossad blew up Mohammed Boudia in Paris on June 28th, 1973.

COMMANDO BOUDIA

Records that I have obtained confirm that Ilich Ramirez flew from Heathrow to Paris using his legal passport on July 24th. Catching a coach to Orly, he then brought a false passport into play.

As he approached passport control at Orly to board a direct flight to Beirut he had become a Chilean citizen, José Adolfo Muller Bernal. Careful examination of his passport would have resulted in his immediate arrest. It was riddled with errors. His supposed Chilean birthplace, Quillota, was incorrectly spelt. The forged stamps that showed the bearer had in theory travelled from Chile to Madrid on 10th June 1973 recorded a physical impossibility. Further forged entries indicated the holder was in Kuwait at precisely the time he was presenting his passport for examination at Orly. Fortunately for Ilich Ramirez, Orly was full of holidaymakers that day. His passport was duly stamped and he climbed onto the plane. It was hardly the most promising of starts for a man who was planning to persuade Wadi Haddad that he was the person to fill the vacancy created by Mossad. What makes his carelessness even more inexcusable is that this is a man, as Peter Boock told me, with a self-professed interest in such fine details.

'Carlos always had a weakness for the kind of people who were logistic experts. Those who knew what flights were available from point A to point B. How one could enter a certain country undetected. This interest stemmed from his many connections with a wide range of secret services and the multifarious roles he played with those secret services.'

Boock was the Baader-Meinhof member who was closer to Wadi Haddad than any other non-Arab, a fact that was confirmed to me by several Arab members of the Haddad group. Their relationship spanned most of the 1970s. His opinion, therefore, on the likelihood of Carlos being handed the mantle of Mohammed Boudia is particularly pertinent.

'I am convinced that Carlos did not take over from Boudia. Haddad simply would not have entertained the idea. Having Carlos do a particular operation or even a number of operations, that was one thing, but running an organization, never. Wadi Haddad's view of Carlos was so clearly defined that he would never have dreamt of authorizing him to have control over a complete branch of the organization.'

Popular Front sources who were close to Haddad during this period confirmed just how accurate that evaluation by the young German was.

'Sure Carlos came out to Beirut in the summer of 1973 and when he met Wadi Haddad he tried to persuade the Old Man to let him take over the Paris operation. Wadi Haddad laughed. Laughed in his face. "You're little more than a boy," he told him. "It's men I need."'

Undeterred, Ramirez continued to argue his case. Eventually Haddad agreed to let him become a full-time member of the Paris unit, working under and strictly taking orders from its new leader, Michel Moukharbel, but before he became a full-time member there would be a test of his ability. A target would be selected for him, he would be advised, given a gun, then it was up to him.

Carlos Two scored excellent marks for his accuracy of the account he had given me of how Ramirez had become a full-time member of the Haddad section of the Popular Front. This begs so many questions. I was told repeatedly by many in the Middle East, including Abu Iyad and Abu Nidal, that Mossad never succeeded in penetrating Wadi Haddad's bases in Beirut, Aden or Baghdad. In Europe, as the killing of Boudia demonstrates, they achieved very successful infiltration, but never in the three main bases. Had another intelligence service succeeded where even Mossad had failed? How could Carlos Two have been so accurately briefed? Was the real Carlos a party to the disinformation exercise that targeted me?

On September 25th, 1973, Carlos flew back from Beirut to Orly. Arriving at Orly he again switched passports. He proffered the false Chilean document that indicated his name was José Adolfo Muller Bernal to the Customs, again he encountered no problems. He then caught a flight to London and a British Immigration Officer (339) obligingly stamped a six-month visa into the false passport. Courtesy of French and British Customs he now had a legal visa and a new identity.

As autumn moved into early winter Nydia detected a change in Ramirez.

'He became worried. Something that I did not understand was making him tense. We went on a marathon of meals, luncheons, cafés, wines, dances, pints of beer. Then, one afternoon, after a trivial chat with two pints of beer in front of us, he told me, "Nydia I have formed a group. I need your help."'

Without waiting for her reply he launched into a monologue which began to seem endless. In essence a justification for violent revolutionary struggle, an explanation of the fact that he was about to leave the armchair and take arms against a sea of capitalistic troubles. Eventually, several bottles of wine later, when he had subsided into silence and she could get a word in, she told him that she was in agreement with his aims and would join him. Refilling their glasses he said,

'Nydia, I am not Ilich. I have stopped being him. My name is Carlos . . . simply Carlos. From now on you will call me Carlos.'

As far as British Customs were concerned, he was José Adolfo Muller Bernal from Chile, which indicates how confusing life was about to get for those around Ilich Ramirez Sanchez.

More significantly, the fact that before he had carried out his test, his first operation for Haddad, he was already talking of having formed a group indicates the kind of problems that lay in the future for his Paris boss, Michel Moukharbel.

In November 1973 Nydia was with him at the Phillimore Court apartment when Senor Ramirez Navas telephoned from Venezuela. What followed was not without poignancy. His father told him that he had just won a big legal case. Ramirez Navas would often take legal work on a contingency basis, particularly with regard to marriage settlements or estate disputes. A straight fifty per cent of any settlement.

'I've just won this case. A big one. I've got five hundred thousand Bolivars [approximately 125,000 dollars]. They're yours my son. Come back and spend them.'

'Daddy. I can't leave this place. Don't get sad. I love you a great deal. I'm not going back and you have to understand that. It was you who showed me what life was about.'

After the phone call Ramirez became depressed.

'My poor old man. I know he'd be happy if he could have us all together in Venezuela. What would I do there? Drive fast in a big trendy car and be chased by all the ambitious girls. Get frustrated as I multiplied his money? That's not one of my life's ambitions. It would weigh on my conscience. That is not my world.'

A few days later he left for what was his world – a briefing from Michel Moukharbel, a briefing on his first target. This time he used yet another passport. Now indeed he was Carlos. Specifically Carlos Martinez Torres, a Peruvian economist. While in Paris he telephoned Nydia asking her to join him. He was waiting for her at Orly airport. He took her to a café on rue de L'Ancienne-Comédie called the Parrot's Tavern. They were on their first Martinis when a slim man of medium height approached; he looked for all the world like a waiter. He was Michel Moukharbel. Born in Lebanon of a well connected family. Well educated, including degrees from the Sorbonne. Totally dedicated to the Palestinian cause.

Nydia observed of him, 'He was a very obsessive man and capable of engaging in anything for that cause, even not considering those around him. People were not important, he was only concerned with moving them around like chess pieces.'

As Ramirez had done, Moukharbel began to discuss the revolutionary struggle for the Latin Americans, the Vietnamese, the people of Chile, and particularly for the Palestinians. 'It is the struggle of a people for a land that belongs to them and from which they have been expelled.'

Later he said to her,

'It must be very clear to you that, no matter what, I am called André.'

The need for war names, the moving in and out of identities – such an essential part of groups like Haddad's – was a particularly confusing aspect of the exercise for Nydia, as I discovered during my interviews with her. So many names. So many games.

From that moment on Nydia became involved in, as she put it, 'Tasks that I had not foreseen on my agenda. A part-time housewife. A centre that provided a home. The woman who dealt with their small problems. Who decided where we should go. What shopping needed to be done.'

While in Paris, the life she had known in London with Ramirez began to be replicated. Parties. Meals. Discos. She recalled:

'One evening the three of us were in the Latin Quarter. Suddenly, at a square near St Stephen's Church, we found a group of Latin musicians who, despite the fact that they were playing so enthusiastically, were being ignored by the passersby. No-one put any money in their hat. I said to the two men, "Come on, let's do something, let's shout or dance because they need help." So Carlos and I started to dance a tango, followed by a cumbia. People began to stop and take notice. Michel passed the hat around. The group had enough for their dinner.'

What a charming picture it presents. When Ramirez left Paris for London with Nydia he was carrying the gun that Moukharbel had given him. He also had been given his first assignment. The murder of Edward Sieff.

Others too had their assignments. Before they had left Paris Carlos had pointed out at a party a particular man, a Turk, yet another with many names. Nydia was told he was known as Abub. Carlos told her that he was planning a big one. He certainly was. French Intelligence sources have confirmed to me that their raid on the headquarters of the Turkish People's Liberation Army forestalled an attempt by the group to assassinate US Secretary of State Henry Kissinger. My research established that Kissinger spent the 18th and 19th of December in Paris and flew to Geneva on the 20th to attend a Middle East peace conference. The Turkish group were planning to assassinate him after his arrival in Geneva on the 20th December, 1973. Before they could leave their base on the outskirts of Paris on that day, the DST pounced. Yet again the man in North Lebanon got full marks.

When Carlos and Nydia returned to London a few days before Christmas 1973, they came back to a city still attempting to recover from a series of IRA attacks. Bombs had gone off near the Home Office in Westminster, near Pentonville Prison and in Hampstead. In Italy at Rome airport thirty people were burned to death and a further forty injured as they sat in a Pan Am 707 – victims of a Palestinian attack. These were violent times. The Venezuelan was about to make his first contribution to them.

Before that event there was time for him to meet, chat up and bed the young Basque woman, Angela Otaola. To Angela this man with the multiplicity of names and nationalities was the Peruvian economist Carlos Martinez Torres. The affair did indeed have the additional bonus of another safe house, but it was from his mother's apartment in Phillimore Court that he set out on Sunday 30th of December to murder Sieff. Again my own research confirmed that the other members of the Ramirez family were away on holiday that Christmas. Among others who confirmed this was Ronald Beet, who was at that time the caretaker of Phillimore Court.

My interview with the man who headed the Special Branch aspect of the police investigation into the attempted murder of Edward Sieff, former Detective Chief Inspector John Hurrell, confirmed for me that the account I had been given by Carlos Two of this attack was clinically accurate. He also confirmed that contrary to all press reports it was indeed a 9 mm Beretta revolver that was used in the shooting. Both would-be killer and victim had unusually good fortune that evening. Edward Sieff's teeth deflected the one bullet that Carlos managed to fire just enough to save his life. His wife had seen their terrified Portuguese manservant coming up the stairs with Carlos, gun pushing into the man's back, prodding him on to the bathroom. She quickly withdrew into her bedroom and telephoned the police. Her call was timed at two minutes past seven. At four minutes past the first patrol responding to the plea for help arrived at the house in St John's Wood. Carlos had gone.

A month before the attack Mr and Mrs Sieff had been among the guests of honour at a reception given by Israeli Prime Minister Golda Meir. Two months after the attempt on his life Edward Sieff accepted the Presidency of the Zionist Federation of Great Britain.

The description that the police issued of the attacker was very accurate. 'Arab looking. Aged about 25. Height five feet eleven inches. Slim build.' At that time Carlos was aged 24. His height was five feet ten inches and he was of slim build.

A few days after the attack, Nydia Tobon told me, Carlos recounted the full details of his attempt to murder Sieff to her. He was particularly chagrined about the misfiring bullets. He also said to her,

'This operation was a test that Wadi Haddad and Moukharbel put me through to test my courage and loyalty. It seems that they are satisfied.'

Indeed they were. By Haddad's view of the world – terror yet more terror – he could be tolerant about what was in the final analysis a bungled attempt at murdering one of Great Britain's leading Jews. In England talk of death lists of other prominent Jews abounded. Armed guards became again for many of them the order of the day, each tightening of the terror screw giving the man in Aden an additional bonus.

When Carlos suggested a daylight bombing of an Israeli bank in the City of London, Haddad gave his immediate approval. No-one died or was seriously injured when, parking the Ramirez family car directly outside the bank, Carlos opened the double doors and threw a box containing plastic-explosive bombs at the counter. Carlos had held the double doors of the bank open with one hand as he raised the other and threw the box. This action had caused him to relax the arm holding the doors, they came back on to him, hitting the box of bombs as he was about to throw it. His throw was deflected and the box slipped across the polished floor before it exploded.

Two botched operations but a great deal of terror.

A pattern was now emerging through my continuing research. When Carlos Two talked of attacks or operations his information was very accurate. As it undoubtedly originated from the intelligence files of a number of countries, that was to be expected. If, for example, his masters were Mossad, the Israeli secret service would have access not only to their own intelligence-gathering services but to a host of others. They share intelligence data with the French, with the British, with the Americans, with the Germans. This interchange is two-way. Equally, a number of Arab countries have similar ongoing arrangements with all of the above-mentioned countries. Unknown until now is the fact that the Israelis also have such an arrangement with Syria; not perhaps to the same degree, but despite the fact that these two countries have been officially in a state of war with each other for many years there has also existed a hidden agenda. Discreet meetings, invariably in a third country, are a regular feature of this hidden agenda.

To record just a few examples of many that I acquired: In March 1988, Uri Lubrani, Israel's main negotiator

429

on Lebanon, conducted secret talks with President Asad's close adviser, Ala Adin Abedin, in Bucharest.

In November 1988, Syria's deputy foreign minister, Youssef Shakur, met Lubrani, who conveyed a personal request from Prime Minister Shamir asking for Syria's help in preventing guerrilla penetration from South Lebanon into Israel. This meeting took place in Vienna.

In January 1989, back in Bucharest again, two members of Syrian Intelligence, Colonel Ibrahim Sabouh and Major Naim Zanika, were given intelligence information by Lubrani and David Jocoby on two of Asad's most dangerous rivals, Muslim Brotherhood leaders Saad Adin and Munzer Watar.

There is not merely a hidden agenda between these two countries that are publicly at each other's throats. There is also a secret peace settlement, brokered by the United States; the bottom line – no acts of war on the Golan Heights. Syria, to all intents and purposes, has accepted the permanent loss of the Golan. The rest is public posturing for the benefit of the Syrian people.

When Carlos Two talked to me of returning to Beirut in early February to plan with Moukharbel and Haddad the next operations, the information he gave me was embellished by intelligence shared sources and probably also by the fruits of continuing infiltration of Palestinian factions by secret agents. They were not able to infiltrate Haddad's inner sanctums in Beirut, Baghdad and Aden, but both Israeli and Syrian agents have undoubtedly infiltrated the PLO, the Popular Front of George Habash and a great many more.

The intelligence data-based information that Carlos Two was in essence sharing with me proved again and again to be established as accurate during my own long hunt for the truth. When he talked of bombing newspapers in Paris, attacking an Embassy in Holland, a café in Paris and other outrages, again and again what he told me checked out. One senior member of French Military Intelligence who continued to be extremely helpful and co-operative over a long period of time remarked to me,

'You know, David, I've come to the conclusion that you have had previous access to our files on this Carlos.'

He was absolutely right. Courtesy of Carlos Two, indirectly I had.

Significantly, it was in the areas that are not covered in such files that Carlos Two and his masters made most of their mistakes. Errors that could not possibly be eliminated without direct access to some of the people whom I have interviewed. For example, Carlos Two had been adamant that his 'father' knew nothing of his secret life and was ignorant of his 'work' on behalf of the Palestinians until the events of rue Toullier and its aftermath in late June 1975 revealed the reality.

His father, however, contradicts this:

'Lenin always knew exactly what his brother was up to. I did not know until Lenin returned to Venezuela in 1973. He had come back temporarily to organize his University degree in this country. From 1973 I knew what Ilich was doing.'

Senor Navas subsequently recounted details of his 1974 visit to Europe during which Ilich Ramirez spent several weeks with his father, in Paris and London. On the last night of the father's stay his eldest son took him out for the evening. It was destined to be the last time in their lives when they could meet openly and publicly, though neither knew that at the time. Retrospective significance apart, the father's account throws a very different light on the question of who in the Ramirez family knew exactly what concerning the secret life of Ilich Ramirez. It also reinforces the demolition of what Carlos Two had said to me on this subject.

'We went out to the El Sombrero (a nightclub below Phillimore Court). We stayed out very late. When we came back to the apartment all the lights were on and everybody was still up. The family were worried sick that something had happened to both myself and Ilich. They all knew of Ilich's involvement with the Popular Front

431

and they had been fearful that something had happened to him.'

Carlos Two, of course, could know none of this. Neither did he know that the real Carlos spent time with his father in Paris. His father's recall of his time with Ilich Ramirez inevitably dwelt on the everyday. Buying a postcard and writing a message of endearment for a friend to carry to Cuba in the hope that it would reach his former love and mother of his daughter, Sonia. On another occasion buying a parcel of children's clothes destined for his child. Ramirez together with his father went several times to the Cuban Embassy in attempts to locate Sonia, who continued to ignore the cards and letters he wrote. He persevered in his attempts to re-establish contact with this woman whom he loved. Those attempts were to have, in mid 1975, bizarre influence on at least one member of the French government.

In London, Ilich took his father on a number of occasions to the Playboy Club. The would-be big time gambler, who would boast to some in his circle of his exploits at the poker table, liked to watch the action at the Club. He also had an eye for the Bunnies.

Apart from continuing to play the roles of dutiful son, penitent lover, man about town and would-be leader of Haddad's European operations, Ramirez had other strands in a hectic existence. He was busy, always busy, making contacts. With the Turks. With the Corsicans. With the Germans. With a wide variety of Arab secret services. He would move in on relationships that Moukharbel had carefully nurtured over a number of years with Boudia and attempt to hijack these elements to his own corner, his own version of the revolution. It was cause for increasing friction between Ramirez and Moukharbel.

Ramirez, the boy whose teachers considered he talked too much and knew too little, had become a man who thought he knew everything. He also considered that he was God's gift to women, an opinion that was at some variance with the men I talked to who knew him well at this time. The Palestinians were scathing. A member of Haddad's group said to me:

'Most of us felt that he was better suited to running a brothel than being involved in our struggle. He spent so much time in the company of prostitutes I became convinced that he was pimping.'

It was an opinion strongly echoed by Peter Boock.

'As far as women were concerned he always thought he was irresistible. This was contrary to the opinion of most of the women I knew who had met him. They thought he was puke. In view of the fact that his affairs often took place in the same circles that we moved in, it was even said, "It does not seem quite clear, but has Carlos opened a brothel?" That seemed to be his scene in any case. The majority of women around who were not on the game did not particularly want to have anything to do with him.'

The majority perhaps, but there were exceptions. Among them a twenty-one-year-old blonde from Copenhagen, Inger Weille.

In May 1974 Carlos was having a drink with Moukharbel at the latter's apartment on Avenue Claude Vellefaux in the 10th Arrondissement. They ran out of ice. Carlos walked across the passage, knocked on the door and asked Inger for some ice cubes. She was invited to join the party and the Carlos chat-up went into operation. He told her he was Lebanese and that his name was Johnny. This name was much used by Carlos at the time. The chat led to arak on the rocks and tapes of Arabic music and very rapidly to bed. Inger became his mistress.

'He told me he wanted to show me the wonders of the Middle East. I fell in love with him the same night.'

To Inger, this 'impeccable dresser, who favoured expensive restaurants and on the dance floor had a great sense of rhythm' was 'a businessman who travelled a lot'.

Their affair lasted six months, until October 1974, at which time she decided to move to Los Angeles. Predictably, Carlos asked her for the use of her Paris apartment, but she declined. Ever the thoughtful lover, he drove her to Charles de Gaulle airport and kissed her goodbye. Later he wrote to say that he had paid her electricity bill and to wish her a Merry Christmas. During their affair he never did get around to showing her the 'wonders of the Middle East' but Inger did get to see some of the 'wonders' of Paris.

'We would make night-time tours of the Parisian demimonde. We frequently visited kinky subterranean clubs. I was shocked at the unrestrained sexual activity. Johnny just stood and looked. He never mistreated me, he was a gentleman, very quiet, very generous.'

His generosity seems to have been boundless. Apart from Inger from Denmark, there was Amparo Silva Masmela from Colombia. She was also the recipient of thoughtful little gifts from Carlos, a pretty tablecloth that his mother had given him, a box of hand grenades and a carton of guns that Haddad sent over with a courier, and a baby. This latter gift was less welcome and Carlos paid for her to have an abortion. There were the fellow Venezuelans, Nancy Sanchez and Maria Teresa Lara. In London there was the Basque Angela Otaola and the ever constant Nydia Tobon. There were undoubtedly others. His German and Palestinian comrades might well be dismissive of his prowess but the man clearly had something going for him. Many women, not former lovers, members of the Venezuelan community resident in London for example, who knew him still talk of his charm, his politeness. To them he was courteous and thoughtful. A good son, a generous host. Appropriately, many men lurked inside this man with so many names.

At Easter 1974 Ramirez chanced to meet another of his former teachers from the Central Polytechnic. Frank Esterkin was holidaying in Paris when he happened upon the Venezuelan strolling the streets. Ramirez gave him a message for the woman whose Russian lessons he had continually disrupted with his talk of the need for revolution.

'Tell Lorissa I've started.'

Self-advertisement was a constant weakness with Ramirez. As the man who replaced him in the affections of Angela Otaola, Barry Woodhams, observed,

'I'm surprised that he didn't walk around with a T-shirt that had written on the front, "I am a terrorist".'

Some of Carlos's women friends, such as Inger Weille and Nancy Sanchez, would have been very surprised at such a slogan on his T-shirt.

One of Nydia's functions that Carlos Two had neglected to talk to me about, because he did not know of it, was to serve as a willing donkey, someone who takes the risk of going through Customs with illegal objects.

In early July, when a member of the Japanese Red Army attached to Haddad's group, Takomoto Takahashi, had brought a very large consignment of weapons, ammunition and explosives through French customs and into France, Carlos Two had recounted to me how he and Moukharbel had dispersed them to various places. Some were easily moved to the exclusive art gallery in rue de Verneuil, others were taken by donkey to Geneva. There had been no mention of Tobon's role in this affair.

Nydia Tobon enlarged on this area of her activities:

'At the beginning of July 1974 I was asked in Paris by Carlos to take a black suitcase with me to London. It weighed a lot. Carlos told me to look after it well and that I should not put it anywhere near a fire as that could be dangerous. Carlos gave no explanation and I did not ask for one.'

In view of the instructions any explanation was, of course, superfluous. Nydia's idea of a safe place was a flat in Knightsbridge. She left the case of arms and explosives in a wardrobe, then sublet the room to a Colombian friend and went to Cambridge for the summer. With accomplices like Nydia it is amazing that Carlos was not exposed and arrested long before the affair at rue Toullier.

Nydia, again acting under instructions from Carlos, telephoned Angela Otaola and arranged a meeting. At Snows Bar in Piccadilly, Angela handed over to the

Colombian woman a heavy metal case; more weapons and bombs to be stored in the wardrobe at Knightsbridge.

When I had questioned Carlos Two about the multiple bombings of the newspaper office in Paris and the attack on the French Embassy in Holland, he had been very forthcoming. He had, for example, told me that he had returned from Holland to prepare for the attack on Le Drugstore on Friday, the 13th of September. My own research established that this was correct. Using the Chilean passport, Carlos Andreas Martinez Torres caught Air France Flight 917 at 21.35 from Amsterdam. There had been, however, one story about which he had rather coyly declined to enlighten me. It concerned one of his former comrades in arms, Antonio Pereira.

'I will just tell you that Antonio Pereira vanished. If you want to know how then ask the DST. I think perhaps they will be too embarrassed to tell you.'

It was one of a number of tasks that Carlos Two threw at me. All part of a brilliantly rehearsed performance. It had added powerfully to the credibility. 'Don't give it all to him on a plate, make him hunt a little but control his hunt. It will preoccupy him and certainly distract him from other areas where we might be vulnerable.' As previously noted after the death of Samir in Beirut I took nothing as fact, everything was checked out. This inevitably included those areas where Carlos Two and his masters were only too happy for me to probe. The affair of Antonio Pereira was one such area.

He was right about the DST, the serving members that is. Certain retired agents were more frank. In view of the fact that for a long time I suspected the Brazilian Pereira and the Ecuadorian Anton Bouvier were one and the same, my investigation into Pereira went deeper and deeper. The hunt for the truth took me from Brazil to Chile to Algeria to France and to Italy.

On March 3rd 1969 in Brazil, Pereira was arrested for the 'crime' of being a 'dangerous intellectual'. He was held for nearly two years. He was never charged, never tried, never sentenced. His story is told in full in Appendix Three. Here it is enough to record that on December 7th, 1970 a group of guerrillas seized the Swiss Ambassador to Brazil and demanded the release of seventy prisoners, including Pereira.

They were flown to Chile the following January. Behind him Pereira had left his wife and daughter; the Brazilian regime had refused to allow them to leave.

From Chile, via Algeria, Pereira and some of his fellow prisoners had by March 1971 reached Paris, where the French government eventually granted them the right to remain as political exiles. He began to create a new life. By 1973 he was involved with a wealthy Brazilian woman, Mohammed Boudia and Moukharbel, the Japanese Red Army and an exclusive art gallery. Exactly what the owner of the gallery, Jean-Charles Lignel, knew, I have been unable to establish. Like the Brazilian who worked for him, Lignel, the son of a wealthy and politically powerful family from Lyons, has vanished.

Certainly by early 1974 the art gallery functioned as a safe house where letters could be left to be forwarded and arms and guns stored, with or without Monsieur Lignel's knowledge or permission.

When Japanese Red Army member Yamada was arrested complete with his interesting variety of passports and thousands of counterfeit dollars, Carlos and Pereira headed the operation to obtain his release, resulting in the attack and hostage taking at the French Embassy in The Hague and subsequently the hand grenade attack on Le Drugstore. There is an irony in Pereira's involvement in the operation on the Embassy. While he was busily planning and liaising with other Red Army members, Yamada, the man they were trying to free, was singing his head off to French Intelligence. Among the other things he told them about was Pereira's involvement in the Haddad group. For good measure he also gave them the address of the art gallery. By the time the DST acted upon this information the attacks in The Hague and at Le Drugstore had taken place. It was the beginning of 'the embarrassment' to which Carlos Two had referred. It got worse.

A squad of DST officers led by Commissioner Herranz squealed to a halt in the fashionable rue de Verneuil, rushed into an art gallery and began interrogating the proprietor in front of his clientele. It took some time before Herranz was satisfied and, rubbing his chin in bemusement, left. He had been sure that the information was first-class. The cars roared away.

Herranz had raided the wrong art gallery – Galeries Verneuil – just a few doors away from where Pereira stood in the window of his own gallery watching.

By the time Herranz had sorted himself out, Pereira had disappeared with his latest girlfriend. My information, from French Intelligence sources and individuals who had been close to Pereira at this time, is that he went to Milan, forgot all about world revolution and settled down with his latest mistress, a Contessa.

At about the same time as Antonio Pereira vanished into the mists of Milan, Nydia Tobon had also decided to find a new address. She moved to Hampstead, to Downshire Hill, a quiet road off Rosslyn Hill, just a few moments' walk from the local police station. She brought with her to her furnished room, rented from one of her lecturers at the LSE, the suitcase of guns and explosives she had brought over from Paris and the black metal case containing a further variety of arms and explosives that she had taken from Angela.

In October the IRA began to give a further demonstration that Ramirez and his colleagues did not have a monopoly when it came to acts of mindless horrific violence. Their new campaign caused Nydia concern.

'Apart from the IRA bombing campaign, my son used to invite his friends around to my room. Also the police had stepped up their patrols and surveillance in the area. I got in touch with Carlos who advised me to move the suitcase of weapons to a safer place.'

In view of the fact that apart from other services she

supplied to Carlos she also acted as a London banker for him, her next course of action was bizarre.

'The taxi journey between Hampstead and Hans Road used to cost about six pounds at that time. It was not expensive but I was short of money so I decided to go by tube. I had to walk a fair distance with the case. I went down Rosslyn Hill past the police station. Once I arrived at Belsize Park tube station I saw at the entrance that there were several policemen posted who were searching any suspicious looking parcels. It was impossible for me to turn back. Controlling my nerves I stood next to them while waiting for the lift which was to take me underground. I finally arrived at Hans Road and left the suitcase in the wardrobe. At that time Guban, a Turkish student, was staying there and I asked him to look after the suitcase until I could find a flat somewhere nearby.'

Soon after this extraordinary performance, Tobon told me, Carlos came to London. Her memory was accurate. I established that he attended a diplomatic reception at the Venezuelan Embassy in London during October. Either before or after drinking chilled white wine and talking politely to the Naval Attaché, Ramirez came round to Nydia's Knightsbridge room. Evidently the Turk was out for the evening.

'He asked for the suitcase. He needed to check the contents, air them and lubricate the parts. When he opened it and took out the black metallic box he smiled like a child. He stared at me and said with affection, "Look, my love, this beauty is a Czech pistol, an M52 high speed automatic. It's great." Carlos drew it to his mouth and blew. It was done very gently, like the first kiss of love.'

Nydia then recounted how he gave her lessons in how to use the hand grenades. She recalled that he caressed his guns and then justified his behaviour.

'He said, "Look, I have to take care of this because it is an extension of my arms. My life depends on them working well, my duty is to love them, take good care of them. The worst that can happen to one is that it jams when you most need it." '

This was less than a year after just such an occurrence had saved the life of Edward Sieff.

That attempted murder had been his 'test of courage', his initiation rite into the Haddad group. Then he only merited a very old Beretta and five bullets, most of them duds. Now, a mere ten months later, he was delivering lectures to Tobon on the art of killing; for hand props he had the full range, from new Czech automatics to hand grenades. He had graduated.

During this visit he gave Nydia one thousand pounds to bank on behalf of Moukharbel. When the group was exposed after rue Toullier, allegations would be made that she handled vast sums on behalf of the organization. Nydia denied this emphatically to me and insisted that the entire amount she handled between the autumn of 1973 and the summer of 1975 was no more than two thousand pounds in total. Analysis of Moukharbel's obsessive jottings covering the expenditure of a few francs would tend to confirm this. In those pre-automatic, twenty-four withdrawal days Nydia represented immediate access in London to money for emergency use. The theory was excellent. Nydia ensured that the practice left something to be desired. The monies that she was given to hold were passed on by her to a fellow Colombian, Anna Pugsley, who held on her behalf a bank account in Canadian dollars. Hardly immediate access, particularly over a weekend.

THE INTELLIGENCE CONNECTION

Research suggested that the CIA and French Intelligence had intervened more than once to protect this man with an ever increasing tally of murders to his name. If it were true it painted a truly horrific and cynical portrait of world affairs.

One of my sources was a former member of French Intelligence, the other a former member of the Latin American Desk of the CIA. I am acutely aware of the inherent dangers of relying on such sources. After my experiences on this particular investigation it would be extraordinary if I were not. Both sources assured me that their information was based on documentary evidence, both declined to make that evidence available. There is, however, external evidence that supports these allegations. It came to me from many sources, Palestinian, Italian, German, Syrian and Saudi Arabian. It concerned the deep relationships that had been fostered over the years by Carlos with many intelligence services. Carlos Two had certainly been briefed on this aspect. More to the point, Carlos himself, through the mouth of one of France's most famous lawyers, confirmed in 1982 that he did indeed have such 'an understanding' with French Intelligence.

An understanding that has allowed him to continue with his appalling work. An understanding that explains why today he is still alive. I asked the former CIA agent why Carlos had been protected by the Agency.

'Looking after one of their own.'

Abu Iyad confirmed the duplicity of Carlos to me:

'Carlos had and still has many masters. To my certain knowledge he has carried out operations for nearly one dozen intelligence agencies. I'll name them for you and some of the jobs he did for them.'

'Do they include the CIA?'

'The CIA regard Carlos as an asset. You tell me what they mean by that.'

Peter Boock was equally revealing on another 'understanding':

'I know for a fact that Carlos had an agreement with the French Secret Service. It began in 1974. The agreement he had with them was that he would not be touched on French territory, whether in France or in any of the French colonies, as long as he did not step out of line. Carlos of course did step out of line but the agreement still held. I know for sure that at that time and onwards from then, he must have been dozens of times in France and certainly not in any sort of undercover way. It was almost as if he were spending a holiday there and nothing ever happened to him. There were similar agreements between the French and other groups.'

What Peter Boock told me was independently confirmed by a number of individuals, members and former members of terrorist groups. Unlike Boock they have asked not to be publicly identified. Boock takes a more sanguine view. He is after all serving three life sentences. Abu Iyad was another who considered Carlos was safe from retaliation:

'The French frequently had champagne receptions where the really top people in the Secret Service had a close look at the top terrorists and the top terrorists had a look at them. The Secret Service would make use of these relationships at a later date. In the interests of France.'

Boock was also familiar with these get-togethers. 'These functions took place near Paris. Almost like State Receptions. Carlos was at these functions and so were members of the Red Army.'

These two men, Abu Iyad and Peter Boock. One in a maximum security prison in Germany, the other surrounded by his own version of maximum security in Tunisia. Neither knowing what the other had said to me. No contact with each other – I checked that with German Security. Each confirmed again and again what the other had said.

'There was a similar arrangement with the Italians, with the Greeks. With the Germans? Yes and no,' stated Boock and then went on to elaborate. He explained that the BND, the West German Secret Service, attempted a number of times to establish a relationship with the PLO. The thrust of their negotiations was the offer of an agreement between the two organizations that would give the PLO the responsibility of controlling the other Palestinian groups, the Popular Front, Abu Nidal, Ahmed Jibril and the other splinter groups, to ensure that they did not carry out actions on West German soil. In return the West Germans offered a range of intelligence data. It was a wildly optimistic proposition. The PLO has never been able to exercise full control over people like Nidal and Jibril. West German Intelligence had but to consider what had happened when the Spanish Secret Service had tried to formulate a similar agreement. Abu Nidal promptly broke it and continued to target Israelis and Israeli facilities based on Spanish soil.

If British Intelligence has a similar agreement they have been more successful at keeping it hidden. What is beyond doubt is the overwhelming evidence I have been given that British Intelligence does have placed in the very highest echelons of the PLO a number of Palestinians who are, and have been for many years, British agents.

With regard to German involvement in these highly questionable activities and Boock's enigmatic 'yes and no', subsequent research and direct contact with the East German Secret Service, Stasi, established that part of the 'yes' referred to East Germany; like virtually every other Warsaw Pact country their secret service had deep relationships with a wide range of terrorist organizations in general and with Ilich Ramirez Sanchez in particular.

If the West German Intelligence Agencies enjoyed less than complete success in arriving at a secret accommodation with the PLO, they were more successful with the groups controlled by Syria. Christian Lochte, having confirmed that French accommodation with a large range of terrorist groups including Iranian-controlled units continues to the present day, turned his attention to secret accommodations between Germany and Syria.

'The Government have an agreement with Asad. No actions on German soil. He accepted that, thus German loans destined for Syria were released and diplomatic relations could continue. This does not of course prevent Syrian-controlled groups from planning terrorist operations on German soil and perpetrating them in another country or indeed breaking the agreement they have with us.

'We have a similar arrangement with the Iranians. They have of course broken it. One of their pilots defected, bringing his plane. The Iraqis paid him one million

443

dollars. The Iranians murdered him in Hamburg. A second pilot was shot in Geneva, also by the Iranians. As for our arrangement with the Syrians – they sent a commando unit to murder a Muslim student based in Aachen. We caught them in a hotel in Bonn. No arrest. No trial. They were put on a plane back to Damascus.'

Once again the question came to mind, 'Who guards the guards?' What kind of world do we live in when the very men and women whose sworn duty is to protect society from terrorism actively consort with the terrorists?

How can it be that Ramirez, frequently referred to as 'The World's Most Wanted Man', is protected, given sanctuary by those who in theory, but not in practice, are hunting him?

RAMIREZ AND BOUVIER

When Carlos Two had talked of the two rocket attack operations at Orly airport in January 1975, his highly detailed account omitted one very significant fact. He had told me of the German Weinrich and his involvement, of the Algerian leader of the commando group, of his Palestinian comrades. There had been no mention of another German. At the time of the interviews I had no knowledge of his presence at Orly; more to the point, neither did Carlos Two. In view of the fact that this man was not merely a long-time friend of Ramirez's but also his most important link to the German groups, that omission was to me further proof that I had pulled another brick out of such a carefully constructed Chez Carlos. The other German who accompanied Ramirez on these two operations was Wilfried Böse. His name does not appear on any intelligence data that I have seen on the Orly attacks, which is perhaps why Carlos Two had no knowledge of his presence at the airport. My own sources for this information are a former member of Haddad's group and Nydia Tobon.

Shortly before these attacks Böse had travelled from Frankfurt to Paris to see Carlos and do a little business with some Austrian airline tickets.

444

Accompanying Böse on this trip was yet another German, Joachim Klein. Meeting the Venezuelan at Moukharbel's apartment on Avenue Claude Vellefaux, he was initially underwhelmed.

'I thought at the time he was an American Mafioso.'

He became more impressed when Böse subsequently told him that Ramirez, 'Fought in the war in Jordan as the only foreigner there and led a commando unit in Paris.'

During that first meeting, Carlos, in a scene reminiscent of the one that he had played out in Nydia's Knightsbridge room a few months earlier, displayed and played with some of his lethal toys.

'In the evening he showed us some of his guns. The Scorpion, it's a very small Czech machine gun, 7.65 calibre. It can be carried in the pocket like a pistol when you fold it up. He also showed us some pistols. Egyptian secret pistols. This was all done by Carlos with great calm, as if he was showing us his stamp collection.'

Klein was another whom Carlos Two neglected to talk to me about when recalling various events of January 1975. Like Böse, Klein would prove before the end of that year trustworthy enough to play a part in the Vienna operation.

A second meeting with Böse and Klein in Paris during February 1975 had also escaped the memory of Carlos Two. Present this time was Moukharbel. The item under discussion was the freeing of the Baader-Meinhof group leaders, currently languishing in a West German prison. Carlos Two had indeed talked to me of the plan, involving wholesale carnage in Germany. The operation envisaged attacking a foreign embassy, kidnapping a wide range of diplomats, blowing up the Chase Bank in Frankfurt and *Quick* magazine in Munich and, if the German government was still proving obdurate, a further bomb outrage involving twenty kilograms of high explosive and a luxury hotel. An operation that potentially involved the murder of hundreds of people to free a few psychopaths.

Wadi Haddad began to put the pieces together for this appalling sequence of events. His desire to get the

Baader-Meinhof leaders out of prison was not in the slightest way motivated by the plans of Baader-Meinhof to create anarchy followed by revolution in Germany. Haddad never did anything, never involved his group in any operation that did not have in his mind some advantage, some gain in his war against Israel. With the Japanese Red Army now reduced to insignificance in his operations, he needed replacements if he was to continue that war. Germany offered rich potential for recruitment. Weinrich, Böse, Klein and a number of others were already committed; if he could unlock the prison cells of the Baader-Meinhof leaders he would not only have them as additional pawns with which to play, the propaganda value would be enormous. Every German revolutionary, be he or she RAF, 2nd of June or Baader-Meinhof, would rally to his cause, to his war. There was also another reason why freeing the Baader-Meinhof leaders got priority treatment – money.

The German operation called for a very substantial financial budget. Not only the best personnel but the best equipment. Haddad needed to get his hands on a large amount of money very quickly.

Exactly where all the money that Wadi Haddad continued to collect throughout the 1970s went remains a mystery. Running his Paris-based European HQ was costly, mounting the wide variety of terrorist attacks was expensive, but his kitty was very large. It included so many donors. Frightened Arab rulers like the Kuwaiti and Saudi Royal families weighed in with annual donations running to millions of dollars. The very threat of assassination or kidnap was more than sufficient to ensure they paid on time. Equally prompt with their payments were three European airlines and one American airline; between them they turned over millions each year. At least one European airline paid over a million dollars per year to European terrorists to ensure that its aircraft were not attacked. A substantial part of this was passed on to Haddad. State subsidy of terrorism. For Haddad the words 'I have adequate funds' did not feature in his lexicon, hence the fund-raising operation in April 1975 of kidnapping the United Arab Emirates Ambassador to Great Britain, Mohammed Mahdi al-Tajir.

Investigation of what Carlos Two had told me of this operation established that it was correct in every detail except one. Ilich Ramirez Sanchez and Anton Bouvier are not the same person.

The most persuasive piece of evidence that Carlos and Bouvier are two different men and not, as Carlos Two insisted to me, one and the same came from one of Britain's top plastic surgeons, who subjected photographs of the two men to a detailed scientific analysis. Point by technical point he destroyed the claim that had been made to me. To the lay eye there is indeed considerable similarity; to the professional a range of differences, some small, others significant, left him in no doubt. Two different men.

Carlos Two had made a mistake, a fundamental one. Having established beyond all scientific doubt that Anton Dages Bouvier did indeed have a life force of his own, I thought through the possibilities. Was it possible that Bouvier was indeed a senior KGB officer? Carlos's controller? This had been the claim made by a number of writers. Then there was the problem of why Carlos Two had made such a mistake. He was so well briefed on the life and activities of the man he was impersonating, how had *his* controllers got that one wrong?

From a number of sources, ranging from British police to Nydia Tobon, I established at least part of the story of Bouvier. Later Peter Boock and a former member of the Haddad group known as Khalid helped other pieces of the puzzle fall into place. What emerged was not the hand of the KGB but that of Wadi Haddad.

When I showed Peter Boock a photograph of Bouvier he said,

'Yes, I know who that is. He was a member of the Haddad group. I only ever saw that man in South Yemen.'

Khalid was more informative.

447

'I knew him [Bouvier] well. I'm sorry but I cannot tell you his name, his real name. I have no idea where he is now and I will do nothing that might lead to his or any comrade's arrest. He was highly regarded by Wadi Haddad, a trusted man. That is why Haddad sent him to London. Even then [early 1975] the Old Man had his suspicions about Carlos, did not fully trust him. Remember there were millions of dollars involved in this kidnap. I believe that Haddad was making sure that he saw all of the ransom money.'

Examination of just a few of the facts on Bouvier quickly reduce the allegation that he was a senior KGB officer controlling Carlos on behalf of Moscow to fantasy. Bouvier flew into London from South Yemen in early April 1975. Like all Haddad operatives his journey was deliberately broken to mask his original point of departure. Bouvier changed planes in Paris and was met at the Cromwell Road Terminal by Nydia Tobon. She had been given the job of 'minding' Bouvier while he was in the British capital. There was an excellent reason for this, Bouvier did not speak a word of English. There are of course plenty of KGB officers in that category, but what would make this one unique was the passport on which he was travelling – a false Ecuadorian one and a very poor forgery at that. It was identical to many to which Haddad's group had access. In a few months' time the French police would find six false Ecuadorian passports at a Carlos safe house in Paris. That a senior KGB officer, or indeed a junior one, would be travelling on such a risky document beggars belief. The KGB have access to genuine passports from a number of countries.

Bouvier had two roles in the planned kidnap. The first was to keep an eye on Carlos and any ransom money. The second was to function as negotiator. A fluent Arabic speaker able to talk to al-Tajir's embassy was vital for the operation.

Bouvier initially stayed with Nydia Tobon at her Earls Court flat. Then, posing as her husband, he signed the

448

lease on the Comeragh Mews apartment that was destined to be the Ambassador's temporary prison. While the final details of the lease were being resolved Nydia Tobon and her 'husband' spent three days at the Victoria Garden Hotel in Westbourne Terrace before taking up residence at their very smart mews flat. When the plan to kidnap al-Tajir was aborted Bouvier returned to South Yemen. His false Ecuadorian passport was left with Nydia Tobon in case the kidnap plan was reactivated. Bouvier used his genuine passport for his return to the Middle East. The false passport has been the source of much delight to writers over the years as they wove elements of KGB involvement into their tales of Carlos. Antonio Dages Bouvier – would the KGB be so dumb as to allow one of their operatives to use a middle name that is non-existent in Ecuador?

As for why Carlos Two made such a mistake – the answer I believe can be found within the files of Special Branch and Scotland Yard. It is clear that after the British police arrested Nydia Tobon and linked her not only with Carlos but with the false Bouvier passport, notwithstanding what they told the British media, they were privately convinced that Carlos and Bouvier were indeed one and the same. The following extract from one of the many interrogations to which Nydia Tobon was subjected illustrates this.

The police officer is Chief Inspector David Munday.

'Why is it that you told us it was Bouvier who gave you the passport and later you said it was Ilich?'

'I made a mistake.'

'Are you sure it was Bouvier?'

'Yes, and not Ilich.'

'You are lying to us.'

'No, that's the truth.'

'Why did he give you the passport?'

'I don't know. He asked me to keep it.'

'Was there a photograph in Bouvier's passport?'

'Yes.'

'He doesn't wear glasses, does he?'

'No . . . well . . . he sometimes does.'

'It was Ilich and not Bouvier who gave you the pass-port, right?'

'No, it was Bouvier.'

'He looks like Ilich, yes or no?'

'Yes, they look alike.'

'If he shaves the moustache off and takes off his glasses Bouvier could become Ilich, right?'

There was no response from Nydia Tobon. The police drew their own conclusions and noted them in their reports. I believe that whoever trained Carlos Two obtained access to those reports and drew the same conclusions.

During the time that Carlos stalked Ambassador al-Tajir in April 1975 the tensions between him and Moukharbel were moving towards a violent confron-tation. The Venezuelan, never a man who modestly held back from expressing his opinion, was virulently critical of his boss. He told Nydia Tobon that under no circumstances should she take any instructions or orders from Moukharbel without first checking them with him. He considered his Lebanese leader to be arrogant, wilful, uncaring about the risks that he ordered members of the group to take. He raged about Moukharbel.

'He is a man without scruples, capable of throwing us into any adventure to satisfy his ego. The guy is mad. He's going too fast. We will have a trial. I will state the case against him because it is extremely serious. To play with comrades' lives is treason, whether they belong to our organization or others that help us.'

Nydia managed to interject while Carlos drew breath.

'Don't you think you're exaggerating?'

'Go to hell. When will you wake up. You're fucked.'

Not much of the charm and graciousness so much admired by the Venezuelan set in that interchange.

When Carlos gave vent to that diatribe his boss, Michel Moukharbel, had less than two months to live.

THE RUE TOULLIER AFFAIR

The other members of the Ramirez family had by now left London. Lenin had returned to Caracas in the previous September. Lenin who has now 'forgotten' so much, including according to his father the fact that, as 1974 was drawing to a close, he was deeply concerned that his elder brother's increasing activities on behalf of Wadi Haddad were going to lead sooner or later to danger for the rest of the family if they remained in England. Also doubtless 'forgotten' by Lenin but recalled for me by his mother's close friend Deborah Herrara was Elba's panic when after yet another IRA bomb attack in West London her Phillimore Gardens apartment was suddenly full of police officers. It was merely a precautionary security check of the entire building but Elba remained on a knife edge while they checked out her flat. With her dear son Ilich one never knew what he might have tucked away in a wardrobe.

In February 1975 Elba Sanchez and Vladimir returned to Venezuela, in their case by an unusual route, via Amsterdam. One final meeting with Ilich, the son she was so close to?

I have already drawn on my long interview with Barry Woodhams in an earlier chapter. Some of Barry Woodhams's observations are also very relevant to an understanding of Ramirez.

'I'd met him a few times well before I moved in with Angela. He'd come to Garway Road when she lived there, my flat was next door. I'd also seen him and talked to him a few times in a Paddington drinking club called Angelo's. I've no recollection that he ever talked about his family. He was all for the good time. Used to talk of going down to Churchill's Club, of his big time poker schools. His English was very good, very precise, clipped, but very good. To Angela he invariably spoke in Spanish. He would like to be regarded as an extrovert but I didn't think he was. He was very money orientated. There was something about his behaviour. I'm not talking about after I looked into his suitcase, before that. I could not put my finger on it but that is why I opened that case, because of my suspicions.

'But in that period before the shootings in Paris if I had any thoughts about Carlos being involved in the terrorist scene I thought he was probably working for the Israelis.'

The Venezuelan, having aroused Woodhams's suspicions, albeit in the wrong direction, would stroll out of Angela's Bayswater flat and rejoin his commando group.

Nydia Tobon:

'On one occasion a police patrol car stopped the car we were travelling in for excess speeding in the centre of London. Our driver wanted to get his gun out and shoot our way through. Carlos jumped like a tiger to stop our comrade, then he jumped out of the car in a friendly and jovial manner and apologized to the police. Back in the car he lectured the driver. "This must never happen again. We have to remain calm, be cold-blooded. Remember that a firm pulse depends on a cold head."'

Excellent advice, but not something he always practised himself. Nydia recounted how every day they drove along High Street Kensington. One particular shop, a boutique called 'Che', always provoked the Venezuelan.

'Every time he passed it Carlos would shout, "Bastards! You sons of a bitch! To call a commercial place after a guerrilla fighter. I want to blow the place up. Teach them a lesson. To do business with the name of the greatest revolutionary in the world."'

The sequence of events that culminated in Carlos killing Michel Moukharbel, two members of the DST and seriously wounding a third has been fully recounted in an earlier chapter. That account, based not only on what I was told by Carlos Two but also my own research, stood up very well when after Samir's death in Beirut I began again at the beginning. I would have been very surprised if it had not done so. Carlos Two and his controllers had done their homework on this affair very well. If the second investigation of this period in the life of Ramirez threw up no obvious contradictions, it did, however, shed further light on the man and his deeds.

Ramirez, the real Carlos, talked much in the interview with El-Jundi of his betrayal by Moukharbel. Betrayal there most certainly was, but not by the Lebanese. The betraying was done by Ramirez. His ego, his arrogance, his inability to practise what he had preached in London to 'remain calm, be cold-blooded' ensured that Wadi Haddad's European centre was destroyed, not temporarily but permanently.

There were no signs of that calmness much prized by Ramirez when he telephoned Nydia Tobon at midnight on the 15th of June.

'There was a sound of alarm in his voice. He told me of André's [Michel Moukharbel] arrest in Beirut, said I must get out of the Comeragh Mews flat immediately. He was worried about CIA and Mossad involvement in this affair.'

Whatever disciplines and self-control applied to Moukharbel's group from the time of Boudia's killing in June 1973, they all dissolved within the space of a few weeks. Moukharbel's own stupidity in flying direct from Beirut to Paris with a caseload of compromising documents was but the first of a series of fatal mistakes: his premature contacting of Carlos, at a time when common sense should have told him that he might well be under DST surveillance; his flight to London to hide with Nydia; Carlos's determination that now was the moment for him to seize control of Haddad's European centre of operations; his series of panic phone calls to Nydia.

'Don't do anything he [Moukharbel] tells you without confirming with me. Remember this man is mad. He can get you into trouble without you knowing it.'

That, Nydia Tobon recounted to me, was one of his milder observations when Carlos telephoned her from Paris on June 20th to warn her that Moukharbel was on his way to London. Two days later the rising panic of

Ramirez was clearly discernible when, again telephoning Nydia, he learned that his boss had vanished.

'Shit! I'll call the old man because this has to be sorted out.'

The summoning of Böse to Paris from the relative safety of London, an instruction that virtually ensured the arrest of Böse, was yet another error. Nydia Tobon also told me that when she then went in turn to Paris, just days before the bloody climax of this affair, Carlos not only declined to come back to London with her but also attempted to persuade her to stay in Paris, permanently.

All of these incidents overwhelmingly establish that cool calm judgement had gone out of the window long before Ilich Ramirez did the same at rue Toullier.

There is no doubt in my mind that the DST officers were indeed unarmed when they went to the rue Toullier, the clearest possible evidence that Moukharbel had not betrayed Ramirez. Indeed, Ramirez's subsequent actions make it abundantly plain that his allegations about his dead comrade were merely his own attempts to cover his appalling ineptitude. Ramirez would not have rushed directly into the arms of his mistress Amparo Silva Masmela at the rue Amélie apartment if he had had the slightest suspicion that he had been betrayed. Moukharbel also used that safe house, indeed it was where his accounts and his incriminating diary were eventually discovered by a highly incompetent French Secret Service. Peter Boock shed an interesting light on these facts.

'There were so many things that Carlos was involved in that did not succeed, precisely for the reason that he was incapable of operating within a collective. He was never punctual. He would never adhere to the rules. For example, when he was retreating from the rue Toullier he did not adhere to the agreed escape route. A route created by Wadi Haddad. Instead he went off and climbed into bed with his mistress.'

Boock declined to enlighten me about the agreed escape route. He was, though, very informative about

Moukharbel and the likelihood that he had betrayed Carlos.

'It is inconceivable. Firstly because of the general assessment of the man [Moukharbel]. He had such a stable reputation that you cannot imagine him doing something like that without concrete evidence. Secondly the way that Wadi Haddad behaved. It was clear from the various investigations that he caused to be made that he believed Carlos had a hidden agenda. One of those agreements he was so good at making. Namely that the French Secret Service had an agreement with Carlos, knew all about him, accepted his presence in France.

'If that is correct then it explains why the DST went to the apartment unarmed. Now, if Moukharbel had been ignorant of that agreement, and with Carlos that is a strong possibility, then through a blunder by the French security, bringing him into that apartment, he suddenly became aware of it . . .'

That Carlos panicked is a fact, whatever reasons induced that panic. The catalyst was realizing that he would have to accompany Herranz and his men down to DST headquarters. Carlos was aware that the interrogation of Moukharbel both in the Lebanon and in France had not been confined to polite questions and answers, physical violence had been used. There was a very good chance it would be used on him.

Peter Boock:

'There is something which has always been absolutely clear about Carlos. He has this tremendous fear of physical violence and this is one of the reasons why he has always in this situation been the first to pull out a gun and the first to use it.'

'So he is a physical coward?'

'Yes.'

None of these various aspects of course was considered when Carlos leapt out of the rue Toullier apartment and directly onto the front pages of the world's press. They were unknown and uninvestigated at that time, they have remained obscured and hidden until now.

Instead a myth was created. A myth of a cold-blooded, highly professional killer. Carlos the Jackal. A man whose ultimate masters were the KGB. A man who had been unleashed by the Soviets in the mid 1960s. A man responsible for virtually every act of terrorism that had occurred from that time to the moment of triple murder in rue Toullier.

16

· THE TRUTH – PART TWO

Across Boulevard St Michel, along Boulevard St Germain, onwards to rue Amélie, to his mistress, Amparo Silva Masmela. His panic and sweating fear, his mad irrationality increasing with every moment . . .

Wadi Haddad had planned for moments like this. Emergency escape routes, alternative courses of action, these were second nature to Dr Haddad. For Carlos that route involved contacting the Algerians, directly. He chose instead a very unsafe house, an apartment crammed with guns and bombs, an apartment that had been used by the now late Michel Moukharbel. He poured out a story of self-justification to Amparo; the account failed to satisfy his need to convince not only her but many other people that he was a much wronged man. He phoned London, attempting to contact Nydia Tobon. His first call to her at about 9.30 pm London time must have been made within minutes of his arrival at the rue Amélie apartment.

Nydia was out, dining with Venezuelan friends in Bayswater. A young friend of her son's, a Colombian named Juanito, who had never met Carlos, took the call. When Nydia returned at eleven he gave her the message.

'Carlos phoned, just after nine. He said to tell you that André [Moukharbel] is dead. You should not leave the house until he calls you back. You are to stay calm and not to worry too much.'

As she waited for his next call Nydia Tobon began to work her way through the file of documents connected with this dark side of her life. Letters, photographs,

Bouvier's passport. Those that would be of use in the future, like the passport, were placed in envelopes, others were tossed into the waste basket.

Carlos was equally busy. He telephoned his mother in Caracas and told his tale, a story of justification. Breaking every Haddad rule, he telephoned the Middle East: a series of Popular Front members were woken up and given the same tale, and eventually he contacted Haddad, determined that his version should be the first that would be heard by 'The Old Man'. Haddad said little, other than instructing Carlos to take 'the agreed route'. There would be plenty of time for the post mortem later.

Carlos wrote a number of letters, one was to the Special Branch at Scotland Yard, another was to the DST. He accused the British and French police of a variety of criminal and treasonable activities. The British police, Carlos alleged, as he named a number of officers, functioned as little more than CIA and Mossad agents. The letter to the DST accused six named officers of being under 'the absolute control of the CIA and Mossad'. It also accused the same six men of collaborating in the assassinations of the former PLO representative in Paris, Mahmud Hamchari, and Iraqi Popular Front member Dr Basel Kubaisi.

Two letters were also sent to Angela Otaola in London.

Dear Angela,
As you know things have gone badly here and I am off. I didn't telephone you because I had to tear up your card. I am sending you this letter twice, at your house and at the bistro, so that if anything happens to me and if I got the address wrong, one of them will get there. Don't call my girl friend any more, I am going away for an unknown amount of time but I hope to be back soon. As for the 'chiquitin' I have sent him to a better world for his betrayal.

The letter that went to the bistro was wrongly addressed. It would soon end up in the hands of the British police, who until that moment had remained ignorant of Nydia Tobon's involvement. A few questions to Angela, who had said nothing about Tobon so far, and her resistance broke. The letter from Carlos led directly to Nydia's arrest.

It was by now three in the morning, the 28th of June. Carlos telephoned Nydia once more. Again the need to get his version heard first. Again the self-justification of the unjustifiable.

'I had to do it. I told you he was a coward. You know that the police caught him. He told them about us. He took the police to Nancy's flat. I had to shoot my way out. I couldn't avoid it. I killed André and several men fell. Remember what I told you about him. About his cowardice?'

There was a great deal more in similar vein. Eventually Nydia asked for instructions.

'What do I do with the envelopes you asked me to keep, the papers, the passport [Bouvier's] and the other things?'

'Each envelope is already addressed, just buy stamps and post them first thing in the morning. You can destroy the other papers. Take the passport out from your house immediately. Don't worry, you have to be strong, remember never to look back, because if you do you get scared.'

A moment later he was gone. During their conversation she had told him he must get out of Paris at once and asked if he would come to London. He had failed to respond, merely continued to blame everyone else for the situation in which he was now enmeshed. He also failed to grasp even a fragment of his own culpability.

'I am going to contact somebody because I have to get out of here fast. I must tell my friends. I can't allow all the work that has been done to collapse. We've got to prevent people getting caught. Help them escape while this mess is cleared up. Moukharbel just fucked it.'

Moukharbel had plenty of company.

Nydia sent the Bouvier passport to fellow Latin American, Anna Pugsley. Unfortunately for her, Tobon incorrectly addressed the envelope. In a few days' time, after the Post Office had failed to locate what was a non-existent address, the letter would be opened and the Ecuadorian passport forwarded to that country's London embassy. Realizing immediately that it was a rather poor forgery, the embassy officials would then send it to Scotland Yard. Anna Pugsley was due for a visit.

As dawn broke in Paris, Carlos was still writing letters of self-justification. Another was sent to the woman he had just spoken to, Nydia Tobon. All around him as he wrote were vital tasks left unfulfilled. Moukharbel's diary, his accounts, the plans they had created before the multiple bombing of the newspaper offices the previous year, a large range of false passports, including six blank Ecuadorian and an international selection that Carlos used.

He made no attempt either to destroy this mountain of incriminating evidence or to move it to safer quarters. The hand grenades, originally stolen by members of the Baader-Meinhof group (evidence that the DST would eventually link to the Japanese Red Army, to the Turks and to Carlos himself), were left in the apartment, so were machine guns, so was an enormous amount of ammunition. Ignoring the implications of all of this, Carlos, the man soon to be hailed as a crack agent of the KGB, continued to behave like some latter-day Kafkaesque figure, caught up in mysterious unjustified accusations, crimes that obviously had nothing to do with him.

I do not know how his mistress Amparo Silva Masmela responded to this bizarre performance. Long before I began my investigation she was beyond talking to anyone. Men who were close to Carlos and Haddad during the 1970s have insisted to me, as Peter Boock did, that the Venezuelan preoccupied himself for at least part of the night with lovemaking.

For a man who had stated during his phone conversation with Nydia in the small hours that he 'had to prevent people getting caught, had to help them escape', Carlos showed as scant a regard for the jeopardy of others as he did for his own continuing freedom. The famous 'cool head' was increasingly conspicuous by its absence. Amparo Silva should have been put on the first plane out, instead she was demonstrably told by her lover to 'carry on as normal, go to work at the bank on Monday. If Maria Lara should call, tell her to ask for political asylum when she gets to Algiers'. These instructions ensured that Amparo's days of liberty were severely numbered.

Shortly before noon Carlos strolled around the corner to the air terminal to check out the various flight times. There he met Angela Armstrong, who instead of contacting the police dutifully obeyed the instructions that Carlos had given her, 'Contact Nancy, tell her to stay in Venezuela.' At first she attempted to get a friend in London to send a cable to Nancy. His parents had heard the news, the friend told her, and would never allow him to send the cable. Like Angela, however, he did not pick up the phone and talk to Scotland Yard.

The following day, Sunday the 29th of June, she telephoned Nancy's home in Caracas and left the warning with Nancy's family, then paranoia set in. Travelling across Paris to discuss 'the problem' with a girlfriend, she felt she was being followed. Looking out of the friend's flat she saw three men on the opposite pavement. She was certain that one of them was writing right to left in a notebook and deduced he must be Arabic. Convinced by now that she was next on the death list, she immediately caught a plane to London, to get away from Carlos, to get away from a nightmare. By doing so she flew directly into the epicentre of what had become a mobile horror. Carlos was in London.

How he came I do not know. That he did there is no doubt. He did not use, as Carlos Two claimed to me, his genuine passport – that was found at the rue Amélie apartment. Where he spent that Saturday night also remains a mystery; French sources have confirmed that it was not at Amparo's apartment.

On Sunday evening at approximately 10 pm, Carlos was in West London. There was no master plan; indeed, by not going directly from Paris to Algiers, he had disobeyed Haddad. He acted instead like a child seeking comfort, searching for his Linus blanket. He returned to that part of the city he knew so well. He wandered down Knightsbridge, past Phillimore Court. Flat four, the last Ramirez family residence in London, was now empty – no sanctuary there. He went instead to Basil Street, to number 22, a block of exclusive flats and apartments, and rang the bell of 'Fuentes'.

Delia Fuentes knew the Ramirez family well. She had been a frequent visitor to Phillimore Court and, like a number of fellow compatriots, had become good friends with Elba. A young widow, she lived alone in a one-bedroomed apartment in Basil Street. She greeted Carlos, who of course was known to her only as Ilich Ramirez Sanchez, with mixed reactions. At that point she was ignorant of his involvement in the rue Toullier murders. Like Elba's other friends she had been told by his mother that Ilich 'was working abroad'. Carlos asked her to let him stay at the flat for a while. She told him that she was tired and apart from that, 'I'm not allowed to have visitors overnight.' After chatting at the door for a while he left. Returning to the living room the image on the television screen transfixed Delia. It was a photograph of Carlos. When the bell had rung she had turned the sound down, now she hurried to the set, but the item had finished. How curious, after not seeing him for months he was at her door and on her TV simultaneously; she wondered why.

The next morning, Monday 30th of June, when Delia arrived at the Venezuelan Consulate where she worked she asked her colleagues if they had seen 'Ilich on TV last night. I wonder why he was on. It's so strange because yesterday evening he came to see me.' The effect was dramatic. The Consul's secretary promptly went into hysterics. Those who had not seen the news item had heard about it from their colleagues. As an astounded Delia attempted to digest what they told her, with others simultaneously urging her to see the Consul at once, the

Venezuelan Consulate was transformed into a bedlam. Delia, fearing for her life, rushed straight to the home of a girlfriend as the Vice Consul was telephoning Scotland Yard. The Special Branch officers who were immediately assigned to the investigation then took an extraordinary decision. They suppressed from the general public the indisputable fact that an armed multiple killer was loose in London.

On Wednesday, July 2nd, having spent the entire interim period with her friend, who was also an embassy employee, Delia plucked up sufficient courage to venture back to her own apartment to collect some clothes. She opened the door to be confronted by a total stranger pointing a gun at her. The flat was completely wrecked. As she started to scream she was thrown into a chair and other strange men entered to subject her to 'a brutal interrogation'.

'Where's your husband?'

'Where is he hiding? What have you done with him?'

'You realize you will be facing very serious charges. Probably get a life sentence unless you co-operate. Now come on, where is he?'

It went on for some time before Delia realized that these were not madmen sent to kill her but members of an organization whose function was, in theory, to protect law-abiding citizens – Special Branch officers from Scotland Yard. The bizarre line of questioning about her 'husband' stemmed from the fact that her telephone was listed as belonging to D. Ramirez. Dora Ramirez, a previous occupant, no relation.

For Delia Fuentes, the nightmare had only just begun. It continued for months with Special Branch officers following her everywhere she went. Carlos, meanwhile, continued to move, unmolested, around London.

By Wednesday, July 2nd, the *Guardian* had been contacted by Barry Woodhams and given a once-in-a-lifetime scoop. The British press and television were carrying lead stories complete with photographs of 'Carlos Martinez'. The photographs were genuine even if the name was not. Scotland Yard continued to suppress his true identity. Armed police officers had immediately taken up residence in Delia's flat. Her phone was bugged, as were a number of other lines, including, without the Ambassador's knowledge or permission, lines into the Embassy. On the previous Monday, a few hours after he had left Delia's apartment, Carlos was sighted again, this time below Angela Otaola's Bayswater flat. Carlos still had over twenty-four hours before Barry Woodhams would learn of the events in the rue Toullier and open a case full of guns, bombs and false passports. Carlos was seen by Fred Emmett, manager of the local self-service laundry, at 1 pm on Monday afternoon. He was seen again the following evening at the late night drinking club, Angelo's, also in the Bayswater area. A club that he had used with both Barry and Angela. A club that was regularly used by off-duty plainclothes police officers. If ever a criminal should have been caught, it was this one.

The police continued their policy of suppressing the fact that a man who would shoot to kill on the slightest provocation was running loose through the streets of London. They also continued to suppress the facts of his true identity. In effect they continued to play God with the lives of an unsuspecting public. Headlines asked 'Where is Killer Carlos?' The men in Scotland Yard knew the answer. All that was preventing the arrest of Carlos was the men hunting him. A full and frank press conference at Scotland Yard, the release of the true facts, would almost certainly have led, in those early days of the hunt, to the Venezuelan's arrest. He changed his clothes more than once and wandered unhindered through the streets. More than two weeks after the Paris murders he was still in London.

While the French police continued to stake out various bars and restaurants in Paris, the man they wanted continued to walk and travel about London. Mrs Beet, the wife of the caretaker at Phillimore Court, told me of her own sighting of Carlos, three weeks after rue Toullier.

'I saw him in High Street Kensington. He recognized me too. He wasn't disguised in any way. He was walking up towards the Post Office. Just strolling. I went into a shop and I remember thinking how odd it was to see him in London, how could I see him here?'

Mrs Beet rationalized the sighting away. Others did not. Others waited in dread for his knock on their door. Elba's close friend Deborah Herrera was one.

'I was terrified. The family were very frequent visitors to my home. Ilich said a number of times to me, "You have a very big loft. You are such a kind person. If one day I need to, I know just the place to hide." I used to laugh, then the shootings in Paris happened, I stopped laughing. My daughter said that if he came I would have to tell the police. They came, with lots of photographs. I thank God that he didn't.'

Indeed the police were very active. An armed team from Special Branch continued twenty-four-hour occupation of Delia's flat; the surrounding area was kept under continuous surveillance. By Wednesday investigating officers had established the address where Nydia should have sent the Bouvier passport, to the banker who was holding funds for Carlos, Anna Pugsley.

The police never discovered the secret Tobon bank account which contained some twelve hundred Canadian dollars. After being held for two days Anna was released. She had clearly lied not only to them but also to her husband about precisely what she knew of Nydia and Carlos. She was fortunate not to be charged. At her request her husband closed the bank account. Nydia, by now awaiting trial, screamed at him when he visited her in Brixton prison that he had defrauded her. He had deducted removal expenses incurred when clearing out her furniture from the Colherne apartment, another little task the Colombian women had asked him to perform.

On the 7th of July Carlos called the Venezuelan Embassy. It was one of a series of bizarre calls that he made to staff. In one he claimed to be a security officer working at the French Embassy and aggressively demanded to know which address he should come to for an Embassy party. Subsequently he phoned to threaten the lives of Ambassador Carlos Perez de la Cova and the naval attaché, Captain Carlos Porras. What provoked these calls remains a mystery, unless he had realized that the Embassy had called in Scotland Yard after his visit to Delia.

His photograph, one lifted from the false passport in the name of Carlos Martinez, continued to stare out from every newspaper while the headlines shouted 'Jackal On The Run'.

While the British police persisted in maintaining the fiction that Martinez was his real name and that wherever he was, he was not in London, Carlos continued to do his best to get arrested.

Nelly Isaacs is another who saw him in central London during July. She had good cause to remember the man who had been a witness at her wedding in 1971 – on his death list was the name of her husband, Lionel. Paying one of her regular visits to the laundromat, she became aware of a figure sitting on the other side of the shop. He wore dark glasses, so she could not see the eyes, a brand new pair of jeans and a black leather jacket. Clothes that others saw him wearing during many London sightings.

It was the way he fiddled with his fingers, a mannerism curiously reminiscent of Ilich. The laundry was close to the BBC and ITN in Portland Place. The police had been following Nelly on a regular basis since their visit to her home, but they must have been otherwise engaged on that day.

If some of these sightings could be rationalized away, some of these fleeting contacts explained on the basis of people's imaginings, one other contact that has the quality of Delia's experience could not. It involved the woman who had taken Carlos to task for disrupting her Russian lessons at the Central Polytechnic, Lorissa Kovalyova, but well before that, Scotland Yard's policy of suppressing the truth had collapsed.

On Sunday the 6th of July, the *Observer* newspaper revealed Carlos's true identity. Though the police still refused to confirm the facts, a little of the truth was getting over to the general public. There was a further sighting of Carlos the same day, again in the Kensington area, again by a family friend. This one was reported in the press and Scotland Yard were obliged to confirm it as 'firm'.

They also revealed that they were searching for an as yet unidentified additional safe house. So was Carlos.

By mid July Bouvier's photograph from the fake passport was released to the press, triggering the predictable headlines, 'Hunt for Jackal No. 2'. Later it would be stated that he had managed to slip the net. In fact he had been back at Wadi Haddad's Aden headquarters since early May. As for Carlos, more than two weeks after they had first learned that he was in London, Scotland Yard officers warned the public that he was dangerous and should not be approached.

The number of arrests mounted, in London, in Paris, in Geneva, in Frankfurt. There was one arrest still outstanding, still eluding the best efforts not only of Scotland Yard but of police forces throughout the world. Carlos had been sighted nearly everywhere, in a dozen European countries, in Latin America, in the Middle East. At about the time of a positive sighting in Beirut, during the second half of July, Carlos was in fact in a prosaic suburb of London, Arnos Grove.

In the mid 1970s Lorissa Kovalyova lived in that area with her daughter Marina, who towards the latter part of July was off school with a mild illness. She received a phone call from someone who did not identify himself and seemed anxious to learn exactly who apart from Lorissa and her daughter was currently staying at the flat. When telling her mother of the conversation, Marina dismissed the caller as 'a nutter'. Lorissa had a different view; from what the caller had said it seemed to her that it might have been Carlos. He had given enough away when talking to the young girl. Carlos would.

Some days later, during the evening, Lorissa received another phone call. It was Carlos. He wanted to come and stay with her. Some of his comments, including that he had seen Marina walking around in her nightdress during the day, could only have been made by a man keeping close surveillance on the flat. She declined the opportunity to take in as a guest a man who was now on the most wanted list of every police force in the world. Displaying considerable courage she contacted the police and subsequently made a full statement not only covering the phone calls but detailing her earlier knowledge of Carlos. This overwhelming proof that the man was in suburban London, like his visit to Delia, has never been made public. Instead the police leaked the assertion that if he was indeed in London then he most certainly did not have either the funds or the documents to get to the Middle East.

That was another problem that Carlos was actively working on.

Carlos Two told me his version of how 'he' escaped from London but, having, I believe, already amply demonstrated that this man was an impostor, reference to such a source will be negligible. I believe that Wadi Haddad arranged for a diplomatic passport to be made available to Carlos, either Yemeni or Algerian, and that this document, together with money, came to London in a diplomatic pouch, but I can't prove it. What is beyond doubt is that by early August Carlos had evaded the efforts of the British police to catch him. He was in Algeria.

French Intelligence, smarting from the pounding it had taken in the newspapers, had been extremely active since the rue Toullier killings. In early August, with Carlos in Algiers still nerving himself for an encounter with Wadi Haddad, the SDECE obtained positive proof that their quarry was in the Arab capital. The British were not advised and armed officers from Scotland Yard continued to sit in the Knightsbridge flat of Delia Fuentes and at a number of other locations. The suppression of information by the French was not brought about on this occasion because of collusion with Carlos or the Popular Front. The French wanted to deal with the problem in their own particular way. The SDECE received a very explicit order from their political masters. 'Kill the Jackal.' Which Government Minister gave the instruction I have been unable with total certainty to identify; undoubtedly the then President of France, Giscard D'Estaing, was consulted and approved this solution to 'l'affaire rue Toullier'.

In early August Carlos was positively sighted in the Algiers suburb of Saint-Eugène, in a night club called 'Dar Salme'. He was in the company of very high-ranking Algerian security officers. Carlos was seen by French under-cover agents in the club on a number of occasions but an attack was ruled out. It would have had to be a suicide mission. The club was owned by President Boumedienne's brother. It had a very exclusive clientele: Ministers, heads of security, senior officers. When the agents asked their head, Alexandre de Marenches, if such a mission should be undertaken, he conferred directly with the President. The instruction went back to 'wait and watch'. By then there was little to watch, Carlos had vanished. French Intelligence assumed he was in another part of the country and would surface again soon, perhaps this time at a more convenient killing point. In fact Carlos had flown to Aden, to Wadi Haddad. His initial meeting with the 'Old Man' was indeed difficult. Haddad had already caused wide-ranging investigations to be made about what was from his position the débâcle in Paris and London, long before Carlos tentatively stepped off the plane in South Yemen. When Carlos appeared clutching his press cuttings Haddad had already rightly concluded that much of the responsibility for the destruction of his carefully constructed European bases could be laid at the door of the Venezuelan. When Carlos attempted to defend himself by accusing Moukharbel of betrayal he was close to signing his own death warrant. Haddad considered putting Carlos on trial which, ironically, is precisely what Carlos had wanted to do to Moukharbel in April 1975. There were just two reasons why he did not follow that course of action.

Haddad was already acutely aware, before Carlos reappeared with press cuttings in a variety of languages, that a myth had been created around the Venezuelan. His hotheaded impetuousness had been transformed in a thousand articles and a hundred TV newscasts into the legend of the ice-cold professional. When the disinformation campaign added to the myth and made Carlos a KGB Cuban- and Russian-trained agent, the reality of what Haddad perceived as appalling incompetence was buried, like Moukharbel, six feet deep.

Haddad knew a propaganda weapon when he saw one. Though it seemed derisory to him, he realized that the legend of Carlos the Jackal had only to be invoked for terror and fear to spread like a bush fire. And for Wadi Haddad the only way that Palestine could be regained was the way it had been lost, through terror and fear. Within weeks he had received powerful confirmation of this view. It came from senior figures of the ruling Baath party in Iraq, and subsequently from the man who, although he had the title of Vice President, was in effect already the unquestioned ruler of Iraq, Saddam Hussein.

President Boumedienne of Algeria had already been seduced by the myth, hence the powerful protection accorded Carlos in that country. Now another Arab leader gave very clear indication of just how quickly and potently that myth had taken hold. Saddam Hussein desired a particular commando operation to take place. He told Haddad that every logistical piece of support necessary would be provided. Money, weapons, information. Above all information. Hussein was, with one exception, unconcerned about the composition of the commando. The exception was the identity of its leader – it had to be Carlos.

Hussein reasoned that with Carlos at the head of this attack the terror and fear that his name would generate would ensure the operation was successful. Hussein and

Haddad are very much two of a kind – when Haddad was told by the Iraqi leader of the details of the desired operation he readily agreed with Hussein's thinking. Yes, fear and terror would be essential if the operation was to have a successful conclusion. Without those elements the operation might well be doomed to fail. With them Presidents and Kings and other Heads of State would know to a certainty that if they did not comply there would be a carnage, a massacre that would include in its number some of the most powerful and important people on the planet.

The plan that Hussein and his closest advisers outlined to Haddad was in its concept chilling. They wanted a Carlos-led team to attack the OPEC headquarters in Vienna during a meeting of the Oil Ministers. Everyone within the Conference was to be seized. Carlos was to demand that a plane be put at his disposal. The Austrian Government was to be told that all the Ministers would be released when the plane landed in the Middle East and after each Minister had made a public statement rejecting any dialogue or negotiations with Israel on the Palestinian issue. The operation was merely a political exercise to promote the Palestinian cause. That was the full extent of the operation that would be stated to the Austrian government during the negotiations to ensure that the plane was provided. There was, however, Saddam Hussein explained, a hidden agenda. With Hussein there always has been.

Once clear of Austrian air space the plane would set course for Aden. Upon arrival all the Ministers were to be freed. Except two. Sheik Ahmed Zaki Yamani of Saudi Arabia and Dr Jamshid Amouzegar of Iran were to be shot.

It was a plan that delighted Haddad. Through the use of fear and terror his view of the Palestinian issue would be given massive worldwide publicity. Saddam Hussein knew his man well. Wadi Haddad found the suggestion irresistible, particularly when Hussein revealed that, like the skin of an onion, the operation had yet another layer.

The Iraqi leader was preparing for war, not against Israel but neighbouring Iran. It was, he told Haddad, a war to revenge 'a national humiliation'. The humiliation had occurred earlier that year and was personally experienced by Saddam Hussein. At its heart were two elements – the Kurdish people and oil.

The Kurds have much in common with the Palestinians. Both races have spent the best part of the twentieth century fighting for an independent homeland. Both have been betrayed by the West. Both have been pawns in the East/West confrontation. Historically the Kurdish region reaches into four countries in the shape of a crescent, parts of Syria, Turkey, Iraq and Iran. The territory that the Kurds lay claim to contains some of the richest oil fields in the world, an excess of mineral wealth designed to concentrate the minds of many. In 1974 full-scale warfare broke out yet again between the Iraqi forces and the Kurds. The Iraqis, recently supplied with a vast array of Soviet weapons, resolved to crush the rebellion once and for all. Baghdad committed virtually its entire fighting force to the war: eight divisions (some 120,000 men), 750 tanks, their entire air force and a twenty thousand-strong police force. The Kurds, descendants from the ancient warlike Medes, fought ferociously against an army that was superior in every respect save one, spirit. The fighting increased in savagery; no prisoners are taken when Iraqi fights Kurd. The Kurds fled to the mountainous regions and into neighbouring Iran. The Shah began to give increasing support and by January 1975 his forces had taken a direct hand in assisting the Kurds. Since the early 1970s the Kurdish cause had also been supported by Israel and the United States. President Nixon had allocated sixteen million dollars of secret aid, cutting out his own State Department. The CIA were given the task of ensuring that arms and money reached the Kurds. By early 1975, though severely pressed, the Kurds were continuing to tie down much of the Iraqi war machine, casualties were numbered in thousands and the cost to the country was 2.5 million dollars per day. If the Kurds could persuade Iran to step up aid or escalate what was already a significant Iranian active participation, then an honourable settlement with the regime was more than just a possibility. It was at this point that the Shah, with United States blessing, pulled the plug, or more accurately, closed the door. Among the many areas of contention between Iran and Iraq was the Shatt al-Arab waterway, a Gulf outlet vital to both nations. It had long been the subject of bitter dispute between the two countries. Under a treaty of 1937 Iran had no legal access to the deeper parts of the waterway and had been attempting without success to persuade Iraq to revise the treaty to allow equal use of the area. Iraq declined and continued to demand that all Iranian vessels pay entry tolls to the Iraqi port authority. In April 1969 Iran had unilaterally torn up the treaty claiming that it had been forcibly imposed by the British. Relations had gone downhill very quickly after that. Then came an OPEC conference in Algiers in March 1975.

To the amazement of all present and subsequently to many knowledgeable observers, the irreconcilable was resolved. It was announced that there was an agreement between Iraq and Iran over access to the Shatt al-Arab. Henceforth the border would run along the Thalweg Line, the deepest point of the waterway, instead of along the Iranian bank (as required in the 1937 treaty). Iraq also agreed to stop aiding an Arab secessionist movement that had been causing the Shah considerable trouble within his country and to cut off aid to revolutionary and Muslim elements that operated both inside and outside Iran. In return for all this Iran undertook to cut off all aid to the Kurds and close its borders to them, effectively sealing their escape route and dooming the Kurdish uprising. With nowhere to run they were duly slaughtered in their thousands.

At the close of the Algiers OPEC meeting the Shah of Iran and Vice President Saddam Hussein shook hands and then embraced and kissed. Those gathered rose to their feet and gave both men a standing ovation. When two leaders in the Middle East embrace and kiss, one should not be standing about clapping, the best course of action would be to dive in the nearest trench. This particularly public gesture of friendship was no exception to the rule. The seeds of the Iraqi-Iranian war were planted that day in Algiers.

Cut off from their escape routes and from financial and military backing, the Kurds soon ceased to be a problem to Saddam Hussein and his fellow Baathists. But the anger and humiliation within them, and particularly within Hussein, burned very deeply. The solution to the problem had been achieved at a price they were not prepared to pay. The decision to wage war against Iran and to tear up the Algiers accord was taken even before it was signed. Taken well before Saddam Hussein flew to Paris in September 1975 to discuss with French Prime Minister Jacques Chirac the purchase of a nuclear reactor. When critics of the transaction pointed out that the reactor was powerful enough to make plutonium for a nuclear bomb comparable to the one dropped on Nagasaki, the French assured them that of course Iraq only wanted the reactor to generate electricity.

During the second week of September, while in Paris, Saddam Hussein and the other members of the Iraqi delegation heard first-hand details of the extraordinary exploits of a certain Carlos. The media myth was by now in top gear. An idea began to form in the Iraqi Vice President's mind. To pay for the war as well as an ambitious five-year plan involving vast economic development for the country was going to require billions of dollars. Iraq's main source of revenue is oil. Estimates of oil revenues for 1975 were in the region of eight billion. The five-year plan called for twenty billion, and there would also be the cost of the war with Iran. The price of oil had to be forced up. The main obstacle to that strategy was Saudi Arabia and particularly its Oil Minister, Sheik Yamani, who had dominated the OPEC meetings for a number of years. The Saudis had on numerous occasions prevented the price of oil going sky-high. But now King Faisal was dead, assassinated just three weeks before the

OPEC meeting in Algiers. The Saudis were in disarray, but they would still resist an oil hike. Unless Yamani was removed, permanently. His removal would create a vacuum in the power politics of oil, which might well be filled by the Iranians, and particularly by their Oil Minister, Jamshid Amouzegar. But if he was removed at the same time as Yamani, the Iraqi point of view in the OPEC group might well prevail.

As the planning evolved it took on delightful Arabesque touches. To ensure that none would subsequently point the finger at the guilty, a number of other countries must be unwittingly involved. The hijacked plane should stop at several Arab countries, and at each stop the Oil Minister of that country would be forced to make a speech denouncing the Israeli/Egyptian accord before being released. This charade would of course be played out at Baghdad International Airport, as well as a number of others. Who would then be able to identify Saddam Hussein as the mastermind behind the outrage?

The Iraqi Vice President soon saw further confirmation of the need to launch an attack on OPEC. At that time a freeze on crude oil prices was in operation, which was due to continue until the following June. The leading advocates of the freeze had been the Saudis, led by Yamani. At an OPEC meeting in Vienna in late September 1975, it was Yamani again who led the opposition to any increase in the price of oil. Other members had different ideas, particularly Iraq and Iran who argued vehemently for a 30 per cent increase. The atmosphere became extremely heated. Yamani was later quoted as describing it as 'violent'.

The increase was finally held to 10 per cent. Yamani's efforts to ensure stability removed from Saddam Hussein's mind any lingering doubts about unleashing Wadi Haddad. The Sheik had in effect signed his own death warrant.

During a 1963 OPEC meeting Yamani had been accused by the Iraqi oil minister of representing a country which was no more than an agent for the American oil companies. Yamani demanded an apology which, when it was not forthcoming, led to the Saudis boycotting further meetings at ministerial level. Eventually the Iraqis apologized and their accusations were expunged from the minutes, but they had been humiliated in front of the entire membership of OPEC. Now, in 1975, Vice President Saddam Hussein had been obliged to lose face and kiss the Shah's. When Sheik Yamani compounded this by resisting Iraqi demands for a massive price increase, a Carlos-led attack at the next OPEC meeting became inevitable in the minds of the leaders of the regime in Baghdad.

During the summer Carlos had arrived from Algiers in very bad physical shape. Always inclined since childhood towards overweight, his over-indulgence in the night clubs and restaurants of Algiers had resulted in his body blowing up like a balloon. Peter Boock recalled, 'At the time I met Carlos his face was swollen up like someone who had been on the razzle for weeks. The Palestinians put him on a diet because he had become so bloated he couldn't take part in training. He was totally out of shape. He looked like his head was a melon on top of a huge balloon. The Palestinians told us that it was a regular joke, they said he needed a size nine brassiere. When I first saw him it really knocked me out. He needed two chairs to sit on.'

Haddad was more than equal to the challenge, in a manner reminiscent of a football manager or an athletics coach preparing his team for a major event. He had only until December to get them match fit. Strenuous daily exercise was organized as well as a strict diet for Carlos while he began to select other team members. Peter Boock told me:

'At the time we were asked if we, RAF, would like to take part in this operation but the Red Army didn't want to know about it. The background was a bit nebulous as far as we were concerned and nobody really wanted to go, so Haddad had no choice but to look among the foreigners who were there, and the only others were the Japanese, for example, and the 2nd of June group. Of course the Japanese did not belong in a place like Vienna so they contacted the 2nd of June group, because of the German language as much as for anything else.'

Haddad selected a mixed team: three Palestinians, two Germans and Carlos. One of the Palestinians, Khalid, was appointed by Haddad as Carlos's number two. As with Samir, one of the three Palestinian survivors of the Munich Olympic Games massacre, Abu Iyad had reached out on my behalf and plucked Khalid from his Middle Eastern home. There was, it transpired, a link between these two attacks, a lesson learned by Wadi Haddad. Khalid explained:

'Wadi Haddad was not involved in any way in the Munich Games operation. I know Abu Iyad has given you all the details of that attack and that you've spoken to Samir. Therefore you already know that, apart from Israeli intransigence, the reason the operation failed was because the first of the commandos to die was the leader. Because of security he had been the only one to know all the details of the plan, including where and to which country the Israeli athletes were to be taken. Once he was killed the operation was doomed. Haddad was aware of this. If Carlos should be killed in Vienna, then I was to take over. I knew all the details of the second stage of the plan. The part that would occur after we had left Austrian air space.'

Each of the team selected a *nom de guerre* thus Carlos being Carlos chose two. He was to be known at all times as 'Salem' or 'Johnny' until of course he made his announcement to the hostages of his real identity. Apart from the training already recorded above there was weapon training. A member of the team selected by Haddad who showed particular aptitude in this area was a female member of 2nd of June, *nom de guerre* Nada, real name Gabriele Kröcher-Tiedemann. She had in fact been getting regular military training in South Yemen since March of that year, under the watchful eye of Wadi Haddad, who knew a psychopath when he met one.

The other German selected by Haddad was a man

already known to Carlos. Indeed he had been a member of the team that had gathered in London in April 1975 to kidnap Ambassador El Tajir. In late 1975 Hans Joachim Klein was back in Frankfurt. Klein had had the benefit of military training in the German army and Haddad considered there was no need to bring him out to Aden for further training. He was contacted by Wilfried Böse and gave his agreement in principle to taking part in the operation. For Khalid and the other Palestinians there was no need to seek assurances, as Khalid explained to me.

'It was an honour to be selected.'

During December 1975 the commando began to gather in Vienna. Klein was at the hotel Am Stephenplatz with a member of the back-up team, Wilfried Böse. The back-up team consisted of six Germans. Among their duties was the provision of two safe houses and surveillance. Carlos completed the last leg of his journey from the South Yemen by catching a Zürich-Vienna train. He then booked into the Vienna Hilton. The next to arrive was Gabriele Tiedemann, and then finally the three Palestinians. In the interim Klein was experiencing one of the problems that I had discussed with Khalid and Boock – language. Carlos spoke only a few words of German and Klein only his native language. Wilfried Böse was obliged to act as interpreter as Carlos outlined the two-part operation. The first part, the seizure of the OPEC building and demands that a political statement be read out over the radio and a plane put at their disposal, he described to Klein as 'a military operation'. The second phase, the murder of Yamani and Amouzegar 'which is for us the start of the operation', he described as 'political'.

Still using Böse as his interpreter, Carlos left Hans Joachim Klein under no illusions about the Wadi Haddad doctrine of terror and fear.

'I am the leader of the commando. My deputy is a Palestinian comrade who will take charge if anything happens to me. We will obtain two machine guns, six pistols, eight hand grenades and sufficient fuses and explosives to blow up the entire OPEC building if that becomes necessary. Also I am waiting for a member of the Iraqi delegation, who will give me the inside information. The security arrangements. That sort of thing. Now for the treatment of the hostages. Whoever resists will immediately be shot. Whoever does not immediately obey an order will be shot. Whoever tries to escape will be shot. If a member of the commando does not obey my orders or does not carry out his previously agreed instructions and thereby endangers the operation, he will be shot.'

To Klein this seemed to indicate that there was going to be 'a bit too much shooting'. He yelled at Carlos, 'Don't you know that you can wound someone with a gun as well as killing them?'

Unlike Tiedemann, Klein would not have been a first choice for this operation if Wadi Haddad had been given the opportunity of conducting a personal evaluation; a man who balked at mass killings would undoubtedly have been considered a liability. Prior to the Vienna operation Klein was a dabbler in such activities. A small-time petty crook who had drifted towards the revolutionary cells in Germany rather than marching with arrogant confidence, he was known around Frankfurt as 'Klein Klein'. Small Klein. His main claim to fame before Vienna was having once acted as chauffeur to Jean-Paul Sartre when the French philosopher had come to visit the imprisoned leaders of Baader-Meinhof. It had hardly been the ideal preparation for a potential bloodbath. Klein balked at the murder of Sheik Yamani; he had no problem with the killing of the Iranian Oil Minister whom he considered to be the evil controlling figure behind the Shah's secret service, Savaak, but the murder of the Saudi Arabian seemed inexplicable even though Carlos stated that he and he alone would be killing the two Oil Ministers.

Carlos continued to stroll around Vienna as the group waited for the arms to come into the city in an Iraqi diplomatic pouch. He was totally unarmed for two weeks yet that same unawareness of any potential risk that had been such a feature of his actions earlier in the year was again in evidence. He dined at the best restaurants,

479

ordered Napoleon brandy to his room in the Hilton, went shopping to purchase a beret, à la Che Guevara. The crash fitness course in the desert had worked well. He was thinner and fitter than at any time in his adult life. He had grown what passed for a beard; with his long trench coat and beret he would have stood out in any crowd, yet this most wanted of men behaved with a complete lack of concern. Contrary to what many others have written, his face had not undergone plastic surgery.

By Friday the 19th of December Klein and some of the others were beginning to twitch. The arms had not yet arrived and Carlos was still lacking vital information concerning the security arrangements and the physical layout at OPEC. That evening Carlos and Khalid went to the Iraqi Embassy in Vienna. Khalid told me what happened.

'At our meeting we were given the arms and the information, all the intelligence information we needed. The weapons and the other things had come the previous day on a direct flight from Baghdad. They came on the same plane that carried the Iraqi Minister of Oil, Tayeh Abdul Karim, and his entire delegation. The original plan had been to attack the following day, the first day of the conference. The Iraqi suggested that we should delay the attack until the second day of meetings (Sunday, the 21st). That would ensure that Yamani and Amouzegar were present.

In view of the fact that Carlos had at his disposal a back-up team of six Germans, his choice of transportation to the OPEC building on Karl Luger Ring was bizarre. Any of the six could have driven the commando team there in either hired or stolen cars. They made the journey by tram. They carried with them the tools of their trade, the guns, the hand grenades, the explosives, the ammunition, in sports bags. Other weapons were stuffed in their pockets, so much weaponry that they could barely walk the few yards from the tram to the OPEC building. At the entrance there was one solitary policeman, Inspector Hermann Ceasar. Carlos, wearing his long white trench coat and brown beret, simply walked past, but Klein greeted the officer. 'Good day Inspector.' Ceasar returned the greeting and saluted. He didn't ask for any identification or to search the bags they were struggling with. His sole function was to 'regulate those driving up to and away from OPEC'. Ceasar, then, knew his place, which is probably why he is still alive. 'It was not my job to control people.' The uncontrollable, in the shape of a rag bag of international terrorists, was about to hit OPEC.

The strange-looking group entered the building. It was 11.40 am. One hour earlier some thirty reporters had gathered on the pavement and inside the entrance. The press had soon established that on that Sunday little of the stuff of headlines was going to be discussed or argued about. Now, as the Carlos group entered, just four reporters remained huddled inside the doors, away from the biting cold, the others had drifted away.

Definitely a slow news day.

Seeing the group one of the reporters joked, 'Here comes the Angolan delegation.' Carlos asked one of the others, 'Has the conference begun yet?' Advised that it had, the commando strode past the lifts and began to walk up the far flight of stairs that led directly to the OPEC reception area.

On the first floor, standing chatting to a few members of oil delegations who had slipped out of the main conference hall for a cigarette, were two police officers, Anton Tichler and Josef Janda. They represented the Austrian government's response to the OPEC request made before this meeting for 'adequate security precautions'. Two armed police officers had indeed proved adequate on numerous occasions in the past. As not the slightest whisper of the planned attack had leaked, the OPEC officials had been content to have just two men on duty on this occasion.

Carlos, followed by the others, burst through the door into the reception area, machine gun in his hands. Though the group had been given full details of the layout by their Iraqi contact, Klein approached receptionist Edith Heller and asked, 'Where's the conference room?'

As if to underline the fact that the question did not require an answer, Carlos began to move in the direction of the room where the OPEC members were gathered. Actions began to occur simultaneously. Edith Heller began to dial the Vienna police headquarters. Klein raised his gun and began to fire at the switchboard. Heller persisted and Klein drilled the telephone that was in her hands. She ducked below the reception desk and, grabbing another phone, with great courage redialled the number.

Tichler moved towards Carlos and grabbed his machine gun. He almost succeeded in wrenching it from the Venezuelan. Breaking free, Carlos turned to continue as Gabriele Tiedemann shot Tichler from close range in the neck. She pushed his body into a lift and, pressing the button, sent the dying Tichler to the ground floor.

One of the Iraqi bodyguards was in the reception area when the group burst in. Though armed he made no attempt to draw his gun. He motioned to Klein that he needed to go to the toilet, urgently. Klein nodded and the Iraqi, hands still raised in the air, began to move in the direction of the stair exit. Tiedemann turned and, seeing the Iraqi, Al Khafali, moving away, rushed at him. As she stuck her pistol in his chest he instinctively went from defensive to offensive. Grabbing her in a bear hug he began to drag her towards the stair exit. Klein stood mesmerized watching as they disappeared through the door. A moment later there was a shot. Klein came to life and ran out to the head of the stairs. The Iraqi was at his feet, choking to death on his own blood, shot in the face. His jacket was open, exposing a gun inside a special quick draw holster. Al Khafali had had plenty of time to draw the gun and use it but had elected instead to leave quietly, actions that indicate a prior knowledge of the attack. When Tiedemann rushed at him and pushed a gun into his chest, he must have believed he was about to be shot, yet still his gun had remained in his holster and he chose instead to attempt to drag her outside. For a quiet word?

A reassurance that he was in on the plan? Apart from her torn coat Tiedemann, who had now murdered two men in less than thirty seconds, was unscathed.

Carlos, meanwhile, had encountered a member of the Libyan delegation, senior civil servant Yousef Ismirli, who showed the same extraordinary courage as Tichler – he grabbed at the machine gun. He wrenched at it with such violence that if Carlos had not been wearing a shoulder strap the Libyan would have had the weapon; the strap was yanked down to his wrist, but held. Pulling a pistol from his waist, Carlos fired twice at point blank range. A moment before firing the Libyan, anticipating what was going to happen, spun round and turned his back to Carlos, who pumped two bullets directly into his shoulder. The force of the shots spun Ismirli completely around, he was now face to face again with the Venezuelan, who showed once more the insane rage that had possessed him in rue Toullier. The Libyan was unarmed and seriously wounded, he no longer represented the slightest threat. That fear, which many have talked to me about, an abnormal fear of suffering the slightest pain, welled up within Carlos and triggered greater anger. He fired at the Libyan three times, twice into the body, once into the throat. So close was he to Ismirli that one of the bullets passed right through the man's body and wounded a Kuwaiti on the other side of the room in the arm.

Carlos, Khalid and Yussef controlled the conference room. As they had entered bursts of machine gun fire had demolished the lights in the corridors. Further bursts were fired into the ceiling of the conference room. Carlos shouted at the Ministers and at everyone else to, 'Get down. Get down. Lie on the floor.' Everyone in the room dropped to the floor, face down. The bursts continued. Many laid out on the floor were convinced that it was going to be a wholesale massacre. Everyone was going to be killed. Valentin Hernandez Acosta, the Venezuelan Oil Minister, told me:

'I felt what I thought were bullets hitting my back, my shoulders. Someone next to me was holding my hand.

Pressing it. In that moment I thought it was my last. That I was near to death. I thought, "It's all right, this is my moment, I am ready." I was thinking about my wife, my children, the only thing I hoped was not to suffer too much. To be killed very quickly. Then the firing stopped. Later I realized that what I had felt was bits of the ceiling hitting me as they shot them off. Their leader was standing in the middle of the room, then he spoke.'

'My name is Carlos. You may have heard of me.'

In one of the outer offices, Janda, the surviving Austrian police officer, had slipped into a side room. He reached for the phone. An OPEC staff member, Enis Attar, was doing the same. The calls hit the Vienna police headquarters virtually together.

'This is OPEC here. We have a shooting. Please send someone here quickly. In the OPEC. Karl Luger Ring. Quickly please.'

On the police tape the listener can hear the bursts of firing, some single, some automatic. What one is listening to is three men dying.

The calls are timed at 11.44 and 50 seconds. Carlos and his group had in less than five minutes seized absolute control of a group that included eleven oil ministers who dealt with the single most important product on the planet.

In terms of the national assets that those eleven men represented, Carlos was holding the richest group of hostages in the history of the world. The minimum collected revenue for the year that was drawing to a close was fifty-five billion pounds, or more than one hundred billion dollars.

Treading over the shattered glass and the plaster Carlos called out to Khalid, 'Where's Yamani?' He had already identified Amouzegar. Then he said, 'Yussef, put down the explosives.' At the mention of Yamani's name the Oil Minister from Gabon looked at Yamani with pity. A moment later and Carlos was looking down at the Saudi minister; he gave an ironic salute with his hand as he announced his discovery to the others.

The telephone calls for help brought a quick response. In less than five minutes an eight-man unit from the Einsatzkommando – Special Command – was at the OPEC building. Four of them fanned out to prevent an escape and the other three stormed into the building, their Uzi machine guns at the ready. They were led by Kurt Leopolder. The first thing they saw was the body of Tichler, lying half out of the open lift. He was dead. Using the same route up the staircase that Carlos had trod a mere ten minutes earlier, Leopolder discovered on the first-floor landing the dying Iraqi. Klein, still organizing the movement of OPEC staff into the conference hall while guarding the area, began firing. Leopolder, lying next to the dying man, returned the fire. Then, calling to his colleagues to move the Iraqi, he dived into the reception area. Again he and Klein exchanged fire, this time one of Leopolder's bullets ricocheted from Klein's gun barrel and drilled him in the stomach. Another bullet hit him in the leg. He began to make for the kitchen. Inside he examined his stomach, just a small neat hole, no blood flowing, it didn't look serious. Klein lit a cigarette and showed the wound to Joseph, who called out for Carlos. Carlos came out of the conference hall, glanced at Klein, then turned to Joseph. 'Throw a grenade.' With that Carlos returned to the conference hall. Joseph hurled a grenade at the three members of the riot squad. The sound was deafening but, astonishingly, no-one was injured. Leopolder lay already wounded by one of Klein's bullets on the reception floor.

While this battle raged Carlos, like a grotesque master of ceremonies at a surprise party, was organizing affairs in the conference room.

Yussef had already laid a series of explosive charges around the conference room. If the riot squad had succeeded in shooting their way past Klein the charges would have been immediately detonated.

When the attack had begun Yamani was certain that he was going to die, he had immediately begun to recite verses from the Koran as he lay on the conference floor.

485

'To the righteous soul will be said: O thou soul, in complete rest and satisfaction. Come back to thy Lord, well content thyself and well pleasing unto Him. Enter thou, then among my devotees. Yea, enter thou my Heaven.'

That certainty of impending death became all the greater when he realized who led this group. Among the names on the death lists that had been found in the safe houses during the summer had been Sheik Zaki Yamani. He began to pray harder.

His fellow Minister, Dr Valentin Hernandez Acosta, felt a hand gently tapping his ankle, then someone spoke to him in Spanish.

'Dr Hernandez you can get up. You are quite safe.'

It was Carlos. Moments before he had brutally murdered the Libyan, now he was showing the greatest respect to Hernandez Acosta. He helped him to his feet. Other ministers were being placed into three groups. Carlos began to chat amiably.

'I know you very well, Doctor.'

'Who are you?'

'I'm Ilich Ramirez Sanchez from Venezuela. We're dividing everybody into three groups. The friends, the neutrals and the enemies. You of course will be with the other neutrals.'

As if he had just bumped into an old friend, Carlos led his fellow countryman to a chair, then, sitting near him, chatted about how during his years in London and his contacts on the Latin American diplomatic circuit he had often heard tell of the Minister. 'One of my mother's closest friends, Deborah Herrera, often talked of you.'

As he pleasantly conversed, the seventy people who had so far survived were being segregated. The 'enemy' consisted of the delegations from Saudi Arabia, Iran, Abu Dhabi and Qatar, they were directed to the top of the room. The 'friends', consisting of Iraqis, Algerians, Libyans and Kuwaitis, were placed by the windows that looked out on to Karl Luger Ring. There was undoubtedly a downside to being one of Carlos's friends, for Yussef was busily engaged in wiring that entire wall

486

with high explosives. If there were another attack from the Austrian riot squad who had taken up positions in the street, there was an excellent chance of the 'friends' being the first to be shot by the would-be rescuers, that was if they were not blown up first by Yussef.

The neutrals, those from Gabon, Nigeria, Ecuador, Venezuela and Indonesia, were allocated the wall opposite. A fourth group, which Carlos categorized as Austrians, but which also included two Britons, was directed to the opposite end of the room to the enemy, again one of the most vulnerable positions, as they were on the same wall as the entrance doors. Three Palestinians, like the Austrians all local OPEC staff, were asked to join the friends by Carlos, who said to them, 'While we are all here, we will be your guests.'

Breaking off from his walk down memory lane with Hernandez Acosta, Carlos got down to the business of negotiating his way out of Vienna. He gave Grizelda Carey, the English secretary to OPEC's Secretary General, a handwritten list of demands and ordered her to copy it.

The original written by Carlos read:

We are holding hostage the delegations to the OPEC Conference. We demand the lecture of our communiqué on the Austrian Radio and Television Network every two hours, starting two hours from now. A large bus with windows covered by curtains must be prepared to carry us to the Airport of Vienna tomorrow at 7.00, there a full-tanked DC9 with a crew of three must be ready to take us and our hostages to our destination.

Any delay, provocation or unauthorized approach under any guise will endanger the life of our hostages.
The Arm of the Arab Revolution
Vienna 21/XII/75

Among those requests was one that contained the cause of the ultimate failure of the entire operation.

While Grizelda Carey was copying this, another OPEC secretary was released. She was told that the group required a wireless and that if it was not supplied within thirty minutes more people would die. The wireless arrived well within the allotted time. It was the first of a series of demands made by Carlos, who was clearly revelling in the situation. He was no longer the shy boy in the Fermin Toro playground, no longer the butt of his classmates' jokes. He was creating international theatre with himself in the leading role. Throughout the various negotiations with the Austrians the leader mentality that is such an essential part of his character was very evident. Here in Vienna there was no Moukharbel to overrule him. During the siege he frequently talked to hostages about the democratic ethos of his group; it was in fact just another spin on the myth of Carlos. His version of democracy during this operation was simple. 'All decisions will be taken democratically by me, any who disagree will be shot.'

Carlos instructed Grizelda to take the demands and a copy of the communiqué in French out of the building. She was also told by the Venezuelan:

'As you go out of reception you will see an injured policeman on the floor. He is free to leave the building on condition that there is no further firing.'

The petrified secretary collected the wounded Leopolder and, continually shouting 'Nicht schiessen bitte – Please don't shoot', arrived shaking in the street.

The communiqué she carried was, as Khalid told me, 'Just a trick. A device. It had only one purpose, to convince Kreisky that we were merely a group of Palestinian fanatics seeking publicity for our cause. If he was convinced of that then we had our ticket out of Austria.'

'And if he didn't give you that ticket out?'

'Then we intended to blow up the building.'

'With everyone, the Ministers and all the other people, still in it?'

'Of course.'

38-40. *Above left* Emotion at the end of the Entebbe hijack. Unknown to the Israelis, Carlos eluded capture by less than two hours. The attack drove another wedge into the relationship between Haddad (*above right*) and Habash (*below*).

41. Carlos in 1979; contrary to all reports, without the benefit of plastic surgery.

42-4. *Above left* Magdalena Kopp. Because of her arrest, the world's most wanted man declared war on France in the letter shown below. *Above right* The only man who seriously rivals Carlos's title of 'most wanted', Abu Nidal.

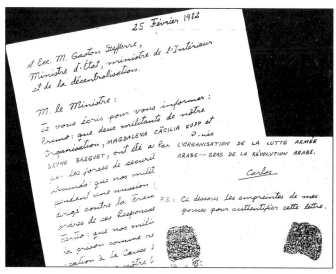

25 Février 1982

A Exc. M. Gaston Defferre,
Ministre d'État, ministre de l'Intérieur
et de la décentralisation.

M. le Ministre :

Je vous écris pour vous informer :
Primo : que deux militants de nôtre
Organisation, MAGDALENA CÄCILIA KOPP et
BRUNO BREGUET, ont été a Par
par les forces de securi
Secundo : que nos milit
rendent une mission
dirigé contre la Fran
ables de ses Responsa
Tertio : que nos mili
la prison comme re
...ation à la Cause
...nôtre l

L'ORGANISATION DE LA LUTTE ARMÉE
ARABE — BRAS DE LA RÉVOLUTION ARABE.

Carlos

P.S.: Ci dessous les empreintes de mes
pouces pour authentifier cette lettre.

45-6. After the declaration came the war: *above* the wreckage of the Paris-Toulouse express: *below* the immediate aftermath of the bombing at St Charles railway station, Marseilles.

47. 'History is written by winners': Menachem Begin kissing the flag of the outlawed terrorist group Irgun.

48. Some of Begin's work before collecting his Nobel Peace Prize. Deir Yassin, 1948.

49. Al-Karameh, 1968. The birth of a legend, but was it also the birth of a myth?

50. In August 1976 at least 2,576 Palestinians were slaughtered at Tel al-Za'atar.

51. The Intifada. Young boys with stones have achieved in a few short years immeasurably more than the entire Palestinian leadership.

52-3. Sabra and Chatila: a slaughter that shocked the world.

The communiqué, laying out the manifesto of this 'Arm of the Arab Revolution', a name created by Haddad especially for this attack, trod the familiar ground of those hardline Arab States that rejected all treaties, all talks of peace with Israel. The Egyptian Army was described as 'heroic' and the text called for it to lead a war of liberation with the armies 'of the north-east front'. These, the text explained, comprised Syria, Iraq and the Palestinian resistance. Oil was to feature as a major weapon in this war of liberation and the current fighting in Lebanon was denounced as a 'great Zionist reactionary-American plot'.

While Grizelda Carey had been preparing the document other aspects of the drama continued to unfold.

In a line straight out of a theatrical farce Carlos came into the conference room and asked, 'Is there a doctor in the room?'

Fortunately for Klein there was, the Minister from Nigeria, Akobo. He examined the wounded German, who was losing only a surprisingly small amount of blood. Akobo pronounced that Klein could not travel and needed surgery at once. Carlos arranged for his immediate removal. In view of the injuries he had sustained, it was astonishing that Klein actually walked out of the OPEC building. Austrian police officers were initially bemused and asked him if he was a hostage. Covering his face from nearby press photographers, Klein replied, 'My name is Angie,' his *nom de guerre* borrowed from a Rolling Stones song. He then collapsed and was rushed to hospital. He should have been dead. At Vienna's Allgemeines Krankenhaus hospital the surgeons discovered that Leopolder's bullet had pierced the German's colon, pancreas and duodenal artery. He was sent straight into the operating theatre.

At the time that the Carlos group had struck, many of the Austrians who would be called upon to make crucial decisions in the next few hours were scattered throughout the country enjoying the start of the Christmas holiday. Chancellor Kreisky was in the ski resort of Lech nearly four hundred miles from the capital in the far south of the country. The head of Vienna's police force, Hofrat Liebhardt, was doing what much of the nation was doing, watching TV and cheering local man Hinterseer to a victory in the slalom race. While Kreisky began the long journey back to Vienna, first by helicopter and then by plane, Liebhardt was at OPEC headquarters taking charge of the police operation within one hour. By the time he arrived the shooting had stopped and the casualties had been removed. When Liebhardt learned that the man he was dealing with was Carlos, he immediately gave a series of orders to all police units. They were forbidden to take any personal risk or act on their own initiative, the greatest care and attention should be paid to all movements. As the siege settled down to an uneasy truce Liebhardt explained to his colleagues some of the background to Carlos. He was well informed on the Venezuelan and knew from studying French intelligence data very precisely what he was confronting. Equally aware of the importance of the hostages, Liebhardt soon concluded that the solution to this situation was going to have to be made by the politicians.

Carlos demanded that the Libyan Ambassador, Al-Ghadamsi, should act as mediator between him and the Austrians. After the Vienna operation was concluded, allegations would be made, initially by Egypt, that Colonel Qathafi had masterminded the entire attack. If he had done, then his preparations left something to be desired. His Ambassador Ghadamsi was also Libya's representative to Czechoslovakia. When Carlos demanded that Al-Ghadamsi be brought to the OPEC headquarters immediately the Austrians were unable to comply – Al-Ghadamsi was in Prague.

While the Austrians began the convoluted process of contacting the Libyan Ambassador, a dangerous vacuum existed. It could have lasted for an indeterminate amount of time. Meanwhile seventy lives hung in the balance. At this point the Iraqi Chargé d'Affaires, Riyadh Al-Azzawi, offered his services. He was later to say that he 'just happened to be passing the OPEC building' and 'just happened to hear shooting'. Quite why he was just passing by was never explained. His office was on the opposite side of Vienna, his home even further away near Esterhazy Park. With his curious appearance the vacuum was filled. The Iraqi repeatedly strolled unconcernedly in and out of OPEC. Liebhardt got a less favourable reaction when he asked to be allowed in to talk to Carlos.

'If a policeman comes in he will not be talked to, he will be shot at.' Carlos was revelling in the situation. At his first meeting with the Iraqi he declared,

'Tell them I'm from Venezuela and my name is Carlos. Tell them I'm the famous Carlos. They know me.'

Back in the main OPEC conference room he moved from group to group telling his hostages that everything was going to be all right. Calling Yamani to a side room for a chilling tête à tête, he told the Oil Minister how he planned to kill him if the Austrians did not broadcast the manifesto, of how he personally controlled a crack team of over forty commandos that he had trained to attack anywhere in the world, of how he had graduated from Patrice Lumumba University with the highest honours ever won by a student, of how some of his operations had been controlled by Moscow. Perhaps the amphetamines that they had all taken before launching the attack, a drug that would ensure they remained awake, caused his euphoria, his need to make such childish boasts; there was also another motivation.

Carlos was acutely aware that though he held the power of life and death over these people, he was not dealing with men of straw. Each of these oil ministers was a man of substance, a man of power. Highly intelligent, sophisticated, each one was in his own way a survivor. These men were prime ministers, ambassadors. In the world of oil politics a country sends only its best men into the conference room. Once the initial terror subsided they displayed an unnerving calmness. There was no panic. Kreisky would not be back in Vienna until 6 pm. As they waited they reacted to their ordeal in a variety of ways but at no time did they appear to wilt. The Iranian Oil Minister, one of the two that the group planned to murder before this affair had reached its conclusion, observed that his Venezuelan colleague, Valentin Hernandez Acosta, had been pressed into service by Carlos as a negotiator, translator and middleman. Amouzegar motioned for him to come over to the enemy group and asked Hernandez Acosta to brief him.

'By this time I had been talking to Carlos for quite a while. He had told me that this attack was part of the Third World War. He told me that he had trained and controlled over four hundred men in South Yemen, that he had trained them in Yemen and Syria. When all the other Ministers had been dropped off, he said, Yamani and Amouzegar would be taken to South Yemen and killed. When I talked to Zaki Yamani and Jamshid Amouzegar I told them these things. Amouzegar said, "Ask him how much. Ask him how much money he wants." When I went back to Carlos I put this to him, he said, "I have been very well paid. I don't need money. I'm not asking for money to spare them."'

Despite that response Valentin Hernandez Acosta remained convinced that money was indeed the quest at the very heart of the OPEC attack. He debated the issue with Carlos, particularly when Carlos shifted his ground and talked of asking the Iranian Shah and the Saudi King 'for something'.

' "Carlos, you ask those governments for something and you could finish being very disappointed. They will not be nice to you. These people, the Saudis and the Iranians, are technocrats. You are not dealing with family. The links, the infrastructure, are different. These men whose lives you threaten are not members of Royal families." Carlos laughed and said, "You see through their systems don't you?" I said, yes I do.'

Carlos had been advised that his demands could not be considered until Kreisky returned to Vienna. He accepted this and filled in the time by alternating between being a leader of a commando group and genial mine host to those he held captive. When Tiedemann had first told him that she had shot and killed two his response in front of Yamani was, 'Quite right. I killed one myself.' The Saudi shuddered. To Hernandez Acosta he showed another side of his character. A side instilled by his mother Elba.

'He behaved like the kind of gentleman who if you met him in the street you would see at once that he was a good candidate for your daughter. A charming, gentle person. Making every effort to be well educated and refined, and yet the balance, there was something wrong with that. On the one hand he chatted pleasantly about how he had taken the name of Carlos to honour our Venezuelan President Carlos Andreas Perez who he said was a good friend of his father's. Then he popped over to where Yussef was playing with the wires to the detonator while holding a grenade. Having given Yussef further instructions he returned to me, apologized for the unseemly interruption and explained that he had let the two British employees of OPEC leave because, "I have been very happy in England. I feel great admiration for the British people, they have been very kind to me." Then moments later he said to me, "Dr Hernandez, if we manage this situation well, all will stay alive, if something goes wrong we are going to kill everybody."'

This deadly mixture contained within one person has bemused many. A young man, so charming that one would have no qualms about leaving him with one's wife and daughters. A young man who could kill and maim one's wife or daughter at the drop of a hand grenade.

When Hernandez Acosta gently pointed out that a number of the hostages were hungry, Carlos was profuse in his apologies. Through the ever busy Iraqi Al-Azzawi the host sent out an order for sandwiches and soft drinks. The Austrians duly obliged with ham sandwiches to a group comprised largely of Muslims. So embarrassing for the host. Again Hernandez Acosta smoothed over the little difficulty, he recalled that a banquet had been prepared at the Hilton for the OPEC members. The Hilton promptly joined Vienna's take-away services.

As the deadline for the first broadcast of the communiqué approached the tension reasserted itself. Carlos had told the Austrians that if the manifesto was not broadcast the killing would recommence. It was more black theatre. Böse had by this time phoned the press in Switzerland, guiding them to a copy of the manifesto that Carlos had previously hidden in a Geneva toilet. During his private talk with Yamani Carlos had told him that if the communiqué was not broadcast at 6.00 pm Yamani would be the first to be shot. Later, during the afternoon, Carlos varied the threat. The first to die would now be the Saudi deputy minister, Abdul Aziz Al-Turki. He was ordered to sit away from the others. Isolated, with the sure knowledge that he would shortly be shot and thrown out of the window, he displayed great courage as he sat calmly awaiting his fate.

The first broadcast went on air at 6.20 pm. Twenty minutes past the deadline, it was deliberately read out in appalling French. Al-Turki's life was spared only to be threatened again by Carlos as he negotiated for the bus to the airport.

'And the bus must have curtains.'

'No, they don't have a bus with curtains. I will ask for a bus without curtains.'

'The next time you try to change the conditions I have set I will throw the first body out of the window.'

At that point Carlos ordered the Saudi deputy to sit at the head of the table again.

'Why?'

'Because you will be the first that I will throw out of the window.'

Then he turned back to the Iraqi Chargé d'Affaires.

'Now go and tell them that.'

Carlos told the delegates that if Kreisky acceded to his demands they would fly out of Vienna on the following morning and that their first stop would be Tripoli.

In the Federal Chancellery, less than a mile from the OPEC building, the Austrian Chancellor, Bruno Kreisky, sat in emergency session with his Cabinet.

Bruno Kreisky had been here before, it was the 1973 hostage crisis over Schönau Castle being re-run, this time for much higher stakes. Then the Chancellor had held in his hands the lives of four, now there were seventy people who would die if Kreisky miscalculated. To the Austrian leader the fact that a considerable number of the hostages were very powerful men was not relevant.

'At the time of Schönau the decision I made was to ensure that three poor Russian Jews and an Austrian customs official should live. At the time of the OPEC attack there were indeed additional factors but the eminence of some of the hostages was not in my mind a factor. All human life is sacred. You don't play games with people's lives.'

The additional factors included the problem of mounting an attack on the OPEC headquarters, which had Embassy status in Austria. It enjoyed the same privileges and inviolability that foreign embassies have throughout the world. Before launching an attack Kreisky would require the permission of the Secretary General of OPEC, who was one of the hostages.

In the light of that fact Chancellor Kreisky contacted the diplomatic representatives of the OPEC member states, the various Ambassadors based in Vienna. They unanimously asked him to submit to the demands that Carlos had made. By early evening Bruno Kreisky was also getting calls from the Heads of State of those countries, again the message was the same. 'Give him what he wants. Whatever it takes. Money. A plane. Anything.'

Three men had already lost their lives during this attack. Kreisky entertained no doubts that an attack launched by Austrian forces would end in a bloodbath. Saddam Hussein had chosen well when he had insisted to Haddad that Carlos should lead the assault on OPEC. His mythical reputation had indeed gone before him.

In the no-win situation that confronted him Chancellor Kreisky made the best of a very poor hand. Through the Iraqi mediator he told Carlos that a plane would be made available but that the doctors attending Klein insisted that to move him from intensive care would probably mean he would die. Under those circumstances Klein should stay in Vienna until fit enough to travel, at which time the Chancellor undertook to put him on a plane to a destination of his choice. Kreisky also insisted that he wanted the written consent of all hostages that they were agreeable to going on the plane and leaving Austria. He also demanded that all OPEC employees resident in Austria should be freed and that all of the hostages taken should be freed immediately the plane landed at its destination.

When these demands were put to Carlos by the Iraqi Chargé d'Affaires, the arrogance within the Latin American exploded.

'I command Kreisky and everybody else here,' he shouted. 'I decide who shall go and who shall stay.'

Then in an instant he was Elba's little boy again.

'I don't intend to take them. But I don't want people to tell me who to take and who to leave.'

The problem of Klein gave the Venezuelan further pause for thought. Told the full extent of the German's injuries and of the likelihood of his dying if moved, Carlos displayed for the first time an uncertainty.

'Our orders are that he must come with us.'

Then he hesitated as the Iraqi assured him that Klein would die if moved. Carlos called over the other members of his group and explained to the Iraqi that they intended to reach a democratic decision on the problem. An innovation from a man who had been behaving like an Emperor throughout the day. They were unanimous. Turning back to Al-Azzawi Carlos said, 'I don't care if he dies on the flight. We came together and we will leave together.'

Resuming his autocratic role, Carlos continued, 'Tell Kreisky to take care, I know all the tricks.'

Throughout the entire siege Carlos had deferred on a number of occasions to Valentin Hernandez Acosta. The Minister, who considered that each minute, each hour that he lived beyond those terrifying opening minutes was a wonderful bonus, displayed a rare presence of mind. It had been he, only minutes after being helped to his feet by Carlos, who had suggested that one of the Austrian secretaries who had gone into hysterics should be allowed to leave.

'If you keep her here, Carlos, she might trigger off the others into hysterics. Best let her go.'

Carlos had seen the wisdom of that and the woman went to freedom. It had been Hernandez Acosta who had suggested the food and then, when darkness fell, fearing that the Austrian police might try to shoot out the lights, suggested getting some candles. He was constantly on the alert seeking ways to keep the situation calm. He had suggested to Carlos that all of the hostages should be allowed to write a letter to their loved ones. Again Carlos saw the logic of that and in a magnanimous gesture stated that he was a man of honour who did not intend to read other people's private letters. A man of honour who had murdered one man and praised Gabriele Tiedemann after she had murdered two more. Late in the evening Hernandez Acosta again intervened. With the basic agreement to his demands having been made, Carlos relaxed. Removing his automatic gun from his waistband he placed it on a table and strolled to the other side of the room to get a coffee. He had put the gun down in front of Hernandez Acosta who for a moment stared at it, then crossing the room spoke to Carlos.

'Your gun, Carlos. You've left it on the table.'

'I can be confident of you. I trust you.'

'Perhaps, but pick it up anyway.'

Carlos obliged.

When Hernandez Acosta recounted that incident to me my mind flicked back to precisely the same scene in North Lebanon and the interchange between Carlos Two and myself. Such a clever touch.

It was nearly midnight before the Libyan Ambassador finally got to the OPEC building. By that time the crucial negotiations had been concluded and the various details of the transfer from the building to the waiting bus, the drive to the airport and the plane's departure all agreed upon. He accompanied the Iraqi who had conducted these negotiations to the first floor. There was for Carlos still one question to which he required an answer. Which Arab countries would accept the Austrian plane?

It was also a question that was greatly preoccupying Chancellor Bruno Kreisky. Carlos had talked of flying directly to Tripoli. There was just one problem with that destination. When Bruno Kreisky telephoned the Libyan leader, Qathafi flatly refused to let the DC9 land at Tripoli airport.

'He was outraged that what he called a group of criminals had attacked OPEC headquarters, and when I told him that a member of his delegation had been killed he said that the group should be arrested and put on trial.'

'Do you think that was a sincere response or was he putting on an act?'

'I know Qathafi well. It was no act.'

Another of Kreisky's Arab friends came to the rescue – President Boumedienne of Algeria. He was prepared to accept the plane. Other Arab countries prevaricated, among them Iraq.

While some slept the ever-busy Carlos began to separate those who were coming from those who were staying: some thirty-five locally based staff were taken into the OPEC library and told that they should remain there until the police came. Thirty-five hostages, comprising eleven Oil Ministers and their respective delegations, boarded the bus shortly before 7.00 am. The destination sign read Sonderfahrt – special trip.

At 9.14 am Carlos, sitting next to the pilot, Manfred Pollack, said, 'OK, let's roll out onto the runway.'

Minutes later flight OS 5950 took off from runway 12. The first part of the Vienna operation had reached, from

Wadi Haddad's point of view, a successful conclusion. Phase two would now begin.

Austria's Chancellor had been conned. Carlos had no intention of releasing all of the hostages at their first touchdown. The Saddam Hussein plan called for the murder of Sheik Zaki Yamani and Jamshid Amouzegar in Aden, the eventual final destination. But although Bruno Kreisky had indeed played with a weak hand, Fate had also dealt him a couple of jokers.

President Boumedienne of Algeria had not merely offered to let the plane land in his country, he had insisted upon it. This 'invitation' was communicated to Carlos while he was still playing God in the OPEC headquarters in Vienna; it came via the Algerian Oil Minister, Belaid Abdesselam, who like Hernandez Acosta had played a vital role in constantly attempting to defuse the situation while the negotiations hung in the balance. He was one of a number of senior Algerian politicians attempting to act as honest brokers, another was the Algerian Foreign Minister, Bouteflika. They saw the whole affair as a frontal attack on OPEC and concluded that loss of life at ministerial level would result in a serious disruption of the organization and possibly an explosive situation in the Arab world.

Before my interview with him, Dr Kreisky told me, he had never revealed anything about his long conversation with President Boumedienne.

'Boumedienne assured me that he would be at the airport in Algiers and that he would ensure that all the hostages were released at that point and that there would be no further loss of life.'

Boumedienne was the first joker that Kreisky held.

At the back of the plane on a stretcher lay the injured Klein. He had brought unrequited terror into the lives of many before being wounded, but the treatment he had received at the hands of the Austrians had been in marked contrast. In other countries he would have undoubtedly been left to die in a hospital corridor. In Vienna skilled surgeons had fought to save his life with emergency operations, intensive care and now his own physician.

A refugee from Iraq, a Kurdish refugee, Dr Wiriya Rawenduzy, busied himself with the oxygen, plasma and glucose that were being fed by tubes to his patient. Saddam Hussein had initiated the OPEC operation after having in his mind suffered public humiliation as part of the price of resolving his struggle to put down Rawenduzy's people. Now the man who had introduced himself to Carlos as 'a Kurdish revolutionary' used all his very considerable skills to keep a man who saw himself as a German revolutionary alive. Just in case the doctor needed any help he had Gabriele Tiedemann constantly hovering by the stretcher.

Tiedemann, who a few short hours earlier had cold-bloodedly murdered two men, was going through one of her Mother Teresa moods. During the siege Hernandez Acosta and the other hostages had only been treated to the bitch killer side of this woman. She had behaved at all times in a cold, hostile, threatening manner. Her gun had been ever ready, now she murmured softly to the barely conscious Klein and frequently mopped the perspiration from his brow. A touching scene.

Another equally strange cameo was being played out by Carlos further up the plane. He too had murdered in the OPEC building. Now that was all behind him. Just a bad dream, except for the dead Libyan. Carlos apologized to the Libyan Oil Minister just as Tiedemann had done to the Iraqi Minister.

'Perhaps your countryman thought I was Jewish. It's my nose you know. People often think I'm a Jew.'

He wandered up and down the aisle, he was again the host anxious to ensure that everyone was having a good time. Hernandez Acosta had pointed out to him that being forced to travel without passport or money presented a problem.

'Dr Acosta. If you want some money, I'll give you some. It's not a problem. How much would you like? A thousand, two thousand dollars?'

'I think not, Carlos. If I borrow money from you I'll have to meet you to return it. I'd rather not have that meeting.'

Carlos laughed and tapped him playfully on the shoulder then wandered over to have a chat with the Nigerian Oil Minister, Dr M. T. Akobo, who asked him for his autograph. Just the kind of request that Carlos loved. He duly obliged. 'Ilich Ramirez Sanchez. Vienna–Algiers. 22nd December.' Later he gave the pilot a couple of cigars, declaring that they had been a present from Fidel Castro. Another Oil Minister, Jaime Duenas-Villavicencio, asked to be photographed with Carlos; the Venezuelan was instantly agreeable, but unfortunately he had forgotten to demand a camera from the Austrians. Returning to Hernandez Acosta, Carlos handed him a letter and asked him very politely if he would deliver it to his mother in Caracas. The Minister promised to act as unpaid postman.

Asked by Yamani why they were going to Algiers when Carlos had told him that the first stop would be Tripoli, Carlos responded with a flash of honesty.

'I could not refuse their invitation. They are not part of this operation but they cannot obstruct my plan. We will not be in Algiers more than two hours. I will release some of the ministers there whom I had planned to set free in Libya and ask them to broadcast my statement.'

Yamani gained the impression that Carlos expected problems in Libya, he questioned his captor about this. The honesty was replaced with braggadocio.

'On the contrary. The Prime Minister will be at the airport to greet us. There will also be a Boeing 707 waiting for us which can take us to Baghdad non-stop after I have released some more Ministers. We will then go to our final destination. Aden.'

Asked by Yamani if they would be landing in Damascus, Carlos was adamant. 'I gave you my opinion respecting the Syrians. They have become deviationists and dangerous and I will not set foot on their soil.'

Spoken like a very loyal supporter of Iraq's Saddam Hussein. With regard to his rather grandiose vision of the welcome that awaited him in Tripoli Carlos was heading for a surprise.

He could not, however, have had any complaints about his reception at Algiers. Thirty minutes before landing he had brought the Algerian Oil Minister into the pilots' cabin. He had requested that an ambulance be standing by to rush Klein to intensive care. Captain Pollack was given clearance to land without delay and the plane was talked into the parking place normally reserved for the Algerian President's plane.

Carlos left the plane unarmed and was escorted to the VIP lounge by the Foreign Minister, Bouteflika. There waiting, as he had promised Kreisky he would be, was President Boumedienne. The Austrian Chancellor's first joker was now in play.

As the plane had landed the hostages had been ordered to pull down their blinds and keep them down. When the minutes began to tick away without any sign of Carlos returning, Hernandez Acosta moved quietly to Khalid. Previously Acosta had been told that he would be leaving the plane at Algiers with the other neutrals. After landing he had put on his hat and coat only to be told by Carlos to take them off again.

'I shall need you to negotiate with the Algerians.'

Now it seemed to the Oil Minister that Khalid was becoming increasingly agitated. Dr Acosta spoke to him.

'What's happened?'

'Something has gone wrong. Carlos told me that if he was not back in one hour the plane and all its passengers was to be blown up. That was forty minutes ago.'

Acosta's pulse began to race. If he had known at that moment of the notorious unpunctuality of Carlos it would have gone into overdrive.

'Look Khalid, before you blow up the plane and all of us on it don't you think it would be a good idea to double-check with Carlos. He might have forgotten the time, gone to the toilet, anything.'

As Khalid conceded it might be a good idea, Dr Hernandez recalled his very last conversation with Carlos before he had left the plane.

'Are you sure that it's not too risky leaving the plane?'

'Don't worry, Dr Hernandez. There's no risk. Look, it would be very difficult for me or my group to do anything against Algeria, the people of this country. But against Boumedienne and Bouteflika, that would not be a problem.'

'What do you mean?'

'If something happens to me then Boumedienne and Bouteflika are dead men and they know it. I have total confidence that if something goes wrong then my group will kill the President and his Foreign Minister.'

Something had gone wrong. President Boumedienne and his government were attempting to persuade Carlos to release all of the hostages. Carlos put the blowing up of the plane on hold as he continued to argue that he would only release the neutrals at this stop and that the remainder would be released at various stop-overs. Boumedienne was particularly concerned about the fates of just two of 'the remainder', Yamani and Amouzegar. Khalid elaborated for me.

'Carlos. Always he talked too much. By the time we got to Algiers quite a number of people knew what we were planning for Yamani and Amouzegar. Boumedienne attempted to extract a guarantee from Carlos that the Saudi and the Iranian would not be harmed. Carlos was at first insistent. He told the Algerians that he had his orders and that he had to obey them. He did however promise to contact Haddad after we had landed at Tripoli to establish if Haddad wanted to change the plan.'

'Was that a genuine offer?'

'No, no. It was to get the Algerians from his back.'

The 'neutrals' were given their freedom, including Dr Hernandez.

'As I left the plane Carlos gave me two bullets as souvenirs. I still have them. He told me that he had intended to use them to kill me. I said to him, "Would

503

you really have killed me, Carlos?" "Dr Hernandez, I promise you. You would have been the very last person to be shot."'

With Carlos back on the plane Captain Pollack asked if he and his co-pilot were now going to be freed.

'First we fly to Tripoli and then Baghdad.'

'We can't fly from Tripoli to Baghdad non-stop. We'll have to touch down either at Beirut or Damascus.'

The plane was re-fuelled and, after more than five hours of long drawn out negotiations, was about to take off. It was at this point that the Algerian joker again popped out of the pack. Among those who had been released was the Algerian Oil Minister, Belaid Abdesselam. Now he reappeared and insisted on continuing the journey with the remaining hostages. Boumedienne reasoned that his Oil Minister's presence might give Yamani and Amouzegar some small insurance; it would also mean that the Libyans would be left under no illusions about the ultimate plan that called for a double murder in Aden. Carlos, fully alert to the implications, attempted to 'persuade' Abdesselam to leave the plane again. Courageously the Algerian refused and took his seat.

Carlos's boast to Yamani of the royal reception awaiting his group at Tripoli was revealed as yet another of his little fantasies as they entered Libyan air space. Air traffic control at Tripoli airport refused to give the plane permission to land and dismissed with contempt the request that Prime Minister Major Jalloud should be awaiting their pleasure.

The Libyan Oil Minister, Ezzedin Ali Mabruk, was taken into the pilots' cabin. In a trembling voice he advised air traffic control, 'The situation on this plane is very dangerous. These men are well armed and will undoubtedly kill us all unless you obey them. We must be allowed to land and I demand that the Prime Minister be summoned to the airport as a matter of grave urgency.'

It was 7.10 pm local time when the plane eventually landed. The majority of the occupants were approaching their second sleepless night. Carlos and his group kept going on amphetamines, the others on their own private reserves of strength.

There was no Presidential parking place for the Austrian plane this time, instead they were instructed to stop on a runway a considerable distance from the airport building. Prime Minister Jalloud was not there to greet them. It took a further ninety minutes before he arrived at the airport. Carlos was told that under no circumstances was he to set foot on Libyan soil. It was hardly the welcome he had described to Yamani.

Full of his own self-importance, the Venezuelan was furious. He was also impotent. Khalid was despatched to negotiate with the Libyans, taking with him the Algerian and Libyan Oil Ministers. Reminded again by the pilot that they could not make Baghdad without a stop-over Carlos told him he would demand that they stop at Tobruk. When Pollack countered that he did not have any navigation charts for Tobruk Carlos told him that he would demand a bigger plane from the Libyans, something that he had airily told Yamani was already fuelled and waiting at Tripoli. It was not.

While Carlos sat on the plane behaving like a temperamental prima donna telling all and sundry that he deserved better treatment and bitterly complaining about the unco-operative Libyans, Khalid was coping with reality in the airport building.

'It was very difficult. Jalloud refused to give us a bigger plane.'

'But Carlos had already told Yamani on the flight from Vienna to Algiers that the Libyans would be putting a Boeing at your disposal. Why had they gone back on that agreement?'

'There was no agreement, that was just Carlos talking big. He was always talking big. It was only after we had left Vienna in the Austrian DC9 that Carlos learned the plane did not have the range to fly non-stop from Tripoli to Baghdad. He talked to the pilot who told him the DC plane would have to stop somewhere on the way from Tripoli or he would have to change planes. He assumed that the Libyans would give him one.'

'On what did he base that assumption?'

'That the Libyans would come to the support of the operation because Qathafi was a man who supported revolutionary movements.'

'That was just a belief. Was there an understanding before the operation that Qathafi would indeed support you?'

'No. Libya was not involved in the plan. It was an Iraqi operation from first to last.'

As Khalid talked to me it became clear that Wadi Haddad had made a serious miscalculation. The master of logistics had failed to appreciate that the maximum flying distance of the plane he had had Carlos demand from Kreisky was 1,200 nautical miles. The distance from Tripoli to Baghdad is 1,700 nautical miles. If Carlos had demanded a bigger plane from the Austrians, Yamani and Amouzegar would have been dead men; now their lives hung in the balance, totally dependent on Qathafi's reaction. Ironically, at the time of the OPEC meeting in Vienna, far from pushing for a higher oil price, Qathafi had reversed his traditional position. Due to an oil glut, the Libyan leader who a few years earlier had been responsible for breaking the rigid price freeze imposed by the Seven Sisters, the oil cartel, had by late 1975 placed Libya very firmly on the side of the OPEC moderates like Saudi Arabia. Now he was being asked to assist in murdering the leading moderate, Sheik Zaki Yamani.

'Jalloud told me that Qathafi was outraged by the Vienna attack. Furious that one of his own delegation had been killed by Carlos and furious that we had dragged Libya into the operation by landing at Tripoli.'

Oblivious of this as he sat on the plane, Carlos continued to talk airily to Captain Pollack of getting a bigger plane from the Libyans. He told Yamani that the reason he had remained on the plane was 'because of the attitude of the Libyans who have demanded that the negotiations be handled by an Arab'.

Jalloud was walking a delicate tightrope as he talked to Khalid. Qathafi had demanded that the Haddad group should release all the hostages and then leave his country, but as always in the Arab world, loss of face was of prime importance. Revolutionary leaders are supposed to support revolutions. After the Libyan Prime Minister had explored a variety of solutions with Khalid for over an hour the two men, accompanied by the Libyan Oil Minister, came onto the plane.

Jalloud moved among the hostages, greeting them in a friendly manner. Stopping to talk to Yamani and Amouzegar, he reassured them, 'Your lives are not in danger.'

Moving to the front of the plane, he sat down next to Carlos and began to demonstrate some of the guile of Arab negotiations.

'Well, yes, we can let you have a bigger plane, a Boeing 737, but I'm afraid it's at Tobruk airport and as I understand that you wish to then fly on to Baghdad I'm afraid that the 737 is of no use to you, it does not have the range. You need a Boeing 707. We do not have one of those available at the moment. My people are trying to charter one for you from another airline. By the way, Carlos, we've just heard from Baghdad. They've refused permission to land.'

One has to see this kind of technique first-hand to appreciate just how good Arab leaders are at it. The idea that any airline on earth would happily charter a multi-million-dollar piece of equipment to the Haddad group stretches credulity to breaking point, something that does not appear to have occurred to the man who had boasted in Vienna, 'I know all the tricks.'

Leaving the entire Carlos group on the plane, Jalloud left, again promising that the plane would be made available 'as soon as possible'.

It was now very late on Monday evening. The OPEC attack had begun before noon on Sunday. Carlos and his team had hardly slept on the Saturday night, all that sustained them now were the amphetamines. Carlos was showing clear signs of anxiety. Tiedemann came forward to join him and burst into tears. Khalid began to vomit. It was all falling apart. By midnight there was still no sign of either Jalloud or the replacement plane.

The plane left Tripoli. Before departing, Carlos had allowed another group of hostages to leave the plane, but it still carried ten hostages; four of the oil ministers and six members of their delegations. It was getting down to the wire.

As they flew the Venezuelan brooded. He considered he had been betrayed by the Libyans. His mental state alternated between the grandiose and the paranoid.

Khalid recalled:

'To Carlos everyone was now conspiring against him. I heard him talking to Al-Kazemi [OPEC minister for Kuwait]. He began by criticizing the Baader-Meinhof group whom he called incompetents. He said he could not understand why Haddad was so concerned at freeing them from German prisons and that the next Haddad action would be to kidnap a European prime minister and hold him as hostage against the release of the Baader-Meinhof leaders. He told Al-Kazemi that the West German Government was paying 2.5 million Deutschmarks a year to the Baader-Meinhof group successors to ensure that there were no attacks on German airports or Lufthansa planes. Then he stated that Qathafi had financed the OPEC attack and also the attack at the Munich Olympic Games.'

'Was any of it true?'

'Only the statement about the Germans paying protection money.'

'The OPEC operation was financed by whom?'

'By the country that conceived the plan.'

'Iraq?'

'Exactly.'

'And the attack at Munich?'

'What has Abu Iyad told you?'

'That he conceived and planned that attack. That it was financed by the PLO.'

'That is also my understanding.'

Then Carlos turned his attention to the Algerians to whom he was returning to try to obtain a larger plane. Perhaps they too would betray him. It was now two thirty in the morning. As Captain Pollack flew the plane over the Tunisian border Carlos suddenly ordered him to land at Tunis airport. The pilot radioed Tunisian flight control informing them he was being forced to land at their airport. The Tunisians had other ideas. They advised Pollack that permission to land was refused and then stated that the Tunisian government had ordered the immediate closure of the airport. Pollack, who in his many conversations with Carlos had found him 'very cool, very polite', suddenly saw another Carlos.

'He became infuriated. As we flew over the city of Tunis he ordered me to land, with or without permission. I protested, told him that they would almost certainly have blocked the runway with vehicles and that they might also attack the plane with rockets.'

'Don't worry about them firing at you, Captain. They don't have rockets. I know about these things. I want you to fly very low over Tunis to frighten them and then land.'

At the start of the flight from Vienna, when discussing details of the flight with Pollack, Carlos had remarked, 'Don't worry Captain, I've hijacked plenty of planes.' He hadn't, just more Latin American bravado. Now he was asking the pilot of a commercial airliner to behave like a stunt pilot at an air festival. There was little he could do but obey. As the plane began to curve to the left and lose height his co-pilot, Herrold, told Carlos to take a look out of the window at the runway below. At precisely this moment someone in air traffic control had the presence of mind to switch off all illumination at the airport. In a moment there was just blackness.

Forced to abandon his plans to land, Carlos ordered the plane to head for Algiers. He railed against the Tunisians.

'The bastards. I will eventually show them who is the boss.'

Arriving over Algiers the plane was forced to circle for nearly an hour. Carlos had been so enraged by his treatment at Tripoli that when he left the Libyan capital he had forgotten about the Algerian Oil Minister Belaid Abdesselam, one of his key negotiators when they had first stopped at Algiers. Abdesselam had been unwittingly left at Tripoli, shades of the murderous fiasco of rue Toullier.

They circled Algiers while other members of the Algerian government were summoned to the airport in the middle of the night. The plane eventually landed at 3.40 am.

This time Khalid was left in control of the plane while Carlos returned to the VIP suite at the airport and demanded a larger plane.

For Yamani and Amouzegar this was their moment of truth. Whether they lived or died now depended entirely on the Algerians.

The Algerians, like the Libyans, were more than a match for Carlos. 'We will try to get you a Boeing 707, but it's the middle of the night. These things take time.' Rocking with fatigue, time was something that Carlos did not have limitless quantities of. The Algerians began to turn on the heat. 'We could let you have a 727 but of course you know already you cannot fly non-stop from here to Baghdad in a 727.'

Making things hotter, they continued, 'Look Carlos, have you considered all the implications if you carry out Haddad's orders? The Saudis and the Iranians will come after you. Who will be able to protect you? Saddam Hussein? Perhaps for a while, but as you already know the Iranians have infiltrated Iraq for many years, and how could Saddam Hussein be seen to protect you when here in Algiers, just a few months ago, he kissed the Shah and signed a peace treaty? Wadi Haddad? If the Saudis bring pressure on South Yemen they will give you up to the Saudis. They'll give you a fair trial then behead you.

Just as they did to Faisal's murderer. There is however an alternative.'

They outlined a much more attractive end to the Vienna operation. As Carlos listened he warmed to their proposals. As he warmed to their suggestions any last vestige of ideals concerning the Palestinian cause dribbled away. Cynics say that every man has his price. Cynics will always have men like Carlos that they can point to.

The Algerian President, Boumedienne, offered Carlos sanctuary in his country. There he would be safe from reprisals from Iran, Saudi Arabia and, if it came to it, from Wadi Haddad. Then Boumedienne upped the ante. Not only a Presidential guarantee of his safety but money. A large amount of money. Instead of killing Yamani and Amouzegar why not demand a ransom to spare their lives? We have a direct line to the Shah, we've had it since before he came here in March. I can also call King Khalid directly. How much?

Carlos was no longer demanding big planes, he was haggling like any tourist in the souk. He haggled well, the figure eventually arrived at was ten million dollars. Per life.

Calls were made to Teheran and to Riyadh. The Shah of Iran accepted the demand, so did the King of Saudi Arabia. Carlos, ever suspicious, demanded a guarantor. Boumedienne had the answer to that.

'The State National Bank of Algeria will undertake to act as guarantor for the entire twenty million dollars.'

Carlos had a deal. He also had a problem.

Waiting on the plane at the very limits of their energies were his four comrades. They waited, not for news of a ransom but news of a Boeing 707. The Algerians had sold Carlos on their solution, now he had to sell it to Khalid and the others. The Haddad plan called for double murder in Aden not double indemnity in Algiers. Carlos retraced his steps to the plane then approached Yamani and Amouzegar. 'I have a problem and I am unsure what to do. You two are my problem. What to do with you. I am a democrat and you two do not

511

know the meaning of democracy. I shall have a meeting now with my colleagues and consult with them on what to do about you both. I shall inform you later about the decision that is taken.'

Yamani and Amouzegar peered anxiously forward, straining their ears to catch what was being said while whether they lived or died was put to a 'democratic discussion'.

Though the two Oil Ministers could not hear what was said, others could. Either through the pilot's talkback system or by their own direct bugging, the Algerians in the airport building were able to listen to the discussion.

Khalid and Tiedemann were particularly incensed at the suggestion that the operation should be aborted in return for a ransom. They were adamant that both Yamani and Amouzegar must be killed. Carlos continually protested.

'But if we kill them I won't get the money.'

He argued that the money was far more important. With additional funds of that magnitude Wadi Haddad would be able to mount dozens of spectacular operations, all in the name of Palestine. Carlos neglected to tell his colleagues that he had insisted to the Algerians that the money should be paid not to Haddad in Aden but to Carlos in Algiers. Khalid recalled the situation for me:

'If I had known that as we argued on the plane, I would have killed Carlos there and then. He was betraying Haddad, the Palestinians, everything.'

The arguments between the group raged on; all the time Yussef kept an automatic gun trained on Yamani and Amouzegar.

From his earliest training with the Palestinians in Jordan in mid 1970 Carlos had developed an increasing leader mentality. Many complained of it. If he was working with German revolutionaries Carlos would continually attempt to place himself at the head of the group. Moukharbel had seen the arrogance, so had many others. Dr Bruno Kreisky, recalling for me this 'democratic meeting' at the head of the plane, cited it as a justification of his opinion that Carlos only worked for Carlos.

'He is a condottiere. A mercenary. During that meeting with the others, which took place in a variety of languages including Arabic, English and German, he was obsessed with the money. It was his only concern.'

Khalid confirmed this.

'He went on and on saying how he would not get paid if we killed the two. Get paid! My people are without their country and all he could think of was money.'

Eventually Khalid and the others were outflanked by the Venezuelan. Khalid explained:

'Wadi Haddad's orders concerning any operation decision were very clear. Whatever instruction or order is given by the leader of the commando must be obeyed without question. We argued with Carlos that what he wanted to do countermanded Haddad's own orders to him. He said that was his affair and he would take full responsibility. We had to obey him.'

With his 'democratic' meeting over Carlos strolled back to the waiting ministers.

'We have decided to release you by mid-day and with that decision your lives are completely out of danger.'

When asked why he needed to wait until mid-day Carlos said he wanted to prolong the excitement a little longer. In fact he was waiting for the ransom money to be transferred.

Reverting to his best charm school manner Carlos added,

'Now why don't we turn the cabin lights off for a while? It will help you sleep.'

The hostages were given pillows, coffee, sweets.

When Carlos had turned on the charm, Gabriele Tiedemann was unable to control her anger. She screamed at Carlos, 'Fuck you.'

Yamani was convinced that he would die on that plane. He did not take into account Algerian guile or know that Carlos had already sold out the operation. A little later the Algerians called Carlos on the talkback. He left, and was advised that the money had already been placed by the Algerians into a bank account in his name. In view of the volatile situation on the plane they dared not wait for the transfers from Iran and Saudi Arabia. They also told Carlos that they had monitored the group's meeting and suggested a solution to him.

Khalid elaborated:

'When he returned he told us that the Algerians had listened in to our discussion. If either Yamani or Amouzegar were harmed we were all going to be killed. Right there, at the airport.'

Shortly before 6 am it was all over. After haranguing Yamani and Amouzegar, Carlos and his four colleagues walked from the plane. A short while later the hostages stepped onto Algerian soil as free men.

In the airport building the Oil Ministers and their various delegations began to recover from the ordeal. Nearby the Carlos group conversed with Algerian security, like a group of travellers waiting to be called for their flight.

Khalid managed to get over to where Yamani was quietly chatting to Bouteflika. He began to harangue Yamani. With eyes dilated, he vowed that Yamani's time on this earth was short.

'You will die much sooner than you think.'

Khalid told me of his intentions:

'Yes, I was carrying a shoulder gun. I planned to kill him right there. Then Bouteflika gave me a glass of orange juice. The next minute I was surrounded by Algerian security and disarmed. They prevented me carrying out the death sentence.'

Kreisky's two jokers, the Algerians and the Libyans, had turned up trumps. That was not how the media would tell the tale, but then the media had not the slightest idea of the truth of this Vienna operation.

Inevitably those far removed from what had confronted Bruno Krcisky were scathing in their denunciation of the Austrian Chancellor. Many were the editorials and articles that accused him of weakness, of striking the flag. The 'no deals with terrorists' brigade in Britain and the United States had a field day. This was in pre-Irangate scandal days and before the murder of PC Yvonne Fletcher outside the Libyan Embassy in London, when the Iron Lady, Margaret Thatcher, allowed the entire Libyan Embassy staff to leave the country without let or hindrance.

The Algerians too came in for a hostile press, a critical editorial in the *Washington Post* caused especial anger in Algiers. Bouteflika observed during a closed Cabinet meeting:

'The Americans would have talked out of the other side of their mouths if Kissinger had been among the hostages.'

Apart from fighting terrorism from the safety of a newspaper office, the media inevitably began to cast about for the mastermind behind the attack. The list of culprits is extraordinary.

Yamani got that particular game off to an excellent start when he pointed the finger at Israel. On the basis of who gains, it was an interesting choice of villain. Disruption of a largely Arab-controlled group handling the precious commodity of oil was certainly in Israel's interests. Initially the Egyptian press agreed with the Saudi Oil Minister. 'Israelis using Arab names', ran the headline in one Cairo newspaper. In Teheran they had another villain, 'The CIA and other Western Intelligence Agencies are behind the attack', declared one semi-official newspaper.

The PLO and the Popular Front both denounced the attack without offering any clues in the hunt for the mastermind. In London some of the City's right-wing press saw the Soviet Union's hand in the affair. Thus, uniquely, both the KGB and the CIA were being blamed. When the French government was confronted with the truth that Carlos had led the attack and that he was wanted in their country for a series of appalling crimes, it evolved a classic French technique for dealing with the problem of asking for his extradition from Algiers.

They planted a story, largely through *Le Monde,* that Carlos could not possibly have led the attack because he had been killed in the Middle East during the summer. When it was established that the 'dead' Carlos had given Dr Hernandez Acosta a letter to his mother, the French were more than equal to that. They declared that this was 'disinformation', that no such letter existed. More significantly, his girlfriend, Amparo Silva Masmela, who had been in prison since the murders at rue Toullier awaiting trial, was released on bail within days of the OPEC attack. Subsequently all charges against her were quietly dropped. Eventually, when a week after the attack the evidence overwhelmingly confirmed that Carlos had led the raid, French Intelligence planted a number of stories that he was now in Libya. In reality he was still in Algeria.

The Egyptians, meanwhile, had found a new mastermind – Colonel Mu'Ammar Qathafi. The newspaper *Akhbar El-Yom* promised that within days official documents would be published that would prove 'irrefutably' that Qathafi was behind the attack and had financed it. Seventeen years later those documents and that proof, irrefutable or otherwise, have yet to be published. In the interim period Qathafi's 'guilt' has become a 'fact'. No-one has ever pointed the finger at the real culprit, President Saddam Hussein. It was also announced in a wide variety of newspapers that the Carlos group had left Algeria and returned 'to their base in Libya'. In fact Khalid, Tiedemann, Joseph and Yussef were flown non-stop from Algiers to Aden and returned to Haddad's headquarters in South Yemen on December 28th. Carlos remained in Algiers until Klein was fit to travel. Initially it was planned that they would remain for a number of weeks. By the 1st of January Carlos, who had grown increasingly incapable of staying too long in any one place, wanted out. Klein was declared fit to travel and the two of them left the same day for South Yemen and for a very turbulent reunion with Wadi Haddad.

While stories of the millions that Qathafi had bestowed on Carlos and the odd one hundred thousand pounds he had given to Klein were filling papers, the truth was being closely examined by Wadi Haddad. Haddad was a very angry man.

His post mortem on the Vienna operation lasted longer than the actual attack. There were so many questions to which he demanded answers. He was critical of the wounded Klein. In Haddad's opinion, he should have opened fire and killed the OPEC telephonist, the Austrian Tichler, the Iraqi Al Khafali and a number of other people, but Klein got brownie points for staying at his position after being wounded. Joseph got a roasting for failing to back up Klein during the initial stages of the attack, he had got distracted in the main conference hall. Khalid was subjected to harsh criticism for failing magically to produce a Boeing 707 in Tripoli. Tiedemann was criticized for getting too close to the Iraqi before killing him. So it continued hour after hour. The harshest criticism was reserved for the man who 'knew all the tricks', for Carlos.

Khalid continued his story:

'In my mind and in the minds of the other members of the commando, it was not only obvious that Carlos had sold out but we believed that he had probably sold out a lot earlier than when he called off the operation at Algiers airport. I think he had it in mind to sell out before the operation began in Vienna. You have to understand, Mr David – and this is basic to understanding Carlos – he was and is bourgeois. A revolutionary only with his mouth, never with his heart. He loved big cars and Hiltons, that was where his heart has always been. If he ever had any ideals they were gone long before OPEC.'

Khalid talked to me at great length about Haddad's post mortem on the Vienna operation. So did Peter Boock:

'Wadi Haddad was beside himself with rage. There was talk of putting Carlos on trial. Others wanted simply to kill him without benefit of trial. Others, including some of the Palestinians, said that to kill him would reflect badly on the entire group, that they had employed him, used him and that he should be accepted for what he was. Some close to Haddad believed that in Carlos they had created a monster that was now uncontrollable.'

In his defence Carlos argued that he had had little choice. No long-distance plane from the Libyans, no access to Baghdad airport even with a long-distance plane. If he had allowed the murders of Yamani and Amouzegar to take place they would have all died alongside the Oil Ministers; as it was they had lived to fight another day. Haddad's response to that had been:

'Better to die with honour than to live with dishonour.'

Each of the extraordinary boasts that Carlos had made, ranging from his 'I've hijacked plenty of planes' to Captain Pollack, to his little gem to Yamani that 'I made an agreement with the Israelis in Switzerland. A non-aggression pact. I guaranteed not to attack them in Israel. They guaranteed not to attack me anywhere else in the world', was examined. Wadi Haddad raised no objection to the many wild and false claims that Carlos had made. In his mind they had probably increased the atmosphere of terror. There was however one exception: the Carlos boast to the Kuwaiti minister concerning the highly profitable blackmail of the West German Government. It happened to be true and for that revelation Carlos was again bitterly attacked.

Over and above all other aspects was one that particularly incensed Haddad. The money. The twenty million dollars. Haddad knew all about it long before Carlos returned to Aden. He was as enthusiastic about acquiring money as he was about creating terror. Money was the oil that kept the Haddad group rolling.

The story of the vast ransom for the lives of Yamani and Amouzegar had an ironic postscript. The Saudis had duly paid. The Shah of Iran had reneged.

As soon as the hostages had been released the Shah had cancelled the order to transfer ten million dollars to an Algerian account opened for Carlos. Advised of this 'perfidy' by the Algerians Carlos had rapidly countered. The Saudi Royal family again found themselves getting phone calls from Algiers. Anxious to ensure that OPEC survived (they were indifferent to Amouzegar's fate), the Saudis had made up the balance: a further ten million dollars was paid into the Algerian account. At this stage the Algerians got in on the act. 'Handling charges' would have to be levied. Five million dollars' worth. That left a balance of fifteen million. Exactly how Carlos and Haddad split that remains a mystery. Each person I interviewed who might have had the answer gave me their figures. The trouble is that those figures differed from person to person. That Carlos got to keep a substantial amount is beyond doubt. That Haddad also got his hands on a sizeable part of the ransom is also indisputable. It was the only way that Carlos could ensure that he lived beyond the post mortem.

Haddad's inquiry was merciless, he wanted every fragment, all were diligently noted and filed.

For Carlos it did indeed become almost a court martial. Among those present during what became an ever larger humiliation were Klein, Tiedemann, Wilfried Böse, Khalid and Brigitte Kuhlmann, but there was no need to be in the room. Haddad was convinced that Carlos had been functioning with a secret agenda, probably with Saudi contacts, well before the group assembled in Vienna. Haddad had never particularly liked the Venezuelan, he had always considered him an actor. A man with a super-ego, forever attempting to give the impression of his own invincible hardness. A man who had already demonstrated in Paris that he was incapable of group work. The sole reason that he had placed Carlos in charge of the Vienna operation had been the insistence of the Iraqi leadership. If that was what the client wanted, that was what he got.

When Carlos had returned with Klein from Algiers it had been in the Presidential plane of Rubayyi Ali. They had been met in Aden by virtually the entire Yemeni Cabinet, a film crew recorded their arrival. A full military band had played them to a welcoming dais. A private audience with President Ali had followed. It was for all the world as if a truly heroic figure had stepped on to the red carpet. Now, back at Haddad's base, Carlos was experiencing a different reception.

Peter Boock provided the details:

'Wadi Haddad gave him such a blasting. In front of everybody. He constantly accused him of betrayal, of being a mercenary, a liar, a cheat. This could be heard all over the neighbourhood.'

Others, including Khalid and Abu Iyad, have talked to me of the beatings and imprisonment to which Carlos was subjected. What saved Carlos from peremptory execution was Haddad's pragmatism.

From the moment that Carlos had led the group into the OPEC headquarters Wadi Haddad had been carefully monitoring the media response throughout the world. The myth that he had watched grow after the rue Toullier murders was now doubled, then re-doubled. Yet again it was confidently asserted that Carlos was controlled by the KGB, yet again every conceivable criminal act, both in the past and in the future, was laid at the door of the Venezuelan. He was about to demolish an atomic plant in West Germany. He was on the verge of killing the Shah and King Hussein in Switzerland. This flawed young man was now omnipotent. Singlehandedly he had sown the seeds of hostility, suspicion and fear around the globe. The Austrians were condemned, the Algerians vilified, the Libyans libelled. This last unlooked-for bonus gave Haddad particular delight. He considered Qathafi to be as empty as Carlos. Now he read, with growing amusement, account after account that placed Carlos in Qathafi's protection. Still no-one pointed the finger at Saddam Hussein.

Airports were on full alert, oil rigs under armed guard. Heads of State were being given maximum protection. NATO heads were in emergency session. Confidential dossiers on the 'Carlos Terror Network' were being assembled in capitals throughout the world. Qathafi had given him millions, the Algerians fifty million (a report that confusingly coincided with another that said

Carlos was about to blow up the Algerian embassy in Belgium). He was planning to kidnap a handful of top Egyptian politicians. He was ruling Libya and giving Qathafi orders. He was about to kill General Pinochet of Chile. He was poised to murder six Western Ambassadors. He had atom bombs at his disposal, and nerve gas, and hydrogen bombs.

All of this and a great deal more was asserted as fact during the early months of 1976. Haddad had, with international media assistance, created an extraordinary phenomenon. Yet again the myth saved Carlos, that and the millions of dollars that the Venezuelan was 'persuaded' to part with. Haddad and his senior Palestinian advisers concluded that to execute the man who had come to epitomize terror would be a public relations error and would damage their cause. It is difficult to understand such thinking but then to understand Haddad's entire rationale is difficult.

Having demonstrated at great length during January and early February 1976 precisely who ran his wing of the Popular Front, Wadi Haddad closed his files on the OPEC operation and turned his attention to planning more horror spectaculars. Carlos might have further use in the future, but never again would he be trusted to lead a commando.

From time to time he kept Carlos on his toes by threatening to send him to Baghdad, something that the chastened Venezuelan did all in his power to avoid. He was deeply concerned about the reaction of the Baathist leaders of Iraq. Haddad was fully aware of their reaction but chose not to share their response to the aborted double murder plan with Carlos.

Among the leadership in Baghdad there had at first been a great panic at the reaction to the Vienna attack in the Arab world. It had aroused enormous hostility. When the operation concluded in Algiers without further bloodshed Saddam Hussein and his colleagues were deeply relieved. That relief turned to delight when the world's media, led by an Egyptian propaganda exercise, blamed

Qathafi for the attack. Emboldened, the Iraqis went back onto the attack at the next OPEC meeting. Yamani had flatly refused to return to Vienna, consequently the meeting took place in Bali under massive security.

The Iraqis went in looking for a 25 per cent increase in the price of oil. For good measure their delegation launched a vicious personal attack on Yamani during the conference, accusing him of being 'an agent of the imperialists'. Yamani stalked out and refused to attend any further meeting until the Iraqis apologized. They duly did, and the Saudis were successful in keeping the next round of price increases to well under 10 per cent. Saddam Hussein was forced to postpone his plan to attack neighbouring Iran until he had pushed the price of oil up even higher and got rid of Iraq's President Al Bakr. The President eventually left office in July 1979, and within a year President Saddam Hussein had torn up the agreement he had been forced to make at Algiers and declared war on Iran.

Carlos, initially unaware of the Iraqi reaction, made every effort to mollify Haddad. When his period confined to barracks ended and he was again allowed to join the intimates around the doctor he demonstrated great enthusiasm for one particular operation – a plan to kidnap Pope Paul.

While Haddad remained sceptical, Carlos argued that there was no bigger target in Europe that they could snatch and barter for the freedom of the Baader-Meinhof leaders. The idea came from members of the 2nd of June movement then training in South Yemen. Haddad sanctioned preparatory research, and a mixed surveillance team that included Wilfried Böse, Brigitte Kuhlmann and 2nd of June members, among them Gabriele Tiedemann, spent over a month in Austria and Italy in early 1976.

The proposed kidnap was eventually called off by Haddad, who had concluded that kidnapping the Pope would result in such international uproar it might well become a suicide mission.

Haddad's terror factory continued to dream up other

plans. Some, like the killing of Simon Wiesenthal and the kidnapping of the entire assembled gathering of European Ministers, never got off the drawing board. Others, such as extracting money from international airlines, did. In April 1976 a demand to Japanese Airlines for five million dollars was followed by an attempt to blow up one of their planes in mid-flight. An observant air stewardess, spotting the unattended bag, removed it from the flight. It exploded on a luggage carousel; miraculously no-one was injured.

By April 1976 the OPEC débâcle was behind Carlos, he felt confident enough of his reception to go to Baghdad. With a touch of his former arrogance he demanded that Sushu, one of Haddad's aides, should find him an open-top Thunderbird car in which to drive around the city. He returned to Algiers and began to establish a permanent residence in that country. He enjoyed the direct protection of President Boumedienne, who viewed him with great affection. History was repeating itself: Boumedienne's predecessor, Ben Bella, had been much taken with Mohammed Boudia.

During the same month a meeting took place in Teheran that indicates how Carlos continued to pre-occupy the thinking of Intelligence agencies on both sides of the Iron Curtain. On April 14th Guennady Kazankin, the Second Secretary of the Russian Embassy, had lunch with John D. Stempel, Political Officer at the American Embassy.

Kazankin is a KGB agent, Stempel a CIA officer. This was a typical keeping-in-touch-with-the-other-side meeting, so beloved by agents during the Cold War. Over a meal in the Pizza Roma restaurant their discussion was wide-ranging: Soviet arms for Egypt, Vice President Nelson Rockefeller's recent visit to Iran, and terrorism. In his subsequent Confidential report Stempel observed:

'He then asked what I thought about the OPEC raid and whether I had any idea who Carlos really was. I said Carlos was a Venezuelan who seemed to be very much in the clutches of the Libyans. Kazankin said he thought the Western powers had been supporting

Carlos's OPEC kidnappings to fragment OPEC unity. I laughed and replied that this was bull crap, nothing could have been better designed to reinforce OPEC unity. Everything I had seen suggested the operation had Libyan backing, adding puckishly that if the KGB and the CIA really wanted to do something useful they should eliminate all these warts on the face of progress. Kazankin laughed and, surprisingly, agreed.'

Carlos, meanwhile, was settling into a villa in Oran, dining with President Boumedienne, Foreign Minister Bouteflika, and getting to know senior members of Algerian Intelligence. The man with a taste for good wines, Havana cigars and Hiltons could still talk a good revolution.

In May, back in South Yemen, both at Haddad's house in Aden and at the training camp outside the city, Carlos was being fed a constant supply of stories served up by the international press. The Venezuelan sat reading accounts of a massive security operation in Canada, an exercise mounted because of government fear that Carlos was planning an attack on the Olympic Games in Montreal. It was another fantasy, comparable to his alleged involvement in the Munich Olympic Games attack in 1972. He also read that he was not in Canada, but in Paris, assassinating Bolivian Ambassador Joaquin Zenteno. Under the Aden sun, his ego was growing as rapidly as his waistline. Talking to Peter Boock and other Germans he remarked,

'The revolution is all right for you youngsters. I'm not interested any more. I just want the hard stuff.'

'What did he mean, "hard stuff"?'

'Money. Big cars. Women and drink.'

Haddad flew into a rage when told what Carlos had said. He ordered that he was to stay in South Yemen 'until I decide you can leave'.

Carlos then gave an impressive demonstration of how far his influence had spread. Peter Boock told me:

'He contacted one or two embassies, had a meeting with the Minister of the Interior and suddenly Carlos had his passport again. At that time, when we went to South Yemen, you had to hand in your passport on arrival. They only gave it back after they had consulted with the Palestinians. Getting in was easy. Getting out without permission, impossible. Except for Carlos. He walked a very narrow edge for a long time. Such a balancing artist! Always he had some cover in reserve.'

Hard stuff or not, Carlos also maintained an active interest in pursuing his dreams to create his own global commando. He dared not poach any Haddad elements but he aspired to create his own worldwide infrastructure. He contacted the international revolutionary cells based in Germany, but those who had no first-hand working knowledge of him checked with those who did and declined his advances. Haddad, meanwhile, had conceived yet another plan to obtain the release of the Baader-Meinhof clique languishing in Stammheim prison in West Germany. Another plane was to be hijacked. Carlos, a man ever intrigued with the logistics and planning of operations, was one of a number of people that Haddad employed in the research for this attack.

The man that Haddad placed in overall charge of this particular hijack was Anton Bouvier. Every detail was meticulously checked and re-checked. The commando team was dispersed to a variety of locations, including Singapore and Bahrain. On the target day they would all converge on Athens. The guns and hand grenades for the team were smuggled into the transit lounge by ground staff. Before the attack the team had undergone extensive training and rehearsal in the Habbanijah Camp, a former British base eighty kilometres from Baghdad. During the intensive training period at Habbanijah Camp, the Italian media bestowed upon both Carlos and Bouvier the ability to be in two places at one time when, in Genoa, Attorney General Francesco Coco was assassinated and Carlos and Bouvier were held to be responsible. In fact they were both in Iraq, busily engaged in drawing up an extensive list of people imprisoned in many countries. These were to be exchanged, if Bouvier's plan was successful, for the plane's passengers, more than 250 men, women and children.

On June 27th Air France Flight 139 from Tel Aviv to Paris was hijacked soon after it left Athens. Haddad and Bouvier used a mixed team of Arabs and Germans, the commando leader was Wilfried Böse. After forcing the plane to land at Benghazi, it then landed at an airport whose name has stood as an example of Israeli ingenuity, courage and daring ever since. Entebbe. An Israeli commando raid succeeded in freeing all but one of the passengers; it also killed Böse and his entire group of hijackers including his mistress, Brigitte Kuhlmann. But the Israelis missed what would have been for them a far greater prize.

During the six days that the plane and its hostages were at Entebbe airport, Böse and his seven colleagues regularly conferred with and took orders from three men. Just forty-five minutes before the Israeli commando team struck, the three men had left the airport to drive into nearby Kampala for a late-night meal, thus escaping the fate of the eight hijackers. The three men were Wadi Haddad, Anton Bouvier and Carlos. Their presence at Entebbe was confirmed to me by a number of sources, including Abu Jihad, Abu Iyad and Peter Boock.

The one passenger whom the Israelis could not reach was an elderly woman, Dora Bloch. She had been allowed to go into the city hospital for a minor throat injury. That fish bone cost her her life. Enraged that he had been outwitted by the Israelis, Ugandan leader Idi Amin burst into the hospital ward where Mrs Bloch was recovering and strangled her with his bare hands.

Haddad subsequently recounted this obscene act to Klein, still recovering from his wounds in Aden. As Haddad and his remaining Germans planned 'revenge' and railed against Israel, Carlos for once took a more balanced position. He was full of admiration for the Israeli action.

'When the enemy retaliates with such devastating brilliance you should acknowledge their ability.'

With his friend Böse in the grave, Carlos saw a potential opening. He re-doubled his efforts to persuade a number of German cells to accept him as their leader. In September, accompanied by Klein to act as his interpreter, he flew from what was now his full-time home in Algeria to Yugoslavia. Courtesy of his good friend the head of Algerian military security, Commander Taihibi, he had acquired yet another identity, as indeed had Joachim Klein.

Carlos was now an Algerian Professor of Archaeology, George Osharan. Klein had become an Algerian television technician. Their trip had been arranged at the highest level, President Boumedienne having obtained permission from, and personally made the arrangements with, President Tito.

Like many a media-created star Carlos had by now made the serious mistake of believing his own publicity; his plans and schemes had become increasingly grandiose. Before his flight from Algiers Carlos had proposed to President Boumedienne that he should carry out on his behalf the assassinations of King Hassan of Morocco and the King's Prime Minister, Osman. Diplomatic relations between the two countries had been broken off in March. Boumedienne thought this an excellent suggestion and further Algerian funds were allocated to the Venezuelan while he carried out a feasibility study. Carlos had concluded that the extremely well protected Moroccan King could only be killed by a larger squad than he could then muster, hence the trip to Yugoslavia. The impresario was on a recruiting mission. Shrewdly choosing non-aligned Yugoslavia as his starting point in Europe, he then travelled via green borders, unofficial points of entry, to Italy, Austria and Germany. He wined, dined and entertained prospective recruits and, with Klein acting as interpreter, attempted to enlist members of 2nd of June, RAF, the Red Brigades and the German Revolutionary Cells. This was at precisely the same time as the West German government was offering a reward of fifty thousand Marks for the capture of any of a list of fourteen 'extremists'.

On the list were Klein, Gabriele Tiedemann and Carlos who, somewhat peeved that he had only been given equal billing with the others, told Klein that he was considering writing a letter of complaint to the West German government. He consoled himself with the observation that Saudi Arabia knew his true worth. There the price on his head was one million *pounds*.

The German periodical *Der Spiegel* had, only a short while before this scouting mission, been publishing extracts from Colin Smith's book on Carlos. The Venezuelan collected them and had them translated. Like so many before and since, he was fascinated by his publicity. His vanity grew by the day. When one of Haddad's close colleagues had suggested that such huge exposure merited plastic surgery Carlos declined the offer to have his face altered. He was however interested in surgery that might remove his flabby breasts. A habit that psychiatrists might make much of was a preoccupation, almost a fetish, with his personal hygiene – constantly taking showers, constantly dusting his body with talcum powder.

The various terrorist groups that he attempted to recruit were largely unimpressed. They knew that the continuing stories of his responsibility for a vast array of attacks were just fantasy. When he was accused of the murder of Attorney General Francesco Coco and two of his bodyguards, the Red Brigades knew the accusation was absurd. When the French and British press pointed the finger at Carlos after the Bolivian Ambassador Joaquin Zenteno was gunned down, groups such as the various Corsican freedom movements, the Carlos Committee and NAPAP (Noyau Armé pour L'Autonomie Populaire – Armed Nucleus for Popular Autonomy) knew he was not involved: the murder had been committed by members of NAPAP. When the German press linked him with the Peter Lorenz kidnapping, the 2nd of June movement knew it was ridiculous, after all they were the group responsible for that, and when the press throughout the world talked of a national alert in Canada, with thousands of photographs of the Venezuelan being displayed, even the Algerian Intelligence officers laughed: some of them were part of the rota *guarding* Carlos from potential assassins.

While a number of countries sought the extradition of Carlos and Klein from Yugoslavia and that country put out a totally false report that the Algerian professor and his TV technician friend had flown out on a flight to Baghdad, Carlos and Klein continued their European talent-spotting and recruitment tour. Though still under thirty years of age, Carlos was confronted with a younger, less respectful group, second-generation terrorists who were as unimpressed with Carlos as the surviving members of first-generation groups were. He won a few converts, most notably Johannes Weinrich, a colleague from the Orly débâcle, but largely the response was 'While Wadi Haddad is around why do we need you?' As for killing the King of Morocco, the European groups showed a marked lack of interest in getting involved in the Algerian-Moroccan dispute about the Sahara.

Even his constant companion Joachim Klein would have no part of Carlos's plans for 'world revolution'. By the end of the year the German had detached himself from the Venezuelan and taken up residence north of Milan. He wanted out, but out is harder than in. Today, in 1993, Klein is still on the run, still in hiding, though now living, if my information is correct, back in his home town of Frankfurt.

If 1976 was proving to be a frustrating year for the world's most wanted man, some of the women who had featured in his life were finding it equally difficult.

Having finished her prison sentence, Angela Otaola was promptly deported from England to her native Spain. The same treatment was accorded to Nydia Tobon. In her case she fought a bitter battle against deportation, to her such treatment was very unjust. Still moaning, she was put on a plane to Bogotá. In France Amparo Silva Masmela made no protest when she too was placed on a plane to Colombia, perhaps she should have. On Wednesday, 24th November 1976, while driving through the streets of Bogotá, she was murdered, shot from a passing car. Her killers were not seeking her, but the man at the wheel, who also died. His name was Alfonso Romero Buj, the former husband of Nydia Tobon. At the time of her death Amparo was four months pregnant. Their murders, part of an internecine feud, were carried out by a guerrilla organization called Leon Arboleda. Both Amparo and her new lover were very actively involved in trade union politics, too actively involved in the eyes of Leon Arboleda.

French Intelligence, in the shape of the SDECE, was planning a similar fate for Carlos. They knew precisely where he lived in Algeria and had concluded he was untouchable in that country. With typical French ingenuity they had evolved a plan to lure him away, not only from Algeria but from his boltholes in Europe.

In early 1976 two agents of the SDECE were despatched to Venezuela. Careful research had established that apart from himself Carlos retained the deepest affection for his parents. One of the French agents took up residence in the town of San Cristobal, the home of Jose Altagracia Ramirez Navas. Slowly, casually, he formed a friendship with the elderly man. The friendship blossomed and the agent became a regular caller. The second agent took a direct route. He knocked on the front door and told the father that he was a great admirer of his son and his various exploits. Over a period of time he too became a regular caller. At the end of 1976, the commander of the two agents, Jean-Baptiste Menuet, flew from France and took up residence in the Colombian town of Cucuta, on the Venezuelan border and only a few miles from San Cristobal. The trap was ready to be sprung.

It called for one of the father's new 'friends' to poison him, the method a dose of concentrated Hepatitis A virus; if necessary a Virus B inoculation would be injected after initial unconsciousness. With the father seriously ill, the French agents reasoned that word would reach Carlos, and that come hell or high water he would reach his father's bedside. At that point he would be kidnapped, rushed over the border to Menuet, placed on a waiting light aeroplane, flown to Guyana, then transported to France to stand trial. The three agents waited, poised to strike. They requested the go-ahead from their boss, Alexandre de Marenches. Because of the political implications, not least the illegal abduction from a foreign country, Marenches sought approval for the kidnap from President Giscard d'Estaing. It had previously met with the approval of the Minister of the Interior, Michel Poniatowski, but in view of the fact that he had left office in early 1977, Marenches, shrewdly wishing to protect his back, went to the Elysée Palace. In a country already suffering almost daily terrorist outrages from a number of groups the possibility of what might occur if Carlos was snatched and brought to Paris was too much for the President to contemplate. He aborted the entire operation immediately. It was a graphic example of how the myth had supplanted the reality. Wadi Haddad would most certainly not have moved to help Carlos and without Haddad's approval it is unlikely in the extreme that anyone else would have. The myth of Carlos was now stronger than any desire to see him brought to justice. For France he had become the world's most unwanted man.

The President's response undoubtedly saved at least one life, that of Senor Navas. The virus would probably have killed him.

Like Carlos himself, many, including an ever increasing number of Heads of State, were not interested in his reality, they found the myth so much more beguiling.

President Boumedienne would casually introduce Carlos to small select gatherings at intimate dinner parties and bask in the reflected glory. President Tito took a more pragmatic view, an Arab view – draw your enemy to you. Carlos was allowed to create a base on Yugoslavian soil. The payment? No attacks on Yugoslavian citizens or property, anywhere in the world. An additional benefit for Tito was the intelligence information that Carlos supplied, particularly on Middle Eastern politics. Another who, in late 1976 and early 1977, found Carlos useful was Syria's ruler, Asad. A series of attacks occurred in Syria. The Semiramis Hotel in Damascus was bombed, then the Inter Continental, then there was an attempt to assassinate Vice President Khaddam. The Syrians indicated that a renegade Palestinian group called Black June were responsible and leaked the fact that this group's leader was Carlos. Such a useful deflection. All of the attacks had been carried out by the Muslim Brotherhood based in Syria. It could have been dangerous to admit to his people that he was confronted with such a potent internal challenge to his dictatorship, far better to blame the notorious Carlos. Abu Nidal was particularly bemused, he was the actual head of Black June.

The myth, like the man himself, had by now become unstoppable and it made his life much easier. Not only did he acquire freedom of entry and departure to country after country, when he felt like adding to his bank balance all it took was the suggestion that an Arab millionaire should donate a million dollars, 'as insurance you understand, we live in such violent times, full of kidnappings and murders', and the money was rapidly paid. At least four million dollars were extorted in this fashion during 1977. Carlos was by now borrowing so many leaves from Haddad's book that the doctor might well have been tempted to sue for breach of copyright.

Frightened millionaires who paid at the drop of the Che Guevara beret. Heads of State who found a variety of uses for him. Governments that, if by some great misfortune they employed honest men who arrested him, duly intervened.

Entering Austria he was stopped and held for a day and a half then quietly released. Entering Sweden, this time posing as an Iraqi diplomat in August 1978, he was again arrested. It is highly unusual to detain or arrest anyone travelling on a diplomatic passport, it occurred because on this occasion Carlos had been a little over-zealous: he was carrying two Iraqi diplomatic passports, in different names, and a third that indicated he was someone quite different, a South Yemeni diplomat. The Iraqi embassy in Stockholm, contacted by Carlos through the Swedish customs officials, promptly complained to the Swedish government that one of their most respected members of government had suffered the indignity of arrest. Carlos was released.

As that incident shows Carlos was by this time very much in favour with yet another President – Saddam Hussein. The unfortunate conclusion to the OPEC attack was mentioned no more. Carlos had in fact created another base, this time in Baghdad, in early 1977. Ever a man looking if not to the future then to his own peace of mind, it was obvious to him that President Boumedienne could not live for long. By mid 1977 the President was already exhibiting to those close to him the onset of senile dementia. The Venezuelan concluded that with Boumedienne slipping away a wind of change might blow through Algeria after his death. When he became aware that Wadi Haddad was suffering from leukaemia, Carlos positioned himself to fill the potential vacuum that would follow Haddad's death. There were constant trips to Iraq, to Yemen, to the Gulf States, so that he could nurse his possible constituency.

The ailing Haddad meanwhile was preparing grimly for yet another attempt to free the surviving leaders of Baader-Meinhof. Another hijack.

Clearly Haddad was not a superstitious man. He trained the commando team where Wilfried Böse and his group trained before Entebbe, at the Habbanijah Camp outside Baghdad. He borrowed, courtesy of Saddam Hussein, a Boeing 737. It happened to be the same type of plane as that used by Lufthansa on their Majorca to Frankfurt flights.

Members of the Iraqi army chauffeured the team between their training camp and Haddad's Baghdad headquarters.

On October 13th 1977 a Lufthansa Boeing 737 flying from Majorca to Frankfurt was hijacked by a Haddad team. Five days later the hijack was over and three of the team dead after a combined German/British squad stormed the plane at Mogadishu in Somalia. The same day Andreas Baader, Gudrun Ensslin and Jan-Carl Raspe killed themselves in Stammheim prison. Ulrike Meinhof had left this life by the same door in May 1976. So many had died and suffered because of the continuing attempts to free these four, now they were gone. But the group they had given birth to, RAF, lived on to continue the killing.

The hijack that ended at Mogadishu represented a dual defeat for Haddad. His team had failed, but more significantly, with their original leadership dead, RAF turned inward. It abandoned its claim to be a support group for liberation struggles throughout the Third World; after Mogadishu it decided to confine its activities to West Germany. No longer would Wadi Haddad be able to call on his German colleagues in his war with Israel. With the Japanese Red Army very largely a spent force and his European infrastructure failing to recover from the activities of Carlos in 1975, Haddad's dreams of a Palestinian homeland achieved through a campaign of unmitigated terror were melting away. Carlos, for once justifying the title of The Jackal, sensed a mortally wounded creature.

In less than a week after Mogadishu there were press reports that Carlos had murdered Haddad by poison and had taken over. It was a scenario that would undoubtedly have appealed to the Venezuelan but, like so much that has been written about the man, it was fantasy. Haddad was ill, but not that ill.

While in late 1977 Carlos waited for the inevitable in Baghdad, his protégée Gabriele Tiedemann again emerged in Europe to spread further terror in the city where she had already murdered two men. In November 1977 she led a 2nd of June commando on a fund-raising expedition. They kidnapped Walter Palmers, the Austrian textile millionaire. He was held to ransom in a safe house on the outskirts of Vienna. After nearly two million dollars had been paid he was released. None of this money, of course, ever found its way to a homeless Palestinian, any more than the millions that Haddad and Carlos had extorted from the Saudis had done. These actions and many others might be cloaked with mouthed aspirations like 'bringing revolution to each and every country', a phrase that frequently dropped from the lips of Carlos, but the reality was different.

Crime Incorporated with branches in all major capitals.

In the month following the Palmers kidnap Tiedemann and Christian Moller, another 2nd of June member, attempted to enter Switzerland illegally through one of its green borders with France, a method much favoured by Carlos when not carrying one of his ever increasing quantity of diplomatic passports. Apprehended by border police, Tiedemann yet again demonstrated her pathological hatred of police officers. Drawing a gun she seriously wounded two customs officers. She and Moller were subsequently arrested. He was sentenced to eleven years imprisonment, Tiedemann to fourteen years.

During the same month that Tiedemann was arrested, December 1977, Carlos sat in Wadi Haddad's Baghdad headquarters listening to a proposition to murder, not a couple of border guards, but a Head of State. The target was Anwar Sadat, President of Egypt. The man seeking his assassination was Yuri Andropov, head of the KGB.

The myth of Carlos had now come full circle. The KGB knew full well that Carlos was not one of theirs, they had been attempting since mid 1975 to establish precisely who the Venezuelan answered to. The conversation, previously recorded, between a KGB agent and a member of the CIA in Teheran in April 1976 was but one of many attempts Russian Intelligence made to establish the truth of Carlos. They concluded rightly that whatever he had been and whatever cause he had initially espoused, after OPEC he was anyone's, if the price was right.

Giving covert assistance through the sale of arms and the supply of training facilities to freedom movements, revolutionaries and guerrilla groups had long been an official part of Soviet Union policy. Actively to sponsor and orchestrate a terrorist action, such as the assassination of a head of state, was a startlingly new departure, whatever the cold war warriors might think to the contrary. What had caused Andropov to move from the passive to the active was Brezhnev's fear that the domino theory was about to apply in the Middle East, particularly the Gulf States. Brezhnev had become President of the Soviet Union in June 1977. In October a joint US-USSR declaration on the continuing Israeli-Palestinian problem stated the necessity of a settlement which would take into account the national rights of the Palestinians. The statement was not followed by any joint superpower initiative but it was followed by an act that stunned Brezhnev and many members of his Politburo, including the then Chairman of the KGB, Andropov. President Sadat went to Israel and in Jerusalem, speaking to the Knesset, launched his own initiative in the quest for a lasting peace between Israel and her Arab neighbours.

Brezhnev saw a developing nightmare. If Egypt, the most powerful Arab nation in military terms, sued for peace, then the rest of the Arab world might well follow down the same path. Even client states such as Syria might not be immune if this initiative gathered momentum. If the Gulf States went the same way then Brezhnev's grand design for the region would be destroyed. His target was the Persian Gulf and the oil. Cheap oil for the Soviet Union and control of the quantity of black gold that came to the West. The Soviets controlled Afghanistan, South Yemen and had close relations with other countries in the region, but if rapprochement became in vogue between Israel and the Arab world, if ends could no longer be played against the middle . . .

President Sadat had spoken in Jerusalem on November 20th, the following month Menachem Begin went to Egypt. In the eyes of many in the Arab world, particularly the Palestinians, Sadat was guilty of treason. Acting on direct orders from Andropov, senior KGB officers convened a meeting at Haddad's Baghdad base. Among those attending were Wadi Haddad, Abu Nidal and Carlos. All present agreed that Sadat was indeed betraying the Arab cause, that it was all part of an Israeli-US plot, that something had to be done. The Soviets had very specific ideas as to what that something should be. They offered five million dollars for the assassination of Anwar Sadat and five million more for the assassination of each and every Arab leader who indicated a desire to follow Sadat to Jerusalem.

Carlos instantly rejected the proposal, left the meeting and caught a flight from Baghdad to Algiers. His response owed nothing to ideals but to self-preservation. It was one thing to boast to the oil ministers during the OPEC attack of his worldwide commando groups numbering forty to four hundred depending on which minister he had been talking to. He might well adore the myth, but he also knew the reality. The handful of Europeans at his disposal could never mount such an attack. He was not in a position to oblige Boumedienne with the murder of King Hassan, not without Algerian military help, which was not forthcoming, and he certainly lacked the wherewithal to launch an assassination attempt on the President of Egypt. From the OPEC attack onwards Carlos had repeatedly been linked not only with the KGB but also with the Libyan leader, Colonel Qathafi. A clearer example of just how specious these allegations were would be hard to find. KGB officers do not reject an order. The KGB does not make lucrative propositions to its own. As for Qathafi, there is no doubt that long before Sadat went to Jerusalem, relations between the two leaders were bitter. Sadat had constantly accused Qathafi of harbouring Carlos and declared that the prime reason was to bring about the Egyptian President's death. Qathafi would have shed no tears if Sadat had been murdered, indeed he danced with delight when Sadat was eventually killed by fundamentalist Muslims in October 1981. If Carlos had been based in Tripoli and under Qathafi's protection and support, then the Soviet proposition would have had frightening potential. The simple truth is he was not, hence the instant rejection and the flight to his sanctuary in Algeria.

Haddad did have the infrastructure but he told the KGB officers, 'I am not in the business of killing Arab leaders.' The leukaemia within his body was tightening its grip. Apart from niceties of not biting the hand that feeds you, Haddad was well aware that his time on earth was short.

Abu Nidal accepted the proposition with as much alacrity as Carlos had rejected it. Nidal immediately began to make contact with elements of the Muslim Brotherhood in Egypt and with his own contacts in the Italian Red Brigades and the German Revolutionary Cells. In April 1978, a mixed group of twenty Palestinians and Europeans, part of the Nidal cell, were arrested in Egypt in connection with a plot to kill President Sadat. The plotting and the attempts would continue until October 1981 when members of the Muslim Brotherhood successfully assassinated Sadat.

Haddad had been right about the limited time left to him. He died in an East Berlin hospital on April 1st, 1978. Carlos flew to Baghdad at once. He attended the funeral service and watched as the Greek Orthodox Haddad was lowered into the ground in an Anglican cemetery. He listened as Haddad's eleven-year-old son made an impassioned oration, then joined in the fifteen-minute ovation that was led by Habash and other leading Palestinians. It was, thank God, the end of a truly murderous era. Haddad's various operations had been directly responsible for thousands of deaths and an even greater number of casualties. His organization had bombed, shot and hijacked its way around the planet. One action alone, the multiple hijacking that had ended at Dawson's Field in Jordan, had led directly to civil war in Jordan, a Black September that saw the slaughter of thousands of Palestinians. He had extorted millions in many currencies from three European airlines and one American airline, though after the Entebbe hijack in June 1976 one of the carriers stopped paying the protection money. The projected kidnap of Ambassador al Tajir in London was aborted, but others were successful, from the Haddad point of view, disbursing yet more millions into his coffers.

The millions paid to avoid terror only created more terror, if not for those who took out the Haddad insurance policy, then for others. Some of these airlines paid with the full knowledge of their respective governments, a tacit acknowledgement of their helplessness when confronted by a man and an organization that stood as a definitive example of terror and terrorism. And for what? Not one inch of Palestinian soil had been liberated. The birth of Israel had in no small measure been brought about by the use of terror. Haddad had sought the re-birth of his country by going the same route. He had failed, but waiting at that funeral service was another Palestinian who had already embarked on the same journey. Such men are like buses, when one leaves another is sure to come along sooner or later. If Carlos was to win his struggle to inherit the Haddad mantle he would have to overcome some formidable adversaries, not least the man who had sat next to him when the Russians had made their proposition, the man who now stood next to him in the Anglican cemetery, Abu Nidal.

Ultimately neither man won the struggle. Many of Haddad's extreme wing of the Popular Front drifted back into the mainstream of the Palestinian movements, some went to augment Nidal's group, the remainder coalesced around a new leader, a lecturer at university known to me only as 'The Silent One'. Subsequent events established that not only was he untalkative, he was not predisposed to Haddad's philosophy of terror and violence. In reality Haddad's group died with him.

Carlos's lack of success in convincing members of the Haddad group to rally to his particular flag had a simple explanation, one I heard from a number of Palestinians including Abu Iyad: 'Wadi Haddad controlled Carlos to the last day of his life. Whether he was in Algeria, Yugoslavia or wherever, Haddad set his limits. He threw Carlos out of his group and yet still determined what he could do or indeed where he could go. The people around

Wadi Haddad not only believed that Carlos had betrayed their cause but also that he was empty, no ideals, just a bourgeois gangster, posing as a revolutionary.'

Carlos consolidated his links with the Iraqi regime. He paid his rent for this base by killing a number of Saddam Hussein's Syrian opponents. He continued his attempts to dominate the German Revolutionary Cells, to persuade members of the Algerian Secret Service to join with him in an assassination attempt on the Moroccan King. The Algerians, aware that Boumedienne was another who was not long for this world, declined to indulge the fantasies of their elderly leader or this upstart Venezuelan. He amused himself in the Algerian nightspots and enjoyed the favours of women who had been hand-picked by Algerian Intelligence. He continued to move around Europe without let or hindrance. On both sides of the Iron Curtain. There were trips to Paris, Belgrade, East Berlin, Prague. A Carlos safe house was maintained in each of these cities.

In May 1978 he was sighted in London. Home Secretary Merlyn Rees denied there was any evidence to justify the report. What the Home Secretary did not tell the public, because Scotland Yard did not tell him, was what had actually happened after the sighting.

An unmarked police car squealed to a stop near Victoria Station. A group of plain clothes officers seized a man, bundled him into the car and roared away. At a central London police station the bemused and very frightened man was confronted by a senior officer.

'You are Ilich Ramirez Sanchez, otherwise known as Carlos. You are being held pending a large number of very serious charges being brought against you. Now why don't you tell me all about yourself.'

'My name is Omar Tovar and I am executive employed by CVG, the Confederation of Venezuelan Iron & Steel Industries.'

'So you admit you're Venezuelan?'

'Of course.'

'And your real name is Ilich Ramirez Sanchez.'

'No.'

It went on. It went on for hours, then days, then nights, until eventually . . . 'Look, we're terribly sorry about this Senor Tovar. You see you do look like Carlos.'

Finally Omar Tovar was given a letter by the Commissioner of Scotland Yard. It formally states that the bearer is not Carlos.

Later the same year the British police tried again. They had been tipped off that Carlos was living in a safe house near Chelsea football ground.

They cordoned off the entire area around Billing Street. Armed officers, guns at the ready, kicked down the front door in a dawn raid. They burst into the bedroom. Sure enough they found a naked man, predictably with an equally naked woman. In Spanish he was ordered not to move. He did not have a clue what they were talking about because he did not speak a word of the language and his name was not Ramirez.

While Special Branch officers continued to hunt Carlos in England, the man they sought was in Baghdad, anxiously watching events to the south of Iraq. Civil war had broken out in South Yemen, and on June 26th, President Salem Rubayya Ali was murdered in a military coup. Suddenly there was one less Presidential plane for Carlos to whistle up as he had done after the OPEC attack. The new regime was even more pro-Soviet, which was bad news for the Venezuelan. The Soviets' antipathy towards Carlos, a fact of life from his Patrice Lumumba University days on, had hardened after his rejection of their proposal in Baghdad to outright hostility. At least in the short term, Aden could not be counted upon as a safe haven.

In July 1978 the British police tried yet again to get their hands on Carlos. This time they arrested not one but two men at Birmingham airport. They were held for five days on the basis that one or the other was most definitely Carlos. In this instance neither was Venezuelan let alone the world's most wanted man. He, in fact, was in Yugoslavia. In August, Joachim Klein, still on the run, gave an interview to the German magazine *Der Spiegel*.

Among other 'revelations', Klein asserted that Carlos had quit terrorism in May 1976. A few months after that observation Carlos was called upon by Yugoslavian Intelligence to pay his Belgrade rent. He obliged. He journeyed to Paris and awaited the arrival of Yugoslavian exile Bruno Busic, a journalist who worked with an exile group that called for independence for Croatia, Tito's homeland. In mid October he was shot dead by Carlos.

Some details of the Baghdad terror summit meeting reached President Sadat. The one error in the Egyptian information was that Carlos had accepted the five-million-dollar contract. This, combined with the additional factual evidence that Carlos had been arrested in Sweden in August and then allowed to continue on his way, was more than enough for President Sadat. He was due in Oslo in December to accept the Nobel Peace Prize. He declined to go.

Sadat was unaware that, as of late December 1978, Carlos had problems of his own. Assassinating the President of Egypt was not on his agenda, particularly when he had just lost the protection of another Arab president. On December 28th Boumedienne died.

When the dust had settled Algeria's new President was named as Colonel Bendjedid Chadli. He had previously been commander of the Oran region, which was unfortunate for Carlos: his Algerian safe house had been in Oran. The Colonel knew him well and did not approve either of the man or his exploits. Bouteflika, retained as Foreign Minister, attempted to intercede on behalf of Carlos, but a desire for change was prevalent among the new regime. Offering sanctuary to terrorists was deterring foreign investment. Yet again Carlos found himself packing and catching a plane as the perpetually open Algerian door became permanently closed to him. South Yemen was still difficult, but there was always Iraq and his chain of European safe houses. There was also, of course, Beirut, but an event that took place in that city on January 22nd 1979 demonstrated to Carlos that the Lebanese capital was not without its attendant dangers for a man who still in theory if not practice espoused the Palestinian cause.

On January 22nd Mossad finally caught up with a man who had not veered from that cause in his entire life. Ali Hassan Salameh, the man the Israelis had dubbed The Red Prince, the man whom they wrongly considered to be the mastermind behind the Munich Olympic Games attack in 1972, was murdered. A remote control bomb, triggered by Mossad agent Erika Chambers, killed Salameh, his four bodyguards and a number of passersby, including a British secretary working in Beirut, Susan Wareham.

At least Baghdad still represented a relatively safe haven for Carlos. The vacuum caused by Haddad's death had been filled. Not by any of the contenders for the role of Godfather of Terror but by a man uho had broken with Haddad precisely because he disapproved of such tactics – Dr George Habash. For Carlos, Abu Nidal and others who believed in the power of the gun and the hand grenade, Habash represented a retrograde step. He approved of attacks within Israel but nowhere else. Attacking their perceived enemy head-on was not part of the philosophy of Carlos. He has never to my knowledge engaged in an operation on Israel within its borders. He survived by attacking soft targets, not hard ones.

In March 1979, still on his global recruiting tour, Carlos ventured back into South Yemen; there were no takers, either among the resident Palestinians or the Yemeni. Back in Baghdad he wrote a long letter to his teenage hero, Douglas Bravo. He told Bravo that he was setting up an international revolutionary movement and invited him to join. Bravo, by now reorientated into Venezuelan society, declined the invitation. He wrote back to Carlos declaring, 'I do not believe in any type of vanguardist movement. They are bound to lead to defeat.'

Undeterred, Carlos returned to Europe, still travelling on his South Yemen diplomatic passport. His constant companion now was Johannes Weinrich, who fulfilled a variety of functions for Carlos, ranging from interpreter to procurer. The Venezuelan's sexual appetite remained as large as ever. As Germans like Peter Boock and Palestinians like Abu Iyad had previously observed, it was largely satisfied by sleeping with prostitutes. Highly appropriate – he sold his expertise, they sold theirs. In April 1979 Weinrich and Carlos could be found in East Berlin; in May in Sofia and then Budapest. Carlos's stay in Hungary lengthened from weeks into months. With the direct approval of the Hungarian President János Kádár he brought many of the tools of his trade into the Hungarian capital – a stockpile of guns of all kinds, landmines, hand grenades, Semtex. In June 1979 Carlos read in the international press that the Iranians were negotiating with him. Ayatollah Sadegh Khalkhali, regarded as the leading revolutionary Court Judge in Iran, indicated that Carlos was about to be sent to Mexico to kill the deposed Shah.

Later that year, while visiting Beirut, Carlos gave the myth further impetus when talking about his life to el-Jundi. Bassam Abu Sharif told me that the interviews had occurred quite casually.

'El-Jundi was complaining about having no money. Of his need to support his family. Carlos said, "I'll talk to you. You can sell the story."'

Published initially in the Arab magazine *Al Watan Al Arabi*, extracts of the interviews were subsequently published around the world. There was however a chilling sequel, as the editor of the Arab magazine told me.

'We published, as you know, three extracts. We were very pleased with the impact. We asked el-Jundi for a fourth piece. He refused, saying that under no circumstances would he write another word about Carlos. We asked why. El-Jundi told us that after publication Carlos had reappeared at his home. He was enraged. Something in the articles had angered him. He got out a gun and shot el-Jundi in the shoulder and said, "Next time, here." He was pointing between his eyes.'

I do not know if this story is merely apocryphal. When I heard it I was filled with a mixture of fear and anger. To have established the truth of this act might have deflected me from my hunt, made me pause in my quest. I had no desire for such deflection. The Carlos I have come to understand is more than capable of such an act.

In November 1979 it was reported that Carlos had masterminded the seizure by Iranian students of the American Embassy in Teheran.

In September 1980 Latin American intelligence services declared their belief that Carlos was responsible for the assassination of the former Nicaraguan dictator Anastasio Samoza Debayle. Carlos was most certainly involved in violent activities at that time but they were of a less political nature. Further extortion of wealthy Arab businessmen, in Kuwait and Lebanon, then back to his European bases and his prostitutes. He changed his clients as frequently as the women he slept with changed theirs. By 1981 Carlos's main Middle East base was no longer Baghdad and his main Arab protector no longer Saddam Hussein. He had gone to work for Hussein's most implacable enemy, President Hafiz al-Asad of Syria.

Asad was fighting what amounted to civil war against the Muslim Brothers in Syria. In March 1981 Carlos led an attack on the leader-in-exile of the Muslim Brothers, Isam al-Attar, who lived in Aachen in West Germany. When the front door was opened not by al-Attar but by his wife, he did not stop to ask for her husband, merely murdered her on the doorstep and vanished.

In September he obliged the Syrian leader by murdering the French Ambassador to the Lebanon, Louis Delamare. Demonstrating his ingratitude for the comfort and support previously given to him by President Saddam Hussein, he also disposed of a number of Iraqis on behalf of the Syrian President.

One particular area that Asad and his regime were particularly sensitive on was press criticism. It did not happen within the confines of Syrian borders, within the country all press was government-controlled. Beyond Syria the regime exercised another form of censorship that was equally effective. They killed the journalists. In Jordan and in Lebanon men died because of what they had written. Carlos was fully prepared to oblige in this area too. The Syrians wanted a particular Arab magazine silenced. The magazine was *Al Watan Al Arabi,* which was financed with Iraqi regime money and published in Paris. In late 1981 Carlos flew from Damascus back to his European bases. In his safe house in Bucharest he began to formulate a plan with Weinrich. This was at precisely the same time as the CIA-inspired disinformation campaign had him crossing the Mexican border and entering the United States on his way to the White House with the intention of killing President Reagan. The reality underlines just how much of American taxpayers' money has been wasted on its various intelligence services. If one author can establish the truth surely a billion-dollar-funded agency can.

Carlos had played the Haddad connection brilliantly. It had enabled him to set up an extraordinary infrastructure. He had failed to draw on the manpower that Haddad commanded in the Middle East and Europe, but because he himself had been part of that he was able cleverly to build on Haddad's many contacts and connections.

Thus, in Hungary he enjoyed the support of President János Kádár, the Ministry of the Interior and the Hungarian Secret Service. 'The man who dealt with and monitored the Carlos group was Sandor Racz, Deputy Minister of the Interior. My investigations established that Carlos had several bases in the country from 1979 to 1982. When arriving in a conventional manner at Budapest International Airport he used the passport control section marked 'diplomats only' at gate number one. As always Carlos favoured a variety of passports and names. The one that he used most frequently, not only for visits to Hungary but to his other European bases, had been given to him during his visit to South Yemen in March 1979. Number 001 278, it indicated that his name was Ahmed Adil Fawaz. Often his entrance required no passport, however, as he entered through green borders from Romania. Members of the current government have told me that he was 'not so much made welcome but tolerated'. It was toleration at an impressive level. Though not granted training facilities, which other COMECON countries would not have viewed with equanimity, Carlos and his group were allowed 'rest and recreation facilities' as they recovered from their last terrorist outrage or prepared for the next one. In 1981, when Hungary joined Interpol and created its own anti-terrorist squad, the happy carefree days of sunbathing and receiving from Czechoslovakia and other suppliers their next consignment of Semtex, infra-red telescopes and the other trappings of their trade began to draw to a close.

When the Soviets eventually discovered that Carlos had bases in Hungary they brought pressure to bear on President Kádár and his colleagues. To the KGB Carlos was 'a mercenary and a renegade who has no involvement in the Palestinian struggle. We recommend his expulsion.'

It took time. Hungarian Secret Service attempted to reason with Carlos – always a difficult exercise. They told him that he must liquidate his bases and move on, that his various 'operations' were in danger of being compromised and 'your activities threaten the People's Republic of Hungary'. They left him in no doubt that the threat came from Moscow. Carlos, ever a man to sit down and write letters at a moment of acute crisis, put pen to paper and wrote to President Kádár.

The letter, written in 1981, thanked the President for his hospitality; Elba would have been gratified to learn that her eldest son had retained his good manners. It continued: 'We have been able to expand our international contacts with the revolutionaries of all nations of the world from Hungarian territory, without being prevented by the Hungarian authorities.' Forgetting that he was in the country under the name of Fawaz, the Venezuelan signed it 'Carlos'. Having told the Minister of the Interior that he never stayed where he was not wanted, Carlos left Budapest in a fit of pique. That was followed by at least a partial reconciliation. He was still moving in and out of the country as late as 1985. A stock of the tools of his trade remains in Hungary as of now.

In Romania, with the direct approval and permission of President Ceauşescu, Carlos maintained bases in Bucharest from 1980 onwards. Wadi Haddad had never been impressed by Ceauşescu, on one occasion observing to Khalid that the Romanian leader was 'as crazy as Qathafi'. Carlos held a far more tolerant opinion, one shared in the late seventies and eighties by many a Western country. The Romanian leader was an honoured guest at the White House, Buckingham Palace and the Elysée Palace at a time when the intelligence agencies of the United States, Britain and France were very aware of the appalling conditions under which the ordinary people lived in Ceauşescu's Romania. Another who enjoyed Ceauşescu's hospitality at this time was Abu Nidal.

Like many a dictator before him, President Nicolae Ceauşescu was a paranoid. He maintained excellent relations with Israel, the only Warsaw Pact country during the Cold War to do so. He became convinced that his state airline, Tarom, was being targeted by Carlos, particularly on the Bucharest–Tel Aviv routes. If his secret service, the DIE, had been functioning efficiently, it would have been able to advise him that Carlos had long ago abandoned the Palestinian cause and that well before 1980 he had become a very expensive gun for hire.

The Romanian leadership, anxious to prevent non-existent plans to hijack Tarom passenger planes coming to fruition, gave Carlos carte blanche: arms, safe houses, training facilities, money.

In early 1981 the DIE advised Carlos that Ceauşescu, like many a landlord before him, had upped the rent. The target that the President had in mind for his house guest was Radio Free Europe. The CIA-funded station based in Munich had been a thorn in Ceauşescu's side for many years. One of its regular features had been the broadcasting of programmes by Romanian exiles that were highly critical of Ceauşescu, his wife and the inner circle of power in Bucharest. The Ceauşescus, like Asad of Syria, were not the sort to take kindly to criticism. Carlos was also advised that there were a number of Romanians living in France who were in need of his attention.

Shortly after Carlos had discussed the issue of how sensitive President Ceauşescu was to criticism he delivered the Romanian leader's response to his critics. Three parcel bombs, posted in Spain, were delivered to the homes of Romanian dissidents living in Paris.

In February 1981, in an operation planned at his East Berlin base, Carlos sent Weinrich into West Germany. On February 21st the Carlos group blew up 'Radio Free Europe', demolishing the radio station that had so enraged Ceauşescu and seriously injuring four people in the process.

If Boumedienne was dead and Saddam Hussein no longer on the favoured client list, they had indisputably been replaced with an international range of powerful protectors. By May 1981, when his protector in Yugoslavia, Marshal Tito, died, Carlos had the backing and support of several regimes and their leaders. Presidents Asad of Syria, Honecker of East Germany, Kádár of Hungary, Ceauşescu of Romania, Hoxha of Albania, Zhivkov of Bulgaria, Husák of Czechoslovakia. The fact that the leaderships changed in Yugoslavia and South Yemen made no difference. Carlos continued to have a base in Belgrade and to carry a South Yemeni diplomatic passport. What brought about the collapse of much of this infrastructure can be traced, not to Gorbachev's perestroika and glasnost, but to Carlos himself. As he had almost singlehandedly destroyed Haddad's European infrastructure in 1975, so in early 1982 he began to bring about a comparable destruction of his own network.

This second destruction was triggered by the innate weaknesses that are within Carlos. The arrogance, the

Latin American machismo, the pathological inability to hold emotions in check, above all the rage when his point of view is seriously threatened.

It began with the 'request' from the Syrian regime that he should silence a minor irritant – the magazine *Al Watan Al Arabi*. Carlos was up for that, they had published el-Jundi's interview with him that had provoked him into shooting the writer.

At the Palast Hotel in East Berlin, at his safe houses in Bucharest and Budapest, he began to put the pieces of the operation together. With him were Weinrich and other members of his group, including Magdalena Kopp. There was a certain piquancy about Kopp's presence. From 1973 she had been Weinrich's lover; this was two years before Weinrich was hiring cars on behalf of Carlos to launch his rocket attack at Orly airport. At some time between then and early 1982 she had transferred her affections from Weinrich to Carlos. It had no apparent effect on the friendship or working relationship between the two men. Weinrich has remained loyal to the Venezuelan to this day.

The relationship between Carlos and Magdalena grew from a one-night stand at the Palast Hotel (which was duly tape-recorded by Honecker's secret police) into something far more significant. Just how significant a great many people were soon to discover.

Magdalena Kopp had, from the early 1970s, been drawn to the revolutionary movements in Germany. Born in Ulm in 1948, she had subsequently trained as a professional photographer. Well educated and demure, there was more than a touch of Gabriele Tiedemann. Though she had been a close friend of, among others, Wilfried Böse, the petite Kopp with the big brown eyes and the shoulder-length brunette hair had until now largely contented herself with being a drawing-room revolutionary.

When Carlos was selecting a unit to carry out the attack in Paris his mistress prevailed upon him. She wanted to be part of the action. In a clear indication of how few rallied to the Carlos version of revolutionary action, the Venezuelan agreed.

In Paris on the 16th of February 1982 the attention of an underground car park attendant was drawn to two people. They were behaving oddly. Leaving his box by Avenue George V, the attendant went to investigate. It transpired that the couple did not have parking permission. An elementary mistake. The attendant told the man and the woman, the apparent owners of an elderly Peugeot with a very new registration number, that he would like to take down some further details. The man, Bruno Breguet, drew a gun and attempted to shoot the attendant. It failed to fire. Leaping into the car they roared off into the night. A short while later a police patrol picked up the car. Not hard with such a giveaway registration number. Stopping the Peugeot, the officers approached. Again Breguet tried to shoot, again his gun failed to fire. I would suspect it was something to do with the safety catch still being on. Breguet and his companion, Magdalena Kopp, were arrested. After years of flirting with the various revolutionary movements Kopp had blown it on her first active operation. In the car police found two full gas bottles, five kilos of 'Penthrit' explosive and detailed maps with a variety of markings. It would later be alleged that the potential target for the two was the Hôtel de Ville or the office of the Prime Minister. Both allegations were wrong: this attack had only one target, ordered by the Syrian regime and within a short walking distance of that underground car park, the offices of *Al Watan Al Arabi* on rue Marbeuf, immediately off Avenue George V.

Breguet and Kopp were not talking, but then they had been so careless there was hardly any need. The car and its contents and their own possessions spoke eloquently. The elderly Peugeot had previously been owned by the brother of one of the leaders of the FLNC, the National Front for the Liberation of Corsica, a group with long-established contacts with Carlos. The false passports were expertly created. In Breguet's West Berlin flat a treasure trove of documents was found which all linked Breguet with Carlos and Weinrich. It was like a replay of the rue Toullier affair without the mindless violence – yet.

Breguet was no stranger to revolutionary incompetence. In June 1970 he disembarked at the Israeli port of Haifa. What particularly attracted the attention of the Israeli officials was the fact that, despite the near stifling heat, Breguet was wearing a heavy overcoat. Extremely heavy. The Israelis found two kilograms of explosive. He got fifteen years for his efforts to help the Popular Front. He had been released prematurely after serving only seven. His early release was due to persistent lobbying by a Swiss banker, François Genoud, who had frequently acted as a financial adviser for the PLO.

At the time of their arrest no-one connected Breguet and Kopp with the world's most wanted man, indeed *Newsweek* and the *New York Post* were just two of many which coincidentally carried reports of Carlos still residing in a seaside villa in Tripoli while he arranged Qathafi's security on foreign trips.

The Venezuelan had other problems than checking out hotel rooms in Vienna for the Libyan leader. The French were holding his girlfriend and all of his machismo welled up from within. Sitting in his Budapest safe house he yet again penned a letter, but this time with a difference. It was a declaration of war on France.

The letter, written in Spanish, was couriered to Holland. There it was dropped in the postbox of the French Embassy. The same Embassy that a few years earlier had been taken over by the Japanese Red Army intent on obtaining a colleague's release from a French prison. This time Carlos did not send in a commando unit, just a single page of writing. The letter arrived on March 1st, 1982, less than two weeks after the arrests of Kopp and Breguet. It was addressed to Gaston Defferre, the Interior Minister.

25 February 1982
Minister of State, Minister for the Interior and Decentralization

M. le Ministre

I am writing to inform you

First: That two soldiers from our Organization, Magdalena Cecilia Kopp and Bruno Breguet, have been arrested in Paris by the French Security forces.

Second: That our soldiers have been arrested while carrying out the orders of those who are accountable for them for a mission which was not directed against France.

Third: That our soldiers do not deserve prison as retribution for their dedication to the Revolutionary Cause.

Fourth: That our Organization will never abandon our soldiers.

Following the decision of our Central direction I give you the following warning. We will not accept our comrades being in prison. We will not tolerate our comrades being extradited to any country, no matter which.

We demand:

1 An immediate halt to all interrogation of our soldiers.

2 The release of our soldiers within 30 days of the date of this letter.

3 That our soldiers should be released with all the correct documents.

4 That our soldiers should be allowed to travel together by a regular airline to a country and by the route of their choice. They should have a French permit to leave.

We are not at war with Socialist France and I beg of you not to force us to be so.

I assure you that the contents of this letter are considered to be a secret of the Organization. However we have no objection to it being made public.

We hope that this business can be brought to an early and satisfactory ending.

By the Organization of the Armed Arab Struggle – arm of the Arab Revolution.

Carlos.

PS: I enclose below my fingerprints in order to identify this letter.

The French Cabinet went into emergency session. The possibility of quietly releasing the two was given serious consideration. A member of Defferre's staff did not agree with the decision that he saw about to be made. He believed that terrorism should be fought, that there should never be any concessions. No deals. He leaked the contents of the Carlos letter to Agence France Presse, thereby pre-empting any deal. Once the threat had become public knowledge and then international knowledge the French Government dug in. There would be no deal.

On March 29th, precisely one month after the Carlos ultimatum, a Carlos group blew up the 'Capitole', the trans-Europe express from Paris to Toulon. The train, known as 'the Chirac train' because Jacques Chirac used it frequently, was travelling at over one hundred miles an hour when a bomb ripped apart the compartment normally reserved for Chirac. Five people died and a further twenty-seven were injured. The casualty figures could easily have been much higher. The train, carrying over four hundred people, miraculously stayed on the track as the first carriage fragmented.

On April 3rd an Israeli diplomat, Yakov Barsimantov, was murdered, shot in the lobby of his Paris apartment.

On April 16th a French Embassy official, Guy Cavallot, and his pregnant wife, Caroline, were murdered in their West Beirut apartment. The killers had masked their guns under a bouquet of flowers.

Three days later, Carlos directed his venom at French property in Vienna. A bomb blast wrecked the offices of Air France. A second bomb simultaneously exploded at the French Embassy in Vienna.

On April 22nd he bombed the French News Agency in Beirut, and then minutes before the trial of Kopp and Breguet was due to start in Paris he hit the target that they had themselves been sent to Paris to attack.

This second, successful attempt originated from the Venezuelan's safe haven in Hungary. A member of the Carlos group, Christa Frohlich, using a false Swiss passport and forged documentation, hired an Opel car in Budapest. It was driven to a safe house in the city, where Carlos constructed a bomb. The number plates were changed, the new ones indicated that the car came from Vienna. Frohlich then drove the car through Europe to its final destination, the offices of *Al Watan Al Arabi* in rue Marbeuf, Paris. As the prosecutor got to his feet to outline the case against Kopp and Breguet, the timing device, previously set by Frohlich, triggered a fearful explosion. The fashionable street was transformed in a moment to Beirut. A passerby, yet another pregnant woman, was killed instantly, sixty more people were injured.

None of this could be rationalized as part of the Palestinian struggle. A terror campaign had been orchestrated in the name of Carlos's love for Magdalena Kopp. The ultimate obscenity. People were dying, being wounded, being terrorized, because one little fat man wished to be reunited with his girlfriend. Fascism of the heart.

The French authorities, in an action reminiscent of their response to the Carlos atrocity at Le Drugstore in 1974, declined to connect any of these attacks with Carlos. The attack on the Arab magazine was attributed to Syrian opposition to the periodical. The French Government subsequently expelled two Syrian diplomats. It was another echo of the rue Toullier, when the French had fastened on Cuban diplomats. They were wrong then, they were wrong now. It was true that the Asad regime had wanted the magazine destroyed or at least intimidated, but that was before

Kopp's arrest. The actual attack had nothing to do with the Syrians. This was personal. One man's war against the State.

President Mitterrand summoned what one of his Ministers described to me as 'an emergency war cabinet meeting'. The President and the entire French Government were under massive twenty-four-hour protection. Democracy was also under siege as the trial of Kopp and Breguet began.

The leading lawyer for the defence was the man who, if Carlos is ever brought to the bar of justice in France, will almost certainly defend him, Jacques Vergès. Over the years his clients have ranged from the far left, in the shape of Palestinian terrorists, to the far right, in the person of Klaus Barbie, a Third Reich terrorist.

Vergès was in no doubt that Breguet had been beaten and tortured after his arrest. He had independent medical evidence confirming sustained beatings and deprivation of sleep. This had occurred in the headquarters of the first territorial brigade on the 16th and 17th of February. He was equally certain that even if found guilty neither Breguet nor Kopp would serve their full sentences. Vergès based this belief on his knowledge of the 'accommodation' that existed between Germany, Switzerland and a number of other countries. An agreement that many Arab groups and Israeli killer squads had with various governments. Immunity from arrest and imprisonment in return for the promise not to initiate attacks within the nation's borders.

Before the start of the trial Minister Gaston Defferre had stated that only twenty people had known the contents of the Carlos letter before it had been deliberately leaked and that whoever had been responsible would bear the responsibility for any blood that was spilt. It had been the clearest indication that the French government was prepared to do a deal with Carlos. Now, with the revelation of the threats and the series of attacks during the pre-trial period, the Government had concluded that all deals were off.

Evidently defence lawyer Vergès remained unconvinced that the French government would maintain its hard-line posture. During the trial he said to the presiding judges:

'These are soldier-prisoners engaged in a noble cause. They know that their friends will not rest while they are in prison. It is not possible that France should keep them in her hands. Will they remain in prison forty hours, one month, three months? The question of when they will be released poses the question of how much blood will be shed before they are freed.'

Vergès then, in a moment of extraordinary indiscretion, indiscreet that is from the French government's point of view, lifted a corner of the veil that for years had covered a secret unwritten agreement between Carlos and successive French governments. Freedom of travel and transit for foreign terrorists on their way to a killing. He concluded:

'Carlos merely asks that this agreement should be honoured.'

Ignoring the revelation, the court sentenced Breguet to five years and Kopp to four years for the possession and transportation of arms and explosives. The potentially far more serious charge of attempted murder lay unprocessed and for that Breguet could thank his inability to use an automatic gun.

With his mistress and Breguet duly sentenced during the last week of April, the French government braced itself for a response from Carlos. A telephone threat to blow up a French Riviera express train during the holiday period ensured armed patrolling guards and teams of bomb disposal experts with metal detectors on every train going south. The Venezuelan considered his options and flew to Beirut.

On the 24th of May a car parked just inside the main French Embassy compound in Beirut exploded. Eleven people were killed, twenty-seven more seriously injured. It was the Venezuelan's first response to the Paris court's verdict and sentence. There would be others.

After Israel had mounted a full-scale invasion into Lebanon in June 1982 there were continuous reports in the news media that Carlos was trapped in Beirut. He was certainly in the Arab capital arranging the final details of his murderous onslaught on the French Embassy a few weeks earlier, but as for being trapped, that was just another part of the continuing myth, he was only a car journey away from his Damascus home and by June Carlos was back in his main Romanian base in Bucharest. Giving Christa Frohlich her final instructions, he drove her to Bucharest International Airport and saw her, complete with a suitcase of high explosives, on to a plane to Rome. Her instructions were to continue her journey to France by train and blow up a holiday express. For once Carlos had underrated the opposition. Frohlich was arrested at Rome airport.

The implications of holding yet another member of the Carlos group were not lost on a number of governments. To my knowledge Christa Frohlich has yet to answer for the carnage for which she was personally responsible in the rue Marbeuf.

Having tried unsuccessfully to intimidate the French government to release his lover, after the arrest of Frohlich Carlos attempted a different approach. Perhaps quiet negotiation might achieve what high explosives had failed to bring about? Vergès attempted to persuade the government 'to see reason'. After all the killings and woundings, President Mitterrand and his colleagues were not inclined to see the Carlos version of reason. Kopp and Breguet remained in prison.

During the summer of 1983 Carlos yet again attempted to bomb Magdalena Kopp out of prison. Using some of the large quantity of high explosive stored exclusively for his use at the Syrian Embassy in East Berlin, another bomb was created. The man selected to plant the bomb was Lebanese, Mustafa Ahmad El-Sibai, a link man between the Carlos group and an Armenian organization, 'Asala'. With the East German Secret Service, STASI, monitoring his every move, El-Sibai crossed the border into West Berlin. The target was the French Cultural Centre. When the bomb went off it killed a young man who was in the process of delivering a petition to the French centre which contained a list of signatures – members of the public protesting against French nuclear tests in the South Pacific. A further twenty-three people were injured.

The government in Paris did not yield and Carlos now had what he considered to be another problem that required his own special solution. The German government indicated in early 1983 that they were preparing formal charges against Gabriele Tiedemann, then still serving out her fifteen-year sentence of imprisonment in a Swiss prison. There was talk that she would be extradited to Cologne where she had last lived a legal existence in the dim recesses of 1973. The Cologne Court wanted to put her on trial for the two murders she had committed during the OPEC attack. Carlos had made no attempt to force the Swiss government to release Tiedemann, but then, they had not concerned themselves with the OPEC attack, just the small matter of Tiedemann attempting to murder a couple of their border guards. A trial that fully examined the OPEC events was something else. Carlos reached again for pen and paper.

While the world's press, inspired by an anonymous article in the *Sunday Telegraph,* told its readers that 'Carlos trains 189 Gaddafi [sic] gunmen', Carlos took time off from the work he was doing for President Asad to write a letter to the German government. This was his response to the Cologne Public Prosecutor who had announced in July 1983 that Tiedemann would be extradited from Switzerland to stand trial in Germany. Though she still had a substantial part of her Swiss prison sentence to serve she was to be 'loaned' to the Germans for the duration of her trial. It was also revealed that the trial would commence on January 24th, 1984.

1st September 83
Federal Minister of the Interior
Dear Excellency
In the name of the central leadership:

1 We destroyed on 25 August at 11.50 hours the French Consulate in West Berlin. This operation belongs in the frame of the armed conflict which was forced on us by the French government. A drawing and some explanations regarding the operation are attached.

2 That we choose West Berlin is a warning for you to desist from activities which were initiated by your predecessors. Frau Gabriele Kröcher-Tiedemann who was never a member of our organization is scheduled for extradition because she is suspected by the German Federal Republic to have been involved in the OPEC operation on 21.12.75.

Any judicial or police measure against Frau Kröcher-Tiedemann (or against any other person) for alleged or actual relations to activities of our organization will be considered as malevolent aggression to which we will respond accordingly.

For the Organization of Armed Arab Fighters – Branch of the Arab Revolution

Carlos

The German government received the letter at their Embassy in Jeddah, Saudi Arabia, during the first week of September. News of its contents did not leak until mid November. Perhaps the thumb prints that again authenticated the writer as Carlos had caused the government to reflect on the implications of the impending trial.

Comprehensive security measures were announced in Cologne and preparations for the trial continued.

The letter writer, meanwhile, who had given new meaning to 'malevolent aggression', turned his attention back to France.

The arrest of Christa Frohlich in June had caused the threat to bomb a holiday express to be unfulfilled. There was no question of Carlos personally carrying out such an attack. The days when he led from the front had, like his revolutionary ideals, been long forgotten. Like any leader of a crime syndicate Carlos led from the back.

Again drawing on some of his stock of Semtex held at the Syrian Embassy in East Berlin Carlos and Weinrich started to create two suitcase bombs destined for France and a third that was to be taken to Lebanon.

At 5.29 pm on New Year's Eve 1983 the Marseilles/Paris express pulled out of Marseilles St Charles Station. It was less than half full. The majority of French holidaymakers had already gathered at whatever locale they planned to raise a glass and see the New Year in, but not all. There was, for example, in the centre of the second carriage, Bernard Berite and his wife Jeanne travelling home to join their two children for a family gathering. They chatted to a travelling companion, Michele Johannes, wife of a doctor from Montélimar, travelling to Paris to join her family for a midnight party. Just over two hours later, with the train travelling at over one hundred miles an hour, one of Carlos's suitcase bombs exploded in the second carriage killing all three. Twenty-five minutes later a second suitcase exploded at St Charles station, killing a further two. Over fifty more people were injured in these two attacks, some very seriously.

On January 1st, 1984, the third suitcase prepared in East Berlin, again with the full knowledge of the East German secret service, exploded at the French Cultural Centre in the northern Lebanese city of Tripoli.

A variety of people with a variety of motives claimed 'credit' for the three attacks. Carlos, never a man to let others take the credit for his work, felt obliged to clarify the situation. Letters in the name of the Arab Armed Struggle Organization, a *nom de guerre* first used by the Venezuelan at the time of the OPEC attack, were released in Lebanon and Paris. To make absolutely sure that everyone got the point Carlos again put pen to paper as he sat in the Palast Hotel, East Berlin. He wrote to Agence France Presse in West Berlin accepting responsibility for the attacks but justifying them with a new rationale. They were in revenge, he claimed in the letter, for French Air Force raids the previous November on Hezbollah strongholds in Baalbek, Lebanon.

'We will not tolerate our children being the only ones to cry for the blood of the martyrs of Baalbek.'

The attack had nothing to do with Iranian martyrs and everything to do with the continued imprisonment of Magdalena Kopp. Hezbollah leaders in Lebanon had insisted there had been no casualties. The devastated railway station is located in the town in which Gaston Defferre was mayor.

What was never appreciated by the French authorities, because their Intelligence Services were themselves un-aware of it, was the relationship that existed between the woman they were holding and Carlos. It might not have affected their judgement and indeed perhaps it should not have, but if they had been for one moment aware that she was, to all intents, save for the formality of a ceremony, the wife of Carlos, then they would have known that to talk of her relationship with his lieutenant Weinrich was to talk of something that had been over long before she took a trip to Paris.

If these latest outrages left the French government unmoved they most certainly had the desired effect on the German government. Less than two weeks after these attacks it was announced that the trial of Gabriele Tiedemann had been postponed 'sine die'. Concurrent with this announcement a variety of govern-ment ministers rejected the accusations that they had bowed to the threats of Carlos.

At precisely the same time, on the 10th of January 1984, the East German government was strenuously denying reports that Carlos was in East Berlin. These had been inspired by a very simple fact: the letter to Agence France Presse had been posted in East Berlin. Surely Carlos would not be so stupid or arrogant as to make such an elementary error? The question is rhetorical – of course he would. It was the kind of mistake, the type of error of judgement that had been such a feature of his life. His obsession with freeing Kopp and this final arrogant gesture which turned an unwelcome light on Honecker's Germany were the last provocation for many of his protectors.

When Carlos began to exploit the Haddad infrastructure in the late 1970s, the secret services of the Warsaw Pact countries where he was attempting to set up bases had been given the green light by their superiors. Kádár of Hungary, Tito of Yugoslavia and Husák of Czechoslovakia believed in assisting all aspects of the Palestinian struggle, whether to the far right, such as Arafat, or to the far left of Habash and Haddad. Carlos sold himself to such men as being a part of the struggle. The fact that he had sold them a false bill of goods speaks well of his powers of persuasion. Others, such as Honecker of East Germany and Ceauşescu of Romania, recognized Carlos for what he then was, something close to their own reality, something that could be used for their own ends. By 1984 there was another player on the field, the Soviet Union. The KGB file on Ramirez records his various attempts between 1980 and 1984 to enter the Soviet Union. It also records that he was refused entry on every occasion. Not content with keeping him out of their own territory, they tightened the screw. For some time they had been bringing increasing pressure on the countries that offered Carlos safe havens to expel the Venezuelan. By 1984 that pressure had intensified. Abu Iyad outlined the situation:

'In 1984, while I was in East Berlin, Carlos came to see me. He was spluttering with rage. He demanded that I should intercede on his behalf with the Soviets. He said that every time he got established in a Socialist Democratic country and the Soviets discovered he was there, they brought pressure on that government to kick him out. By 1984 they were trying to freeze him out of every Warsaw Pact country.'

'Why?'

'I am very sure that the Soviets hate him. Fundamentally they are opposed to terrorism. He was not a Communist, he was a socialist who became corrupted. He loves to live the bourgeois life. He loves women. He loves all the materialistic aspects of life. This hatred was mutual, they hated him, he hated them. Always, long before this time in East Berlin, he spoke of them in angry negative terms. He led such a bourgeois life, even in East Berlin a suite of rooms in a hotel. The Soviets really despised him.'

'Why didn't they just have him arrested and handed over to the West?'

'I don't know. But then I don't know why the West never applied for his extradition at this time, I'm talking between 1980 and 1984. They knew very precisely where he was.'

'Are you sure?'

'Ask your German friends.'

Abu Iyad was right. At least, based on what I was subsequently told by not only West German counter espionage but also their colleagues in France, he was right. Between 1980 and 1984 German intelligence had very accurately pinpointed Carlos bases in Prague, Budapest, Bucharest and East Berlin. German intelligence sources told me that they had shared this information 'across Europe and also with Langley'. As to why no attempt was made by any Western government to have Carlos extradited, one of the senior German intelligence agents with whom I discussed this offered the following:

'Look, a number of Western countries tried in 1975 when we positively identified Carlos entering Yugoslavia. What was the Yugoslavian response then? "What Carlos? We haven't seen him. No, he's not in Yugoslavia." During the early 80s we again to a certainty identified his East European safe houses. The various governments concerned would have probably said much the same.'

'But surely the attempt should have been made.'

'That was up to our bosses. They were advised. They did nothing.'

'By bosses you mean the German government?'

'Of course. Not only my government, yours as well, and the French, and the Americans. All of them. No action.'

Thus Carlos was given freedom to bomb, shoot, murder and terrorize not only by the East but also the West. Little wonder that he wrote such bombastic letters threatening Ministers and declaring war on countries that had the temerity to uphold the rule of law and order. A would-be revolutionary of gross incompetence in his ghastly chosen profession is transformed by disinformation and media myth into the ultimate professional killer. The myth is embraced not only by the general public but by the man himself. It becomes his reality. In the school of terror he moved inexorably from 'shows promise, must talk less and try harder' to 'graduated with honours'. And throughout his awful progress he is accorded every privilege, every protection by governments motivated by self interest, by governments motivated by fear. Truly an anti-hero of and for our times.

By April 1984 Carlos had, in the eyes of his East European protectors, overreached himself. When the Soviets turned the screw harder, Honecker in East Germany could no longer justify the continued presence of Carlos on Berlin soil with arguments that he was assisting the Palestinian struggle by giving Carlos safe haven. Neither could Husák in Czechoslovakia nor Kádár in Hungary. His attacks in France and throughout Europe and the Middle East, attacks solely designed and carried out to obtain the freedom of his mistress, could not be seen by any sane person as being part of the Palestinian struggle for natural justice. To suggest otherwise is to libel and slander the Palestinian peoples.

Shortly before Easter 1984 a top-level meeting between representatives of a number of East European countries took place in East Germany. A variety of secret services attended as well as government ministers. Among other topics debated was the continuing problem of the Carlos group. It had never been particularly big; intelligence estimates vary, but the average figure quoted to me was ten. This was the hard-core group. For certain operations it had been augmented with Syrians and Lebanese. With such a relatively small number Carlos, ably assisted by Johannes Weinrich, had succeeded in continually throwing entire nations into total panic. Nearer to home, in his safe havens, his presence had also been felt. As the secret services compared notes a clear pattern emerged.

Carlos was very prone to boast not only about the size and power of the group that he commanded but also about their discipline. 'They are all professionals,' he would say. Like his stories of how large and effective they were, the statement of professionalism was another lie.

There was nothing professional about the extraordinary number of prostitutes that consorted with the group. Each woman represented a security risk, particularly as virtually all of them had been hand-picked by that country's secret service. There was the drunkenness, picking fights with the locals, roaring through red lights, shooting up hotel ceilings, the constant transgressions of promises given about when and where explosives and guns could be brought in. The group were drunk not only on the alcohol they bought with hard currency but also on what they considered their successes. They considered themselves all-powerful and invincible. They were beginning to dabble in the internal politics of the various countries. Enough was enough. The meeting took a unanimous decision. The wide-ranging facilities that had been offered to the Carlos group were to be withdrawn. No further operations would be planned and launched from the safe havens. Right of entry was withdrawn.

The various decisions were communicated to Carlos. Inevitably he argued, he resisted, he bought a little time here, gained a concession there, but the party was over.

His power bases were now reduced to two: Syria and South Yemen. The Carlos version of Crime Incorporated began to pay increasing attention to the Middle East, not to the cause that he had betrayed long ago but to the pursuit of profit. Royal Princes and wealthy businessmen in Kuwait, Bahrain, Qatar, the United Arab Emirates and Oman suddenly found themselves getting a business proposition. The method of contact varied but the proposition always came from the same man, Carlos. He had moved into security and protection. The Mafia had come to the desert. His fees were high, very high, but in view of the identity of the man offering the service his offer was invariably irresistible.

In 1974, when Joachim Klein had first met Carlos, he thought he was a Mafioso. In 1975 Carlos appeared one day at Angela Otaola's Bayswater flat excitedly brandishing a newspaper. The headline story dealt with an armed hold-up of an American Express office in Kensington. He discussed the crime with Barry Woodhams and said,

'God! I wish I'd been with them.'

Before the year was out, courtesy of the OPEC payout, he was not with 'them', he was past them, in a league of his own. From that time on he had pursued 'the hard stuff', criminality carried out in the name of the revolution. The only thing that got revolutionized was his bank account.

From his Damascus base Carlos turned his attention to drugs. The young man who had moralized to Nydia Tobon about smoking dope had become in his thirties a man who desired part of the action in the drug world. Still travelling on diplomatic passports, he made trips in late 1984 and early 1985 to Panama and Nicaragua. Staging posts are crucial in the world of international drugs. Apart from what was coming out of Colombia there was also, virtually sitting on his Syrian doorstep, the Lebanese drug industry. Buying and selling – it had become such an essential part of his life from the OPEC attack onwards.

Magdalena Kopp was released from her French prison on the 4th of May, 1985. She had served three years and four months of her four-year sentence, her full term less remission for good behaviour. The French on this occasion had stood resolute. The cost for that resolution had been fearful.

Much to the chagrin of her lawyer, Jacques Vergès, she

was expelled to West Germany. He clearly feared a further arrest and trial for Kopp. He underrated the power, both real and illusory, of Carlos. Kopp was interrogated by the West Germans for a few days. 'Carlos. Yes, I did know him, but that was all such a long time ago.' They released her, gave her new documents, and within the month she was reunited with Carlos in Damascus.

There were no more Carlos-inspired attacks in France; Breguet, also earning full remission, was released in September 1985. By then Carlos and Magdalena Kopp were married. The witnesses at the wedding ceremony included her former lover, Johannes Weinrich.

During 1985, as in every previous year since the OPEC attack, the world's media continued to bolster the Carlos myth. He had been hired by Sikh extremists to assassinate the Indian Prime Minister Rajiv Gandhi. He was going to murder Pope John Paul II in Venezuela. He had masterminded the *Achille Lauro* hijacking.

Carlos was meanwhile addressing himself to the problem of increasing his bank balance. Unlike his father Carlos was a millionaire many times over, in any currency, but he wanted more.

His most significant criminal action in 1986 brought an echo from an earlier time, of early 1975 and the Wadi Haddad plan to kidnap the United Arab Emirates ambassador to Great Britain, Mohammed Mahdi al-Tajir. As the Carlos protection racket expanded, a substitute for that aborted kidnap came into Carlos's sights. It would also serve as a powerful demonstration to his 'clients'. The target was al-Tajir's brother, Sadiq. He lived in an area well known to Carlos, Knightsbridge. Sadiq was kidnapped on January 6th and released after the Ambassador had paid a ransom of three million dollars, payable by bank draft. The bank draft was cashed by Carlos in Beirut. He has never been linked with the crime by Scotland Yard's anti-terrorist branch. Perhaps they should confer with Lebanon's intelligence services.

The following month, February 1986, the Mossad-inspired story that Carlos had been murdered and buried in the Libyan sands broke. If the story of his death left me unconvinced, many others fell for it, not least a number of Western intelligence agencies. In 1987 David Atlee Phillips, a very experienced CIA operative of some twenty-five years service which included covert work in Lebanon and South America and Head of CIA operations in the Western hemisphere, stated that he believed Carlos to be dead. It illustrates the danger of how even a highly experienced secret agent can fall out of touch. At the time Phillips made this observation, September 1987, he had already retired from the CIA. He really should have checked with his colleagues still in the service. At virtually the same time as Phillips had Carlos under the Libyan desert the CIA had him on the phone. He had flown from Damascus to Latin America to hold meetings with members of the Colombian Medellín drug cartel. Items on the agenda were cocaine and marijuana. Carlos was representing his Syrian business partners, who included Monzer Al Kasser. The Colombian cartel was represented by two of its most powerful members, Jorge Ochoa and Gonzales Rodriguez Gacha. The meetings took place in Rio de Janeiro and Buenos Aires and finally in Medellín. The proximity of Colombia's border with his home country proved an irresistible lure to Carlos. Crossing at one of the many green borders, he drove to the coastal city of Maracaibo. Using a public phone box he telephoned his father to set up a meeting just over the border on Colombian soil. The CIA, who were running a tap on the father's phone, contacted their colleagues in Venezuela. They moved quickly. Carlos moved quicker. There was no sign of the world's most wanted man when scores of armed security agents and soldiers moved in on the designated meeting place in Cucuta.

He returned to Damascus, to his wife and to his sole protector, President Hafiz al-Asad.

This, then, based upon my research and personal investigation, is the truth about Ilich Ramirez Sanchez.

None of it relies on the mixture of information and disinformation that Carlos Two had given to me, though yet again a great deal of what that man had said subsequently proved to be uncannily accurate. The impostor had also been wrong just too many times. Then there were the deliberately planted pieces of disinformation. Qathafi's alleged masterminding of the OPEC operation was one, but another, I was quite sure, held the key. The old rule of 'who gains' is an excellent one to follow when confronted with disinformation. During the years that I had been occupied in the hunt not only for the man but for the truth of the man I had given much thought to this. I became convinced that the entire disinformation exercise had been set up for just one reason – to destroy Yasser Arafat in the eyes of his people and in the eyes of the entire Arab world. Many would gain from the Palestinian leader's destruction but one country and one leader stood to gain much more than any other. Not Israel, but the country for which I was now heading – Syria.

I had established a great deal of this, but by no means all, before making a final journey to the Middle East in October 1989. Some of the facts were not established until after I had returned from that trip. Some of the information only came to hand after I had the answer to the question that above all other questions I was determined to resolve. On October 11th, 1989, I caught a flight from London to Paris, and then another one to Damascus. Before I caught any return flight I hoped against hope to find the answer. Was Carlos in Damascus?

PART THREE

17

DAMASCUS

I arrived in Damascus in the late evening. If my conclusions were correct, then somewhere in this city Carlos
was getting ready to celebrate his fortieth birthday on
the following day. A quiet dinner party perhaps? Just
a few friends round to join him and Magdalena. The
ever-faithful Johannes Weinrich would undoubtedly be
there, but who else? His Syrian business associate Monzer
Al Kasser? Members of Syrian Intelligence? My musings
were rudely cut short. If as I believed this was the most
significant journey since my odyssey began in 1983, then
it had started with a wonderful anticlimax. Air France had
lost my luggage, all of it. 'Breakfast in London. Dinner in
Damascus. Luggage in Kuwait.'

My clothes I could replace, the contents of a brown
suitcase were quite another matter. My research material.
A distillation of six years' work. It was a case, bought
years earlier, that had been chosen with particular care:
just small enough to be classified as walk-on luggage,
but large enough to hold a great deal of material. For
years there had never been a problem, but this time an
officious Air France receptionist at check-in at Heathrow
had insisted that this case accompany the rest of my
luggage in the hold. I had argued, told them to measure,
assured them it conformed to cabin luggage size, quoted
IATA regulations, then, still steaming, handed over the
case.

The 'lost' luggage, apart from inducing recurring
bouts of internal panic, presented me with an additional problem. In that brown case was material for

a series of interviews. Original copies of all the documents and photographs were safely stored in London but without the material I could not begin my attempts to get those interviews.

Between visits to the airport and phone calls to London where my wife was playing hunt the case, I reviewed the game plan.

Bassam Abu Sharif, one of the men who had confirmed to me that Carlos was based in Damascus, had said: 'It will be for you I believe very dangerous, particularly if they were to learn that you know Carlos is there. Don't tell them that, whatever you do. Say that you believe him to be in the Bekaa Valley. Then they might move him out there for you to talk to on Lebanese soil. For them to admit that he is with them in Syria would be too shameful for them to do. If they agree to you seeing him they will want it to be Lebanon's shame.'

Bassam, like Abu Iyad, had given me names. So had the former Syrian Minister whom I had met in Libya. From all three men the names had been the same. Again like Bassam, Abu Iyad, the Minister and Yasser Arafat had expressed deep misgivings about this trip and left me under no illusions about the inherent dangers which ranged from arrest to an unfortunate accident. Charming.

Equally charming were some of my fellow residents in this city. There was Carlos, enjoying, if my information was correct, full privileges and maximum protection by the grace of President Asad, who extended the same courtesies to a number of other men who also featured on the world's most wanted lists. There was Alois Brunner, a Nazi war criminal, who assisted Eichmann in the deportation of the Jews from Vienna in 1938, who deported over forty-six thousand Jews trom Salonika to Auschwitz in 1943, and then later twenty-four thousand Jews from a French transit camp at Drancy. My Syrian friend in Libya, the ex Minister, had told me that Brunner had been in Damascus since 1960, that he lived in George Haddad Street, only a short walk from the hotel where

I was staying. The West Germans and the French had applied for Brunner's extradition but the Syrians had ignored the demands.

There was Abu Nidal, who when not in Libya often stayed in Damascus. I planned to talk to members of his group while I was here. It just might lead to Carlos.

There was Ahmed Jibril, who had been accused within hours of the Pan Am airliner explosion over the Scottish town of Lockerbie of ultimate responsibility for the carnage. Jibril was another I wanted to talk to.

There was Monzer Al Kasser, considered by many of the intelligence sources that I had spoken to over the years of this manhunt to be one of the world's leading drug dealers and arms merchants. Al Kasser could lead me to Carlos. German Intelligence had told me that they were business partners. If only I could get to Al Kasser.

There was Elie Houbeika. Many, including an official Israeli Commission of Inquiry, had identified him as bearing the major responsibility for the massacres of hundreds, possibly thousands, of Palestinians in Sabra and Chatila. Houbeika had never spoken in depth to anyone on the record about the massacres at the camps. Arafat had said to me that the Syrians would never let me talk to him. I was sure that Houbeika held the key not only to those awful killings but to the alleged complicity that Carlos Two had insisted upon – Arafat's own bloody responsibility.

The names of Ahmed Jibril and Elie Houbeika had been on the list that I had submitted to the Syrian Government during the summer. It would be interesting to see how the Syrians responded to the request for interviews with them, and with others who, I had been assured, could if they so wished lead directly to Carlos: Vice President Abd al-Halim Khaddam, Colonel Mohammed Al-Khuly, Ali Duba and Colonel Haytham Ahmed Sa'id. So many names. The one name I lacked was Carlos's current alias, but I was working on that.

One week, four suitcases and thirty-seven phone calls later, I had made some progress. As well as haunting the offices of the Ministry of Information I had started fishing in other waters.

At the official level when dealing with Zuheir Jannan, the Director of the Ministry of Information, I talked only generally about the various interviews I was officially seeking. Jannan was particularly concerned about my desire to interview Al-Khuly, Ali Duba and Haytham Sa'id. These men were so secret, I was told, that their wives hardly knew of their existence. 'How did I know about them? It would be difficult.' It always was.

I had contacted 'a friend of a friend', one of the media fixers that are such an essential feature in Lebanon and Syria. Salwah Orstwani's English was rusty, but her mind was sharp. An attractive woman in her late thirties, she carried a few extra pounds, a black leather ensemble, a considerable range of jewellery, and her contacts book, which included the name Ali Duba. She brought with her to that first meeting a young man who had no problem with my native language, a Palestinian named Samir Khatib. His command of English was so good that from time to time he acted as official interpreter for the President. I decided to tell them about a man called Carlos and my meetings with Carlos Two north of Beirut. On the 'who gains' premise I gave the account an additional spin and told them how the man I had met had been very critical of Syria, made many accusations against Asad and members of his regime, of my conviction that the man was an impostor created by a power or an intelligence agency obviously hostile to Syria and its leaders, of my hunt for the truth and my desire to expose the plot. I had previously concluded that the Syrians would not let me get to the real Carlos unless they saw a significant advantage in such a meeting. The scenario I laid before Salwah and Samir contained, I hoped, a powerful reason why Syrian Intelligence should open the door to their Venezuelan house guest. The first word that Salwah had uttered to me was 'welcome', a charming trait much used by Syrians when greeting a stranger. I wanted to hear General Ali Duba say it. Coming from the head of Syrian Military Intelligence it would have a particular resonance. Or from Colonel Mohammed Al-Khuly, head of Air Force Intelligence. Or from Colonel Haytham Sa'id, one of Al-Khuly's most trusted colleagues. While I continued to seek access to these men, who led lives so secret that just the mere mention of them was sufficient to make the Director of the Ministry of Information blanch, I simultaneously turned my attention to other individuals with slightly higher profiles. My first interview in Damascus was with Abu Mousa, a Palestinian who since 1983 has become distracted from his lifelong fight against Israel, and taken to fighting fellow Palestinians.

Human blood ran as a constant theme through our conversation. It was inevitable. The son of conservative religious farmers, Mousa was born near Al Quds, east of Jerusalem, in 1927, and educated at a village school under the British Mandate. From a very early age this tall, quietly spoken man in his lightweight Chairman Mao tunic had seen the spilling of blood and the taking of life. He recalled the great Arab Rebellion against the British between 1936 and 1939, a period that contained terror from three sources, Palestinian, Jewish and British. The Palestinians blew up trains and oil lines. The Jews threw bombs into crowded buses. The British blew up large sections of Jaffa 'for town planning purposes'. Eventually a British Commission determined the underlying cause for the disturbances was the Palestinian desire for national independence and their fear that the Jews were going to be given a national home on Palestinian land. The British solution was to propose the partition of Palestine into a Jewish state, a Palestinian state to be merged with TransJordan, and British mandatory enclaves. Under these recommendations the Jews, who at that time owned 5.6 per cent of Palestine, were to be given 33 per cent of the country, and any Palestinians living in those areas were to be forcibly expelled.

Abu Mousa recalled the fighting in 1948 in which he took part. He bought his own gun, a First World War rifle. 'The Palestinians were forbidden to own a gun, a knife, a fired bullet even. Forbidden by the British. If they found a man with a knife his home was demolished.'

He remembered Deir Yassin. How the few elderly survivors of that massacre were paraded by the Irgun and Stern Gang through the streets of his village. 'The Jews made a victory parade of it. From the survivors we learned what the Jews were celebrating. That massacre, that atrocity took place under the very eyes of the British. Under the "protection" of the British Mandate.'

For Abu Mousa a direct line could be traced from the massacre at the village of Deir Yassin to those of Sabra and Chatila. 'To spread panic. To spread terror. In 1948 to make the Palestinian fly from his homeland. In 1982 to make him fly not just from Beirut but from all of Lebanon.'

He cited other massacres in which the sole variations were the nationalities of the killing machine. Israel in the 1960s. Jordan and Israel and Lebanon in the 70s and the 80s. And Sabra and Chatila?

It would be wrong for the reader to conclude that Abu Mousa was preoccupied with these appalling atrocities. His responses came from my questions. It was I who had the preoccupation. To wade through so much blood. How else to find the truth of Sabra and Chatila? I had felt sure that I would be able to predict Abu Mousa's response when I asked him for an opinion on men like Carlos and Abu Nidal.

Abu Mousa is a professional soldier. In 1973 he was General Commander of all the Palestinian forces in South Lebanon. Such men of any race or nationality hold very similar views on people like Carlos.

'Carlos has not assisted the Palestinian cause. He was trained by Fatah in Jordan, to fight as a soldier. But what has that training to do with the OPEC attack? Carlos works for regimes, not for the Palestinian cause. Our enemy is within the borders of Israel. Not in the planes, airports and cities of the rest of the world. During the first ten days of total war in 1973 we carried out three hundred and thirty operations inside the occupied land. In Israel, that is where Carlos and Abu Nidal should strike.'

We talked of Mousa's break with Arafat. The final rupture had occurred in 1982 when, with Beirut in the hands of the Israeli forces and their allies, Arafat and his fighters were forced from Lebanon. Mousa had argued passionately that instead of Tunis they should go to Syria and unoccupied parts of Lebanon, so much nearer to the ultimate enemy. We also talked of Sabra and Chatila and, without revealing from where the accusation had originated, I expounded to him the allegations of Arafat's collusion. Even allowing for his alienation from the mainstream of the PLO, Mousa's response and the reasons he gave for it shook me. It made an interview with Elie Houbeika vital.

My daily visits to the Ministry had borne fruit, but not the kind I was in the market for. A slim, elegantly dressed young man appeared at my hotel one evening in response to promptings from the Director of Public Relations. He wanted to interview me on Syrian TV. I told Rezk Abou Okdeh that he had obviously been given the wrong end of the stick from his friends in the Ministry: I had not come to Damascus to be interviewed but to conduct interviews. Rezk had been told that I was researching a book on the Middle East, particularly on the Israeli-Palestinian conflict. He wanted me to come on to his programme 'Focus' and tell his viewers all about it.

With a firm idea in my mind of the enthusiasm with which this would be received in certain Syrian quarters, I explained to the insistent Rezk that I never talk about work in progress. He countered. He had read my last book. Just my luck. 'Please come on the show and tell us all about the murder of the Pope and Vatican corruption.' I declined politely.

I started to throw the net a little wider. Re-establishing contact with the Syrian newspaper editor whom I had met in Tripoli, I discussed with him the problem of getting to Ali Duba. His strong recommendation was to talk to the Minister of Information, one Mohammed Sulman. The names were piling up even if the interviews were not.

Returning from a meeting later, I found Rezk waiting in the hotel foyer, accompanied by a friend who had an important uncle – Ali Duba. Some instant horse trading took place. The friend would talk to Uncle Duba on my behalf if I agreed to perform in front of the cameras for Rezk and talk about my previous book. I agreed.

Curious how the 'who gains' system works. Within twenty-four hours of that conversation the men at the Ministry advised me that I could interview Elie Houbeika. For two weeks they had told me that such an interview was impossible, thereby confirming Arafat's prediction. Now, I was advised the interview was on.

The possibility of reaching Duba grew somewhat after further conversations with Salwah. She had reached not Duba but men close to him. My request for a meeting was going forward. Samir, meanwhile, was attempting to place me in front of Ahmed Jibril. He was another on the Ministry's list of 'impossibles' but Samir had his own routes to Jibril. Every time I met this young man I was reminded of another Samir who had given me so much help and protection in Beirut in 1985 before his shocking death on the street outside the Sabra camp. An arranged death perhaps. I still wondered about that.

For a man living under Syrian protection, Houbeika is a very careful man, even in the heart of suburban Damascus. Ten young men, all with the ubiquitous Kalashnikov, guard his home. All are Lebanese. I spent many hours with Houbeika; he was spectacularly indiscreet about a number of subjects. Whether he also displayed spectacular honesty is a moot point. I recalled some of Abu Iyad's observations on Houbeika.

'Elie Houbeika worked closely with the Israelis for a long time. The main reason he switched sides is that the Israeli inquiry into what happened in Sabra and Chatila placed the responsibility for the massacres on Houbeika's shoulders. Since then he is a creature of the Syrians. He will lie to you, tell you a fake story.'

I wanted time to consider the implications of what he had said to me followed by a second conversation. When he mentioned that he would be in Beirut in seven days' time I suggested a second meeting there. I was already planning a trip to the Lebanese capital because I wanted to visit the Sabra and Chatila camps and I wanted to make a phone call, one that Syrian Intelligence could not listen to. Houbeika agreed to see me again at his home in West Beirut. The only remaining problem was to persuade the Syrians to let me go to Beirut.

They were not happy about the idea at all, wanted me to wait 'until the situation in Beirut is stable'. A man could die waiting for stability in Beirut. Many thousands already had.

The men from the Ministry said my request would be given immediate and urgent consideration. My heart sank when I heard that. A man could also die in the Arab world while he waited for that kind of consideration, probably of old age.

Salwah advised me that the same kind of consideration was being given to my request to establish that Ali Duba was not a figment of someone's imagination. On Monday October 23rd both Salwah and Samir brought me the news that, according to some of their Palestinian contacts, and they had a great many, Carlos was in Libya.

The following day at the Ministry I got the good news bad news routine. The good news: 'Yes, we will let you go into Beirut.' That was good news? The bad news: 'An interview with Ahmed Jibril is out of the question. He is talking to no-one.'

Back at the hotel Samir was waiting for me. Jibril had agreed to talk to me the following evening. Fully aware that I could not ask the Ministry to supply an interpreter, I asked Samir to fill the gap.

My preparations for the Jibril interview were interrupted by the arrival of Rezk and Duba's nephew. They had come to collect the rent. Before I talked to Jibril I was going to have to talk to Rezk, in a TV studio.

On the following day, October 24th, I was hurtling in a taxi to the centre of the city and the studios. My constant reassurances to the driver in fractured Arabic that 'we had plenty of time' were interpreted as 'Go faster. Go faster.'

The personality cult, so predominant in the Arab world, is in garish evidence in Syria. In Libya the Colonel, in a variety of costumes and uniforms, is everywhere. In Jordan the King watches your every move. In Syria the President is always with you, even in the toilets at the studios. For some inexplicable reason, Asad's visage watching me piss aggravated me.

'Why do you have him there? Why is he everywhere?' I asked Rezk.

He found the question extremely mysterious.

'Why?'

'Yes, why? I wouldn't mind if it was out of genuine affection, out of love for the man. But come on. You haven't had free elections in this country since 1954. He's got over a quarter of a million people locked up as political prisoners. You have total press censorship . . .'

His gestures stopped me, he was waving his arms frantically, simulating either a fit or a seizure. He grabbed me and took me out of his dingy basement office into the corridor.

'Please David. You must not say these things.'

'The office bugged as well then?'

The interview was a good one, Rezk had obviously read my last book closely.

'David, thank you so much. That was fascinating. I would like you to stay there for a second interview. Are you agreeable to that?'

'Certainly.'

'Good.' He turned to camera. 'In next week's programme I shall be talking to David Yallop about another author, Salman Rushdie, and his book *The Satanic Verses*.'

This in a country that is ninety per cent Muslim, many many millions of them deeply devout. In a city where the man I was due to talk to in a few hours, Ahmed Jibril, had publicly announced that he was going to kill Rushdie and thus carry out the sentence of death imposed by Iran's Ayatollah Khomeini.

I drank a glass of water, took a deep breath and waited for the crew to begin recording.

Later that evening I was in downtown Damascus with Samir and Ahmed Jibril. He began by telling me that he had hesitated long before agreeing to this interview, given it a great deal of thought. He had been very reluctant to talk ever again, he said, to any writer.

His image in the Western media had never been good. After he broke with Habash's Popular Front in 1967 and formed the PFLP-GC (Popular Front for the Liberation of Palestine–General Command) it deteriorated. The first attack laid at his door, through press accusations unsupported by evidence, was the mid-air explosion of a Swissair passenger plane in which forty-seven people had died. No-one ever 'claimed' responsibility. Over the years the Syrian former Army Captain and his group had been blamed, rightly or wrongly, for a number of attacks. The latest had been the destruction of a Pan Am flight over Scotland that resulted in two hundred and seventy deaths – the Lockerbie disaster.

Born in a village three kilometres from Jaffa in February 1938, the story of Jibril's early life had a familiar ring. For a Palestinian living under the British Mandate it did not matter if one was a member of a farming family like Abu Mousa or an influential wealthy family such as Jibril's – the same restrictions applied, the same taxes were levied. Jibril's family owned large citrus orchards, his Syrian mother belonged to a powerful well-connected family, her father was Vice President of Syria at one time and Prime Minister at another, but her husband was Palestinian with the attendant disadvantages.

The powerful Syrian connections certainly helped when, like hundreds of thousands of others, the Jibril family were forced to flee.

While the majority ran, walked and shuffled out of Palestine, Ahmed Jibril and the other members of his family, after a series of phone calls from the Presidential palace in Damascus to the British administration in

Palestine, flew from Lod airport to Damascus before settling, in October 1947, near the Golan Heights at the town of Qunaytra. A town with a clear view of his homeland. Twelve years later, having been trained both in Syria and at an Egyptian Military Academy, Jibril was back on that same border – Syrian officer during the day, Palestinian guerrilla fighter at night. He perfected his own form of land mine and when off duty would slip over the border with other like-minded Palestinians. Many of the explosions that occurred to the north of Lake Tiberius in the late 1950s and early 1960s were, Jibril told me, his work.

The near-anarchy that prevailed in Jordan in the late 1960s, largely caused by Palestinians, Jibril blamed on the sudden influx of volunteers who joined the PLO after the battle of Karameh.

'Before that my group was about two hundred and fifty. Arafat's about two hundred. Suddenly, in less than one year, there were thousands of fedayeen. They were inexperienced, they were undisciplined. Under Israeli attack they would retreat to the cities. And the city spoils the freedom fighter.'

I was interested in the battle of Karameh. It had been crucial, as I have recorded earlier, in demonstrating to the entire Arab world that the Israelis were not invincible. It had proved to be an historic rallying point. A small, poorly equipped Palestinian force had, with Yasser Arafat at its command, stood its ground and fought a column of some fifteen thousand Israeli troops who were supported by armour and helicopters. Though losing most of their three hundred fighters, the Palestinians had inflicted what were by Israeli standards heavy casualties and driven them back. Within seventy-two hours Fatah had over five thousand new recruits. It was a story of Palestinian heroism against appalling odds. Ahmed Jibril had another version.

As Samir translated it to me tears welled up in his eyes, then ran down his cheeks. With good reason. If the account of Karameh that Jibril was giving me was accurate

584

then Fatah and the PLO and, more specifically, Yasser Arafat, had gulled the Arab world with an extraordinary myth. If the Jibril account was accurate.

Although on that evening I did not have untrammelled access either to the files of Syrian Intelligence or the inner thoughts of the Syrian regime, I was fully aware that this small, chubby man sitting next to me certainly did. His views, his statements would undoubtedly be influenced by such sources. Of the late President Sadat, he said,

'He spent most of his life smoking hashish cigarettes. Sadat was recruited to the CIA payroll during the time of Nasser's presidency. Recruited by the brother-in-law to the Saudi King Faisal, Kamal Khaddam.'

On King Hussein of Jordan:

'Our information is that he was originally employed by British Intelligence and that he defected to the CIA in 1958. In that year he started to work for the CIA.'

On the man I had recently interviewed, Elie Houbeika, the man that the world in general and Israel in particular accused of being at the very heart of the conspiracy that led to the slaughter in Sabra and Chatila, Jibril said: 'He was not only trained by the CIA, he was also trained by the Israeli Mossad. Many times he visited Israel.'

This last accusation I knew to be completely accurate.

On Wadi Haddad:

'Haddad refused to accept the Marxist doctrine and kept faith with the Pan-Arab doctrine. That is why he and Habash split. We were of the opinion that we had the potential to fight the enemy on the battlefield. It seemed to Wadi Haddad that hijacking planes was an easier way. This was done to collect money and to attract world attention to the Palestinian cause. We have never attacked a civilian target. Certainly not by intention.'

'Do I understand you correctly? The various attacks that you have been blamed for, or credited with, depending where one stands, which begin, I believe, with the blowing up of the Swissair plane in mid-flight in

February 1970 – are you saying that that attack or any since have nothing to do with you or your group?'

'I remember when that incident took place, exactly, the Swissair plane. We were in Jordan and we were short of money. One of the international insurance companies contacted us to say that if we claimed responsibility for that attack, the blowing up of the Swiss airliner, they would slip beneath the table about three or four million dollars.'

'Can you remember the name of the company?'

'No. The people who came to see us in Jordan were mediators acting on behalf of the company and the airline. We declined the offer.'

I asked him to list the operations and attacks for which he did accept responsibility.

'With one exception we have not carried out any actions outside the occupied territories. The exception was the holding of an American officer in June 1975. Colonel Ernest Morgan. That happened by accident, he was passing through a checkpoint. He was asked to show his identity card. He was held for a short time. Never interrogated and exchanged for two hundred tons of rice and the same amount of sugar. That went to a slum area of Beirut, Al Káratina, virtually destroyed by Phalangist shelling, without food. Other than that nothing. No outside operations or attacks.'

This brought us very neatly to the Lockerbie disaster. As previously recorded, long before there had been any forensic examination of the wreckage, Jibril and his group had been accused throughout Western media of perpetrating this atrocity. The accusations had persisted, inspired by the CIA and other Western intelligence agencies with their leaks, debriefings, background conversations and thousands and thousands of column inches. Hour upon hour of airtime. In depth analysis followed 'searching probe' – all had come to the same conclusion. The group responsible was Jibril's. Acting, so the allegations said, on behalf of Iran. An act of revenge for the shooting down of a civilian airliner by a US warship in July 1988.

Also previously recorded are my own attempts to warn British Intelligence of a major attack on an American target. I had been told that the attack would be Syrian inspired. Now in Damascus I was talking to the man whom the world believed had made the attack a reality. But perhaps two and two do not always make four.

'The United States should count her enemies. I can list almost fifty. Consecutive American administrations and the CIA have engaged in a very dirty war against the Third World countries. You may be amazed, Mr David, to learn that all the Third World countries were very delighted at the earthquake that hit San Francisco . . . We were accused of the Lockerbie bombing even before the American experts had arrived in Scotland. Where is the evidence? I defy them to produce it. General Command had nothing to do with the Lockerbie bombing. They persist in charging that we are responsible. Very recently the Syrian Foreign Minister, Farouk al-Sharaa, met James Baker, the US Secretary of State. Baker asked him, "What have you done with the GC people?" Farouk al-Sharaa was confused, did not know what he was talking about. Baker elaborated, "I mean Ahmed Jibril." The Minister pointed out to him that eleven months had elapsed since the Lockerbie bombing. "You have made plenty of accusations against Jibril, but where is the evidence?" Baker insisted that the United States did indeed have the evidence, "incontrovertible evidence" he called it. He promised to provide it. That was three weeks ago, we are still waiting.'

I asked him what firm evidence against his group had come from other countries, from Germany and from Britain.

'The same Minister, Farouk al-Sharaa, has recently had meetings in West Germany with their Minister of the Interior. He asked him point blank for any evidence that links my group with Lockerbie. He was told categorically that neither West Germany, Britain nor the United States has evidence that links my group with that bombing.'

I went at it a number of ways, examined the various allegations. I was not looking for a candid admittance, I am not that naïve. My conclusion was that if Ahmed Jibril cared to, he could make a great deal of work for libel lawyers in many countries and that he would probably win every case.

From discussing many deaths I turned to one that, according to reports, Jibril had stated he would be happy to bring about. That of the author Salman Rushdie. He clarified his position.

'We are prepared to carry out the ruling of the Islamic law against Salman Rushdie because he is a Muslim. That is if we are in a position to do that. He should of course appear before a court. If he is then sentenced to death, I would carry out the death sentence. The man has abused our prophets.'

Late in the six-hour interview I casually asked about Carlos.

'I have not heard of Carlos for a long time. I've no idea where he is.'

I did not indicate to Ahmed Jibril that I was convinced that Carlos was right there in Damascus, but I did wonder if Jibril would be equally ready to execute the man I was seeking if such a sentence was ever passed in one of the many countries where Carlos had not 'abused prophets', just murdered and maimed. Somehow I doubted it.

The following day I learned from three different sources that Ali Duba was 'outside'. Not my hotel but Damascus. Five of his relations had been killed in a car accident obliging him to take a short trip. Initially my response to this news was to adopt a cynical approach and assume it part of an exercise to fob me off. Later the same day Duba's nephew confirmed the accuracy of the story and advised me that 'Uncle will be back by the time you return from Beirut.' That at least had a positive ring to it. At least there was one person who thought I would be coming back. Others were less certain.

A colleague of Jibril's paid me a visit with copies of photographs taken during the interview. He also gave me a letter from Jibril addressed to his members in Lebanon ordering them to protect me and ensure my safe passage. When he handed me this he strongly advised me against my proposed trip.

'It is not safe for you. It is very dangerous. I recommend you do not go to Beirut.'

I thanked him for his concern but said there were reasons why the trip was essential without elaborating.

The Ministry advised me that one of their staff would accompany me, to act as an interpreter. Ahmed Hariri's command of English was all right but he would be less than useless if there were a problem. Ahmed is a hypochondriac. I could just imagine what would occur if some members of Hezbollah appeared by our car. 'I would like to help you, David, but you see, it's my back, or my legs, or these headaches.' I was also advised that I would be staying in the Summerland Hotel, in the heart of West Beirut. I knew exactly where it was, in a section of the city teeming with fundamentalist Iranians. The Ministry also advised me that I would have to pay for a taxi there and back. 'The car is broken.' The car? And this is the Arab country most feared by Israel?

My requests to see and to talk to the mysterious Duba were by now having some response, if only in the interest that was being paid to me by Syrian Muhabarrat-Intelligence. They have a wide selection of secret agents in Syria. A group for each of the three armed services. A fourth group for the Vice President. A fifth for the President and a sixth so secret no-one knows who they work for and answer to. Each appeared to be regularly represented in the foyer of the Sheraton Hotel. The majority wore very scruffy suits and sat at all hours in the lounge continuously drinking coffee and appearing to study their newspapers. Whenever I was meeting someone, one or two would detach themselves from the pack and sit nearby. They looked to be very poorly paid, which may explain the low calibre.

On Thursday, October 26th, the eve of my trip to Beirut, Salwah and Samir contacted me. Her information was that Carlos was definitely in Libya. Over a coffee and out of earshot of Syrian Intelligence she then proceeded to tell me of her conversation on my behalf with Abu Nidal's deputy in Damascus. It was he who had stated that the man I was looking for was in Tripoli. He had also indicated that he had further information for me. There were, he insisted, three men who were Carlos. She elaborated. It was not a version that I had ever heard before but the idea that Carlos was a multiple personality was not new to me.

The Israelis have long believed there might be as many as four men who operated as Carlos. Qathafi had talked to me of his belief that the original was dead and that others used his name. It was interesting that this view was shared by members of the Israeli military, including men like Colonel Raanan Kissin. Salwah advised me that the one I was seeking, Ilich Ramirez Sanchez, was in Libya, and that the others were dead.

Later, as I pondered on a roomful of overweight Venezuelans, my wife called from London. She had been in touch with a contact, Robert Farah, a senior member of the Lebanese Forces who was at that time in Washington. I had been seeking certain names and phone numbers connected with my trip to Beirut. He had readily supplied them. He had also given Anna some advice for me.

'He said that under no circumstances should you go through the Bekaa Valley tomorrow. There is an Iranian visiting there. A former Minister called Ali Akbar Mohtashemi. He's a hardliner and has great influence and control over Hezbollah. Robert said they would like nothing more than to snatch you while he's visiting.'

In the many years that I have known her I have never heard such fear in her voice. I reassured her. I was confident that the Syrians would not let anything happen to me, far too embarrassing. At least I think I was confident. I had to make the trip; there were at least two men in Beirut who could give me the answers I was failing to get in Damascus.

The following morning I joined Nabi Berri for breakfast. The Amal Shiite leader discussed the situation in Beirut, where General Michel Aoun and his followers were disagreeing with Syrian peace initiatives. The disagreement took the traditional Lebanese form, heavy fighting had been going on for months. Berri's last words to me were, 'I'm glad that I am not in Beirut at the moment.' I did not bother to tell Berri where I was headed.

It is difficult to convey to the reader the fear and apprehension of trips like this. As these words are being written Terry Anderson, John McCarthy, Terry Waite, Edward Tracy, Brian Keenan and all of the other Western hostages are, thankfully, free men. In October 1989 they were not. That month Waite went past the one thousand day mark in his captivity; Edward Tracy and John McCarthy were about to 'celebrate' their fourth birthdays as hostages; Terry Anderson was 'celebrating' his fifth birthday as a hostage on the very day that I was setting out to drive through the Bekaa and then on to Beirut, the two areas where to a certainty the hostages were being held by 'The Party of God'.

The journey would have been impossible without Syrian approval. Even with it there were a number of checkpoints and control posts where commanders attempted to turn us back. On each occasion Ahmed produced a letter signed by a member of the Syrian Government. I never enquired as to its contents but it was certainly effective. Inside Lebanon we drove to a Syrian command post at El Masna. It was here, Ahmed explained, that we would pick up an armed escort. At El Masna there was a complication. The Syrian officer who had been advised of my journey had been summoned to Damascus for an urgent meeting. His second-in-command plied me with coffee while he and Ahmed engaged in a long excitable conversation in Arabic. Some time later we were on our way. The escort, a jeep in front and an unmarked car behind, appeared to be a mix of army and intelligence. Aware from previous outings with Ahmed that unless he ate regularly he experienced 'much dizziness', I suggested that we stop for lunch on the way. When we did, it was at Bar Elias, right in the middle of the Bekaa. The restaurant was fairly crowded as the three vehicles screamed to a halt, and the armed escort fanned out as if we were going to launch a commando raid on the clientele.

'Look Ahmed, could you have a word with them. A bit more low-profile perhaps.'

'They are obeying their orders.'

'I appreciate that. Look, tell them I'd like to buy them lunch.'

The offer reduced the number who waited outside, giving every impression that they were about to attack anyone who even vaguely looked like a Muslim Fundamentalist, to just two. The remainder piled into the restaurant.

The maitre d' approached the table.

'Would you care for some Beaujolais Nouveau?'

'In October? You've got that here quickly.'

He beamed.

'I have had it since August.'

A very enterprising race the Lebanese, 89 Beaujolais in mid summer. It was excellent, so the maitre d' assured me. But then, how could I tell?

We were soon in the centre of the war zone. Gas stations sandbagged, civilians taking an afternoon walk, no dog just a Kalashnikov, wrecked deserted villages, Syrian tanks in offensive positions forty kilometres from Beirut.

Dropping down from the mountainous roads we drove through Armoun on the outskirts of the city. Newly built and newly destroyed. Swinging onto the coast road we headed for the heart of West Beirut. Huge photographs of the Ayatollah Khomeini and Rafsanjani adorned the buildings. The effect of the Arak on Ahmed was obviously wearing off.

'This is a crucial moment for you, David.'

I tried to make light of it.

'Good to know that they are still selling Total petrol and that the Mercedes agent is open.'

Then in the suburb of Ozey.

'Car bombs usually go up here.'

He was not the easiest of travelling companions.

We had come to a halt in a typical Beirut traffic jam. Right in the middle of Hezbollah-controlled territory. The armed guard behind opened their car doors and two of their number ran to our taxi. Flinging open the front doors and standing on the door of the car, they shouted at Talib to drive on. He revved the engine, swung the car half off the road, then, with a highly dextrous display of driving, continued. Through the Janah area where a massive explosion had previously occurred. I could feel the fear in the car.

The powers that be had evidently decided the Summerland Hotel was just a little too close to Hezbollah, yet the distance between the Summerland and the Beau Rivage where I stayed is a very short walk, less than three quarters of a mile. An interesting comment on clearly delineated fiefdoms, or perhaps on Syrian optimism.

I remembered the Beau Rivage. During my forays into the city in 1985 Samir and I had drunk coffee on the terrace by the swimming pool. The area had hummed with life then. It had reminded me of Rick's Bar in the movie *Casablanca*. There had been lots of wheeling and dealing, mysterious propositions being initiated or finalized. A guide book might have given it a couple of stars. Now, in October 1989, it was sans stars, windows and customers. In an effort to improve the flow of fresh air in the hotel various armies had blasted shells through a number of its walls, the foyer was sandbagged to the ceiling, the empty swimming pool looked as if it had taken a direct hit. One of the cleaners was meticulously dusting a number of wall signs that proclaimed, 'To the Pool', 'To the Restaurant', 'To the Bar'. Well, the signs were clean, even if all three amenities were closed. The management had been thrilled when Ahmed and I appeared, we had doubled the number of guests staying there that weekend.

Before booking in we confirmed our safe arrival to the Syrian officer in charge of West Beirut, General 'Ali'. I did not catch his second name. In view of the fact that he was currently holding down one of the most unenviable positions on the planet his attitude towards me was understandable. He could not understand how I had obtained permission to come to Beirut or indeed why I should want to. No, under no circumstances could I cross the green line and go to East Beirut, to do so would put my life at extreme risk, the General told me. I begged to disagree. In my mind the extreme risk was here, in the western sector of the city, within nodding distance of Hezbollah. Over the green line General Michel Aoun and his followers were making their last stand against the Syrians, not a stubborn Irishman. With diplomatic relations between Syria and Great Britain still non-existent I had assumed my other nationality for this trip. English or Irish, it mattered little to General Ali. I was a white European.

'You are worth a great deal of money to certain groups in this city. Crossing the green line is out of the question. It would be one of the areas where they would attempt to kidnap you. I must also insist that you do not leave the Beau Rivage without an escort. Under no circumstances are you to go out at night. Welcome to Beirut.'

It posed an interesting problem. There were members of Lebanese security, names given to me by the man in Washington, whom I needed to talk to. Phoning from the hotel was out of the question. I had to assume that all calls from there would be tapped.

I temporarily put that to one side. Tomorrow morning there would be a further meeting with Elie Houbeika and then Sabra and Chatila. It was highly appropriate to talk to Houbeika again before visiting the camps: his name and what took place in those camps in September 1982 will be for ever linked.

A massacre, a bloody, unremitting evil massacre was carried out in the Palestinian refugee camps of Sabra and Chatila. Millions of words have been written. Countless allegations made. A Lebanese Government Inquiry concluded that the 'Israelis are legally responsible'. An Israeli Government Inquiry blamed its 'Lebanese allies, the Phalangist Militia', but it also apportioned varying degrees of responsibility to a wide range of Israelis, from Prime Minister Begin down. Some men's careers were destroyed, others had their ambitions at least temporarily halted. None of this mattered one single jot to the people who had been murdered. Officialdom cannot even agree on precisely how many were slaughtered in these camps between Wednesday September 15th and Saturday September 18th. The obscenity of the murders was followed by many other obscenities, including the numbers game. With the Israeli army and its Phalange allies entirely surrounding the camps, men, be they Lebanese, be they Israeli, entered and began to torture, rape and murder. They had entered, so Minister of Defence General Ariel Sharon declared, 'because there are two thousand terrorists hiding in the camps'. If that be so one can only express astonishment that so few entered Sabra and Chatila to hunt 'the terrorists'. The hunters were according to official Israeli figures but one hundred and fifty. How many did they kill? The Israelis put the number as 'between 700 and 800'. The Palestinian Red Crescent put the number as 'over two thousand'. Death certificates were issued for more than 1,200 by the International Red Cross but many could not come to claim that piece of paper. Entire families were slaughtered then scooped up in bulldozers and buried in mass graves. Bassam Abu Sharif, who based his figures on PLO records involving cash allowances and food allowances given by the PLO both before and after the massacres, put the number of deaths at 'over seven thousand'. Any estimate should also include the truckloads of the still living who were transported from the camps to unknown destinations from which they have not returned. The population of the two camps on the eve of the massacres was a minimum of twenty thousand people. Within two days that figure, based on an analysis of every estimate, had been permanently reduced by at least three thousand, but the numbers that were murdered, like the subsequent conclusions of exactly who was responsible, are of no concern to the dead.

Sharon was right to talk of 'terrorists in Sabra and Chatila', his error was in calling them Palestinians. The terrorists were the men that he allowed into the camps while his own army stood, watched, listened and then claimed to have seen nothing, heard nothing and done nothing.

In November 1984, in a restaurant in Paris, when my hunt for Carlos was in its relative infancy, I had mentioned Sabra and Chatila to men whose help I was seeking in my hunt. I had told them that the killings that had taken place in those camps in September 1982 had caused me to re-evaluate my own attitude towards Israel. By Paris 1984 I had come some distance from a carefree, unthinking holiday I had enjoyed with Anna on a Moshav in the Sinai in 1978. By the time I sat in Beirut in October 1989 I had come much further. Apart from discovering for myself the reality of the Israeli-Palestinian issue I believe that that chance remark in a Paris restaurant held the key to what subsequently happened during my hunt. Held the key to who had created Carlos Two and to why someone had gone to such inordinate lengths to convince me that this creation was genuine, was indeed Ilich Ramirez Sanchez.

The timing of that 'breakthrough' in Paris also held the key as to why this particular author had been targeted. I had been looking for Carlos since the autumn of 1983. I had pressed every imaginable button, contacted every conceivable source available and drawn a continuing blank until November 1984. In June 1984 my last book, *In God's Name*, had been published. By November it had been translated and published in nearly forty countries. It had been at the top of the best-seller lists around the world. It has sold to date nearly six million copies.

I am certain that success was the key to why a bizarre disinformation exercise had been created. I must have seemed to its creators the perfect target. If I could be convinced by persuasive evidence to accept their point of view, then there would be an excellent chance that my potential readers would also be convinced. What was at work here was the Hitler Syndrome – 'If you tell a lie long enough and loud enough, it becomes the truth.'

The story I had been told by Carlos Two about Sabra and Chatila was powerful. It was compelling and very nearly convincing. As I sat in that Beirut hotel I was certain of one thing. The plot, the plan, to use me to discredit the Palestinian leadership was Syrian-inspired. Asad and the men surrounding him were determined to destroy Arafat's extraordinary influence over his people. When I had not rushed to publish after those two meetings in North Lebanon, whichever branch of Syrian Intelligence was responsible for orchestrating this exercise must have concluded that, for whatever reason, they had lost the game they were playing with me. My appearance in Damascus had clearly reactivated the game. If they were not prepared to risk putting Carlos Two in front of me again, after all there was this tiresome demand concerning fingerprints, others could be wheeled forward. Others totally under Syrian control could run with the same baton, for precisely the same ultimate aim, to destroy Arafat. I was under no illusions. The Syrians were only letting me talk to those they wished me to talk to. The little games they played concerning, for example, my requests to interview Abu Mousa, Ahmed Jibril and Elie Houbeika. In theory I had circumvented their refusals, but none of those men would have talked to me without previous approval from Syrian Intelligence. I talked of many things to these three men but one particular theme ran through all three interviews – Yasser Arafat. That theme produced from all three an extraordinary symmetry.

Abu Mousa:

'I do not have any concrete evidence that there was collusion between Arafat and those who perpetrated the Massacre of Sabra and Chatila, the Phalange, but Arafat was happy about the massacre. He feels that such events may bring about a sympathy, a world sympathy, for the Palestinian cause. The Jews were killed by the Nazis, the whole world sympathized with them. Massacres of Palestinians are in Arafat's mind fruitful. Sabra and Chatila is not the first such example.

'For example, in 1976 the Palestinian camp of Tel al Za'atar in Beirut was besieged by Lebanese forces for months. At that time I and my forces were stationed in South Lebanon. I had a large force under my command. We were not engaging the enemy down there. I proposed to Arafat that I had the capacity of breaking through the siege, we could then have chosen either to evacuate the camp or to remain within and defend the camp. Arafat rejected this proposal, despite the general assessment he was given by all of us that without such a counter attack the camp would fall.'

'How many Palestinians were killed in Tel al Za'atar?'

'Not less than two thousand five hundred persons.'

'What reasons did Arafat give for refusing to allow you to relieve the siege?'

'To relieve the camp my forces would have to pass through Baabda [the seat of the Lebanese Government where the Presidential Palace stood]. This was unacceptable to Arafat, who considered that this might offend Lebanese sensibilities. When Arafat declined my offer I tried to do it anyway. I moved my forces by night. I got as far as Aley and rested the soldiers. Arafat learned I was there, he sent Major Abu Sharar with a written order. In effect it said that if I did not return to the South with my forces I would be dismissed and put on trial.'

'If you still have it, I would like a copy of that order.'

'Certainly.'

He subsequently gave it to me. It reads:

The Palestinian Movement for National Liberation 'Fatah'

By Hand / Very Secret on 1/4/76 at 11.30

From: The Commander General [Yasser Arafat]
To: The Commander of the 'Castel' forces [Abu Mousa]

I gather that you have moved some of your forces to Al-Jabal [the Lebanese mountain area] without telling me. What is the reason for this move? It not only disturbs our security, but also the military plan that we agreed on together with Major Boutary in the South.

How has this move happened without informing the Commander General and obtaining his approval?

I ask you to return this force now to its previously agreed place to conform with our accepted military plan.

I'm sorry that this has happened without you informing the Commander General. This is a very serious precedent in the military work of our revolutionary military forces and you must bear the consequences.

ABU AMAR [Yasser Arafat]
The Commander General
1/4/76

Abu Mousa, although unable to offer what he called 'concrete proof' that global sympathy derived from Palestinian massacres was an essential part of Yasser Arafat's philosophy – 'He did not utter it. He's not that stupid' – insisted that his close relationship with Arafat over many years had convinced him that it was indeed a belief that for the sake of a Palestine state, Palestinian people must be sacrificed.

Ahmed Jibril:

'From 1965 I was of the opinion that Arafat was not serious in his expressed desire to fight Israel. He wanted to be a movie star . . . The only reason we won the battle of Karameh is because the Jordanians refused to obey their king. He had agreed with Israel that his troops would offer no resistance to the Israeli forces if they came over the border to kill the Palestinians. They disobeyed their orders and opened fire on the Israeli forces. It was their revenge for the king having withdrawn his forces from the West Bank after they had suffered heavy losses . . . Before the battle Arafat and Abu Iyad wanted to retreat with help from the Iraqis. I refused. Said we should stand and fight . . . I can tell you very frankly that none of the Israeli armour or tanks was destroyed in the camp of El Karameh. In one hour the Iraqis penetrated the camp and Arafat and Abu Iyad were forced to flee, they were the first to do so, to the mountains where I had men deployed. Arafat ran away but told his people to stay in the camp. In that camp seventy young people surrendered to the Israelis, these were unarmed people. They walked forward. The Israelis put them against a school wall and killed them, every one.'

To Ahmed Jibril what occurred at Karameh was 'either absolute military stupidity or a conspiracy to gain sympathy from the West'. At the time he had been uncertain. 'But now I can confirm that it was not military stupidity, especially after the massacres perpetrated in Tel al Za'atar, Sabra and Chatila and other places.'

To Jibril the conspiracy was more subtle than meetings and arrangements. He believes that the Israelis have a clear perception of Arafat's view on the need for massacres, the need for sacrifices on a massive scale, and that they are more than ready to oblige.

'The Israelis have learned a lot from the massacre at Deir Yassin, they had in mind to perpetrate a similar massacre at Sabra and Chatila. They believed that it would intimidate the survivors and they would be forced to leave, to flee the Lebanese territories. According to the investigations carried out by the special committee the Israelis and the Lebanese front were involved in this massacre, but I do not rule out the possibility of CIA involvement in this affair. To say that the massacres were carried out as an act of revenge after the assassination of Bashir Gemayel, as some have said, is without foundation. A pointless pretext. We have information that Sharon and Rafael Eitan conducted talks with Bashir Gemayel concerning this massacre and we have confirmation that Bashir Gemayel said he would turn Sabra and Chatila into a zoo.'

That leaves the man considered by the majority who have written on the subject to be the zoo keeper – Elie Houbeika.

When discussing with Houbeika the siege and subsequent slaughter of Tel al Za'atar in which he had played an active role, I told him of my interview with Abu Mousa and his allegations concerning an Arafat-inspired conspiracy to ensure that the siege ended in a massacre. He displayed great interest in the details and stated that it was the first time he had heard of Abu Mousa's conflict with Arafat over the siege of Tel al Za'atar.

'The opponents that we faced in Tel al Za'atar, they were not Fatah, they were the Popular Front, these were the fighters we were facing and I don't think that we could have destroyed their defences if there was no, let's say, treason from the inside. We were heavily outnumbered, we were some one hundred and fifty, we had no artillery, they had artillery. We had no overall tactics, just small groups fighting by their own tactics or strategy. I don't know how we managed to get into that camp. We couldn't do it by ourselves. We were facing three or four thousand fighters. I know that Bashir Gemayel, who was our commander, had talks, negotiations with Palestinian leaders from inside the camp. This camp was the backbone of the Popular Front. Maybe Arafat wanted to get rid of them.'

Based on other research that I have carried out there is little doubt that the PLO High Command ordered those trapped within Tel al Za'atar not to surrender and that in issuing that order the PLO leadership was fully aware that they were dooming many to die. There are even allegations that during the closing stage of the siege the PLO leadership instructed artillery units based outside the camp to turn their guns on to the survivors. For the massacres at Sabra and Chatila, however, I have not discovered any independent evidence that supports the allegations Carlos Two made to me of an Arafat-inspired conspiracy to bring about a massacre of his own people. Those who controlled Carlos Two had clearly concluded that in my eagerness to publish a book based on my interviews with Carlos I would not seek out such independent evidence. In that they misjudged their target. What I did seek out, and indeed establish, was clear evidence that the Syrians had not put all their eggs in one basket. A major disinformation exercise was but one part of their strategy. One way and another the Syrian regime had been attempting to destroy the Arafat leadership for many years. Arafat had been persona non grata in Syria since 1983. The fact that Yasser Arafat refused to let Asad dominate Palestinian policy, the fact that after being forced out of Beirut just weeks before the Sabra and Chatila massacres he had chosen Tunis rather than Syria as his headquarters – these and other events had provoked the Syrian leadership into direct action. They inspired an inter-Palestinian rebellion, drawing the Jibril and Abu Mousa factions away from the fold. In 1985, when the Arafat faction was again a force to be reckoned with in Lebanon, this had resulted in open warfare between the cliques. At precisely the time I sat in that Paris restaurant and made my first major breakthrough in my search for Carlos, the Syrian leadership had very high on its agenda the destruction of Arafat. They were failing in their attempts to kill him physically; I firmly believe that in attempting to use me they were attempting to destroy him spiritually in the eyes of his people. In the so-called 'war of the camps' that erupted in 1985 the fiercest opposition to the Arafat supporters and fighters in Beirut came from the Syrian-supported Amal militia. It was a murderous struggle. Arafat, pouring PLO funds into Beirut, was quite literally buying back the loyalty of Palestinian factions that had been pro-Syrian. The time, trouble and expense of the disinformation exercise that I was exposed to was but a fragment of the commitment the Syrians were making to destroy the entire PLO leadership.

One small factor, more than any other, convinced me that Syrian Intelligence controlled Carlos Two. I repeatedly asked myself how it could be that not once but three times during 1985 I had been able to enter and leave Beirut without visas and without troubling security control at Beirut airport. It had happened earlier, once at Algiers, clearly orchestrated by someone who was either a member of Algerian Intelligence or had excellent contacts in that area. How could it happen three times in Beirut?

I put the question to Wadi Haddad, not the man who had controlled Carlos but another with the same name, a Lebanese who was the chief national security adviser to Lebanese President Amine Gemayel between 1982 and 1984.

'At the time you are talking of, early 1985 to late 1985, when you made those three visits, the airport and the surrounding area were totally controlled by Amal militia. The only way that you could have entered and left in that manner would have been with Amal approval. Amal, of course, as you know, are controlled by Syria.'

It explained not only Samir's ability to get me in and out, it also explained why we never had any trouble at the many checkpoints. Meeting the Amal leader Nabi Berri over breakfast in a Damascus hotel in 1989 merely underlined the continuing closeness of his relationship with the Syrian regime. Now, if I got lucky in Beirut, I would then be returning to the very city where the disinformation plan to target me had been created. It was an interesting situation. Before that there was unfinished business with Houbeika and Sabra and Chatila.

At the time I had my meetings with Elie Houbeika he was thirty-three years of age. He was very bright and in excellent physical condition. Born into the Maronite Christian community, he received, as I did, a Catholic education.

'In 1974, when I was seventeen to eighteen years old, I got my first rifle, from the Phalangist party. They had been given weapons by President Franjieh.'

I commented that at the time he had taken up arms many saw Lebanon, particularly Beirut, as the playground of the Middle East.

'It was the brothel of the Middle East. Arabs, Saudis for example, who had acquired great wealth but lacked the education or culture to go abroad to France or the United States treated Lebanon as the Americans treated Cuba before Castro.'

He told me he had become aware at the age of fourteen, that there were too many Palestinians in Lebanon when he watched a huge demonstration of Palestinians marching through Beirut.

'They broke windows, doors, beat up Lebanese policemen. I felt a growing danger to the State of Lebanon and the Lebanese entity. I decided to join the Phalange party the same day. I had to wait three years until I was old enough. By 1973, when I joined, there were something like eight hundred thousand Palestinians living in Lebanon, many in battlefield dress, many with weapons. The number continued to grow until 1982. Then it greatly diminished.'

It certainly did. I wanted to learn exactly how Houbeika had assisted that reduction of numbers and of his military and intelligence training. His first training had been at a commando school run by the Lebanese army in the Mettan area near Bikfaria. This illegal Phalange force received great assistance not only from the official army but the Christian community, particularly the churches and the monasteries.

'The religious men gave us great help. Complete support. Our weapons were stored in the churches and the monasteries. Many of our training camps were based in the monasteries. For us it was like the continuation of the Crusades.'

'Is this the view the Church took of what you were doing?'

'Yes, of course, of course. When we went for absolution we would be given fresh guns and ammunition after confession by the priests. All the time they were telling us, "This is a sacred war, it is not a crime to kill, it's a matter of self-defence." The monks were the main backbone, their leaders were more extremist than Bashir [Gemayel] himself. The training in Lebanon was basic, how to shoot, how to camouflage. In Israel we did specialized training. Street fighting, very sophisticated techniques. This was from 1976 onwards. It was negotiated by Bashir with the Israelis. We were trained by the Israelis in the Galilee area. These negotiations were with a range of people. Perez, Begin, Rabin, Sharon, Eitan. The Israelis wished to create a Christian army in Lebanon that would ultimately bring about a Christian state with a mutual defence policy with Israel.'

Houbeika was a fast learner. By 1980 Bashir Gemayel had appointed him as Head of Intelligence and he began to build his own organization.

Houbeika started from scratch with men who had to be trained in this highly specialized work. He had previously developed contacts with Mossad and Shin Bet but was wary of continuing deep involvement.

'They were dealing with us as if we were their agents. They wanted to know the identity of my various agents and would then attempt to run them as if they were their own personal assets. They wanted to debrief my people and channel them towards areas of intelligence work that preoccupied Israel, information on the Syrian army, technical information on Syrian Mig fighter planes. Our preoccupations were different. Infiltrating the Palestinian groups. The Americans came and they wanted very badly to work with us. With Bashir's approval I sent men to be trained by the CIA in Washington. The American I liaised with was Jack Coogan. I had read somewhere that an intelligence agency should not just have deep relations with one major intelligence organization, we needed another, so we went to the French. I had meetings with Admiral Lacoste, who was head of French Intelligence. We began to build. With each new relationship our power grew. Our expertise improved with the training and the techniques my people were taught by a number of countries. The British refused to have a direct relationship, but as they are responsible for Oman's intelligence services we went there and established an indirect relationship with the British through Oman intelligence.'

Houbeika elaborated on the other contacts he forged and the benefits it brought to his intelligence agency. The French, the Germans, the Americans and the Italians not only offered training facilities for Houbeika's men in their own countries, they also sent specialists to the Lebanon to train and to liaise with his organization. The Germans taught his people how to analyse and evaluate information. The Americans and the French trained his officers in how to acquire the raw intelligence material. His people were trained at CIA headquarters at Langley, in Paris, in Frankfurt, in Hamburg. Since Sabra and Chatila in September 1982, Houbeika and his group of intelligence officers and men have borne in the eyes of the world the responsibility for the massacres. If that verdict is the right and proper one then others should be placed in the dock with Houbeika and his men: those who trained them, not just in the ways of espionage, but in the ways of killing, also bear the guilt for what took place in those camps.

This training and liaison with foreign agencies continued right up to the time of the massacres. And it was a two-way street.

'The CIA wanted to know everything we had or obtained on Israel. The French and the Germans wanted all we could get on the Armenian terrorist group ASALA, both countries have a significant Turkish population, particularly the Germans. The Italians wanted information on the Red Brigades. All of them wanted maximum information on the Palestinian terrorist groups. The British as well. The Germans and the French reciprocated and fed us their intelligence information. The CIA never. They gave us training, equipment. When the Israelis discovered this they went mad. Bashir of course still had a continuing close relationship with Israel. The Israelis said to him, "Look, this cannot continue. What are the Americans doing for you compared to what we are doing? We send in planes to protect you and your people, we give you weapons, we train you. We want intelligence co-ordination, not co-operation." I declined to co-operate with the Israelis so Bashir set up a second intelligence unit under Elie Wazin, nicknamed Abas, to co-operate with Mossad.'

As a man with wide-ranging contacts, Houbeika was in an excellent position to evaluate the rival secret services.

'The Americans have a very good "Elint", electronic intelligence. Human intelligence not so good. The British were the best in this area. Regarding Lebanon, the Germans and the British were the best. The French? They were like the Lebanese militias. They were fighting each other in Lebanon. I know that a few years ago some of their intelligence people were killed in Beirut and they put the blame on Hezbollah and other factions. It was their own struggle, they were killing each other. But by far the best were the Mossad. A lot of intelligence and, security-wise, very active. They could send aeroplanes, they could send snipers. Mossad not only dealt with the gathering of intelligence, they also responded. The Head of Mossad at that time, Hofi [Major General Yitzhak Hofi], he was the best. He had a very good close relationship with Begin. They were part of a very powerful team, Begin, Hofi, Sharon, Eitan. Israel's Military Intelligence? That was another matter, they thought the Lebanese Christians were the worst kind of Arabs they could face. There was therefore an intelligence split within Israel.'

If Elie Houbeika told me the truth as we discussed the events leading up to Israel's invasion of Lebanon in 1982, then a clear conspiracy had existed for some considerable time before the Israeli forces came over the border. A conspiracy that had many parties to it, including the man who would be President, Bashir Gemayel. He and other Lebanese sat on one side of the table and the Israeli government sat on the other.

'In 1981 Sharon flew into Jounieh by helicopter. Usually the Israelis came by boats and the meetings were held on them out at sea, but by 1981 the Mossad had an operational safe house in Jounieh. I was present during this meeting. The first thing Sharon said to Bashir was, "We in Israel [the Cabinet] are discussing what to do if one day the Palestinians carry out a terrorist attack. We are weighing how we should respond. If, for example, a Palestinian group should infiltrate the Israeli border, go to a kibbutz and kill a child we cannot confine our retaliation to an air strike. We want to go inside Lebanese territory and destroy their camps. What's your reaction to that?" Bashir said, "If you do that you will endanger us, because afterwards the Palestinians will retaliate against us." Sharon said, "OK, we'll discuss this matter later on, but are you ready to help us if something like this happens, or to change the course of the operation in a way that will help you?" And Bashir said, "Of course." Later, after Sharon left, Bashir said to us, "They will come and we have to be ready for them. To assist them." He gave an order to conscript every student. In less than a year we had an army of twelve thousand people and meeting after meeting with the Israelis. Sometimes in Jounieh, sometimes in Tel Aviv. Among those taking part were Begin, Sharon, Hofi and Eitan. Early in 1982, at one of these meetings Sharon said, "OK, the terrorist scenario. If it happens, we will go forty kilometres into Lebanon and we will destroy all Palestinian camps within that area." Bashir said, "This may help you. It doesn't help us. To help us you will have to stay there for at least six months. If you don't we will not be able to resist the Syrians when you pull out." Sharon said, "OK, it's not a problem, we know how the first round will be shot, we never know how it will end. We went to Sinai for one month. We remained eleven years. Six months in Beirut is not a problem for Israel. We will begin with the first forty kilometres. That will be the first shot."

'During the first 1981 meeting the Israelis asked Bashir for every conceivable document that would assist them during the invasion. They wanted to know about the electricity, the telephones, the whole communications system, the whole infrastructure of the government of Lebanon. Bashir gave them tons and tons of papers, of maps, technical drawings, data concerning every conceivable institution in Lebanon. I am sure that up to the present day the Israelis know exactly what's happening in Lebanon, even down to the smallest detail of the smallest institution in this country. That's because of the material that Bashir Gemayel made available to them in 1981.'

Houbeika told me that the Reagan administration were kept fully informed of these plans for the invasion of Lebanon. With regard to that first shot that triggered the Israeli forces over the border – the attempted murder of Ambassador Argov in London by an Abu Nidal group – Houbeika, the head of Bashir Gemayel's Intelligence, the man who had established an intimate relationship with the intelligence agencies of many countries, was certain that he knew who was behind the attack on Argov.

'The Mossad. You know, when the Israelis move they leave nothing to chance. It's calculated very accurately. If their Ambassador was hit at that time that means it was *planned* by the Israelis to happen when it did. Because their invasion of Lebanon was also planned to happen when it did. They needed two months from June to July, these were the months when they could move, troops, heavy artillery, the whole infrastructure of an invading army. After that time they would have faced many problems. In the Bekaa valley the terrain would be very difficult for the tanks to move after the rains came. With the kind of rain we get at that time, so heavy the mud could swallow a tank. Not only the rains; with the continuous cloud their infantry troops would not have been able to get air support. You can bomb from high altitude because of infra red sighting but for direct air support for infantry you must have a clear view. Abu Nidal's group was and still is very heavily infiltrated by Mossad. I had confirmation of this from many intelligence sources. From Europe, from the South, our sources in the South. Many of Nidal's group would be constantly going into Israel for meetings. Putting the Mossad involvement at its very lowest, they would have been fully aware before the attack in London of the date, the time and the place. Therefore they could have easily prevented it.'

On the third of June 1982, the Israeli Foreign Minister, Yitzhak Shamir, called for the elimination of the PLO so that the Camp David Agreement could be 'advanced'. Hours later Ambassador Argov was shot in London. The following day the Israeli invasion of Lebanon began with the air force carrying out repeated bombing raids over South Lebanon and West Beirut. All the secret meetings between Bashir Gemayel and the Israeli leaders for the invasion, the date of which had been postponed at least five times while the Israelis waited for a 'terrorist attack' that would serve as an acceptable provocation to their American allies, all of this planning now reached fruition.

Elie Houbeika:

'So when the Israelis had advanced forty kilometres, Sharon came to Beirut and saw Bashir and said to him, "Now what?" And Bashir said, "You have to reach Damour." Sharon said, "I'll try, but there is the Syrian army, we will have to manoeuvre. We'll see what we can do." When Sharon and his army reached Damour he again came to see Bashir. "We have reached Damour, now why don't you go and make the sparkle in Beirut, it will help us to come in deeper. You have to take your own part in this war. You have to invade West Beirut." Bashir said, "I can't, it's too strong at present, you will have to come closer. Come to Hadeth." So the Israelis came to Hadeth. Again Bashir drew Sharon closer to Beirut. "We will have to link our forces at Kfarshima.

If you don't link with us there we will do nothing." So they linked, then Sharon and his army came into East Beirut and to Baada. Bashir ordered some of his military forces to make a move against the Technical College at Hadeth. It was being held by Amal Shi'ites. There was a small clash between something like twenty Amal and two platoons of Lebanese forces, that's all. Then Bashir says to Sharon, "I've paid the price." Sharon and the other Israelis went mad. "Don't be ridiculous! That's unbelievable." This was just a relatively minor skirmish, they were still looking for Bashir to give them the sparkle. The invasion of West Beirut. The destruction of the Palestinian camps. Particularly they desired the death of Yasser Arafat. Sharon tried many times to kill him while he was still in West Beirut, especially during the continuous bombing. I'll give you just one example. During the last days of the war, I received a phone call from the director of my old school, Frères Bon Lasad. The director, Frère Bernabay, told me he needed my help, he said that Israeli soldiers were destroying everything in the school, were stealing radios, typewriters, everything. I went to the school to see if I could help. The Israelis had taken over a large section of it, they were using it as a base. Sharon was there, Eitan, Drori and Amos Yaron. They had a television set rigged up. There was a large quantity of champagne in the room. They told me afterwards that the television set was linked to a particular bomb in one of their aeroplanes with a camera on it. They had been given information that Arafat was having a meeting in one of his multiple headquarters and this bomb was destined to hit him while the meeting was in progress. The TV pictures showed a high aerial view of Beirut and then moments later the picture cut out as the bomb exploded. They opened up the champagne and toasted the fact that Arafat was dead. In fact Arafat had left the apartment just three or four minutes before the bomb had exploded.

'Bashir talked again to the Israelis. "Every time Israel makes war it wins the war and loses the peace. If you really want to win this war I will have to be elected

President of Lebanon. If you can reach my school at Jamhour above the Presidential Palace at Baada then I can make my election as President a reality. When that is done, then we can make treaties of mutual defence, strategical treaties, every kind of accord."'

Gemayel's insistence that the Israeli forces should take his former school was not through any mystical super-stitious belief. The school and the high ground around it dominates the Presidential Palace below. It was oc-cupied by Syrian forces. No deputy would dare come to the Presidential Palace for the elections while Syrian forces occupied a position from which they could de-stroy the Palace. The Israelis yet again obliged. In the event the election that took place on August 23rd, 1982, occurred not in the Palace but in the Lebanese Army's military academy at Fayadiye. On the second vote Bashir Gemayel was elected President of Lebanon.

Before the election Gemayel had discussed the compo-sition of his government with his allies, the Israelis. How broadly based would it be? Would it be a government of national reconciliation? Houbeika said:

'I remember hearing Rafael Eitan [Lieutenant General, Israeli Chief of Staff] say, "How wide will the government be? How small will it be? It makes no difference, Bashir. We're talking about a big coffin or a small coffin. Within that coffin you will ensure that the Government, the Min-isters, will be like a corpse. Deal with them in any way you want." After he had been elected Bashir went for a secret meeting at night with Begin, Sharon and Shamir. It took place in Nahariya [a town in northern Israel, close to the Lebanese border]. It began at 11.00 pm on September 1st and continued to three the following morning. Begin said to him, "Now you are elected I cannot call you my son any more. I will have to call you Mr President. But because you are Mr President and I am Prime Minister of Israel we can now sign those treaties that we have agreed on in the past." Bashir responded, "I cannot. I am newly elected. I have to form a government and they will discuss such treaties with you." Sharon interjected at

that. "We were talking about a government in Lebanon."
Bashir said, "I cannot accept that. My dignity rejects it.
I have to form a broadly based government. That is
democracy. I have to have a balance with the Muslims.
With the Arab States. I don't want to open one window
and close twenty-one doors. Just give me time." Begin
flew into a tremendous rage, and called him a liar and a
cheat. He swore at him. "Just who do you think you are?
It's not your army in Jerusalem. It's mine in Lebanon.
I can smash you just like that."'

Back in Beirut the President-elect told his closest colleagues of his belief that a bilateral relationship with
Israel would be very dangerous.

'We have to bring in the Americans and bring them
in substantially, in strength. A tripartite agreement. In
addition I would like to have an open door with Syria.'

The secret meeting was followed by another. On
September 12th Sharon and Bashir Gemayel reviewed
their plans.

September 1st, the date of Bashir Gemayel's secret
midnight meeting with Israel's leaders, and September
12th, the date of his meeting with Sharon, have particular
significance, as can be seen from a brief chronology of
key events that had taken place.

On the 6th of June the Israeli invasion of Lebanon
began. By the 14th of June the Israeli forces were already
occupying a number of Beirut suburbs; on the same day
President Reagan's special envoy, Phillip Habib, arrived
in Lebanon for the first round of peace talks. By the 25th of
June the Israeli forces had Beirut completely surrounded.
By the 19th of August negotiations were completed for
the complete evacuation of PLO forces from Beirut. On
the 23rd of August Gemayel was elected President. At
precisely the same time the international peace keeping
force was arriving and taking up strategic positions around
the capital. By the 1st of September the evacuation of the
PLO forces from Beirut and from Lebanon had been completed. Before his departure Yasser Arafat had negotiated
and been given a written agreement by Habib that the

civilian Palestinians would be protected after his troops departed, yet as early as the 12th of September the entire international peace keeping force had been withdrawn and departed. It was a scenario for a massacre. Without the Americans, the Italians, and the French, who was to protect the people of Sabra and Chatila? The Phalange forces of Gemayel? The Israelis?

By the 14th of September the President-elect of Lebanon, Bashir Gemayel, had had the door to Syria opened to him. Houbeika played a significant role. A secret dialogue began, this time not with the Israelis but with elements of the country most bitterly opposed to it, Syria. Houbeika quietly began to arrange a meeting between Bashir Gemayel and the Syrian President's brother, Rif'at. It was scheduled to take place in North Lebanon at the village of Aaqoura on the 17th of September. To ensure that Bashir's presence in the area would not be detected, Houbeika told me, he had arranged a bizarre disguise. The President-elect would travel to the meeting place wearing a mask, a replica of France's President, François Mitterrand.

The final details of the meeting were put in place on the 11th of September. On the 14th Bashir Gemayel was chairing a meeting at the Phalange HQ in Beirut when an electronically controlled bomb exploded killing Gemayel and twenty-five party workers. Some, like Houbeika, pointed the finger at the Palestinians, others at Syria, others at Israel. The man who activated the device, Habib Chartouny, a twenty-six-year-old Lebanese Christian, was soon arrested by Houbeika. He talked to me of this assassination at great length, attempting to convince me that Chartouny had links with the Palestinians. Understandable perhaps – this conversation was taking place in Damascus. It might well have been difficult for Houbeika to admit that Chartouny was a member of the Syrian Social Nationalist Party, that the man who gave him the bomb and his instructions, Nabil 'Alam, immediately took refuge in

Syria, and that 'Alam is a Syrian Intelligence agent controlled by the elusive Ali Duba.[1]

If Houbeika's account of the planned meeting between Gemayel and President Asad's brother is accurate, there would appear to have been a breakdown in communications between Ri'fat and Duba. What was about to happen in Sabra and Chatila would be widely interpreted as Phalange revenge for the murder of their leader. It was not. It was part of an agenda agreed long before his death. Houbeika told me:

'After Bashir's death Sharon came with Eitan. They had a meeting with Fadi Frem [Commander of Lebanese Forces], Fouad Abounader and Zahi Bustani. The Israelis said, "You know about the sparkle we agreed with Bashir?" They said that yes, they did know. Sharon said, "Well it's the time. We cannot leave the main infrastructure of the Palestinians in Beirut intact. We have to go in but we cannot go in to an Arab capital, it will be the first time something like that has been done. Worldwide it would not be acceptable, so you have to help us." Fadi said, "We cannot do that without the approval of Sheikh Pierre [Sheikh Pierre Gemayel, founder of the Phalangist Party, and Bashir's father]." So Fadi, Fouad and Zahi went to see Sheikh Pierre. They told him that Bashir had agreed on a sparkle with the Israelis and that the Israelis were now here to ask for it. Sheikh Pierre was in very bad shape, this is shortly after Bashir's death. He told them, "Everything that Bashir decided must happen." Fadi advised the Israelis accordingly, then they too went to Sheikh Pierre to hear it from him directly. This was Sharon and Eitan. Sheikh Pierre said to them, "Look, consider Bashir is still living, me and Amine [Amine Gemayel] will follow the same line." So Fadi immediately gave the orders to some of his troops that were already based in the airport to march against the camps. Not only

[1] During a subsequent interview with Ahmed Jibril in late 1992 he admitted to me that he had made the bomb which killed Bashir Gemayel.

those, people from the Shi'ites, Amal troops from the area of Bourj al Barajneh. Also troops from the South were brought up. Troops under the control of Major Saad Haddad. All of these people entered the camps.'

The joint Israeli-Lebanese Army operation to enter West Beirut started on Wednesday 15th of September at six in the morning. It had been previously agreed that the Israeli forces would not enter the camps; that task would be performed by the Phalangists. By Thursday afternoon the Palestinian refugee camps of Sabra and Chatila were surrounded on three sides by Israeli forces and on the fourth side by their Phalange allies. At five in the afternoon, with the Israeli High Command carefully monitoring their movements, the Phalange forces began their entry of Chatila camp. The Israeli forward command post was located on the roof of the five-storey Kuwaiti Embassy, less than two hundred metres from Chatila.

On the morning of Saturday the 18th of September 1982, author and journalist Robert Fisk, under the eyes of the still-watching Israeli officers, entered Chatila. With him were three colleagues: Loren Jenkins, Karsten Tveit and William Foley. I had planned to write my own account of what these men and others found inside the camps until Robert Fisk published his book *Pity the Nation*. I am deeply grateful for his kindness in allowing me to quote verbatim from his work. Not least because it comes not second- or third-hand, but from an eye-witness.

It was the flies that told us. There were millions of them, their hum almost as eloquent as the smell. Big as bluebottles, they covered us, unaware at first of the difference between the living and the dead. If we stood still, writing in our notebooks, they would settle like an army – legions of them – on the white surface of our notebooks, hands, arms, faces, always congregating around our eyes and mouths, moving from body to body, from the many dead to the few living, from corpse to reporter, their small green bodies panting with excitement as they found new flesh upon which to settle and feast.

If we did not move quickly enough, they bit us. Mostly they stayed around our heads in a grey cloud, waiting for us to assume the generous stillness of the dead. They were obliging, these flies, forming our only physical link with the victims who lay around us, reminding us that there is life in death. Someone benefits. The flies were impartial. It mattered not the slightest that the bodies here had been the victims of mass murder. The flies would have performed in just this way for the unburied dead of any community. Doubtless it was like this on hot afternoons during the Great Plague.

At first, we did not use the word massacre. We said very little because the flies would move unerringly for our mouths. We held handkerchiefs over our mouths for this reason, then we clasped the material to our noses as well because the flies moved over our faces. If the smell of the dead in Sidon was nauseating, the stench in Chatila made us retch. Through the thickest of handkerchiefs we smelled them. After some minutes, *we* began to smell of the dead.

They were everywhere, in the road, in laneways, in back yards and broken rooms, beneath crumpled masonry and across the top of garbage tips. The murderers – the Christian militiamen whom Israel had let into the camps to 'flush out terrorists' – had only just left. In some cases, the blood was still wet on the ground. When we had seen a hundred bodies, we stopped counting. Down every alleyway, there were corpses, women, young men, babies and grandparents – lying together in lazy and terrible profusion where they had been knifed or machine-gunned to death. Each corridor through the rubble produced more bodies. The patients at a Palestinian hospital had disappeared after gunmen ordered the doctors to leave. Everywhere, we found signs of hastily dug mass graves. Perhaps a thousand people were butchered; probably half that number again.

Even while we were there, amid the evidence of such savagery, we could see the Israelis watching us. From the top of the tower block to the west – the second building on the Avenue Camille Chamoun – we could see them staring at us through field-glasses, scanning back and forth across the streets of the corpses, the lenses of the binoculars sometimes flashing in the sun as their gaze ranged through the camp. Loren Jenkins cursed a lot. I thought it was probably his way of controlling his feelings of nausea amid this terrible smell. All of us wanted to vomit. We were *breathing* death, inhaling the very putrescence of the bloated corpses around us. Jenkins immediately realized that the Israeli defence minister would have to bear some responsibility for this horror. 'Sharon!' he shouted. 'That fucker Sharon! This is Deir Yassin all over again.'

What we found inside the Palestinian Chatila camp at ten o'clock on the morning of 18 September 1982 did not quite beggar description, although it would have been easier to re-tell in the cold prose of a medical examination. There had been massacres before in Lebanon, but rarely on this scale and never overlooked by a regular, supposedly disciplined army. In the panic and hatred of battle, tens of thousands had been killed in this country. But these people, hundreds of them, had been shot down unarmed. This was a mass killing, an incident – how easily we used the word 'incident' in Lebanon – that was also an atrocity. It went beyond even what the Israelis would have in other circumstances called a *terrorist* atrocity. It was a war crime.

Jenkins and Tveit and I were so overwhelmed by what we found in Chatila that at first we were unable to register our own shock. Bill Foley of AP had come with us. All he could say as he walked round was 'Jesus Christ!' over and over again. We might have accepted evidence of a few murders; even dozens

618

of bodies, killed in the heat of combat. But there were women lying in houses with their skirts torn up to their waists and their legs wide apart, children with their throats cut, rows of young men shot in the back after being lined up at an execution wall. There were babies – blackened babies because they had been slaughtered more than 24 hours earlier and their small bodies were already in a state of decomposition – tossed into rubbish heaps alongside discarded U.S. army ration tins, Israeli army medical equipment and empty bottles of whisky.

Where were the murderers? Or, to use the Israelis' vocabulary, where were the 'terrorists'?

Fisk's question still demands an answer. The murderers, the 'terrorists' were in many places. Some were back in their barracks in East Beirut, others had been flown back to South Lebanon by the Israelis. Their accomplices were in other places – on the Israeli forward command position, in the corridors of power in Tel Aviv and Jerusalem.

Prime Minister Menachem Begin was much given to recalling the past. Prone to talk in dramatic images of the Holocaust. Susceptible to uttering phrases like 'Never again'. Begin, the man who had kissed the outlawed flag of the Irgun, picked up the gun and the bomb and murdered during the 1940s. Begin, the Nobel Peace Prize winner. Begin's 'Never again' referred of course not to his own acts of terrorism but to the horror and evil of the Final Solution, but were there some softly spoken qualifying words that came from the same mouth? Words that found safe haven in the darkness of the souls of at least some of his listening audience. 'Never again. Except to the Palestinians.'

Elie Houbeika: 'On Saturday [September 18th, 1982][1]

[1] Houbeika, 10 years after the event, thought this meeting took place on Saturday September 18th. The Kahan Report records the meeting as having taken place on September 17th, 1982.

we had a meeting. Eitan [Israeli Chief of Staff General Eitan] came and said, "Well, it was a perfect operation. We congratulate the groups of the Lebanese forces who were extremely efficient."'

Houbeika's account continued with the statement that a day later, when world opinion was beginning to react, the Israelis returned. 'We have a catastrophe on our hands,' Sharon allegedly stated, followed by, 'You have to bear the consequences, take it on yourselves.'

One question above all others deeply concerned me as I talked to Elie Houbeika.

'Is it your understanding that, before Lebanese troops went into the camps, this "sparkle" the Israelis were seeking was in fact the massacre?'

'Yes. One of the deals between Amine and between Bashir and the Israelis was to get all the Palestinians to the Bekaa. So this could only be done with a massacre. It would stampede them to the Bekaa.'

'The same as Deir Yassin?'

'I don't know about Deir Yassin.'

Perhaps not, but others did. When questioned on his own involvement Houbeika was insistent – he had no involvement in the massacres of Sabra and Chatila, he stated firmly that during the entire period his major preoccupation, indeed his sole preoccupation, was his interrogation of the man who had murdered Bashir Gemayel, the Syrian agent Chartouny. He recounted his movements for the period in considerable detail. He told me of his hunts in various parts of Beirut for the remote control device that Chartouny had used and of his meetings with Amine Gemayel, a man now grooming himself to step into his dead brother's shoes and become President of Lebanon, something that became a reality within days. With regard to the various allegations, first made within days of the massacre and subsequently repeated and enlarged upon during the Israeli Government's Kahan Commission hearings on the events that Fisk rightly calls a war crime, Houbeika, speaking for the first time, denied any involvement. With regard to the testimony given by Israeli officers to the Kahan Commission that placed Houbeika on the roof where the Israeli forward command position was located, Houbeika flatly denied being on that roof during the period of time when the massacres were taking place, denied urging the men already murdering within the camps to 'Do the will of God'.

'At that time my own organization consisted of thirty guys. We were not military troops. We worked solely on intelligence . . . When the Israelis named me as the man responsible I went to Fadi Frem, I said to him, "Look Fadi, I don't know if this is serious," because at that time nobody took it seriously, you know, OK Palestinians, Israelis, who cares? We had been having fights with the Palestinians for ten years, so one massacre less, one massacre more . . . I told him, "What about this?" He said, "Don't even think about it." I went to see Johnny Abdul, who was at that time the chief of intelligence of Sarkis [President Elias Sarkis]. I said, "What should I do?" He said, "Do nothing." CIA people came and said, "Well, Elie, we have to cut our relations with you, official ones, but they will continue unofficially."'

Houbeika told me that he went to many people, the kingmaker, Sheikh Pierre Gemayel, his surviving son Amine. The word was the same from them all. Do nothing, there is nothing to worry about.

'If you were not in command of those men, who went into the camps who was?'

'Busi Ashkar. He was the commander-in-chief of Beirut Command.'

Amine Gemayel succeeded his brother as President of Lebanon on September 21st. Just one week after Bashir's murder and three days after the massacres in Sabra and Chatila had stopped. The same week that Amine was elected he received an urgent request for a meeting with General Ariel Sharon and Israel's Defence Minister, Yitzhak Shamir.

Elie Houbeika:

'This meeting took place two or three days after

Amine's election at Maison de Future in Beit Al-Mustakbal. Sharon and Shamir spoke to him of Sabra and Chatila. Amine said, "That is something of the past. There is no problem." But to Sharon and Shamir it was a problem, a big one, they were asking him to give them a name, any name. They said, "Look, just state that your forces entered into Sabra and Chatila, don't mention anything about massacres but put the responsibility of the actions there on yourself." Amine said, "No way, we had nothing to do with Sabra and Chatila." They said, "How come? Pierre Gemayel was present, he gave the approval for it. Fadi Frem was present." Fadi said, "Yes we have done it," and Amine said, "Look, I am newly elected, I cannot help you if I am burned with this affair, you know this is a matter of the past, leave it in the past. We will deal with the future."'

Many were not prepared to leave 'it' in the past. The expressions of horror, the condemnations, were worldwide, from Jews and Gentiles alike. On Saturday the 25th of September came the most significant reaction of them all. It came from within Israel. It came from the very soul of the country. That evening the people took to the streets of Tel Aviv. New immigrants, old immigrants, liberal, orthodox, survivors of the Holocaust, serving soldiers, they came from every walk of life. Estimates of their numbers vary between three and five hundred thousand. In a country with a population of approximately four million this demonstration was by any criteria significant. The biggest demonstration in the country's history. They demanded the withdrawal of Israeli forces, not just from Beirut but from Lebanon. They demanded a full independent public inquiry into the massacres. They demonstrated that as well as the darkness within the hearts and minds of some of their political leaders there was a morality, a goodness within the hearts of many in Israel. They established that the soul, the conscience, was alive and well. They demanded justice for what had been done in Sabra and Chatila.

'By the rivers of Babylon, there we sat down, yea we wept when we remembered Zion.'

This demonstration led directly to the establishing of the Kahan Commission which, despite all its pejorative language, such as Palestinians being constantly referred to as 'terrorists', and despite all of its flaws, such as the fatal inability to set the massacres within the context of the entire Israeli invasion of Lebanon, was a sincere attempt to arrive at least at some partial truths. Some of Israel's leaders suffered as a result of the Commission's conclusions, others benefited. If Begin was destroyed, Shamir's star rose. Drori, Sharon, Eitan, Yaron and Saguy were all considered to varying degrees to be men who bore some blame, some guilt. Sharon may have been forced out of one Cabinet position but he soon acquired another. Major General Yehoshua Saguy, Israel's Director of Military Intelligence, was one of a number to be dismissed. Saguy's name, the reader may recall, appeared earlier in this tale – it was he who inspired the 'Carlos is dead' story in 1986.

Subsequently President Amine Gemayel set up a Lebanese Government inquiry into the massacres. It conducted its investigations in secret and concluded that the massacres had been carried out 'by persons unknown'. No-one has ever been charged with crimes arising from what was perpetrated in Sabra and Chatila between Thursday September 16th and Saturday September 18th, 1982.

Houbeika's allegations had such serious implications that it was crucial to interview two men: President Amine Gemayel and Israel's Minister of Defence, Ariel Sharon.

When I interviewed the former Lebanese President in Paris in January 1993, he confirmed as accurate and true a great deal of Houbeika's evidence: Israel's secret arming and training of the Phalange, including the covert supply of oil; Sharon's secret trip to Jounieh in 1981 to forge an alliance with Bashir Gemayel; the 1981 conspiracy between the Phalange party, General Sharon and other leading Israelis to orchestrate the invasion of Lebanon by Israel, an invasion that would follow what Sharon called 'a hypothetical terrorist attack'; Bashir Gemayel's continuing attempts to ensure that the Israeli army came ever deeper into Lebanon until they were in Beirut. Perhaps most damning of all, Amine Gemayel confirmed that the massacres in Sabra and Chatila were 'supposed to happen before the death of Bashir. It was supposed to happen with the help of the Lebanese forces during the operations'. Amine Gemayel told me that he was aware from February 1982 not only that an Israeli invasion of his country was imminent, but that part of the plan involved Lebanese forces doing 'the dirty work, the sparkle'.

The former President elaborated: 'It could have been a disaster for the Israelis to reach Beirut and to have allowed the Palestinian infrastructure in the camps of West Beirut to remain. It could have been a political disaster for Sharon's career to reach Beirut and to keep the PLO infrastructure alive. So I'm talking, you know, realpolitik. That's why for sure somebody in Israel was aware and it could have been a real disaster not to clean the camps and this job should have been done by somebody. And they brought the Lebanese, the army of South Lebanon, Haddad's people, came from the south to be in Beirut at that time. And I heard they were in Sabra and Chatila at that time.'

Amine Gemayel also advised me that he was aware that *prior* to the massacres, Israel had a number of undercover agents living in the Sabra and Chatila camps and that Israel 'knew everything that was going on in the camps'. If this is true, then the Israeli high command, including General Sharon, would have known that their claims that even after the PLO withdrawal from Beirut there were still some two thousand armed terrorists in the camps were specious.

Amine Gemayel also confirmed that Elie Houbeika's account of the secret meeting between his brother and Menachem Begin in September 1982 was accurate.

There were only two areas where the former Lebanese President took issue with Houbeika's evidence. First,

624

he denied that his brother, Bashir Gemayel, was a willing party to the proposed sparkle, and second, while confirming Sharon's visit to the Gemayel family home on September 15th, some 24 hours before the massacres began, Amine Gemayel denied that there was any conversation at that time between his father and the Israeli general concerning the proposed entry by Lebanese forces into the Sabra and Chatila camps. Finally, he confirmed the secret meeting that took place with Sharon and Shamir at the House of the Future shortly after he was elected President, and confirmed how Israel's Foreign Minister and Minister of Defence had come seeking a scapegoat to blame for the massacres.

As for General Sharon, I have made a number of requests to interview him. By letter I advised him that in this book 'some of the comments made to me about you were of a highly critical nature and I wish to be as fair to you as I can by giving you an opportunity to respond to these various comments'. At the time of going to press, the former Israeli general had yet to respond to these requests.

I left Elie Houbeika in his seventh-floor apartment in West Beirut and with my Syrian minders drove the short distance to the Sabra and Chatila camps. To go directly from one to the other seemed very appropriate. We drove through an area known locally as Coca-Cola, named after a factory dispensing one of America's favourite drinks, or rather the remnants of a factory: most of it had been destroyed with American bombs dropped by the Israelis in 1982. The city looked much as I had seen it four years earlier. Attempts to rebuild were constantly halted and thwarted by renewed warfare. The sports complex at Matina Reatia with its wrecked stadium, bombed fly-overs leading nowhere, and everywhere litter and waste, including unwanted humanity, refugees from the latest round of madness between the troops of General Michel Aoun and the Syrian forces, people clustered in shacks and hovels.

The camps of Sabra and Chatila were reminiscent of

Gaza City but the conditions were much worse. Open sewerage running down the earth roads, children playing in it cheek by jowl with a lock-up selling meat and other food, the car having constantly to detour around massive bomb craters. I told Ahmed to stop the car, and under the ever-watchful eyes of the Syrian soldiers we began to wander through Sabra and Chatila and talk to some of the survivors.

These people had by any definition the right to be called survivors. Some that I spoke to had been living there for nearly forty years; they had survived all the carnage that had preceded the massacres and the carnage that followed. September 1982 had not been the end of the ordeal for these people. That had been followed by the camp wars, lasting from 1985 to 1988, continuous outbreaks of fighting, sieges, and then further fighting. They talked to me of the bombing that had continued without pause in 1982 for more than eighty days, of the cluster bombs that had fallen on the camps causing dreadful injuries and many deaths. They told me how they felt secure and safe after Phillip Habib had brokered the peace and Arafat's forces had left Lebanon. 'There was no reason for fear. There was a guarantee.' They became aware of heavy Israeli troop movements around the camps on Wednesday September the 14th. They assumed that this was normal activity. The Israelis gave every impression to the inhabitants that everything was fine.

'It started at four o'clock on the Thursday afternoon. They intensified their movements into the camps after six when it was dark. The Israeli forces' task at that time was just to illuminate the area. There were continuous Israeli flares during the darkness. These were fired from around the perimeter. It was quite obvious that those actually implementing the massacre were the Lebanese forces because we could easily identify that from their uniforms, their badges. They may have had Israelis amongst them dressed as Lebanese, who could tell? Difficult to concentrate on their identities with what was going on.'

And what was going on beggars belief.

A grocer with an artificial leg. They broke it off then shot him in the chest. An eighteen-year-old offering assistance to a wounded woman. Five bullets in his chest. A handful of elderly people appealing to the Israeli forces at the camp entrance. Six old people asking the occupying force for assistance. Ordered to return inside. Ordered to return to their deaths. The survivors insisted that these six were not killed by Lebanese but by Israeli forces. Survivors who were born in Galilee, in Aka, in Haifa.

'Seventy per cent of the killings were carried out with knives and axes. They preferred that technique. The silent killings. It gave them access to more and more victims. Shots alert. My son and a lady were at the entrance of the camp. They were allowed to leave because ten others were approaching. Shots would have alerted the ten. They let two go to kill ten. The killing was indiscriminate. Whole families from the babies to the old.'

They showed me the site of two mass graves and insisted that those who lay below had not figured in any Red Cross count. They talked of hundreds being herded into the nearby sports stadium. 'Some were shot. Others were buried alive.'

These survivors put the number that died at a minimum of five thousand. As for the figures that Bassam Abu Sharif had given me, based on PLO payments both before and after the massacres, they were quietly dismissive of PLO assistance.

'The PLO were not giving us any financial help from 1982 until the Intifada started in December 1987. Not a penny. After that, yes. Before that, no.'

How do they survive still? They find work where they can, though under Lebanese law they are officially forbidden to do so. United Nations relief is available to just 3 per cent of the camp population. 'The aid is sufficient to survive for three days out of thirty in the month. The aid is only available for the disabled or the completely disadvantaged people.'

Of course the others who live in this place are so advantaged.

After much arguing and many phone calls the Lebanese Army eventually and with great reluctance allowed Ahmed and me onto the roof of what had been the Israeli forward command post at the time of the massacres. A position from which, according to the Kahan Commission report, 'it was impossible to see what was happening within the alleys of the camp, not even with the aid of the 20 × 120 binoculars that were on the command post roof'.

I stood where Sharon and the others had stood. With my naked eyes I could see over a large section of the camps. I could see the colour of the washing hanging on the lines. I could see old men reading their newspapers, stirring their tea. When binoculars were handed to me I could identify what newspapers they were reading. It was four in the afternoon, the time that the killings had started. It was a month later, if anything the light would have been slightly worse than that afternoon in September 1982. Came the darkness, came the Israeli flares. The Lebanese officer standing beside me told me that with flares the visibility from where we stood would have been excellent.

I walked back the one hundred or so metres into the camps, past the playground under which a countless number lay buried. As I walked back deeper into the camps I suddenly heard a blast of music that sounded familiar. I rounded a corner. Sitting on a pile of debris was a young Palestinian boy, perhaps twelve years of age. Next to him was a huge ghetto blaster, clearly a prized possession in this land of duty free. He was playing a Bruce Springsteen cassette. It was the particular track that had caught my attention.

We made a promise we swore we'd always remember
   no retreat no surrender
Like soldiers in the winter's night with a vow to defend, no retreat no surrender

Now young faces grow sad and old and hearts of fire
grow cold, we swore blood brothers against the
wind. I'm ready to grow young again and hear
your sister's voice calling us home across the open
yards, well maybe we could cut someplace of our
own with these drums and these guitars
Blood brothers in the stormy night with a vow to
defend, no retreat no surrender
Now on the street tonight the lights grow dim, the
walls of my room are closing in
There's a war outside still raging
You say it ain't ours anymore to win
I want to sleep beneath peaceful skies in my lover's
bed with a wide open country in my eyes and these
romantic dreams in my head

I stood transfixed by the image. He had been looking
at me as the song roared out over the squalor and the
numbing devastation all around. As Springsteen went into
his next song I wondered whether the young Palestinian
had any awareness of the words in relation to his life,
to his surroundings. I did not wonder for long. He
smiled at me then held up his two hands. His fingers
formed two V-for-victory gestures.

Back at my hotel I thought about the day. About my
conversations with Houbeika and then the residents of
Sabra and Chatila. I had waited for a number of years
to walk through those camps. To see. To question. To
listen. To bear some form of personal witness, not for
others but for myself in my attempts to understand how
and why so much unremitting evil had been unleashed
in these places. The reality had been what I had always
known it would be. Merely symbolic, not enlightening.
One of the tasks that I had set myself for this particular
trip to Beirut had been fulfilled. I turned my attention
back to the other. To Carlos.

There were men I needed to talk to on the other side
of this city. I could not get to them and I wondered if they

could get to me. The problem was making contact other than through a Syrian-army-monitored switchboard. I made a call that I did not mind them listening in to. To Amin Doughan, the feisty newspaper editor whom I had met in Tripoli. He was in. He would be delighted to see me. Ahmed reminded me of the injunction given by the Syrian High Command. Under no circumstances must I leave the hotel after dark and it was now night time. Amin, as I knew he would, came to the rescue. He would come by car and collect me. Unfortunately Ahmed insisted on coming with me.

At Amin's home we were made welcome with typical Lebanese charm. As we ate and drank and discussed Michel Aoun's last stand, I quietly asked Amin if there might be a phone somewhere. Alone in Amin's study, I placed a number of telephone numbers and names on the desk and began dialling. They were the names that my wife had been given by the Lebanese officer based in Washington. I struck lucky with the second call. Points of reference were exchanged and the man I was talking to relaxed. He could not, regrettably, get over the green line that separated the city at that time of night, but he was happy to talk freely on the phone. In view of the fact that he was a senior member of Lebanese Intelligence I assumed the line was clean. I explained to him a little of the background and my reason for going to Damascus. I also told him of the problems that I was encountering.

'Of course. They will never admit he is there.'

'Yes, I realize that. Look, do you know what name he is now using and a precise location?'

'You should make some discreet enquiries for a Mexican business-man named Michel Assaf. He lives in the Mezze district. Al Akram street.'

'And this gentleman can lead me to the man I'm looking for?'

'David. This gentleman *is* the man you are looking for.'

Later, back at the hotel, I checked out the address on my maps. It was only a short distance from the Sheraton hotel. I had been sitting virtually on the doorstep of Carlos for nearly three weeks. Apart from the false name I had also foolishly been looking for a false reality – a man still living at least partially what in his mind was a revolutionary life with revolutionary contacts. I should have been looking quite simply for a businessman. What was it he said to Peter Boock and the others in Yemen in 1976? About going after 'the hard stuff'. Materialism. The consumer society. I wondered ruefully if I could not have saved myself a great deal of time by checking out Wall Street and the London Stock Exchange and leafing through the Names at Lloyds.

Michel Assaf. Michel. In Gaza City Samir's relation Omar had talked of a 'Michel'.

By Sunday evening, 29th October, I was back in Damascus. By the following morning I had worked out a game plan. A discreet visit to the Mezze district had established that whoever lived on Al Akram street merited special protection, including a number of armed uniformed guards, probably members of Syrian Intelligence. This is not an unusual feature of life in Damascus. Houbeika, Abu Mousa, Jibril, Habash and a number of other guests of President Asad all merit such protection.

On one corner was a military college, at the other end of the road a mosque. In between there were modern blocks of flats; everywhere there were armed guards. Whatever else lived in this road close to the main highway to Beirut, a great deal of power and influence resided here.

Assuming that the Syrians might think it decidedly odd if I suddenly abandoned my attempts to see Ali Duba and others on my shopping list I continued to attempt to obtain official access to these people. These attempts included discussing my needs with the Minister for Foreign Information, Mohammed Sulman. With regard to my request to talk to Vice President Khaddam, the Minister told me that the Vice President was currently confined to bed. 'A severe cold.'

With regard to Ali Duba, Sulman confirmed that he

was still in Latahia coping with the aftermath of the car accident that had cost five of his relations their lives. He was due back by the end of the week. In the interim, Sulman promised to try and arrange a meeting with one of Duba's senior colleagues.

As I prepared for an interview with Nayef Hawatmeh, leader of yet another Palestinian group that had splintered from the Popular Front, to form in this case the Popular Democratic Front, the PDF, my attention was constantly drawn to the larger task. How to reach Carlos. I was not seeking a long extensive interview with him. Undoubtedly he would have given an undertaking to the Syrian regime not to grant such an interview. In terms of the facts, the truth, of Ilich Ramirez Sanchez, such an interview was by this time irrelevant. My hunt, not only for the man but his reality, had well established that reality before this trip. All I was now seeking was definitive proof that the man I had previously met was indeed an impostor and that this man Michel Assaf was beyond any doubt the real Carlos, was in fact Ilich Ramirez Sanchez. I had come to Damascus well prepared for this task.

All I needed was one brief meeting with Michel Assaf. That was all. A man who, if he was indeed Ramirez, was, in the view of Nayef Hawatmeh,

'A terrorist. A man without any political outlook. A man who like his leader Wadi Haddad merely served to further the aspirations of Iraq. The Haddad group were Iraq's child.'

Through other Palestinian contacts that I had by now made in the city I indicated my desire to talk to the leaders of yet another splinter group of the PLF. This was the key to the game plan that I had evolved. A meeting was set up for Thursday afternoon. A few hours before I set off for this interview I received news that in terms of irony gave me the most ironic moment of this entire story. It came from Salwah. She had not only made contact with Military Intelligence but had spoken on my behalf to Colonel Haytham Ahmed Sa'id, a gentleman who could

54-5. Who was responsible for the Sabra and Chatila slaughter? Two of the candidates are seen here with the author: Yasser Arafat (*below*) and Elie Houbeika (*above*).

56-7. *Above* Lockerbie: an atrocity the author tried to prevent. *Below* with the man considered by the United States and Great Britain to be responsible - Ahmed Jibril.

58-9. Colonel Mu'ammar Qathafi, and his home after the 1986 bombing.

60. Raafat's home, the morning after Reagan had done 'what he had to do'.

61. Raafat Ghussein; educated in Britain, murdered in Tripoli.

62. *Left to right from top* The protectors of the world's most wanted man: Houari Boumedienne; Saddam Hussein; Salem Rubayya Ali; Tito; Gustav Husák; Nicolae Ceauşescu; Janos Kádár; Erich Honecker. And then there was one – only President Hafiz al-Asad of Syria continues to give Carlos sanctuary.

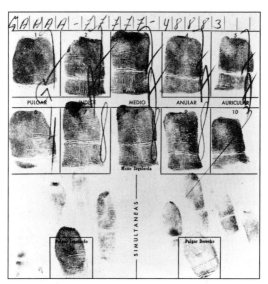

63-4. *Top* The fingerprints of Ilich Ramirez Sanchez. *Above* His residence in Damascus. He and his family live on the top floor.

The People's Democratic Republic of Yemen

MINISTRY OF FOREIGN AFFAIRS

DIPLOMATIC PASSPORT

005004

MR. NAGI
ABUBAKER AHMED

65-8. *Clockwise from top left*
Elba Maria Sanchez;
Magdalena Kopp; Carlos's
false passport that worried
Libyan intelligence;
Johannes Weinrich.

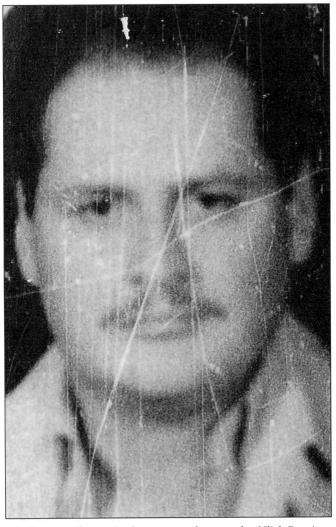

69. Portrait of a criminal: a current photograph of Ilich Ramirez Sanchez.

if he so wished throw much light on a number of terrorist attacks in Europe, particularly in West Germany.

'They refuse to meet you.'

'Why?'

'They are convinced you are an agent for the Mossad.'

I considered for a moment the years I had expended, not merely to establish the truth of Carlos but the truth of the Israeli-Palestinian issue. I remembered my experiences and my feelings in the West Bank and Gaza. Samir burst into an angry argument with his friend in Arabic. I waited until it had subsided then looked enquiringly at him.

'They are fools. They think you are the Mossad. They think you are the same as Farzad Bazoft.'

I shook my head in a quiet despair. If the Syrians believed that, then there would be no interviews with Duba, Said, Al-Khuly or any member of Syrian Intelligence.

Farzad Bazoft, an Iranian-born journalist employed by the *Observer,* had been arrested in Iraq about a month before I had flown to Damascus. Near the end of his Iraqi government-sponsored trip, Bazoft had gone to investigate reports of a massive explosion at a defence establishment to the south of Baghdad. He and his companion, British nurse Daphne Parish, had been arrested. Before my trip John Major, then British Foreign Minister, had officially raised their case with his Iraqi opposite number, Tariq Aziz, focusing in particular on the fact that the British were being denied consular access to the couple.

Now, Samir explained, there had been a new development. Bazoft had just gone on Iraqi TV and confessed to being on a spying mission for Israel. He had 'confessed' to having been recruited by Israeli Intelligence while in London in 1987. I pointed out to Samir and Salwah that it must be transparently obvious to anyone with half a brain that poor Bazoft had had his alleged confession beaten and tortured out of him. It was a madness. Now another madness was being perpetrated here in Damascus.

Just as I was convinced that the real Carlos was in this city, so I was by now equally convinced that the intelligence agency that had targeted me, attempted to manipulate me, was of Syrian origin. If what I was now being told were true then they must have concluded that they had been attempting to turn a Mossad agent. It was unreal, yet if they had arrived at that conclusion at the very start, then it might well explain why they had not simply trotted out the authentic version, always assuming he would have played their game. If I was from Mossad they dared not take the risk of producing the real Carlos in North Lebanon. Where one Mossad agent goes, others are not far behind. In the city of Jounieh, a relatively short journey from my all-night meetings with Carlos Two, the area was riddled with Mossad agents. I had not known that then, it was something that Elie Houbeika and others had told me, long after those meetings.

I began to feel that my life was taking on a surreal quality as I set out with Samir to talk to the men from the PLF. We drove down Kuwatly Street past the Defence Ministry complex where, if my information was correct, Ali Duba and his men plotted and conspired. I wondered how long I would be able to hold out if they decided to let me in there, not to ask but to answer questions. How long would it be before I made a return visit to the television studios to talk not of murder in the Vatican or Salman Rushdie but of my work on behalf of Israeli Intelligence?

The particular PLF faction that I went to talk to was known as the Abu Nidal Group. I was assured during my meeting that they had no connection with *the* Abu Nidal, just a desire to use a title that means 'Father of the Struggle', but Nidal was not the man I was seeking in Damascus.

'The Al Kasser brothers are of course known to you?'

'Yes, Gassan was collaborating with Wadi Haddad and Monzer with Abu Abbas. But now both are businessmen.'

'Yes, of course. I am anxious to make contact with a

business colleague of theirs. Michel Assaf.'

'What do you want with him?'

'I have a message for him. From his father. I promised to deliver it to him personally. Do you know him?'

'I think he is a business colleague of the brothers. Monzer may not be here but Gassan is.'

'Well, if you could ask him either to see me or to arrange for me to meet this Michel Assaf, I would be most grateful.'

'I will try. Do you have a letter of introduction, something like that?'

'Yes, I do.'

I handed him an envelope, sealed, addressed simply to Michel Assaf. Then I calmly turned to the various internal politics of the Palestinian movements and drank another cup of café Arabi. Sources in West German and French Intelligence had told me long before my trip to Damascus of links between the Al Kasser brothers and Carlos. Monzer is a multi-millionaire businessman who deals in arms and drugs. Intelligence agents believe that Carlos's trips to Latin America had been on behalf of Monzer Al Kasser, who also has close links with Abu Abbas. Monzer is banned for life from the United Kingdom, has been sentenced *in absentia* in France to eight years' imprisonment and is also banned from Austria and Germany. For good measure he has also been linked with Ahmed Jibril. His brother Gassan, as indicated above, also has links with Palestinian splinter groups.

Later, back in the hotel, I replayed the conversation many times. Had I been casual enough? There was no doubt that the name Michel Assaf had struck a chord with Ali Aziz, the man to whom I had been speaking. Now I could only wait. I had planned to give him a 'letter of introduction' even before he had asked for it. It would be interesting to see if the contents provoked a response. This meeting had taken place on Thursday the 2nd of November. Later that evening, checking through my diary, I realized that it had been the anniversary of the Balfour Declaration. The day that the Israeli-Palestinian issue became a political reality. I just hoped against hope that the men at the PLF were not quite as paranoid as Syrian Intelligence; if they were, then undoubtedly great significance might be read into this unfortunate coincidence.

The following day, from a friend of Ali Duba's nephew, I received confirmation of what Salwah had already told me. The nephew had been severely reprimanded for ever talking to me. I was being placed in quarantine. They feared that any contact I might have directly with any member of Syrian Intelligence might mean that in the course of any discussion I might have with them I would learn invaluable secrets, highly sensitive information and that I would then rush straight back to my Mossad masters. In the privacy of my room I alternated between rage and uncontrollable laughter. If the room, like the telephone, was bugged they might well have concluded they were dealing with a madman.

For the next few days I stayed close to the hotel, hoping for a telephone call from a number of people. The calls did not come. I began to take walks in a nearby park, Tishreen Park. At least there I was free from the gaze of the men in the foyer with their dirty, crumpled suits. I took another walk in the park on Sunday, November the 5th. My thoughts were very much of London, my wife and my young children – at dusk they would be having a fireworks party, minus one father. The park was much like any open pleasant space on a Sunday afternoon. Families. Young lovers. Friends out walking. Perhaps they all took Sunday off as well as Friday.

'Mr Yallop?'

I had drawn level with one of the park benches, slightly set back from the path, partially masked. I stopped and stared nonplussed at the smartly dressed Arab who was beckoning me. There was something familiar, very familiar about him, yet he was a total stranger. I walked to him and he extended his hand.

'I am Michel Assaf.'

He was too. It was the heavy moustache that had

confused me, that and the fact that he was older, heavier. His thinning hair too, much lighter than I'd imagined. He produced the contents of the envelope that I had given to Ali Aziz.

'How did you get this?'

'It was given to me by the man who wrote it.'

'Really, from my father?'

'Yes, but I need to be sure.'

The piece of paper he held was a page from the textbook written a lifetime ago by Jose Altagracia Ramirez Navas. A textbook on the Venezuelan Constitution, written at the behest of his eldest son, Ilich Ramirez Sanchez. It would be so typical of that son to meet me in such a manner. Like a scene from a bad movie.

The face bore no signs of plastic surgery. The ears, those oh so distinctive ears, were identical to every photograph I had. He looked for all the world like a Syrian businessman out for a stroll in the park. This time I wanted to be sure. Too many years. Too much aggravation had gone down the line. We sat on the bench.

'You have a message from my father?'

'Yes, but I want to be sure that I'm giving it to the right man. It's a very simple message but to Senor Altagracia an important one. I'd like to ask you a few questions.'

'There can be no interview.'

The accent was extraordinary. Precisely the same as I had heard in North Lebanon on two occasions, yet this was not the man I had met there.

'Of course not, but you know I'm a writer?'

'Yes, they told me.'

'They?'

'My friends.'

I didn't ask him who his friends were. It was not relevant.

'Is your memory good?'

'It's excellent.'

'In 1971, you attended a wedding in London. You were one of the official witnesses. Signed the certificate. What was the bride's name?'

637

He smiled. He was beginning to enjoy this. I had thought he might. 'Nelly. Nelly Arteaga. She married Lionel Isaacs.'

'Earlier, when you came back from the Middle East. You obtained a new passport at your country's embassy in Amsterdam. In the passport photo you're wearing a jumper. Who gave it to you?'

He stared at me.

'Who told you about that?'

'Your father. Who gave it to you?'

'George Habash.'

'Your parents had a baby daughter. Born prematurely. She died at less than three months of age. What name was she known by?'

'Natasha.'

He was caught up in it now. Like a man on a TV quiz show.

'What brand of cigarettes did your father smoke when you were a boy?'

'He never smoked. From the day I was born he stopped. For the sake of my health.'

'One of the songs you once sang at Fermin Toro begins, "God rules in the sky". What's the next line?'

'En la tierra los christianos . . . Christians rule on earth.'

He clapped his hands delightedly. Chubby well manicured hands. Hands that had killed so many.

'That's fine. The message from your father is, as I said, a simple one. "Tell Ilich that I love him. I always have done and I always will and when he is permanently settled in a socialist democratic country I wish to come and join him and spend the rest of my life with him."'

He sat silently for a moment, then stood.

'I am grateful to you. Thank you.'

I watched him as he walked away. That was Carlos. He had got a perfect score on the questions I had asked him. I watched as he left the park, an expensive-looking car stopped by him. He entered and it drove away. From the distance it looked like a Mercedes.

The message I had given him had been genuine. One that his father had given to my interpreter in San Cristobal. I wondered how he would respond to it, whether he would send for his father. Only the future would tell. For myself, it was time to go home.

EPILOGUE

A cynical observer of the late twentieth century might well observe that if Carlos had not existed we would have invented him; that his creation was essential because he so perfectly epitomizes many of the fundamental elements of our age and our various societies. Not for the first time would the cynical observer have been nearer the truth than he knew. The Carlos described in the prologue to this book does not exist. He never did.

This Carlos has been created by many men. The information contained in the prologue has been acquired from two sources: the world's media and published books, many of whose authors have cited among their sources the intelligence files of a number of countries.

There is not a single shred of truth in the account of this man's life that is recorded in the prologue of this book.

It is a fantasy, but a fantasy that has impressively succeeded in its aim – to make the Cold War between East and West even colder; to ensure that a peaceful resolution of the Palestinian issue remains an unattainable dream; to spread the seeds of suspicion and hostility across borders; to create an evil mischief. As the myths surrounding Carlos grew, they presented various governments with a chance that they seized: to justify the unjustifiable, to explain the inexplicable and to deflect from the truth. As the reader will discover in Appendix One, entitled 'The Hitler Syndrome,' the story of Carlos is the story of a disinformation exercise without parallel in modern peacetime.

*　　*　　*

What occurred within days of my meeting with Carlos is without doubt the sweetest aspect of the entire story. Ilich Ramirez Sanchez who as a young man had dreamed of revolution found himself the victim of another revolution. An historic and dramatically successful one. Earlier that year the then president of the Soviet Union, Mikhail Gorbachev, declared:

'Let us consign the Cold War to oblivion.'

Quite suddenly in November 1989, Berlin was no longer a divided city. Now it is no longer a divided country.

The wall is down; so is the curtain.

Honecker was swept away, one sanctuary less for Carlos. By the end of December 1989 the Venezuelan had lost another of his safe houses: Ceauşescu had been overthrown. So too in Bulgaria, Czechoslovakia, Hungary. Safe house after safe house collapsed, like a house of cards. While Carlos and his revolutionary dreams had merely created a nightmare for the many that they touched, the Cold War order had been swept away to be replaced with the potential for a better way of life for the entire planet.

It is still a case of run, Carlos, run – but where to? The world's most wanted man has achieved a unique double: he is simultaneously the world's most unwanted man. How many heads of state still have a vacancy for an ageing terrorist with a gun?

Ramirez, as this book has demonstrated, became a pawn in the Cold War, used by the West to sow even greater seeds of hostility and suspicion than already existed. Now even that disgusting use of this man has been rendered obsolete. In what we have since 1945 called the East, where Carlos was used by various Eastern regimes as an in-house terrorist, the dictators that employed the Venezuelan mercenary are either dead or deposed.

In March 1990, the poor wretched Farzad Bazoft whose arrest and torture and subsequent confession in neighbouring Iraq caused me moments of anxiety in Syria, was executed by the Iraqi regime. My own research has established that, far from being an Israeli

Mossad agent, he was spying on behalf of MI6. Part of his intelligence brief had been to acquire information on the super gun that scientist Gerald Bull was developing for Saddam Hussein. Bull himself was subsequently murdered by a Mossad agent in Brussels.

Two months after the farce of the Bazoft trial in Baghdad another farcical trial reached its inevitable end. If it was a foregone conclusion that Bazoft was going to be found guilty, it was equally predictable that Gabriele Tiedemann, when finally brought before a very fearful bar of German justice in Cologne charged with murdering two men during the OPEC attack of December 1975, would be acquitted. The verdict, delivered on May 22nd, 1990 had been a dreadful inevitability from the moment that witness after witness, including all the surviving OPEC ministers, had refused to give evidence. The shadow of Carlos had loomed very large over the proceedings. That shadow ensured a travesty of justice. This creature, Tiedemann, had cold-bloodedly murdered two men. The evidence is irrefutable, but that evidence was never laid before the Cologne Court. The moral is clear: if you want to get away with murder, then become a friend of Carlos. Perhaps when the facts that are contained within this book are considered – facts rather than the myth – individuals as well as governments will summon up the courage to bring Ilich Ramirez Sanchez to the bar of justice. Perhaps then we will finally bury the myth of this man.

On August 14th, 1990, less than two weeks after Iraq invaded Kuwait, that myth was yet again in evidence. Headlines proclaimed that Carlos was in Baghdad, summoned by Saddam Hussein to a top-level meeting of terrorists. Stories were run stating that Carlos was to be unleashed on the West by the Iraqi president. He must have had great trouble with the leash. No such attacks came – one of the reasons being that Carlos continued to lead a life of indolent ease in Damascus.

That President Hussein did indeed try to play the terrorist card there is no doubt. It just did not involve Carlos.

It did, however, involve lesser luminaries, including Abu Nidal, but the Iraqi president had not fully considered the Palestinian card. He had Yasser Arafat in his pocket, but other members of the PLO took a different view. They believed that it was an act of lunacy for the PLO to align itself with Iraq's aggression. Among this latter group was Abu Iyad. Every time that Hussein attempted to activate, with Palestinian extremists, an act of terrorism, it was thwarted by Iyad. In supreme control of PLO intelligence, he was perfectly placed to prevent sleepers who were sympathetic to Hussein being activated. Such an irony – the Godfather of Black September using all of his guile on behalf of a Western alliance that included Israel. Abu Iyad, who had freely admitted to me that he planned the Black September attack on the Munich Olympics and a number of other outrages, had by January 1991 successfully stopped every Iraqi terrorist operation from reaching fruition. On January 14th, 1991 he paid for those achievements with his life. Murdered on the direct orders of President Saddam Hussein, he was shot down in Tunis by a member of the Abu Nidal group, a member who, unlike others to whom he had introduced me, he had failed to identify.

As we moved inexorably towards a war with Iraq I had wondered just how high a price we had paid to ensure that Syria come into the hostilities on the side of the West. Great Britain's resumption of diplomatic relations was part of the price. Another part concerned the Lockerbie affair. For two years the Western finger had pointed unerringly and continuously at Syria and specifically at the Jibril group. The reader will recall Jibril quoting to me the words of United States Secretary of State James Baker addressed to the Syrian Foreign Minister in late 1989.

'We have the proof. We have the incontrovertible evidence.'

Suddenly in late 1990 some of this 'incontrovertible evidence' was made public. The problem was we were no longer blaming our 'ally' Syria but Qathafi's Libya.

By early 1992 there was much talk of 'ultimate sanctions' against Libya unless it complied with our demands. I have seen this movie before.

I was very conscious of the dramatic changes occurring in Europe as the research for this book continued and the writing was begun and completed. Yet again life was being extremely well written. The Cold War was melting away. Carlos and his life, particularly since the late 1960s, are in a curious way very much a part of that Cold War. Used by both sides, he became the archetypal bogey man. Every country has such a creature within its culture: in his native Spanish they frighten little children with talk of 'coco'; in Italy, 'spauracchio'; in Russia, 'gombore domovoy'; in France 'croque-mitaine'; in Germany 'der schwarze Manni'. Now, thanks to one Venezuelan, we have a universal word that crosses all linguistic barriers – Carlos.

Ilich Ramirez Sanchez had been attracted to the Palestinians' cause, to their fight for an independent State but the attraction waned to be replaced with something he found infinitely more desirable, what he called 'the hard stuff'. The one-time Marxist turned capitalist betrayed his original political philosophy as easily as he betrayed the Palestinian cause. The child of the petite bourgeoisie became in manhood bourgeoisie personified. In terms of personal ethics, morality, integrity, he held an 'everything-must-be-sold closing-down sale' decades ago.

Ramirez and others like him have over the years been a propaganda gift not to Palestinian aspirations but to the Israeli hardliners. Each mindless act of violence, of terrorism, has been seized upon by Israel's extreme right wing not merely to justify the 'no land' approach but also to justify Israel's own mindless acts of violence and terrorism.

I am neither Arab nor Jew.

I hold no brief for Yasser Arafat and the men around him any more than I do for Yitzhak Shamir or his successors, Rabin and Peres; neither do I support the men of violence who stalk the Israeli-Palestinian issue. I despise these men who are consumed with hatred and yet more hatred. Nidal or Netanyahu are merely two sides of the same coin.

My commitment in this issue is to the ordinary Palestinian and the ordinary Israeli. Both deserve peace. Israel is the country of the Jews; it is also the homeland of the Palestinians. That the talents and genius of both races have not been not harnessed for mutual benefit for these past one hundred years will stand for eternity as an example of mankind's stupidity. This particular evolutionary clock stands at a minute to midnight. If the current generation on both sides fail to negotiate a just settlement that is acceptable to the majority of both peoples, they will hand to their next generations an awful legacy. The bloodbath that will come will make the last one hundred years look like a picnic.

'Tell Ilich that I love him. I always have and I always will.'

His father's poignant message, including the plea to be allowed to join his son, haunted me as I wrote this book. I often wondered how the son had responded. Late in 1991 I had the answer. He had sent not for his father but for Elba, his mother, the woman who always knew so much more than Senor Jose Altagracia Ramirez Navas about their eldest child.

Nearly two years after I had met him, with his world visibly shrinking before his eyes, it suddenly got even smaller. His pleasant sojourn in Damascus with his wife Magdalena, their daughter, Rosa, his ever-faithful companion Johannes Weinrich, and two or three like-minded companions came to an end. As President Asad moved Syria into the Western fold he decided to clean up his act.

In late September 1991 a Syrian Airlines Boeing 707 landed at Tripoli. It carried a highly unusual cargo that included Yemeni diplomat Nagi Abu Baker Ahmed, his wife and child, his mother – travelling on a Moroccan diplomatic passport – and three male friends, all travelling on Yemeni diplomatic passports. The Libyans listened while

Nagi Ahmed explained that they were all Palestinians who, having been forced to leave Syria, wished to take up residency in Libya. The Libyan officials were unimpressed, especially when they opened up Nagi Ahmed's luggage. It included two Beretta pistols, two hand grenades, one million dollars in bills, and a large quantity of jewellery. Syrian embassy officials were called to the airport. They could throw little light on the group of diplomats. They were refused entry and sent immediately back to Damascus. The Syrians were not amused. Their response was to blow up a Libyan Airlines plane at Damascus International Airport.

The Libyans had secretly photographed the group. Subsequent examination of the photographs established that Nagi Ahmed, complete with moustache, was Ilich Ramirez Sanchez. The Libyans further established that other members of the group included his wife, Magdalena Kopp, and his mother, Elba Sanchez.

If Carlos had indeed been working for Qathafi at the time of the attack on the OPEC headquarters in Vienna, or indeed at any other time, it is very difficult to accept that he would have needed such a weight of false passports to gain entry into Libya and even more difficult to believe that he would have been thrown out.

The Syrians have subsequently advised through discreet contacts with Western Intelligence that the party were promptly flown out again to the Yemen. Not so. Carlos and his diminishing entourage have taken up residency again in Damascus, where any of the Western governments who are all so totally committed to fighting terrorism can easily find them.

Run, Carlos. Run.

In March 1992 the man who in the mid-1940s had a ten-thousand-pound price put on his head by the British government, who organized the blowing up of the King David Hotel, killing ninety-one people, and the following year in 1947 ordered his Irgun gang to hang two kidnapped British sergeants, died. One obituary described Menachem Begin as 'an unrepentant terrorist who won the Nobel Peace Prize, then launched another war.' In the following month, inspired by the United States, United Nations sanctions on Libya began. Their purpose was to force Colonel Qathafi to hand over two Libyans suspected of being involved in the Lockerbie bombing. The sanctions included a total air embargo of Libya. Throughout the remainder of 1992, no planes landed or took off in Libya and the two suspects remained in their home country, as did the actual perpetrators of the Lockerbie bombing – some in Damascus and some in Teheran.

During the first week of June 1992, Carlos was sentenced by a French court to life imprisonment for the murder of two members of the DST in rue Toullier in 1975. The one small problem for the French was that Carlos was not in the courtroom. He continues to live in Damascus with his wife Magdalena, their two children, and Weinrich, under a regime that under subtle Western pressure has attempted to clean up its act. In late 1991, President Asad announced the release of three and a half thousand political prisoners, many of whom had been detained without trial for over a decade. There are least a further five thousand political prisoners also being held without benefit of a trial. The majority are allowed no contact with the outside world. Since Asad came to power, thousands of detainees have died from maltreatment and torture. Syria, our 'ally', remains on the United States' list of countries supporting terrorism.

The myth of Carlos continues to exercise a powerful effect on the media For example, in a *Sunday Times* article on Carlos in mid-1992, the disinformation referred to Ramirez's teenage training in Cuba and his 'masterminding' of the 1972 machine-gun attack at Lod airport.

In Israel, Shamir, another unrepentant terrorist, was replaced by the bone-breaking Rabin. It was a step in the right direction. But could the bone-breaker become a peace-maker? Anything had to be better than Shamir. During an unguarded moment in June 1992 Shamir said, 'I would have carried on autonomy talks for ten years and meanwhile, we would have reached half a million people in Judea and Samaria [West Bank].'

Ten years? With the clock one minute from midnight?

With the Cold War consigned to history, the military arms complex of the West was in urgent need of a new threat to ensure continuing output and sales of its merchandise. By the end of 1992, the favourite for this role was Iran. In the US the strategy reaped immediate benefits, including a five-billion-dollar defence deal for seventy-two new F-15E ground-attack aircraft, thus guaranteeing thousands of jobs at McDonnell-Douglas, and a further multi-billion-dollar deal for Patriot and Hawk missile air-defence systems to Kuwait and Qatar, thus ensuring a similar situation for Raytheon. Other Western countries were not far behind. China and Russia, meanwhile, were playing both ends against the middle, by selling missiles to Iraq and Syria as well as to Saudi Arabia, and for good measure also to Iran. Predictably, at the end of 1992, the US Justice Department began to issue arrest warrants for terrorists whom it identified as Iranian, and who it claimed were guilty of killing US hostages in Lebanon and of hijacking an American airliner – crimes that first the Reagan administration and subsequently the Bush White House had previously attributed to Qathafi's Libya.

In Lebanon the estimated nearly half a million Palestinians living there were confronted with a new threat. In September 1992, Lebanon's interior minister, Sami Khatib, announced plans to resettle the Palestinians where they were. Khatib's government proposed to take 'a census in Lebanon and other parts of the world where Palestinian refugees live with a view to resettling them and giving them the citizenship of host countries.' If this plan were to be put into effect, the majority of Palestinians would be denied forever the right of return to their homeland: a people who have been waiting in their millions since the late 1940s to return to their country doomed to live forever in foreign lands; a policy that meets with wholehearted Israeli approval. During the same year, Yitzhak Shamir had stated categorically that while all Jews would have in perpetuity the right of return to Israel, this would be denied also in perpetuity to Palestinians. Ethnic cleansing takes many forms. One other member of the current Lebanese government who still has very fixed ideas on how to solve the Palestinian problem is Elie Houbeika. He is currently the Lebanese minister in charge of returning displaced persons to their homes.

Hezbollah's 'holy war' against Israeli occupation in Southern Lebanon continued to pose a threat. The Party of God killing and being killed by God's Chosen People.

By late 1992, the Cold War had indeed been consigned to oblivion. Unfortunately, Gorbachev had gone with it. The totalitarian regimes in some of Eastern Europe had been replaced by an appalling cocktail ranging from neo-Fascism in former East Germany to ethnic cleansing in what had been Yugoslavia. The Bosnians of Yugoslavia are now referred to as 'the new Palestinians'. It was beginning to appear as if the Palestinians had either moved into history or, in the words of Golda Meir, 'do not exist'.

The election of President Clinton augured well for Israel. The three-billion-dollar-a-year aid package for Israel was set to continue. Prior to his election, Clinton had uttered a number of remarks destined to set alarm bells ringing among the Palestinians. Playing to the Israeli lobby, the man who at that time aspired to the White House described Jerusalem as the capital of a united Israel. Clinton was also critical of Bush for linking the ten-billion-dollar loan guarantees to Israel with a freeze on settlements in the occupied territories.

Governor Mario Cuomo of New York, visiting Israel just two months before the presidential elections, re-assured Prime Minister Yitzhak Rabin that, if elected, Clinton would be 'probably the most supportive' US leader in modern history.

I happened to be in Israel during Cuomo's visit, a visit that did not include any trips to the Gaza Strip or the Palestinian refugee camps on the West Bank or any meetings with any of the Palestinian leaders, or indeed a single Arab. Cuomo gave a number of startlingly clear indications of where his concerns and priorities are in the Israeli/Palestinian issue. He described the Arab boycott of Israel as 'an economic boycott against New York State'. He also reminded his listeners that Israel was New York's thirteenth-largest trading partner. Of the three-billion-dollar annual aid package, Cuomo observed, 'We need Israel. The aid which Israel receives from the United States is not a gift, but an investment in a strong ally.' Of Clinton, Governor Cuomo observed, 'In the modern political history of the United States, no American politician has made statements more supportive of Israel than Democratic presidential Candidate Bill Clinton.' Speaking to reporters in Jerusalem, he added that, 'The Democratic Party does not accept the [Bush] administration's land for peace formula. Clinton's position is that we want to work as an honest broker to help Israel achieve peace on terms decided upon by Israel and not by the United States.'

And presumably not by the Palestinians?

Of Prime Minister Rabin, the man who while Defence Minister in Shamir's government had urged the Israeli army to 'break more, yet more limbs of the Palestinians', a man who justified the switch to plastic bullets in the occupied territories by explaining that the purpose of this new weapon was to 'increase the number of casualties among those who take part in violent activities, but not to kill them,' a man who had observed of the Israeli army brutality in those same territories: 'Israel has nothing to hide from because we are not ashamed of what we are doing,' Governor Cuomo spoke of 'the beauty, the special particular beauty of Rabin. His early establishment of credentials as a military analyst and a heroic military leader gives him the capacity to do things diplomatically that someone without that reputation would not be able to do.'

Clinton's presidency looked like becoming a long hard winter for the Palestinians.

On Rosh Hashanah, the Jewish New Year, on September 29, 1992, I watched as every single Arab attempting to drive from the West Bank into Jerusalem was refused entry and turned back at gunpoint. The green line border continued to determine who could and who could not have the right to return. Less than five Palestinians shot dead and fifty injured still constituted a quiet week in the Gaza Strip. Suddenly imposed curfews continued both in the West Bank and Gaza Strip. During the 1992 academic year, 40 per cent of Palestinian school-days were lost through Israeli closures. Nearly 50 per cent of the Gaza Strip continued to be reserved for the Israeli military or Jewish settlers. More than fifteen hundred Palestinians have been killed since the Intifada erupted in 1987. More than a hundred Israelis have also died. The peace talks continued to meander on with an increasing air of unreality, while a bloody future beckoned. The Islamic resistance movement, Hamas, the largest militant Islamic faction in the occupied territories, continued to increase its influence. It was rapidly approaching the point where it would have the wholehearted support of more than 50 per cent of the Palestinians living in the occupied territories. With money and arms available from Iran, it clearly demonstrated the awful alternative if the current peace talks were not successfully concluded. After invading Lebanon in 1982, Israel discovered her own Vietnam, but it was only the first act of what awaited Israeli forces in the occupied territories if those peace talks failed. During this late 1992 visit I discussed these implications not only with some of the leaders of Hamas, but also with senior members of the Israeli Defence Force. I discovered that they shared my forebodings. One senior military adviser to Prime Minister Rabin said:

'I and others have made it abundantly clear to the Prime Minister that there can be no military solution for Israel with regard to the Gaza Strip and West Bank. The solution will have to be political.'

Shortly after these comments were made to me, Rabin's government gave a demonstration that they still believed in a military option.

In mid-December 1992, members of Hamas abducted and murdered an Israeli soldier. Israel's response was swift. Sixteen hundred Palestinians were immediately arrested. Within forty-eight hours, 418 of these men, blindfolded and handcuffed, were dumped in South Lebanon. The remainder were held without trial. The 418 were suspected of supporting Hamas. No charges were brought, no trials took place. When the Lebanese government refused them entry, they were doomed to remain in no man's land, in freezing conditions, with the minimum of food and shelter.

In January 1993, with virtually every country except the United States condemning the expulsions, the Israeli government demonstrated that Machiavelli was alive and well. While the Rabin government continued to publicly denounce the PLO, it opened up a secret dialogue with members of Yasser Arafat's organization. A series of meetings began to take place in Norway. Reality within Israeli/Palestinian politics had arrived.

For Rabin, the catalyst had been the awareness that the expulsions of the Hamas members and sympathizers had not stopped the Intifada. Israelis and Palestinians were continuing to die. Finally, after all the years of bloodshed, an Israeli prime minister was prepared to consider a political solution.

For Arafat, stripped of prestige and a significant proportion of revenue after backing Saddam Hussein's invasion of Kuwait, there was the same awareness that Hamas had now become the dominant force, particularly in the Gaza Strip.

Prime Minister Rabin took good care to distance himself from this initiative. He was content to leave the running to his foreign minister, Shimon Peres. If the talks ended in failure and news of them leaked out, Rabin intended to ensure that it was Peres and not him who would be subjected to the predictable criticism for having talked to the PLO in the first place. If the talks ended in success there would always be time to grab the credit. Very few people outside the immediate participants knew of these secret negotiations. The Clinton administration, like the Israeli and Palestinian negotiating teams at the official peace conference, were not on the 'need-to-know' list.

In February 1993, a little more than one month after these talks had begun, the Clinton administration and indeed the entire country were given a demonstration at home of just how violent Middle Eastern politics can get. The World Trade Center bombing in New York killed six and injured many hundreds. It destroyed the myth that the American mainland is safe from a major terrorist attack. What happened that day in New York could easily happen again, anywhere in the United States. To offer a reward of $2 million for the arrest of the chief suspect, Ramzi Ahmed Yousef, as the State Department did, is to display an extraordinary ignorance of the enemy. Applying capitalistic thinking to a Muslim fundamentalist group dedicated to the overthrow of Egypt's President Mubarak is an absurdity. There will be no takers.

In the days after the Trade Center bombing, the Carlos myth yet again showed its indestructibility. He was an early media candidate for chief perpetrator. But the truth is far more frightening than a chubby middle-aged businessman. The bombing was one aspect of United States foreign policy coming home to roost. Mubarak is perceived by an overwhelming majority in the Middle East to be no more than an American puppet. If you want to change the puppet it is sometimes more effective to gain the attention of the puppet master.

By mid 1993 the official Middle East peace talks were drifting aimlessly while their highly secret counterpart had reached a critical stage. The Israelis had offered a degree of autonomy to the Palestinians in Gaza and to their astonishment, Arafat had rejected it. If he was to sell the deal to his own people, there had to be at least a part of the West Bank on the table. He suggested a 'Gaza and Jericho First' scenario. While Prime Minister

Rabin pondered, Israel yet again made one of her own unique contributions to the peace talks, both official and secret. She went to war. The proclaimed target was Hezbollah militants based in south Lebanon. The aim, in Prime Minister Rabin's words, was 'to create a massive refugee problem for Lebanon.' This from the leader of a nation created largely because of a refugee problem. A sustained land, sea and air bombardment of south Lebanon in midsummer killed over one hundred and fifty, injured hundreds more, and caused over a quarter of a million people to flee northward. The Israeli government announced that it was 'delighted'. As in December 1992, when the illegal deportations of over four hundred Palestinians took place, it was only after Israel had been subjected to international condemnation that President Clinton very reluctantly proffered a word or two of criticism. Governor Cuomo had indeed uttered a basic truth when he had talked of Clinton's pro-Israel position. It speaks volumes for the determination of the Palestinian side that peace should prevail, that they continued to secretly negotiate under such provocation.

In the last week of August 1993 Shimon Peres flew to California for a meeting with US Secretary of State Warren Christopher. They talked for at least four hours. This senior member of the most pro-Israeli administration for decades listened astonished and open-mouthed as Peres outlined the deal that Israel had concluded with the PLO. The reader will find the full text recorded in Appendix Four. It can, I believe, be summarized in three words: Land for Peace.

If the spirit of this agreement prevails, and if the seed that has been planted is allowed to grow to fruition, then what has occurred is as momentous a moment as that night in Berlin in November 1989 when the Wall began to come down. What lies in the immediate future for both Arab and Jew is, appropriately enough, a very Biblical battle. A fight between good and evil. By early September the opinion polls both in Israel and the occupied territories were showing a majority in favour of the peace deal.

But there were always going to be men who would oppose this deal. Who would, in truth, oppose any deal.

By early September it seemed to me that one sound above all others could be clearly heard. It was a political and media screeching of brakes as global opinion went into reverse on Arafat and the PLO. Thus a man whom Rabin had described as evil and the State Department had labelled a terrorist stood on the White House lawn on Monday, September 13, 1993 surrounded by a galaxy of political heavyweights and protected by United States security. And as Arafat stood on that lawn, men were already being trained in the Lebanese cities of Tyre and Sidon to assassinate him. Abu Nidal and Ahmed Jibril have already offered one million dollars reward for the man who pulls the trigger and ends the life of Yasser Arafat. It is to be devoutly hoped that he lives long enough to see this fragile plant grow a little. The alternative, an alternative much desired by some on the extreme right within Israel and others on the far left in Gaza, Sudan, Damascus and a dozen other places, is too awful to contemplate.

Towards the end of 1983 I set out to discover the truth and the reality of two major world problems. One was terrorism, the other was the Palestinian issue. I leave it for you, the reader, to judge how well I have succeeded with these tasks. With regard to the truth and reality of Ilich Ramirez Sanchez, I have discovered far more than I ever anticipated. After this book was published in Germany, I initiated a dialogue with Chancellor Kohl's office, urging among other aspects that Germany apply to Syria for the extradition of Ramirez Sanchez. This the German government have now done. It remains to be seen just how much longer the Syrian regime will protect this man. The running may or may not be nearly at an end for the Venezuelan, but the final moment of truth is undoubtedly now confronting both the Israelis and the Palestinians.

APPENDIX ONE
THE HITLER SYNDROME

The men he had murdered in the shabby one-room apartment at nine rue Toullier were not in their graves when the world's press, like Apaches running wild, began building the myth of Carlos. It was to become a definitive example of what I choose to call the Hitler Syndrome: 'If you tell a lie long enough and loud enough, it becomes the truth.'

Within days he was not only here there and everywhere, he was also everyone. In his native Venezuela the newspapers declared, 'based on information from Interpol', that Carlos was Douglas Bravo. In Italy he was likened to James Bond. In Peru, the media declared that Carlos was a CIA invention. In Great Britain the papers gave him a variety of titles including 'The Cocktail Party Revolutionary', but it was 'The Jackal' that was destined, like the man to whom they gave it, to run and run.

Barry Woodhams told me, 'Even that stuff that was written about a copy of Forsyth's *The Day of the Jackal* being found among his possessions was wrong. A copy of the book was in the bookcase. They were all my books, including that one.'

For the world's media it was a story that had every single ingredient they could desire. Every new revelation gave it fresh impetus. The discovery of the safe houses in London and Paris. Guns, bombs, false passports. The revelations, as a result of an increasing number of arrests, of an international line-up of female 'accomplices'. The ladies from Colombia, Venezuela, Spain, South Africa. The increasing number of terrorist outrages that were linked to his name. His association with every conceivable terrorist group. Throw that into the pot and add 'The Jackal' and one has a cordon bleu concoction that will appeal to millions of palates.

The meal was initially too rich for certain sections of the French press who suspected it had been prepared by a chef employed by the French Secret Service. At first some observers simply could not believe that The Jackal could be so inept, but with each fresh sensational revelation healthy French scepticism gave way to a desire to follow the pack.

The French Secret Service began to bestir itself. It saw in the situation a unique opportunity for anti-Soviet propaganda. The disinformation wheels began to turn.

The periodical *Minute,* in an issue dated 9th July, stated, 'Our inquiry informed us that during the summer of 1973 Carlos was in Bucharest. He was the oracle of a fashionable café in the Romanian capital, the Scala. In the evening he went home, a building occupied by Chilean communists seeking refuge in the East after the government coup of Pinochet. Three years after having been ignominiously chased out of the Soviet Union, Carlos was living in a satellite country, i.e. Romania. So who has lifted the prohibition of séjour?' The magazine also revealed that Carlos 'had lived in Moscow for six years'.

The facts, as already recorded earlier, establish that Carlos spent part of the summer of 1973 in London and the remainder in the Middle East. He had not lived in Moscow for six years but for a little over a year and a half.

In the same issue *Minute* quoted the manager of the Lloyds Bank branch where Amparo Silva Masmela had been employed. 'I have been trembling since the Carlos affair began. We had total trust in Miss Silva Masmela, who was dealing with very confidential files.'

During my investigation a senior member of the personnel department of Lloyds contacted on my behalf his colleagues in Paris. Subsequently he wrote to me:

'. . . our Paris branch can shed no light on the alleged

statement by a senior member of its staff concerning Miss Silva . . . she was employed between 24.3.1975 and 30.6.1975 and held a junior post in the Correspondence Department.'

When French Minister of the Interior, Michel Poniatowski, announced on the 11th of July 1975 the expulsion of three Cuban diplomats that he linked to 'the Carlos affair', joy among the cold war warriors was unconfined. The Minister had only to hint at Soviet involvement for it to become fact.

The truth, that these three men were innocent of any terrorist activities either directly or indirectly, was never considered by either the French or their international colleagues.

My own investigations established that the three Cubans were involved primarily not with Ramirez but with the women of nine rue Toullier, not merely the residents but a variety of women who passed through the door. To be expelled for such activities from France of all countries has a certain piquancy. Carlos's major preoccupation with the Cubans was to try and obtain news of his Cuban lover Sonia and their daughter.

A French military intelligence source reported to me:

'Look, the government had to do something. It was a very embarrassing situation. Three members of DST gunned down by one man who escapes. A member of the Popular Front, in their custody, therefore in theory under their protection, also shot. Arms caches all over the place. Herranz and his men displayed gross incompetence, not for the first time, don't forget the affair of Antonio Pereira. When they went to rue Toullier they even rang the wrong bell. Such ineptness. Poniatowski needed to deflect the criticism. We had been made to look very foolish and by we I mean the whole damn secret service, not just the poor amateurs that ended up bleeding to death on that floor. Then to compound the ineptness Carlos escaped from Paris. The Cubans fitted the bill, perfectly.'

Less than two weeks later the French periodical *Valeurs*

Actuelles added to the already over-rich myth of Carlos.

The writer was political commentator François Lebrette. His article headed 'The Man of the Tri-Continental' left its readers in no doubt as to who ultimately controlled Carlos. It was subtitled, 'The background to the Carlos affair: the taking in hand of small-time terrorist groups by Cubans who are themselves instruments of the Russian KGB.'

The writer declared that the Cuban diplomats had been expelled for taking part in setting up a network of terrorism and sabotage in Europe, North Africa and the Near East which was organized to act only on the orders of Moscow.

He traced the source of this international conspiracy to the Tri-Continental meetings in Havana during January 1966, meetings he saw as 'the first attempt to co-ordinate the activities of all revolutionary groups throughout the world, be they Trotskyist, Maoist or pro-Soviet'.

The Carlos group was 'manipulated by the Russian KGB'. After outlining at some considerable length how the KGB used Cuban surrogates to perform tasks that the Soviet Union, officially pursuing a policy of detente, could not do themselves, Lebrette continued:

'That Carlos and Moukharbel are members of a network controlled by the KGB is not really in doubt, if only because of the methods used.'

These methods included, in the mind of Lebrette, the fact that Carlos was an ex-student of Patrice Lumumba University and that the first person he had shot in rue Toullier was his boss, Moukharbel, thus 'applying the KGB's golden rule: no pity, shoot whoever can talk'.

The fact that Moukharbel kept an accounts book was to Lebrette damning proof of KGB involvement. 'All KGB agents are asked to be able to justify at all times their activities and their expenses to travelling controllers, who can at any moment come and ask for these accounts.'

In conclusion Lebrette asserted, 'The Western [secret] services know that Cubans have organized in all the

Mediterranean ports, from Marseilles to Beirut and from Piraeus to Alexandria "dormant networks" of sabotage which are only waiting for the green light.'

The Soviet Union really should have addressed itself to the problem of its traffic lights. Eighteen years later they are still presumably stuck on red.

Nowhere in the article is there a fragment of hard fact or evidence upon which to base such amazing conclusions but then by its very definition disinformation is not concerned with hard facts or evidence.

Eight days after that French Secret Service-inspired article their colleagues across the Channel added to the brew. Enter the anonymous 'Special Correspondent' with unlimited access to *The Times* newspaper. His article headed 'Is the Jackal a Moscow-trained terrorist who has broken out of control?' appeared on July 29th.

Fundamentally it posed the question that had already been asked by the Soviet Union about Carlos. 'Who benefits?' The Moscow Radio broadcast had concluded that the answer could be found among the cold war hawks, those who saw reds not only underneath the beds, but behind the curtains, in the wardrobes and virtually queuing at the front door. The anonymous correspondent came to a different conclusion.

Having incorrectly stated that Carlos left the Patrice Lumumba University in Moscow in 1969, the writer described his view of the University. He talked of the Russians processing Third World students through the University 'for training in terrorism, sabotage and guerrilla war techniques in training camps in Odessa, Baku, Simferopol and Tashkent'.

Moving on from what the writer clearly considered to be such an irrefutable fact that evidence to support it was superfluous, he observed,

'Although full details of his place of training are not yet known, Carlos would have been given intensive training, probably at one of the camps mentioned, in firearms proficiency, the use of aliases, changes of address, clandestine communications and safe houses.'

661

Again no evidence firm or otherwise was offered to support this assertion. Thus with one bound, rather than the hero being free the villain had been shackled in perpetuity to the KGB. The invisible conductor of this particular orchestra had, at least in the mind of the 'Special Correspondent', been identified.

Seizing on Poniatowski's statements both on and off the record the article repeated the French Minister's observations about the links between the Russian Secret Service and the DGI. The article then placed Carlos in Marseilles during what is called 'communist-inspired anti-fascist riots' and for good measure threw in the involvement of the 'intensely pro-Soviet Colombian Communist Party' through Nydia Tobon and her ex-husband Alfonso Romero Buj.

The writer observed,

'The trouble is that it is relatively easy to train terrorists, but far more difficult to keep them under control.'

If it is that easy to train terrorists, it must be wondered how, if they had the slightest involvement with him, the KGB could have made such an appalling job of training Carlos or indeed Nydia Tobon.

At no point did the anonymous author address himself to the problems posed to his thesis by the reality of the fatal ineptness of Carlos, but then the purpose of the exercise was to sow seeds of hostility and suspicion, to use Carlos as a gift from God, given to Western security for propaganda purposes.

As the French Secret Service provided its disinformation to Lebrette, the British Secret Service were doing precisely the same to their man who shrewdly preferred to keep his name secret. A device he had used many times in the past and one he was destined to use again in the future. His name is Brian Crozier.

Two months before writing this article Crozier had testified before a United States Senate Committee hearing evidence on national and international terrorism. The Chairman, Senator Strom Thurmond, introducing Crozier to the Committee, observed,

'Our first witness is Mr Brian Crozier, Director of the Institute for the Study of Conflict in London, who has a deserved reputation as one of the free world's foremost experts on international terrorism.'

For the benefit of the Committee, David Martin, described as 'senior analyst', put on the record Crozier's qualifications that justified the Senator's description.

They were deeply impressive. More than twenty years' study of the use of violence for political purposes. As a journalist he had covered 'violent situations' in Indo-China, Indonesia, Algeria, Cyprus, the former Congo and Latin America. He had written for the *New York Times*, *Time* magazine, Reuters, *The Economist* and the *Sunday Times*. In 1960 he had written a book, *The Rebels*, which Martin described as 'a comparative study, pioneering in its field, of revolutionary methods all over the world. And it is my understanding that this study formed the basis for the first counter-insurgency course at Fort Bragg, Mr Chairman, and that it is required reading in military and defense colleges in many countries.'

The committee was told that Crozier was the founder of the Institute for the Study of Conflict in London and that he had set up that organization in 1970 with the collaboration of Professor Leonard Schapiro and Sir Robert Thompson and 'a number of distinguished Britons who have had experience or possess expertise in this special area'.

Subsequently Brian Crozier had published another book, A *Theory of Conflict*.

It was indeed an impressive introduction. It was followed by a speech and various readings into the record that clearly also left their mark on the listening committee.

Crozier's discourse was global. Much of it was devoted to alleged Soviet involvement in terrorism, for as Crozier saw it: 'By far the greatest subversive centre in the world is the USSR, which is actively supported by Eastern Europe, especially by East Germany, Czechoslovakia, and Bulgaria.'

The Tri-Continental meetings of January 1966 inevitably came in for comment, as did Cuba in general: 'Castro has likewise exported subversion and terrorism to most other countries in Latin America . . .' But Crozier's main target, one that he returned to repeatedly, was the Soviet Union. Patrice Lumumba University was reduced to a processing plant for 'freedom fighters' on their way to specialized training courses for 'Sabotage, terrorism, assassination, and other kinds of clandestine and violent warfare in training camps in Simferopol, in Baku, in Tashkent, and in Odessa.'

Crozier also stated that 'The USSR spends enormous, but obviously incalculable, sums on subversion all over the world.'

His final observation on this part of his testimony that had painted a picture of terrorist reds under the beds of the entire free world was:

'I should add in fairness that the Russians hold ambiguous views on terrorism. They are on record as opposing the hijacking of international airliners, for instance, not least because this kind of action has happened in the USSR itself. But they are in the terrorist business on a large scale, and this fact should be remembered at a time when "detente" is supposed to be the order of the day.'

Crozier might also have added 'in fairness' that the Russian method of 'opposing' terrorism was brutally simple. When the Soviets caught a terrorist they took him out and shot him.

There were also one or two facts about Crozier himself that 'in fairness' might have assisted that Senate Committee as they evaluated his testimony, including his longstanding links with the CIA.

Virtually the first thing that catches a visitor's eye as one walks into the marble hallway of the CIA's headquarters in Langley is an inscription. The words were borrowed by the then Director of the CIA, Allen Dulles, from the Bible. 'And ye shall know the truth and the truth shall make you free.' Goebbels and Hitler would have enjoyed that. Like the former Nazi party, the CIA knows the value of lies and disinformation. Another former Director, William Colby, claimed that the Agency rarely planted a completely false story because it was necessary to develop and maintain a reputation for reliability. By 1975 the CIA had spent over seventy-five million dollars in its efforts to prevent the election of a Communist government in Italy. Over half of that amount went in propaganda exercises involving newspapers, radio, posters and books. CIA media manipulation in Chile, brought about the overthrow of Allende and his replacement by Pinochet. During a three-year period, 1970 to 1973, *El Mercurio,* one of the most influential newspapers in Chile, received from the CIA over three and a half million dollars. It also received and printed a minimum of one story a day during that period that had either been written by the CIA or was based on Agency-provided comment. The CIA call such tactics 'theme guidance'.

Since the Agency's inception after the Second World War more than two thousand books have been produced, subsidized or sponsored by the CIA, over 25 per cent of them in the English language.

Within the files of the covert action department at Langley is a thoughtful document on the value of controlling the content of books. It is stamped 'SECRET' but I would not be at all surprised to learn that at some time in the past a copy of it had found its way to those members of Syrian Intelligence who had decided to target me in 1984. It reads in part:

'Books differ from all other propaganda media, primarily because one single book can significantly change the reader's attitude and action to an extent unmatched by the impact of any other single medium . . . this is, of course, not true of all books at all times, but it is true significantly often enough to make books the most important weapon of strategic (long range) propaganda.'

The writer then addresses himself to that most vexatious of tasks, controlling the author.

'The advantage of our direct contact with the author

is that we can acquaint him in great detail with our intentions; that we can provide him with whatever material we want him to include and that we can check the manuscript at every stage. Our control over the writer will have to be enforced, usually by paying him for the time he works on the manuscript or at least advancing him sums which he might have to repay . . . The Agency must make sure the actual manuscript will correspond with our operational and propaganda intention.'

There has never been a recorded example of any author ever repaying the CIA for work carried out on their behalf. This area of the CIA's work was described in 1976 by the House Select Committee on Intelligence (Pike Committee). They concluded that media and propaganda projects were probably 'the largest single category of covert action projects undertaken by the CIA'.

Among the many top secret memos in CIA files that detail these covert activities is one written in May 1968. It is addressed to the Director of the CIA, Richard Helms. It gives 'an operational summary' of a CIA propaganda unit based in London called Forum World Features, FWF.

'In its first two years, FWF has provided the United States with a significant means to counter Communist propaganda, and has become a respected feature service well on the way to a position of prestige in the journalism world.' The memo also informed Helms that Forum was 'run with the knowledge and co-operation of British Intelligence'.

The CIA had created and funded FWF in 1966 as a commercial news service selling weekly packets of features stories to newspapers throughout the world. Within two years it was placing CIA material into over fifty newspapers. One of its case officers ensuring that Forum repaid the substantial CIA investment was Robert Gene Gately. When it was exposed as a CIA front in 1975 the man running the agency promptly closed it down. His name was Brian Crozier.

Five years earlier in 1970 Crozier had created the Institute for the Study of Conflict (ISC) which was indirectly and directly, at least in its infancy, also part-funded by the CIA. The ISC, like Forum, had close links with both the CIA and British Intelligence.

The ISC has a number of aims, they include the study of urban terrorism and guerrilla warfare. It attempts to explain the actions of 'the more important extremist groups', consider 'revolutionary challenges' and, perhaps its most continuing preoccupation, to analyse 'subversion and political violence'. Over the years its Council members have included numerous people with intelligence connections. The majority of members could be fairly described as ultra right-wing conservatives.

In the light of Brian Crozier's vast experience both as a journalist and a recognized authority on subversion it would be difficult to think of anyone alive who was better placed to recognize a disinformation exercise when he saw one. Notwithstanding his very close relations with a number of secret services I do not believe he was a willing party to the disinformation exercise that was mounted around Carlos. That he was unwittingly used is beyond doubt. That he not only fully trusted his intelligence sources but also assumed they were incapable of a cynical manipulation of the truth is apparent from various statements he made to me. Given his excellent contacts he was the perfect target for British intelligence. Any information given to him stood an excellent chance of subsequently appearing in *The Times*, much of it did, and if not in that august newspaper then in Crozier's weekly newsletter to a highly selective clientele or in the annual review that the ISC published.

In the annual review for 1975–76, Crozier, in a long essay entitled 'Russia's Revolutionary Base', wrote:

AID FOR TERRORISM

Soviet involvement in support for terrorism has consistently been recorded in this Annual, and where appropriate in other publications of this Institute. The dividing line between terrorism and guerrilla war is not always easy to trace, and this article gives examples of clandestine arms-running to Angola and other places. However, the year also brought two interesting examples of Soviet involvement with 'pure' terrorism:

1 The 'Jackal' case. Ilich Ramirez Sanchez – known as Carlos and also as The Jackal (from *The Day of the Jackal*, the best selling novel by Frederick Forsyth about a hired gunman whose target was General de Gaulle) – studied at the Patrice Lumumba University in Moscow, which he left in 1969, aged 21. Third world students are processed there for training, usually elsewhere, in terrorism, sabotage and guerrilla war *(The Times*, London, 29 July 1975).

The reader will doubtless note that yet again no evidence is offered to justify the claim that Ramirez had undergone terrorist training while attending the University and indeed yet again Crozier incorrectly states the only verifiable fact that he records on Ramirez, the date when the Venezuelan left Patrice Lumumba. Citing *The Times* as his source would undoubtedly impress anyone who was unaware that by doing so he was citing himself as his source. This curious habit is a feature not only of Crozier's writings but of a great many right-wing 'experts' on subversion and terrorism. By the following year his intelligence contacts had furnished Crozier with more 'facts'. The Vienna operation led by Carlos had occurred. The British Secret Service and the CIA now took the view that Crozier and his readers were ripe for further disinformation on Carlos. The following quote is from the Annual for 1976–77.

INTERNATIONAL TERRORISM

The year brought fresh evidence of the large-scale Soviet involvement in terrorism. The fact that 'Carlos' – the name commonly used for the Venezuelan terrorist, Ilich Ramirez Sanchez – was trained in the USSR has been known since mid-1975 (see the 1975–76 edition of this Annual, p.22). New details, however, came to light during Carlos's trip to Yugoslavia in September 1976. He was reported to have attended a meeting of Communist-supported terrorist organizations at which KGB agents were present *(The Economist's Foreign Report*, 22 September 1976).

Despite advance warning to the Yugoslav authorities from the United States no attempt was made to arrest him, and a formal American letter of protest followed. According to the Cairo newspaper *Al Akhbar*, Carlos had come into possession of a small nuclear bomb.

Police and intelligence files show that Carlos was originally recruited by the KGB in Venezuela, studied under the KGB Colonel Victor Simenov at Camp Matanzas outside Havana (Cuba) and was sent to the Patrice Lumumba Friendship University in Moscow for further training in 1968. Aged 22 or 23, he also attended four special institutions run by the Soviet secret police near Moscow, for courses in political indoctrination, sabotage, the use of weapons and killer karate. Carlos later spread the story that he had been expelled from Moscow in 1969 for anti-Soviet attitudes and immorality; but these are stock Soviet cover stories to protect KGB agents.

The Economist's Foreign Report referred to was at that time edited by Crozier. It was, and still is, largely based on material supplied from intelligence sources. The 'small nuclear bomb' is a delightful invention of the Egyptian Secret Service propaganda machine. Though a fiction when it was reported in the *Foreign Report* it immediately became a 'fact' in the minds of the exclusive clientele that received the newsletter.

When I interviewed Brian Crozier I was totally unaware of his close relationship with British Intelligence and the CIA. My only reason for talking to him was to establish if it was indeed he who had written the *Times* article of July

29th 1975 and to establish if he had copies or had read the police and intelligence files that he had apparently quoted from in his 1976 article.

'This *Times* article of July 29th, 1975, linking Carlos with the KGB, did you write it?'

'No, I don't think I did. Of course I've written so many it's difficult to identify them all, but that's not one of mine.'

'What evidence would you put before me to say "This is why I believe he [Carlos] was a KGB agent"? I know he went to Lumumba.'

'Well the fact that he went to Lumumba is terribly important. You say that your evidence makes it doubtful that he was trained by the KGB.'

'It does, strongly.'

'I don't know. You see, I'm basically a journalist, I'm not an academic, and I have a lot of sources, international sources and I've obviously sources in the intelligence world and all I can say is that I'm going by a particular intelligence source that has never been proved wrong, that's all I can say.'

Crozier then stated that in the case of Africans and others he had seen documentary evidence and statements that they had been trained in KGB camps. But as for Carlos:

'In the case of Carlos it's certainly word of mouth, but it convinced me at the time and I've seen nothing that has caused me to change my mind.'

'Word of mouth', one of the crucial tools of trade of every investigative writer, but a tool that should always be handled with the greatest care, particularly when dealing with a source from the world of intelligence and counter-intelligence. Who gains? Is there an independent secondary source? Has the Hitler Syndrome been applied? It certainly was by Crozier's source in British Intelligence. How, for example, could Carlos have undergone KGB training in Cuba when the documentary evidence establishes beyond all doubt, reasonable or otherwise, that at precisely that time he was attending school in the Earls

Court Road, London? For the record, Brian Crozier did in fact write that *Times* article.

The importance of Crozier, of what he genuinely believed and what he sincerely wrote, cannot be overstated. He talked to me of the newsletter that he had run for about seven years.

'It was a high level kind of thing, read by Mrs Thatcher and Ronald Reagan and others, and I had a very, very restricted list, only about 160 people in about 15 countries, all decision makers. And I can tell you without boasting that time and again either Mrs Thatcher or Reagan or people round them would say, "Well you know, we haven't got hold of this stuff from anywhere else, where did you get it from?" Well, the simple answer is that we were asking the right questions. Foreign offices don't. They ask conventional questions which they've always asked and I wasn't interested in those questions at all.'

Crozier most certainly was not boasting when he said that to me. My subsequent investigations confirmed that over many years Crozier and his colleagues did indeed have the ear of virtually every leader in the Western world, and more than the ear, the mouth as well. His protégé, author and journalist Robert Moss, was for a number of years one of Prime Minister Thatcher's most trusted speech writers. Crozier, Moss and their inner circle have from the mid 1960s up to and including the present day directly influenced foreign policy on an extraordinary range of issues. Detente and their collective desire to frustrate and undermine it being but one.

The extraordinary potential this presented to a variety of secret services was not lost on Western Intelligence. If they could not get their view of the world, or rather their view of what the world should become, through the front door of number ten Downing Street and the White House and accepted by the respective occupants then they used the back door. An Intelligence-inspired Crozier report here, a memorable Moss line there. The Enemy Within?

One of the earliest examples of the desire of the CIA to come to the disinformation party that the SDECE

(French External Intelligence) and MI6 were enjoying occurred only days after the Carlos-led attack on the OPEC headquarters in Vienna. In the first days of January 1976 the CIA targeted the State Department. Officials in the department were fed the same lies that had been fed to Crozier in London. The CIA also used their excellent media contacts. One was the influential *Time* magazine, which in the first issue in the new year carried a full page article headed, 'The Man Known As Carlos'. The article contains all of the disinformation originally fed to the unwitting Crozier. Like the man who the previous year had been introduced to a Senate Committee as 'one of the free world's foremost experts on international terrorism', the editors at *Time* magazine were equally trusting. No original research was initiated, no cross-checking effected. After all, why bother with the irksome task of original research if the man from State or the contact at Langley is giving you the information?

The disinformation exercise on Carlos that Western Intelligence agencies on both sides of the Atlantic mounted was an unparalleled success. They conned every single aspect of the media, including one of their most important targets, the authors of books.

First to walk into the minefield was Colin Smith. At the time he wrote *Carlos, Portrait of a Terrorist* he was the *Observer*'s Chief Roving Reporter. In his opening pages Smith states that 'there is more than a shadow of suspicion that he [Carlos] is somehow connected with the Russians', and that 'The DGI [Cuban Intelligence] were probably his immediate bosses'.

Unable to trace any hospital records for Ramirez in London between June 1969 and February 1970, Smith concludes that the ulcer was a fiction 'concocted either by Ilich or his employers [the KGB]'. He speculates that during this period Carlos possibly received terrorist training either in the Middle East or Cuba. The author subsequently dismisses the expulsion of Ramirez as a disinformation exercise arranged by the KGB. He might well have drawn a different conclusion if he had discovered that twenty Venezuelan students were simultaneously expelled.

Undoubtedly Smith did considerable research before writing and he avoids a number of the intelligence traps. But in many areas, when dealing with the activities of Ramirez, he is grossly inaccurate, not least in one of the final conclusions that Carlos's 'other employers, the men in Dzerhinsky Square [KGB headquarters] who probably told the Cubans to get him out of Paris cannot be displeased at the chaos he has caused in the West'. Nowhere does Smith confront the blinding contradiction of an alleged KGB agent regularly performing in such a grossly incompetent manner.

By comparison with what was to come, however, it would appear that Colin Smith only accepted a part of the disinformation that the Intelligence services were pumping out. He rejected, for example, allegations that Qathafi had masterminded the OPEC operation. MI6, the CIA and Mossad, who by now had also joined in this particular game, concluded that they had to try harder. They did, with very effective results.

By the time that the second book on Carlos was published during the first half of 1977 the various secret services that were involved in this disinformation exercise had conned virtually the entire international news media. The fantasy portrait of Carlos had been accepted then reproduced by reporter after reporter. The speculative linking of Ramirez with terrorist training in the Soviet Union that Crozier had floated in mid 1975 had by early 1976 become an unquestioned 'fact'.

Time Magazine, 5th January 1976:

'He [Carlos] also attended four special institutes run by the Soviet secret police near Moscow, where he took courses in political indoctrination, sabotage, the use of weapons and killer karate.'

Like Crozier before them, the periodical had not a shred of evidence to justify those statements and, again like Crozier, their intelligence source persists in feeding out the wrong date of the departure of Carlos from the Soviet Union.

Newsweek, in an issue published the same week as the *Time* article, broke new ground. They had Mohammed Boudia and Carlos becoming 'fast friends' at Patrice Lumumba University and for good measure asserted that Carlos 'collaborated with Japanese Red Army leader Fusak Shigenobu to plan the pro-Palestinian massacre at Israel's Lod Airport'. During the time Ramirez was at Patrice Lumumba University, Mohammed Boudia was living and working in Paris. At the time of the Lod massacre, Ramirez was living and studying in London; his first terrorist action, the attempted murder of Edward Sieff, was still over one and a half years away.

In Europe, *Le Figaro* in France and *La Tribune de Lausanne* in Switzerland stated their conviction that Carlos 'belongs to the KGB'.

In March 1977 *The Carlos Complex. A Pattern of Violence* by Christopher Dobson and Ronald Payne was published. The authors were foreign correspondents who, as they said in their introduction, had 'covered virtually every war since the end of the Second World War'. They were also staff reporters for the London *Sunday Telegraph,* a paper of an ultra conservative shade.

To discuss every factual error that is contained within the pages of their book would take a book entirely devoted to them. I believe the following examples are more than sufficient to illustrate just how completely two very experienced reporters were duped by the intelligence sources they trusted.

The CIA in particular was much driven by the idea of using Ramirez not only in their propaganda war against the Soviets but against an enemy much closer to home, the Cubans. It was this Intelligence Agency that was responsible for feeding the non-existent 'Cuban connection' to the two authors. Thus:

'Carlos left school [in Caracas] in 1966 and his father sent him abroad to finish his education. He travelled in the Caribbean and went to Mexico and then, late in the year, arrived in Cuba to attend one of Castro's training camps for young guerrillas . . .'

'Carlos went through his training at Camp Matanzas, one of three such camps around Havana. He was one of a hundred young Venezuelans being educated in the art of subversion. Their professor was the notorious General Victor Simenov of the KGB who had been posted to Havana to become the operational boss of the Cuban secret service . . .'

'Carlos's involvement in this scene of international communist skulduggery is known because when Castro Hidalgo defected from the Cuban Embassy in Paris and was debriefed by the CIA, he named Carlos as one of the Venezuelan "students" in Cuba.'

Payne and Dobson go on to recount how, in early 1968, the Cubans sent Carlos with a team of insurgents who landed in Venezuela, that he was picked up 'almost immediately', questioned by the police and then released 'to flee back to Cuba'.

Then:

'Later that same year the Cubans tried again, Carlos was sent back to Venezuela to help stir up trouble at the University of Caracas in imitation of the student revolt in Paris. But again he failed. He was arrested for the second time and on this occasion the police grilled him for twelve hours. He was released only after the intervention of his father.'

As has already been recorded in an earlier chapter, based on a large number of interviews, access to school records, access to Customs files and Venezuelan police records, Carlos left Venezuela during August 1966, flew directly to London with his mother and two brothers, and lived continuously in that city continuing his education there until October 1968, at which point he flew directly to Moscow and started his education at Patrice Lumumba University.

General Simenov did not take over responsibility for overseeing Cuban Intelligence until 1970. That is a matter of public record. And Castro Hidalgo? It would have been quite extraordinary if Hidalgo had named one totally un-known, obscure Venezuelan out of the alleged hundred he is supposed to have seen being trained at Camp Matanzas. The fact is that Hidalgo did no such thing.

There is no mention of Ramirez in Hidalgo's CIA debriefing. There is no mention in Hidalgo's CIA-sponsored book *Spy for Fidel*. There is no mention of Ilich Ramirez Sanchez in any testimony Hidalgo has ever given either to the CIA, the Senate Sub-Committee on Terrorism or to anyone else. It would have been remarkable if there had been. Hidalgo was posted from Havana to Paris in March 1967. He was based at the Cuban Embassy in the French capital until he defected on March 31st 1969. During that time and prior to that, while living in Cuba, he never once set foot in the training camp at Matanzas.

Doubtless if his CIA interrogators in 1969 had wanted to insert the name of Ramirez into Castro's debriefing it would have gone in. But they had no knowledge, at that time, of the young Venezuelan, nor indeed of the so-called Ecuadorian Anton Bouvier, another individual whom American intelligence, in their conversations with Payne and Dobson, obligingly 'placed' in Cuba. Thus Bouvier magically became, according to the authors, one of Carlos's instructors.

The Cuban connection to the Venezuelan had of course raised its head when France expelled three of Castro's diplomats. It got a further push when, during Nydia Tobon's trial in London in the autumn of 1975, various newspapers reporting her case stated that 'Carlos had been educated in Cuba'.

I asked Nydia Tobon's defence counsel, Cheryl Drew, about this. The remark had been attributed to her.

'The press coverage of the trial was grossly inaccurate. I particularly remember that *The Times* and the *Telegraph* were very inaccurate. I have no recollection of ever saying anything like that.'

Lenin Ramirez Sanchez confirmed the inaccuracy of the Cuban connection:

'Up to the end of 1973 I can state with total conviction

that Ilich had never been to Cuba. I saw less of him after that time so obviously I cannot comment on his precise movements after that date.'

So too did Nydia Tobon:

'We talked of Castro and Che very often. It was very obvious that certainly up to the time of my arrest in the summer of 1975 he had never set foot in Cuba.'

Quite why Christopher Dobson and Ronald Payne chose to accept the Cuban connection as expounded to them by the CIA when basic research would have established that at the time the Agency had Ramirez cavorting around Cuba and then invading Venezuela he was in fact attending a school in Earls Court remains a mystery. One of a number connected with their book.

Equally culpable in this disinformation exercise perpetrated on these two authors was British Special Branch which advised Payne and Dobson in 'off the record' briefings that Bouvier had a London bank account under his middle name of 'Dages' and had given Carlos financial assistance. There is no evidence that Bouvier did have a British bank account under any of his three names or that he ever gave Carlos financial assistance.

The authors talk of 'persistent reports from a number of sources that he [Carlos] returned to Russia in 1974 with a PFLP group undergoing special training at a Russian camp. Some of these reports come from Arab terrorists who have been captured by the Israelis and swear that they saw Carlos in the camp.'

Israeli intelligence, which was the source of this canard, did not specify to Payne and Dobson the name of the camp or more significantly the date of this alleged additional training in 1974. If the reader cares to turn back a few chapters it will be seen that 1974 was a busy year for Carlos, it left precious little time for a training course in the Soviet Union. That training could not have taken place in January, Carlos was in London attempting to kill Edward Sieff then preparing and carrying out the bomb attack on Bank Hapoalim. It could not have taken place in February, he flew to the Middle East, to

Aden for planning meetings on the next series of attacks. In March and April a wide variety of witnesses place Ramirez in London. In April a further witness places Ramirez in Paris. In May he began a six-month affair with a woman in Paris which with a variety of other relationships placed him in France, with only temporary absences, until October. Apart from increasing the number of the women in his life he was also during this time blowing up newspaper offices in Paris; assisting in the seizure of the French Embassy in Holland; throwing a hand grenade into a Parisian store; and organizing, again from Paris, the movement of arms via donkeys into a variety of countries. In October and November witnesses place Ramirez in London and finally in December 1974 and January 1975 when he was planning the first rocket attack at Orly at least one dozen witnesses place him in Paris for the entire two months. Perhaps he did this additional training at night school?

Payne and Dobson, like Colin Smith before them, saw great potential in the entries that French intelligence leaked from Moukharbel's diary or account book. All three authors asserted that the entry 'Marseilles. 12 August, train tickets and hotel 500 francs' covered a trip that Carlos and Moukharbel had made to Marseilles in August 1973, to observe French anti-Algerian riots. Smith states they stayed at the French sea port for 'almost four weeks' having probably been sub-contracted by a 'foreign power' who wanted a first-hand report on the riots. Payne and Dobson go several better by contending that both Carlos and Moukharbel were arrested and after being released fled back to Paris.

Documentary evidence establishes that Carlos flew to the Middle East on July 24th and did not return until September 25th.

In 1973, even assuming that Carlos, ever a man with a Hilton mentality, had travelled with Moukharbel by second class fare to Marseilles, the return tickets would have been a minimum of 472 francs. The balance of 28 francs would have been insufficient at even the cheapest hotel for two people to spend one night.

My purpose here is not to castigate other writers but to condemn the intelligence agencies that fed this material to them. They knew very precisely the implications of what they were perpetrating and their aims are abundantly clear. To destroy any hopes of detente between East and West. To destroy the dreams of the Palestinian people. To sow hostility and suspicion between nations. They succeeded on every count. The lies were being told long and loud. They were becoming the truth. Before this disinformation exercise would run its course they would be the truth. They would influence attitudes and official foreign policy in a variety of countries including Great Britain and the United States.

With regard to the attack on the OPEC headquarters, Payne and Dobson asserted 'the Vienna raid was carried out to satisfy several different aims and to satisfy a number of different clients'.

The list of 'clients' that they record is impressively long, it ranges from Carlos himself, the rest of his commando group, the Popular Front, Iraq, Libya, Algeria and behind them all the Soviet Union. Perhaps the authors were working on the principle that if you accuse enough elements and countries you must by the law of averages hit the right one. Rather like the racehorse tipster who names every runner and in the following day's newspaper only quotes his favourable comment about the eventual winner.

As far as that OPEC attack was concerned, the men in Mossad were particularly effective when it came to planting false information on Payne and Dobson. The authors asserted in the book as they had previously done in their February 1976 newspaper article that Carlos was paid one million pounds by Colonel Qathafi for the OPEC raid and that Klein who was a member of the commando was paid one hundred thousand pounds as compensation for being wounded. The only 'evidence' they offer for such statements is their assertion that the then Saudi Arabian Oil Minister Sheik Yamani 'has no doubt that it was

679

Gaddafi [sic] who financed the OPEC affair and, while he still refuses to blame the Libyan President publicly, he threatens that he will do so when the time is ripe'.

Other than Yamani's original accusation of Israeli involvement, that ripening time has yet to happen.

Apart from creating a minor industry for themselves, Payne and Dobson have continued to quote extensively from their book on Carlos in subsequent works and are now widely regarded as experts on terrorism. The intelligence agencies responsible for the Carlos disinformation exercise reaped a very rich harvest.

In 1978 the BBC transmitted a current affairs special programme entitled 'Terror International'. It was an examination by reporter Tom Mangold of the Wadi Haddad infrastructure. Special advisers on the programme were Ronald Payne and Christopher Dobson. Later, in the United States, CBS transmitted the programme. On April 26th, 1978, Senator Eagleton had the entire transcript of the CBS transmission read into the record. In 1984 the book *Terrorism: The Soviet Connection* by Ray S. Cline and Yonah Alexander was published. Cline was Deputy Director of the CIA from 1962 to 1966, another internationally recognized expert on terrorism. Among the sources that Cline and Alexander quote to justify their joint assertion that the Soviet Union was at the very heart of an international terrorist infrastructure is the Congressional record covering the CBS programme. In another part of the book Cline quotes himself as a source and in a further part cites Brian Crozier as a source. In yet another part of the book Payne and Dobson are cited as specific sources for the contention that Carlos was trained in Cuba and subsequently given terrorist training at Patrice Lumumba University. Thus lies that had in part originated from the CIA are now quoted by a former Director of the CIA as irrefutable evidence.

In July 1975, when Cuban diplomats were summoned to the Quai d'Orsay and advised that three members of their embassy had been declared persona non grata, they demanded a full explanation. The French government advised them that it was at that time 'unable to give any explanation as to the facts of the charges against the three'. They were assured that one would be forthcoming. Three years later the Cubans were still waiting.

When in 1978 Michel Poniatowski wrote a book *L'Avenir n'est écrit nulle part* which dealt with his period in office as Minister of the Interior during 1975 the Cubans might well have thought that now, finally, if in a rather public manner, they were going to get 'the facts'. Poniatowski had been the Minister responsible for the expulsions.

The Minister did indeed cover 'the Carlos Affair' within his book. He gave a definitive example of just how successful the disinformation campaign centred on Carlos had become. He tells his readers that Carlos at the age of seventeen went to Cuba where 'he underwent terrorist training, automatic arms, plastic bombs, mines, destruction of pipe-lines, decoding, photography, falsification of documents, etc at the camp of Matanzas near Havana'. There was not a single word of truth in it.

Warming to the fabrication that his own Secret Service had in part created, Poniatowski told of how Carlos made two vain attempts to enter Venezuela to indulge in subversive activities. The fiction continues with the observation that Carlos was expelled in 1969 from Patrice Lumumba University, an error that is a telling giveaway about the Minister's sources. Like Payne and Dobson before him he quotes the 'continual reports placing him in training camps in Russia in 1974'. Among the crimes he attributes to Carlos he includes the Lod airport massacre of 1972 and the Lufthansa hijacking to Mogadishu in 1977. Carlos had not the slightest involvement in either outrage.

Of his expulsion of the Cuban diplomats, not a word. The greatest coup for those men in Langley, Tel Aviv and London who had orchestrated the disinformation exercise was now about to take place – they were about to convince the Director of the CIA, the United States Secretary of State, the President and Vice President of the United States, and through these men Prime Minister Margaret Thatcher, that their lies were the unvarnished truth. The groundwork had been brilliantly laid. All that was needed was an American author gullible enough to swallow the story whole. Cometh the hour, cometh the woman. Enter Claire Sterling.

Outside the worlds of Edward Lear and Lewis Carroll it would be difficult to find so much nonsense gathered between the covers of one book as that contained in *The Terror Network* written, though compiled would be a more accurate description, by Sterling.

In her introduction she says, 'I had no access at all to the CIA while writing this book.' No witting access perhaps. Unwittingly she had continuous access not only to the CIA but also to MI6 and Mossad and the disinformation campaign that they had run so superbly. For an author much preoccupied with disinformation I cannot find a single instance in her book acknowledging what even a cursory study of the subject would confirm, the existence of Western disinformation, yet her book is a monument to the achievements of a wide number of Western Intelligence agencies in this field.

The premise of her book is that terrorism is 'Russia's Ultimate Weapon'. The final words of her introduction are, 'This is not a book of fiction. It deals with facts.'

The majority of her sources for her facts in her chapter on Carlos will by now have a familiar ring. Authors Payne, Dobson, Smith, Crozier, and for good measure the former French Minister Poniatowski, whose sources of course were Crozier, Payne and Dobson. Of the seventeen different sources she cites for this chapter only two are not from previously published works. Those two are unnamed and unidentified 'intelligence sources'. There is an obvious inherent danger in relying solely on such sources, Western or Eastern, Israeli or Arab. In my own work I have checked and cross-checked every single reference, and always from more than one source. If French Intelligence contacts, for example, independently confirm, as they did, information previously given to me by

Peter Boock, which is then independently confirmed to me by Bassam Abu Sharif, I believe it not unreasonable to conclude that what I am confronted with is a fact, is truth. Based on Sterling's methodology one source should apparently suffice.

Her chapter on Ilich Ramirez Sanchez, relying as it does so heavily on other authors who to a greater or lesser degree had been gulled by Western intelligence agencies, inevitably walks onto the same landmines. The early training of Carlos at Camp Matanzas by DGI and KGB officers. His 'case officer' Anton Bouvier. His subsequent terrorist training in the Soviet Union, based originally by Crozier on mere verbal information from intelligence. It is all depressingly familiar.

Sterling had the additional bonus of being able to consider and test statements made by Carlos himself. The el-Jundi interviews with Ramirez had by now been published. Her approach to this material is revealing. Making no attempt to obtain the interviews in the original Arabic, she contented herself with *Le Figaro*'s version, complete with its additional fabricated material. She made no attempt to test the truthfulness of the statements attributed to Carlos. Thus his remarks about his involvement in Caracas with the Young Communist movement and his leadership of a large Communist secret cell are all faithfully recorded and utilized to justify her assertion that Carlos was a KGB officer. Original research in Venezuela would have established that by the time of his conversation with el-Jundi Carlos had become in part an active member of the disinformation team. He had started to believe his own publicity.

Her preoccupation with the albeit fantasy involvement of Carlos the Young Communist is doubly ironic. Claire Sterling, unlike Ramirez, was in her youth a card-carrying member of the Communist Party.

It would be inaccurate to state that Sterling relied entirely on secondhand disinformation. There is at least one instance in this chapter that an unnamed intelligence source took the opportunity to feed a new titbit to this very credulous woman. According to Sterling, 'In April 1973, Israeli forces raided the Lebanese cornice of Ramblatt-el Blida and found themselves able for a while to listen in on messages transmitted by a Soviet KGB officer under diplomatic cover in Beirut. By chance, therefore – they were still in the dark about Carlos, like everybody else – they learned that he was drawing checks on the London bank account of a KGB agent named Antonio Dages Bouvier.'

Sterling cites as her source 'highly responsible intelligence sources – not Israelis as it happens'. Indeed, when I discussed this with a senior Mossad agent, he roared with laughter and dismissed it as a 'fairy tale'. Bouvier did not visit London until 1975. My own 'highly responsible sources' at the Special Branch in London advised me that at no time throughout the 1970s was a bank account operative in this man's name or in any combination of his names. Executives at three of Britain's major banking institutions also could find no trace of a Bouvier bank account for the relevant period. The idea that an Israeli Sayaret Matkal killer team slipped ashore from Israeli patrol boats under cover of darkness on the night of April 9th, 1973, performed their allotted killing tasks and were back at sea in less than an hour, yet found time to monitor Soviet embassy signals, stretches credulity to breaking point.

Her statement that Carlos 'retired soon after the OPEC attack' would have come as a particular surprise to Carlos who in fact has killed considerably more people since that date than he had done before it, a fact that makes equal nonsense of her conclusion that after Vienna he was 'simply recalled to Russia as a blown agent with a swelled head'.

Sterling places Mohammed Boudia at the Patrice Lumumba University in 1969; like others before her she claims that Boudia was a KGB agent and the man who recruited Ramirez during his time at the University.

Original research by the author would have established that Boudia was working full time as administrator at the

TOP theatre in Paris from 1968 until 1971. As for the possibility that Boudia warmly recommended Carlos to Habash, Bassam Abu Sharif denied it.

'You don't seriously believe that if Carlos had arrived out here with a letter of introduction from Boudia he would have been sent to one of the summer camps for students do you?'

Like others before her, Claire Sterling pulled in one particular resident of Paris as she sought to expose what she saw as the Soviet hand in virtually every act of terrorism. The gentleman in question was an Egyptian Jew named Henri Curiel. As a self-declared Communist since his early twenties and a man who immersed himself in a wide variety of revolutionary movements during his many years in Paris, Curiel proved to be a gift for Sterling. He also had, as Payne and Dobson noted before her, a cousin called George Blake, who unlike Curiel was indeed a KGB officer. The fact that Blake's only known contact with Curiel was during his childhood and then only for a few years did not deter Miss Sterling from extraordinary speculation about an ongoing treasonable relationship. In her mind both were part of this global Soviet conspiracy.

Another who could not be left out was, inevitably, the Libyan leader, Colonel Qathafi. Analysis of the chapter on Qathafi entitled 'The Daddy Warbucks of Terrorism' leads the reader to the inescapable conclusion that Qathafi was working hand in glove with the Soviets to destabilize the entire free world. Sterling asserts that after the OPEC attack in Vienna, the commando group returned to Libya and that Carlos 'was given a handsome seaside villa, complete with staff, car and chauffeur'. She also asserts, 'Hans-Joachim Klein, wounded hero of the Carlos raid on OPEC, wrote that on getting back to Libya he was "toasted at dinner with the foreign minister, travelled in the president's private jet, dined with the head of the secret service, and was assigned a bodyguard".'

Just to make sure the reader gets her drift, Sterling has,

in her earlier chapter on Carlos, observed of the OPEC operation:

'All the necessary inside information could be had from Colonel Qaddafi [sic]. It was his idea, after all, as Hans-Joachim Klein conceded obliquely after the event . . .'

Nowhere in the interviews that Klein has given, nor in his autobiography, does he state, obliquely or otherwise, that the OPEC attack was Qathafi's brainchild. Nor does Klein state that after the Vienna operation and his initial recuperation in Algeria either he or Carlos went to Libya. He is most careful to avoid identifying either the mastermind or the country where he was treated so regally.

Like Crozier and Robert Moss, Sterling had friends in very high places. Like them she had attended a conference on international terrorism at the Jonathan Institute in Jerusalem in July 1979. Seated nearby as they listened to Prime Minister Menachem Begin urging them all to expose 'Soviet Terrorism' was George Bush. Near him was former Deputy Director of the CIA, Ray Cline, and next to him George Keegan, former head of United States Air Force Intelligence. Four former heads of Israeli Ministry Intelligence were also in the room. In the minds of those attending it the conference confirmed, as Jacques Soustelle observed, that 'the Soviets pull all the strings behind international terrorism'. Just over one year later Claire Sterling had finished her book. That was in October 1980.

On November 2nd, 1980, the Sunday before the Presidential election, the influential *New York Times* carried in its magazine section an article entitled 'Terror: a Soviet Export'. The author was Robert Moss, protégé of Brian Crozier.

Moss had indisputably been drinking at the same well as Messrs Crozier, Payne, Dobson and Sterling. Referring to the expulsion of Ramirez from the Patrice Lumumba University he wrote, 'However, West European intelligence sources maintain that this story [expulsion because of loose living and indiscipline] was a blind intended to camouflage the fact that Carlos had been recruited

686

by the KGB as a link man with international terrorist groups, especially the PFLP. These sources also contend that Carlos had received training in Cuba under KGB Colonel Victor Simenov at Camp Matanzas even before his arrival in the Soviet Union.'

A month later the Reagan/Bush team won the Presidential election. Among the appointments made by the new President during December was that of General Alexander Haig as his Secretary of State and William Casey as Director of the CIA.

Sterling's book was not due for publication until April 1981. A copy of the galley proofs of the book found their way, by what route I do not know, into the hands of Haig.

On January 26th, 1981, less than a week after the inauguration, President Reagan held his first Cabinet meeting. Haig was much occupied with the problem of terrorism. The hostage crisis in Teheran had mercifully come to a happy conclusion the previous week, but Haig clearly believed the worst was yet to come. He wheeled out the State Department's terrorism expert, Anthony Quainton, to address the Cabinet. Quainton commanded everyone's complete attention when he declared, 'This country is not immune from direct terrorist attack. The United States is vulnerable.'

Among those listening was William Casey.

The following day Haig held his first press conference at the State Department. The Reagan administration's foreign policies in key areas were not long in coming. The Soviet Union was accused by Haig of 'the training, funding and equipping of international terrorists'. Unable to resist a sarcastic reference to President Carter's human rights campaign, Haig observed,

'International terrorism will take the place of human rights . . . The greatest problem to me in the human rights area today is the spread of rampant international terrorism. The Soviets are today involved in conscious policies, in programmes if you will, which foster and expand this activity.'

Apart from grabbing the headlines with these statements, Haig's accusation, made before he had warmed his seat, astonished many of his colleagues in the State Department. After the press conference, Ronald I. Spiers, head of the Department's Intelligence branch, attempted to reason with his new boss, a formidable task. Spiers protested that the accusations could not be sustained in the light of current intelligence reports. Haig produced his ace – his sole source of information upon which he had based his remarks at the press conference, remarks which had clearly indicated that detente was dead and buried. He held up a copy of the galley proofs of Sterling's *The Terror Network*. Confronted with these Spiers ducked for cover. Agreeing with his Secretary of State that it was possible Sterling had indeed acquired new and compelling evidence, he requested William Casey at the CIA to make a Special National Intelligence Estimate, SNIE, an intelligence analysis designed to give the best assessment of the collective wisdom of all United States intelligence agencies on the subject. It was the first such analysis to be undertaken by the Director. It was to become one of his major preoccupations. Another that he shared not only with Haig but with virtually every other member of the Cabinet was Qathafi.

On March 1st, the *New York Times* magazine published a long article by Claire Sterling, 'Terrorism, Tracing the International Network'. It was an adaptation of material contained in her forthcoming book with one or two additional lines, direct quotes from Haig's press conference, quotes that had of course been inspired, without attribution, by her book. Sterling was clearly dismayed that the new Secretary of State was apparently not being taken seriously in certain quarters.

'Journalists who interviewed Government intelligence experts – including some CIA aides – quoted officials to the effect that there was no hard evidence to support Mr Haig's accusations. And many Americans shook their heads despairingly at what sounded to them like nothing more than an old cold warrior's refrain, a broadside political attack against a safe and familiar target.'

Having told her readers about her two and a half years' research, 'talking to government officials and police in ten countries from Sweden to Lebanon, examining court records and interviews in the public prints . . .' she now knew how right Haig was. She then proceeded to share the fruits of her labours, kicking off with an account of the Japanese Red Army attack on the French Embassy at The Hague. There were a number of things missing from the account, not least a shred of evidence that the attack had been perpetrated on the orders of Moscow.

The head of the CIA was as impressed with the article as he had been by the book, the Hitler Syndrome was in full flower by now.

'If you tell a lie long enough and loud enough, it becomes the truth.'

What Casey could not understand, and said so loudly and clearly to senior members of the CIA, was how Sterling had so much better data than the CIA. He demanded an explanation. A number of his senior members of staff immediately offered one.

'All her book contains is very largely disinformation that we and other intelligence services have pushed out in the first place.'

Casey refused to accept that. He wanted to believe, therefore he believed.

The top intelligence experts at Langley and some of their best operation staff were put on the case. The more they studied her book the more convinced they became. The quantum leaps it contained, the 'guilty by association' reasoning. They continued to fail in their hunt for the smoking gun. They continued to ask 'where's the beef?'

The national intelligence officer for the Soviet Union, the most senior Soviet analytic post in the US intelligence agencies, agreed with his colleagues at Langley. His draft report to Casey dismissed Sterling's 'facts'. It concluded that there was little or no evidence of Soviet involvement in terrorism. It was not a conclusion Casey wanted to hear. He handed the draft report back to its author with the observation, 'Read Claire Sterling's book. Forget about this crap.'

He waved his copy of *The Terror Network* in the face of the senior Soviet analyst.

'I paid $13.95 for this and it told me more than you bastards who I pay fifty thousand a year to.'

Thus the 'bastards' were put back to work again to re-study a book claiming to be fact that should have been published as fiction. It should not be thought that Casey stood alone at Langley surrounded by a sea of scepticism. His Deputy Director, Bobby Inman, was convinced that Sterling was right and the entire collective opinion of the experts at Langley was wrong. Another who was equally convinced was General Tighe, head of Defense Intelligence Agency, the DIA, which reports directly to the Defense Department – the cancer was spreading.

Another who considered that the Langley experts might have got it wrong was Lincoln Gordon, former President of the Johns Hopkins University and one of a three-man panel whose function was to review CIA evaluations. The head of the CIA, hoping for more positive conclusions, instructed Gordan to undertake his own investigation of Sterling's allegations. His draft report to Casey went straight down the middle. Yes, the Soviets supported 'wars of liberation'. No, they were not masterminding global terrorism. The report cited several instances where the Soviets had acted to prevent a terrorist attack by warning the Americans.

Gordan's conclusion was that there was no evidence to justify Sterling's thesis and therefore none to justify Secretary of State Haig's press conference accusations. Predictably General Tighe, who had been totally convinced of a global Soviet terrorist conspiracy before he had read Sterling's book, did not agree with Gordan's conclusions. Eventually Gordan's point of view prevailed and his secret estimate concluding that the Soviets were innocent of the charges made against them in *The Terror Network* went to the President.

The recommendations in the report included some excellent observations, not least that less reliance should be placed on high-tech satellite intelligence and more on the human element, including the penetration of terrorist organizations.

Apparently Gordan found in Sterling's book one clear-cut example of the author unwittingly using CIA disinformation. Given greater time I am sure he would have found, as I have, many more.

The accusations that Haig had made were never publicly withdrawn. The record was never corrected. Casey and a great many others within the Administration remained convinced that Sterling was right and the Langley experts wrong.

The head of the CIA did not conduct a similar detailed analysis on the many other allegations that abounded in the Sterling book and in at least one instance – Sterling's assertions about Qathafi – he merely embraced them. At the time that he had received the initial request from the State Department to investigate Sterling's allegations on 'Russia's Ultimate Secret Weapon – Terrorism', he was already studying a secret SNIE report compiled by his predecessor, Admiral Stansfield Turner. It was headed 'Libya: Aims and Vulnerabilities'. Qathafi had proved to be an increasing irritation to the Carter Administration which, while desiring to curb his 'adventurism', particularly in neighbouring countries like Chad, was conscious of the fact that it had to balance its responses to the Libyan leader's attempts to export his vision of revolution against the dependence of the United States on its imports of high quality Libyan oil. At the time Reagan assumed office 10 per cent of imported United States oil came from Libya. A ban on this source of supply, the secret report noted, 'would result in a serious gasoline shortage on the US East Coast'.

The report discussed the possibilities of removing Qathafi from power and concluded that the likelihood of a successful coup by any organized group of Libyan exiles was remote. One of its conclusions noted: 'Barring an assassination, he could continue in power for many years.'

Simultaneously with his study of this report Casey was reading in Sterling's book of 'The Daddy Warbucks of Terrorism'. It included the categoric statements that Qathafi had provided 'the funds, arms and training for the Olympic Games massacre in 1972', that 'he undertook to bankroll the Carlos network in Paris' and that the attack on the OPEC headquarters in Vienna had been 'his idea'.

The last two allegations are dealt with in other parts of this book. With regard to the first, the Munich Games attack, as can be seen from the following interchange of letters, Israel's government held the same view as Claire Sterling.

27 April 1989
Mr Yitzhak Shamir
Prime Minister
Kaplan Street
Jerusalem, Israel

Dear Prime Minister

I have been researching for the past five years material for my next book. This book deals with a number of Middle East issues, including what is now widely called the Palestinian issue. With regard to this particular area, I have concentrated my research on a number of elements. One of these concerns acts of terrorism.

On 20 November 1986 at the United Nations in New York the representative for Israel made a speech defending the USA attack on Libya that had occurred on 15 April 1986. During the course of this speech he said:

Libya's relationship with the terrorist Palestinian Liberation Organisation (PLO) deserved special attention. Qaddafi bankrolled some of the most

horrendous crimes committed by Palestinian terror-
ists. It (Libya) had granted $5 million to the Fatah
(Black September) group for the murder of eleven
Israeli athletes at the 1972 Munich Olympics.
Qaddafi had financed the PFLP's seizure of the
Organization of Petroleum Exporting Countries
(OPEC) building in Vienna in 1975, in which four
people were killed. In January of this year he had
given $13 million to Abu Nidal for mass murder
– the massacre of innocent tourists in Rome and
Vienna on 27 December 1985.

I have attempted to make my research as diligent
and as meticulous as is humanly possible and I am sure
if you have enquiries made you will find confirmation
of that fact from some of your colleagues. I include
among these the senior spokesman for the IDF and
Uri Lubrani.
I would like to receive from you any documentary
evidence that supports and sustains the allegations
made by your country's representative at the United
Nations. I give you my firm undertaking that all such
evidence will be utilized and quoted in my book.
I await the favour of an early reply.
Yours faithfully
DAVID A. YALLOP

Ministry of Foreign Affairs
Jerusalem
August 7, 1989

Dear Mr Yallop
I am writing to you on behalf of Mr H. Z. Hurvitz,
Adviser to Prime Minister Shamir, in reply to your
letter of April 27.
The Israeli representative's speech at the UN on
November 20, 1986 was based on the enclosed paper
which was distributed by the Israeli Information
Center.

On Page 6 it states that, according to the West German newspaper *Bild am Sonntag*, Kaddafi promised to provide the Abu Nidal group with $12.7 million annually for terrorist operations. At a meeting in Libya, the first payment of $4.7 million was made by the late Colonel Ashkal.

On Page 7 the report states that Libya granted $5 million to the FATAH group 'Black September' which murdered 11 Israeli athletes at the Munich Olympics. The perpetrators used Libya's diplomatic mail to receive their weapons in Germany (a former Libyan Minister, Mr Mahaishi, told the *Daily Telegraph*, 19.3.76).

The report also states (page 7) that 'Libya financed the terrorist operation in Vienna in which Habash Front terrorists seized an OPEC building and took as hostages the OPEC oil ministers meeting there.'

In addition to the Israeli Information Center's report, I hereby enclose a Fact Sheet prepared by the US Department of State and an overview which was written by the Canadian Alderman Mark Maloney. Both these papers prove clearly Kaddafi's *direct* support for terrorism.

I trust that the enclosed material will be of assistance in your search.

Sincerely yours,
Talya Lador-Fresher
Information Division

encl: 3
cc: H. Z. Hurvitz, Adviser to Prime Minister Shamir

15 March 1991
Mr Yitzhak Shamir
Prime Minister
Kaplan Street
Jerusalem, Israel

Dear Prime Minister
    I am enclosing with this letter for your benefit copies

of earlier correspondence so that you may refresh your memory before responding to me.

Since receiving the response of August 7 1989 from your Ministry of Foreign Affairs, among the tasks I have subsequently undertaken is a detailed investigation of the material that came from that Department.

My initial reaction on studying that material was one of astonishment that a representative of Israel should get to his feet in the United Nations on 20 November 1986 and make the statement quoted in my earlier letter to you based on such truly pathetic source material as the West German newspaper *Bild am Sonntag* and the British newspaper the *Daily Telegraph*.

With regard to your United Nations assertions concerning Libya's relationship with Palestinian terrorists, analysis of the material sent to me plus research, investigations and interviews establishes that without exception it is undocumented, highly speculative and does not contain a shred of real evidence. It is riddled with 'the US suspects involvement by Libyan sympathizers'; 'it is believed that these attacks . . .'; 'strongly suspected'; 'involvement by Libyan sympathizers is suspected'; 'there may have been Libyan involvement', etc, etc.

For your IDF spokesman to assert that Libya financed the terrorist operation in Vienna on 21 December 1975 is, based upon the evidence that I have carefully researched during the past seven years, totally inaccurate. I know full well who financed the attack on OPEC, who planned the operation, what its real purpose was and the identities of the individuals who perpetrated this outrage. It may well have suited the political aspirations of a number of countries to lay the blame for this attack at the door of Mu'Ammar Qathafi but the concepts of honesty and truth have been appallingly served by such allegations . . . If your country's posture towards Libya and its leader is based upon, and solely based upon, such fallacious material, then I am afraid Prime Minister there is something very rotten in the State of Israel.

I hold no brief for Colonel Mu'Ammar Qathafi, but I do hold pursuit of truth as an absolutely sacred tenet. The 'evidence' that your government has sent me would not justify hanging a dog, let alone a Head of State.

I would ask you again, as I asked you in my letter of 27 April 1989, for any *documentary evidence* that supports and sustains the allegations made by your country's representative at the United Nations. Yet again I give you my firm undertaking that all such *evidence* will be utilized and quoted in my book.

Yours sincerely
DAVID A. YALLOP

Prime Minister's Bureau
Jerusalem
April 19, 1991
141–14

Dear Mr Yallop

I am writing on behalf of the Prime Minister, Mr Yitzhak Shamir, to acknowledge your letter of 15 March 1991.

You may rest assured that the appropriate Israel authorities base their assessments on a great deal more than press information – especially in regard to the Libyan dictator Qaddafi and his role in support of terrorism.

We are not in the habit of sharing such information with private individuals. If you are particularly interested in this subject you will, I am sure, eventually get the true picture.

Yours sincerely
H. Z. Hurvitz
Adviser to the Prime Minister

In my attempts 'to get the true picture' concerning

the Munich Olympic Games attack, I talked to a variety of people, including a senior officer currently working for the Mossad, who stated, 'This was purely a Black September operation. We have no information that he [Qathafi] took part in the planning or logistics.'

I tried again, this time during my interviews with Abu Iyad.

'You were the Godfather, the creator of Black September?'

'Yes.'

'The attack on the Olympic Games at Munich in 1972. Who paid for it? Who planned it?'

'I planned it in conjunction with other members.'

'Members of El Fatah?'

'Yes. It was financed from our central funds. El Fatah funds.'

'What was Colonel Qathafi's role?'

'He had no role, either in financing the operation or planning it. His only involvement was to bury the members of the commando who died during the action and to receive the three survivors after they were released by the Germans. They then returned to Lebanon as Samir has told you.'

If DCI Casey had let his Langley team of experts loose on these particular allegations concerning the Munich attack and the Vienna OPEC attack, they would undoubtedly have again demonstrated that Claire Sterling had moved into a realm of fantasy. He declined to conduct the exercise and instead began to preoccupy both himself and other key members of the Reagan Administration with the task of removing the Libyan leader. Bob Woodward[1] has graphically recounted how this was to become a major obsession for the President and those around him. It is an obsession that continues to this day with the Clinton administration.

In April 1981, a month before the CIA top secret report

[1] *Veil: The Secret Wars of the CIA 1981–1987*, Bob Woodward, Simon & Schuster, 1987

that dismissed her allegations of a Soviet global terrorist conspiracy went to President Reagan, Claire Sterling found herself with a far more sympathetic audience. At the same time as the publication of her book, she testified before the Senate Sub Committee on Security and Terrorism.

Unlike the experts at Langley, the Sub Committee was ill equipped to test her sweeping assertions, particularly those concerning Carlos. Their Chairman, Senator Denton, was later to express his dismay 'that at this meeting of a very important committee of the Congress not one member of the committee had any idea who Carlos was'.

In his opening statement on April 24th, Senator Denton described Claire Sterling as 'an international journalist, a lady of great prestige in her profession and with a profound background in the subject we are addressing today'.

Having been sworn in Sterling then proceeded to share some of her 'profound background' with the Committee.

During her testimony Sterling was asked by Senator Leahy: 'The question that kept recurring to me throughout the reading of your book is, do you feel that the CIA can substantiate the facts and the conclusions contained in your book?'

'Well I am not really in a position to answer that question, Senator.'

'Maybe I should say it this way, do you feel they should be able to?'

'I would certainly feel they should be able to. As I explain in the book, I had no information at all from the CIA.'

She elaborated on that by explaining that she understood the CIA was not permitted to speak with journalists and then observed,

'I did speak with all other Western intelligence services.'

As the Senator retorted,

'Many of whom get their information from the CIA.'

A short while later Sterling said more about her sources.

'I can only say that my information is not based primarily on intelligence service information either from the CIA or from any country. The overwhelming evidence has come from sources accessible to the public.'

And that, in a single sentence, demonstrates the appalling danger to which Claire Sterling had unwittingly exposed herself. If a writer relies primarily on what other journalists, other authors, have previously written on a subject, then errors will be carried forward, lies given fresh life and the original disinformation will live on. A few minutes later she gave a powerful example of how effectively the Hitler Syndrome had contaminated her book. Cuba and the Tri-Continental Conference of 1966 were under discussion. Sterling turned to the training camps which she stated had 'started in 1968 and 1969'.

'Some of the most important people on the terrorist scene in the 1970s were trained there. For example, Carlos the Jackal, the most notorious I suppose of all the figures in the world scene in terrorism during the 1970s, trained in Camp Matanzas in Cuba in 1966. In fact he came in 1966 directly after the Tri-Continental Conference. He was sent by the Communist Party of Venezuela; he had his first training there. There he studied under the man who became his KGB control when he was operating as a terrorist leader in Europe, Antonio Dages Bouvier, with the fake Ecuadorian name.

'From there he went on; from the Camp Matanzas training he was sent on by the Venezuelan Communist Party to the Patrice Lumumba University in Moscow for two years. This is not made up, but it does not come from the intelligence services, he has said so himself in an interview granted in November 1979 to an Arab weekly, which is published in my book.'

It is made up. Apart from the reference to Carlos's sponsorship at the University none of it is contained in his el-Jundi interviews, nor is it even contained within the distorted *Le Figaro* version of that interview which Sterling relied upon. Disinformation that began in the offices of the CIA, MI6, Mossad and the SDECE was now being given its final seal of approval through the mouth of a witness giving sworn testimony to a Senate Committee.

The life force of the disinformation campaign that surrounds this man Carlos has been unending. Just as the secret services that created it had hoped. In book after book, in country after country, in Sweden, France, in Great Britain, in the United States, in works purporting to be serious academic studies, again and again one finds among the sources quoted the same names whose works have been examined in this appendix.

And the Western secret services begat Crozier and François Lebrette; and Crozier and Lebrette begat Smith, Payne and Dobson; and Smith, Payne and Dobson begat Claire Sterling and Sterling begat General Alexander Haig and William Casey . . .

For Claire Sterling there was a sting in the tail concerning the allegations she had made about Henri Curiel.

Curiel was murdered in Paris in May 1978, nearly three years before *The Terror Network* was published. After the book's publication his widow and a former associate, Joyce Blau, sued Claire Sterling. Part of her defence was that there had been errors made in the French translation, but the main thrust of her defence was that she was not accusing Curiel of being a KGB agent, she was merely presenting a hypothesis. What had been asserted by the author on publication to be 'not a book of fiction. It deals with facts' was now reduced by that same author to mere hypothesis. The court handed down a split decision; they accepted her plea that her suppositions should not be regarded as having been an assumption of truth, but she was fined for the comments she had made about Joyce Blau and the court ordered that two passages of her book should be blacked out. Sterling and her French publisher were also ordered to pay for the publication in two French newspapers of the court's findings.

Before this court case Henri Curiel's family had been attempting since his murder to obtain access to a 1977

Government investigation into Curiel. Despite a court order the Minister of the Interior refused to hand the family a copy of the report. In June 1981 a new French government and a new Minister of the Interior obliged. The report fully exonerated Henri Curiel and stated that all allegations made by the previous government about Curiel, that he was involved in subversion and gave assistance to pro-Arab terrorists, were 'without foundation'.

As 1981 progressed so did the Reagan Administration's preoccupation with Colonel Qathafi. Millions of dollars of aid, at Haig's and Casey's instigation, were funnelled to Chad Rebel Defence Minister Habre to assist him in his battle against Libyan forces that the Libyan leader had sent into Chad to assist the ruling government. News of this action leaked in the form of 'A Plan to Overthrow Qathafi'. The White House issued a denial, though of course the ultimate aim of such covert action was perfectly described in that *Newsweek* headline.

By July, Casey and his colleagues were convinced that Qathafi had designs on Niger, not least for its uranium yellowcake. Overt action joined covert – a US naval exercise in territorial waters claimed by the Libyan leader culminated in August in US fighter jets shooting down two Libyan air force planes. The pressure was stepped up with a series of belligerent statements. A few days after the downing of the Libyan planes Qathafi was in Ethiopia; during a conversation with the country's leader Qathafi allegedly declared that he was going to have President Reagan killed. The National Security Agency, NSA, allegedly subsequently intercepted the Libyan leader uttering similar threats during a telephone conversation. Security in the United States went on maximum alert. A week later, with no assassination attempt, the Administration relaxed, with the exception of CIA chief Casey.

In October he persuaded the President to send a mixed team of Pentagon, State and CIA officials to Morocco to assist King Hassan after guerrillas in the country had attacked a garrison. Libyan-backed guerrillas, or so the CIA believed.

The reports that Qathafi was planning to have the President of the United States assassinated became a veritable flood. Casey does not appear for one moment to have addressed himself to the question that they begged. If one Head of State was proposing to have another murdered, how come the world and his wife knew about it? Neither did the CIA chief ever ponder the curious fact that virtually all of these reports only began to emerge after he had issued a global directive to all CIA bureau chiefs requesting the initiating of a disinformation campaign against Qathafi.

Casey sought not confirmation but affirmation. He got it in spades.

It came from New Delhi from 'the relative of a Libyan diplomat' who wrote an anonymous letter. It came from a 'casual informant' with 'excellent access to senior Libyan military officers'; this particular source also stated that the Libyans were planning to murder US Ambassador Rabb in Rome.

In September 1981 Casey received a 'report' that the Libyans were planning a kamikaze-style attack on the aircraft carrier USS *Nimitz*. In October a series of reports to Casey, again allegedly from 'an informant with access to senior Libyan intelligence' put every US embassy throughout the world on maximum alert. A Libyan hit squad, according to the information, had been unleashed. It was either a very big squad or one with the capacity to move at the speed of light, its simultaneous targets were the US embassies in Paris, Rome, Athens, Beirut, Tunis, London and Madrid.

The Reagan Administration was fond, overly fond, of describing Colonel Qathafi as 'paranoiac'; by late October many of its members were demonstrating acute paranoia. They were convinced that Qathafi was about to attack, the problem was that they were not sure where. Ambassador Rabb was rushed onto a plane at Milan and flown home without being given time to pack a suitcase, 'for his own protection'. A Libyan hit team was reported to be in Rome, then a further report from Italian intelligence declared that they had moved on, destination unknown.

Another informant, this time claiming to have 'just left a Libyan training camp', described details of the training exercises. These, the informer alleged, included simulated attacks on a Presidential car convoy. For good measure this man also stated that during training they had been told that if Reagan proved too difficult a target then Vice President Bush, Secretary of State Haig and Defense Secretary Weinberger were to be assassinated.

By late November 1981 White House staff were routinely sending out decoy car caravans around Washington while the President took to travelling in an unmarked car. A ring of surface ground-to-air missiles was placed around the White House. A team of crack snipers and marksmen took up positions on the roof of the White House. A siege mentality gripped the Reagan Administration.

Vice President George Bush gave clear evidence that cool thinking was in short supply when he launched a verbal attack on Qathafi which included chastising him for protecting 'The Ugandan Madman, Idi Amin'. If Bush really believed that, then it was further evidence that Casey's intelligence-gathering left a great deal to be desired. Amin had been living under the protection of the Saudi Arabian rulers for several years.

Crisis meetings of the National Security Council became the order of the day. During the first week of December the marriage of disinformation, and these many reports of Qathafi-inspired terrorism were nothing more than that, reached its perfect climax. The *Washington Post*, the *New York Times* and then the rest of the American media carried stories that a Libyan hit team was attempting to enter the United States. Target: the President. Further reports elaborated the theme – there were now two hit teams, both controlled by Carlos the Jackal.

Composite pictures of five of the 'killers' were carried by press and TV. Reagan's top aides, Meese, Baker and

Deaver, caught the paranoia and were given twenty-four-hour Secret Service armed guards. A secret service car tailed Deaver's daughter as she journeyed to and from school. The President decided that the risk was too great to turn on the Christmas tree lights in Pennsylvania Avenue. He did it by remote control from the Oval Office.

Reagan not only turned on the lights but turned up the heat on Qathafi. America's oil companies were ordered to pull out employees working in Libya, some 1,500 personnel. Visa restrictions for anyone wishing to travel to Libya were announced. Libya was declared off limits for Americans.

Every border control point, particularly those on the Mexican border, was put on maximum alert. Then it was leaked that the hit squads would come over the Canadian border. If members of the Senate Sub Committee that Claire Sterling had testified in front of had not been too sure who Carlos was, the American public was very quickly informed. The newspapers were full of his exploits, many of them grossly inaccurate, but it all assisted in increasing the fear and hostility that was being directed towards Qathafi.

Speaking from his Tripoli base on ABC Television, Colonel Qathafi denounced Reagan as a liar and accused the American Administration of waging terrorism against Libya, 'militarily, economically and psychologically'. He challenged Reagan to produce the evidence. For good measure he also denied harbouring Carlos.

Senate Intelligence Committee Vice-Chairman Moynihan, a man well placed to know the truth, recounted,

'It's Qathafi that's the liar, and a mad dictator. We have concrete evidence that there have been officials of the United States government targeted.'

The President weighed in.

'I would not believe a word Qathafi says if I were you. We have the evidence and he knows it.'

To the President the evidence was 'irrefutable'. Reagan

would in the coming years talk frequently of 'irrefutable evidence' concerning Qathafi's alleged terrorist activities.

Meanwhile, the President's Secretary of State, Haig, had not been idle. In the intelligence reports of Carlos-led Libyan hit squads he saw powerful confirmation of Sterling's allegations not only about Carlos but also about 'The Daddy Warbucks of Terrorism'. He approved a series of covert operations involving the Defense Department, the CIA and US and Egyptian forces against Qathafi. Everything short of an actual land invasion of Libya was given the green light.

Reagan initiated a feasibility study for 'a military response against Libya in the event of a further Libyan attempt to assassinate American officials or attack US facilities'. The study concluded with five 'graduated responses' that ranged from bombing selected Libyan targets through to a Navy Seal commando-style attack on Libyan vessels anchored in Tripoli.

Shortly after their media interchange Reagan sent a top secret letter to Qathafi. He asserted that he had verifiable information about the planned Libyan attacks and threatened massive retaliation if a Libyan-sponsored attack on a United States official occurred anywhere in the world.

American immigration officials received a further warning from the Administration. 'Carlos is extremely dangerous and will not hesitate to fire.'

Asked by Dan Rather of CBS if the reports of the hit squads were untrue, President Reagan responded,

'No, we had too much information from too many sources and we had our facts straight. We tried to sit on them. We tried to keep that all quiet . . . but our information was valid.'

It was not valid. It was not true. Not a shred of the 'irrefutable evidence' stood up either to CIA analysis or State Department study.

From a CIA report:

'Subsequent reports on actual plans to carry out attacks against senior US Government officials, however, have come from sources with only indirect access, whose credibility is open to question. It is possible that some of the reporting may have been generated because informants are aware that we are seeking this information.'

The State Department conclusion was that the stories of the Carlos-led hit squads were examples of 'disinformation feeding off itself'.

The vast bulk of this disinformation could be traced directly to one CIA source, a wealthy Iranian arms dealer, Manucher Ghorbanifar, a man who fails CIA polygraph tests as regularly as other men change their shirts. William Casey was fully aware of this yet allowed himself and others within the Administration, up to and including the President, to be persuaded of the validity of the reports that Carlos and a dozen killers were making tracks for the White House.

Ghorbanifar is a man of many parts, entirely appropriate for a man who would be at the very heart of the Irangate affair. The CIA might consider him an 'asset', so does the Israeli Mossad, so too does Iran's secret service. He had floated the fantasies about Qathafi and Carlos to serve his friends in Tel Aviv. The fact that he was telling the head of the CIA what he wanted to hear made his task immeasurably easier.

When it was established that the allegations made by Claire Sterling and the earlier writers concerning Carlos and the Soviet 'Terror Network' were the product of a large amount of intelligence disinformation, no apology to the Soviets was made either by Haig or any other member of the Reagan Administration. That same silence followed the conclusions of the CIA and the State Department that they had been very active participants in a disinformation campaign that first targeted Qathafi and then falsely linked him with Carlos.

That is how the Hitler Syndrome works, failure to reveal the facts, the truth, is a crucial element in ensuring that ultimately the Syndrome is effective.

It was applied to Carlos, it was applied to the Cold War. It was applied to Qathafi and Libya.

'Libya is an American problem,' the Soviet Ambassador to the United States, Anatoliy Dobrynin, remarked to Secretary of State General Alexander Haig. That was in early February 1981 at only their second meeting after Ronald Reagan had entered the White House. Haig and the other members of the new Administration fully understood the signal from Moscow contained in the Ambassador's observation. Hostile acts perpetrated against Soviet client states such as Syria or countries such as Iran might elicit from the Soviets an equally hostile response but it was open season on Libya. For the next eleven years the open season has continued.

A decade of American disinformation campaigns aimed at Qathafi. A decade of claims of 'irrefutable evidence' of Libyan involvement in an ever growing number of terrorist acts. The Reagan Administration's pathological obsession with securing the downfall of Qathafi had culminated in the night bombing raids of April 1986. An attack encouraged by people like Lieutenant Colonel Oliver North, a man who according to Constantine Menges's account lived in a dream world of imaginary visits from Henry Kissinger and dinners with high officials of the Reagan Administration. Menges was ideally placed to observe North, employed as he was as a special assistant to the President for national security affairs. He considered that North had 'an overactive ego'. Menges's NSC colleague Jacqueline Tillman is more explicit. Talking to Menges she observed, 'I've worked here at the NSC for some weeks now with Ollie North and I've concluded that not only is he a liar, but he's delusional, power-hungry and a danger to the President and the country.'

There is a considerable body of evidence to justify such a view and there was long before the Irangate Scandal. Colonel North was an active player in the various disinformation exercises that the Reagan Administration and United States Intelligence agencies mounted against the Libyan leader. He was actively involved in the 1981 campaign when President Reagan asserted that he had 'irrefutable evidence' that Qathafi had sent killer assassination squads into the United States to murder the President, the Secretary of State and a whole range of key political figures. The President had no evidence, irrefutable or otherwise, of such squads. What he did have was a barrel of lies created by North, the CIA, the Mossad and a Mossad agent who had failed five lie detector tests.

In November 1985 the bloodiest hijack in aviation history resulted in fifty-seven people dying, most of them when Egyptian commandos, urged on by American advisers, stormed the plane at Luqa airport, Malta. Again the Reagan Administration saw Qathafi's hand in the affair. Again they were wrong. From the evidence I obtained from the then Prime Minister of Malta, Mifsud Bonnici, from members of his staff, from Egyptian Intelligence and from Abu Nidal there is no doubt that the hijack was the work of Abu Nidal members, having been previously planned in Damascus.

In December 1985, after terrorist attacks at Rome and Vienna airports resulted in 19 deaths and many casualties, President Reagan yet again talked of 'irrefutable evidence' that linked Qathafi to the attacks. Building on this, the President then initiated a campaign to persuade his European allies to isolate Qathafi and his regime. This campaign continued despite the fact that Robert Oakley, head of the US State Department's anti-terrorist unit, was forced to admit, less than one month after the attacks, that there was 'little or no evidence to link Qathafi to the attacks'. In February 1987, after a year-long investigation into these two outrages, Italian Prosecutor Domenico Sica concluded that the attacks had in fact been planned in Syria.

These are just three instances, I could cite many others where terrorist attacks were *deliberately* laid at the wrong door, instances where 'irrefutable proof' dissolves away to black propaganda when subjected to analysis.

In early 1986 the Reagan Administration was conducting a series of secret polls. The essential aim was to establish how the people of the United States would respond to a strike against Libya. The polls also served as a useful guide to precisely how successfully the anti-Qathafi campaign was playing to the electorate. Among the privileged recipients of the conclusions arrived at by these polls were NSC staff, including Oliver North. By March 1986 the secret polls showed that public opinion favoured a military strike provided that it was quick and a 'reluctant' response rather than one resulting from United States provocation.

Within one month the proposition became a reality. On March 29th the German-Arab Friendship Society in Berlin was bombed; nine people were injured. On April 5th yet another bomb exploded in Berlin, this time at a night club, the La Belle Disco. Approximately fifty people were injured and two killed, one of the dead was an American serviceman. Yet again the American President talked of 'irrefutable evidence', this time with regard to the attack on the night club in Berlin. Initially this evidence was not shared with the public but only with some European Heads of State and Prime Ministers. A high-level United States delegation led by Vernon Walters toured the corridors of power of Europe. Walters attempted to persuade the West Germans, the French, the Italians, the Spanish and the British to join with the United States in imposing a wide range of sanctions against Libya. The German, Italian, French and Spanish governments remained unimpressed with Reagan's incontrovertible evidence: a series of intercepted messages between the Libyan Bureau in East Berlin and Tripoli that allegedly implicated the Libyans in the night club bombing. The only European leader who was convinced by the evidence was Prime Minister Thatcher.

The planes that attacked Libya at 2.00 am on the 15th of April 1986 came from British bases in the South of England and from the US Sixth Fleet in the Mediterranean. The F-111 bombers from Britain were obliged to fly via the Bay of Biscay. Both the

French and the Spanish refused to grant permission for them to overfly their territories.

The attack was very precisely timed to coincide with the main television news slots in the United States at 7.00 pm. Two hours later President Reagan went on network television to explain to the nation why he had mobilized over thirty billion dollars worth of military hardware to strike at a Third World country. He played garbled fragments of the intercepts with explanatory sub-titles. What had failed to convince Prime Minister Chirac and the others failed to convince me. To this day these tapes have never been handed over for independent evaluation. Under great pressure from the Germans, *copies* of the tapes were handed over to the German Intelligence Service (BND). Fragments talking of a 'wedding', 'a happy event' and 'good work' left the BND unconvinced. They arrived at an interpretation markedly different from the American version, and in view of the fact that it had been the BND who had originally cracked the Libyan code years earlier, the German interpretation must be taken seriously.

According to the American version the tapes were alleged to contain:

4th April. Libyan Bureau to Tripoli. 'Await a development tomorrow morning, as God wills.'

5th April. Libyan Bureau to Tripoli. 'At 1.30 this morning a successful operation was accomplished without leaving a trace of our identity.'

The alleged third intercept was from Tripoli congratulating their colleagues in East Berlin.

The intelligence chiefs in Bonn, Paris, Rome and Tel Aviv did not think the tapes were genuine. Such explicit instructions had never been intercepted before. The ability of satellite surveillance is known to all, including the Libyans. The Libyans, in the view of the intelligence world, have never been responsible for a direct attack on Americans. Reagan's pathological obsession about Qathafi was well known in political circles. The conclusion that the experts, at least the ones I have talked to, have come to is that 'evidence' was deliberately manufactured by members of the National Security Council. Evidence that would be so compelling that it would remove any doubts from the President's mind about unleashing his forces. As of early 1993 the NSA (the US National Security Agency) North African specialists have been denied access to the 'evidence'. The normal intelligence channels for translating and interpreting have therefore been deliberately bypassed and ignored.

Boasting of how good the intercepts were, Defense Secretary Weinberger and Secretary of State Shultz stated that, having monitored the April 4th message, American military police had been fully mobilized and were immediately clearing the bars and discos. Weinberger asserted that the military police were 'just fifteen minutes late' in clearing La Belle Disco.

Major Ruth la Fontaine, deputy chief of West Berlin's military police, has confirmed that there was no mobilization, no clearance of bars and discos, 'It was a normal day for us.'

The attack that occurred at the German-Arab Friendship Society in Berlin on the 29th of March was the work of a Syrian-controlled agent, Ahmed Hasi. He was initially arrested on suspicion of having perpetrated the second attack at the night club. At the same time Nezar Hindawi was arrested in London after attempting to blow up an El Al passenger plane. Hindawi was also a Syrian agent. Hindawi and Hasi are brothers. Two terrorist operations masterminded by Syrian Intelligence and, sandwiched in between, La Belle Disco.

In the wastepaper basket in Ahmed Hasi's Berlin apartment police found a drawing of the dance floor and surrounding area, the alcoves, the exits, of La Belle Disco. The crater caused by the bomb explosion in the German-Arab Friendship Society was virtually identical to that left after the La Belle Disco bombing. According to a police report it was 'identical in dimensions, depth and appearance'.

One of the number of intelligence experts with whom

I discussed the La Belle Disco bombing was Christian Lochte, President of the Hamburg office for the Protection of the Constitution, who said, 'It is quite clear to me that the disco bombing in Berlin was not planned by the Libyans. If one were to point the finger at a particular country, then one should point the finger at Syria.'

He was equally categoric about the attacks at Vienna and Rome airports, 'Based on our own investigation, also the information that Mossad and the Italian services had made available to us, there was absolutely no doubt that it was a question of the Abu Nidal group and that they came from Syria and Lebanon, but not from Libya. The CIA, at least the representatives that we spoke to, didn't want to know. For them it had to be Qathafi. The TWA aircraft that was bombed in mid-air killing four Americans – that was done by a group based in Iraq. The evidence was overwhelming. Again the Americans would not listen. It became clear to us that no matter what happened, or where, the Americans were going to find a line to Qathafi. La Belle was for them an ideal opportunity. Without secret service proof or evidence and after the American people had been emotionally prepared, it was then the ideal opportunity for them to make a raid on Libya. From the investigations we have made and in particular the assistance from our British colleagues in Berlin, we established such a close connection between this attack and the attack on the German-Arab club in Berlin. It was clear that the Syrians had paid for both attacks in order to deal with opponents to their regime. For Asad to make it clear, as he has, that Syria had nothing to do with these attacks is, as far as our experience with the Syrians is concerned, a worthless declaration.'

As for the tapes of the intercepted messages – the sole evidence that the President of the United States produced to justify the attack on Libya – Christian Lochte said,

'They would never dare to present the original tapes to us. The intelligence services, not only of this country, but of others, know the truth. We know that it was Syria and not Libya.'

Notwithstanding that the United States President is forbidden by law to assassinate or attempt to assassinate foreign Heads of State, the attack carried out on April 15th 1986 had as its prime objective the assassination of Colonel Mu'Ammar Qathafi. Although there were secondary targets which included military bases at Benghazi, the prime target of the 1986 attack on Tripoli was the Libyan leader. Colonel North was later to state that the designated targets were 'the command and control center and administrative buildings of El-Aziziya Barracks'. None of them was hit. A member of the United States Air Force intelligence unit who took part in the pre-raid briefing said to me,

'Nine of the eighteen F-111s that left from the UK were specifically briefed for targets within the barracks. Two of those nine were specifically briefed to bomb Qathafi's residence inside the barracks where he was living with his family. His precise whereabouts? We had excellent intelligence confirming he was inside his residence.'

Each of the F-111s carried four 2,000 lb bombs. North was also later to tell colleagues that the intelligence as to precisely where Qathafi was on that night came from Israel, with the last fix on his position coming less than three hours before the first bombs fell. It is common practice in the West, when any country wishes to mask the real source of its intelligence, to attribute it to Israel. The Israelis never object, it serves as excellent PR. As revealed in my account of my second interview with Colonel Qathafi, a far more likely source for this information was the royal palace in Morocco.

In the event the first bomb to drop on Tripoli fell on Qathafi's home. He was sleeping in a different room from his wife, who, troubled by a back injury, was resting in a nearby room. Hana, his adopted daughter aged fifteen months, was killed, his eight other children and his wife Safiya were all hospitalized, some with serious injuries.

The day after the attack Prime Minister Margaret

Thatcher, explaining to the House of Commons why she had given the United States permission to use aircraft bases in the United Kingdom, said, 'The President assured me that the operation would be limited to clearly defined targets related to terrorism, and that the risk of collateral damage would be minimized.' Her explanation continued with the information that using the F-111s 'would provide the safest means of achieving particular objectives with the lowest possible risk both of civilian casualties in Libya and of casualties among United States personnel'.

Thus, if one accepts Thatcher's explanation, she granted permission on humanitarian grounds.

The word 'collateral' is obscene-speak for you, me, our homes and any other target that gets hit accidentally.

Having used thirty billion dollars' worth of military equipment, President Reagan failed in his prime objective: Qathafi lived. There was, however, considerable 'collateral' damage. 41 people were killed, a further 226 were injured. The French Embassy was destroyed. The foreign embassies of six other countries suffered varying degrees of damage. Twenty private residences were obliterated, a further 587 were damaged.

When President Reagan addressed the American nation two hours after the attack, his auto-cue had to be amended. Passages written *before* the start of the raid that justified the killing of Qathafi were deleted. Among the remarks that Reagan did make was:

'Today, we have done what we had to do. If necessary we shall do it again.'

At first the Reagan Administration denied that there were any civilian casualties. Then, when press and television reporters began filing their despatches around the world, this was amended to an assertion that any civilian casualties were caused by the Libyans themselves, the argument presumably being that defence missiles fired at American planes had fallen back directly to earth. When the physical evidence of made in the USA bomb fragments was shown on television the Administration conceded that perhaps one or two bombs had missed their intended targets. The bodyguard of lies flowing from the Administration seemed to be without end.

Among the 'collateral' damage was eighteen-year-old Raafat Bassam Ghussein, a young girl who had returned from her English school to spend the Easter holidays with her family. They lived next to the French Embassy. Four others died in the same building when the house sustained a direct hit.

Raafat's father Bassam, a man still grievously pining for his daughter seven years after her death, told me of watching on the day before the attack as the staff in the French Embassy removed cabinet after cabinet of documents. 'They said the decorators were coming in.' French Embassy staff, like other European Embassy personnel, had been alerted by their respective governments to the imminent bombing raid. No-one told ordinary people like the Ghussein family. Bassam, educated in the United States, working for an American oil company in Libya, with a jewel of a daughter returning from her English school only to be pursued by a plane based in England. Death written most horrifically.

Sleeping in the back of his home was just part of the reason that Qathafi survived, there were others. The thirty-billion-dollar contract on his life failed to deliver principally because the laser-guidance systems on at least four of the nine F-111s briefed to attack Qathafi's home malfunctioned. Those pilots had to turn back. A fifth F-111 dropped its bomb-load on a residential section of Tripoli, killing, among others, eighteen-year-old Raafat. Air Force Intelligence in its top secret debriefing describes this as 'pilot error'.

The Hitler Syndrome was applied with such powerful effect against Qathafi that it was eventually used to justify an act of State terrorism perpetrated by the United States fully aided and abetted by Great Britain. Or is it only an act of terrorism when 'they' do it to 'us'?

As I have observed earlier within this appendix, Claire Sterling, referring to her 'two and a half years' research' for her book, records the fact that she had talked to 'Government officials and police in ten countries from Sweden to Lebanon . . .' One of the Government officials whom she subsequently talked to while investigating the attempt on the life of Pope John Paul the Second was Christian Lochte.

'She once sat in that chair you are sitting in now and we tried with regard to the background on the attempt on the life of the Pope to make it clear to her that the KGB were not involved. It took a long time but we explained it to her very carefully. But she became more and more angry, she didn't want to hear it. Later I was at a conference in Washington and she also appeared there at a reception. I introduced her to a member of the CIA and told her that also in his opinion the KGB had nothing to do with the attempt on the life of the Pope. It was so clear, so obvious.'

Christian Lochte also had an opinion on William Casey, the head of the CIA during the Reagan years.

'Sterling had a great influence on Casey and high ranking people in the CIA. He was a very nice old gentleman. I always imagined him in front of me, sitting in a rocking chair on the verandah somewhere in the Mid West with the natural wisdom of a farmer. And so he's predestined for any kind of nonsense. The main thing was that it had to be something which you had to go around one or two corners with your thoughts to arrive at. That, he and others considered intelligence. Show them a simple explanation and they reject it. It can't be true. Give them a conspiracy involving the Soviets and they'll grab it with both hands.'

So much time, money and effort devoted entirely to black propaganda. Surely the truth about the Soviet Union, Qathafi and Carlos should suffice? Communism as applied and interpreted under a succession of Soviet leaders was not merely Godless, not only evil, but fatally inefficient and had inevitably to self-destruct on economic grounds alone. The Libyan leader has a dangerously naïve vision of world revolution. Through the money, arms and support that he has exported from his country the innocent have died and the blameless have been maimed. This is an indisputable fact. Actions that justify reactions. Why the over-kill? That Carlos is a vicious amoral killer, a mercenary without the comforting cloak of ideals, a man who should most certainly be brought to justice, not a creation of the KGB but a product of our times, is also indisputable fact. No need for fantasies with these three elements. The truth is awful enough.

Why poison the well?

The man I had met twice in Lebanon was without doubt an impostor, but much of what he told me was true. My own research and investigations have established that beyond doubt. His truth was not confined to facts about the real Carlos. It is also true that a disinformation exercise created by the intelligence services of France, Great Britain, the United States and Israel surrounded Carlos within days of his leap to freedom from 9 rue Toullier. It is also true that that disinformation exercise was given a terrible potency by the myths that poured with increasing volume from the popular press. And these aspects are perhaps the greatest obscenity in this man's life, a life that is filled with so many obscenities.

But for the myths and the disinformation, Carlos would have been of no further use to Wadi Haddad. He had destroyed Haddad's European infrastructure. He had killed Moukharbel, caused Nydia Tobon, Angela Otaola and Silva Masmela to be imprisoned. Years of work, of planning, had been wiped out. Haddad would never again have such an operational base in Europe. What saved Carlos from summary execution when he eventually returned to Haddad's base in the summer of 1975 was that the myth of Carlos had so perfectly replaced the tawdry reality. It gave Carlos an enormous value in Haddad's eyes. Above everything Haddad believed in the philosophy of terror. Now he had at his disposal an all-powerful image of terror very largely created by Western Intelligence. He was quick to appreciate the potential. So were others, including Saddam Hussein, who conceived the idea for the attack on OPEC headquarters, who had himself followed the Carlos affair at the rue Toullier and the subsequent press coverage with great interest. Creating a monster which could then be used to perform monstrous acts had not been the intention of the various Intelligence services when they had applied the Hitler Syndrome to Carlos but then in this life you do not always get what you want.

APPENDIX TWO

'Now everything is under control. We've just had a very quiet weekend.'

Israeli Major to author
Monday, 13th February 1989

CHRONICLE OF EVENTS IN THE GAZA STRIP
From Friday 10th February 1989 to Monday 13th February 1989

• FRIDAY

Curfew has been imposed on the following locations:
Jabalia Refugee Camp: 6th consecutive day.
Al Shati' (Beach) Refugee Camp: 6th day.
An-Nasser and Sheikh Radwan suburbs of Gaza City: 3rd day.
Beit Lahia Housing Compound near Gaza: 5th day.
Town of Rafah and nearby Rafah Refugee Camp: 3rd day.
Nusseirat Refugee Camp: 3rd day.
Khan Yunis Refugee Camp and Al Amal suburb of Khan Yunis City: 7th day.
Total general strike has continued all over the Gaza Strip for the fourth consecutive day.

The military authorities placed checkposts on all entrances to Gaza while mechanized and foot army patrols took to the main streets of the city. Some soldiers even took up positions on top of high buildings in the city to monitor events in anticipation of further unrest.

Checkposts were also erected on entrances to Breij Refugee Camp as well as in the city centre of Khan Yunis. Soldiers were seen watching the main mosque in the city from a distance, fearing that demonstrations may break out soon after the Friday prayer.

Fierce clashes erupted between Palestinians and Israeli troops in Rafah Refugee Camp. The demonstrators pelted troops with stones and empty bottles. The soldiers opened fire, and shot rounds of rubber bullets as well. Anwar Suleiman Al Sheikh Eed (15) was hit by a rubber bullet in his left eye, which had to be removed later at the Gaza Ophthalmic Hospital.

SATURDAY

This morning curfew was imposed on the village of Beit Hanoun and on the Al Sabra suburb of Gaza City. Curfews continued in Jabalia, Beit Lahia and Rafah. In Nusseirat, Khan Yunis and Shati' Refugee Camps, the curfew has been lifted. The army also lifted the curfew that was imposed on Sheikh Radwan and An Nasser suburbs in Gaza six days ago.

Demonstrations and clashes broke out this morning in Khan Yunis city and the nearby refugee camp that bears the same name. Demonstrators fought with troops and threw stones at them. The soldiers opened fire, injuring Jum'ah Assar (16) when a plastic bullet hit his face. Khaled Abu Dukka (17) and Ayman Kamel Jbeir (19) were beaten up by soldiers. Both were taken to Nasser Hospital in Khan Yunis where it was established that they had broken limbs as well as bruises all over their bodies.

Shops were re-opened all over the Gaza Strip this morning after a four-day total commercial strike.

A group of Palestinian youths stoned an Israeli military patrol in the market area in Gaza's Omar Al Mukhtar Street. The soldiers used tear-gas canisters and as a result a number of local residents were rushed to Al Ahli and Al Shifa hospitals.

Residents of Rafah Refugee Camp defied the curfew imposed on their camp by the Israeli troops by taking to the streets and holding huge demonstrations. They threw stones at Israeli troops who in return opened fire and used tear-gas canisters. A number of youths were chased by soldiers through the narrow alleyways of the camp.

Four people were admitted to Al Ahli Hospital in Gaza for treatment of injuries sustained when Israeli soldiers roughed them up. The four are Ashraf Kamel Sakik (25) from Al Daraj suburb; Mohammed Ali Shehadeh Zaqout (43) from Shati' Refugee Camp; Rami Mohammed Abu Al Kheir (12) and Yasser Mohammed Al Silk (14) from Al Zaitoun suburb.

Supervised by the military governor of the area, soldiers and security branches conducted a mass-arrest campaign in the village of Beit Hanoun. Soldiers combed the area and nearby fields looking for suspects. More than a dozen youths were arrested. At least eight others had their identity cards confiscated by soldiers and were ordered to report to the military government headquarters. Meanwhile, a curfew was imposed on the village, during which time soldiers stormed some houses and searched them. Soldiers also conducted a massive arrest campaign in the Al Sabra suburb of Gaza.

SUNDAY

Curfew was lifted in Jabalia Refugee Camp and Beit Lahia Housing Compound. The curfew imposed on Rafah four days ago was lifted and so was the curfew clamped on Beit Hanoun village yesterday, during which soldiers arrested a number of suspects.

Demonstrations broke out this afternoon between Israeli soldiers and Palestinians from Shati' Refugee Camp. They followed what local refugees said were provocations by soldiers. The Palestinians threw stones and the soldiers used tear-gas and rubber bullets. Mohammed Al Abed Joudeh (65) was hit in his right eye by a rubber bullet. He was rushed to the Gaza Ophthalmic Hospital for treatment. A number of refugee residents of the camp were beaten up by soldiers and had to be hospitalized. Among them were:

Sami Abdul Karim Matar, 24
Fakhri Awad, 40
Ra'fat Al Ajrami, 15
Nazira Mohammed Abu Odeh, 29 (female)
Samir Abed Issa, 45
Abdul Mun'em Sidki Yunis, 15
Mohammed Yousef Abu Odeh, 35

At noon clashes erupted between Israeli soldiers and Palestinian demonstrators in Rafah when Arab youths stoned an army patrol. Soldiers used rubber bullets and tear-gas and consequently a number of people were injured. Among them were:

Mas'ad Daoud Yassin, 14, hit in the right hand by a rubber bullet.
Amal Atiyeh Abu Ideh (female), 19, hit in the head by a rubber bullet.

The army confiscated three private cars, Peugeot made, from their owners in Jabalia Refugee Camp and threw them into a water pool (sic).

Palestinian youths attacked two army patrols in Jabalia Refugee Camp, pelting them with stones until the soldiers were forced to leave the area. Later the youths attacked an army post in the camp. The soldiers, meanwhile, chased the youths into the narrow alleyways of the camp but failed to arrest any of them.

MONDAY

Israeli soldiers last night broke into several houses in Jabalia Refugee Camp and searched them; some of the residents had their identity cards confiscated and were ordered to report to the military government headquarters for questioning.

Demonstrations broke out this morning in Rafah

Refugee Camp near the UNRWA preparatory schools after soldiers harassed a number of students. The students pelted the soldiers with stones and the troops used tear-gas canisters. A few canisters were shot inside one of the UNRWA-run schools. A wave of demonstrations later spread all over the city and the neighbouring refugee camp. The army then used live ammunition and a number of people were reported injured, either by bullets or from tear-gas inhalation. Ahmad Khalil Al Yazouri (14) was one of those wounded, when he was hit in the head by a steel marble. He was rushed to Nasser Hospital in Khan Yunis but, due to his critical condition, he was then transferred to Tal Hashomeir Hospital in Tel Aviv where he died of his wounds. Ahmad's brother, Basel, was among the first wave of Palestinians killed by Israeli troops at the beginning of the uprising. He was shot dead on January 9th, 1988. Abdul Aziz Dandoul (15) was also shot in the head with a steel marble and taken to Tal Hashomeir Hospital in Tel Aviv. Soon after the clashes the army clamped a curfew on the Rafah Refugee Camp.

An arbitrary wave of arrests was carried out by Israeli troops in the Sabra suburb of Gaza City. Those arrested were between 15 and 22 years old.

Palestinian students stoned Israeli soldiers stationed at the army post inside Jabalia Refugee Camp. Soldiers opened fire and chased a group of students into one of the UNRWA-run vocational training centres. The soldiers, wielding batons in their hands, beat up a number of people, among them Shadi Bader Abu Dhaher (16), who was hit in the head by a steel marble and whose injury was described as moderate, and Fahimeh Dheeb, a 34-year-old woman who was beaten by soldiers and suffered a broken arm. All the wounded were taken to the UNRWA clinic in the camp.

There were renewed clashes in the Shaboura suburb of Rafah Refugee Camp. Israeli soldiers used live ammunition and tear-gas to disperse the demonstrators. Mohammed Ahmad Mahmoud (15) was hit in the right thigh by a rubber bullet. He was taken to Nasser Hospital in Khan Yunis. Kahdijeh Abdul Hadi Nusrani, a 28-year-old woman, was rushed to hospital after she fainted on inhaling tear-gas.

Demonstrations broke out early in the morning in Shati' Refugee Camp. The army opened fire and Ahmad Mohammed Rashed (17) was wounded in the right hand. Others were beaten up, including Ra'ed Atiyeh Abdul Mu'ti (20); Hamad Mu'een Al Masri (29), and Omar Safi Salameh (23). They were taken to Shifa Hospital in Gaza.

APPENDIX THREE

ANTONIO PEREIRA'S STORY
A case history of one man's journey into terrorism

What follows is based on information acquired from a variety of sources, French and Brazilian Intelligence, Amnesty International, The International Association of Democratic Jurists, interviews, most notably with Pereira's former Brazilian lawyer, Annina de Cavalho, French, Belgian and Italian legal sources.

Antonio Expedito Carvalho Pereira was born in January 1931 into a poor family in Itagui in the province of Rio Grande do Sul, Brazil.

As a result of great effort and no little talent he obtained an excellent education and graduated in law. Further study resulted in more qualifications and he obtained a University professorship; he combined this post in Sao Paulo with an active law practice.

Between 1961 and 1964 Brazil experienced a fertile period of political and social expression. Different sectors of society achieved remarkable progress, in organizing their respective institutions, their trade unions and in their aspirations to carry out democratic reforms. Agrarian reforms began to take place, the national wealth started to be more fairly distributed, the country was beginning to move away from its almost complete reliance in so many areas on the United States. Like Carlos's native Venezuela, Brazil has had a history of dictatorships, political repression and torture; between 1960 and 1964 it was going through a period of democratic rule. Enter the Generals. In April 1964 democracy was forcibly replaced with a military dictatorship. In 1968, after four years of increasingly repressive rule, there was a 'coup within a coup' and, while still under a military regime, the country tilted even further to the right. Added to a long list of already existing curtailments to civil rights came new proclamations. The concept of Habeas Corpus was abolished, the already stringent censorship became draconian. Violence towards the individual, particularly the individual who publicly objected to this state of affairs, became institutionalized. There were Government Death Squads. Disappearances became everyday events. Guerrilla activity increased as any utterance against a government action, whether domestic or foreign, was considered by the regime to be 'an act of subversion'. All 'political offences' were tried by one of the military tribunals.

This was the reality of life for Pereira and his fellow citizens. As one of the ever-diminishing number of lawyers who took on the defence of clients accused of 'political offences', he was a marked man. He was double-marked for teaching law at Sao Paulo University. This placed him in the regime's category of 'dangerous intellectuals'. As a lawyer who also defended students, workers with left-wing sympathies and, on one occasion, the guerrilla leader Carlos Lamarca, it was only a matter of time before the regime came for him. They came on March 3rd, 1969.

At ten in the morning fifteen officers, Army sergeants and members of the Political Police forced their way into his office in Sao Paulo. Another squad surrounded the building. The Brazilian standard method of arrest circa 1969 was then applied: he was handcuffed, badly beaten up, then dragged unconscious out into the street, Calle del Riachuelo, and taken to the barracks of the Army police. He was held there for seventeen days.

During each and every one of those seventeen days he was tortured. The police wanted to know his relationship and dealings with all his clients. He refused to tell them. On the first day he was suspended by his feet for seven hours, beaten continuously, kept constantly wet, subjected to electric shocks in the mouth, ears, nape of the neck, genital organs and tendons. When he lost consciousness Sergeant Roberto of the Army police pushed one electrified wire into his urethra and another into his rectum.

These tortures continued, with a number of variations. Among them was a device known as 'the Armchair of the Dragon'. The victim is sat in an armchair similar to that found in many hairdressers; it is equipped with metal arms and legs through which an electric current is passed.

Pereira continued to refuse to give his captors what they wanted. His wife, Nazareth Oliveira Pereira, was brought in, and Antonio was forced to watch while she was stripped and then tortured; she in turn was forced to watch while he was tortured. Next they brought in his three brothers, Joao, José and Francisco. All were tortured in his presence. Then they brought in his secretary, Celia Hatsumi Heto, and his driver, Lazaro, who were stripped and subjected to the same treatment. Finally they arrested his ten-year-old daughter, Teresa Cristina. Again Antonio Pereira was forced to watch while she was tortured under the direction of Army Captain Antonio Carlos Pivatto.

I have the full names and ranks of thirteen other creatures – I cannot call them men – who participated in these torturing sessions, as well as the names of two Commissioner-Judges who also took part, Fernandez and Simonetti. Pivatto commanded one team of torturers, another was commanded by General Luis Felipe.

On March 18th, 1969, with Pereira still refusing to oblige with either a confession or incriminating statements about his clients, he was transferred to DOPS (State Department for Political and Social Order) Central Police Station. During his two-day ordeal at this place he was subjected to the Armchair of the Dragon on at least four occasions and underwent sustained torture.

On March 20th he was brought back to the barracks and the Army police tried again for a further two weeks.

He was then moved back to the central police station, where he was held in complete isolation for four months. He was subsequently transferred to the penal colony at Tiradentes. After a total of eleven months he was again interrogated before a military tribunal presided over by a judge. He was not tried but eventually returned to the Tiradentes prison. He had been held for nearly two years when a group of guerrillas seized the Swiss ambassador to Brazil, M. Giovanni Enrico Bucher, on December 7th 1970 and demanded the release of seventy prisoners. Among those named was Antonio Pereira. He had never been charged, never tried, never sentenced.

In late January 1971, Pereira, along with the other sixty-nine prisoners, flew to Chile. Behind he had left his wife and daughter: the Brazilian regime had refused to allow them to leave and they had not been on the list of demands.

From Chile, via Algeria, Pereira and some of his fellow prisoners had by March 1971 reached Paris, where the French government eventually granted them the right to remain as political exiles. He began to create a new life. By 1973 he was involved with a wealthy Brazilian woman, Mohammed Boudia and Moukharbel, the Japanese Red Army and an exclusive art gallery. The same year he met Carlos.

APPENDIX FOUR

DECLARATION OF PRINCIPLES ON INTERIM SELF-GOVERNMENT ARRANGEMENTS

Signed by representatives of Israel and the P.L.O., Washington, D.C., September 13, 1993

The Government of the State of Israel and the P.L.O. team (in the Jordanian-Palestinian delegation to the Middle East Peace Conference) (the 'Palestinian Delegation'), representing the Palestinian people, agree that it is time to put an end to decades of confrontation and conflict, recognize their mutual legitimate and political rights, and strive to live in peaceful coexistence and mutual dignity and security and achieve a just, lasting and comprehensive peace settlement and historic reconciliation through the agreed political process. Accordingly, the two sides agree to the following principles:

Article I

AIM OF THE NEGOTIATIONS

The aim of the Israeli-Palestinian negotiations within the current Middle East peace process is, among other things, to establish a Palestinian Interim Self-Government Authority, the elected Council (the 'Council'), for the Palestinian people in the West Bank and the Gaza Strip, for a transitional period not exceeding five years, leading to a permanent settlement based on Security Council Resolutions 242 and 338.

It is understood that the interim arrangements are an integral part of the whole peace process and that the negotiations on the permanent status will lead to the implementation of Security Council Resolutions 242 and 338.

Article II

FRAMEWORK FOR THE INTERIM PERIOD

The agreed framework for the interim period is set forth in this Declaration of Principles.

Article III

ELECTIONS

1. In order that the Palestinian people in the West Bank and Gaza Strip may govern themselves according to democratic principles, direct, free and general political elections will be held for the Council under agreed supervision and international observation, while the Palestinian police will ensure public order.
2. An agreement will be concluded on the exact mode and conditions of the elections in accordance with the protocol attached as Annex I, with the goal of holding the elections not later than nine months after the entry into force of this Declaration of Principles.
3. These elections will constitute a significant interim preparatory step toward the realization of the legitimate rights of the Palestinian people and their just requirements.

Article IV

JURISDICTION

Jurisdiction of the Council will cover West Bank and Gaza Strip territory, except for issues that will be negotiated in the permanent status negotiations. The two sides view the West Bank and Gaza Strip as a single territorial unit, whose integrity will be preserved during the interim period.

Article V

TRANSITIONAL PERIOD AND PERMANENT STATUS NEGOTIATIONS

1. The five-year transitional period will begin upon the withdrawal from the Gaza Strip and Jericho area.
2. Permanent status negotiations will commence as soon as possible, but not later than the beginning of the third year of the interim period, between the Government of Israel and the Palestinian people representatives.
3. It is understood that these negotiations shall cover remaining issues, including: Jerusalem, refugees, settlements, security arrangements, borders, relations and cooperation with other neighbors, and other issues of common interest.
4. The two parties agree that the outcome of the permanent status negotiations should not be prejudiced or preempted by agreements reached for the interim period.

Article VI

PREPARATORY TRANSFER OF POWERS AND RESPONSIBILITIES

1. Upon the entry into force of this Declaration of Principles and the withdrawal from the Gaza Strip and the Jericho area, a transfer of authority from the Israeli military government and its Civil Administration to the authorized Palestinians for this task, as detailed herein, will commence. This transfer of authority will be of a preparatory nature until the inauguration of the Council.
2. Immediately after the entry into force of this Declaration of Principles and the withdrawal from the Gaza Strip and Jericho area, with the view to

promoting economic development in the West Bank and Gaza Strip, authority will be transferred to the Palestinians in the following spheres: education and culture, health, social welfare, direct taxation, and tourism. The Palestinian side will commence in building the Palestinian police force, as agreed upon. Pending the inauguration of the Council, the two parties may negotiate the transfer of additional powers and responsibilities, as agreed upon.

Article VII

INTERIM AGREEMENT

1. The Israeli and Palestinian delegations will negotiate an agreement on the interim period (the 'Interim Agreement').

2. The Interim Agreement shall specify, among other things, the structure of the Council, the number of its members, and the transfer of powers and responsibilities from the Israeli military government and its Civil Administration to the Council. The Interim Agreement shall also specify the Council's executive authority, legislative authority in accordance with Article IX below, and the independent Palestinian judicial organs.

3. The Interim Agreement shall include arrangements, to be implemented upon the inauguration of the Council, for the assumption by the Council of all of the powers and responsibilities transferred previously in accordance with Article VI above.

4. In order to enable the Council to promote economic growth, upon its inauguration, the Council will establish, among other things, a Palestinian Electricity Authority, a Gaza Sea Port Authority, a Palestinian Development Bank, a Palestinian Export Promotion Board, a Palestinian Environmental Authority, a Palestinian Land Authority and a Palestinian Water Administration Authority, and any other authorities agreed upon, in accordance

with the Interim Agreement that will specify their powers and responsibilities.

5. After the inauguration of the Council, the Civil Administration will be dissolved, and the Israeli military government will be withdrawn.

Article VIII

PUBLIC ORDER AND SECURITY

In order to guarantee public order and internal security for the Palestinians of the West Bank and the Gaza Strip, the Council will establish a strong police force, while Israel will continue to carry the responsibility for defending against external threats, as well as the responsibility for overall security of Israelis for the purpose of safeguarding their internal security and public order.

Article IX

LAWS AND MILITARY ORDERS

1. The Council will be empowered to legislate, in accordance with the Interim Agreement, within all authorities transferred to it.
2. Both parties will review jointly laws and military orders presently in force in remaining spheres.

Article X

JOINT ISRAELI-PALESTINIAN LIAISON COMMITTEE

In order to provide for a smooth implementation of this Declaration of Principles and any subsequent agreements pertaining to the interim period, upon the entry into force of this Declaration of Principles, a Joint Israeli-Palestinian Liaison Committee will be established in order to deal with issues requiring coordination, other issues of common interest, and disputes.

Article XI

ISRAELI-PALESTINIAN COOPERATION IN ECONOMIC FIELDS

Recognizing the mutual benefit of cooperation in promoting the development of the West Bank, the Gaza Strip and Israel, upon the entry into force of this Declaration of Principles, an Israeli-Palestinian Economic Cooperation Committee will be established in order to develop and implement in a cooperative manner the programs identified in the protocols attached as Annex III and Annex IV.

Article XII

LIAISON AND COOPERATION WITH JORDAN AND EGYPT

The two parties will invite the Governments of Jordan and Egypt to participate in establishing further liaison and cooperation arrangements between the Government of Israel and the Palestinian representatives, on one hand, and the Governments of Jordan and Egypt, on the other hand, to promote cooperation between them. These arrangements will include the constitution of a Continuing Committee that will decide by agreement on the modalities of admission of persons displaced from the West Bank and Gaza Strip in 1967, together with necessary measures to prevent disruption and disorder. Other matters of common concern will be dealt with by this Committee.

Article XIII

REDEPLOYMENT OF ISRAELI FORCES

1. After the entry into force of this Declaration of Principles, and not later than the eve of elections for the Council, a redeployment of Israeli military forces in the West Bank and the Gaza Strip will

take place, in addition to withdrawal of Israeli forces carried out in accordance with Article XIV.

2. In redeploying its military forces, Israel will be guided by the principle that its military forces should be redeployed outside populated areas.

3. Further redeployments to specified locations will be gradually implemented commensurate with the assumption of responsibility for public order and internal security by the Palestinian police force pursuant to Article VIII above.

Article XIV

ISRAELI WITHDRAWAL FROM THE GAZA STRIP AND JERICHO AREA

Israel will withdraw from the Gaza Strip and Jericho area, as detailed in the protocol attached as Annex II.

Article XV

RESOLUTION OF DISPUTES

1. Disputes arising out of the application or interpretation of this Declaration of Principles, or any subsequent agreements pertaining to the interim period, shall be resolved by negotiations through the Joint Liaison Committee to be established pursuant to Article X above.

2. Disputes which cannot be settled by negotiations may be resolved by a mechanism of conciliation to be agreed upon by the parties.

3. The parties may agree to submit to arbitration disputes relating to the interim period, which cannot be settled through reconciliation. To this end, upon the agreement of both parties, the parties will establish an Arbitration Committee.

Article XVI

ISRAELI-PALESTINIAN COOPERATION CONCERNING REGIONAL PROGRAMS

Both parties view the multilateral working groups as an appropriate instrument for promoting a 'Marshall Plan,' the regional programs and other programs, including special programs for the West Bank and Gaza Strip, as indicated in the protocol attached as Annex IV.

Article XVII

MISCELLANEOUS PROVISIONS

1. This Declaration of Principles will enter into force one month after its signing.
2. All protocols annexed to this Declaration of Principles and Agreed Minutes pertaining thereto shall be regarded as an integral part hereof.

Annex I

PROTOCOL ON THE MODE AND CONDITIONS OF ELECTIONS

1. Palestinians of Jerusalem who live there will have the right to participate in the election process, according to an agreement between the two sides.
2. In addition, the election agreement should cover, among other things, the following issues:
    a. the system of elections;
    b. the mode of the agreed supervision and international observation and their personal composition; and
    c. rules and regulations regarding election campaigns, including agreed arrangements for the organizing of mass media, and the possibility of licensing a broadcasting and TV station.
3. The future status of displaced Palestinians who were registered on 4th June 1967 will not be prejudiced

because they are unable to participate in the election process due to practical reasons.

Annex II

PROTOCOL ON WITHDRAWAL OF ISRAELI FORCES FROM THE GAZA STRIP AND JERICHO AREA

1. The two sides will conclude and sign within two months from the date of entry into force of this Declaration of Principles, an agreement on the withdrawal of Israeli military forces from the Gaza Strip and Jericho area. This agreement will include comprehensive arrangements to apply in the Gaza Strip and the Jericho area subsequent to the Israeli withdrawal.

2. Israel will implement an accelerated and scheduled withdrawal of Israeli military forces from the Gaza Strip and Jericho area, beginning immediately with the signing of the agreement on the Gaza Strip and Jericho area and to be completed within a period not exceeding four months after the signing of this agreement.

3. The above agreement will include, among other things:
   a. Arrangements for a smooth and peaceful transfer of authority from the Israeli military government and its Civil Administration to the Palestinian representatives.
   b. Structure, powers and responsibilities of the Palestinian authority in these areas, except: external security, settlements, Israelis, foreign relations, and other mutually agreed matters.
   c. Arrangements for the assumption of internal security and public order by the Palestinian police force consisting of police officers recruited locally and from abroad (holding Jordanian passports and Palestinian documents issued by Egypt). Those who will participate in the Palestinian

      police force coming from abroad should be trained as police and police officers.

d. A temporary international or foreign presence, as agreed upon.

e. Establishment of a joint Palestinian-Israeli Co-ordination and Cooperation Committee for mutual security purposes.

f. An economic development and stabilization program, including the establishment of an Emergency Fund, to encourage foreign investment, and financial and economic support. Both sides will coordinate and cooperate jointly and unilaterally with regional and international parties to support these aims.

g. Arrangements for a safe passage for persons and transportation between the Gaza Strip and Jericho area.

4. The above agreement will include arrangements for coordination between both parties regarding passages:

a. Gaza–Egypt; and

b. Jericho–Jordan.

5. The offices responsible for carrying out the powers and responsibilities of the Palestinian authority under this Annex II and Article VI of the Declaration of Principles will be located in the Gaza Strip and in the Jericho area pending the inauguration of the Council.

6. Other than these agreed arrangements, the status of the Gaza Strip and Jericho area will continue to be an integral part of the West Bank and Gaza Strip, and will not be changed in the interim period.

Annex III

PROTOCOL ON ISRAELI-PALESTINIAN COOPERATION IN ECONOMIC AND DEVELOPMENT PROGRAMS

The two sides agree to establish an Israeli-Palestinian Continuing Committee for Economic Cooperation, focusing, among other things, on the following:

1. Cooperation in the field of water, including a Water Development Program prepared by experts from both sides, which will also specify the mode of cooperation in the management of water resources in the West Bank and Gaza Strip, and will include proposals for studies and plans on water rights of each party, as well as on the equitable utilization of joint water resources for implementation in and beyond the interim period.

2. Cooperation in the field of electricity, including an Electricity Development Program, which will also specify the mode of cooperation for the production, maintenance, purchase and sale of electricity resources.

3. Cooperation in the field of energy, including an Energy Development Program, which will provide for the exploitation of oil and gas for industrial purposes, particularly in the Gaza Strip and in the Negev, and will encourage further joint exploitation of other energy resources. This program may also provide for the construction of a petrochemical industrial complex in the Gaza Strip and the construction of oil and gas pipelines.

4. Cooperation in the field of finance, including a Financial Development and Action Program for the encouragement of international investment in the West Bank and the Gaza Strip, and in Israel, as well as the establishment of a Palestinian Development Bank.

5. Cooperation in the field of transport and communications, including a Program, which will define guidelines for the establishment of a Gaza Sea Port Area, and will provide for the establishing of transport and communications lines to and from the West Bank and the Gaza Strip to Israel and to other countries. In addition, this Program will provide for carrying out the necessary construction of roads, railways, communications lines, etc.

6. Cooperation in the field of trade, including studies, and Trade Promotion Programs, which will encourage local, regional and inter-regional trade, as well as a feasibility study of creating free trade zones in the Gaza Strip and in Israel, mutual access to these zones, and cooperation in other areas related to trade and commerce.

7. Cooperation in the field of industry, including Industrial Development Programs, which will provide for the establishment of joint Israeli-Palestinian Industrial Research and Development Centers, will promote Palestinian-Israeli joint ventures, and provide guidelines for cooperation in the textile, food, pharmaceutical, electronics, diamonds, computer and science-based industries.

8. A program for cooperation in, and regulation of, labor relations and cooperation in social welfare issues.

9. A Human Resources Development and Cooperation Plan, providing for joint Israeli-Palestinian workshops and seminars, and for the establishment of joint vocational training centers, research institutes and data banks.

10. An Environmental Protection Plan, providing for joint and/or coordinated measures in this sphere.

11. A program for developing coordination and cooperation in the field of communication and media.

12. Any other programs of mutual interest.

Annex IV

PROTOCOL ON ISRAELI-PALESTINIAN COOPERATION CONCERNING REGIONAL DEVELOPMENT PROGRAMS

1. The two sides will cooperate in the context of the multilateral peace efforts in promoting a Development Program for the region, including the West Bank and the Gaza Strip, to be initiated by the G-7. The parties will request the G-7 to seek the participation in this program of other interested states, such as members of the Organization for Economic Cooperation and Development, regional Arab states and institutions, as well as members of the private sector.

2. The Development Program will consist of two elements:
   a. an Economic Development Program for the West Bank and the Gaza Strip.
   b. a Regional Economic Development Program.

   A. The Economic Development Program for the West Bank and the Gaza Strip will consist of the following elements:
      1. A Social Rehabilitation Program, including a Housing and Construction Program.
      2. A Small and Medium Business Development Plan.
      3. An Infrastructure Development Program (water, electricity, transportation and communications, etc.).
      4. A Human Resources Plan.

741

5. Other programs.

B. The Regional Economic Development Program may consist of the following elements:
  1. The establishment of a Middle East Development Fund, as a first step, and a Middle East Development Bank, as a second step.
  2. The development of a joint Israeli-Palestinian-Jordanian Plan for coordinated exploitation of the Dead Sea area.
  3. The Mediterranean Sea (Gaza)–Dead Sea Canal.
  4. Regional Desalinization and other water development projects.
  5. A regional plan for agricultural development, including a coordinated regional effort for the prevention of desertification.
  6. Interconnection of electricity grids.
  7. Regional cooperation for the transfer, distribution and industrial exploitation of gas, oil and other energy resources.
  8. A Regional Tourism, Transportation and Telecommunications Development Plan.
  9. Regional cooperation in other spheres.

3. The two sides will encourage the multilateral working groups, and will coordinate towards their success. The two parties will encourage intersessional activities, as well as pre-feasibility and feasibility studies, within the various multilateral working groups.

AGREED MINUTES TO THE DECLARATION OF PRINCIPLES ON INTERIM SELF-GOVERNMENT ARRANGEMENTS

A. GENERAL UNDERSTANDINGS AND AGREEMENTS

Any powers and responsibilities transferred to the Palestinians pursuant to the Declaration of Principles prior to the inauguration of the Council will be subject to the same principles pertaining to Article IV, as set out in these Agreed Minutes below.

B. SPECIFIC UNDERSTANDINGS AND AGREEMENTS

Article IV

It is understood that:

1. Jurisdiction of the Council will cover West Bank and Gaza Strip territory, except for issues that will be negotiated in the permanent status negotiations: Jerusalem, settlements, military locations, and Israelis.
2. The Council's jurisdiction will apply with regard to the agreed powers, responsibilities, spheres and authorities transferred to it.

Article VI (2)

It is agreed that the transfer of authority will be as follows:

1. The Palestinian side will inform the Israeli side of the names of the authorized Palestinians who will assume the powers, authorities and responsibilities that will be transferred to the Palestinians according to the Declaration of Principles in the following fields: education and culture, health, social welfare, direct taxation, tourism and any other authorities agreed upon.
2. It is understood that the rights and obligations of these offices will not be affected.

743

3. Each of the spheres described above will con-
    tinue to enjoy existing budgetary allocations
    in accordance with arrangements to be mutu-
    ally agreed upon. These arrangements also
    will provide for the necessary adjustments re-
    quired in order to take into account the taxes
    collected by the direct taxation office.
4. Upon the execution of the Declaration of Prin-
    ciples, the Israeli and Palestinian delegations
    will immediately commence negotiations on
    a detailed plan for the transfer of auth-
    ority on the above offices in accordance
    with the above understandings.

Article VII(2)
The Interim Agreement will also include arrangements for coordination and cooperation.

Article VII(5)
The withdrawal of the military government will
not prevent Israel from exercising the powers and
responsibilities not transferred to the Council.

Article VIII
It is understood that the Interim Agreement will
include arrangements for cooperation and coordination between the two parties in this regard. It
is also agreed that the transfer of powers and
responsibilities to the Palestinian police will be
accomplished in a phased manner, as agreed in
the Interim Agreement.

Article X
It is agreed that, upon the entry into force
of the Declaration of Principles, the Israeli
and Palestinian delegations will exchange the
names of the individuals designated by them as
members of the Joint Israeli-Palestinian Liaison
Committee. It is further agreed that each side will

have an equal number of members in the Joint Committee. The Joint Committee will reach decisions by agreement. The Joint Committee may add other technicians and experts, as necessary. The Joint Committee will decide on the frequency and place or places of its meetings.

Annex II
It is understood that, subsequent to the Israeli withdrawal, Israel will continue to be responsible for external security, and for internal security and public order of settlements and Israelis. Israeli military forces and civilians may continue to use roads freely within the Gaza Strip and the Jericho area.

DONE at Washington, D.C., this thirteenth day of September, 1993.

For the Government of   For the P.L.O.:
Israel:
   Shimon Peres   Mahmoud Abbas

Witnessed By:

Warren Christopher   Anatole Kozyrev
The United States   The Russian Federation
of America

INDEX

749

766

A SELECTION OF RELATED TITLES
AVAILABLE FROM CORGI BOOKS

THE PRICES SHOWN BELOW WERE CORRECT AT THE TIME OF
GOING TO PRESS. HOWEVER TRANSWORLD PUBLISHERS RESERVE
THE RIGHT TO SHOW NEW RETAIL PRICES ON COVERS WHICH MAY
DIFFER FROM THOSE PREVIOUSLY ADVERTISED IN THE TEXT OR
ELSEWHERE.

❐ 12138 X	THE HOLY BLOOD AND THE HOLY GRAIL		
		Baigent, Leigh & Lincoln	£5.99
❐ 13182 2	THE MESSIANIC LEGACY	Baigent, Leigh & Lincoln	£5.99
❐ 13596 8	THE TEMPLE AND THE LODGE	Baigent & Leigh	£5.99
❐ 13878 9	THE DEAD SEA SCROLLS DECEPTION	Baigent & Leigh	£4.99
❐ 13818 5	INSIDE THE BRITISH ARMY	Anthony Beevor	£6.99
❐ 13337 X	THE PROVISIONAL IRA	Patrick Bishop & Eamonn Mallie	£4.99
❐ 13679 4	REBELS	Peter de Rosa	£5.99
❐ 13296 9	VICARS OF CHRIST	Peter de Rosa	£5.99
❐ 13898 3	THE TAKING OF THE STONE OF DESTINY		
		Ian R Hamilton QC	£4.99
❐ 13892 4	FIFTY YEARS IN THE SYSTEM	Jimmy Laing	£5.99
❐ 13727 8	THE VIEW FROM NO.11	Nigel Lawson	£9.99
❐ 13831 2	THE HOLY PLACE	Henry Lincoln	£4.99
❐ 13311 6	MOSSAD	Ronald Payne	£4.99
❐ 99533 9	GROTESQUE LIBELS	Adam Raphael	£5.99
❐ 13847 9	THE PLUMBER	Joseph Salerno & Stephen Rivele	£4.99
❐ 13058 3	THE MARILYN CONSPIRACY	Milo Speriglio	£3.99
❐ 13950 5	JESUS THE MAN	Barbara Thierling	£5.99
❐ 12858 9	JACK THE RIPPER	Colin Wilson & Robin Odell	£4.99
❐ 13590 9	HOLY FACES, SECRET PLACES	Ian Wilson	£5.99
❐ 99349 2	THE LOCH NESS STORY	Nicholas Witchell	£6.99
❐ 13452 X	THE DAY THE LAUGHTER STOPPED	David Yallop	£6.99
❐ 13288 8	IN GOD'S NAME	David Yallop	£5.99
❐ 13451 1	TO ENCOURAGE THE OTHERS	David Yallop	£4.99
❐ 13454 6	DELIVER US FROM EVIL	David Yallop	£5.99

All Corgi Books are available at your bookshop or newsagent, or can be ordered from
the following address:
Corgi Books
Cash Sales Department
P.O. Box 11, Falmouth, Cornwall TR10 9EN

UK and B.F.P.O. customers please send a cheque or postal order (no currency) and
allow £1.00 for postage and packing for the first book plus 50p for the second book
and 30p for each additional book to a maximum charge of £3.00 (7 books plus).

Overseas customers, including Eire, please allow £2.00 for postage and packing for the
first book plus £1.00 for the second book and 50p for each subsequent title ordered.

NAME (Block letters) ....

ADDRESS ....